THE 1662 BOOK OF COMMON PRAYER
INTERNATIONAL EDITION

THE BOOK OF COMMON PRAYER

*and Administration of the
Sacraments and Other Rites
and Ceremonies of the Church*

TOGETHER WITH THE PSALTER OR
PSALMS OF DAVID, POINTED AS THEY
ARE TO BE SUNG OR SAID IN CHURCHES;
AND THE FORM OR MANNER OF MAKING,
ORDAINING, AND CONSECRATING OF
BISHOPS, PRIESTS, AND DEACONS

IVP ACADEMIC
DOWNERS GROVE, ILLINOIS

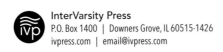

InterVarsity Press
P.O. Box 1400 | Downers Grove, IL 60515-1426
ivpress.com | email@ivpress.com

InterVarsity Press® is the publishing division of InterVarsity Christian Fellowship/USA®. For more information, visit intervarsity.org.

Cover design: David Fassett

ISBN 978-1-5140-0699-3

Printed in China ∞

Library of Congress Cataloging-in-Publication Data
A catalog record for this book is available from the Library of Congress.

30 29 28 27 26 25 24 23 | 13 12 11 10 9 8 7 6 5 4 3 2 1

This is an international edition of the 1662 text of The Book of Common Prayer and Administration of the Sacraments and Other Rites and Ceremonies of the Church, together with the Psalter and Ordinal. It employs less archaic spelling and punctuation, modestly updates obscure expressions, and includes prayers for civil authorities that may be used regardless of nation or polity.

Table of Contents.

CONTENTS

The Preface.

I T hath been the wisdom of the Church of England, ever since the first compiling of her public liturgy, to keep the mean between the two extremes of too much stiffness in refusing and of too much easiness in admitting any variation from it. For, as on the one side common experience showeth that where a change hath been made of things advisedly established (no evident necessity so requiring) sundry inconveniences have thereupon ensued, and those many times more and greater than the evils that were intended to be remedied by such change; so on the other side, the particular forms of divine worship, and the rites and ceremonies appointed to be used therein, being things in their own nature indifferent and alterable, and so acknowledged, it is but reasonable that upon weighty and important considerations, according to the various exigency of times and occasions, such changes and alterations should be made therein as to those that are in place of authority should from time to time seem either necessary or expedient. Accordingly we find that in the reigns of several princes of blessed memory since the Reformation, the church, upon just and weighty considerations her thereunto moving, hath yielded to make such alterations in some particulars as in their respective times were thought convenient. Yet so as that the main body and essentials of it (as well in the chiefest materials, as in the frame and order thereof) have still continued the same unto this day, and do yet stand firm and unshaken, notwithstanding all the vain attempts and impetuous assaults made against it by such men as are given to change and have always discovered a greater regard to their own private fancies and interests than to that duty they owe to the public.

By what undue means and for what mischievous purposes the use of the liturgy (though enjoined by the laws of the land, and those laws never yet repealed) came, during the late unhappy confusions, to be discontinued is too well known to the world, and we are not willing here to remember. But when, upon His Majesty's happy restoration, it seemed probable that, amongst other things, the use of the liturgy also would return of course (the same having never been legally abolished), unless some timely means were used to prevent it, those men who under the late usurped powers had made it a great part of their business to render the people disaffected thereunto saw themselves in point of reputation and interest concerned (unless they would freely acknowledge themselves to have erred, which such men are very hardly brought to do) with their utmost endeavours to hinder the restitution thereof. In order whereunto divers pamphlets were published against the Book of Common Prayer, the old objections mustered up, with the addition of some new ones, more than formerly had been made, to make the number swell. In fine, great importunities were used to His Sacred Majesty that the said book might be revised, and such alterations therein, and additions thereunto made, as should be thought requisite for the ease of tender consciences; whereunto His Majesty, out of his pious inclination to give satisfaction (so far as could be reasonably expected) to all his subjects of what persuasion soever, did graciously condescend.

In which review we have endeavoured to observe the like moderation as we find to have been used in the like case in former times. And therefore of the sundry alterations proposed unto us, we have rejected all such as were either of dangerous consequence (as secretly striking at some established doctrine or laudable practice of the Church of England, or indeed of the whole catholic church of Christ) or else of no consequence at all, but utterly frivolous and vain. But such alterations as were tendered to us (by what persons, under what pretences, or to what purpose soever so tendered) as seemed to us in any degree requisite or expedient, we have willingly and of our own accord assented unto, not enforced so to do by any strength of argument convincing us of the necessity of making the said alterations. For we are fully persuaded in our judgements (and we here profess it to the world) that the book, as it stood before established by law, doth not contain in it anything contrary to the word of God, or to sound doctrine, or which a godly man may not with a good conscience use and submit unto, or which is not fairly defensible against any that shall oppose the same, if it shall be allowed such just and favourable construction as in common equity ought to be allowed to all human writings, especially such as are set forth by authority, and even to the very best translations of the holy Scripture itself.

THE PREFACE

Our general aim therefore in this undertaking was not to gratify this or that party in any their unreasonable demands, but to do that which to our best understandings we conceived might most tend to the preservation of peace and unity in the church, the procuring of reverence and exciting of piety and devotion in the public worship of God, and the cutting off occasion from them that seek occasion of cavil or quarrel against the liturgy of the church. And as to the several variations from the former book, whether by alteration, addition, or otherwise, it shall suffice to give this general account, that most of the alterations were made, either first, for the better direction of them that are to officiate in any part of divine service, which is chiefly done in the calendars and rubrics; or secondly, for the more proper expressing of some words or phrases of ancient usage in terms more suitable to the language of the present times, and the clearer explanation of some other words and phrases that were either of doubtful signification or otherwise liable to misconstruction; or thirdly, for a more perfect rendering of such portions of holy Scripture as are inserted into the liturgy, which in the epistles and gospels especially and in sundry other places are now ordered to be read according to the last translation; and that it was thought convenient that some prayers and thanksgivings fitted to special occasions should be added in their due places, particularly for those at sea, together with an office for the baptism of such as are of riper years, which although not so necessary when the former book was compiled, yet by the growth of Anabaptism, through the licentiousness of the late times crept in amongst us, is now become necessary, and may be always useful for the baptizing of natives in our plantations and others converted to the faith.

If any man who shall desire a more particular account of the several alterations in any part of the liturgy shall take the pains to compare the present book with the former, we doubt not but the reason of the change may easily appear.

And having thus endeavoured to discharge our duties in this weighty affair as in the sight of God, and to approve our sincerity therein (so far as lay in us) to the consciences of all men, although we know it impossible (in such variety of apprehensions, humours, and interests as are in the world) to please all, nor can expect that men of factious, peevish, and perverse spirits should be satisfied with anything that can be done in this kind by any other than themselves, yet we have good hope that what is here presented, and hath been by the convocations of both provinces with great diligence examined and approved, will be also well accepted and approved by all sober, peaceable, and truly conscientious sons of the Church of England.

Concerning the Service of the Church.

THERE was never anything by the wit of man so well devised or so sure established which in continuance of time hath not been corrupted, as among other things it may plainly appear by the common prayers in the church, commonly called divine service. The first original and ground whereof, if a man would search out by the ancient Fathers, he shall find that the same was not ordained but of a good purpose and for a great advancement of godliness. For they so ordered the matter that all the whole Bible (or the greatest part thereof) should be read over once every year, intending thereby that the clergy, and especially such as were ministers in the congregation, should (by often reading and meditation in God's word) be stirred up to godliness themselves, and be more able to exhort others by wholesome doctrine and to confute them that were adversaries to the truth; and further, that the people (by daily hearing of holy Scripture read in the church) might continually profit more and more in the knowledge of God and be the more inflamed with the love of his true religion.

But these many years passed this godly and decent order of the ancient Fathers hath been so altered, broken, and neglected by planting in uncertain stories and legends, with multitude of responds, verses, vain repetitions, commemorations, and synodals, that commonly when any book of the Bible was begun, after three or four chapters were read out, all the rest were unread. And in this sort the Book of Isaiah was begun in Advent, and the Book of Genesis in Septuagesima, but they were only begun and never read through. After like sort were other books of holy Scripture used.

And moreover, whereas Saint Paul would have such language spoken to the people in the church as they might understand, and have profit by hearing the same, the service in this Church of England these many years hath been read in Latin to the people, which they understand not, so that they have heard with their ears only, and their heart, spirit, and mind have not been edified thereby.

And furthermore, notwithstanding that the ancient Fathers have divided the Psalms into seven portions, whereof every one was called a nocturn, now of late time a few of them have been daily said and the rest utterly omitted.

Moreover, the number and hardness of the rules called the *Pie,* and the manifold changings of the service, was the cause that to turn the book only was so hard and intricate a matter that many times there was more business to find out what should be read, than to read it when it was found out.

These inconveniences therefore considered, here is set forth such an order whereby the same shall be redressed. And for a readiness in this matter, here is drawn out a calendar for that purpose, which is plain and easy to be understood, wherein (so much as may be) the reading of holy Scripture is so set forth that all things shall be done in order, without breaking one piece from another. For this cause be cut off anthems, responds, invitatories, and such like things as did break the continual course of the reading of the Scripture.

Yet, because there is no remedy but that of necessity there must be some rules, therefore certain rules are here set forth, which as they are few in number, so they are plain and easy to be understood. So that here you have an order for prayer and for the reading of the holy Scripture much agreeable to the mind and purpose of the old Fathers, and a great deal more profitable and commodious than that which of late was used. It is more profitable, because here are left out many things, whereof some are untrue, some uncertain, some vain and superstitious; and nothing is ordained to be read but the very pure word of God, the holy Scriptures, or that which is agreeable to the same, and that in such a language and order as is most easy and plain for the understanding both of the readers and hearers. It is also more commodious, both for the shortness thereof and for the plainness of the order, and for that the rules be few and easy.

And whereas heretofore there hath been great diversity in saying and singing in churches within this realm – some following Salisbury Use, some Hereford Use, and some the Use of Bangor, some of York, some of Lincoln – now from henceforth all the whole realm shall have but one Use.

And forasmuch as nothing can be so plainly set forth but doubts may arise in the use and practice of the same, to appease all such diversity (if any arise) and for the resolution of all doubts concerning the manner how to understand, do, and execute the things contained in this book, the parties that so doubt or diversely take anything shall alway resort to the bishop of the diocese, who by his discretion shall take order for the quieting and appeasing of the same, so that the same order be not contrary to anything contained in this book. And if the bishop of the diocese be in doubt, then he may send for the resolution thereof to the archbishop.

THOUGH it be appointed that all things shall be read and sung in the church in the English tongue, to the end that the congregation may be thereby edified, yet it is not meant but that when men say Morning and Evening Prayer privately they may say the same in any language that they themselves do understand.

And all priests and deacons are to say daily the Morning and Evening Prayer either privately or openly, not being let by sickness or some other urgent cause.

And the curate that ministereth in every parish church or chapel, being at home, and not being otherwise reasonably hindered, shall say the same in the parish church or chapel where he ministereth, and shall cause a bell to be tolled thereunto a convenient time before he begin, that the people may come to hear God's word and to pray with him.

Of Ceremonies, Why Some Be Abolished & Some Retained.

OF such ceremonies as be used in the church, and have had their beginning by the institution of man, some at the first were of godly intent and purpose devised and yet at length turned to vanity and superstition. Some entered into the church by undiscreet devotion and such a zeal as was without knowledge, and for because they were winked at in the beginning, they grew daily to more and more abuses, which not only for their unprofitableness, but also because they have much blinded the people and obscured the glory of God, are worthy to be cut away and clean rejected. Other there be which, although they have been devised by man, yet it is thought good to reserve them still, as well for a decent order in the church (for the which they were first devised) as because they pertain to edification, whereunto all things done in the church (as the apostle teacheth) ought to be referred. And although the keeping or omitting of a ceremony, in itself considered, is but a small thing, yet the wilful and contemptuous transgression and breaking of a common order and discipline is no small offence before God.

'Let all things be done among you', saith Saint Paul, 'in a seemly and due order.' The appointment of the which order pertaineth not to private men. Therefore no man ought to take in hand, nor presume to appoint or alter, any public or common order in Christ's church, except he be lawfully called and authorized thereunto.

And whereas in this our time, the minds of men are so diverse that some think it a great matter of conscience to depart from a piece of the least of their ceremonies, they be so addicted to their old customs; and again on the other side, some be so newfangled that they would innovate all things, and so despise the old that nothing can like them but that is new; it was thought expedient not so much to have respect how to please and satisfy either of these parties, as how to please God and profit them both. And yet lest any man should be offended whom good reason might satisfy, here be certain causes rendered why some of the accustomed ceremonies be put away and some retained and kept still.

Some are put away because the great excess and multitude of them hath so increased in these latter days that the burden of them was intolerable, whereof Saint Augustine in his time complained that they were grown to such a number that the estate of Christian people was in worse case concerning that matter than were the Jews. And he counselled that such yoke and burden should be taken away as time would serve quietly to do it.

But what would Saint Augustine have said if he had seen the ceremonies of late days used among us, whereunto the multitude used in his time was not to be compared? This our excessive multitude of ceremonies was so great, and many of them so dark, that they did more confound and darken than declare and set forth Christ's benefits unto us.

And besides this, Christ's gospel is not a ceremonial law (as much of Moses' law was), but it is a religion to serve God, not in bondage of the figure or shadow, but in the freedom of the Spirit, being content only with those ceremonies which do serve to a decent order and godly discipline, and such as be apt to stir up the dull mind of man to the remembrance of his duty to God by some notable and special signification whereby he might be edified.

Furthermore, the most weighty cause of the abolishment of certain ceremonies was that they were so far abused, partly by the superstitious blindness of the rude and unlearned and partly by the unsatiable avarice of such as sought more their own lucre than the glory of God, that the abuses could not well be taken away, the thing remaining still.

But now as concerning those persons which peradventure will be offended for that some of the old ceremonies are retained still: If they consider that without some ceremonies it is not possible to keep any order or quiet discipline in the church, they shall easily perceive just cause to reform their judgements. And if they think much that any of the old do remain, and would rather have all devised anew, then such men granting some ceremonies convenient to be had, surely where the old may be well used, there they cannot reasonably reprove the old only for their age without bewraying of their own folly. For in such a case they ought rather to have reverence unto them for their antiquity, if they will declare themselves to be more studious of unity and concord than of innovations and newfangleness, which (as much as may be with the true setting forth of Christ's religion) is always to be eschewed. Furthermore, such shall have no just cause with the ceremonies reserved to be offended. For as those be taken away which were most abused and did burden men's consciences without any cause, so the other that remain are retained for a discipline and order, which (upon just causes) may be altered and changed, and therefore are not to be esteemed equal with God's law. And moreover, they be neither dark nor dumb ceremonies, but are so set forth that every man may understand what they do mean and to what use they do serve. So that it is not like that they in time to come should be abused as other have been. And in these our doings we condemn no other nations, nor prescribe anything but to our own people only. For we think it convenient that every country should use such ceremonies as they shall think best to the setting forth of God's honour and glory, and to the reducing of the people to a most perfect and godly living, without error or superstition; and that they should put away other things which from time to time they perceive to be most abused, as in men's ordinances it often chanceth diversely in divers countries.

The Order How the Psalter Is Appointed to Be Read.

THE Psalter shall be read through once every month, as it is there appointed both for Morning and Evening Prayer. But in February it shall be read only to the twenty-eighth or twenty-ninth day of the month.

And whereas January, March, May, July, August, October, and December have one and thirty days apiece, it is ordered that the same psalms shall be read the last day of the said months which were read the day before, so that the Psalter may begin again the first day of the next month ensuing.

And whereas the 119th Psalm is divided into twenty-two portions and is overlong to be read at one time, it is so ordered that at one time shall not be read above four or five of the said portions.

And at the end of every psalm, and of every such part of the 119th Psalm, shall be repeated this hymn,

*Glory be to the Father, and to the Son, * and to the Holy Ghost;*
*As it was in the beginning, is now, and ever shall be, * world without end. Amen.*

Note that the Psalter followeth the division of the Hebrews and the translation of the Great English Bible set forth and used in the time of King Henry the Eighth and Edward the Sixth.

The Order How the Rest of Holy Scripture Is Appointed to Be Read.

THE Old Testament is appointed for the first lessons at Morning and Evening Prayer, so that the most part thereof will be read every year once, as in the calendar is appointed.

The New Testament is appointed for the second lessons at Morning and Evening Prayer and shall be read over orderly every year thrice, besides the epistles and gospels, except the Apocalypse, out of which there are only certain lessons appointed at the end of the year and certain proper lessons appointed upon divers feasts.

And to know what lessons shall be read every day, look for the day of the month in the calendar following (p. xxxiv), and there ye shall find the chapters and portions of chapters that shall be read for the lessons both at Morning and Evening Prayer, except only the movable feasts, which are not in the calendar; and the immovable, where there is a blank left in the column of lessons, the proper lessons for all which days are to be found in the table of the proper lessons (p. xxix).

And note that whensoever proper psalms or lessons are appointed, then the psalms and lessons of ordinary course appointed in the Psalter and calendar (if they be different) shall be omitted for that time.

Note also that the collect, epistle, and gospel appointed for the Sunday shall serve all the week after where it is not in this book otherwise ordered.

Tables & Rules

for the movable and immovable feasts, together with the days of fasting and abstinence, through the whole year.

Rules to Know When the Movable Feasts and Holy Days Begin.

Easter Day (on which the rest depend) is always the first Sunday after the full moon which happens upon or next after the twenty-first day of March; and if the full moon happens upon a Sunday, Easter Day is the Sunday after.

Advent Sunday is always the nearest Sunday to the Feast of St. Andrew, whether before or after.

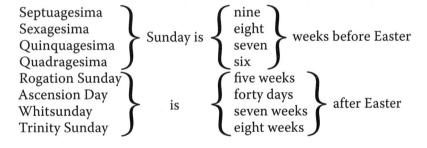

Septuagesima		nine	
Sexagesima	Sunday is	eight	weeks before Easter
Quinquagesima		seven	
Quadragesima		six	
Rogation Sunday		five weeks	
Ascension Day	is	forty days	after Easter
Whitsunday		seven weeks	
Trinity Sunday		eight weeks	

A Table of All the Feasts
that are to be observed throughout the year.

All Sundays in the year

The days of the feasts of:

The Circumcision of our
　　Lord JESUS CHRIST
The Epiphany
The Conversion of St. Paul
The Purification of
　　the Blessed Virgin
St. Matthias the Apostle

The Annunciation of
　　the Blessed Virgin
St. Mark the Evangelist
St. Philip and St. James
　　the Apostles
The Ascension of our
　　Lord JESUS CHRIST

St. Barnabas	St. Simon and St. Jude
The Nativity of St. John	the Apostles
the Baptist	All Saints
St. Peter the Apostle	St. Andrew the Apostle
St. James the Apostle	St. Thomas the Apostle
St. Bartholomew the Apostle	The Nativity of our Lord
St. Matthew the Apostle	St. Stephen the Martyr
St. Michael and All Angels	St. John the Evangelist
St. Luke the Evangelist	The Holy Innocents

Monday and Tuesday in Easter Week
Monday and Tuesday in Whitsun Week

A Table of the Vigils, Fasts, and Days of Abstinence
to be observed in the year.

The evens or vigils before:

The Nativity of our Lord	St. John the Baptist
The Purification of the	St. Peter
Blessed Virgin Mary	St. James
The Annunciation of the	St. Bartholomew
Blessed Virgin	St. Matthew
Easter Day	St. Simon and St. Jude
Ascension Day	St. Andrew
Pentecost	St. Thomas
St. Matthias	All Saints

Note that if any of these feast days fall upon a Monday, then the vigil or fast day shall be kept upon the Saturday, and not upon the Sunday next before it.

Days of fasting or abstinence:

I. The forty days of Lent
II. The Ember Days at the four seasons, being the Wednesday, Friday, and Saturday after: the first Sunday in Lent, the feast of Pentecost, September 14, and December 13
III. The three Rogation Days, being the Monday, Tuesday, and Wednesday before Holy Thursday, or the Ascension of our Lord
IV. All the Fridays in the year, except Christmas Day

TABLES AND RULES

A Table to Find Easter Day

from the present time till the year 2199 inclusive,
according to the following calendar.

Golden Number	Day of the Month	Sunday Letter
	Mar. 21	C
XIV	22	D
III	23	E
	24	F
XI	25	G
	26	A
XIX	27	B
VIII	28	C
	29	D
XVI	30	E
V	31	F
	Apr. 1	G
XIII	2	A
II	3	B
	4	C
X	5	D
	6	E
XVIII	7	F
VII	8	G
	9	A
XV	10	B
IV	11	C
	12	D
XII	13	E
I	14	F
	15	G
IX	16	A
XVII	17	B
VI	18	C
	19	D
	20	E
	21	F
	22	G
	23	A
	24	B
	25	C

This table contains as much of the calendar as is necessary for the determining of Easter. To find which, look for the Golden Number of the year in the first column of the table, against which stands the day of the Paschal full moon. Then look in the third column for the Sunday Letter, next after the day of the full moon, and the day of the month standing against that Sunday letter is Easter Day. If the full moon happens upon a Sunday, then (according to the first rule) the next Sunday after is Easter Day.

To find the Golden Number, or Prime, add one to the year of our Lord, and then divide by 19. The remainder, if any, is the Golden Number; but if nothing remaineth, then 19 is the Golden Number.

To find the Dominical or Sunday Letter according to the calendar until the year 2099 inclusive, add to the year of our Lord its fourth part, omitting fractions; and also the number 6. Divide the sum by 7, and if there is no remainder, then A is the Sunday Letter; but if any number remaineth, then the letter standing against that number in the small annexed table is the Sunday Letter. For the next following century, that is, from the year 2100 till the year 2199 inclusive, add to the current year its fourth part, and also the number 5, and then divide by 7, and proceed as in the last rule.

0	A
1	G
2	F
3	E
4	D
5	C
6	B

Note that in all bissextile or leap years, the letter found as above will be the Sunday Letter from the intercalated day exclusive to the end of the year.

TABLES AND RULES

A Table of the Movable Feasts
according to the several days that Easter can possibly fall upon.

Easter Day	Sundays after Epiphany	Septuagesima Sunday	The First Day of Lent	Rogation Sunday	Ascension Day	Whitsunday	Sundays after Trinity	Advent Sunday
Mar. 22	1	Jan. 18	Feb. 4	Apr. 26	Apr. 30	May 10	27	Nov. 29
23	1	19	5	27	May 1	11	27	30
24	1	20	6	28	2	12	27	Dec. 1
25	2	21	7	29	3	13	27	2
26	2	22	8	30	4	14	27	3
27	2	23	9	May 1	5	15	26	Nov. 27
28	2	24	10	2	6	16	26	28
29	2	25	11	3	7	17	26	29
30	2	26	12	4	8	18	26	30
31	2	27	13	5	9	19	26	Dec. 1
Apr. 1	3	28	14	6	10	20	26	2
2	3	29	15	7	11	21	26	3
3	3	30	16	8	12	22	25	Nov. 27
4	3	31	17	9	13	23	25	28
5	3	Feb. 1	18	10	14	24	25	29
6	3	2	19	11	15	25	25	30
7	3	3	20	12	16	26	25	Dec. 1
8	4	4	21	13	17	27	25	2
9	4	5	22	14	18	28	25	3
10	4	6	23	15	19	29	24	Nov. 27
11	4	7	24	16	20	30	24	28
12	4	8	25	17	21	31	24	29
13	4	9	26	18	22	June 1	24	30
14	4	10	27	19	23	2	24	Dec. 1
15	5	11	28	20	24	3	24	2
16	5	12	Mar. 1	21	25	4	24	3
17	5	13	2	22	26	5	23	Nov. 27
18	5	14	3	23	27	6	23	28
19	5	15	4	24	28	7	23	29
20	5	16	5	25	29	8	23	30
21	5	17	6	26	30	9	23	Dec. 1
22	6	18	7	27	31	10	23	2
23	6	19	8	28	June 1	11	23	3
24	6	20	9	29	2	12	22	Nov. 27
25	6	21	10	30	3	13	22	28

TABLES AND RULES

Note that in a bissextile or leap year, the number of Sundays after Epiphany will be the same as if Easter Day had fallen one day later than it really does. And for the same reason one day must in every leap year be added to the day of the month given by the table for Septuagesima Sunday, and the like must be done for the First Day of Lent (commonly called Ash Wednesday) unless the table gives some day in the month of March for it, for in that case the day given by the table is the right day.

A. apostle	*Hag.* Haggai	*Pet.* Peter
Ab. abbot	*Heb.* Hebrews	*Phil.* Philippians
Archb. archbishop	*Hos.* Hosea	*Phlm.* Philemon
Archd. archdeacon	*Isa.* Isaiah	*Prov.* Proverbs
Bar. Baruch	*Jas.* James	*Ps.* Psalm
Bel Bel & the Dragon	*Jdt.* Judith	*Rev.* Revelation
B. bishop	*Jer.* Jeremiah	*Rom.* Romans
C. confessor	*Josh.* Joshua	*Sam.* Samuel
Col. Colossians	*Judg.* Judges	*Sg. III* Song of the
Cor. Corinthians	*K.* king	3 Children
Dr. doctor	*Kgs.* Kings	*Sir.* Sirach
Dan. Daniel	*Lam.* Lamentations	*Song* Song of
D. deacon	*Lev.* Leviticus	Solomon
Deut. Deuteronomy	*M.* martyr	*Sus.* Susanna
E. evangelist	*Macc.* Maccabees	*Thess.* Thessalon-
Eccl. Ecclesiastes	*Mal.* Malachi	ians
Eph. Ephesians	*Matt.* Matthew	*Tim.* Timothy
Esd. Esdras	*Mic.* Micah	*Tob.* Tobit
Esth. Esther	*Nah.* Nahum	*Tr.* translation
Exod. Exodus	*Neh.* Nehemiah	*V.* virgin
Ezek. Ezekiel	*Num.* Numbers	*Wis.* Wisdom of
Gal. Galatians	*Obad.* Obadiah	Solomon
Gen. Genesis	*P.* presbyter	*Zech.* Zechariah
Hab. Habakkuk	or priest	*Zeph.* Zephaniah

Proper Lessons

*to be read at Morning and Evening
Prayer on the Sundays and other
holy days throughout the year.*

Lessons Proper for Sundays.

Sundays	Mattins		Evensong	
	1 Lesson	2 Lesson	1 Lesson	2 Lesson
Of Advent				
1	Isa. 1	-	Isa. 2	-
2	5	-	24	-
3	25	-	26	-
4	30	-	32	-
After Christmas				
1	37	-	38	-
2	41	-	43	-
After Epiphany				
1	44	-	46	-
2	51	-	53	-
3	55	-	56	-
4	57	-	58	-
5	59	-	64	-
6	65	-	66	-
Septuagesima	Gen. 1	-	Gen. 2	-
Sexagesima	3	-	6	-
Quinquagesima	9:1-19	-	12	-
In Lent				-
1	19:1-29	-	22	-
2	27	-	34	-
3	39	-	42	-

LESSONS PROPER FOR SUNDAYS

Sundays	Mattins		Evensong	
	1 Lesson	2 Lesson	1 Lesson	2 Lesson
4	Gen. 43	-	Gen. 45	-
5	Exod. 3	-	Exod. 5	-
6	9	Matt. 26	10	Heb. 5:1-10
Easter Day	12	Rom. 6	14	Acts 2:22-47
After Easter				
1	Num. 16	-	Num. 22	-
2	23–24	-	25	-
3	Deut. 4	-	Deut. 5	-
4	6	-	7	-
5	8	-	9	-
After Ascension	12	-	13	-
Whitsunday	16:1-17	Acts 10:34-48	Isa. 11	19:1-20
Trinity Sunday	Gen. 1	Matt. 3	Gen. 18	1 John 5
After Trinity				
1	Josh. 10	-	Josh. 23	-
2	Judg. 4	-	Judg. 5	-
3	1 Sam. 2	-	1 Sam. 3	-
4	12	-	13	-
5	15	-	17	-
6	2 Sam. 12	-	2 Sam. 19	-
7	21	-	24	-
8	1 Kgs. 13	-	1 Kgs. 17	-
9	18	-	19	-
10	21	-	22	-
11	2 Kgs. 5	-	2 Kgs. 9	-
12	10	-	18	-
13	19	-	23	-
14	Jer. 5	-	Jer. 22	-
15	35	-	36	-
16	Ezek. 2	-	Ezek. 13	-

LESSONS PROPER FOR HOLY DAYS

Sundays	Mattins		Evensong	
	1 Lesson	*2 Lesson*	*1 Lesson*	*2 Lesson*
17	Ezek. 14	-	Ezek. 18	-
18	20	-	24	-
19	Dan. 3	-	Dan. 6	-
20	Joel 2	-	Mic. 6	-
21	Hab. 2	-	Prov. 1	-
22	Prov. 2	-	3	-
23	11	-	12	-
24	13	-	14	-
25	15	-	16	-
26	17	-	19	-

Lessons Proper for Holy Days – Mattins.

Day	1 Lesson	2 Lesson
St. Andrew	Prov. 20	-
St. Thomas the Apostle	23	-
Nativity of Christ	Isa. 9:1-7	Luke 2:1-14
St. Stephen	Prov. 28	Acts 6:8–7:29
St. John	Eccl. 5	Rev. 1
Innocents' Day	Jer. 31:1-17	-
Circumcision	Gen. 17	Rom. 2
Epiphany	Isa. 60	Luke 3:1-22
Conversion of St. Paul	Wis. 5	Acts 22:1-21
Purification of the V. Mary	9	-
St. Matthias	19	-
Annunciation of our Lady	Sir. 2	-
Wednesday before Easter	Hos. 13	John 11:45-57
Thursday before Easter	Dan. 9	13
Good Friday	Gen. 22:1-19	18
Easter Even	Zech. 9	Luke 23:50-56
Monday in Easter Week	Exod. 16	Matt. 28

LESSONS PROPER FOR HOLY DAYS

Day	1 Lesson	2 Lesson
Tuesday in Easter Week	Exod. 20	Luke 24:1-12
St. Mark	Sir. 4	-
St. Philip and St. James	7	John 1:43-51
Ascension Day	Deut. 10	Luke 24:44-53
Monday in Whitsun Week	Gen. 11:1-9	1 Cor. 12
Tuesday in Whitsun Week	1 Sam. 19:18-24	1 Thess. 5:12-23
St. Barnabas	Sir. 10	Acts 14
St. John the Baptist	Mal. 3	Matt. 3
St. Peter	Sir. 15	Acts 3
St. James	21	-
St. Bartholomew	24	-
St. Matthew	35	-
St. Michael	Gen. 32	Acts 12:1-19
St. Luke	Sir. 51	-
St. Simon and St. Jude	Job 24–25	-
All Saints	Wis. 3:1-9	Heb. 11:32–12:6

Lessons Proper for Holy Days – Evensong.

Day	1 Lesson	2 Lesson
St. Andrew	Prov. 21	-
St. Thomas the Apostle	24	-
Nativity of Christ	Isa. 7:10-16	Titus 3:4-8
St. Stephen	Eccl. 4	Acts 7:30-54
St. John	6	Rev. 22
Innocents' Day	Wis. 1	-
Circumcision	Deut. 10:12-22	Col. 2
Epiphany	Isa. 49	John 2:1-11
Conversion of St. Paul	Wis. 6	Acts 26
Purification of the V. Mary	12	-
St. Matthias	Sir. 1	-
Annunciation of our Lady	3	-

PROPER PSALMS

Day	1 Lesson	2 Lesson
Wednesday before Easter	Hos. 14	-
Thursday before Easter	Jer. 31	-
Good Friday	Isa. 53	1 Pet. 2
Easter Even	Exod. 13	Heb. 4
Monday in Easter Week	17	Acts 3
Tuesday in Easter Week	32	1 Cor. 15
St. Mark	Sir. 5	-
St. Philip and St. James	9	-
Ascension Day	2 Kgs. 2	Eph. 4:1-16
Monday in Whitsun Week	Num. 11:16-29	1 Cor. 14:1-25
Tuesday in Whitsun Week	Deut. 30	1 John 4:1-13
St. Barnabas	Sir. 12	Acts 15:1-35
St. John the Baptist	Mal. 4	Matt. 14:1-12
St. Peter	Sir. 19	Acts 4
St. James	22	-
St. Bartholomew	29	-
St. Matthew	38	-
St. Michael	Dan. 10:5-21	Jude 6-15
St. Luke	Job 1	-
St. Simon and St. Jude	42	-
All Saints	Wis. 5:1-16	Rev. 19:1-16

Proper Psalms on Certain Days.

Day	Mattins	Evensong
Christmas Day	19, 45, 85	89, 110, 132
Ash Wednesday	6, 32, 38	102, 130, 143
Good Friday	22, 40, 54	69, 88
Easter Day	2, 57, 111	113, 114, 118
Ascension Day	8, 15, 21	24, 47, 108
Whitsunday	48, 68	104, 145

JANUARY – MATTINS

January hath 31 days			1 Lesson	2 Lesson
1	A	*Circumcision of our Lord*	—	—
2	B		Gen. 1	Matt. 1
3	C		3	2
4	D		5	3
5	E		7	4
6	F	*Epiphany of our Lord*	—	—
7	G		9	5
8	A	Lucian, P. & M.	13	6
9	B		15	7
10	C		17	8
11	D		19	9
12	E		21	10
13	F	Hilary, B. & C.	23	11
14	G		25	12
15	A		27	13
16	B		29	14
17	C		31	15
18	D	Prisca, Roman V. & M.	33	16
19	E		35	17
20	F	Fabian, B. of Rome & M.	38	18
21	G	Agnes, Roman V. & M.	40	19
22	A	Vincent, Spanish D. & M.	42	20
23	B		44	21
24	C		46	22
25	D	*Conversion of St. Paul*	—	—
26	E		48	23
27	F		50	24
28	G		Exod. 2	25
29	A		4	26
30	B		6:1-13	27
31	C		8	28

January hath 31 days			1 Lesson	2 Lesson
1	A	*Circumcision of our Lord*	—	—
2	B		Gen. 2	Rom. 1
3	C		4	2
4	D		6	3
5	E		8	4
6	F	*Epiphany of our Lord*	—	—
7	G		12	5
8	A	Lucian, P. & M.	14	6
9	B		16	7
10	C		18	8
11	D		20	9
12	E		22	10
13	F	Hilary, B. & C.	24	11
14	G		26	12
15	A		28	13
16	B		30	14
17	C		32	15
18	D	Prisca, Roman V. & M.	34	16
19	E		37	1 Cor. 1
20	F	Fabian, B. of Rome & M.	39	2
21	G	Agnes, Roman V. & M.	41	3
22	A	Vincent, Spanish D. & M.	43	4
23	B		45	5
24	C		47	6
25	D	*Conversion of St. Paul*	—	—
26	E		49	7
27	F		Exod. 1	8
28	G		3	9
29	A		5	10
30	B		7	11
31	C		9	12

February hath 28 (or 29) days			1 Lesson	2 Lesson
1	D	*fast*	Exod. 10	Mark 1
2	E	*Purification of Mary the Blessed V.*	—	2
3	F	Blasius, Armenian B. & M.	12	3
4	G		14	4
5	A	Agatha, Sicilian V. & M.	16	5
6	B		18	6
7	C		20	7
8	D		22	8
9	E		24	9
10	F		33	10
11	G		Lev. 18	11
12	A		20	12
13	B		Num. 11	13
14	C	Valentine, B. & M.	13	14
15	D		16	15
16	E		20	16
17	F		22	Luke 1:1-38
18	G		24	1:39-80
19	A		27	2
20	B		31	3
21	C		35	4
22	D		Deut. 1	5
23	E	*fast*	3	6
24	F	*St. Matthias, A. & M.*	—	7
25	G		5	8
26	A		7	9
27	B		9	10
28	C		11	11
29			13	Matt. 7

FEBRUARY – EVENSONG

February hath 28 (or 29) days			1 Lesson	2 Lesson
1	D	*fast*	Exod. 11	1 Cor. 13
2	E	*Purification of Mary the Blessed V.*	—	14
3	F	Blasius, Armenian B. *&* M.	13	15
4	G		15	16
5	A	Agatha, Sicilian V. *&* M.	17	2 Cor. 1
6	B		19	2
7	C		21	3
8	D		23	4
9	E		32	5
10	F		34	6
11	G		Lev. 19	7
12	A		26	8
13	B		Num. 12	9
14	C	Valentine, B. *&* M.	14	10
15	D		17	11
16	E		21	12
17	F		23	13
18	G		25	Gal. 1
19	A		30	2
20	B		32	3
21	C		36	4
22	D		Deut. 2	5
23	E	*fast*	4	6
24	F	*St. Matthias, A. & M.*	—	Eph. 1
25	G		6	2
26	A		8	3
27	B		10	4
28	C		12	5
29			14	Rom. 12

MARCH – MATTINS

			1 Lesson	2 Lesson
1	D	David, Archb. of Menevia	Deut. 15	Luke 12
2	E	Cedde, or Chad, B. of Lichfield	17	13
3	F		19	14
4	G		21	15
5	A		24	16
6	B		26	17
7	C	Perpetua of Mauritania, M.	28	18
8	D		30	19
9	E		32	20
10	F		34	21
11	G		Josh. 2	22
12	A	Gregory *Magnus*, B. of Rome *&* C.	4	23
13	B		6	24
14	C		8	John 1
15	D		10	2
16	E		24	3
17	F		Judg. 2	4
18	G	Edward, K. of the West Saxons	4	5
19	A		6	6
20	B		8	7
21	C	Benedict, Ab.	10	8
22	D		12	9
23	E		14	10
24	F	*fast*	16	11
25	G	*Annunciation of Mary*	—	12
26	A		18	13
27	B		20	14
28	C		Ruth 1	15
29	D		3	16
30	E		1 Sam. 1	17
31	F		3	18

MARCH – EVENSONG

			1 Lesson	2 Lesson
1	D	David, Archb. of Menevia	Deut. 16	Eph. 6
2	E	Cedde, or Chad, B. of Lichfield	18	Phil. 1
3	F		20	2
4	G		22	3
5	A		25	4
6	B		27	Col. 1
7	C	Perpetua of Mauritania, M.	29	2
8	D		31	3
9	E		33	4
10	F		Josh. 1	1 Thess. 1
11	G		3	2
12	A	Gregory *Magnus*, B. of Rome *&* C.	5	3
13	B		7	4
14	C		9	5
15	D		23	2 Thess. 1
16	E		Judg. 1	2
17	F		3	3
18	G	Edward, K. of the West Saxons	5	1 Tim. 1
19	A		7	2–3
20	B		9	4
21	C	Benedict, Ab.	11	5
22	D		13	6
23	E		15	2 Tim. 1
24	F	*fast*	17	2
25	G	*Annunciation of Mary*	—	3
26	A		19	4
27	B		21	Titus 1
28	C		Ruth 2	2–3
29	D		4	Phlm.
30	E		1 Sam. 2	Heb. 1
31	F		4	2

April hath 30 days			1 Lesson	2 Lesson
1	G		1 Sam. 5	John 19
2	A		7	20
3	B	Richard, B. of Chichester	9	21
4	C	Ambrose, B. of Milan	11	Acts 1
5	D		13	2
6	E		15	3
7	F		17	4
8	G		19	5
9	A		21	6
10	B		23	7
11	C		25	8
12	D		27	9
13	E		29	10
14	F		31	11
15	G		2 Sam. 2	12
16	A		4	13
17	B		6	14
18	C		8	15
19	D	Alphege, Archb. of Canterbury	10	16
20	E		12	17
21	F		14	18
22	G		16	19
23	A	St. George, M.	18	20
24	B		20	21
25	C	St. Mark, E. & M.	—	22
26	D		22	23
27	E		24	24
28	F		1 Kgs. 2	25
29	G		4	26
30	A		6	27

APRIL – EVENSONG

April hath 30 days			1 Lesson	2 Lesson
1	G		1 Sam. 6	Heb. 3
2	A		8	4
3	B	Richard, B. of Chichester	10	5
4	C	Ambrose, B. of Milan	12	6
5	D		14	7
6	E		16	8
7	F		18	9
8	G		20	10
9	A		22	11
10	B		24	12
11	C		26	13
12	D		28	Jas. 1
13	E		30	2
14	F		2 Sam. 1	3
15	G		3	4
16	A		5	5
17	B		7	1 Pet. 1
18	C		9	2
19	D	Alphege, Archb. of Canterbury	11	3
20	E		13	4
21	F		15	5
22	G		17	2 Pet. 1
23	A	St. George, M.	19	2
24	B		21	3
25	C	*St. Mark, E. & M.*	—	1 John 1
26	D		23	2
27	E		1 Kgs. 1	3
28	F		3	4
29	G		5	5
30	A		7	2 & 3 John

May hath 31 days			1 Lesson	2 Lesson
1	B	*St. Philip & St. James, A. & M.*	—	—
2	C		1 Kgs. 8	Acts 28
3	D	Invention of the Cross	10	Matt. 1
4	E		12	2
5	F		14	3
6	G	St. John the Evangelist *ante*	16	4
7	A	*portam Latinam*	18	5
8	B		20	6
9	C		22	7
10	D		2 Kgs. 2	8
11	E		4	9
12	F		6	10
13	G		8	11
14	A		10	12
15	B		12	13
16	C		14	14
17	D		16	15
18	E		18	16
19	F	Dunstan, Archb. of Canterbury	20	17
20	G		22	18
21	A		24	19
22	B		Ezra 1	20
23	C		4	21
24	D		6	22
25	E		9	23
26	F	Augustine, Archb. of Canterbury	Neh. 2	24
27	G	Venerable Bede, P.	5	25
28	A		8	26
29	B		10	27
30	C		Esth. 1	28
31	D		3	Mark 1

MAY – EVENSONG

May hath 31 days			*1 Lesson*	*2 Lesson*
1	B	*St. Philip & St. James, A. & M.*	—	Jude
2	C		1 Kgs. 9	Rom. 1
3	D	Invention of the Cross	11	2
4	E		13	3
5	F		15	4
6	G	St. John the Evangelist *ante*	17	5
7	A	*portam Latinam*	19	6
8	B		21	7
9	C		2 Kgs. 1	8
10	D		3	9
11	E		5	10
12	F		7	11
13	G		9	12
14	A		11	13
15	B		13	14
16	C		15	15
17	D		17	16
18	E		19	1 Cor. 1
19	F	Dunstan, Archb. of Canterbury	21	2
20	G		23	3
21	A		25	4
22	B		Ezra 3	5
23	C		5	6
24	D		7	7
25	E		Neh. 1	8
26	F	Augustine, Archb. of Canterbury	4	9
27	G	Venerable Bede, P.	6	10
28	A		9	11
29	B		13	12
30	C		Esth. 2	13
31	D		4	14

June hath 30 days			1 Lesson	2 Lesson
1	E	Nicomede, Roman P. & M.	Esth. 5	Mark 2
2	F		7	3
3	G		9	4
4	A		Job 2	5
5	B	Boniface, B. of Mainz & M.	4	6
6	C		6	7
7	D		8	8
8	E		10	9
9	F		12	10
10	G		14	11
11	A	*St. Barnabas, A. & M.*	—	—
12	B		16	12
13	C		19	13
14	D		21	14
15	E		23	15
16	F		26–27	16
17	G	St. Alban, M.	29	Luke 1
18	A		31	2
19	B		33	3
20	C	Tr. of Edward, K. of the West	35	4
21	D	Saxons	37	5
22	E		39	6
23	F	*fast*	41	7
24	G	*Nativity of St. John the Baptist*	—	—
25	A		Prov. 1	8
26	B		3	9
27	C		5	10
28	D	*fast*	7	11
29	E	*St. Peter, A. & M.*	—	—
30	F		9	12

JUNE – EVENSONG

June hath 30 days			1 Lesson	2 Lesson
1	E	Nicomede, Roman P. & M.	Esth. 6	1 Cor. 15
2	F		8	16
3	G		Job 1	2 Cor. 1
4	A		3	2
5	B	Boniface, B. of Mainz & M.	5	3
6	C		7	4
7	D		9	5
8	E		11	6
9	F		13	7
10	G		15	8
11	A	*St. Barnabas, A. & M.*	—	—
12	B		17–18	9
13	C		20	10
14	D		22	11
15	E		24–25	12
16	F		28	13
17	G	St. Alban, M.	30	Gal. 1
18	A		32	2
19	B		34	3
20	C	Tr. of Edward, K. of the West	36	4
21	D	Saxons	38	5
22	E		40	6
23	F	*fast*	42	Eph. 1
24	G	*Nativity of St. John the Baptist*	—	—
25	A		Prov. 2	2
26	B		4	3
27	C		6	4
28	D	*fast*	8	5
29	E	*St. Peter, A. & M.*	—	—
30	F		10	6

JULY – MATTINS

July hath 31 days			1 Lesson	2 Lesson
1	G		Prov. 11	Luke 13
2	A	Visitation of the Blessed V. Mary	13	14
3	B		15	15
4	C	Tr. of St. Martin, B. & C.	17	16
5	D		19	17
6	E		21	18
7	F		23	19
8	G		25	20
9	A		27	21
10	B		29	22
11	C		Eccl. 1	23
12	D		3	24
13	E		5	John 1
14	F		7	2
15	G	Swithun, B. of Winchester, Tr.	9	3
16	A		11	4
17	B		Jer. 1	5
18	C		3	6
19	D		5	7
20	E	Margaret, V. & M. at Antioch	7	8
21	F		9	9
22	G	St. Mary Magdalen	11	10
23	A		13	11
24	B	*fast*	15	12
25	C	*St. James, A. & M.*	—	13
26	D	St. Anne, Mother of the Blessed	17	14
27	E	V. Mary	19	15
28	F		21	16
29	G		23	17
30	A		25	18
31	B		27	19

July hath 31 days			1 Lesson	2 Lesson
1	G		Prov. 12	Phil. 1
2	A	Visitation of the Blessed V. Mary	14	2
3	B		16	3
4	C	Tr. of St. Martin, B. & C.	18	4
5	D		20	Col. 1
6	E		22	2
7	F		24	3
8	G		26	4
9	A		28	1 Thess. 1
10	B		31	2
11	C		Eccl. 2	3
12	D		4	4
13	E		6	5
14	F		8	2 Thess. 1
15	G	Swithun, B. of Winchester, Tr.	10	2
16	A		12	3
17	B		Jer. 2	1 Tim. 1
18	C		4	2–3
19	D		6	4
20	E	Margaret, V. & M. at Antioch	8	5
21	F		10	6
22	G	St. Mary Magdalen	12	2 Tim. 1
23	A		14	2
24	B	*fast*	16	3
25	C	*St. James, A. & M.*	—	4
26	D	St. Anne, Mother of the Blessed	18	Titus 1
27	E	V. Mary	20	2–3
28	F		22	Phlm.
29	G		24	Heb. 1
30	A		26	2
31	B		28	3

AUGUST – MATTINS

August hath 31 days			1 Lesson	2 Lesson
1	C	Lammas Day	Jer. 29	John 20
2	D		31	21
3	E		33	Acts 1
4	F		35	2
5	G		37	3
6	A	Transfiguration of our Lord	39	4
7	B	Name of Jesus	41	5
8	C		43	6
9	D		45–46	7
10	E	St. Laurence, Archd. of Rome & M.	48	8
11	F		50	9
12	G		52	10
13	A		Lam. 2	11
14	B		4	12
15	C		Ezek. 2	13
16	D		6	14
17	E		13	15
18	F		18	16
19	G		34	17
20	A		Dan. 2	18
21	B		4	19
22	C		6	20
23	D	*fast*	8	21
24	E	*St. Bartholomew, A. & M.*	—	22
25	F		10	23
26	G		12	24
27	A		Hos. 2–3	25
28	B	St. Augustine, B. of Hippo, C., Dr.	5–6	26
29	C	Beheading of St. John the Baptist	8	27
30	D		10	28
31	E		12	Matt. 1

August hath 31 days			*1 Lesson*	*2 Lesson*
1	C	Lammas Day	Jer. 30	Heb. 4
2	D		32	5
3	E		34	6
4	F		36	7
5	G		38	8
6	A	Transfiguration of our Lord	40	9
7	B	Name of Jesus	42	10
8	C		44	11
9	D		47	12
10	E	St. Laurence, Archd. of Rome & M.	49	13
11	F		51	Jas. 1
12	G		Lam. 1	2
13	A		3	3
14	B		5	4
15	C		Ezek. 3	5
16	D		7	1 Pet. 1
17	E		14	2
18	F		33	3
19	G		Dan. 1	4
20	A		3	5
21	B		5	2 Pet. 1
22	C		7	2
23	D	*fast*	9	3
24	E	*St. Bartholomew, A. & M.*	—	1 John 1
25	F		11	2
26	G		Hos. 1	3
27	A		4	4
28	B	St. Augustine, B. of Hippo, C., Dr.	7	5
29	C	Beheading of St. John the Baptist	9	2 & 3 John
30	D		11	Jude
31	E		13	Rom. 1

xlix

SEPTEMBER – MATTINS

September hath 30 days			*1 Lesson*	*2 Lesson*
1	F	Giles, Ab. & C.	Hos. 14	Matt. 2
2	G		Joel 2	3
3	A		Amos 1	4
4	B		3	5
5	C		5	6
6	D		7	7
7	E	Evurtius, B. of Orleans	9	8
8	F	Nativity of the Blessed V. Mary	Jonah 1	9
9	G		4	10
10	A		Mic. 2	11
11	B		4	12
12	C		6	13
13	D		Nah. 1	14
14	E	Holy Cross Day	3	15
15	F		Hab. 2	16
16	G		Zeph. 1	17
17	A	Lambert, B. & M.	3	18
18	B		Hag. 2	19
19	C		Zech. 2–3	20
20	D	*fast*	6	21
21	E	*St. Matthew, A., E., & M.*	—	22
22	F		8	23
23	G		10	24
24	A		12	25
25	B		14	26
26	C	St. Cyprian, Archb. of Carthage	Mal. 2	27
27	D	& M.	4	28
28	E		Tob. 2	Mark 1
29	F	*St. Michael & All Angels*	—	2
30	G	St. Jerome, P., C., & Dr.	4	3

1

SEPTEMBER – EVENSONG

September hath 30 days			1 Lesson	2 Lesson
1	F	Giles, Ab. & C.	Joel 1	Rom. 2
2	G		3	3
3	A		Amos 2	4
4	B		4	5
5	C		6	6
6	D		8	7
7	E	Evurtius, B. of Orleans	Obad.	8
8	F	Nativity of the Blessed V. Mary	Jonah 2–3	9
9	G		Mic. 1	10
10	A		3	11
11	B		5	12
12	C		7	13
13	D		Nah. 2	14
14	E	Holy Cross Day	Hab. 1	15
15	F		3	16
16	G		Zeph. 2	1 Cor. 1
17	A	Lambert, B. & M.	Hag. 1	2
18	B		Zech. 1	3
19	C		4–5	4
20	D	*fast*	7	5
21	E	*St. Matthew, A., E., & M.*	—	6
22	F		9	7
23	G		11	8
24	A		13	9
25	B		Mal. 1	10
26	C	St. Cyprian, Archb. of Carthage	3	11
27	D	& M.	Tob. 1	12
28	E		3	13
29	F	*St. Michael & All Angels*	—	14
30	G	St. Jerome, P., C., & Dr.	6	15

OCTOBER – MATTINS

October hath 31 days			1 Lesson	2 Lesson
1	A	Remigius, B. of Rheims	Tob. 7	Mark 4
2	B		9	5
3	C		11	6
4	D		13	7
5	E		Jdt. 1	8
6	F	Faith, V. & M.	3	9
7	G		5	10
8	A		7	11
9	B	St. Denys the Areopagite, B. & M.	9	12
10	C		11	13
11	D		13	14
12	E		15	15
13	F	Tr. of K. Edward the C.	Wis. 1	16
14	G		3	Luke 1:1-38
15	A		5	1:39-80
16	B		7	2
17	C	Etheldreda, V.	9	3
18	D	*St. Luke, E.*	—	4
19	E		11	5
20	F		13	6
21	G		15	7
22	A		17	8
23	B		19	9
24	C		Sir. 2	10
25	D	Crispin, M.	4	11
26	E		6	12
27	F	*fast*	8	13
28	G	*St. Simon & St. Jude, A. & M.*	—	14
29	A		10	15
30	B		12	16
31	C	*fast*	14	17

OCTOBER – EVENSONG

October hath 31 days			1 Lesson	2 Lesson
1	A	Remigius, B. of Rheims	Tob. 8	1 Cor. 16
2	B		10	2 Cor. 1
3	C		12	2
4	D		14	3
5	E		Jdt. 2	4
6	F	Faith, V. & M.	4	5
7	G		6	6
8	A		8	7
9	B	St. Denys the Areopagite, B. & M.	10	8
10	C		12	9
11	D		14	10
12	E		16	11
13	F	Tr. of K. Edward the C.	Wis. 2	12
14	G		4	13
15	A		6	Gal. 1
16	B		8	2
17	C	Etheldreda, V.	10	3
18	D	*St. Luke, E.*	—	4
19	E		12	5
20	F		14	6
21	G		16	Eph. 1
22	A		18	2
23	B		Sir. 1	3
24	C		3	4
25	D	Crispin, M.	5	5
26	E		7	6
27	F	*fast*	9	Phil. 1
28	G	*St. Simon & St. Jude, A. & M.*	—	2
29	A		11	3
30	B		13	4
31	C	*fast*	15	Col. 1

November hath 30 days			*1 Lesson*	*2 Lesson*
1	D	*All Saints' Day*	—	—
2	E		Sir. 16	Luke 18
3	F		18	19
4	G		20	20
5	A		22	21
6	B	Leonard, C.	24	22
7	C		27	23
8	D		29	24
9	E		31	John 1
10	F		33	2
11	G	St. Martin, B. & C.	35	3
12	A		37	4
13	B	Britius, B.	39	5
14	C		41	6
15	D	Machutus, B.	43	7
16	E		45	8
17	F	Hugh, B. of Lincoln	47	9
18	G		49	10
19	A		51	11
20	B	Edmund, K. & M.	Bar. 2	12
21	C		4	13
22	D	Cecilia, V. & M.	6	14
23	E	St. Clement I, B. of Rome & M.	Bel	15
24	F		Isa. 2	16
25	G	Catherine, V. & M.	4	17
26	A		6	18
27	B		8	19
28	C		10	20
29	D	*fast*	12	21
30	E	*St. Andrew, A. & M.*	—	Acts 1

November hath 30 days			1 Lesson	2 Lesson
1	D	*All Saints' Day*	—	—
2	E		Sir. 17	Col. 2
3	F		19	3
4	G		21	4
5	A		23	1 Thess. 1
6	B	Leonard, C.	25:1-12	2
7	C		28	3
8	D		30:1-17	4
9	E		32	5
10	F		34	2 Thess. 1
11	G	St. Martin, B. & C.	36	2
12	A		38	3
13	B	Britius, B.	40	1 Tim. 1
14	C		42	2–3
15	D	Machutus, B.	44	4
16	E		46:1-19	5
17	F	Hugh, B. of Lincoln	48	6
18	G		50	2 Tim. 1
19	A		Bar. 1	2
20	B	Edmund, K. & M.	3	3
21	C		5	4
22	D	Cecilia, V. & M.	Sus.	Titus 1
23	E	St. Clement I, B. of Rome & M.	Isa. 1	2–3
24	F		3	Phlm.
25	G	Catherine, V. & M.	5	Heb. 1
26	A		7	2
27	B		9	3
28	C		11	4
29	D	*fast*	13	5
30	E	*St. Andrew, A. & M.*	—	6

DECEMBER – MATTINS

December hath 31 days			*1 Lesson*	*2 Lesson*
1	F		Isa. 14	Acts 2
2	G		16	3
3	A		18	4
4	B		20–21	5
5	C		23	6
6	D	Nicholas, B. of Myra in Lycia	25	7:1-29
7	E		27	7:30-60
8	F	Conception of the Blessed V. Mary	29	8
9	G		31	9
10	A		33	10
11	B		35	11
12	C		37	12
13	D	Lucy, V. & M.	39	13
14	E		41	14
15	F		43	15
16	G	*O Sapientia*	45	16
17	A		47	17
18	B		49	18
19	C		51	19
20	D	*fast*	53	20
21	E	*St. Thomas, A. & M.*	—	21
22	F		55	22
23	G		57	23
24	A	*fast*	59	24
25	B	*Christmas Day*	—	—
26	C	*St. Stephen, First Martyr*	—	—
27	D	*St. John, A. & E.*	—	—
28	E	*Innocents' Day*	—	25
29	F		61	26
30	G		63	27
31	A	Silvester, B. of Rome	65	28

DECEMBER – EVENSONG

December hath 31 days			1 Lesson	2 Lesson
1	F		Isa. 15	Heb. 7
2	G		17	8
3	A		19	9
4	B		22	10
5	C		24	11
6	D	Nicholas, B. of Myra in Lycia	26	12
7	E		28	13
8	F	Conception of the Blessed V. Mary	30	Jas. 1
9	G		32	2
10	A		34	3
11	B		36	4
12	C		38	5
13	D	Lucy, V. & M.	40	1 Pet. 1
14	E		42	2
15	F		44	3
16	G	*O Sapientia*	46	4
17	A		48	5
18	B		50	2 Pet. 1
19	C		52	2
20	D	*fast*	54	3
21	E	*St. Thomas, A. & M.*	—	1 John 1
22	F		56	2
23	G		58	3
24	A	*fast*	60	4
25	B	*Christmas Day*	—	—
26	C	*St. Stephen, First Martyr*	—	—
27	D	*St. John, A. & E.*	—	—
28	E	*Innocents' Day*	—	5
29	F		62	2 John
30	G		64	3 John
31	A	Silvester, B. of Rome	66	Jude

The Order for Morning Prayer
Daily Throughout the Year.

¶ *At the beginning of Morning Prayer the minister shall read with a loud voice one or more of these sentences of the Scriptures that follow. And then he shall say that which is written after the sentences.*

WHEN the wicked man turneth away from his wickedness that he hath committed, and doeth that which is lawful and right, he shall save his soul alive. *Ezekiel 18:27.*

I acknowledge my transgressions, and my sin is ever before me. *Psalm 51:3.*

Hide thy face from my sins, and blot out all mine iniquities. *Psalm 51:9.*

The sacrifices of God are a broken spirit; a broken and a contrite heart, O God, thou wilt not despise. *Psalm 51:17.*

Rend your heart and not your garments, and turn unto the LORD your God, for he is gracious and merciful, slow to anger and of great kindness, and repenteth him of the evil. *Joel 2:13.*

To the Lord our God belong mercies and forgivenesses, though we have rebelled against him, neither have we obeyed the voice of the LORD our God, to walk in his laws which he set before us. *Daniel 9:9-10.*

O LORD, correct me, but with judgement; not in thine anger, lest thou bring me to nothing. *Jeremiah 10:24; Psalm 6:1.*

Repent ye, for the kingdom of heaven is at hand. *St. Matthew 3:2.*

I will arise and go to my father, and will say unto him, 'Father, I have sinned against heaven and before thee, and am no more worthy to be called thy son.' *St. Luke 15:18-19.*

Enter not into judgement with thy servant, O Lord, for in thy sight shall no man living be justified. *Psalm 143:2.*

If we say that we have no sin, we deceive ourselves, and the truth is not in us; but if we confess our sins, he is faithful and just to forgive us our sins, and to cleanse us from all unrighteousness. *1 John 1:8-9.*

DEARLY beloved brethren, the Scripture moveth us in sundry places to acknowledge and confess our manifold sins and wickedness, and that we should not dissemble nor cloak them before the face of almighty God our heavenly Father, but confess them with a humble, lowly, penitent, and obedient heart, to the end that we may obtain forgiveness of the same, by his infinite goodness and mercy. And although we ought at all times humbly to acknowledge our sins before God, yet ought we most chiefly so to do, when we assemble and meet together to render thanks for the great benefits that we have received at his hands, to set forth his most worthy praise, to hear his most holy word, and to ask those things which are requisite and necessary, as well for the body as the soul. Wherefore I pray and beseech you, as many as are here present, to accompany me with a pure heart and humble voice, unto the throne of the heavenly grace, saying after me,

MORNING PRAYER

¶ *A general confession to be said by the whole congregation after the minister, all kneeling.*

ALMIGHTY and most merciful Father, We have erred and strayed from thy ways like lost sheep. We have followed too much the devices and desires of our own hearts. We have offended against thy holy laws. We have left undone those things which we ought to have done; And we have done those things which we ought not to have done; And there is no health in us. But thou, O Lord, have mercy upon us, miserable offenders. Spare thou those, O God, who confess their faults. Restore thou those who are penitent, According to thy promises declared unto mankind In Christ Jesu our Lord. And grant, O most merciful Father, for his sake, That we may hereafter live a godly, righteous, and sober life, To the glory of thy holy name. Amen.

¶ *The absolution or remission of sins to be pronounced by the priest alone, standing, the people still kneeling.*

ALMIGHTY God, the Father of our Lord Jesus Christ, who desireth not the death of a sinner, but rather that he may turn from his wickedness and live, and hath given power and commandment to his ministers to declare and pronounce to his people, being penitent, the absolution and remission of their sins: He pardoneth and absolveth all those who truly repent and unfeignedly believe his holy gospel; wherefore let us beseech him to grant us true repentance and his Holy Spirit, that those things may please him which we do at this present, and that the

3

rest of our life hereafter may be pure and holy, so that at the last we may come to his eternal joy, through Jesus Christ our Lord.

¶ *The people shall answer here and at the end of all other prayers,* Amen.

¶ *Then the minister shall kneel and say the Lord's Prayer with an audible voice, the people also kneeling and repeating it with him, both here and wherever else it is used in divine service.*

OUR Father, who art in heaven, Hallowed be thy name. Thy kingdom come. Thy will be done, On earth as it is in heaven. Give us this day our daily bread. And forgive us our trespasses, As we forgive those who trespass against us. And lead us not into temptation, But deliver us from evil. For thine is the kingdom, the power, and the glory, For ever and ever. Amen.

¶ *Then likewise he shall say,*

O Lord, open thou our lips.

Answer.   And our mouth shall show forth thy praise.

Priest.   O God, make speed to save us.

Answer.   O Lord, make haste to help us.

¶ *Here, all standing up, the priest shall say,*

Glory be to the Father, and to the Son, and to the Holy Ghost;

Answer.   As it was in the beginning, is now, and ever shall be, world without end. Amen.

Priest. Praise ye the Lord.
Answer. The Lord's name be praised.

¶ *Then shall be said or sung this psalm following, except on Easter Day, upon which another anthem is appointed (p. 135), and on the nineteenth day of every month, when it is read in the ordinary course of the Psalms.*

Venite, exultemus Domino. Psalm 95.

O COME, let us sing unto the LORD; * let us heartily rejoice in the strength of our salvation.

Let us come before his presence with thanksgiving, * and show ourselves glad in him with psalms.

For the LORD is a great God, * and a great king above all gods.

In his hand are all the corners of the earth, * and the strength of the hills is his also.

The sea is his and he made it, * and his hands prepared the dry land.

O come, let us worship and fall down, * and kneel before the LORD our maker.

For he is the Lord our God, * and we are the people of his pasture and the sheep of his hand.

Today if ye will hear his voice – 'Harden not your hearts * as in the provocation, and as in the day of temptation in the wilderness,

When your fathers tempted me, * proved me, and saw my works.

Forty years long was I grieved with this generation and said, * "It is a people that do err in their hearts, for they have not known my ways",

Unto whom I sware in my wrath * that they should not enter into my rest.'

Glory be to the Father, and to the Son, * and to the Holy Ghost;

As it was in the beginning, is now, and ever shall be, * world without end. Amen.

¶ *Then shall follow the Psalms in order as they are appointed (p. 362). And at the end of every psalm throughout the year shall be repeated,*

Glory be to the Father, and to the Son, * and to the Holy Ghost;

Answer. As it was in the beginning, is now, and ever shall be, * world without end. Amen.

¶ *Then shall be read distinctly with an audible voice the first lesson, taken out of the Old Testament as is appointed in the calendar (p. xxxiv), except if proper lessons are assigned for that day (p. xxix). And he who readeth shall so stand and turn himself as to be best heard by those who are present. And after that shall be said or sung, in English, the hymn called Te Deum laudamus, daily throughout the year.*

¶ *Note that before every lesson the minister shall say,* Here beginneth *such a* chapter *(or verse of such a* chapter*) of such a book; and after every lesson,* Here endeth the first *(or the second)* lesson.

Te Deum laudamus.

WE praise thee, O God; * we acknowledge thee to be the Lord.

All the earth doth worship thee, * the Father everlasting.

To thee all angels cry aloud, * the heavens and all the powers therein;

To thee cherubim and seraphim * continually do cry,

'Holy, holy, holy, * Lord God of Sabaoth;

Heaven and earth are full of the majesty * of thy glory.'

The glorious company of the apostles * praise thee.

The goodly fellowship of the prophets * praise thee.

The noble army of martyrs * praise thee.

The holy church throughout all the world * doth acknowledge thee:

The Father * of an infinite majesty;

Thine honourable, true, * and only Son;

Also the Holy Ghost, * the Comforter.

THOU art the king of glory, * O Christ.

Thou art the everlasting Son * of the Father.

When thou tookest upon thee to deliver man, * thou didst not abhor the Virgin's womb.

When thou hadst overcome the sharpness of death, * thou didst open the kingdom of heaven to all believers.

Thou sittest at the right hand of God * in the glory of the Father.

We believe that thou shalt come * to be our judge.

We therefore pray thee, help thy servants, * whom thou hast redeemed with thy precious blood.

Make them to be numbered with thy saints * in glory everlasting.

O LORD, save thy people, * and bless thine heritage.
Govern them, * and lift them up for ever.
Day by day * we magnify thee,
And we worship thy name, * ever world without end.
Vouchsafe, O Lord, * to keep us this day without sin.
O Lord, have mercy upon us, * have mercy upon us.
O Lord, let thy mercy lighten upon us, * as our trust is in thee.
O Lord, in thee have I trusted; * let me never be confounded.

¶ *Or this canticle.*
Benedicite, omnia opera.

O ALL ye works of the Lord, bless ye the Lord: * praise him and magnify him for ever.

O YE angels of the Lord, bless ye the Lord: * praise him and magnify him for ever.
O ye heavens, bless ye the Lord: * praise him and magnify him for ever.
O ye waters that be above the firmament, bless ye the Lord: * praise him and magnify him for ever.
O all ye powers of the Lord, bless ye the Lord: * praise him and magnify him for ever.
O ye sun and moon, bless ye the Lord: * praise him and magnify him for ever.
O ye stars of heaven, bless ye the Lord: * praise him and magnify him for ever.
O ye showers and dew, bless ye the Lord: * praise him and magnify him for ever.

O ye winds of God, bless ye the Lord: * praise him and magnify him for ever.

O ye fire and heat, bless ye the Lord: * praise him and magnify him for ever.

O ye winter and summer, bless ye the Lord: * praise him and magnify him for ever.

O ye dews and frosts, bless ye the Lord: * praise him and magnify him for ever.

O ye frost and cold, bless ye the Lord: * praise him and magnify him for ever.

O ye ice and snow, bless ye the Lord: * praise him and magnify him for ever.

O ye nights and days, bless ye the Lord: * praise him and magnify him for ever.

O ye light and darkness, bless ye the Lord: * praise him and magnify him for ever.

O ye lightnings and clouds, bless ye the Lord: * praise him and magnify him for ever.

O LET the earth bless the Lord: * yea, let it praise him and magnify him for ever.

O ye mountains and hills, bless ye the Lord: * praise him and magnify him for ever.

O all ye green things upon the earth, bless ye the Lord: * praise him and magnify him for ever.

O ye wells, bless ye the Lord: * praise him and magnify him for ever.

O ye seas and floods, bless ye the Lord: * praise him and magnify him for ever.

O ye whales, and all that move in the waters, bless ye the Lord: * praise him and magnify him for ever.

O all ye fowls of the air, bless ye the Lord: * praise him and magnify him for ever.

O all ye beasts and cattle, bless ye the Lord: * praise him and magnify him for ever.

O ye children of men, bless ye the Lord: * praise him and magnify him for ever.

O LET Israel bless the Lord: * praise him and magnify him for ever.

O ye priests of the Lord, bless ye the Lord: * praise him and magnify him for ever.

O ye servants of the Lord, bless ye the Lord: * praise him and magnify him for ever.

O ye spirits and souls of the righteous, bless ye the Lord: * praise him and magnify him for ever.

O ye holy and humble men of heart, bless ye the Lord: * praise him and magnify him for ever.

O Ananias, Azarias, and Misael, bless ye the Lord: * praise him and magnify him for ever.

Glory be to the Father, and to the Son, * and to the Holy Ghost;

As it was in the beginning, is now, and ever shall be, * world without end. Amen.

¶ *Then shall be read in like manner the second lesson, taken out of the New Testament. And after that the hymn following, except when it shall happen to be read in the chapter for the day or for the gospel on Saint John the Baptist's Day.*

Benedictus. St. Luke 1:68-79.

Blessed be the Lord God of Israel, * for he hath visited and redeemed his people,

And hath raised up a mighty salvation for us * in the house of his servant David,

As he spake by the mouth of his holy prophets, * which have been since the world began:

That we should be saved from our enemies, * and from the hand of all that hate us,

To perform the mercy promised to our forefathers, * and to remember his holy covenant,

To perform the oath which he sware to our forefather Abraham: * that he would give us,

That we, being delivered out of the hand of our enemies, * might serve him without fear,

In holiness and righteousness before him * all the days of our life.

And thou, child, shalt be called the prophet of the Highest, * for thou shalt go before the face of the Lord to prepare his ways,

To give knowledge of salvation unto his people, * for the remission of their sins,

Through the tender mercy of our God, * whereby the dayspring from on high hath visited us,

To give light to them that sit in darkness and in the shadow of death, * and to guide our feet into the way of peace.

Glory be to the Father, and to the Son, * and to the Holy Ghost;

As it was in the beginning, is now, and ever shall be, * world without end. Amen.

MORNING PRAYER

¶ *Or instead Jubilate Deo, Psalm 100.*

¶ *Then shall be sung or said the Apostles' Creed by the minister and the people standing, except on such days as the Creed of Saint Athanasius is appointed to be read (p. 27).*

I BELIEVE in God the Father almighty, Maker of heaven and earth; And in Jesus Christ his only Son our Lord, Who was conceived by the Holy Ghost, Born of the Virgin Mary, Suffered under Pontius Pilate, Was crucified, dead, and buried. He descended into hell. The third day he rose again from the dead. He ascended into heaven, And sitteth on the right hand of God the Father almighty. From thence he shall come to judge the quick and the dead. I believe in the Holy Ghost, The holy catholic church, The communion of saints, The forgiveness of sins, The resurrection of the body, And the life everlasting. Amen.

¶ *After that, these prayers following, all devoutly kneeling, the minister first pronouncing with a loud voice,*

        The Lord be with you.

Answer.   And with thy spirit.

¶ *Minister.*
Let us pray.

Lord, have mercy upon us.
Christ, have mercy upon us.
Lord, have mercy upon us.

MORNING PRAYER

¶ *Then the minister, clerks, and people shall say the Lord's Prayer with a loud voice.*

OUR Father, who art in heaven, Hallowed be thy name. Thy kingdom come. Thy will be done, On earth as it is in heaven. Give us this day our daily bread. And forgive us our trespasses, As we forgive those who trespass against us. And lead us not into temptation, But deliver us from evil. Amen.

¶ *Then the priest, standing up, shall say,*

O Lord, show thy mercy upon us.

Answer. And grant us thy salvation.

Priest. O Lord, save them that rule.

Answer. And mercifully hear us when we call upon thee.

Priest. Endue thy ministers with righteousness.

Answer. And make thy chosen people joyful.

Priest. O Lord, save thy people.

Answer. And bless thine inheritance.

Priest. Give peace in our time, O Lord.

Answer. Because there is none other that fighteth for us, but only thou, O God.

Priest. O God, make clean our hearts within us.

Answer. And take not thy Holy Spirit from us.

¶ *Then shall follow three collects: The first of the day, which shall be the same that is appointed at the Communion (p. 49); the second for peace; the third for grace to live well. And the two last collects shall never alter, but daily be said at Morning Prayer throughout all the year, as followeth, all kneeling.*

13

The Second Collect, for Peace.

O GOD, who art the author of peace and lover of concord, in knowledge of whom standeth our eternal life, whose service is perfect freedom: Defend us thy humble servants in all assaults of our enemies, that we, surely trusting in thy defence, may not fear the power of any adversaries, through the might of Jesus Christ our Lord. *Amen.*

The Third Collect, for Grace.

O LORD, our heavenly Father, almighty and everlasting God, who hast safely brought us to the beginning of this day: Defend us in the same with thy mighty power, and grant that this day we fall into no sin, neither run into any kind of danger, but that all our doings may be ordered by thy governance, to do always what is righteous in thy sight, through Jesus Christ our Lord. *Amen.*

¶ *In choirs and places where they sing, here followeth the anthem. Then these four prayers following are to be read here, except when the Litany is read (p. 31), and then only the last two are to be read, as they are there placed.*

A Prayer for All Those in Civil Authority.

A LMIGHTY God, whose kingdom is everlasting and power infinite: Have mercy upon this whole land, and so rule the hearts of all in authority, [*especially* —,] that they, knowing whose ministers they are, may above all things seek thy honour and glory; and that we and all the people, duly considering whose authority they bear, may faithfully and obediently honour them, according to thy blessed word and ordinance, through Jesus Christ our Lord, who with thee and the Holy Ghost liveth and reigneth, ever one God, world without end. *Amen.*

¶ *Or this.*

ALMIGHTY Father, whose kingdom is everlasting: We beseech thee of thy mercy to direct and prosper the counsels of all those who bear authority in this land, that in humility and honesty they may faithfully serve the people committed to their charge. And grant, we pray thee, that religion and piety, peace and unity, truth and justice, may be established among us for all generations, through Jesus Christ our Lord. *Amen.*

A Prayer for the Clergy and People.

ALMIGHTY and everlasting God, who alone workest great marvels: Send down upon our bishops and pastors, and all congregations committed to their charge, the healthful Spirit of thy grace; and that they may truly please thee, pour upon them the continual dew of thy blessing. Grant this, O Lord, for the honour of our advocate and mediator, Jesus Christ. *Amen.*

A Prayer of Saint Chrysostom.

ALMIGHTY God, who hast given us grace at this time with one accord to make our common supplications unto thee, and dost promise that when two or three are gathered together in thy name, thou wilt grant their requests: Fulfil now, O Lord, the desires and petitions of thy servants, as may be most expedient for them, granting us in this world knowledge of thy truth, and in the world to come life everlasting. *Amen.*

2 Corinthians 13:14.

T HE grace of our Lord Jesus Christ, and the love of God, and the fellowship of the Holy Ghost, be with us all evermore. *Amen.*

¶ Here endeth the order of Morning
Prayer throughout the year.

¶ *Instead of* O Lord, save them that rule *may be said* O Lord, save the King.
¶ *Instead of the prayer for civil authorities may be said the prayers for the King's Majesty and the royal family (p. 48).*

The Order for Evening Prayer Daily Throughout the Year.

¶ *At the beginning of Evening Prayer the minister shall read with a loud voice one or more of these sentences of the Scriptures that follow. And then he shall say that which is written after the sentences.*

WHEN the wicked man turneth away from his wickedness that he hath committed, and doeth that which is lawful and right, he shall save his soul alive. *Ezekiel 18:27.*

I acknowledge my transgressions, and my sin is ever before me. *Psalm 51:3.*

Hide thy face from my sins, and blot out all mine iniquities. *Psalm 51:9.*

The sacrifices of God are a broken spirit; a broken and a contrite heart, O God, thou wilt not despise. *Psalm 51:17.*

Rend your heart and not your garments, and turn unto the LORD your God, for he is gracious and merciful, slow to anger and of great kindness, and repenteth him of the evil. *Joel 2:13.*

To the Lord our God belong mercies and forgivenesses, though we have rebelled against him, neither have we obeyed the voice of the LORD our God, to walk in his laws which he set before us. *Daniel 9:9-10.*

O LORD, correct me, but with judgement; not in thine anger, lest thou bring me to nothing. *Jeremiah 10:24; Psalm 6:1.*

Repent ye, for the kingdom of heaven is at hand. *St. Matthew 3:2.*

I will arise and go to my father, and will say unto him, 'Father, I have sinned against heaven and before thee, and am no more worthy to be called thy son.' *St. Luke 15:18-19.*

Enter not into judgement with thy servant, O Lord, for in thy sight shall no man living be justified. *Psalm 143:2.*

If we say that we have no sin, we deceive ourselves, and the truth is not in us; but if we confess our sins, he is faithful and just to forgive us our sins, and to cleanse us from all unrighteousness. *1 John 1:8-9.*

D EARLY beloved brethren, the Scripture moveth us in sundry places to acknowledge and confess our manifold sins and wickedness, and that we should not dissemble nor cloak them before the face of almighty God our heavenly Father, but confess them with a humble, lowly, penitent, and obedient heart, to the end that we may obtain forgiveness of the same, by his infinite goodness and mercy. And although we ought at all times humbly to acknowledge our sins before God, yet ought we most chiefly so to do, when we assemble and meet together to render thanks for the great benefits that we have received at his hands, to set forth his most worthy praise, to hear his most holy word, and to ask those things which are requisite and necessary, as well for the body as the soul. Wherefore I pray and beseech you, as many as are here present, to accompany me with a pure heart and humble voice, unto the throne of the heavenly grace, saying after me,

¶ *A general confession to be said by the whole congregation after the minister, all kneeling.*

ALMIGHTY and most merciful Father, We have erred and strayed from thy ways like lost sheep. We have followed too much the devices and desires of our own hearts. We have offended against thy holy laws. We have left undone those things which we ought to have done; And we have done those things which we ought not to have done; And there is no health in us. But thou, O Lord, have mercy upon us, miserable offenders. Spare thou those, O God, who confess their faults. Restore thou those who are penitent, According to thy promises declared unto mankind In Christ Jesu our Lord. And grant, O most merciful Father, for his sake, That we may hereafter live a godly, righteous, and sober life, To the glory of thy holy name. Amen.

¶ *The absolution or remission of sins to be pronounced by the priest alone, standing, the people still kneeling.*

ALMIGHTY God, the Father of our Lord Jesus Christ, who desireth not the death of a sinner, but rather that he may turn from his wickedness and live, and hath given power and commandment to his ministers to declare and pronounce to his people, being penitent, the absolution and remission of their sins: He pardoneth and absolveth all those who truly repent and unfeignedly believe his holy gospel; wherefore let us beseech him to grant us true repentance and his Holy Spirit, that those things may please him which we do at this present, and that the rest of our life hereafter may be pure and holy, so that at the last we may come to his eternal joy, through Jesus Christ our Lord. *Amen.*

¶ *Then the minister shall kneel and say the Lord's Prayer, the people also kneeling and repeating it with him.*

OUR Father, who art in heaven, Hallowed be thy name. Thy kingdom come. Thy will be done, On earth as it is in heaven. Give us this day our daily bread. And forgive us our trespasses, As we forgive those who trespass against us. And lead us not into temptation, But deliver us from evil. For thine is the kingdom, the power, and the glory, For ever and ever. Amen.

¶ *Then likewise he shall say,*

O Lord, open thou our lips.

Answer. And our mouth shall show forth thy praise.
Priest. O God, make speed to save us.
Answer. O Lord, make haste to help us.

¶ *Here, all standing up, the priest shall say,*

Glory be to the Father, and to the Son, and to the Holy Ghost;

Answer. As it was in the beginning, is now, and ever shall be, world without end. Amen.
Priest. Praise ye the Lord.
Answer. The Lord's name be praised.

¶ *Then shall be said or sung the Psalms in order as they are appointed (p. 362). Then a lesson from the Old Testament, as is appointed (pp. xxix, xxxiv). And after that Magnificat (or the song of the Blessed Virgin Mary) in English, as followeth.*

Magnificat. St. Luke 1:46-55.

MY soul doth magnify the Lord, * and my spirit hath rejoiced in God my saviour.

For he hath regarded * the lowliness of his handmaiden.

For behold, from henceforth * all generations shall call me blessed.

For he that is mighty hath magnified me, * and holy is his name.

And his mercy is on them that fear him * throughout all generations.

He hath showed strength with his arm; * he hath scattered the proud in the imagination of their hearts.

He hath put down the mighty from their seat, * and hath exalted the humble and meek.

He hath filled the hungry with good things, * and the rich he hath sent empty away.

He remembering his mercy hath holpen his servant Israel, * as he promised to our forefathers, Abraham and his seed for ever.

Glory be to the Father, and to the Son, * and to the Holy Ghost;

As it was in the beginning, is now, and ever shall be, * world without end. Amen.

¶ *Or Cantate Domino, Psalm 98, except on the nineteenth day of the month, when it is read in the ordinary course of the Psalms.*

¶ *Then a lesson of the New Testament, as it is appointed. And after that Nunc dimittis (or the song of Simeon) in English, as followeth.*

Nunc dimittis. St. Luke 2:29-32.

LORD, now lettest thou thy servant depart in peace, * according to thy word.

For mine eyes have seen * thy salvation,

Which thou hast prepared * before the face of all people,

To be a light to lighten the Gentiles, * and to be the glory of thy people Israel.

Glory be to the Father, and to the Son, * and to the Holy Ghost;

As it was in the beginning, is now, and ever shall be, * world without end. Amen.

¶ *Or else Deus misereatur, Psalm 67, except on the twelfth day of the month.*

¶ *Then shall be said or sung the Apostles' Creed by the minister and the people, standing.*

I BELIEVE in God the Father almighty, Maker of heaven and earth; And in Jesus Christ his only Son our Lord, Who was conceived by the Holy Ghost, Born of the Virgin Mary, Suffered under Pontius Pilate, Was crucified, dead, and buried. He descended into hell. The third day he rose again from the dead. He ascended into heaven, And sitteth on the right hand of God the Father almighty. From thence he shall come to judge the quick and the dead. I believe in the Holy Ghost, The holy catholic church, The communion of saints, The forgiveness of sins, The resurrection of the body, And the life everlasting. Amen.

EVENING PRAYER

¶ *After that, these prayers following, all devoutly kneeling, the minister first pronouncing with a loud voice,*
        The Lord be with you.
Answer.   And with thy spirit.

        ¶ *Minister.*
        Let us pray.

        Lord, have mercy upon us.
        Christ, have mercy upon us.
        Lord, have mercy upon us.

¶ *Then the minister, clerks, and people shall say the Lord's Prayer with a loud voice.*
Oᴜʀ Father, who art in heaven, Hallowed be thy name. Thy kingdom come. Thy will be done, On earth as it is in heaven. Give us this day our daily bread. And forgive us our trespasses, As we forgive those who trespass against us. And lead us not into temptation, But deliver us from evil. Amen.

¶ *Then the priest standing up shall say,*
        O Lord, show thy mercy upon us.
Answer.   And grant us thy salvation.
Priest.   O Lord, save them that rule.
Answer.   And mercifully hear us when we call upon thee.
Priest.   Endue thy ministers with righteousness.
Answer.   And make thy chosen people joyful.
Priest.   O Lord, save thy people.
Answer.   And bless thine inheritance.

Priest.	Give peace in our time, O Lord.
Answer.	Because there is none other that fighteth for us, but only thou, O God.
Priest.	O God, make clean our hearts within us.
Answer.	And take not thy Holy Spirit from us.

¶ *Then shall follow three collects: The first of the day (p. 49), the second for peace, the third for aid against all perils, as hereafter followeth, which last two collects shall be daily said at Evening Prayer without alteration.*

The Second Collect at Evening Prayer.

O GOD, from whom all holy desires, all good counsels, and all just works do proceed: Give unto thy servants that peace which the world cannot give, that both our hearts may be set to obey thy commandments, and also that by thee, we, being defended from the fear of our enemies, may pass our time in rest and quietness, through the merits of Jesus Christ our Saviour. *Amen.*

The Third Collect, for Aid against All Perils.

L IGHTEN our darkness, we beseech thee, O Lord, and by thy great mercy defend us from all perils and dangers of this night, for the love of thy only Son, our Saviour, Jesus Christ. *Amen.*

———————

¶ *In choirs and places where they sing, here followeth the anthem.*

EVENING PRAYER

A Prayer for All Those in Civil Authority.

ALMIGHTY God, whose kingdom is everlasting and power infinite: Have mercy upon this whole land, and so rule the hearts of all in authority, [*especially —,*] that they, knowing whose ministers they are, may above all things seek thy honour and glory; and that we and all the people, duly considering whose authority they bear, may faithfully and obediently honour them, according to thy blessed word and ordinance, through Jesus Christ our Lord, who with thee and the Holy Ghost liveth and reigneth, ever one God, world without end. *Amen.*

¶ *Or this.*

ALMIGHTY Father, whose kingdom is everlasting: We beseech thee of thy mercy to direct and prosper the counsels of all those who bear authority in this land, that in humility and honesty they may faithfully serve the people committed to their charge. And grant, we pray thee, that religion and piety, peace and unity, truth and justice, may be established among us for all generations, through Jesus Christ our Lord. *Amen.*

A Prayer for the Clergy and People.

ALMIGHTY and everlasting God, who alone workest great marvels: Send down upon our bishops and pastors, and all congregations committed to their charge, the healthful Spirit of thy grace; and that they may truly please thee, pour upon them the continual dew of thy blessing. Grant this, O Lord, for the honour of our advocate and mediator, Jesus Christ. *Amen.*

EVENING PRAYER

A Prayer of Saint Chrysostom.

ALMIGHTY God, who hast given us grace at this time with one accord to make our common supplications unto thee, and dost promise that when two or three are gathered together in thy name, thou wilt grant their requests: Fulfil now, O Lord, the desires and petitions of thy servants, as may be most expedient for them, granting us in this world knowledge of thy truth, and in the world to come life everlasting. *Amen.*

2 Corinthians 13:14.

THE grace of our Lord Jesus Christ, and the love of God, and the fellowship of the Holy Ghost, be with us all evermore. *Amen.*

¶ *Here endeth the order of Evening Prayer throughout the year.*

¶ *Instead of* O Lord, save them that rule *may be said* O Lord, save the King.
¶ *Instead of the prayer for civil authorities may be said the prayers for the King's Majesty and the royal family (p. 48).*

At Morning Prayer.

¶ Upon these feasts, Christmas Day, the Epiphany, Saint Matthias, Easter Day, Ascension Day, Whitsunday, Saint John the Baptist, Saint James, Saint Bartholomew, Saint Matthew, Saint Simon and Saint Jude, Saint Andrew, and upon Trinity Sunday, shall be sung or said at Morning Prayer, instead of the Apostles' Creed, this confession of our Christian faith, commonly called the Creed of Saint Athanasius, by the minister and people, standing.

Quicunque vult.

WHOSOEVER will be saved, * before all things it is necessary that he hold the catholic faith.

Which faith, except every one do keep whole and undefiled, * without doubt he shall perish everlastingly.

And the catholic faith is this: * That we worship one God in Trinity, and Trinity in Unity;

Neither confounding the persons, * nor dividing the substance.

For there is one person of the Father, another of the Son, * and another of the Holy Ghost.

But the Godhead of the Father, of the Son, and of the Holy Ghost is all one; * the glory equal, the majesty co-eternal.

Such as the Father is, such is the Son, * and such is the Holy Ghost:

The Father uncreated, the Son uncreated, * and the Holy Ghost uncreated;

The Father incomprehensible, the Son incomprehensible, * and the Holy Ghost incomprehensible;

The Father eternal, the Son eternal, * and the Holy Ghost eternal.

And yet they are not three eternals, * but one eternal;

As also there are not three incomprehensibles, nor three uncreated; * but one uncreated, and one incomprehensible.

So likewise the Father is almighty, the Son almighty, * and the Holy Ghost almighty.

And yet they are not three almighties, * but one almighty.

So the Father is God, the Son is God, * and the Holy Ghost is God.

And yet they are not three Gods, * but one God.

So likewise the Father is Lord, the Son Lord, * and the Holy Ghost Lord.

And yet not three Lords, * but one Lord.

For like as we are compelled by the Christian verity * to acknowledge every person by himself to be God and Lord,

So are we forbidden by the catholic religion * to say there are three Gods or three Lords.

The Father is made of none, * neither created, nor begotten.

The Son is of the Father alone, * not made, nor created, but begotten.

The Holy Ghost is of the Father and of the Son, * neither made, nor created, nor begotten, but proceeding.

So there is one Father, not three Fathers; one Son, not three Sons; * one Holy Ghost, not three Holy Ghosts.

And in this Trinity none is before or after other; * none is greater or less than another;

But the whole three persons are coeternal together * and coequal.

So that in all things, as is aforesaid, * the Unity in Trinity and the Trinity in Unity is to be worshipped.

He therefore that will be saved * must thus think of the Trinity.

FURTHERMORE, it is necessary to everlasting salvation * that he also believe rightly the incarnation of our Lord Jesus Christ.

For the right faith is that we believe and confess * that our Lord Jesus Christ, the Son of God, is God and man;

God, of the substance of the Father, begotten before the worlds; * and man, of the substance of his mother, born in the world;

Perfect God and perfect man, * of a reasonable soul and human flesh subsisting;

Equal to the Father as touching his Godhead, * and inferior to the Father as touching his manhood;

Who although he is God and man, * yet he is not two, but one Christ;

One, not by conversion of the Godhead into flesh, * but by taking of the manhood into God;

One altogether, not by confusion of substance, * but by unity of person.

For as the reasonable soul and flesh is one man, * so God and man is one Christ,

Who suffered for our salvation, * descended into hell, rose again the third day from the dead.

He ascended into heaven; he sitteth on the right hand of the Father, God almighty, * from whence he shall come to judge the quick and the dead,

At whose coming all men shall rise again with their bodies, * and shall give account for their own works,

And they that have done good shall go into life everlasting, * and they that have done evil, into everlasting fire.

This is the catholic faith, * which except a man believe faithfully, he cannot be saved.

Glory be to the Father, and to the Son, * and to the Holy Ghost;

As it was in the beginning, is now, and ever shall be, * world without end. Amen.

The Litany.

¶ *Here followeth the Litany, or General Supplication, to be sung or said after Morning Prayer upon Sundays, Wednesdays, and Fridays, and at other times when it shall be commanded by the ordinary.*

O GOD the Father of heaven, have mercy upon us miserable sinners.

O God the Father of heaven, have mercy upon us miserable sinners.

O God the Son, Redeemer of the world, have mercy upon us miserable sinners.

O God the Son, Redeemer of the world, have mercy upon us miserable sinners.

O God the Holy Ghost, proceeding from the Father and the Son, have mercy upon us miserable sinners.

O God the Holy Ghost, proceeding from the Father and the Son, have mercy upon us miserable sinners.

O holy, blessed, and glorious Trinity, three persons and one God, have mercy upon us miserable sinners.

O holy, blessed, and glorious Trinity, three persons and one God, have mercy upon us miserable sinners.

REMEMBER not, Lord, our offences, nor the offences of our forefathers; neither take thou vengeance of our sins. Spare us, good Lord; spare thy people, whom thou hast redeemed with thy most precious blood, and be not angry with us for ever.

Spare us, good Lord.

THE LITANY

FROM all evil and mischief; from sin, from the crafts and assaults of the devil; from thy wrath, and from everlasting damnation,

Good Lord, deliver us.

From all blindness of heart; from pride, vainglory, and hypocrisy; from envy, hatred, and malice, and all uncharitableness,

Good Lord, deliver us.

From fornication, and all other deadly sin; and from all the deceits of the world, the flesh, and the devil,

Good Lord, deliver us.

From lightning and tempest; from plague, pestilence, and famine; from battle and murder, and from sudden death,

Good Lord, deliver us.

From all sedition, privy conspiracy, and rebellion; from all false doctrine, heresy, and schism; from hardness of heart, and contempt of thy word and commandment,

Good Lord, deliver us.

By the mystery of thy holy incarnation; by thy holy nativity and circumcision; by thy baptism, fasting, and temptation,

Good Lord, deliver us.

By thine agony and bloody sweat; by thy cross and passion; by thy precious death and burial; by thy glorious resurrection and ascension; and by the coming of the Holy Ghost,

Good Lord, deliver us.

In all time of our tribulation, in all time of our wealth, in the hour of death, and in the day of judgement,

Good Lord, deliver us.

W E sinners do beseech thee to hear us, O Lord God,
and that it may please thee to rule and govern thy
holy church universal in the right way,
We beseech thee to hear us, good Lord.
That it may please thee to rule the heart of thy servant,
—, and all others in authority, that under them we may
lead a quiet and peaceable life in all godliness and honesty,
We beseech thee to hear us, good Lord.
That it may please thee to be their defender and keeper,
We beseech thee to hear us, good Lord.
That it may please thee to endue the *legislators,* and the
ministers of state, with grace, wisdom, and understanding,
We beseech thee to hear us, good Lord.
That it may please thee to bless and keep the *judges* and
magistrates, giving them grace to execute justice and to
maintain truth,
We beseech thee to hear us, good Lord.
That it may please thee to illuminate all bishops, priests,
and deacons, with true knowledge and understanding of
thy word; and that both by their preaching and living they
may set it forth and show it accordingly,
We beseech thee to hear us, good Lord.
That it may please thee to bless and keep all thy people,
We beseech thee to hear us, good Lord.
That it may please thee to give to all nations unity, peace,
and concord,
We beseech thee to hear us, good Lord.
That it may please thee to give us a heart to love and
dread thee, and diligently to live after thy commandments,
We beseech thee to hear us, good Lord.

That it may please thee to give to all thy people increase of grace, to hear meekly thy word, and to receive it with pure affection, and to bring forth the fruits of the Spirit,

We beseech thee to hear us, good Lord.

That it may please thee to bring into the way of truth all such as have erred and are deceived,

We beseech thee to hear us, good Lord.

That it may please thee to strengthen such as do stand, and to comfort and help the weak-hearted, and to raise up those who fall, and finally to beat down Satan under our feet,

We beseech thee to hear us, good Lord.

That it may please thee to succour, help, and comfort all who are in danger, necessity, and tribulation,

We beseech thee to hear us, good Lord.

That it may please thee to preserve all who travel by land, by water, or by air; all women labouring with child, all sick persons, and young children, and to show thy pity upon all prisoners and captives,

We beseech thee to hear us, good Lord.

That it may please thee to defend and provide for the fatherless children, and widows, and all who are desolate and oppressed,

We beseech thee to hear us, good Lord.

That it may please thee to have mercy upon all men,

We beseech thee to hear us, good Lord.

That it may please thee to forgive our enemies, persecutors, and slanderers, and to turn their hearts,

We beseech thee to hear us, good Lord.

That it may please thee to give and preserve to our use

the kindly fruits of the earth, so that in due time we may enjoy them,

We beseech thee to hear us, good Lord.

That it may please thee to give us true repentance; to forgive us all our sins, negligences, and ignorances; and to endue us with the grace of thy Holy Spirit, to amend our lives according to thy holy word,

We beseech thee to hear us, good Lord.

Son of God, we beseech thee to hear us.

Son of God, we beseech thee to hear us.

O Lamb of God, that takest away the sins of the world,

Grant us thy peace.

O Lamb of God, that takest away the sins of the world,

Have mercy upon us.

O Christ, hear us.

O Christ, hear us.

Lord, have mercy upon us.

Lord, have mercy upon us.

Christ, have mercy upon us.

Christ, have mercy upon us.

Lord, have mercy upon us.

Lord, have mercy upon us.

¶ *Then shall the priest and the people say the Lord's Prayer.*

OUR Father, who art in heaven, Hallowed be thy name. Thy kingdom come. Thy will be done, On earth as it is in heaven. Give us this day our daily bread. And forgive us our trespasses, As we forgive those who trespass against us. And lead us not into temptation, But deliver us from evil. Amen.

THE LITANY

Priest. O Lord, deal not with us after our sins,
Answer. Neither reward us after our iniquities.

Let us pray.

O GOD, merciful Father, who despisest not the sighing of a contrite heart, nor the desire of such as are sorrowful: Mercifully assist our prayers that we make before thee in all our troubles and adversities, whensoever they oppress us, and graciously hear us, that those evils which the craft and subtlety of the devil or man worketh against us be brought to nought, and by the providence of thy goodness they may be dispersed, that we thy servants, being hurt by no persecutions, may evermore give thanks unto thee in thy holy church, through Jesus Christ our Lord.
O Lord, arise, help us, and deliver us for thy name's sake.

O GOD, we have heard with our ears, and our fathers have declared unto us, the noble works that thou didst in their days, and in the old time before them.
O Lord, arise, help us, and deliver us for thine honour.

G LORY be to the Father, and to the Son, and to the Holy Ghost;
As it was in the beginning, is now, and ever shall be, world without end. Amen.
From our enemies defend us, O Christ.
Graciously look upon our afflictions.
Pitifully behold the sorrows of our hearts.
Mercifully forgive the sins of thy people.

Favourably with mercy hear our prayers.
O Son of David, have mercy upon us.
Both now and ever vouchsafe to hear us, O Christ.
*Graciously hear us, O Christ; graciously hear us, O Lord
Christ.*

Priest.   O Lord, let thy mercy be showed upon us,
Answer.   As we do put our trust in thee.

Let us pray.

WE humbly beseech thee, O Father, mercifully to look
upon our infirmities, and for the glory of thy name,
turn from us all those evils that we most justly have deserved, and grant that in all our troubles we may put our
whole trust and confidence in thy mercy, and evermore
serve thee in holiness and pureness of living, to thy honour and glory, through our only mediator and advocate,
Jesus Christ our Lord. *Amen.*

A Prayer of Saint Chrysostom.
ALMIGHTY God, who hast given us grace at this time
with one accord to make our common supplications
unto thee, and dost promise that when two or three are
gathered together in thy name, thou wilt grant their requests: Fulfil now, O Lord, the desires and petitions of thy
servants, as may be most expedient for them, granting us
in this world knowledge of thy truth, and in the world to
come life everlasting. *Amen.*

THE LITANY

2 Corinthians 13:14.

THE grace of our Lord Jesus Christ, and the love of God, and the fellowship of the Holy Ghost, be with us all evermore. *Amen.*

¶ *Here endeth the Litany.*

❧

¶ *Instead of the two suffrages beginning* That it may please thee to rule the heart, *&c. (p. 33) may be said the suffrages following:*

That it may please thee to keep and strengthen in the true worshipping of thee, in righteousness and holiness of life, thy servant *CHARLES,* our most gracious King and Governor,

We beseech thee to hear us, good Lord.

That it may please thee to rule his heart in thy faith, fear, and love, and that he may evermore entrust his way to thee, and ever seek thy honour and glory,

We beseech thee to hear us, good Lord.

That it may please thee to be his defender and keeper, giving him the victory over all his enemies,

We beseech thee to hear us, good Lord.

That it may please thee to bless and preserve Queen *Camilla, William* Prince of *Wales,* the Princess of *Wales,* and all the royal family,

We beseech thee to hear us, good Lord.

Prayers & Thanksgivings upon Several Occasions

*to be used before the two final
prayers of the Litany or of
Morning and Evening Prayer.*

Prayers.
For Rain.

O GOD, heavenly Father, who by thy Son Jesus Christ hast promised, to all those who seek thy kingdom and the righteousness thereof, all things necessary to their bodily sustenance: Send us, we beseech thee, in this our necessity, such moderate rain and showers, that we may receive the fruits of the earth to our comfort and to thy honour, through Jesus Christ our Lord. *Amen.*

For Fair Weather.

O ALMIGHTY Lord God, who for the sin of man didst once drown all the world, except eight persons, and afterward of thy great mercy didst promise never to destroy it so again: We humbly beseech thee, that although we for our iniquities have worthily deserved a plague of rain and waters, yet upon our true repentance thou wilt send us such weather, as that we may receive the fruits of the earth in due season, and learn both by thy punishment to amend our lives, and for thy clemency to give thee praise and glory, through Jesus Christ our Lord. *Amen.*

PRAYERS

In a Time of Dearth and Famine.

O GOD, heavenly Father, whose gift it is that the rain doth fall, the earth is fruitful, beasts increase, and fishes do multiply: Behold, we beseech thee, the afflictions of thy people, and grant that the scarcity and dearth, which we now most justly suffer for our iniquity, may through thy goodness be mercifully turned into abundance and plenty, for the love of Jesus Christ our Lord, to whom, with thee and the Holy Ghost, be all honour and glory, now and for ever. *Amen.*

¶ *Or this.*

O GOD, merciful Father, who, in the time of Elisha the prophet, didst suddenly in Samaria turn great scarcity and dearth into plenty and abundance: Have mercy upon us, that we, who are now for our sins punished with like adversity, may likewise find a seasonable relief. Increase the fruits of the earth by thy heavenly benediction, and grant that we, receiving thy bountiful liberality, may use the same to thy glory, the relief of those who are needy, and our own comfort, through Jesus Christ our Lord. *Amen.*

In a Time of War and Tumults.

O ALMIGHTY God, King of all kings, and governor of all things, whose power no creature is able to resist, to whom it belongeth justly to punish sinners, and to be merciful to those who truly repent: Save and deliver us, we humbly beseech thee, from the hands of our enemies. Abate their pride, assuage their malice, and confound their devices, that we, being armed with thy defence, may be preserved evermore from all perils, to glorify thee, who art the only giver of all victory, through the merits of thy only Son, Jesus Christ our Lord. *Amen.*

In a Time of Any General Plague or Sickness.

O ALMIGHTY God, who in thy wrath didst send a plague upon thine own people in the wilderness, for their obstinate rebellion against Moses and Aaron; and also, in the time of King David, didst slay with the plague of pestilence threescore and ten thousand, and yet remembering thy mercy didst save the rest: Have pity upon us miserable sinners, who now are visited with great sickness and mortality, that as thou didst then accept an atonement, and didst command the destroying angel to cease from punishing, so it may now please thee to withdraw from us this plague and grievous sickness, through Jesus Christ our Lord. *Amen.*

In the Ember Weeks.
¶ *To be said every day for those who are
to be admitted into holy orders.*

A LMIGHTY God, our heavenly Father, who hast purchased to thyself a universal church by the precious blood of thy dear Son: Mercifully look upon the same, and at this time so guide and govern the minds of thy servants, the bishops and pastors of thy flock, that they may lay hands suddenly on no man, but faithfully and wisely make choice of fit persons to serve in the sacred ministry of thy church. And to those who shall be ordained to any holy function, give thy grace and heavenly benediction, that both by their life and doctrine they may set forth thy glory, and set forward the salvation of all men, through Jesus Christ our Lord. *Amen.*

¶ *Or this.*

A LMIGHTY God, the giver of all good gifts, who of thy divine providence hast appointed divers orders in thy church: Give thy grace, we humbly beseech thee, to all those who are to be [or *who are this day*] called to any office and administration in the same, and so replenish them with the truth of thy doctrine, and endue them with innocency of life, that they may faithfully serve before thee, to the glory of thy great name, and the benefit of thy holy church, through Jesus Christ our Lord. *Amen.*

A Prayer that May Be Said after Any of the Former.

O GOD, whose nature and property is ever to have mercy and to forgive: Receive our humble petitions, and though we be tied and bound with the chain of our sins, yet let the pity of thy great mercy loose us, for the honour of Jesus Christ, our mediator and advocate. *Amen.*

A Prayer for the Legislature.
¶ *To be read during their session.*

M OST gracious God, we humbly beseech thee, as for this *nation* in general, so especially for the *legislature* at this time assembled, that thou wouldest be pleased to direct and prosper all their consultations, to the advancement of thy glory; the good of thy church; and the safety, honour, and welfare of *this people,* that all things may be so ordered and settled by their endeavours, upon the best and surest foundations, that peace and happiness, truth and justice, religion and piety, may be established among us for all generations. These and all other necessaries, for them, for us, and thy whole church, we humbly beg in the name and mediation of Jesus Christ, our most blessed Lord and Saviour. *Amen.*

A Collect or Prayer for All Conditions of Men.
¶ *To be used when the Litany is*
not appointed to be said.

O GOD, the creator and preserver of all mankind, we humbly beseech thee for all sorts and conditions of men, that thou wouldest be pleased to make thy ways known unto them, thy saving health unto all nations. More especially we pray for the good estate of the catholic church, that it may be so guided and governed by thy good Spirit, that all who profess and call themselves Christians may be led into the way of truth, and hold the faith in unity of spirit, in the bond of peace, and in righteousness of life. Finally, we commend to thy fatherly goodness all those who are any ways afflicted or distressed, in mind, body, or estate, [* *especially those for whom our prayers are desired,*] that it may please thee to comfort and relieve them, according to their several necessities, giving them patience under their sufferings, and a happy issue out of all their afflictions. And this we beg for Jesus Christ's sake. *Amen.*

* *To be said when any desire the prayers of the congregation.*

THANKSGIVINGS

Thanksgivings.

A General Thanksgiving.

ALMIGHTY God, Father of all mercies, we, thine unworthy servants, do give thee most humble and hearty thanks for all thy goodness and loving-kindness to us and to all men, [*particularly to those who desire now to offer up their praises and thanksgivings for thy late mercies vouchsafed unto them]. We bless thee for our creation,

To be said when any who have been prayed for desire to return praise.

preservation, and all the blessings of this life, but above all, for thine inestimable love in the redemption of the world by our Lord Jesus Christ, for the means of grace, and for the hope of glory. And, we beseech thee, give us that due sense of all thy mercies, that our hearts may be unfeignedly thankful, and that we show forth thy praise, not only with our lips, but in our lives, by giving up ourselves to thy service, and by walking before thee in holiness and righteousness all our days, through Jesus Christ our Lord, to whom, with thee and the Holy Ghost, be all honour and glory, world without end. *Amen.*

For Rain.

O GOD, our heavenly Father, who by thy gracious providence dost cause the former and the latter rain to descend upon the earth, that it may bring forth fruit for the use of man: We give thee humble thanks that it hath pleased thee, in our great necessity, to send us at the last a joyful rain upon thine inheritance, and to refresh it when it was dry, to the great comfort of us thy unworthy

44

servants, and to the glory of thy holy name, through thy mercies in Jesus Christ our Lord. *Amen.*

For Fair Weather.

O LORD God, who hast justly humbled us by thy late plague of immoderate rain and waters, and in thy mercy hast relieved and comforted our souls by this seasonable and blessed change of weather: We praise and glorify thy holy name for this thy mercy, and will always declare thy loving-kindness from generation to generation, through Jesus Christ our Lord. *Amen.*

For Plenty.

O MOST merciful Father, who of thy gracious goodness hast heard the devout prayers of thy church, and turned our dearth and scarcity into abundance and plenty: We give thee humble thanks for this thy special bounty, beseeching thee to continue thy loving-kindness unto us, that our land may yield us her fruits of increase, to thy glory and our comfort, through Jesus Christ our Lord. *Amen.*

For Peace and Deliverance from Our Enemies.

O ALMIGHTY God, who art a strong tower of defence unto thy servants against the face of their enemies: We yield thee praise and thanksgiving for our deliverance from those great and imminent dangers with which we were compassed. We acknowledge that it was of thy goodness that we were not delivered over as a prey unto them, beseeching thee still to continue these thy mercies towards us, that all the world may know that thou art our saviour and mighty deliverer, through Jesus Christ our Lord. *Amen.*

For Restoring Public Peace at Home.

O ETERNAL God, our heavenly Father, who alone makest men to be of one mind in a house, and stillest the outrage of a violent and unruly people: We bless thy holy name, that it hath pleased thee to appease the unhappy tumults which have been lately raised up amongst us, most humbly beseeching thee to grant to all of us grace, that we may henceforth obediently walk in thy holy commandments, and, leading a quiet and peaceable life in all godliness and honesty, may continually offer unto thee our sacrifice of praise and thanksgiving for these thy mercies towards us, through Jesus Christ our Lord. *Amen.*

For Deliverance from Plague or General Sickness.

O LORD God, who hast wounded us for our sins, and consumed us for our transgressions, by thy late heavy and dreadful visitation, and now, in the midst of judgement remembering mercy, hast redeemed our souls from the jaws of death: We offer unto thy fatherly goodness ourselves, our souls and bodies, which thou hast delivered, to be a living sacrifice unto thee, always praising and magnifying thy mercies in the midst of thy church, through Jesus Christ our Lord. *Amen.*

¶ Or this.

W E humbly acknowledge before thee, O most merciful Father, that all the punishments which are threatened in thy law might justly have fallen upon us, by reason of our manifold transgressions and hardness of heart, yet seeing it hath pleased thee of thy tender mercy, upon our weak and unworthy humiliation, to assuage the contagious sickness with which we lately have been sore afflicted, and to restore the voice of joy and health into our dwellings. We offer unto thy Divine Majesty the sacrifice of praise and thanksgiving, lauding and magnifying thy glorious name for this thy preservation and providence over us, through Jesus Christ our Lord. *Amen.*

Collects for the King.

ALMIGHTY God, whose kingdom is everlasting and power infinite: Have mercy upon the whole church, and so rule the heart of thy chosen servant *CHARLES,* our King and Governor, that he, knowing whose minister he is, may above all things seek thy honour and glory; and that we and all his subjects, duly considering whose authority he hath, may faithfully serve, honour, and humbly obey him, according to thy blessed word and ordinance, through Jesus Christ our Lord, who with thee and the Holy Ghost liveth and reigneth, ever one God, world without end. *Amen.*

ALMIGHTY and everlasting God, we are taught by thy holy word that the hearts of kings are in thy rule and governance, and that thou dost dispose and turn them as it seemeth best to thy godly wisdom: We humbly beseech thee so to dispose and govern the heart of *CHARLES* thy servant, our King and Governor, that in all his thoughts, words, and works, he may ever seek thy honour and glory, and study to preserve thy people committed to his charge, in wealth, peace, and godliness. Grant this, O merciful Father, for thy dear Son's sake, Jesus Christ our Lord. *Amen.*

A Prayer for the King's Majesty.

O LORD, our heavenly Father, the high and mighty, King of kings, Lord of lords, the only ruler of princes, who dost from thy throne behold all the dwellers upon earth: Most heartily we beseech thee with thy favour to behold our most gracious Sovereign Lord, King *CHARLES;* and so replenish him with the grace of thy Holy Spirit, that he may always incline to thy will and walk in thy way. Endue him plenteously with heavenly gifts; grant him in health and wealth long to live; strengthen him that he may vanquish and overcome all his enemies; and finally, after this life, he may attain everlasting joy and felicity, through Jesus Christ our Lord. *Amen.*

A Prayer for the Royal Family.

A LMIGHTY God, the fountain of all goodness, we humbly beseech thee to bless Queen *Camilla, William* Prince of *Wales,* the Princess of *Wales,* and all the royal family: Endue them with thy Holy Spirit, enrich them with thy heavenly grace, prosper them with all happiness, and bring them to thine everlasting kingdom, through Jesus Christ our Lord. *Amen.*

The Collects, Epistles, & Gospels

to be used throughout the year.

¶ *Note that the collect appointed for every Sunday, or for any holy day that hath a vigil or eve, shall be said at the evening service of the day before.*

The First Sunday in Advent.
The Collect.

ALMIGHTY God, give us grace that we may cast away the works of darkness, and put upon us the armour of light, now in the time of this mortal life, in which thy Son Jesus Christ came to visit us in great humility, that in the last day, when he shall come again in his glorious majesty, to judge both the quick and the dead, we may rise to the life immortal, through him who liveth and reigneth with thee and the Holy Ghost, now and ever. *Amen.*

¶ *This collect is to be repeated every day with the other collects in Advent, until Christmas Eve.*

The Epistle. Romans 13:8-14.

OWE no man anything, but to love one another, for he that loveth another hath fulfilled the law. For this, 'Thou shalt not commit adultery, thou shalt not kill, thou shalt not steal, thou shalt not bear false witness, thou shalt not covet', and if there be any other commandment, it is briefly comprehended in this saying, namely, 'Thou shalt love thy neighbour as thyself.' Love worketh no ill to his neighbour; therefore love is the fulfilling of the law.

And that, knowing the time, that now it is high time to awake out of sleep, for now is our salvation nearer than when we believed. The night is far spent; the day is at hand. Let us therefore cast off the works of darkness, and let us put on the armour of light. Let us walk honestly, as in the day, not in rioting and drunkenness, not in chambering and wantonness, not in strife and envying. But put ye on the Lord Jesus Christ, and make not provision for the flesh, to fulfil the lusts thereof.

The Gospel. St. Matthew 21:1-13.

WHEN they drew nigh unto Jerusalem and were come to Bethphage, unto the Mount of Olives, then sent Jesus two disciples, saying unto them, 'Go into the village over against you, and straightway ye shall find an ass tied, and a colt with her. Loose them, and bring them unto me. And if any man say aught unto you, ye shall say, "The Lord hath need of them", and straightway he will send them.'

All this was done that it might be fulfilled which was spoken by the prophet, saying, 'Tell ye the daughter of Sion, "Behold, thy king cometh unto thee, meek, and sitting upon an ass, and a colt, the foal of an ass."'

And the disciples went and did as Jesus commanded them, and brought the ass and the colt, and put on them their clothes, and they set him thereon. And a very great multitude spread their garments in the way; others cut down branches from the trees, and strawed them in the way. And the multitudes that went before and that followed cried, saying, 'Hosanna to the Son of David: Blessed is he that cometh in the name of the Lord; Hosanna in the highest.'

And when he was come into Jerusalem all the city was moved, saying, 'Who is this?'

And the multitude said, 'This is Jesus, the prophet of Nazareth of Galilee.'

And Jesus went into the temple of God, and cast out all them that sold and bought in the temple, and overthrew the tables of the money-changers, and the seats of them that sold doves, and said unto them, 'It is written, "My house shall be called the house of prayer", but ye have made it a den of thieves.'

The Second Sunday in Advent.
The Collects.

B LESSED Lord, who hast caused all holy Scriptures to be written for our learning: Grant that we may in such wise hear them, read, mark, learn, and inwardly digest them, that by patience and comfort of thy holy word, we may embrace and ever hold fast the blessed hope of everlasting life, which thou hast given us in our Saviour Jesus Christ. *Amen.*

A LMIGHTY God, give us grace that we may cast away the works of darkness, and put upon us the armour of light, now in the time of this mortal life, in which thy Son Jesus Christ came to visit us in great humility, that in the last day, when he shall come again in his glorious majesty, to judge both the quick and the dead, we may rise to the life immortal, through him who liveth and reigneth with thee and the Holy Ghost, now and ever. *Amen.*

The Epistle. Romans 15:4-13.

WHATSOEVER things were written aforetime were written for our learning, that we through patience and comfort of the Scriptures might have hope.

Now the God of patience and consolation grant you to be like-minded one toward another, according to Christ Jesus, that ye may with one mind and one mouth glorify God, even the Father of our Lord Jesus Christ. Wherefore receive ye one another, as Christ also received us, to the glory of God. Now I say that Jesus Christ was a minister of the circumcision for the truth of God, to confirm the promises made unto the fathers, and that the Gentiles might glorify God for his mercy, as it is written, 'For this cause I will confess to thee among the Gentiles, and sing unto thy name.' And again he saith, 'Rejoice, ye Gentiles, with his people.' And again, 'Praise the Lord, all ye Gentiles, and laud him, all ye people.' And again, Isaiah saith, 'There shall be a root of Jesse, and he that shall rise to reign over the Gentiles, in him shall the Gentiles trust.'

Now the God of hope fill you with all joy and peace in believing, that ye may abound in hope, through the power of the Holy Ghost.

The Gospel. St. Luke 21:25-33.

'AND there shall be signs in the sun, and in the moon, and in the stars, and upon the earth distress of nations, with perplexity, the sea and the waves roaring, men's hearts failing them for fear, and for looking after those things which are coming on the earth, for the powers of heaven shall be shaken. And then shall they see the Son of Man coming in a cloud with power and great glory.

'And when these things begin to come to pass, then look up, and lift up your heads, for your redemption draweth nigh.'

And he spake to them a parable, 'Behold the fig tree, and all the trees; when they now shoot forth, ye see and know of your own selves that summer is now nigh at hand. So likewise ye, when ye see these things come to pass, know ye that the kingdom of God is nigh at hand.

'Verily I say unto you, this generation shall not pass away till all be fulfilled. Heaven and earth shall pass away, but my words shall not pass away.'

The Third Sunday in Advent.
The Collects.

O LORD Jesu Christ, who at thy first coming didst send thy messenger to prepare thy way before thee: Grant that the ministers and stewards of thy mysteries may likewise so prepare and make ready thy way, by turning the hearts of the disobedient to the wisdom of the just, that at thy second coming to judge the world we may be found an acceptable people in thy sight, who livest and reignest with the Father and the Holy Spirit, ever one God, world without end. *Amen.*

A LMIGHTY God, give us grace that we may cast away the works of darkness, and put upon us the armour of light, now in the time of this mortal life, in which thy Son Jesus Christ came to visit us in great humility, that in the last day, when he shall come again in his glorious majesty, to judge both the quick and the dead, we may rise to the life immortal, through him who liveth and reigneth with thee and the Holy Ghost, now and ever. *Amen.*

The Epistle. 1 Corinthians 4:1-5.

LET a man so account of us, as of the ministers of Christ, and stewards of the mysteries of God.

Moreover it is required in stewards that a man be found faithful. But with me it is a very small thing that I should be judged of you, or of man's judgement. Yea, I judge not mine own self. For I know nothing against myself, yet am I not hereby justified, but he that judgeth me is the Lord. Therefore judge nothing before the time, until the Lord come, who both will bring to light the hidden things of darkness, and will make manifest the counsels of the hearts, and then shall every man have praise of God.

The Gospel. St. Matthew 11:2-10.

NOW when John had heard in the prison the works of Christ, he sent two of his disciples and said unto him, 'Art thou he that should come, or do we look for another?'

Jesus answered and said unto them, 'Go and show John again those things which ye do hear and see. The blind receive their sight and the lame walk; the lepers are cleansed and the deaf hear; the dead are raised up and the poor have the gospel preached to them. And blessed is he, whosoever shall not be offended in me.'

THE FOURTH SUNDAY IN ADVENT

And as they departed, Jesus began to say unto the multitudes concerning John, 'What went ye out into the wilderness to see? A reed shaken with the wind? But what went ye out for to see? A man clothed in soft raiment? behold, they that wear soft clothing are in kings' houses. But what went ye out for to see? A prophet? yea, I say unto you, and more than a prophet. For this is he of whom it is written, "Behold, I send my messenger before thy face, which shall prepare thy way before thee."'

The Fourth Sunday in Advent.
The Collects.

O LORD, raise up (we pray thee) thy power and come among us, and with great might succour us; that whereas, through our sins and wickedness, we are sore let and hindered in running the race that is set before us, thy bountiful grace and mercy may speedily help and deliver us, through the satisfaction of thy Son our Lord, to whom, with thee and the Holy Ghost, be honour and glory, world without end. *Amen.*

A LMIGHTY God, give us grace that we may cast away the works of darkness, and put upon us the armour of light, now in the time of this mortal life, in which thy Son Jesus Christ came to visit us in great humility, that in the last day, when he shall come again in his glorious majesty, to judge both the quick and the dead, we may rise to the life immortal, through him who liveth and reigneth with thee and the Holy Ghost, now and ever. *Amen.*

THE FOURTH SUNDAY IN ADVENT

The Epistle. Philippians 4:4-7.

REJOICE in the Lord alway, and again I say, rejoice. Let your moderation be known unto all men. The Lord is at hand. Be careful for nothing, but in everything by prayer and supplication, with thanksgiving, let your requests be made known unto God. And the peace of God, which passeth all understanding, shall keep your hearts and minds through Christ Jesus.

The Gospel. St. John 1:19-28.

THIS is the record of John when the Jews sent priests and Levites from Jerusalem to ask him, 'Who art thou?' And he confessed and denied not, but confessed, 'I am not the Christ.'

And they asked him, 'What then? Art thou Elijah?' And he saith, 'I am not.' 'Art thou that prophet?' And he answered, 'No.' Then said they unto him, 'Who art thou? that we may give an answer to them that sent us. What sayest thou of thyself?' He said, 'I am the voice of one crying in the wilderness, "Make straight the way of the Lord", as said the prophet Isaiah.' And they which were sent were of the Pharisees. And they asked him and said unto him, 'Why baptizest thou then, if thou be not that Christ, nor Elijah, neither that prophet?' John answered them, saying, 'I baptize with water. But there standeth one among you whom ye know not: he it is, who coming after me is preferred before me, whose shoe's latchet I am not worthy to unloose.' These things were done in Bethany beyond Jordan, where John was baptizing.

CHRISTMAS DAY

The Nativity of our Lord, or the Birthday of
Christ, Commonly Called Christmas Day.*
The Collect.

ALMIGHTY God, who hast given us thy only-begotten
Son to take our nature upon him, and as at this time
to be born of a pure virgin: Grant that we, being regenerate and made thy children by adoption and grace, may
daily be renewed by thy Holy Spirit, through the same our
Lord Jesus Christ, who liveth and reigneth with thee and
the same Spirit, ever one God, world without end. *Amen.*

The Epistle. Hebrews 1:1-12.

GOD, who at sundry times and in divers manners spake
in time past unto the fathers by the prophets, hath in
these last days spoken unto us by his Son, whom he hath
appointed heir of all things, by whom also he made the
worlds, who, being the brightness of his glory and the express image of his person, and upholding all things by the
word of his power, when he had by himself purged our
sins, sat down on the right hand of the Majesty on high,
being made so much better than the angels, as he hath
by inheritance obtained a more excellent name than they.
    For unto which of the angels said he at any time, 'Thou
art my Son, this day have I begotten thee'? And again,
'I will be to him a Father, and he shall be to me a Son'?
And again, when he bringeth in the first-begotten into
the world, he saith, 'And let all the angels of God worship him.' And of the angels he saith, 'Who maketh his
angels spirits, and his ministers a flame of fire.' But unto

* December 25.

the Son he saith, 'Thy throne, O God, is for ever and ever; a sceptre of righteousness is the sceptre of thy kingdom. Thou hast loved righteousness and hated iniquity; therefore God, even thy God, hath anointed thee with the oil of gladness above thy fellows.' And, 'Thou, Lord, in the beginning hast laid the foundation of the earth, and the heavens are the works of thine hands. They shall perish, but thou remainest; and they all shall wax old as doth a garment, and as a vesture shalt thou fold them up, and they shall be changed; but thou art the same, and thy years shall not fail.'

The Gospel. St. John 1:1-14.

I n the beginning was the Word, and the Word was with God, and the Word was God. The same was in the beginning with God. All things were made by him, and without him was not anything made that was made. In him was life, and the life was the light of men. And the light shineth in darkness, and the darkness comprehended it not.

There was a man sent from God whose name was John. The same came for a witness, to bear witness of the light, that all men through him might believe. He was not that light, but was sent to bear witness of that light. That was the true light, which lighteth every man that cometh into the world. He was in the world, and the world was made by him, and the world knew him not. He came unto his own, and his own received him not. But as many as received him, to them gave he power to become the sons of God, even to them that believe on his name – which were born, not of blood, nor of the will of the flesh, nor of the will of man, but of God. And the Word was made flesh and dwelt among us, and we beheld his glory, the glory as of the only begotten of the Father, full of grace and truth.

Saint Stephen's Day.*
The Collects.

GRANT, O Lord, that in all our sufferings here upon earth for the testimony of thy truth, we may steadfastly look up to heaven, and by faith behold the glory that shall be revealed; and, being filled with the Holy Ghost, may learn to love and bless our persecutors by the example of thy first martyr, Saint Stephen, who prayed for his murderers to thee, O blessed Jesus, who standest at the right hand of God to succour all those that suffer for thee, our only mediator and advocate. *Amen.*

¶ *Then shall follow the collect of the Nativity, which shall be said continually unto New Year's Eve.*

ALMIGHTY God, who hast given us thy only-begotten Son to take our nature upon him, and as at this time to be born of a pure virgin: Grant that we, being regenerate and made thy children by adoption and grace, may daily be renewed by thy Holy Spirit, through the same our Lord Jesus Christ, who liveth and reigneth with thee and the same Spirit, ever one God, world without end. *Amen.*

For the Epistle. Acts 7:55-60.

STEPHEN, being full of the Holy Ghost, looked up steadfastly into heaven, and saw the glory of God and Jesus

* December 26.

standing on the right hand of God, and said, 'Behold, I see the heavens opened, and the Son of Man standing on the right hand of God.' Then they cried out with a loud voice, and stopped their ears, and ran upon him with one accord, and cast him out of the city, and stoned him. And the witnesses laid down their clothes at a young man's feet, whose name was Saul. And they stoned Stephen, calling upon God and saying, 'Lord Jesus, receive my spirit.' And he kneeled down and cried with a loud voice, 'Lord, lay not this sin to their charge.' And when he had said this, he fell asleep.

The Gospel. St. Matthew 23:34-39.

BEHOLD, I send unto you prophets and wise men and scribes. And some of them ye shall kill and crucify, and some of them shall ye scourge in your synagogues, and persecute them from city to city, that upon you may come all the righteous blood shed upon the earth, from the blood of righteous Abel unto the blood of Zechariah son of Barachiah, whom ye slew between the temple and the altar. Verily I say unto you, all these things shall come upon this generation.

O Jerusalem, Jerusalem, thou that killest the prophets and stonest them which are sent unto thee, how often would I have gathered thy children together, even as a hen gathereth her chickens under her wings, and ye would not! Behold, your house is left unto you desolate. For I say unto you, ye shall not see me henceforth till ye shall say, 'Blessed is he that cometh in the name of the Lord.'

SAINT JOHN THE EVANGELIST'S DAY

Saint John the Evangelist's Day.*
The Collects.

MERCIFUL Lord, we beseech thee to cast thy bright beams of light upon thy church, that it, being enlightened by the doctrine of thy blessed apostle and evangelist Saint John, may so walk in the light of thy truth, that it may at length attain to the light of everlasting life, through Jesus Christ our Lord. *Amen.*

ALMIGHTY God, who hast given us thy only-begotten Son to take our nature upon him, and as at this time to be born of a pure virgin: Grant that we, being regenerate and made thy children by adoption and grace, may daily be renewed by thy Holy Spirit, through the same our Lord Jesus Christ, who liveth and reigneth with thee and the same Spirit, ever one God, world without end. *Amen.*

The Epistle. 1 John 1.

THAT which was from the beginning, which we have heard, which we have seen with our eyes, which we have looked upon, and our hands have handled, of the Word of life (for the life was manifested, and we have seen it and bear witness, and show unto you that eternal life, which was with the Father, and was manifested unto us) – that which we have seen and heard declare we unto you, that ye also may have fellowship with us, and truly our fellowship is with the Father and with his Son Jesus Christ. And these things write we unto you that your joy may be full.

* December 27.

This then is the message which we have heard of him and declare unto you, that God is light, and in him is no darkness at all. If we say that we have fellowship with him and walk in darkness, we lie and do not the truth. But if we walk in the light as he is in the light, we have fellowship one with another, and the blood of Jesus Christ his Son cleanseth us from all sin. If we say that we have no sin, we deceive ourselves, and the truth is not in us. If we confess our sins, he is faithful and just to forgive us our sins, and to cleanse us from all unrighteousness. If we say that we have not sinned, we make him a liar, and his word is not in us.

The Gospel. St. John 21:19-25.

JESUS said unto Peter, 'Follow me.' Then Peter, turning about, seeth the disciple whom Jesus loved following – which also leaned on his breast at supper and said, 'Lord, which is he that betrayeth thee?' Peter, seeing him, saith to Jesus, 'Lord, and what shall this man do?' Jesus saith unto him, 'If I will that he tarry till I come, what is that to thee? Follow thou me.' Then went this saying abroad among the brethren that that disciple should not die. Yet Jesus said not unto him, 'He shall not die', but, 'If I will that he tarry till I come, what is that to thee?'

This is the disciple which testifieth of these things and wrote these things, and we know that his testimony is true.

And there are also many other things which Jesus did, the which, if they should be written every one, I suppose that even the world itself could not contain the books that should be written.

THE INNOCENTS' DAY

The Innocents' Day.*
The Collects.

O ALMIGHTY God, who out of the mouths of babes and sucklings hast ordained strength, and madest infants to glorify thee by their deaths: Mortify and kill all vices in us, and so strengthen us by thy grace, that by the innocency of our lives, and constancy of our faith even unto death, we may glorify thy holy name, through Jesus Christ our Lord. *Amen.*

A LMIGHTY God, who hast given us thy only-begotten Son to take our nature upon him, and as at this time to be born of a pure virgin: Grant that we, being regenerate and made thy children by adoption and grace, may daily be renewed by thy Holy Spirit, through the same our Lord Jesus Christ, who liveth and reigneth with thee and the same Spirit, ever one God, world without end. *Amen.*

For the Epistle. Revelation 14:1-5.

I LOOKED, and lo, a Lamb stood on the Mount Sion, and with him an hundred forty and four thousand, having his Father's name written in their foreheads. And I heard a voice from heaven, as the voice of many waters, and as the voice of a great thunder; and I heard the voice of harpers harping with their harps. And they sung as it were a new song before the throne, and before the four living creatures and the elders, and no man could learn that song but the hundred and forty and four thousand which were redeemed from the earth. These are they

* December 28.

which were not defiled with women, for they are virgins. These are they which follow the Lamb whithersoever he goeth. These were redeemed from among men, being the first fruits unto God and to the Lamb. And in their mouth was found no guile, for they are without fault before the throne of God.

The Gospel. St. Matthew 2:13-18.

THE angel of the Lord appeareth to Joseph in a dream, saying, 'Arise and take the young child and his mother, and flee into Egypt, and be thou there until I bring thee word, for Herod will seek the young child to destroy him.' When he arose, he took the young child and his mother by night and departed into Egypt, and was there until the death of Herod, that it might be fulfilled which was spoken of the Lord by the prophet, saying, 'Out of Egypt have I called my Son.'

Then Herod, when he saw that he was mocked of the wise men, was exceeding wroth, and sent forth and slew all the children that were in Bethlehem, and in all the coasts thereof, from two years old and under, according to the time which he had diligently inquired of the wise men. Then was fulfilled that which was spoken by Jeremiah the prophet, saying, 'In Ramah was there a voice heard, lamentation and weeping and great mourning, Rachel weeping for her children, and would not be comforted, because they are not.'

The Sunday after Christmas Day.
The Collect.

ALMIGHTY God, who hast given us thy only-begotten Son to take our nature upon him, and as at this time to be born of a pure virgin: Grant that we, being regenerate and made thy children by adoption and grace, may daily be renewed by thy Holy Spirit, through the same our Lord Jesus Christ, who liveth and reigneth with thee and the same Spirit, ever one God, world without end. *Amen.*

The Epistle. Galatians 4:1-7.

NOW I say, that the heir, as long as he is a child, differeth nothing from a servant, though he be lord of all, but is under tutors and governors until the time appointed of the father. Even so we, when we were children, were in bondage under the elements of the world. But when the fulness of the time was come, God sent forth his Son, made of a woman, made under the law, to redeem them that were under the law, that we might receive the adoption of sons. And because ye are sons, God hath sent forth the Spirit of his Son into your hearts, crying, 'Abba, Father'. Wherefore thou art no more a servant, but a son; and if a son, then an heir of God through Christ.

The Gospel. St. Matthew 1:18-25.

THE birth of Jesus Christ was on this wise: When as his mother Mary was espoused to Joseph, before they came together, she was found with child of the Holy Ghost. Then Joseph her husband, being a just man and not willing to make her a public example, was minded to put her away privily. But while he thought on these things, behold, the angel of the Lord appeared unto him in a dream, saying, 'Joseph, thou son of David, fear not to take unto thee Mary thy wife, for that which is conceived in her is of the Holy Ghost. And she shall bring forth a son, and thou shalt call his name JESUS, for he shall save his people from their sins.' Now all this was done, that it might be fulfilled which was spoken of the Lord by the prophet, saying, 'Behold, a virgin shall be with child, and shall bring forth a son, and they shall call his name *Emmanuel*', which being interpreted is 'God with us'. Then Joseph, being raised from sleep, did as the angel of the Lord had bidden him, and took unto him his wife, and knew her not till she had brought forth her firstborn son. And he called his name JESUS.

The Circumcision of Christ.*
The Collect.

ALMIGHTY God, who madest thy blessed Son to be circumcised and obedient to the law for man: Grant us the true circumcision of the Spirit, that, our hearts and all our members being mortified from all worldly and carnal lusts, we may in all things obey thy blessed will, through the same thy Son Jesus Christ our Lord. *Amen.*

The Epistle. Romans 4:8-14.

'BLESSED is the man to whom the Lord will not impute sin.' Cometh this blessedness then upon the circumcision only, or upon the uncircumcision also? for we say

* January 1.

that faith was reckoned to Abraham for righteousness. How was it then reckoned? When he was in circumcision or in uncircumcision? not in circumcision, but in uncircumcision. And he received the sign of circumcision, a seal of the righteousness of the faith which he had yet being uncircumcised, that he might be the father of all them that believe, though they be not circumcised, that righteousness might be imputed unto them also; and the father of circumcision to them who are not of the circumcision only, but also walk in the steps of that faith of our father Abraham, which he had being yet uncircumcised. For the promise, that he should be the heir of the world, was not to Abraham, or to his seed through the law, but through the righteousness of faith. For if they which are of the law be heirs, faith is made void and the promise made of none effect.

The Gospel. St. Luke 2:15-21.

AND it came to pass, as the angels were gone away from them into heaven, the shepherds said one to another, 'Let us now go even unto Bethlehem, and see this thing which is come to pass, which the Lord hath made known unto us.' And they came with haste and found Mary and Joseph, and the babe lying in a manger. And when they had seen it, they made known abroad the saying which was told them concerning this child. And all they that heard it wondered at those things which were told them by the shepherds. But Mary kept all these things and pondered them in her heart. And the shepherds returned, glorifying and praising God for all the things that they had heard and seen, as it was told unto them.

And when eight days were accomplished for the circumcising of the child, his name was called JESUS, which was so named of the angel before he was conceived in the womb.

¶ *The same collect, epistle, and gospel shall serve for every day until the Epiphany.*

The Epiphany, or the Manifestation
of Christ to the Gentiles.*
The Collect.

O GOD, who by the leading of a star didst manifest thy only-begotten Son to the Gentiles: Mercifully grant that we, who know thee now by faith, may after this life have the fruition of thy glorious Godhead, through Jesus Christ our Lord. *Amen.*

The Epistle. Ephesians 3:1-12.

F OR this cause I, Paul, the prisoner of Jesus Christ for you Gentiles – if ye have heard of the dispensation of the grace of God which is given me to you-ward, how that by revelation he made known unto me the mystery (as I wrote afore in few words, whereby, when ye read, ye may understand my knowledge in the mystery of Christ), which in other ages was not made known unto the sons of men, as it is now revealed unto his holy apostles and prophets by the Spirit: that the Gentiles should

* January 6.

be fellow-heirs, and of the same body, and partakers of his promise in Christ, by the gospel, whereof I was made a minister, according to the gift of the grace of God given unto me by the effectual working of his power. Unto me, who am less than the least of all saints, is this grace given, that I should preach among the Gentiles the unsearchable riches of Christ, and to make all men see what is the fellowship of the mystery, which from the beginning of the world hath been hid in God, who created all things by Jesus Christ, to the intent that now unto the principalities and powers in heavenly places might be known by the church the manifold wisdom of God, according to the eternal purpose which he purposed in Christ Jesus our Lord, in whom we have boldness and access with confidence by the faith of him.

The Gospel. St. Matthew 2:1-12.

WHEN Jesus was born in Bethlehem of Judea in the days of Herod the king, behold, there came wise men from the east to Jerusalem, saying, 'Where is he that is born king of the Jews? for we have seen his star in the east, and are come to worship him.' When Herod the king had heard these things, he was troubled, and all Jerusalem with him. And when he had gathered all the chief priests and scribes of the people together, he demanded of them where Christ should be born. And they said unto him, 'In Bethlehem of Judea, for thus it is written by the prophet, "And thou Bethlehem, in the land of Judah, art not the least among the princes of Judah, for out of thee shall come a governor that shall rule my people Israel."'

Then Herod, when he had privily called the wise men, inquired of them diligently what time the star appeared. And he sent them to Bethlehem and said, 'Go and search diligently for the young child. And when ye have found him, bring me word again, that I may come and worship him also.'

When they had heard the king, they departed; and lo, the star which they saw in the east went before them, till it came and stood over where the young child was. When they saw the star, they rejoiced with exceeding great joy. And when they were come into the house, they saw the young child with Mary his mother, and fell down and worshipped him; and when they had opened their treasures, they presented unto him gifts: gold and frankincense and myrrh. And being warned of God in a dream that they should not return to Herod, they departed into their own country another way.

The First Sunday after the Epiphany.
The Collect.

O LORD, we beseech thee mercifully to receive the prayers of thy people who call upon thee, and grant that they may both perceive and know what things they ought to do, and also may have grace and power faithfully to fulfil the same, through Jesus Christ our Lord. *Amen.*

The Epistle. Romans 12:1-5.

I BESEECH you therefore, brethren, by the mercies of God, that ye present your bodies a living sacrifice, holy, acceptable unto God, which is your reasonable service.

And be not conformed to this world, but be ye transformed by the renewing of your mind, that ye may prove what is that good, and acceptable, and perfect will of God. For I say, through the grace given unto me, to every man that is among you, not to think of himself more highly than he ought to think, but to think soberly, according as God hath dealt to every man the measure of faith. For as we have many members in one body, and all members have not the same office; so we, being many, are one body in Christ, and every one members one of another.

The Gospel. St. Luke 2:41-52.

Now Jesus' parents went to Jerusalem every year at the feast of the Passover. And when he was twelve years old, they went up to Jerusalem, after the custom of the feast. And when they had fulfilled the days, as they returned, the child Jesus tarried behind in Jerusalem, and Joseph and his mother knew not of it. But they, supposing him to have been in the company, went a day's journey, and they sought him among their kinsfolk and acquaintance. And when they found him not, they turned back again to Jerusalem, seeking him. And it came to pass that after three days they found him in the temple, sitting in the midst of the doctors, both hearing them and asking them questions. And all that heard him were astonished at his understanding and answers. And when they saw him, they were amazed. And his mother said unto him, 'Son, why hast thou thus dealt with us? behold, thy father and I have sought thee sorrowing.' And he said unto them, 'How is it that ye sought me? Wist ye not that

I must be about my Father's business?' And they understood not the saying which he spake unto them. And he went down with them and came to Nazareth, and was subject unto them, but his mother kept all these sayings in her heart. And Jesus increased in wisdom and stature, and in favour with God and man.

The Second Sunday after the Epiphany.
The Collect.

ALMIGHTY and everlasting God, who dost govern all things in heaven and earth: Mercifully hear the supplications of thy people, and grant us thy peace all the days of our life, through Jesus Christ our Lord. *Amen.*

The Epistle. Romans 12:6-16.

HAVING then gifts differing according to the grace that is given to us, whether prophecy, let us prophesy according to the proportion of faith; or ministry, let us wait on our ministering; or he that teacheth, on teaching; or he that exhorteth, on exhortation; he that giveth, let him do it with simplicity; he that ruleth, with diligence; he that showeth mercy, with cheerfulness.

Let love be without dissimulation. Abhor that which is evil; cleave to that which is good. Be kindly affectioned one to another with brotherly love, in honour preferring one another; not slothful in business; fervent in spirit, serving the Lord; rejoicing in hope, patient in tribulation, continuing instant in prayer; distributing to the necessity of saints, given to hospitality. Bless them which persecute you; bless, and curse not. Rejoice with them that do rejoice, and weep with them that weep. Be of the same mind one towards another. Mind not high things, but condescend to men of low estate.

The Gospel. St. John 2:1-11.

AND the third day there was a marriage in Cana of Galilee, and the mother of Jesus was there. And both Jesus was called and his disciples to the marriage. And when they wanted wine, the mother of Jesus saith unto him, 'They have no wine.' Jesus saith unto her, 'Woman, what have I to do with thee? mine hour is not yet come.' His mother saith unto the servants, 'Whatsoever he saith unto you, do it.' And there were set there six water pots of stone, after the manner of the purifying of the Jews, containing two or three firkins apiccc. Jesus saith unto them, 'Fill the water pots with water.' And they filled them up to the brim. And he saith unto them, 'Draw out now, and bear unto the governor of the feast.' And they bare it. When the ruler of the feast had tasted the water that was made wine, and knew not whence it was (but the servants which drew the water knew), the governor of the feast called the bridegroom and saith unto him, 'Every man at the beginning doth set forth good wine, and when men have well drunk, then that which is worse. But thou hast kept the good wine until now.' This beginning of miracles did Jesus in Cana of Galilee, and manifested forth his glory, and his disciples believed on him.

The Third Sunday after the Epiphany.

The Collect.

ALMIGHTY and everlasting God, mercifully look upon our infirmities, and in all our dangers and necessities stretch forth thy right hand to help and defend us, through Jesus Christ our Lord. *Amen.*

The Epistle. Romans 12:16-21.

BE not wise in your own conceits. Recompense to no man evil for evil. Provide things honest in the sight of all men. If it be possible, as much as lieth in you, live peaceably with all men. Dearly beloved, avenge not yourselves, but rather give place unto wrath, for it is written, "'Vengeance is mine; I will repay", saith the Lord.' Therefore if thine enemy hunger, feed him; if he thirst, give him drink. For in so doing thou shalt heap coals of fire on his head. Be not overcome of evil, but overcome evil with good.

The Gospel. St. Matthew 8:1-13.

WHEN Jesus was come down from the mountain, great multitudes followed him. And behold, there came a leper and worshipped him, saying, 'Lord, if thou wilt, thou canst make me clean.' And Jesus put forth his hand, and touched him, saying, 'I will; be thou clean.' And immediately his leprosy was cleansed. And Jesus saith unto him, 'See thou tell no man, but go thy way, show thyself to the priest, and offer the gift that Moses commanded, for a testimony unto them.'

And when Jesus was entered into Capernaum, there came unto him a centurion, beseeching him and saying,

'Lord, my servant lieth at home sick of the palsy, grievously tormented.' And Jesus saith unto him, 'I will come and heal him.' The centurion answered and said, 'Lord, I am not worthy that thou shouldest come under my roof, but speak the word only, and my servant shall be healed. For I am a man under authority, having soldiers under me, and I say unto this man, "Go", and he goeth; and to another, "Come", and he cometh; and to my servant, "Do this", and he doeth it.' When Jesus heard it, he marvelled and said to them that followed, 'Verily I say unto you, I have not found so great faith, no, not in Israel. And I say unto you, that many shall come from the east and west, and shall sit down with Abraham and Isaac and Jacob in the kingdom of heaven. But the children of the kingdom shall be cast out into outer darkness: there shall be weeping and gnashing of teeth.' And Jesus said unto the centurion, 'Go thy way, and as thou hast believed, so be it done unto thee.' And his servant was healed in the selfsame hour.

The Fourth Sunday after the Epiphany.
The Collect.

O GOD, who knowest us to be set in the midst of so many and great dangers, that by reason of the frailty of our nature we cannot always stand upright: Grant to us such strength and protection, as may support us in all dangers and carry us through all temptations, through Jesus Christ our Lord. *Amen.*

THE FOURTH SUNDAY AFTER THE EPIPHANY

The Epistle. Romans 13:1-7.

LET every soul be subject unto the higher powers, for there is no power but of God. The powers that be are ordained of God. Whosoever therefore resisteth the power, resisteth the ordinance of God, and they that resist shall receive to themselves judgement. For rulers are not a terror to good works, but to the evil. Wilt thou then not be afraid of the power? do that which is good, and thou shalt have praise of the same. For he is the minister of God to thee for good. But if thou do that which is evil, be afraid; for he beareth not the sword in vain, for he is the minister of God, a revenger to execute wrath upon him that doeth evil. Wherefore ye must needs be subject, not only for wrath, but also for conscience' sake. For for this cause pay ye tribute also, for they are God's ministers, attending continually upon this very thing. Render therefore to all their dues: tribute to whom tribute is due, custom to whom custom, fear to whom fear, honour to whom honour.

The Gospel. St. Matthew 8:23-34.

AND when Jesus was entered into a ship, his disciples followed him. And behold, there arose a great tempest in the sea, insomuch that the ship was covered with the waves, but he was asleep. And his disciples came to him, and awoke him, saying, 'Lord, save us; we perish.' And he saith unto them, 'Why are ye fearful, O ye of little faith?' Then he arose, and rebuked the winds and the sea, and there was a great calm. But the men marvelled, saying, 'What manner of man is this, that even the winds and the sea obey him!'

And when he was come to the other side into the country of the Gergesenes, there met him two possessed with devils, coming out of the tombs, exceeding fierce, so that no man might pass by that way. And behold, they cried out, saying, 'What have we to do with thee, Jesus, thou Son of God? Art thou come hither to torment us before the time?' And there was a good way off from them an herd of many swine, feeding. So the devils besought him, saying, 'If thou cast us out, suffer us to go away into the herd of swine.' And he said unto them, 'Go.' And when they were come out, they went into the herd of swine, and behold, the whole herd of swine ran violently down a steep place into the sea, and perished in the waters. And they that kept them fled, and went their ways into the city, and told everything, and what was befallen to the possessed of the devils. And behold, the whole city came out to meet Jesus; and when they saw him, they besought him that he would depart out of their coasts.

The Fifth Sunday after the Epiphany.
The Collect.

O LORD, we beseech thee to keep thy church and household continually in thy true religion, that those who do lean only upon the hope of thy heavenly grace may evermore be defended by thy mighty power, through Jesus Christ our Lord. *Amen.*

THE FIFTH SUNDAY AFTER THE EPIPHANY

The Epistle. Colossians 3:12-17.

PUT on therefore, as the elect of God, holy and beloved, bowels of mercies, kindness, humbleness of mind, meekness, long-suffering; forbearing one another, and forgiving one another, if any man have a quarrel against any. Even as Christ forgave you, so also do ye. And above all these things put on charity, which is the bond of perfectness. And let the peace of God rule in your hearts, to the which also ye are called in one body, and be ye thankful. Let the word of Christ dwell in you richly in all wisdom, teaching and admonishing one another in psalms and hymns and spiritual songs, singing with grace in your hearts to the Lord. And whatsoever ye do, in word or deed, do all in the name of the Lord Jesus, giving thanks to God and the Father by him.

The Gospel. St. Matthew 13:24-30.

THE kingdom of heaven is likened unto a man which sowed good seed in his field. But while men slept, his enemy came and sowed tares among the wheat, and went his way. But when the blade was sprung up, and brought forth fruit, then appeared the tares also. So the servants of the householder came and said unto him, 'Sir, didst not thou sow good seed in thy field? from whence then hath it tares?' He said unto them, 'An enemy hath done this.' The servants said unto him, 'Wilt thou then that we go and gather them up?' But he said, 'Nay, lest while ye gather up the tares, ye root up also the wheat with them. Let both grow together until the harvest, and in the time of harvest I will say to the reapers, "Gather ye together first the tares, and bind them in bundles to burn them, but gather the wheat into my barn.'"

The Sixth Sunday after the Epiphany.
The Collect.

O GOD, whose blessed Son was manifested that he might destroy the works of the devil, and make us the sons of God, and heirs of eternal life: Grant us, we beseech thee, that, having this hope, we may purify ourselves, even as he is pure, that, when he shall appear again with power and great glory, we may be made like unto him in his eternal and glorious kingdom, where with thee, O Father, and thee, O Holy Ghost, he liveth and reigneth, ever one God, world without end. *Amen.*

The Epistle. 1 John 3:1-8.

B EHOLD what manner of love the Father hath bestowed upon us, that we should be called the sons of God. Therefore the world knoweth us not, because it knew him not. Beloved, now are we the sons of God, and it doth not yet appear what we shall be, but we know that when he shall appear, we shall be like him, for we shall see him as he is. And every man that hath this hope in him purifieth himself, even as he is pure.

Whosoever committeth sin transgresseth also the law, for sin is the transgression of the law. And ye know that he was manifested to take away our sins, and in him is no sin. Whosoever abideth in him sinneth not; whosoever sinneth hath not seen him, neither known him. Little children, let no man deceive you: he that doeth righteousness is righteous, even as he is righteous; he that committeth sin is of the devil, for the devil sinneth from the beginning. For this purpose the Son of God was manifested, that he might destroy the works of the devil.

The Gospel. St. Matthew 24:23-31.

THEN if any man shall say unto you, 'Lo, here is Christ, or there', believe it not. For there shall arise false Christs, and false prophets, and shall show great signs and wonders, insomuch that (if it were possible) they shall deceive the very elect. Behold, I have told you before. Wherefore, if they shall say unto you, 'Behold, he is in the desert', go not forth; 'Behold, he is in the secret chambers', believe it not. For as the lightning cometh out of the east, and shineth even unto the west, so shall also the coming of the Son of Man be. For wheresoever the carcass is, there will the eagles be gathered together.

Immediately after the tribulation of those days shall the sun be darkened, and the moon shall not give her light, and the stars shall fall from heaven, and the powers of the heavens shall be shaken. And then shall appear the sign of the Son of Man in heaven, and then shall all the tribes of the earth mourn, and they shall see the Son of Man coming in the clouds of heaven, with power and great glory. And he shall send his angels with a great sound of a trumpet, and they shall gather together his elect from the four winds, from one end of heaven to the other.

SEPTUAGESIMA SUNDAY

The Sunday Called Septuagesima, or
the Third Sunday before Lent.
The Collect.

O LORD, we beseech thee favourably to hear the prayers
of thy people, that we, who are justly punished for
our offences, may be mercifully delivered by thy goodness, for the glory of thy name, through Jesus Christ our
Saviour, who liveth and reigneth with thee and the Holy
Ghost, ever one God, world without end. *Amen.*

The Epistle. 1 Corinthians 9:24-27.

K NOW ye not that they which run in a race run all, but
one receiveth the prize? So run, that ye may obtain.
And every man that striveth for the mastery is temper-
ate in all things. Now they do it to obtain a corruptible
crown, but we an incorruptible. I therefore so run, not as
uncertainly; so fight I, not as one that beateth the air; but
I keep under my body, and bring it into subjection, lest
that by any means, when I have preached to others, I myself should be a castaway.

The Gospel. St. Matthew 20:1-16.

T HE kingdom of heaven is like unto a man that is an
householder, which went out early in the morning to
hire labourers into his vineyard. And when he had agreed
with the labourers for a penny a day, he sent them into
his vineyard. And he went out about the third hour, and
saw others standing idle in the marketplace, and said unto
them, 'Go ye also into the vineyard, and whatsoever is

right I will give you.' And they went their way. Again he went out about the sixth and ninth hour, and did likewise. And about the eleventh hour he went out, and found others standing idle, and saith unto them, 'Why stand ye here all the day idle?' They say unto him, 'Because no man hath hired us.' He saith unto them, 'Go ye also into the vineyard, and whatsoever is right, that shall ye receive.' So when even was come, the lord of the vineyard saith unto his steward, 'Call the labourers, and give them their hire, beginning from the last unto the first.' And when they came that were hired about the eleventh hour, they received every man a penny. But when the first came, they supposed that they should have received more, and they likewise received every man a penny. And when they had received it, they murmured against the goodman of the house, saying, 'These last have wrought but one hour, and thou hast made them equal unto us, which have borne the burden and heat of the day.' But he answered one of them and said, 'Friend, I do thee no wrong; didst not thou agree with me for a penny? Take that thine is, and go thy way. I will give unto this last, even as unto thee. Is it not lawful for me to do what I will with mine own? Is thine eye evil because I am good?' So the last shall be first, and the first last, for many be called, but few chosen.

SEXAGESIMA SUNDAY

The Sunday Called Sexagesima, or the
Second Sunday before Lent.
The Collect.

O LORD God, who seest that we put not our trust in
anything that we do: Mercifully grant that by thy
power we may be defended against all adversity, through
Jesus Christ our Lord. *Amen.*

The Epistle. 2 Corinthians 11:19-31.

Y E suffer fools gladly, seeing ye yourselves are wise. For
ye suffer if a man bring you into bondage, if a man devour you, if a man take of you, if a man exalt himself, if
a man smite you on the face. I speak as concerning reproach, as though we had been weak.

Howbeit, whereinsoever any is bold (I speak foolishly),
I am bold also. Are they Hebrews? so am I. Are they Israelites? so am I. Are they the seed of Abraham? so am I.
Are they ministers of Christ? (I speak as a fool) I am more
– in labours more abundant, in stripes above measure,
in prisons more frequent, in deaths oft. Of the Jews five
times received I forty stripes save one; thrice was I beaten
with rods; once was I stoned; thrice I suffered shipwreck;
a night and a day I have been in the deep; in journeyings
often, in perils of waters, in perils of robbers, in perils by
mine own countrymen, in perils by the heathen, in perils
in the city, in perils in the wilderness, in perils in the sea,
in perils among false brethren, in weariness and painful-
ness, in watchings often, in hunger and thirst, in fastings
often, in cold and nakedness.

Besides those things that are without, that which cometh upon me daily, the care of all the churches. Who is weak and I am not weak? who is offended and I burn not? If I must needs glory, I will glory of the things which concern mine infirmities. The God and Father of our Lord Jesus Christ, which is blessed for evermore, knoweth that I lie not.

The Gospel. St. Luke 8:4-15.

WHEN much people were gathered together and were come to him out of every city, Jesus spake by a parable: 'A sower went out to sow his seed. And as he sowed, some fell by the wayside, and it was trodden down, and the fowls of the air devoured it. And some fell upon a rock, and as soon as it was sprung up, it withered away, because it lacked moisture. And some fell among thorns, and the thorns sprang up with it, and choked it. And other fell on good ground, and sprang up, and bare fruit an hundredfold.' And when he had said these things, he cried, 'He that hath ears to hear, let him hear.'

And his disciples asked him, saying, 'What might this parable be?' And he said, 'Unto you it is given to know the mysteries of the kingdom of God, but to others in parables, that seeing they might not see, and hearing they might not understand. Now the parable is this: the seed is the word of God. Those by the wayside are they that hear; then cometh the devil and taketh away the word out of their hearts, lest they should believe and be saved. They on the rock are they which, when they hear, receive the word with joy; and these have no root, which for a while believe, and in time of temptation fall away. And that which fell among thorns are they which, when they have heard, go forth, and are choked with cares and riches and pleasures of this life, and bring no fruit to perfection. But that on the good ground are they which in an honest and good heart, having heard the word, keep it, and bring forth fruit with patience.

The Sunday Called Quinquagesima, or
the next Sunday before Lent.
The Collect.

O LORD, who hast taught us that all our doings without charity are nothing worth: Send thy Holy Ghost and pour into our hearts that most excellent gift of charity, the very bond of peace and of all virtues, without which whosoever liveth is counted dead before thee. Grant this for thine only Son Jesus Christ's sake. *Amen.*

The Epistle. 1 Corinthians 13.

T HOUGH I speak with the tongues of men and of angels, and have not charity, I am become as sounding brass or a tinkling cymbal. And though I have the gift of prophecy, and understand all mysteries and all knowledge, and though I have all faith, so that I could remove mountains, and have not charity, I am nothing. And though I bestow all my goods to feed the poor, and though I give my body to be burned, and have not charity, it profiteth me nothing.

Charity suffereth long, and is kind; charity envieth not; charity vaunteth not itself, is not puffed up, doth not behave itself unseemly, seeketh not her own, is not easily provoked, thinketh no evil, rejoiceth not in iniquity, but rejoiceth in the truth; beareth all things, believeth all things, hopeth all things, endureth all things. Charity never faileth.

But whether there be prophecies, they shall fail; whether there be tongues, they shall cease; whether there be knowledge, it shall vanish away. For we know in part, and we prophesy in part. But when that which is perfect is come, then that which is in part shall be done away. When I was a child, I spake as a child, I understood as a child, I thought as a child; but when I became a man, I put away childish things. For now we see through a glass darkly, but then face to face; now I know in part, but then shall I know even as also I am known.

And now abideth faith, hope, charity, these three; but the greatest of these is charity.

The Gospel. St. Luke 18:31-43.

THEN Jesus took unto him the twelve, and said unto them, 'Behold, we go up to Jerusalem, and all things that are written by the prophets concerning the Son of Man shall be accomplished. For he shall be delivered unto the Gentiles, and shall be mocked, and spitefully entreated, and spat on; and they shall scourge him, and put him to death; and the third day he shall rise again.' And they understood none of these things, and this saying was hid from them, neither knew they the things which were spoken.

And it came to pass that as he was come nigh unto Jericho, a certain blind man sat by the wayside begging. And hearing the multitude pass by, he asked what it meant. And they told him that Jesus of Nazareth passeth by. And he cried, saying, 'Jesus, thou Son of David, have mercy on me.'

And they which went before rebuked him, that he should hold his peace. But he cried so much the more, 'Thou Son of David, have mercy on me.'

And Jesus stood and commanded him to be brought unto him, and when he was come near, he asked him, saying, 'What wilt thou that I should do unto thee?' And he said, 'Lord, that I may receive my sight.' And Jesus said unto him, 'Receive thy sight; thy faith hath saved thee.' And immediately he received his sight, and followed him, glorifying God. And all the people, when they saw it, gave praise unto God.

The First Day of Lent, Commonly
Called Ash Wednesday.
The Collect.

ALMIGHTY and everlasting God, who hatest nothing that thou hast made, and dost forgive the sins of all those who are penitent: Create and make in us new and contrite hearts, that we, worthily lamenting our sins and acknowledging our wretchedness, may obtain of thee, the God of all mercy, perfect remission and forgiveness, through Jesus Christ our Lord. *Amen.*

¶ *This collect is to be read every day in Lent after the collect appointed for the day.*

ASH WEDNESDAY

For the Epistle. Joel 2:12-17.

"TURN ye even to me', saith the Lord, 'with all your heart, and with fasting, and with weeping, and with mourning.' And rend your heart, and not your garments, and turn unto the LORD your God, for he is gracious and merciful, slow to anger and of great kindness, and repenteth him of the evil. Who knoweth if he will return and repent, and leave a blessing behind him, even a meat offering and a drink offering unto the LORD your God?

Blow the trumpet in Zion; sanctify a fast; call a solemn assembly. Gather the people; sanctify the congregation; assemble the elders; gather the children, and those that suck the breasts. Let the bridegroom go forth of his chamber, and the bride out of her closet. Let the priests, the ministers of the LORD, weep between the porch and the altar, and let them say, 'Spare thy people, O LORD, and give not thine heritage to reproach, that the heathen should rule over them. Wherefore should they say among the peoples, "Where is their God?"'

The Gospel. St. Matthew 6:16-21.

WHEN ye fast, be not as the hypocrites, of a sad countenance, for they disfigure their faces, that they may appear unto men to fast. Verily I say unto you, they have their reward. But thou, when thou fastest, anoint thine head, and wash thy face, that thou appear not unto men to fast, but unto thy Father which is in secret. And thy Father, which seeth in secret, shall reward thee openly.

Lay not up for yourselves treasures upon earth, where moth and rust doth corrupt, and where thieves break through and steal. But lay up for yourselves treasures in heaven, where neither moth nor rust doth corrupt, and where thieves do not break through nor steal. For where your treasure is, there will your heart be also.

The First Sunday in Lent.
The Collects.

O LORD, who for our sake didst fast forty days and forty nights: Give us grace to use such abstinence, that, our flesh being subdued to the Spirit, we may ever obey thy godly motions in righteousness and true holiness, to thy honour and glory, who livest and reignest with the Father and the Holy Ghost, one God, world without end. *Amen.*

A LMIGHTY and everlasting God, who hatest nothing that thou hast made, and dost forgive the sins of all those who are penitent: Create and make in us new and contrite hearts, that we, worthily lamenting our sins and acknowledging our wretchedness, may obtain of thee, the God of all mercy, perfect remission and forgiveness, through Jesus Christ our Lord. *Amen.*

The Epistle. 2 Corinthians 6:1-10.

W E then, as workers together with him, beseech you also that ye receive not the grace of God in vain – for he saith, 'I have heard thee in a time accepted, and in the day of salvation have I succoured thee'; behold, now is the accepted time; behold, now is the day of salvation – giving no offence in anything, that the ministry be not blamed, but in all things approving ourselves as the ministers of

God: in much patience, in afflictions, in necessities, in distresses, in stripes, in imprisonments, in tumults, in labours, in watchings, in fastings; by pureness, by knowledge, by long-suffering, by kindness, by the Holy Ghost, by love unfeigned, by the word of truth, by the power of God, by the armour of righteousness on the right hand and on the left, by honour and dishonour, by evil report and good report; as deceivers, and yet true; as unknown, and yet well known; as dying, and behold, we live; as chastened, and not killed; as sorrowful, yet alway rejoicing; as poor, yet making many rich; as having nothing, and yet possessing all things.

The Gospel. St. Matthew 4:1-11.

THEN was Jesus led up of the Spirit into the wilderness, to be tempted of the devil. And when he had fasted forty days and forty nights, he was afterward an-hungered. And when the tempter came to him, he said, 'If thou be the Son of God, command that these stones be made bread.'

But he answered and said, 'It is written, "Man shall not live by bread alone, but by every word that proceedeth out of the mouth of God."'

Then the devil taketh him up into the holy city, and setteth him on a pinnacle of the temple, and saith unto him, 'If thou be the Son of God, cast thyself down, for it is written, "He shall give his angels charge concerning thee, and in their hands they shall bear thee up, lest at any time thou dash thy foot against a stone."' Jesus said unto him, 'It is written again, "Thou shalt not tempt the Lord thy God."'

Again, the devil taketh him up into an exceeding high

mountain, and showeth him all the kingdoms of the world and the glory of them, and saith unto him, 'All these things will I give thee, if thou wilt fall down and worship me.'

Then saith Jesus unto him, 'Get thee hence, Satan, for it is written, "Thou shalt worship the Lord thy God, and him only shalt thou serve."' Then the devil leaveth him, and behold, angels came and ministered unto him.

The Second Sunday in Lent.
The Collects.

A LMIGHTY God, who seest that we have no power of ourselves to help ourselves: Keep us both outwardly in our bodies and inwardly in our souls, that we may be defended from all adversities which may happen to the body, and from all evil thoughts which may assault and hurt the soul, through Jesus Christ our Lord. *Amen.*

A LMIGHTY and everlasting God, who hatest nothing that thou hast made, and dost forgive the sins of all those who are penitent: Create and make in us new and contrite hearts, that we, worthily lamenting our sins and acknowledging our wretchedness, may obtain of thee, the God of all mercy, perfect remission and forgiveness, through Jesus Christ our Lord. *Amen.*

The Epistle. 1 Thessalonians 4:1-8.

W E beseech you, brethren, and exhort you by the Lord Jesus, that as ye have received of us how ye ought to walk and to please God, so ye would abound more and more. For ye know what commandments we gave you by the Lord Jesus. For this is the will of God, even your sanctification: that ye should abstain from fornication; that every one of you should know how to possess his vessel in sanctification and honour, not in the lust of concupiscence, even as the Gentiles which know not God; that no man go beyond and defraud his brother in any matter, because that the Lord is the avenger of all such, as we also have forewarned you and testified. For God hath not called us unto uncleanness, but unto holiness. He therefore that despiseth, despiseth not man, but God, who hath also given unto us his Holy Spirit.

The Gospel. St. Matthew 15:21-28.

JESUS went thence and departed into the coasts of Tyre and Sidon. And behold, a woman of Canaan came out of the same coasts and cried unto him, saying, 'Have mercy on me, O Lord, thou Son of David; my daughter is grievously vexed with a devil.'

But he answered her not a word. And his disciples came and besought him, saying, 'Send her away, for she crieth after us.'

But he answered and said, 'I am not sent but unto the lost sheep of the house of Israel.'

Then came she and worshipped him, saying, 'Lord, help me.'

But he answered and said, 'It is not meet to take the children's bread, and to cast it to dogs.'

And she said, 'Truth, Lord, yet the dogs eat of the crumbs which fall from their masters' table.'

Then Jesus answered and said unto her, 'O woman,

great is thy faith; be it unto thee even as thou wilt.' And her daughter was made whole from that very hour.

The Third Sunday in Lent.
The Collects.

WE beseech thee, almighty God, look upon the hearty desires of thy humble servants, and stretch forth the right hand of thy Majesty, to be our defence against all our enemies, through Jesus Christ our Lord. *Amen.*

ALMIGHTY and everlasting God, who hatest nothing that thou hast made, and dost forgive the sins of all those who are penitent: Create and make in us new and contrite hearts, that we, worthily lamenting our sins and acknowledging our wretchedness, may obtain of thee, the God of all mercy, perfect remission and forgiveness, through Jesus Christ our Lord. *Amen.*

The Epistle. Ephesians 5:1-14.

BE ye therefore followers of God, as dear children; and walk in love, as Christ also hath loved us, and hath given himself for us, an offering and a sacrifice to God for a sweet-smelling savour.

But fornication, and all uncleanness, or covetousness, let it not be once named amongst you, as becometh saints; neither filthiness, nor foolish talking, nor jesting, which are not convenient; but rather giving of thanks. For this ye know, that no whoremonger, nor unclean person, nor covetous man, who is an idolater, hath any inheritance in the kingdom of Christ and of God.

Let no man deceive you with vain words, for because of these things cometh the wrath of God upon the children of disobedience. Be not ye therefore partakers with them. For ye were sometimes darkness, but now are ye light in the Lord: walk as children of light (for the fruit of the Spirit is in all goodness and righteousness and truth), proving what is acceptable unto the Lord. And have no fellowship with the unfruitful works of darkness, but rather reprove them, for it is a shame even to speak of those things which are done of them in secret. But all things that are reproved are made manifest by the light, for whatsoever doth make manifest is light. Wherefore he saith, 'Awake, thou that sleepest, and arise from the dead, and Christ shall give thee light.'

The Gospel. St. Luke 11:14-28.

JESUS was casting out a devil, and it was dumb. And it came to pass, when the devil was gone out, the dumb spake, and the people wondered.

But some of them said, 'He casteth out devils through Beelzebub, the chief of the devils.'

And others, tempting him, sought of him a sign from heaven. But he, knowing their thoughts, said unto them, 'Every kingdom divided against itself is brought to desolation, and a house divided against a house falleth. If Satan also be divided against himself, how shall his kingdom stand? because ye say that I cast out devils through Beelzebub. And if I by Beelzebub cast out devils, by whom do your sons cast them out? therefore shall they be your judges. But if I with the finger of God cast out devils, no doubt the kingdom of God is come upon you. When a strong man armed keepeth his palace, his goods are in peace. But when a stronger than he shall come upon him, and overcome him, he taketh from him all his armour wherein he trusted, and divideth his spoils. He that is not with me is against me, and he that gathereth not with me scattereth. 'When the unclean spirit is gone out of a man, he walketh through dry places, seeking rest; and finding none, he saith, "I will return unto my house whence I came out." And when he cometh, he findeth it swept and garnished. Then goeth he, and taketh to him seven other spirits more wicked than himself, and they enter in, and dwell there. And the last state of that man is worse than the first.'

And it came to pass, as he spake these things, a certain woman of the company lifted up her voice and said unto him, 'Blessed is the womb that bare thee, and the paps which thou hast sucked.' But he said, 'Yea rather, blessed are they that hear the word of God, and keep it.'

The Fourth Sunday in Lent.
The Collects.

G RANT, we beseech thee, almighty God, that we, who for our evil deeds do worthily deserve to be punished, by the comfort of thy grace may mercifully be relieved, through our Lord and Saviour Jesus Christ. *Amen.*

A LMIGHTY and everlasting God, who hatest nothing that thou hast made, and dost forgive the sins of all those who are penitent: Create and make in us new and contrite hearts, that we, worthily lamenting our sins and acknowledging our wretchedness, may obtain of thee, the God of all mercy, perfect remission and forgiveness, through Jesus Christ our Lord. *Amen.*

The Epistle. Galatians 4:21-31.

TELL me, ye that desire to be under the law, do ye not hear the law? For it is written that Abraham had two sons, the one by a bondmaid, the other by a freewoman. But he who was of the bondwoman was born after the flesh, but he of the freewoman was by promise. Which things are an allegory, for these are the two covenants: the one from the Mount Sinai, which gendereth to bondage, which is Hagar. For this Hagar is Mount Sinai in Arabia, and answereth to Jerusalem which now is, and is in bondage with her children. But Jerusalem which is above is free, which is the mother of us all. For it is written, 'Rejoice, thou barren that bearest not; break forth and cry, thou that travailest not, for the desolate hath many more children than she which hath an husband.' Now we, brethren, as Isaac was, are the children of promise. But as then he that was born after the flesh persecuted him that was born after the Spirit, even so it is now. Nevertheless what saith the Scripture? 'Cast out the bondwoman and her son, for the son of the bondwoman shall not be heir with the son of the freewoman.' So then, brethren, we are not children of the bondwoman, but of the free.

The Gospel. St. John 6:1-14.

JESUS went over the sea of Galilee, which is the sea of Tiberias. And a great multitude followed him, because they saw his miracles which he did on them that were diseased. And Jesus went up into a mountain, and there he sat with his disciples. And the Passover, a feast of the Jews, was nigh.

When Jesus then lifted up his eyes and saw a great company come unto him, he saith unto Philip, 'Whence shall we buy bread that these may eat?' And this he said to prove him, for he himself knew what he would do. Philip answered him, 'Two hundred pennyworth of bread is not sufficient for them, that every one of them may take a little.'

One of his disciples, Andrew, Simon Peter's brother, saith unto him, 'There is a lad here which hath five barley loaves and two small fishes. But what are they among so many?' And Jesus said, 'Make the men sit down.' Now there was much grass in the place. So the men sat down, in number about five thousand. And Jesus took the loaves, and when he had given thanks, he distributed to the disciples, and the disciples to them that were set down, and likewise of the fishes, as much as they would. When they were filled, he said unto his disciples, 'Gather up the fragments that remain, that nothing be lost.' Therefore they gathered them together, and filled twelve baskets with the fragments of the five barley loaves which remained over and above unto them that had eaten.

Then those men, when they had seen the miracle that Jesus did, said, 'This is of a truth that prophet that should come into the world.'

The Fifth Sunday in Lent.
The Collects.

WE beseech thee, almighty God, mercifully to look upon thy people, that by thy great goodness they may be governed and preserved evermore, both in body and soul, through Jesus Christ our Lord. *Amen.*

ALMIGHTY and everlasting God, who hatest nothing that thou hast made, and dost forgive the sins of all those who are penitent: Create and make in us new and contrite hearts, that we, worthily lamenting our sins and acknowledging our wretchedness, may obtain of thee, the God of all mercy, perfect remission and forgiveness, through Jesus Christ our Lord. *Amen.*

The Epistle. Hebrews 9:11-15.

CHRIST being come an high priest of good things to come, by a greater and more perfect tabernacle (not made with hands, that is to say, not of this building), neither by the blood of goats and calves, but by his own blood, he entered in once into the holy place, having obtained eternal redemption for us. For if the blood of bulls and of goats, and the ashes of a heifer sprinkling the unclean, sanctifieth to the purifying of the flesh, how much more shall the blood of Christ, who, through the eternal Spirit, offered himself without spot to God, purge your conscience from dead works to serve the living God?

And for this cause he is the mediator of the new testament, that by means of death, for the redemption of the transgressions that were under the first testament, they which are called might receive the promise of eternal inheritance.

The Gospel. St. John 8:46-59.

JESUS said, 'Which of you convinceth me of sin? And if I say the truth, why do ye not believe me? He that is of God heareth God's words. Ye therefore hear them not, because ye are not of God.

Then answered the Jews and said unto him, 'Say we not well that thou art a Samaritan, and hast a devil?'

Jesus answered, 'I have not a devil, but I honour my Father, and ye do dishonour me. And I seek not mine own glory – there is one that seeketh and judgeth.

'Verily, verily I say unto you, if a man keep my saying, he shall never see death.'

Then said the Jews unto him, 'Now we know that thou hast a devil. Abraham is dead, and the prophets, and thou sayest, "If a man keep my saying, he shall never taste of death." Art thou greater than our father Abraham, which is dead? and the prophets are dead. Whom makest thou thyself?'

Jesus answered, 'If I honour myself, my honour is nothing. It is my Father that honoureth me, of whom ye say that he is your God, yet ye have not known him, but I know him. And if I should say, "I know him not", I shall be a liar like unto you; but I know him, and keep his saying.

'Your father Abraham rejoiced to see my day, and he saw it and was glad.' Then said the Jews unto him, 'Thou art not yet fifty years old, and hast thou seen Abraham?'

Jesus said unto them, 'Verily, verily I say unto you, before

Abraham was, I am.' Then took they up stones to cast at him, but Jesus hid himself, and went out of the temple.

The Sunday next before Easter.
The Collects.

ALMIGHTY and everlasting God, who, of thy tender love towards mankind, hast sent thy Son, our Saviour Jesus Christ, to take upon him our flesh and to suffer death upon the cross, that all mankind should follow the example of his great humility: Mercifully grant that we may both follow the example of his patience, and also be made partakers of his resurrection, through the same Jesus Christ our Lord. *Amen.*

ALMIGHTY and everlasting God, who hatest nothing that thou hast made, and dost forgive the sins of all those who are penitent: Create and make in us new and contrite hearts, that we, worthily lamenting our sins and acknowledging our wretchedness, may obtain of thee, the God of all mercy, perfect remission and forgiveness, through Jesus Christ our Lord. *Amen.*

The Epistle. Philippians 2:5-11.

LET this mind be in you, which was also in Christ Jesus, who, being in the form of God, thought it not robbery to be equal with God; but made himself of no reputation, and took upon him the form of a servant, and was made in the likeness of men; and being found in fashion as a man, he humbled himself and became obedient unto death, even the death of the cross. Wherefore God also hath highly exalted him, and given him a name which is above every name, that at the name of JESUS every knee should bow, of things in heaven, and things in earth, and things under the earth; and that every tongue should confess that Jesus Christ is Lord, to the glory of God the Father.

The Gospel. St. Matthew 27:1-54.

WHEN the morning was come, all the chief priests and elders of the people took counsel against Jesus to put him to death. And when they had bound him, they led him away, and delivered him to Pontius Pilate the governor.

Then Judas who had betrayed him, when he saw that he was condemned, repented himself and brought again the thirty pieces of silver to the chief priests and elders, saying, 'I have sinned in that I have betrayed the innocent blood.' And they said, 'What is that to us? see thou to that.' And he cast down the pieces of silver in the temple, and departed, and went and hanged himself. And the chief priests took the silver pieces and said, 'It is not lawful for to put them into the treasury, because it is the price of blood.' And they took counsel, and bought with them the potter's field to bury strangers in. Wherefore that field was called 'the field of blood' unto this day. Then was fulfilled that which was spoken by Jeremiah the prophet, saying, 'And they took the thirty pieces of silver, the price of him that was valued, whom they of the children of Israel did value; and gave them for the potter's field, as the Lord appointed me.'

And Jesus stood before the governor, and the governor asked him, saying, 'Art thou the king of the Jews?'

And Jesus said unto him, 'Thou sayest.' And when he was accused of the chief priests and elders, he answered nothing. Then saith Pilate unto him, 'Hearest thou not how many things they witness against thee?' And he answered him to never a word, insomuch that the governor marvelled greatly.

Now at that feast the governor was wont to release unto the people a prisoner, whom they would. And they had then a notable prisoner called Barabbas. Therefore when they were gathered together, Pilate said unto them, 'Whom will ye that I release unto you? Barabbas – or Jesus which is called Christ?' For he knew that for envy they had delivered him.

When he was set down on the judgement seat, his wife sent unto him, saying, 'Have thou nothing to do with that just man, for I have suffered many things this day in a dream because of him.' But the chief priests and elders persuaded the multitude that they should ask Barabbas and destroy Jesus. The governor answered and said unto them, 'Whether of the twain will ye that I release unto you?' They said, 'Barabbas.' Pilate saith unto them, 'What shall I do then with Jesus which is called Christ?' They all say unto him, 'Let him be crucified.' And the governor said, 'Why, what evil hath he done?' But they cried out the more, saying, 'Let him be crucified.'

When Pilate saw that he could prevail nothing, but that rather a tumult was made, he took water, and washed his hands before the multitude, saying, 'I am innocent of the blood of this just person; see ye to it.' Then answered all the people and said, 'His blood be on us and on our children.' Then released he Barabbas unto them, and when he had scourged Jesus, he delivered him to be crucified.

Then the soldiers of the governor took Jesus into the common hall, and gathered unto him the whole band of soldiers. And they stripped him, and put on him a scarlet robe. And when they had plaited a crown of thorns, they put it upon his head, and a reed in his right hand; and they bowed the knee before him, and mocked him, saying, 'Hail, king of the Jews.' And they spat upon him, and took the reed, and smote him on the head. And after that they had mocked him, they took the robe off from him, and put his own raiment on him, and led him away to crucify him. And as they came out, they found a man of Cyrene, Simon by name; him they compelled to bear his cross.

And when they were come unto a place called *Golgotha*, that is to say, 'a place of a skull', they gave him vinegar to drink mingled with gall; and when he had tasted thereof, he would not drink. And they crucified him, and parted his garments, casting lots, that it might be fulfilled which was spoken by the prophet, 'They parted my garments among them, and upon my vesture did they cast lots.' And sitting down they watched him there, and set up over his head his accusation written, *This is Jesus, the king of the Jews.* Then were there two thieves crucified with him, one on the right hand and another on the left.

And they that passed by reviled him, wagging their heads and saying, 'Thou that destroyest the temple and buildest it in three days, save thyself. If thou be the Son of God, come down from the cross.' Likewise also the chief priests mocking him, with the scribes and elders, said, 'He saved others, himself he cannot save. If he be the king of Israel, let him now come down from the cross, and we will believe him. He trusted in God; let him deliver him now, if he will have him, for he said, "I am the Son of God."' The thieves also which were crucified with him cast the same in his teeth.

Now from the sixth hour there was darkness over all the land unto the ninth hour. And about the ninth hour Jesus cried with a loud voice, saying, *Eli, Eli, lama sabachthani?* that is to say, 'My God, my God, why hast thou forsaken me?' Some of them that stood there, when they heard that, said, 'This man calleth for Elijah.' And straightway one of them ran and took a sponge, and filled it with vinegar, and put it on a reed, and gave him to drink. The rest said, 'Let be; let us see whether Elijah will come to save him.'

Jesus, when he had cried again with a loud voice, yielded up the ghost. And behold, the veil of the temple was rent in twain from the top to the bottom, and the earth did quake, and the rocks rent. And the graves were opened; and many bodies of saints which slept, arose and came out of the graves after his resurrection, and went into the holy city, and appeared unto many. Now when the centurion and they that were with him, watching Jesus, saw the earthquake and those things that were done, they feared greatly, saying, 'Truly this was the Son of God.'

Monday before Easter.
The Collects.

ALMIGHTY and everlasting God, who, of thy tender love towards mankind, hast sent thy Son, our Saviour Jesus Christ, to take upon him our flesh and to suffer death upon the cross, that all mankind should follow the example of his great humility: Mercifully grant that we may both follow the example of his patience, and also be made partakers of his resurrection, through the same Jesus Christ our Lord. *Amen.*

ALMIGHTY and everlasting God, who hatest nothing that thou hast made, and dost forgive the sins of all those who are penitent: Create and make in us new and contrite hearts, that we, worthily lamenting our sins and acknowledging our wretchedness, may obtain of thee, the God of all mercy, perfect remission and forgiveness, through Jesus Christ our Lord. *Amen.*

For the Epistle. Isaiah 63.

'WHO is this that cometh from Edom, with dyed garments from Bozrah? this that is glorious in his apparel, travelling in the greatness of his strength?' 'I that speak in righteousness, mighty to save.' 'Wherefore art thou red in thine apparel, and thy garments like him that treadeth in the wine vat?' 'I have trodden the wine-press alone, and of the people there was none with me, for I will tread them in mine anger, and trample them in my fury, and their blood shall be sprinkled upon my garments, and I will stain all my raiment. For the day of vengeance is in mine heart, and the year of my redeemed is come. And I looked, and there was none to help, and I wondered that there was none to uphold. Therefore mine own arm brought salvation unto me, and my fury, it upheld me. And I will tread down the people in mine anger, and make them drunk in my fury, and I will bring down their strength to the earth.'

I will mention the loving-kindnesses of the LORD, and the praises of the LORD, according to all that the LORD hath bestowed on us; and the great goodness towards the house of Israel, which he hath bestowed on them according to his mercies, and according to the multitude of his loving-kindnesses. For he said, 'Surely they are my people, children that will not lie'; so he was their saviour. In all their affliction he was afflicted, and the angel of his presence saved them; in his love and in his pity he redeemed them, and he bare them, and carried them all the days of old.

But they rebelled and vexed his Holy Spirit; therefore he was turned to be their enemy, and he fought against them. Then he remembered the days of old, Moses and his people, saying, 'Where is he that brought them up out of the sea with the shepherd of his flock? where is he that put his Holy Spirit within him? that led them by the right hand of Moses, with his glorious arm, dividing the water before them, to make himself an everlasting name? that led them through the deep as an horse in the wilderness, that they should not stumble?' As a beast goeth down into the valley, the Spirit of the LORD caused him to rest; so didst thou lead thy people, to make thyself a glorious name.

Look down from heaven, and behold from the habitation of thy holiness and of thy glory. Where is thy zeal and thy strength, the sounding of thy bowels and of thy mercies towards me? Are they restrained? Doubtless thou art our Father, though Abraham be ignorant of us, and Israel acknowledge us not. Thou, O LORD, art our Father, our Redeemer, thy name is from everlasting.

O LORD, why hast thou made us to err from thy ways, and hardened our heart from thy fear? Return for thy servants' sake, the tribes of thine inheritance. The people of thy holiness have possessed it but a little while: our adversaries have trodden down thy sanctuary. We are thine; thou never barest rule over them; they were not called by thy name.

The Gospel. St. Mark 14.

AFTER two days was the feast of the Passover and of unleavened bread. And the chief priests and the scribes sought how they might take him by craft and put him to death. But they said, 'Not on the feast day, lest there be an uproar of the people.'

And being in Bethany, in the house of Simon the leper, as he sat at meat, there came a woman having an alabaster box of ointment of spikenard, very precious, and she brake the box and poured it on his head. And there were some that had indignation within themselves and said, 'Why was this waste of the ointment made? for it might have been sold for more than three hundred pence, and have been given to the poor.' And they murmured against her. And Jesus said, 'Let her alone; why trouble ye her? she hath wrought a good work on me. For ye have the poor with you always, and whensoever ye will ye may do them good, but me ye have not always. She hath done what she could;

she is come aforehand to anoint my body to the burying. Verily I say unto you, wheresoever this gospel shall be preached throughout the whole world, this also that she hath done shall be spoken of for a memorial of her.'

And Judas Iscariot, one of the twelve, went unto the chief priests, to betray him unto them. And when they heard it, they were glad, and promised to give him money. And he sought how he might conveniently betray him.

And the first day of unleavened bread, when they killed the Passover, his disciples said unto him, 'Where wilt thou that we go and prepare, that thou mayest eat the Passover?' And he sendeth forth two of his disciples and saith unto them, 'Go ye into the city, and there shall meet you a man bearing a pitcher of water. Follow him. And wheresoever he shall go in, say ye to the goodman of the house, "The master saith, 'Where is the guest-chamber where I shall eat the Passover with my disciples?'" And he will show you a large upper room furnished and prepared; there make ready for us.' And his disciples went forth and came into the city, and found as he had said unto them, and they made ready the Passover.

And in the evening he cometh with the twelve. And as they sat and did eat, Jesus said, 'Verily I say unto you, one of you which eateth with me shall betray me.' And they began to be sorrowful, and to say unto him one by one, 'Is it I?' And another said, 'Is it I?' And he answered and said unto them, 'It is one of the twelve, that dippeth with me in the dish. The Son of Man indeed goeth, as it is written of him, but woe to that man by whom the Son of Man is betrayed. Good were it for that man if he had never been born.' And as they did eat, Jesus took bread, and blessed, and brake it, and gave to them, and said, 'Take, eat; this is my body.' And he took the cup, and when he had given thanks he gave it to them, and they all drank of it. And he said unto them, 'This is my blood of the new testament, which is shed for many. Verily I say unto you, I will drink no more of the fruit of the vine until that day that I drink it new in the kingdom of God.'

And when they had sung an hymn, they went out into the Mount of Olives.

And Jesus saith unto them, 'All ye shall be offended because of me this night, for it is written, "I will smite the shepherd, and the sheep shall be scattered." But, after that I am risen, I will go before you into Galilee.' But Peter said unto him, 'Although all shall be offended, yet will not I.'

And Jesus saith unto him, 'Verily I say unto thee, that this day, even in this night, before the cock crow twice, thou shalt deny me thrice.' But he spake the more vehemently, 'If I should die with thee, I will not deny thee in any wise.' Likewise also said they all.

And they came to a place which was named Gethsemane, and he saith to his disciples, 'Sit ye here, while I shall pray.' And he taketh with him Peter and James and John, and began to be sore amazed, and to be very heavy, and saith unto them, 'My soul is exceeding sorrowful unto death. Tarry ye here, and watch.' And he went forward a little and fell on the ground, and prayed that, if it were possible, the hour might pass from him. And he said, '*Abba*, Father, all things are possible unto thee. Take away this cup from me; nevertheless not what I will, but what thou wilt.' And he cometh and findeth them sleeping, and saith unto Peter, 'Simon, sleepest thou? couldest not thou watch one hour? Watch ye and pray, lest ye enter into temptation. The spirit truly is ready, but the flesh is weak.' And again he went away and prayed, and spake the same words. And when he returned, he found them asleep again (for their eyes were heavy), neither wist they what to answer him. And he cometh the third time and saith unto them, 'Sleep on now, and take your rest. It is enough. The hour is come; behold, the Son of Man is betrayed into the hands of sinners. Rise up; let us go. Lo, he that betrayeth me is at hand.'

And immediately, while he yet spake, cometh Judas, one of the twelve, and with him a great multitude with swords and staves, from the chief priests and the scribes and the elders. And he that betrayed him had given them a token, saying, 'Whomsoever I shall kiss, that same is he. Take him and lead him away safely.' And as soon as he was come, he goeth straightway to him and saith, 'Master, master', and kissed him. And they laid their hands on him and took him. And one of them that stood by drew a sword, and smote a servant of the high priest and cut off his ear. And Jesus answered and said unto them, 'Are ye come out as against a thief, with swords and with staves to take me? I was daily with you in the temple teaching, and ye took me not, but the Scriptures must be fulfilled.' And they all forsook him and fled. And there followed him a certain young man, having a linen cloth cast about his naked body, and the young men laid hold on him. And he left the linen cloth and fled from them naked.

And they led Jesus away to the high priest, and with him were assembled all the chief priests and the elders and the scribes. And Peter followed him afar off, even into the palace of the high priest, and he sat with the servants and warmed himself at the fire.

And the chief priests and all the council sought for witness against Jesus to put him to death, and found none. For many bare false witness against him, but their witness agreed not together.

And there arose certain, and bare false witness against him, saying, 'We heard him say, "I will destroy this temple that is made with hands, and within three days I will build another made without hands."' But neither so did their witness agree together. And the high priest stood up in the midst and asked Jesus, saying, 'Answerest thou nothing? what is it which these witness against thee?' But he held his peace and answered nothing. Again the high priest asked him and said unto him, 'Art thou the Christ, the Son of the Blessed?' And Jesus said, 'I am, and "ye shall see the Son of Man sitting on the right hand of power" and "coming in the clouds of heaven."' Then the high priest rent his clothes and saith, 'What need we any further witnesses? ye have heard the blasphemy – what think ye?' And they all condemned him to be guilty of death. And some began to spit on him, and to cover his face, and to buffet him, and to say unto him, 'Prophesy', and the servants did strike him with the palms of their hands.

And as Peter was beneath in the palace, there cometh one of the maids of the high priest. And when she saw Peter warming himself, she looked upon him and said,

'And thou also wast with Jesus of Nazareth.' But he denied, saying, 'I know not, neither understand I what thou sayest.' And he went out into the porch, and the cock crew. And a maid saw him again, and began to say to them that stood by, 'This is one of them.' And he denied it again. And a little after, they that stood by said again to Peter, 'Surely thou art one of them, for thou art a Galilean, and thy speech agreeth thereto.' But he began to curse and to swear, saying, 'I know not this man of whom ye speak.' And the second time the cock crew. And Peter called to mind the word that Jesus said unto him, 'Before the cock crow twice, thou shalt deny me thrice.' And when he thought thereon, he wept.

Tuesday before Easter.
The Collects.

ALMIGHTY and everlasting God, who, of thy tender love towards mankind, hast sent thy Son, our Saviour Jesus Christ, to take upon him our flesh and to suffer death upon the cross, that all mankind should follow the example of his great humility: Mercifully grant that we may both follow the example of his patience, and also be made partakers of his resurrection, through the same Jesus Christ our Lord. *Amen.*

ALMIGHTY and everlasting God, who hatest nothing that thou hast made, and dost forgive the sins of all those who are penitent: Create and make in us new and contrite hearts, that we, worthily lamenting our sins and acknowledging our wretchedness, may obtain of thee, the God of all mercy, perfect remission and forgiveness, through Jesus Christ our Lord. *Amen.*

For the Epistle. Isaiah 50:5-11.

THE Lord GOD hath opened mine ear, and I was not rebellious, neither turned away back. I gave my back to the smiters, and my cheeks to them that plucked off the hair; I hid not my face from shame and spitting. For the Lord GOD will help me; therefore shall I not be confounded; therefore have I set my face like a flint, and I know that I shall not be ashamed. He is near that justifieth me; who will contend with me? let us stand together. Who is mine adversary? let him come near to me. Behold, the Lord GOD will help me; who is he that shall condemn me? lo, they all shall wax old as a garment; the moth shall eat them up. Who is among you that feareth the LORD, that obeyeth the voice of his servant, that walketh in darkness and hath no light? let him trust in the name of the LORD, and stay upon his God. Behold, all ye that kindle a fire, that compass yourselves about with sparks: walk in the light of your fire, and in the sparks that ye have kindled. This shall ye have of mine hand: ye shall lie down in sorrow.

The Gospel. St. Mark 15:1-39.

AND straightway in the morning the chief priests held a consultation with the elders and scribes and the whole council, and bound Jesus, and carried him away, and delivered him to Pilate.

And Pilate asked him, 'Art thou the king of the Jews?' And he answering said unto him, 'Thou sayest it.' And the chief priests accused him of many things, but he answered nothing.

And Pilate asked him again, saying, 'Answerest thou nothing? behold how many things they witness against thee.'

But Jesus yet answered nothing, so that Pilate marvelled. Now at that feast he released unto them one prisoner, whomsoever they desired. And there was one named Barabbas, which lay bound with them that had made insurrection with him, who had committed murder in the insurrection. And the multitude, crying aloud, began to desire him to do as he had ever done unto them.

But Pilate answered them, saying, 'Will ye that I release unto you the king of the Jews?' For he knew that the chief priests had delivered him for envy. But the chief priests moved the people, that he should rather release Barabbas unto them.

And Pilate answered and said again unto them, 'What will ye then that I shall do unto him whom ye call the king of the Jews?' And they cried out again, 'Crucify him.' Then Pilate said unto them, 'Why, what evil hath he done?' And they cried out the more exceedingly, 'Crucify him.' And so Pilate, willing to content the people, released Barabbas unto them, and delivered Jesus, when he had scourged him, to be crucified.

And the soldiers led him away into the hall called *Praetorium*, and they call together the whole band. And they clothed him with purple, and plaited a crown of thorns, and put it about his head, and began to salute him, 'Hail, king of the Jews.' And they smote him on the head with a reed, and did spit upon him, and bowing their knees worshipped him. And when they had mocked him, they took off the purple from him, and put his own clothes on him, and led him out to crucify him. And they compel one Simon, a Cyrenian, who passed by, coming out of the country, the father of Alexander and Rufus, to bear his cross. And they bring him unto the place *Golgotha,* which is, being interpreted, 'the place of a skull.' And they gave him to drink wine mingled with myrrh, but he received it not.

And when they had crucified him, they parted his garments, casting lots upon them, what every man should take. And it was the third hour, and they crucified him. And the superscription of his accusation was written over, *The king of the Jews.* And with him they crucify two thieves, the one on his right hand and the other on his left. And the Scripture was fulfilled which saith, 'And he was numbered with the transgressors.' And they that passed by railed on him, wagging their heads and saying, 'Ah, thou that destroyest the temple, and buildest it in three days, save thyself, and come down from the cross.' Likewise also the chief priests mocking said among themselves, with the scribes, 'He saved others, himself he cannot save. Let Christ the king of Israel descend now from the cross, that we may see and believe.' And they that were crucified with him reviled him.

And when the sixth hour was come, there was darkness over the whole land until the ninth hour. And at the ninth hour Jesus cried with a loud voice, saying, *Eloi, Eloi, lama sabachthani?* which is, being interpreted, 'My God, my

God, why hast thou forsaken me?' And some of them that stood by, when they heard it, said, 'Behold, he calleth Elijah.' And one ran and filled a sponge full of vinegar, and put it on a reed, and gave him to drink, saying, 'Let alone; let us see whether Elijah will come to take him down.' And Jesus cried with a loud voice and gave up the ghost.

And the veil of the temple was rent in twain from the top to the bottom. And when the centurion, which stood over against him, saw that he so cried out and gave up the ghost, he said, 'Truly this man was the Son of God.'

Wednesday before Easter.
The Collects.

ALMIGHTY and everlasting God, who, of thy tender love towards mankind, hast sent thy Son, our Saviour Jesus Christ, to take upon him our flesh and to suffer death upon the cross, that all mankind should follow the example of his great humility: Mercifully grant that we may both follow the example of his patience, and also be made partakers of his resurrection, through the same Jesus Christ our Lord. *Amen.*

ALMIGHTY and everlasting God, who hatest nothing that thou hast made, and dost forgive the sins of all those who are penitent: Create and make in us new and contrite hearts, that we, worthily lamenting our sins and acknowledging our wretchedness, may obtain of thee, the God of all mercy, perfect remission and forgiveness, through Jesus Christ our Lord. *Amen.*

WEDNESDAY BEFORE EASTER

The Epistle. Hebrews 9:16-28.

WHERE a testament is, there must also of necessity be the death of the testator, for a testament is of force after men are dead; otherwise it is of no strength at all while the testator liveth. Whereupon neither the first testament was dedicated without blood, for when Moses had spoken every precept to all the people, according to the law, he took the blood of calves and of goats, with water and scarlet wool and hyssop, and sprinkled both the book and all the people, saying, 'This is the blood of the testament, which God hath enjoined unto you.' Moreover he sprinkled with blood both the tabernacle and all the vessels of the ministry. And almost all things are by the law purged with blood, and without shedding of blood is no remission.

It was therefore necessary that the patterns of things in the heavens should be purified with these, but the heavenly things themselves with better sacrifices than these. For Christ is not entered into the holy places made with hands, which are the figures of the true, but into heaven itself, now to appear in the presence of God for us; nor yet that he should offer himself often, as the high priest entereth into the holy place every year with blood of others, for then must he often have suffered since the foundation of the world, but now once in the end of the world hath he appeared to put away sin by the sacrifice of himself. And as it is appointed unto men once to die, but after this the judgement, so Christ was once offered to bear the sins of many, and unto them that look for him shall he appear the second time without sin unto salvation.

The Gospel. St. Luke 22.

Now the feast of unleavened bread drew nigh, which is called the Passover. And the chief priests and scribes sought how they might kill him, for they feared the people. Then entered Satan into Judas surnamed Iscariot, being of the number of the twelve. And he went his way and communed with the chief priests and captains, how he might betray him unto them. And they were glad and covenanted to give him money. And he promised and sought opportunity to betray him unto them in the absence of the multitude.

Then came the day of unleavened bread, when the Passover must be killed. And he sent Peter and John, saying, 'Go and prepare us the Passover, that we may eat.' And they said unto him, 'Where wilt thou that we prepare?' And he said unto them, 'Behold, when ye are entered into the city, there shall a man meet you, bearing a pitcher of water. Follow him into the house where he entereth in. And ye shall say unto the goodman of the house, "The master saith unto thee, 'Where is the guest-chamber, where I shall eat the Passover with my disciples?'" And he shall show you a large upper room furnished; there make ready.' And they went and found as he had said unto them, and they made ready the Passover. And when the hour was come, he sat down, and the twelve apostles with him. And he said unto them, 'With desire I have desired to eat this Passover with you before I suffer. For I say unto you, I will not anymore eat thereof until it be fulfilled in the kingdom of God.' And he took the cup, and gave thanks, and said, 'Take this, and divide it among yourselves. For I say unto you, I will not drink of the fruit of the vine until the kingdom of God shall come.'

And he took bread, and gave thanks, and brake it, and gave unto them, saying, 'This is my body, which is given for you. This do in remembrance of me.' Likewise also the cup after supper, saying, 'This cup is the new testament in my blood, which is shed for you. But behold, the hand of him that betrayeth me is with me on the table. And truly the Son of Man goeth, as it was determined, but woe unto that man by whom he is betrayed.' And they began to inquire among themselves which of them it was that should do this thing.

And there was also a strife among them, which of them should be accounted the greatest. And he said unto them, 'The kings of the Gentiles exercise lordship over them, and they that exercise authority upon them are called benefactors. But ye shall not be so, but he that is greatest among you, let him be as the younger, and he that is chief, as he that doth serve. For whether is greater, he that sitteth at meat or he that serveth? is not he that sitteth at meat? But I am among you as he that serveth. Ye are they which have continued with me in my temptations. And I appoint unto you a kingdom, as my Father hath appointed unto me, that ye may eat and drink at my table in my kingdom, and sit on thrones judging the twelve tribes of Israel.'

And the Lord said, 'Simon, Simon, behold, Satan hath desired to have you, that he may sift you as wheat, but I have prayed for thee, that thy faith fail not. And when thou art converted, strengthen thy brethren.' And he said unto him, 'Lord, I am ready to go with thee, both into prison and to death.' And he said, 'I tell thee, Peter, the cock shall not crow this day, before that thou shalt thrice deny that thou knowest me.'

And he said unto them, 'When I sent you without purse and scrip and shoes, lacked ye anything?' And they said, 'Nothing.' Then said he unto them, 'But now, he that hath a purse, let him take it, and likewise his scrip. And he that hath no sword, let him sell his garment and buy one. For I say unto you that this that is written must yet be accomplished in me, "And he was reckoned among the transgressors", for the things concerning me have an end.' And they said, 'Lord, behold, here are two swords.' And he said unto them, 'It is enough.'

And he came out and went, as he was wont, to the Mount of Olives, and his disciples also followed him. And when he was at the place, he said unto them, 'Pray that ye enter not into temptation.' And he was withdrawn from them about a stone's cast, and kneeled down and prayed, saying, 'Father, if thou be willing, remove this cup from me; nevertheless not my will, but thine be done.' And there appeared an angel unto him from heaven, strengthening him. And being in an agony he prayed more earnestly, and his sweat was as it were great drops of blood falling down to the ground. And when he rose up from prayer and was come to his disciples, he found them sleeping for sorrow, and said unto them, 'Why sleep ye? rise and pray, lest ye enter into temptation.'

And while he yet spake, behold, a multitude, and he that was called Judas, one of the twelve, went before them and drew near unto Jesus to kiss him. But Jesus said unto him,

'Judas, betrayest thou the Son of Man with a kiss?' When they who were about him saw what would follow, they said unto him, 'Lord, shall we smite with the sword?' And one of them smote the servant of the high priest and cut off his right ear. And Jesus answered and said, 'Suffer ye thus far.' And he touched his ear, and healed him. Then Jesus said unto the chief priests and captains of the temple and the elders who were come to him, 'Be ye come out as against a thief, with swords and staves? When I was daily with you in the temple, ye stretched forth no hands against me. But this is your hour, and the power of darkness.'

Then took they him, and led him, and brought him into the high priest's house; and Peter followed afar off. And when they had kindled a fire in the midst of the hall, and were set down together, Peter sat down among them. But a certain maid beheld him as he sat by the fire, and earnestly looked upon him and said, 'This man was also with him.' And he denied him, saying, 'Woman, I know him not.'

And after a little while another saw him and said, 'Thou art also of them.' And Peter said, 'Man, I am not.' And about the space of one hour after, another confidently affirmed, saying, 'Of a truth this fellow also was with him, for he is a Galilean.' And Peter said, 'Man, I know not what thou sayest.' And immediately, while he yet spake, the cock crew. And the Lord turned and looked upon Peter. And Peter remembered the word of the Lord, how he had said unto him, 'Before the cock crow, thou shalt deny me thrice.' And Peter went out and wept bitterly.

And the men that held Jesus mocked him and smote him. And when they had blindfolded him, they struck him on the face and asked him, saying, 'Prophesy, who is it that smote thee?' And many other things blasphemously spake they against him. And as soon as it was day, the elders of the people and the chief priests and the scribes came together, and led him into their council, saying, 'Art thou the Christ? tell us.' And he said unto them, 'If I tell you, ye will not believe. And if I also ask you, ye will not answer me, nor let me go. Hereafter shall the Son of Man sit on the right hand of the power of God.'

Then said they all, 'Art thou then the Son of God?' And he said unto them, 'Ye say that I am.' And they said, 'What need we any further witness? for we ourselves have heard of his own mouth.'

Thursday before Easter.
The Collects.

ALMIGHTY and everlasting God, who, of thy tender love towards mankind, hast sent thy Son, our Saviour Jesus Christ, to take upon him our flesh and to suffer death upon the cross, that all mankind should follow the example of his great humility: Mercifully grant that we may both follow the example of his patience, and also be made partakers of his resurrection, through the same Jesus Christ our Lord. *Amen.*

ALMIGHTY and everlasting God, who hatest nothing that thou hast made, and dost forgive the sins of all those who are penitent: Create and make in us new and contrite hearts, that we, worthily lamenting our sins and acknowledging our wretchedness, may obtain of thee, the God of all mercy, perfect remission and forgiveness, through Jesus Christ our Lord. *Amen.*

The Epistle. 1 Corinthians 11:17-34.

I N this that I declare unto you I praise you not, that ye come together not for the better, but for the worse.

For first of all, when ye come together in the church, I hear that there be divisions among you, and I partly believe it. For there must be also heresies among you, that they who are approved may be made manifest among you. When ye come together therefore into one place, this is not to eat the Lord's supper. For in eating every one taketh before other his own supper, and one is hungry, and another is drunken. What, have ye not houses to eat and to drink in? or despise ye the church of God, and shame them that have not? What shall I say to you? shall I praise you in this? I praise you not. For I have received of the Lord that which also I delivered unto you, that the Lord Jesus, the same night in which he was betrayed, took bread, and when he had given thanks, he brake it, and said, 'Take, eat; this is my body, which is broken for you. This do in remembrance of me.' After the same manner also he took the cup, when he had supped, saying, 'This cup is the new testament in my blood. This do ye, as oft as ye drink it, in remembrance of me.' For as often as ye eat this bread and drink this cup, ye do show the Lord's death till he come.

Wherefore whosoever shall eat this bread and drink this cup of the Lord unworthily, shall be guilty of the body and blood of the Lord. But let a man examine himself, and so let him eat of that bread and drink of that cup. For he that eateth and drinketh unworthily, eateth and drinketh damnation to himself, not discerning the Lord's body. For this cause many are weak and sickly among you and many sleep. For if we would judge ourselves, we should not be judged. But when we are judged, we are chastened of the Lord, that we should not be condemned with the world.

Wherefore, my brethren, when ye come together to eat, tarry one for another. And if any man hunger, let him eat at home, that ye come not together unto condemnation. And the rest will I set in order when I come.

The Gospel. St. Luke 23:1-49.

T HE whole multitude of them arose and led him unto Pilate.

And they began to accuse him, saying, 'We found this fellow perverting the nation, and forbidding to give tribute to Caesar, saying that he himself is Christ a king.'

And Pilate asked him, saying, 'Art thou the king of the Jews?' And he answered him and said, 'Thou sayest it.' Then said Pilate to the chief priests and to the people, 'I find no fault in this man.' And they were the more fierce, saying, 'He stirreth up the people, teaching throughout all Jewry, beginning from Galilee to this place.'

When Pilate heard of Galilee, he asked whether the man were a Galilean. And as soon as he knew that he belonged unto Herod's jurisdiction, he sent him to Herod, who himself was also at Jerusalem at that time.

And when Herod saw Jesus he was exceeding glad, for he was desirous to see him of a long season, because he had heard many things of him, and he hoped to have seen some miracle done by him. Then he questioned with him in many words, but he answered him nothing. And the chief priests and scribes stood and vehemently accused him. And Herod with his men of war set him at naught and mocked him, and arrayed him in a gorgeous robe, and sent him again to Pilate. And the same day Pilate and Herod were made friends together, for before they were at enmity between themselves.

And Pilate, when he had called together the chief priests and the rulers and the people, said unto them, 'Ye have brought this man unto me as one that perverteth the people, and behold, I, having examined him before you, have found no fault in this man touching those things whereof ye accuse him. No, nor yet Herod, for I sent you to him, and lo, nothing worthy of death is done by him. I will therefore chastise him and release him.' For of necessity he must release one unto them at the feast. And they cried out all at once, saying, 'Away with this man, and release unto us Barabbas' (who, for a certain sedition made in the city and for murder, was cast into prison).

Pilate therefore, willing to release Jesus, spake again to them. But they cried, saying, 'Crucify him, crucify him.'

And he said unto them the third time, 'Why, what evil hath he done? I have found no cause of death in him; I will therefore chastise him and let him go.' And they were instant with loud voices, requiring that he might be crucified; and the voices of them and of the chief priests prevailed. And Pilate gave sentence that it should be as they required. And he released unto them him that for sedition and murder was cast into prison, whom they had desired, but he delivered Jesus to their will.

And as they led him away, they laid hold upon one Simon, a Cyrenian, coming out of the country, and on him they laid the cross, that he might bear it after Jesus. And there followed him a great company of people, and of women, which also bewailed and lamented him. But Jesus turning unto them said, 'Daughters of Jerusalem, weep not for me, but weep for yourselves, and for your children. For behold, the days are coming, in the which they shall say, "Blessed are the barren, and the wombs that never bare, and the paps which never gave suck." Then shall they begin to say to the mountains, "Fall on us", and to the hills, "Cover us." For if they do these things in a green tree, what shall be done in the dry?'

And there were also two others, malefactors, led with him to be put to death. And when they were come to the place which is called Calvary, there they crucified him, and the malefactors, one on the right hand and the other on the left. Then said Jesus, 'Father, forgive them, for they know not what they do.' And they parted his raiment and cast lots. And the people stood beholding; and the rulers also with them derided him, saying, 'He saved others, let him save himself, if he be Christ, the chosen of God.'

And the soldiers also mocked him, coming to him and offering him vinegar and saying, 'If thou be the king of the Jews, save thyself.' And a superscription also was written over him in letters of Greek and Latin and Hebrew, *This is the king of the Jews.*

And one of the malefactors which were hanged railed on him, saying, 'If thou be Christ, save thyself and us.'

But the other answering rebuked him, saying, 'Dost not thou fear God, seeing thou art in the same condemnation? And we indeed justly, for we receive the due reward of our deeds, but this man hath done nothing amiss.' And he said unto Jesus, 'Lord, remember me when thou comest into thy kingdom.' And Jesus said unto him, 'Verily I say unto thee, today shalt thou be with me in paradise.'

And it was about the sixth hour, and there was a darkness over all the earth until the ninth hour. And the sun was darkened, and the veil of the temple was rent in the midst. And when Jesus had cried with a loud voice, he said, 'Father, into thy hands I commend my spirit'; and having said thus, he gave up the ghost.

Now when the centurion saw what was done, he glorified God, saying, 'Certainly this was a righteous man.' And all the people that came together to that sight, beholding the things that were done, smote their breasts, and returned.

And all his acquaintance, and the women that followed him from Galilee, stood afar off, beholding these things.

Good Friday.
The Collects.

ALMIGHTY God, we beseech thee graciously to behold this thy family, for which our Lord Jesus Christ was contented to be betrayed and given up into the hands of wicked men, and to suffer death upon the cross, who now liveth and reigneth with thee and the Holy Ghost, ever one God, world without end. *Amen.*

ALMIGHTY and everlasting God, by whose Spirit the whole body of the church is governed and sanctified: Receive our supplications and prayers, which we offer before thee for all estates of men in thy holy church, that every member of the same, in his vocation and ministry, may truly and godly serve thee, through our Lord and Saviour Jesus Christ. *Amen.*

O MERCIFUL God, who hast made all men, and hatest nothing that thou hast made, nor desirest the death of a sinner, but rather that he should be converted and live: Have mercy upon all Jews, Muslims, unbelievers, and heretics, and take from them all ignorance, hardness of heart, and contempt of thy word; and so fetch them home, blessed Lord, to thy flock, that they may be saved among the remnant of the true Israelites, and be made one fold under one shepherd, Jesus Christ our Lord, who liveth and reigneth with thee and the Holy Spirit, one God, world without end. *Amen.*

ALMIGHTY and everlasting God, who hatest nothing that thou hast made, and dost forgive the sins of all those who are penitent: Create and make in us new and contrite hearts, that we, worthily lamenting our sins and acknowledging our wretchedness, may obtain of thee, the God of all mercy, perfect remission and forgiveness, through Jesus Christ our Lord. *Amen.*

The Epistle. Hebrews 10:1-25.

THE law having a shadow of good things to come, and not the very image of the things, can never with those sacrifices, which they offered year by year continually, make the comers thereunto perfect. For then would they not have ceased to be offered? because that the worshippers once purged should have had no more conscience of sins. But in those sacrifices there is a remembrance again made of sins every year. For it is not possible that the blood of bulls and of goats should take away sins.

Wherefore when he cometh into the world, he saith, 'Sacrifice and offering thou wouldest not, but a body hast thou prepared me; in burnt offerings and sacrifices for sin thou hast had no pleasure. Then said I, "Lo, I come; in the volume of the book it is written of me, 'To do thy will, O God.'"' Above, when he said, 'Sacrifice and offering and burnt offerings and offering for sin thou wouldest not, neither hadst pleasure therein' (which are offered by the law), then said he, 'Lo, I come to do thy will, O God.' He taketh away the first, that he may establish the second. By the which will, we are sanctified through the offering of the body of Jesus Christ once for all.

And every priest standeth daily ministering and offering oftentimes the same sacrifices which can never take away sins. But this man, after he had offered one sacrifice for sins for ever, sat down on the right hand of God, from henceforth expecting till his enemies be made his footstool. For by one offering he hath perfected for ever them that are sanctified. Whereof the Holy Ghost also is a witness to us, for after that he had said before, "'This is the covenant that I will make with them after those days", saith the Lord, "I will put my laws into their hearts, and in their minds will I write them, and their sins and iniquities will I remember no more." Now where remission of these is, there is no more offering for sin.

Having therefore, brethren, boldness to enter into the holiest by the blood of Jesus, by a new and living way, which he hath consecrated for us, through the veil (that is to say, his flesh), and having an high priest over the house of God, let us draw near with a true heart, in full assurance of faith, having our hearts sprinkled from an evil conscience, and our bodies washed with pure water. Let us hold fast the profession of our faith without wavering – for he is faithful that promised – and let us consider one another to provoke unto love and to good works, not forsaking the assembling of ourselves together, as the manner of some is, but exhorting one another, and so much the more as ye see the day approaching.

The Gospel. St. John 19:1-37.

PILATE therefore took Jesus and scourged him. And the soldiers plaited a crown of thorns, and put it on his head, and they put on him a purple robe and said, 'Hail, king of the Jews'; and they smote him with their hands.

Pilate therefore went forth again and saith unto them, 'Behold, I bring him forth to you, that ye may know that I find no fault in him.'

Then came Jesus forth, wearing the crown of thorns and the purple robe. And Pilate saith unto them, 'Behold the man.' When the chief priests therefore and officers saw him, they cried out, saying, 'Crucify him, crucify him.'

Pilate saith unto them, 'Take ye him and crucify him, for I find no fault in him.' The Jews answered him, 'We have a law, and by our law he ought to die, because he made himself the Son of God.'

When Pilate therefore heard that saying, he was the more afraid, and went again into the judgement hall and saith unto Jesus, 'Whence art thou?' But Jesus gave him no answer. Then saith Pilate unto him, 'Speakest thou not unto me? knowest thou not that I have power to crucify thee, and have power to release thee?' Jesus answered, 'Thou couldest have no power at all against me, except it were given thee from above. Therefore he that delivered me unto thee hath the greater sin.' And from thenceforth Pilate sought to release him.

But the Jews cried out, saying, 'If thou let this man go, thou art not Caesar's friend. Whosoever maketh himself a king, speaketh against Caesar.'

When Pilate therefore heard that saying, he brought Jesus forth and sat down in the judgement seat, in a place that is called 'the pavement', but in the Hebrew, *Gabbatha*. And it was the preparation of the Passover, and about the sixth hour, and he saith unto the Jews, 'Behold your king.' But they cried out, 'Away with him; away with him; crucify him.' Pilate saith unto them, 'Shall I crucify your king?'

The chief priests answered, 'We have no king but Caesar.'

Then delivered he him therefore unto them to be crucified, and they took Jesus and led him away. And he, bearing his cross, went forth into a place called 'the place of a skull', which is called in the Hebrew *Golgotha*, where they crucified him, and two others with him, on either side one and Jesus in the midst.

And Pilate wrote a title and put it on the cross. And the writing was, *Jesus of Nazareth, the king of the Jews.* This title then read many of the Jews, for the place where Jesus was crucified was nigh to the city, and it was written in Hebrew and Greek and Latin.

Then said the chief priests of the Jews to Pilate, 'Write not "The king of the Jews", but that he said "I am king of the Jews."' Pilate answered, 'What I have written, I have written.'

Then the soldiers, when they had crucified Jesus, took his garments and made four parts, to every soldier a part, and also his coat. Now the coat was without seam, woven from the top throughout. They said therefore among themselves, 'Let us not rend it, but cast lots for it, whose it shall be', that the Scripture might be fulfilled which saith, 'They parted my raiment among them, and for my vesture they did cast lots.'

These things therefore the soldiers did. Now there stood by the cross of Jesus his mother and his mother's sister, Mary the wife of Clopas, and Mary Magdalene.

When Jesus therefore saw his mother, and the disciple standing by whom he loved, he saith unto his mother, 'Woman, behold thy son.' Then saith he to the disciple, 'Behold thy mother.' And from that hour that disciple took her unto his own home.

After this Jesus, knowing that all things were now accomplished, that the Scripture might be fulfilled, saith,

'I thirst.' Now there was set a vessel full of vinegar, and they filled a sponge with vinegar, and put it upon hyssop, and put it to his mouth. When Jesus therefore had received the vinegar, he said, 'It is finished', and he bowed his head, and gave up the ghost.

The Jews therefore, because it was the preparation, that the bodies should not remain upon the cross on the Sabbath day (for that Sabbath day was an high day), besought Pilate that their legs might be broken, and that they might be taken away. Then came the soldiers and brake the legs of the first, and of the other which was crucified with him. But when they came to Jesus and saw that he was dead already, they brake not his legs. But one of the soldiers with a spear pierced his side, and forthwith came there out blood and water. And he that saw it bare record, and his record is true, and he knoweth that he saith true, that ye might believe. For these things were done that the Scripture should be fulfilled, 'A bone of him shall not be broken.' And again another Scripture saith, 'They shall look on him whom they pierced.'

Easter Even.
The Collect.

GRANT, O Lord, that as we are baptized into the death of thy blessed Son, our Saviour Jesus Christ, so by continually mortifying our corrupt affections we may be buried with him, and that through the grave, and gate of death, we may pass to our joyful resurrection, for his merits, who died and was buried and rose again for us, thy Son Jesus Christ our Lord. *Amen.*

The Epistle. 1 Peter 3:17-22.

IT is better, if the will of God be so, that ye suffer for well-doing than for evil-doing. For Christ also hath once suffered for sins, the just for the unjust, that he might bring us to God, being put to death in the flesh, but quickened by the Spirit – by which also he went and preached unto the spirits in prison, which sometime were disobedient, when once the long-suffering of God waited in the days of Noah, while the ark was a-preparing, wherein few (that is, eight) souls were saved by water. The like figure whereunto, even baptism, doth also now save us – not the putting away of the filth of the flesh, but the answer of a good conscience towards God – by the resurrection of Jesus Christ, who is gone into heaven and is on the right hand of God, angels and authorities and powers being made subject unto him.

The Gospel. St. Matthew 27:57-66.

WHEN the even was come, there came a rich man of Arimathea, named Joseph, who also himself was Jesus' disciple. He went to Pilate and begged the body of Jesus. Then Pilate commanded the body to be delivered.

And when Joseph had taken the body, he wrapped it in a clean linen cloth, and laid it in his own new tomb, which he had hewn out in the rock; and he rolled a great stone to the door of the sepulchre, and departed. And there was Mary Magdalen, and the other Mary, sitting over against the sepulchre.

Now the next day, that followed the day of the preparation, the chief priests and Pharisees came together unto

Pilate, saying, 'Sir, we remember that that deceiver said, while he was yet alive, "After three days I will rise again." Command therefore that the sepulchre be made sure until the third day, lest his disciples come by night, and steal him away, and say unto the people, "He is risen from the dead"; so the last error shall be worse than the first.'

Pilate said unto them, 'Ye have a watch. Go your way; make it as sure as you can.'

So they went and made the sepulchre sure, sealing the stone, and setting a watch.

Easter Day.

¶ *At Morning Prayer, instead of the psalm* O come, let us sing, *&c. (p. 5), these anthems shall be sung or said.*
The Anthems.

CHRIST our Passover is sacrificed for us; * therefore let us keep the feast,

Not with the old leaven, nor with the leaven of malice and wickedness, * but with the unleavened bread of sincerity and truth. *1 Corinthians 5:7-8.*

CHRIST being raised from the dead dieth no more; * death hath no more dominion over him.

For in that he died, he died unto sin once, * but in that he liveth, he liveth unto God.

Likewise reckon ye also yourselves to be dead indeed unto sin, * but alive unto God through Jesus Christ our Lord. *Romans 6:9-11.*

CHRIST is risen from the dead * and become the first fruits of them that slept.

For since by man came death, * by man came also the resurrection of the dead.

For as in Adam all die, * even so in Christ shall all be made alive. *1 Corinthians 15:20-22.*

Glory be to the Father, and to the Son, * and to the Holy Ghost;

Answer. As it was in the beginning, is now, and ever shall be, * world without end. Amen.

The Collect.

ALMIGHTY God, who through thine only-begotten Son Jesus Christ hast overcome death and opened unto us the gate of everlasting life: We humbly beseech thee, that as by thy special grace preventing us thou dost put into our minds good desires, so by thy continual help we may bring the same to good effect, through Jesus Christ our Lord, who liveth and reigneth with thee and the Holy Ghost, ever one God, world without end. *Amen.*

The Epistle. Colossians 3:1-7.

IF ye then be risen with Christ, seek those things which are above, where Christ sitteth on the right hand of God. Set your affection on things above, not on things on the earth. For ye are dead, and your life is hid with Christ in God. When Christ, who is our life, shall appear, then shall ye also appear with him in glory.

Mortify therefore your members which are upon the earth: fornication, uncleanness, inordinate affection, evil concupiscence, and covetousness, which is idolatry – for which things' sake the wrath of God cometh on the children of disobedience, in the which ye also walked sometime when ye lived in them.

The Gospel. St. John 20:1-10.

THE first day of the week cometh Mary Magdalen early, when it was yet dark, unto the sepulchre, and seeth the stone taken away from the sepulchre. Then she runneth and cometh to Simon Peter, and to the other disciple whom Jesus loved, and saith unto them, 'They have taken away the Lord out of the sepulchre, and we know not where they have laid him.'

Peter therefore went forth, and that other disciple, and came to the sepulchre. So they ran both together, and the other disciple did outrun Peter and came first to the sepulchre. And he, stooping down and looking in, saw the linen clothes lying, yet went he not in.

Then cometh Simon Peter following him and went into the sepulchre, and seeth the linen clothes lie, and the napkin that was about his head, not lying with the linen clothes but wrapped together in a place by itself.

Then went in also that other disciple, which came first to the sepulchre, and he saw and believed. For as yet they knew not the Scripture that he must rise again from the dead. Then the disciples went away again unto their own home.

Monday in Easter Week.
The Collect.

A LMIGHTY God, who through thy only-begotten Son Jesus Christ hast overcome death and opened unto us the gate of everlasting life: We humbly beseech thee, that as by thy special grace preventing us thou dost put into our minds good desires, so by thy continual help we may bring the same to good effect, through Jesus Christ our Lord, who liveth and reigneth with thee and the Holy Ghost, ever one God, world without end. *Amen.*

For the Epistle. Acts 10:34-43.

P ETER opened his mouth and said, 'Of a truth I perceive that God is no respecter of persons, but in every nation he that feareth him and worketh righteousness is accepted with him. The word which God sent unto the children of Israel, preaching peace by Jesus Christ – he is Lord of all – that word, I say, ye know, which was published throughout all Judea, and began from Galilee, after the baptism which John preached: how God anointed Jesus of Nazareth with the Holy Ghost and with power, who went about doing good, and healing all that were oppressed of the devil, for God was with him. And we are witnesses of all things which he did, both in the land of the Jews and in Jerusalem, whom they slew and hanged on a tree – him God raised up the third day and showed him openly, not to all the people but unto witnesses chosen before of God, even to us who did eat and drink with him after he rose from the dead. And he commanded us to preach unto the people, and to testify that it is he who was ordained of God to be the judge of quick and dead. To him give all the prophets witness, that through his name whosoever believeth in him shall receive remission of sins.'

The Gospel. St. Luke 24:13-35.

BEHOLD, two of his disciples went that same day to a village called Emmaus, which was from Jerusalem about threescore furlongs. And they talked together of all these things which had happened. And it came to pass that while they communed together and reasoned, Jesus himself drew near and went with them. But their eyes were holden that they should not know him. And he said unto them, 'What manner of communications are these that ye have one to another, as ye walk and are sad?' And the one of them, whose name was Cleopas, answering said unto him, 'Art thou only a stranger in Jerusalem, and hast not known the things which are come to pass there in these days?' And he said unto them, 'What things?' And they said unto him, 'Concerning Jesus of Nazareth, who was a prophet mighty in deed and word before God and all the people; and how the chief priests and our rulers delivered him to be condemned to death, and have crucified him. But we trusted that it had been he which should have redeemed Israel; and besides all this, today is the third day since these things were done. Yea, and certain women also of our company made us astonished, which were early at the sepulchre; and when they found not his body, they came, saying that they had also seen a vision of angels, which said that he was alive. And certain of them which were with us went to the sepulchre, and found it even so as the women had said, but him they saw not.

Then he said unto them, 'O fools, and slow of heart to believe all that the prophets have spoken. Ought not Christ to have suffered these things, and to enter into his glory?' And beginning at Moses and all the prophets, he expounded unto them in all the Scriptures the things concerning himself. And they drew nigh unto the village whither they went, and he made as though he would have gone further, but they constrained him, saying, 'Abide with us, for it is towards evening and the day is far spent.' And he went in to tarry with them. And it came to pass, as he sat at meat with them, he took bread, and bless-ed it, and brake, and gave to them. And their eyes were opened and they knew him, and he vanished out of their sight. And they said one to another, 'Did not our heart burn within us while he talked with us by the way, and while he opened to us the Scriptures?'

And they rose up the same hour and returned to Jeru-salem, and found the eleven gathered together, and them that were with them, saying, 'The Lord is risen indeed, and hath appeared to Simon.' And they told what things were done in the way, and how he was known of them in breaking of bread.

Tuesday in Easter Week.
The Collect.

ALMIGHTY God, who through thy only-begotten Son Jesus Christ hast overcome death and opened unto us the gate of everlasting life: We humbly beseech thee, that as by thy special grace preventing us thou dost put into our minds good desires, so by thy continual help we may bring the same to good effect, through Jesus Christ our Lord, who liveth and reigneth with thee and the Holy Ghost, ever one God, world without end. *Amen.*

For the Epistle. Acts 13:26-41.

MEN and brethren, children of the stock of Abraham, and whosoever among you feareth God, to you is the word of this salvation sent. For they that dwell at Jerusalem, and their rulers, because they knew him not, nor yet the voices of the prophets which are read every Sabbath day, they have fulfilled them in condemning him. And though they found no cause of death in him, yet desired they Pilate that he should be slain. And when they had fulfilled all that was written of him, they took him down from the tree, and laid him in a sepulchre. But God raised him from the dead, and he was seen many days of them which came up with him from Galilee to Jerusalem, who are his witnesses unto the people. And we declare unto you glad tidings, how that the promise which was made unto the fathers, God hath fulfilled the same unto us their children, in that he hath raised up Jesus again, as it is also written in the second psalm, 'Thou art my Son; this day have I begotten thee.' And as concerning that he raised him up from the dead, now no more to return to corruption, he said on this wise, 'I will give you the sure mercies of David.' Wherefore he saith also in another psalm, 'Thou shalt not suffer thine holy one to see corruption.' For David, after he had served his own generation by the will of God, fell on sleep, and was laid unto his fathers, and saw corruption. But he whom God raised again saw no corruption.

Be it known unto you therefore, men and brethren, that through this man is preached unto you the forgiveness of sins; and by him all that believe are justified from all things, from which ye could not be justified by the law of Moses. Beware therefore, lest that come upon you which is spoken of in the prophets, 'Behold, ye despisers, and wonder, and perish, for I work a work in your days, a work which ye shall in no wise believe, though a man declare it unto you.'

The Gospel. St. Luke 24:36-48.

JESUS himself stood in the midst of them and saith unto them, 'Peace be unto you.' But they were terrified and affrighted, and supposed that they had seen a spirit. And he said unto them, 'Why are ye troubled, and why do thoughts arise in your hearts? Behold my hands and my feet, that it is I myself. Handle me and see, for a spirit hath not flesh and bones, as ye see me have.' And when he had thus spoken, he showed them his hands and his feet. And while they yet believed not for joy, and wondered, he said unto them, 'Have ye here any meat?' And they gave him a piece of a broiled fish and of an honeycomb. And he took it, and did eat before them.

And he said unto them, 'These are the words which I spake unto you while I was yet with you, that all things must be fulfilled which were written in the law of Moses, and in the prophets, and in the Psalms concerning me.'

Then opened he their understanding, that they might understand the Scriptures, and said unto them, 'Thus it is written, and thus it behoved Christ to suffer, and to rise from the dead the third day, and that repentance and remission of sins should be preached in his name among all nations, beginning at Jerusalem. And ye are witnesses of these things.'

The First Sunday after Easter.
The Collect.

ALMIGHTY Father, who hast given thine only Son to die for our sins, and to rise again for our justification: Grant us so to put away the leaven of malice and wickedness, that we may alway serve thee in pureness of living and truth, through the merits of the same thy Son Jesus Christ our Lord. *Amen.*

The Epistle. 1 John 5:4-12.

WHATSOEVER is born of God overcometh the world, and this is the victory that overcometh the world, even our faith. Who is he that overcometh the world, but he that believeth that Jesus is the Son of God? This is he that came by water and blood, even Jesus Christ; not by water only, but by water and blood. And it is the Spirit that beareth witness, because the Spirit is truth. For there are three that bear witness, the Spirit, and the water, and the blood; and these three agree in one. If we receive the witness of men, the witness of God is greater, for this is the witness of God, which he hath testified of his Son. He that believeth on the Son of God hath the witness in himself;

he that believeth not God hath made him a liar, because he believeth not the record that God gave of his Son. And this is the record, that God hath given to us eternal life, and this life is in his Son. He that hath the Son hath life, and he that hath not the Son of God hath not life.

The Gospel. St. John 20:19-23.

THE same day at evening, being the first day of the week, when the doors were shut where the disciples were assembled for fear of the Jews, came Jesus and stood in the midst and saith unto them, 'Peace be unto you.' And when he had so said, he showed unto them his hands and his side. Then were the disciples glad when they saw the Lord.

Then said Jesus to them again, 'Peace be unto you. As my Father hath sent me, even so send I you.' And when he had said this, he breathed on them and saith unto them, 'Receive ye the Holy Ghost. Whose soever sins ye remit, they are remitted unto them; and whose soever sins ye retain, they are retained.'

The Second Sunday after Easter.
The Collect.

ALMIGHTY God, who hast given thine only Son to be unto us both a sacrifice for sin and also an example of godly life: Give us grace that we may always most thankfully receive that his inestimable benefit, and also daily endeavour ourselves to follow the blessed steps of his most holy life, through the same Jesus Christ our Lord. *Amen.*

THE SECOND SUNDAY AFTER EASTER

The Epistle. 1 Peter 2:19-25.

THIS is thankworthy, if a man for conscience toward God endure grief, suffering wrongfully. For what glory is it, if, when ye be buffeted for your faults, ye shall take it patiently? But if, when ye do well and suffer for it, ye take it patiently, this is acceptable with God. For even hereunto were ye called, because Christ also suffered for us, leaving us an example, that ye should follow his steps – who did no sin, neither was guile found in his mouth; who, when he was reviled, reviled not again; when he suffered, he threatened not, but committed himself to him that judgeth righteously; who his own self bare our sins in his own body on the tree, that we, being dead to sins, should live unto righteousness; by whose stripes ye were healed. For ye were as sheep going astray, but are now returned unto the shepherd and bishop of your souls.

The Gospel. St. John 10:11-16.

JESUS said, 'I am the good shepherd; the good shepherd giveth his life for the sheep. But he that is an hireling, and not the shepherd, whose own the sheep are not, seeth the wolf coming, and leaveth the sheep, and fleeth; and the wolf catcheth them, and scattereth the sheep. The hireling fleeth because he is an hireling, and careth not for the sheep.

'I am the good shepherd, and know my sheep, and am known of mine. As the Father knoweth me, even so know I the Father, and I lay down my life for the sheep. And other sheep I have which are not of this fold; them also I must bring, and they shall hear my voice, and there shall be one fold and one shepherd.'

The Third Sunday after Easter.
The Collect.

A LMIGHTY God, who showest to those who are in error the light of thy truth, to the intent that they may return into the way of righteousness: Grant unto all those who are admitted into the fellowship of Christ's religion, that they may eschew those things that are contrary to their profession, and follow all such things as are agreeable to the same, through our Lord Jesus Christ. *Amen.*

The Epistle. 1 Peter 2:11-17.

D EARLY beloved, I beseech you as strangers and pilgrims, abstain from fleshly lusts, which war against the soul, having your conversation honest among the Gentiles, that, whereas they speak against you as evildoers, they may, by your good works which they shall behold, glorify God in the day of visitation.

Submit yourselves to every ordinance of man for the Lord's sake; whether it be to the king, as supreme; or unto governors, as unto them that are sent by him for the punishment of evildoers and for the praise of them that do well. For so is the will of God, that with well-doing ye may put to silence the ignorance of foolish men – as free, and not using your liberty for a cloak of maliciousness, but as the servants of God. Honour all men. Love the brotherhood. Fear God. Honour the king.

THE FOURTH SUNDAY AFTER EASTER

The Gospel. St. John 16:16-22.

JESUS said to his disciples, 'A little while and ye shall not see me; and again a little while and ye shall see me; because I go to the Father.'

Then said some of his disciples among themselves, 'What is this that he saith unto us, "A little while and ye shall not see me; and again a little while and ye shall see me"; and "because I go to the Father"?' They said therefore, 'What is this that he saith "A little while"? we cannot tell what he saith.'

Now Jesus knew that they were desirous to ask him, and said unto them, 'Do ye inquire among yourselves of that I said, "A little while and ye shall not see me; and again a little while and ye shall see me?"

'Verily, verily I say unto you that ye shall weep and lament, but the world shall rejoice; and ye shall be sorrowful, but your sorrow shall be turned into joy. A woman, when she is in travail, hath sorrow because her hour is come. But as soon as she is delivered of the child, she remembereth no more the anguish, for joy that a man is born into the world.

'And ye now therefore have sorrow, but I will see you again, and your heart shall rejoice, and your joy no man taketh from you.'

The Fourth Sunday after Easter.
The Collect.

O ALMIGHTY God, who alone canst order the unruly wills and affections of sinful men: Grant unto thy people, that they may love the thing which thou commandest, and desire that which thou dost promise, that so, among the sundry and manifold changes of the world, our hearts may surely there be fixed, where true joys are to be found, through Jesus Christ our Lord. *Amen.*

The Epistle. James 1:17-21.

EVERY good gift and every perfect gift is from above, and cometh down from the Father of lights, with whom is no variableness, neither shadow of turning. Of his own will begat he us with the word of truth, that we should be a kind of first fruits of his creatures.

Wherefore, my beloved brethren, let every man be swift to hear, slow to speak, slow to wrath. For the wrath of man worketh not the righteousness of God. Wherefore lay apart all filthiness and superfluity of naughtiness, and receive with meekness the engrafted word, which is able to save your souls.

The Gospel. St. John 16:5-15.

JESUS said unto his disciples, 'Now I go my way to him that sent me, and none of you asketh me, "Whither goest thou?" But because I have said these things unto you, sorrow hath filled your heart. Nevertheless I tell you the truth; it is expedient for you that I go away. For if I go not away, the Comforter will not come unto you; but if I depart, I will send him unto you. And when he is come, he will reprove the world of sin, and of righteousness, and of judgement: of sin, because they believe not on me; of righteousness, because I go to my Father, and ye see me no more; of judgement, because the prince of this world is judged.

'I have yet many things to say unto you, but ye cannot bear them now. Howbeit when he, the Spirit of truth, is come, he will guide you into all truth. For he shall not speak of himself, but whatsoever he shall hear, that shall he speak, and he will show you things to come. He shall glorify me, for he shall receive of mine and shall show it unto you.

'All things that the Father hath are mine. Therefore said I, that he shall take of mine and shall show it unto you.'

The Fifth Sunday after Easter.
The Collect.

O LORD, from whom all good things do come: Grant to us thy humble servants, that by thy holy inspiration we may think those things that are good, and by thy merciful guiding may perform the same, through our Lord Jesus Christ. *Amen.*

The Epistle. James 1:22-27.

B E ye doers of the word and not hearers only, deceiving your own selves. For if any be a hearer of the word and not a doer, he is like unto a man beholding his natural face in a glass. For he beholdeth himself, and goeth his way, and straightway forgetteth what manner of man he was. But whoso looketh into the perfect law of liberty, and continueth therein, he being not a forgetful hearer but a doer of the work, this man shall be blessed in his deed.

If any man among you seem to be religious, and bridleth not his tongue, but deceiveth his own heart, this man's religion is vain. Pure religion and undefiled before God and the Father is this, to visit the fatherless and widows in their affliction, and to keep himself unspotted from the world.

The Gospel. St. John 16:23-33.

'VERILY, verily I say unto you, whatsoever ye shall ask the Father in my name, he will give it you. Hitherto have ye asked nothing in my name; ask, and ye shall receive, that your joy may be full.

'These things have I spoken unto you in proverbs; the time cometh when I shall no more speak unto you in proverbs, but I shall show you plainly of the Father.

'At that day ye shall ask in my name, and I say not unto you that I will pray the Father for you, for the Father himself loveth you, because ye have loved me and have believed that I came out from God. I came forth from the Father and am come into the world. Again, I leave the world and go to the Father.'

His disciples said unto him, 'Lo, now speakest thou plainly, and speakest no proverb. Now are we sure that thou knowest all things, and needest not that any man should ask thee. By this we believe that thou camest forth from God.' Jesus answered them, 'Do ye now believe? Behold, the hour cometh, yea, is now come, that ye shall be scattered every man to his own, and shall leave me alone. And yet I am not alone, because the Father is with me. These things I have spoken unto you that in me ye might have peace. In the world ye shall have tribulation, but be of good cheer, I have overcome the world.'

The Ascension Day.
The Collect.

G RANT, we beseech thee, almighty God, that like as we do believe thy only-begotten Son our Lord Jesus Christ to have ascended into the heavens, so we may also in heart and mind thither ascend, and with him continually dwell, who liveth and reigneth with thee and the Holy Ghost, one God, world without end. *Amen.*

For the Epistle. Acts 1:1-11.

T HE former treatise have I made, O Theophilus, of all that Jesus began both to do and teach until the day in which he was taken up, after that he through the Holy Ghost had given commandments unto the apostles whom he had chosen: to whom also he showed himself alive after his passion by many infallible proofs, being seen of them forty days, and speaking of the things pertaining to the kingdom of God; and, being assembled together with them, commanded them that they should not depart from Jerusalem, but wait for the promise of the Father, 'which', saith he, 'ye have heard of me. For John truly baptized with water, but ye shall be baptized with the Holy Ghost not many days hence.'

When they therefore were come together, they asked of him, saying, 'Lord, wilt thou at this time restore again the kingdom to Israel?' And he said unto them, 'It is not for you to know the times or the seasons which the Father hath put in his own power. But ye shall receive power, after that the Holy Ghost is come upon you, and ye shall be witnesses unto me both in Jerusalem, and in all Judea, and in Samaria, and unto the uttermost part of the earth.' And when he had spoken these things, while they beheld, he was taken up, and a cloud received him out of their sight. And while they looked steadfastly toward heaven as he went up, behold, two men stood by them in white apparel, which also said, 'Ye men of Galilee, why stand ye gazing up into heaven? This same Jesus, which is taken up from you into heaven, shall so come in like manner as ye have seen him go into heaven.'

The Gospel. St. Mark 16:14-20.

JESUS appeared unto the eleven as they sat at meat, and upbraided them with their unbelief and hardness of heart, because they believed not them which had seen him after he was risen.

And he said unto them, 'Go ye into all the world, and preach the gospel to every creature. He that believeth and is baptized shall be saved, but he that believeth not shall be damned.

'And these signs shall follow them that believe: in my name shall they cast out devils; they shall speak with new tongues; they shall take up serpents; and if they drink any deadly thing, it shall not hurt them; they shall lay hands on the sick, and they shall recover.'

So then after the Lord had spoken unto them, he was received up into heaven, and sat on the right hand of God. And they went forth and preached everywhere, the Lord working with them and confirming the word with signs following.

Sunday after Ascension Day.
The Collect.

O GOD, the king of glory, who hast exalted thine only Son Jesus Christ with great triumph unto thy kingdom in heaven: We beseech thee, leave us not comfortless, but send to us thy Holy Ghost to comfort us, and exalt us unto the same place whither our Saviour Christ is gone before, who liveth and reigneth with thee and the Holy Ghost, one God, world without end. *Amen.*

The Epistle. 1 Peter 4:7-11.

T HE end of all things is at hand; be ye therefore sober and watch unto prayer. And above all things have fervent charity among yourselves, for charity shall cover the multitude of sins. Use hospitality one to another without grudging. As every man hath received the gift, even so minister the same one to another, as good stewards of the manifold grace of God. If any man speak, let him speak as the oracles of God; if any man minister, let him do it as of the ability which God giveth, that God in all things may be glorified through Jesus Christ, to whom be praise and dominion for ever and ever. Amen.

The Gospel. St. John 15:26-16:4.

W HEN the Comforter is come, whom I will send unto you from the Father, even the Spirit of truth, which proceedeth from the Father, he shall testify of me. And ye also shall bear witness, because ye have been with me from the beginning.

These things have I spoken unto you that ye should not be offended. They shall put you out of the synagogues; yea, the time cometh, that whosoever killeth you will think that he doeth God service. And these things will they do unto you, because they have not known the Father, nor me. But these things have I told you, that, when the time shall come, ye may remember that I told you of them.

Whitsunday.
The Collect.

G OD, who as at this time didst teach the hearts of thy faithful people, by sending to them the light of thy Holy Spirit: Grant us by the same Spirit to have a right judgement in all things, and evermore to rejoice in his holy comfort, through the merits of Christ Jesus our Saviour, who liveth and reigneth with thee, in the unity of the same Spirit, one God, world without end. *Amen.*

For the Epistle. Acts 2:1-11.

W HEN the day of Pentecost was fully come, they were all with one accord in one place. And suddenly there came a sound from heaven, as of a rushing mighty wind, and it filled all the house where they were sitting. And there appeared unto them cloven tongues, like as of fire, and it sat upon each of them. And they were all filled with the Holy Ghost and began to speak with other tongues, as the Spirit gave them utterance.

And there were dwelling at Jerusalem Jews, devout men,

out of every nation under heaven. Now when this was noised abroad, the multitude came together and were confounded, because that every man heard them speak in his own language. And they were all amazed and marvelled, saying one to another, 'Behold, are not all these which speak Galileans? And how hear we every man in our own tongue, wherein we were born? Parthians, and Medes, and Elamites, and the dwellers in Mesopotamia, and in Judea, and Cappadocia, in Pontus, and Asia, Phrygia, and Pamphylia, in Egypt, and in the parts of Libya about Cyrene, and strangers of Rome, Jews and proselytes, Cretes and Arabians, we do hear them speak in our tongues the wonderful works of God.'

The Gospel. St. John 14:15-31.

JESUS said unto his disciples, 'If ye love me, keep my commandments. And I will pray the Father, and he shall give you another Comforter, that he may abide with you for ever; even the Spirit of truth, whom the world cannot receive, because it seeth him not, neither knoweth him. But ye know him, for he dwelleth with you, and shall be in you. I will not leave you comfortless; I will come to you.

'Yet a little while and the world seeth me no more, but ye see me. Because I live, ye shall live also. At that day ye shall know that I am in my Father, and ye in me, and I in you. He that hath my commandments and keepeth them, he it is that loveth me. And he that loveth me shall be loved of my Father, and I will love him, and will manifest myself to him.'

Judas saith unto him (not Iscariot), 'Lord, how is it that thou wilt manifest thyself unto us, and not unto the world?'

Jesus answered and said unto him, 'If a man love me, he will keep my words, and my Father will love him, and we will come unto him, and make our abode with him. He that loveth me not keepeth not my sayings, and the word which ye hear is not mine, but the Father's which sent me.

'These things have I spoken unto you, being yet present with you. But the Comforter, which is the Holy Ghost, whom the Father will send in my name, he shall teach you all things, and bring all things to your remembrance, whatsoever I have said unto you.

'Peace I leave with you; my peace I give unto you; not as the world giveth, give I unto you. Let not your heart be troubled, neither let it be afraid. Ye have heard how I said unto you, "I go away, and come again unto you." If ye loved me, ye would rejoice because I said, "I go unto the Father", for my Father is greater than I. And now I have told you before it come to pass, that, when it is come to pass, ye might believe.

'Hereafter I will not talk much with you, for the prince of this world cometh, and hath nothing in me. But that the world may know that I love the Father, and as the Father gave me commandment, even so I do.'

Monday in Whitsun Week.
The Collect.

G OD, who as at this time didst teach the hearts of thy faithful people, by sending to them the light of thy Holy Spirit: Grant us by the same Spirit to have a right judgement in all things, and evermore to rejoice in his holy comfort, through the merits of Christ Jesu our Saviour, who liveth and reigneth with thee, in the unity of the same Spirit, one God, world without end. *Amen.*

For the Epistle. Acts 10:34-48.

THEN Peter opened his mouth and said, 'Of a truth I perceive that God is no respecter of persons, but in every nation he that feareth him and worketh righteousness, is accepted with him. The word which God sent unto the children of Israel, preaching peace by Jesus Christ – he is Lord of all – that word, I say, ye know, which was published throughout all Judea, and began from Galilee, after the baptism which John preached: how God anointed Jesus of Nazareth with the Holy Ghost and with power, who went about doing good, and healing all that were oppressed of the devil, for God was with him. And we are witnesses of all things which he did, both in the land of the Jews and in Jerusalem, whom they slew and hanged on a tree – him God raised up the third day and showed him openly, not to all the people but unto witnesses chosen before of God, even to us who did eat and drink with him after he rose from the dead. And he commanded us to preach unto the people, and to testify that it is he who was ordained of God to be the judge of quick and dead. To him give all the prophets witness, that through his name whosoever believeth in him shall receive remission of sins.'

While Peter yet spake these words, the Holy Ghost fell on all them which heard the word. And they of the circumcision which believed were astonished, as many as came with Peter, because that on the Gentiles also was poured out the gift of the Holy Ghost. For they heard them speak with tongues and magnify God. Then answered Peter, 'Can any man forbid water, that these should not be baptized, which have received the Holy Ghost as well as we?' And he commanded them to be baptized in the name of the Lord. Then prayed they him to tarry certain days.

The Gospel. St. John 3:16-21.

GOD so loved the world that he gave his only-begotten Son, that whosoever believeth in him should not perish, but have everlasting life. For God sent not his Son into the world to condemn the world, but that the world through him might be saved. He that believeth on him is not condemned, but he that believeth not is condemned already, because he hath not believed in the name of the only-begotten Son of God. And this is the condemnation, that light is come into the world, and men loved darkness rather than light, because their deeds were evil. For every one that doeth evil hateth the light, neither cometh to the light, lest his deeds should be reproved. But he that doeth truth cometh to the light, that his deeds may be made manifest, that they are wrought in God.

Tuesday in Whitsun Week.
The Collect.

GOD, who as at this time didst teach the hearts of thy faithful people, by sending to them the light of thy Holy Spirit: Grant us by the same Spirit to have a right judgement in all things, and evermore to rejoice in his holy comfort, through the merits of Christ Jesu our Saviour, who liveth and reigneth with thee, in the unity of the same Spirit, one God, world without end. *Amen.*

For the Epistle. Acts 8:14-17.

WHEN the apostles which were at Jerusalem heard that Samaria had received the word of God, they sent unto them Peter and John, who, when they were come down, prayed for them that they might receive the Holy Ghost (for as yet he was fallen upon none of them; only they were baptized in the name of the Lord Jesus). Then laid they their hands on them, and they received the Holy Ghost.

The Gospel. St. John 10:1-10.

'VERILY, verily I say unto you, he that entereth not by the door into the sheepfold, but climbeth up some other way, the same is a thief and a robber. But he that entereth in by the door is the shepherd of the sheep. To him the porter openeth, and the sheep hear his voice, and he calleth his own sheep by name, and leadeth them out. And when he putteth forth his own sheep, he goeth before them, and the sheep follow him, for they know his voice. And a stranger will they not follow, but will flee from him, for they know not the voice of strangers.'

This parable spake Jesus unto them, but they understood not what things they were which he spake unto them.

Then said Jesus unto them again, 'Verily, verily I say unto you, I am the door of the sheep. All that ever came before me are thieves and robbers, but the sheep did not hear them. I am the door: by me if any man enter in, he shall be saved, and shall go in and out, and find pasture. The thief cometh not but for to steal, and to kill, and to destroy; I am come that they might have life, and that they might have it more abundantly.'

Trinity Sunday.
The Collect.

ALMIGHTY and everlasting God, who hast given unto us thy servants grace, by the confession of a true faith, to acknowledge the glory of the eternal Trinity, and in the power of the Divine Majesty to worship the Unity: We beseech thee that thou wouldest keep us steadfast in this faith, and evermore defend us from all adversities, who livest and reignest, one God, world without end. *Amen.*

For the Epistle. Revelation 4.

AFTER this I looked, and behold, a door was opened in heaven, and the first voice which I heard was as it were of a trumpet talking with me, which said, 'Come up hither, and I will show thee things which must be here-after.' And immediately I was in the Spirit, and behold, a throne was set in heaven, and one sat on the throne. And he that sat was to look upon like a jasper and a sardine stone, and there was a rainbow round about the throne, in sight like unto an emerald. And round about the throne were four and twenty seats, and upon the seats I saw four and twenty elders sitting, clothed in white raiment, and they had on their heads crowns of gold. And out of the throne proceeded lightnings and thunderings and voices.

And there were seven lamps of fire burning before the throne, which are the seven spirits of God. And before the throne there was a sea of glass like unto crystal; and in the midst of the throne, and round about the throne, were four living creatures full of eyes before and behind. And the first creature was like a lion, and the second creature like a calf, and the third creature had a face as a man, and the fourth creature was like a flying eagle. And the four living creatures had each of them six wings about him; and they were full of eyes within; and they rest not day and night, saying, 'Holy, holy, holy, Lord God almighty, which was and is and is to come.' And when those living creatures give glory and honour and thanks to him that sat on the throne, who liveth for ever and ever, the four and twenty elders fall down before him that sat on the throne, and worship him that liveth for ever and ever, and cast their crowns before the throne, saying, 'Thou art worthy, O Lord, to receive glory and honour and power, for thou hast created all things, and for thy pleasure they are, and were created.'

The Gospel. St. John 3:1-15.

THERE was a man of the Pharisees, named Nicodemus, a ruler of the Jews. The same came to Jesus by night and said unto him, 'Rabbi, we know that thou art a teacher come from God, for no man can do these miracles that thou doest, except God be with him.'

Jesus answered and said unto him, 'Verily, verily I say unto thee, except a man be born again, he cannot see the kingdom of God.'

Nicodemus saith unto him, 'How can a man be born when he is old? Can he enter the second time into his mother's womb, and be born?'

Jesus answered, 'Verily, verily I say unto thee, except a man be born of water and of the Spirit, he cannot enter into the kingdom of God.

'That which is born of the flesh is flesh, and that which is born of the Spirit is spirit. Marvel not that I said unto thee, "Ye must be born again." The wind bloweth where it listeth, and thou hearest the sound thereof, but canst not tell whence it cometh and whither it goeth. So is every one that is born of the Spirit.'

Nicodemus answered and said unto him, 'How can these things be?'

Jesus answered and said unto him, 'Art thou a master of Israel, and knowest not these things? Verily, verily I say unto thee, we speak that we do know, and testify that we have seen, and ye receive not our witness. If I have told you earthly things, and ye believe not, how shall ye believe if I tell you of heavenly things? And no man hath ascended up to heaven, but he that came down from heaven, even the Son of Man, who is in heaven. And as Moses lifted up the serpent in the wilderness, even so must the Son of Man be lifted up, that whosoever believeth in him should not perish, but have eternal life.'

The First Sunday after Trinity.
The Collect.

O GOD, the strength of all those who put their trust in thee: Mercifully accept our prayers, and because through the weakness of our mortal nature we can do no good thing without thee, grant us the help of thy grace, that in keeping of thy commandments we may please thee, both in will and deed, through Jesus Christ our Lord. *Amen.*

The Epistle. 1 John 4:7-21.

BELOVED, let us love one another, for love is of God, and every one that loveth is born of God and knoweth God. He that loveth not knoweth not God, for God is love. In this was manifested the love of God towards us, because that God sent his only-begotten Son into the world, that we might live through him. Herein is love, not that we loved God, but that he loved us, and sent his Son to be the propitiation for our sins.

Beloved, if God so loved us, we ought also to love one another. No man hath seen God at any time. If we love one another, God dwelleth in us, and his love is perfected in us. Hereby know we that we dwell in him, and he in us, because he hath given us of his Spirit. And we have seen and do testify that the Father sent the Son to be the saviour of the world. Whosoever shall confess that Jesus is the Son of God, God dwelleth in him, and he in God. And we have known and believed the love that God hath to us. God is love, and he that dwelleth in love dwelleth in God, and God in him. Herein is our love made perfect, that we may have boldness in the day of judgement, because as he is, so are we in this world. There is no fear in love, but perfect love casteth out fear, because fear hath torment. He that feareth is not made perfect in love. We love him because he first loved us. If a man say, 'I love God', and hateth his brother, he is a liar. For he that loveth not his brother whom he hath seen, how can he love God whom he hath not seen? And this commandment have we from him, that he who loveth God love his brother also.

The Gospel. St. Luke 16:19-31.

THERE was a certain rich man, which was clothed in purple and fine linen, and fared sumptuously every day. And there was a certain beggar named Lazarus, which was laid at his gate, full of sores, and desiring to be fed with the crumbs which fell from the rich man's table. Moreover the dogs came and licked his sores.

And it came to pass that the beggar died, and was carried by the angels into Abraham's bosom. The rich man also died, and was buried; and in hell he lifted up his eyes, being in torments, and seeth Abraham afar off, and Lazarus in his bosom. And he cried and said, 'Father Abraham, have mercy on me, and send Lazarus, that he may dip the tip of his finger in water and cool my tongue, for I am tormented in this flame.'

But Abraham said, 'Son, remember that thou in thy lifetime receivedst thy good things, and likewise Lazarus evil things, but now he is comforted, and thou art tormented. And besides all this, between us and you there is a great gulf fixed, so that they who would pass from hence to you cannot, neither can they pass to us, that would come from thence.'

Then he said, 'I pray thee therefore, father, that thou wouldest send him to my father's house, for I have five brethren, that he may testify unto them, lest they also come into this place of torment.'

Abraham saith unto him, 'They have Moses and the prophets; let them hear them.' And he said, 'Nay, father Abraham, but if one went unto them from the dead, they will repent.' And he said unto him, 'If they hear not Moses and the prophets, neither will they be persuaded though one rose from the dead.'

The Second Sunday after Trinity.
The Collect.

O LORD, who never failest to help and govern those whom thou dost bring up in thy steadfast fear and love: Keep us, we beseech thee, under the protection of thy good providence, and make us to have a perpetual fear and love of thy holy name, through Jesus Christ our Lord. *Amen.*

The Epistle. 1 John 3:13-24.

M ARVEL not, my brethren, if the world hate you. We know that we have passed from death unto life, because we love the brethren. He that loveth not his brother abideth in death. Whosoever hateth his brother is a murderer, and ye know that no murderer hath eternal life abiding in him. Hereby perceive we the love of God, because he laid down his life for us, and we ought to lay down our lives for the brethren.

But whoso hath this world's good, and seeth his brother have need, and shutteth up his bowels of compassion from him, how dwelleth the love of God in him?

My little children, let us not love in word, neither in tongue, but in deed and in truth. And hereby we know that we are of the truth and shall assure our hearts before him. For if our heart condemn us, God is greater than our heart, and knoweth all things.

Beloved, if our heart condemn us not, then have we confidence towards God. And whatsoever we ask, we receive of him, because we keep his commandments and do those things that are pleasing in his sight. And this is his commandment, that we should believe on the name of his Son Jesus Christ, and love one another, as he gave us commandment. And he that keepeth his commandments dwelleth in him, and he in him. And hereby we know that he abideth in us, by the Spirit which he hath given us.

The Gospel. St. Luke 14:16-24.

A CERTAIN man made a great supper and bade many, and sent his servant at supper time to say to them that were bidden, 'Come, for all things are now ready.' And they all with one consent began to make excuse.

The first said unto him, 'I have bought a piece of ground, and I must needs go and see it; I pray thee have me excused.' And another said, 'I have bought five yoke of oxen, and I go to prove them; I pray thee have me excused.' And another said, 'I have married a wife, and therefore I cannot come.' So that servant came and showed his lord these things.

Then the master of the house being angry said to his servant, 'Go out quickly into the streets and lanes of the city, and bring in hither the poor, and the maimed, and the halt, and the blind.' And the servant said, 'Lord, it is done as thou hast commanded, and yet there is room.' And the lord said unto the servant, 'Go out into the highways and hedges, and compel them to come in, that my house may be filled. For I say unto you that none of those men which were bidden shall taste of my supper.'

The Third Sunday after Trinity.
The Collect.

O LORD, we beseech thee mercifully to hear us, and grant that we, to whom thou hast given a hearty desire to pray, may by thy mighty aid be defended and comforted in all dangers and adversities, through Jesus Christ our Lord. *Amen.*

The Epistle. 1 Peter 5:5-11.

A LL of you be subject one to another, and be clothed with humility, for 'God resisteth the proud, and giveth grace to the humble.' Humble yourselves therefore under the mighty hand of God, that he may exalt you in due time; casting all your care upon him, for he careth for you.

Be sober; be vigilant; because your adversary the devil, as a roaring lion, walketh about seeking whom he may devour – whom resist, steadfast in the faith, knowing that the same afflictions are accomplished in your brethren that are in the world.

But the God of all grace, who hath called us into his eternal glory by Christ Jesus, after that ye have suffered a while, make you perfect, stablish, strengthen, settle you. To him be glory and dominion for ever and ever. Amen.

THE FOURTH SUNDAY AFTER TRINITY

The Gospel. St. Luke 15:1-10.

THEN drew near unto him all the publicans and sinners for to hear him. And the Pharisees and scribes murmured, saying, 'This man receiveth sinners and eateth with them.'

And he spake this parable unto them, saying, 'What man of you, having an hundred sheep, if he lose one of them, doth not leave the ninety and nine in the wilderness, and go after that which is lost until he find it? And when he hath found it, he layeth it on his shoulders, rejoicing. And when he cometh home, he calleth together his friends and neighbours, saying unto them, "Rejoice with me, for I have found my sheep which was lost." I say unto you that likewise joy shall be in heaven over one sinner that repenteth, more than over ninety and nine just persons which need no repentance. Either what woman having ten pieces of silver, if she lose one piece, doth not light a candle, and sweep the house, and seek diligently till she find it? And when she hath found it, she calleth her friends and her neighbours together, saying, "Rejoice with me, for I have found the piece which I had lost."

'Likewise, I say unto you, there is joy in the presence of the angels of God over one sinner that repenteth.'

The Fourth Sunday after Trinity.
The Collect.

O GOD, the protector of all who trust in thee, without whom nothing is strong, nothing is holy: Increase and multiply upon us thy mercy, that, thou being our ruler and guide, we may so pass through things temporal, that we finally lose not the things eternal. Grant this, O heavenly Father, for Jesus Christ's sake, our Lord. *Amen.*

The Epistle. Romans 8:18-23.

I RECKON that the sufferings of this present time are not worthy to be compared with the glory which shall be revealed in us. For the earnest expectation of the creature waiteth for the manifestation of the sons of God. For the creature was made subject to vanity, not willingly, but by reason of him who hath subjected the same in hope, because the creature itself also shall be delivered from the bondage of corruption into the glorious liberty of the children of God. For we know that the whole creation groaneth and travaileth in pain together until now. And not only they, but ourselves also, which have the first fruits of the Spirit – even we ourselves groan within ourselves, waiting for the adoption, to wit, the redemption of our body.

The Gospel. St. Luke 6:36-42.

'BE ye therefore merciful, as your Father also is merciful. Judge not, and ye shall not be judged; condemn not, and ye shall not be condemned; forgive, and ye shall be forgiven. Give, and it shall be given unto you – good measure, pressed down, and shaken together, and running over, shall men give into your bosom. For with the same measure that ye mete withal, it shall be measured to you again.' And he spake a parable unto them, 'Can the blind lead the blind? Shall they not both fall into the ditch?

'The disciple is not above his master, but every one that is perfect shall be as his master.

'And why beholdest thou the mote that is in thy brother's eye, but perceivest not the beam that is in thine own eye? Either how canst thou say to thy brother, "Brother, let me pull out the mote that is in thine eye", when thou thyself beholdest not the beam that is in thine own eye? Thou hypocrite, cast out first the beam out of thine own eye, and then shalt thou see clearly to pull out the mote that is in thy brother's eye.'

The Fifth Sunday after Trinity.
The Collect.

GRANT, O Lord, we beseech thee, that the course of this world may be so peaceably ordered by thy governance, that thy church may joyfully serve thee in all godly quietness, through Jesus Christ our Lord. *Amen.*

The Epistle. 1 Peter 3:8-15.

BE ye all of one mind, having compassion one of another: love as brethren, be pitiful, be courteous; not rendering evil for evil, or railing for railing, but contrariwise blessing; knowing that ye are thereunto called, that ye should inherit a blessing. For 'he that will love life, and see good days, let him refrain his tongue from evil, and his lips that they speak no guile; let him eschew evil and do good; let him seek peace and ensue it. For the eyes of the Lord are over the righteous, and his ears are open unto their prayers, but the face of the Lord is against them that do evil.'

And who is he that will harm you, if ye be followers of that which is good? But and if ye suffer for righteousness' sake, happy are ye. And be not afraid of their terror, neither be troubled, but sanctify the Lord God in your hearts.

The Gospel. St. Luke 5:1-11.

IT came to pass that as the people pressed upon him to hear the word of God, Jesus stood by the lake of Gennesaret, and saw two ships standing by the lake, but the fishermen were gone out of them and were washing their nets. And he entered into one of the ships, which was Simon's, and prayed him that he would thrust out a little from the land, and he sat down and taught the people out of the ship.

Now when he had left speaking, he said unto Simon, 'Launch out into the deep, and let down your nets for a draught.' And Simon answering said unto him, 'Master, we have toiled all the night and have taken nothing; nevertheless, at thy word I will let down the net.' And when they had this done, they enclosed a great multitude of fishes, and their net brake. And they beckoned unto their partners which were in the other ship, that they should come and help them. And they came and filled both the ships, so that they began to sink.

When Simon Peter saw it, he fell down at Jesus' knees, saying, 'Depart from me, for I am a sinful man, O Lord.' For he was astonished, and all that were with him, at the draught of the fishes which they had taken; and so was also James, and John, the sons of Zebedee, which were partners with Simon. And Jesus said unto Simon, 'Fear not; from henceforth thou shalt catch men.' And when they had brought their ships to land, they forsook all and followed him.

The Sixth Sunday after Trinity.
The Collect.

O GOD, who hast prepared for those who love thee such good things as pass man's understanding: Pour into our hearts such love toward thee, that we, loving thee above all things, may obtain thy promises, which exceed all that we can desire, through Jesus Christ our Lord. *Amen.*

The Epistle. Romans 6:3-11.

K NOW ye not that so many of us as were baptized into Jesus Christ were baptized into his death? Therefore we are buried with him by baptism into death, that like as Christ was raised up from the dead by the glory of the Father, even so we also should walk in newness of life.

For if we have been planted together in the likeness of his death, we shall be also in the likeness of his resurrection – knowing this, that our old man is crucified with him, that the body of sin might be destroyed, that henceforth we should not serve sin. For he that is dead is freed from sin. Now if we be dead with Christ, we believe that we shall also live with him, knowing that Christ being raised from the dead dieth no more; death hath no more dominion over him. For in that he died, he died unto sin once; but in that he liveth, he liveth unto God. Likewise reckon ye also yourselves to be dead indeed unto sin, but alive unto God through Jesus Christ our Lord.

The Gospel. St. Matthew 5:20-26.

JESUS said unto his disciples, 'Except your righteousness shall exceed the righteousness of the scribes and Pharisees, ye shall in no case enter into the kingdom of heaven.

'Ye have heard that it was said by them of old time, "Thou shalt not kill" and "Whosoever shall kill, shall be in danger of the judgement." But I say unto you that whosoever is angry with his brother without a cause shall be in danger of the judgement, and whosoever shall say to his brother *"Raca"* shall be in danger of the council, but whosoever shall say "Thou fool" shall be in danger of hellfire.

'Therefore if thou bring thy gift to the altar, and there rememberest that thy brother hath aught against thee, leave there thy gift before the altar and go thy way. First be reconciled to thy brother, and then come and offer thy gift.

'Agree with thine adversary quickly, whilst thou art in the way with him; lest at any time the adversary deliver thee to the judge, and the judge deliver thee to the officer, and thou be cast into prison. Verily I say unto thee, thou shalt by no means come out thence till thou hast paid the uttermost farthing.'

The Seventh Sunday after Trinity.
The Collect.

LORD of all power and might, who art the author and giver of all good things: Graft in our hearts the love of thy name, increase in us true religion, nourish us with all goodness, and of thy great mercy keep us in the same, through Jesus Christ our Lord. *Amen.*

The Epistle. Romans 6:19-23.

I SPEAK after the manner of men, because of the infirmity of your flesh. For as ye have yielded your members servants to uncleanness, and to iniquity unto iniquity, even so now yield your members servants to righteousness unto holiness. For when ye were the servants of sin, ye were free from righteousness. What fruit had ye then in those things whereof ye are now ashamed? for the end of those things is death. But now being made free from sin, and become servants to God, ye have your fruit unto holiness, and the end everlasting life. For the wages of sin is death, but the gift of God is eternal life, through Jesus Christ our Lord.

The Gospel. St. Mark 8:1-9.

IN those days the multitude being very great, and having nothing to eat, Jesus called his disciples unto him and saith unto them, 'I have compassion on the multitude, because they have now been with me three days and have nothing to eat. And if I send them away fasting to their own houses, they will faint by the way, for divers of them came from far.'

And his disciples answered him, 'From whence can a man satisfy these men with bread here in the wilderness?' And he asked them, 'How many loaves have ye?' And they said, 'Seven.' And he commanded the people to sit down on the ground. And he took the seven loaves, and gave thanks, and brake, and gave to his disciples to set before them, and they did set them before the people. And they had a few small fishes, and he blessed and commanded to set them also before them. So they did eat and were filled, and they took up of the broken meat that was left seven baskets. And they that had eaten were about four thousand. And he sent them away.

The Eighth Sunday after Trinity.
The Collect.

O GOD, whose never-failing providence ordereth all things both in heaven and earth: We humbly beseech thee to put away from us all hurtful things, and to give us those things which are profitable for us, through Jesus Christ our Lord. *Amen.*

The Epistle. Romans 8:12-17.

BRETHREN, we are debtors, not to the flesh, to live after the flesh. For if ye live after the flesh, ye shall die; but if ye through the Spirit do mortify the deeds of the body, ye shall live. For as many as are led by the Spirit of God, they are the sons of God. For ye have not received the spirit of bondage again to fear; but ye have received the Spirit of adoption, whereby we cry, 'Abba, Father'. The Spirit itself beareth witness with our spirit, that we are the children of God, and if children, then heirs – heirs of God, and joint-heirs with Christ, if so be that we suffer with him, that we may be also glorified together.

THE NINTH SUNDAY AFTER TRINITY

The Gospel. St. Matthew 7:15-21.

BEWARE of false prophets, which come to you in sheep's clothing, but inwardly they are ravening wolves. Ye shall know them by their fruits. Do men gather grapes of thorns, or figs of thistles? Even so every good tree bringeth forth good fruit, but a corrupt tree bringeth forth evil fruit. A good tree cannot bring forth evil fruit, neither can a corrupt tree bring forth good fruit. Every tree that bringeth not forth good fruit is hewn down and cast into the fire. Wherefore by their fruits ye shall know them.

Not everyone that saith unto me 'Lord, Lord' shall enter into the kingdom of heaven, but he that doeth the will of my Father which is in heaven.

The Ninth Sunday after Trinity.
The Collect.

GRANT to us, Lord, we beseech thee, the spirit to think and do always such things as are rightful, that we, who cannot do anything that is good without thee, may by thee be enabled to live according to thy will, through Jesus Christ our Lord. *Amen.*

The Epistle. 1 Corinthians 10:1-13.

BRETHREN, I would not that ye should be ignorant, how that all our fathers were under the cloud, and all passed through the sea, and were all baptized unto Moses in the cloud and in the sea, and did all eat the same spiritual meat, and did all drink the same spiritual drink. For they drank of that spiritual rock that followed them, and that rock was Christ. But with many of them God was not well pleased, for they were overthrown in the wilderness. Now these things were our examples, to the intent we should not lust after evil things, as they also lusted. Neither be ye idolaters, as were some of them, as it is written, 'The people sat down to eat and drink, and rose up to play.' Neither let us commit fornication, as some of them committed, and fell in one day three and twenty thousand. Neither let us tempt Christ, as some of them also tempted, and were destroyed of serpents. Neither murmur ye, as some of them also murmured, and were destroyed of the destroyer. Now all these things happened unto them for ensamples, and they are written for our admonition, upon whom the ends of the world are come.

Wherefore let him that thinketh he standeth take heed lest he fall. There hath no temptation taken you, but such as is common to man; but God is faithful, who will not suffer you to be tempted above that ye are able, but will with the temptation also make a way to escape, that ye may be able to bear it.

The Gospel. St. Luke 16:1-9.

JESUS said unto his disciples, 'There was a certain rich man, which had a steward, and the same was accused unto him that he had wasted his goods. And he called him and said unto him, "How is it that I hear this of thee? Give an account of thy stewardship, for thou mayest be no longer steward." Then the steward said within himself, "What shall I do? for my lord taketh away from me the stewardship. I cannot dig; to beg I am ashamed. I am resolved what to do, that when I am put out of the stewardship they may receive me into their houses." So he called every one of his lord's debtors unto him, and said unto the first, "How much owest thou unto my lord?" And he said, "An hundred measures of oil." And he said unto him, "Take thy bill, and sit down quickly, and write fifty." Then said he to another, "And how much owest thou?" And he said, "An hundred measures of wheat." And he said unto him, "Take thy bill, and write fourscore." And the lord commended the unjust steward because he had done wisely, for the children of this world are in their generation wiser than the children of light. And I say unto you, make to yourselves friends of the mammon of unrighteousness, that when ye fail, they may receive you into everlasting habitations.'

The Tenth Sunday after Trinity.
The Collect.

LET thy merciful ears, O Lord, be open to the prayers of thy humble servants, and that they may obtain their petitions, make them to ask such things as shall please thee, through Jesus Christ our Lord. *Amen.*

The Epistle. 1 Corinthians 12:1-11.

CONCERNING spiritual gifts, brethren, I would not have you ignorant. Ye know that ye were Gentiles, carried away unto these dumb idols, even as ye were led. Wherefore I give you to understand that no man speaking by the Spirit of God calleth Jesus accursed, and that no man can say that Jesus is the Lord, but by the Holy Ghost. Now there are diversities of gifts, but the same

Spirit. And there are differences of administrations, but the same Lord. And there are diversities of operations, but it is the same God who worketh all in all.

But the manifestation of the Spirit is given to every man to profit withal. For to one is given by the Spirit the word of wisdom, to another the word of knowledge by the same Spirit, to another faith by the same Spirit, to another the gifts of healing by the same Spirit, to another the working of miracles, to another prophecy, to another discerning of spirits, to another divers kinds of tongues, to another the interpretation of tongues. But all these worketh that one and the selfsame Spirit, dividing to every man severally as he will.

The Gospel. St. Luke 19:41-47.

AND when Jesus was come near, he beheld the city, and wept over it, saying, 'If thou hadst known, even thou, at least in this thy day, the things which belong unto thy peace! but now they are hid from thine eyes. For the days shall come upon thee, that thine enemies shall cast a trench about thee, and compass thee round, and keep thee in on every side, and shall lay thee even with the ground, and thy children within thee; and they shall not leave in thee one stone upon another, because thou knewest not the time of thy visitation.'

And he went into the temple, and began to cast out them that sold therein and them that bought, saying unto them, 'It is written, "My house is the house of prayer", but ye have made it a den of thieves.' And he taught daily in the temple.

The Eleventh Sunday after Trinity.

The Collect.

O GOD, who declarest thy almighty power most chiefly in showing mercy and pity: Mercifully grant unto us such a measure of thy grace, that we, running the way of thy commandments, may obtain thy gracious promises, and be made partakers of thy heavenly treasure, through Jesus Christ our Lord. *Amen.*

The Epistle. 1 Corinthians 15:1-11.

BRETHREN, I declare unto you the gospel which I preached unto you, which also ye have received, and wherein ye stand – by which also ye are saved, if ye keep in memory what I preached unto you, unless ye have believed in vain. For I delivered unto you first of all that which I also received: how that Christ died for our sins, according to the Scriptures, and that he was buried, and that he rose again the third day, according to the Scriptures; and that he was seen of Cephas, then of the twelve; after that, he was seen of above five hundred brethren at once, of whom the greater part remain unto this present, but some are fallen asleep. After that, he was seen of James, then of all the apostles. And last of all he was seen of me also, as of one born out of due time. For I am the least of the apostles, that am not meet to be called an apostle, because I persecuted the church of God. But by the grace of God I am what I am, and his grace which was bestowed upon me was not in vain, but I laboured more abundantly than they all – yet not I, but the grace of God which was with me.

Therefore whether it were I or they, so we preach, and so ye believed.

The Gospel. St. Luke 18:9-14.

JESUS spake this parable unto certain which trusted in themselves that they were righteous, and despised others:

'Two men went up into the temple to pray, the one a Pharisee and the other a publican. The Pharisee stood and prayed thus with himself, "God, I thank thee that I am not as other men are, extortioners, unjust, adulterers, or even as this publican. I fast twice in the week; I give tithes of all that I possess."

'And the publican, standing afar off, would not lift up so much as his eyes unto heaven, but smote upon his breast, saying, "God be merciful to me a sinner." I tell you this man went down to his house justified rather than the other, for every one that exalteth himself shall be abased, and he that humbleth himself shall be exalted.'

The Twelfth Sunday after Trinity.
The Collect.

ALMIGHTY and everlasting God, who art always more ready to hear than we are to pray, and art wont to give more than either we desire or deserve: Pour down upon us the abundance of thy mercy, forgiving us those things whereof our conscience is afraid, and giving us those good things which we are not worthy to ask, but through the merits and mediation of Jesus Christ, thy Son, our Lord. *Amen.*

THE TWELFTH SUNDAY AFTER TRINITY

The Epistle. 2 Corinthians 3:4-9.

SUCH trust have we through Christ to God-ward, not that we are sufficient of ourselves to think anything as of ourselves, but our sufficiency is of God, who also hath made us able ministers of the new testament, not of the letter, but of the spirit, for the letter killeth, but the spirit giveth life. But if the ministration of death, written and engraven in stones, was glorious, so that the children of Israel could not steadfastly behold the face of Moses for the glory of his countenance, which glory was to be done away, how shall not the ministration of the spirit be rather glorious? For if the ministration of condemnation be glory, much more doth the ministration of righteousness exceed in glory.

The Gospel. St. Mark 7:31-37.

JESUS, departing from the coasts of Tyre and Sidon, came unto the sea of Galilee, through the midst of the coasts of Decapolis. And they bring unto him one that was deaf and had an impediment in his speech, and they beseech him to put his hand upon him. And he took him aside from the multitude, and put his fingers into his ears, and he spat, and touched his tongue; and looking up to heaven, he sighed and saith unto him, 'Ephphatha,' that is, 'Be opened.' And straightway his ears were opened, and the string of his tongue was loosed, and he spake plain. And he charged them that they should tell no man. But the more he charged them, so much the more a great deal they published it, and were beyond measure astonished, saying, 'He hath done all things well; he maketh both the deaf to hear and the dumb to speak.'

The Thirteenth Sunday after Trinity.
The Collect.

ALMIGHTY and merciful God, of whose gift alone it cometh that thy faithful people do unto thee true and laudable service: Grant, we beseech thee, that we may so faithfully serve thee in this life, that we fail not finally to attain thy heavenly promises, through the merits of Jesus Christ our Lord. *Amen.*

The Epistle. Galatians 3:16-22.

TO Abraham and his seed were the promises made. He saith not, 'And to seeds', as of many, but as of one, 'And to thy seed', which is Christ. And this I say, that the covenant that was confirmed before of God in Christ, the law, which was four hundred and thirty years after, cannot disannul, that it should make the promise of none effect. For if the inheritance be of the law, it is no more of promise, but God gave it to Abraham by promise.

Wherefore then serveth the law? It was added because of transgressions, till the seed should come to whom the promise was made, and it was ordained by angels in the hand of a mediator. Now a mediator is not a mediator of one, but God is one.

Is the law then against the promises of God? God forbid! for if there had been a law given which could have given life, verily righteousness should have been by the law. But the Scripture hath concluded all under sin, that the promise by faith of Jesus Christ might be given to them that believe.

The Gospel. St. Luke 10:23-37.

'BLESSED are the eyes which see the things that ye see. For I tell you that many prophets and kings have desired to see those things which ye see, and have not seen them; and to hear those things which ye hear, and have not heard them.'

And behold, a certain lawyer stood up, and tempted him, saying, 'Master, what shall I do to inherit eternal life?' He said unto him, 'What is written in the law? how readest thou?'

And he answering said, 'Thou shalt love the Lord thy God with all thy heart, and with all thy soul, and with all thy strength, and with all thy mind; and thy neighbour as thyself.'

And he said unto him, 'Thou hast answered right; this do and thou shalt live.'

But he, willing to justify himself, said unto Jesus, 'And who is my neighbour?' And Jesus answering said, 'A certain man went down from Jerusalem to Jericho, and fell among thieves, which stripped him of his raiment, and wounded him, and departed, leaving him half dead. And by chance there came down a certain priest that way, and when he saw him, he passed by on the other side. And likewise a Levite, when he was at the place, came and looked on him, and passed by on the other side. But a certain Samaritan, as he journeyed, came where he was;

and when he saw him, he had compassion on him, and went to him, and bound up his wounds, pouring in oil and wine, and set him on his own beast, and brought him to an inn, and took care of him. And on the morrow, when he departed, he took out two pence and gave them to the host, and said unto him, "Take care of him, and whatsoever thou spendest more, when I come again, I will repay thee." Which now of these three, thinkest thou, was neighbour unto him that fell among the thieves?' And he said, 'He that showed mercy on him.' Then said Jesus unto him, 'Go and do thou likewise.'

The Fourteenth Sunday after Trinity.
The Collect.

A LMIGHTY and everlasting God, give unto us the increase of faith, hope, and charity; and, that we may obtain that which thou dost promise, make us to love that which thou dost command, through Jesus Christ our Lord. *Amen.*

The Epistle. Galatians 5:16-24.

I SAY then, walk in the Spirit, and ye shall not fulfil the lust of the flesh. For the flesh lusteth against the Spirit, and the Spirit against the flesh; and these are contrary the one to the other, so that ye cannot do the things that ye would. But if ye be led by the Spirit, ye are not under the law. Now the works of the flesh are manifest, which are these: adultery, fornication, uncleanness, lasciviousness, idolatry, witchcraft, hatred, variance, emulations, wrath, strife, seditions, heresies, envyings, murders, drunkenness, revellings, and such like – of the which I tell you before, as I have also told you in time past, that they who do such things shall not inherit the kingdom of God. But the fruit of the Spirit is love, joy, peace, long-suffering, gentleness, goodness, faith, meekness, temperance. Against such there is no law. And they that are Christ's have crucified the flesh with the affections and lusts.

The Gospel. St. Luke 17:11-19.

AND it came to pass, as Jesus went to Jerusalem, that he passed through the midst of Samaria and Galilee. And as he entered into a certain village, there met him ten men that were lepers, which stood afar off. And they lifted up their voices and said, 'Jesus, master, have mercy on us.'

And when he saw them, he said unto them, 'Go show yourselves unto the priests.' And it came to pass that as they went, they were cleansed. And one of them, when he saw that he was healed, turned back, and with a loud voice glorified God, and fell down on his face at his feet, giving him thanks, and he was a Samaritan.

And Jesus answering said, 'Were there not ten cleansed? but where are the nine? There are not found that returned to give glory to God, save this stranger.' And he said unto him, 'Arise, go thy way; thy faith hath made thee whole.'

The Fifteenth Sunday after Trinity.
The Collect.

KEEP, we beseech thee, O Lord, thy church with thy perpetual mercy, and, because the frailty of man without thee cannot but fall, keep us ever by thy help from all things hurtful, and lead us to all things profitable to our salvation, through Jesus Christ our Lord. *Amen.*

The Epistle. Galatians 6:11-18.

YE see how large a letter I have written unto you with mine own hand. As many as desire to make a fair show in the flesh, they constrain you to be circumcised, only lest they should suffer persecution for the cross of Christ. For neither they themselves who are circumcised keep the law, but desire to have you circumcised, that they may glory in your flesh. But God forbid that I should glory, save in the cross of our Lord Jesus Christ, by whom the world is crucified unto me, and I unto the world. For in Christ Jesus neither circumcision availeth anything nor uncircumcision, but a new creature. And as many as walk according to this rule, peace be on them, and mercy, and upon the Israel of God.

From henceforth let no man trouble me, for I bear in my body the marks of the Lord Jesus. Brethren, the grace of our Lord Jesus Christ be with your spirit. Amen.

The Gospel. St. Matthew 6:24-34.

NO man can serve two masters, for either he will hate the one, and love the other; or else he will hold to the one, and despise the other. Ye cannot serve God and mammon.

Therefore I say unto you, take no thought for your life, what ye shall eat or what ye shall drink, nor yet for your body, what ye shall put on. Is not the life more than meat, and the body than raiment? Behold the fowls of the air, for they sow not, neither do they reap, nor gather into barns, yet your heavenly Father feedeth them. Are ye not much better than they? Which of you by taking thought can add one cubit unto his stature? And why take ye thought for raiment? Consider the lilies of the field, how they grow. They toil not, neither do they spin, and yet I say unto you that even Solomon in all his glory was not arrayed like one of these. Wherefore, if God so clothe the grass of the field, which today is, and tomorrow is cast into the oven, shall he not much more clothe you, O ye of little faith? Therefore take no thought, saying, 'What shall we eat?' or 'What shall we drink?' or 'Wherewithal shall we be clothed?' For after all these things do the Gentiles seek; for your heavenly Father knoweth that ye have need of all these things. But seek ye first the kingdom of God and his righteousness, and all these things shall be added unto you. Take therefore no thought for the morrow, for the morrow shall take thought for the things of itself. Sufficient unto the day is the evil thereof.

The Sixteenth Sunday after Trinity.
The Collect.

O LORD, we beseech thee, let thy continual pity cleanse and defend thy church, and, because it cannot continue in safety without thy succour, preserve it evermore by thy help and goodness, through Jesus Christ our Lord. *Amen.*

THE SIXTEENTH SUNDAY AFTER TRINITY

The Epistle. Ephesians 3:13-21.

I DESIRE that ye faint not at my tribulations for you, which is your glory.

For this cause I bow my knees unto the Father of our Lord Jesus Christ, of whom the whole family in heaven and earth is named, that he would grant you, according to the riches of his glory, to be strengthened with might by his Spirit in the inner man, that Christ may dwell in your hearts by faith – that ye, being rooted and grounded in love, may be able to comprehend with all saints what is the breadth and length and depth and height and to know the love of Christ, which passeth knowledge, that ye might be filled with all the fulness of God.

Now unto him that is able to do exceeding abundantly above all that we ask or think, according to the power that worketh in us, unto him be glory in the church by Christ Jesus, throughout all ages, world without end. Amen.

The Gospel. St. Luke 7:11-17.

A ND it came to pass the day after, that Jesus went into a city called Nain, and many of his disciples went with him, and much people. Now when he came nigh to the gate of the city, behold, there was a dead man carried out, the only son of his mother, and she was a widow, and much people of the city was with her. And when the Lord saw her, he had compassion on her and said unto her, 'Weep not.' And he came and touched the bier, and they that bare him stood still. And he said, 'Young man, I say unto thee, arise.' And he that was dead sat up and began to speak.

And he delivered him to his mother. And there came a fear on all, and they glorified God, saying that a great prophet is risen up among us and that God hath visited his people. And this rumour of him went forth throughout all Judea and throughout all the region round about.

The Seventeenth Sunday after Trinity.
The Collect.

LORD, we pray thee that thy grace may always prevent and follow us, and make us continually to be given to all good works, through Jesus Christ our Lord. *Amen.*

The Epistle. Ephesians 4:1-6.

I THEREFORE, the prisoner of the Lord, beseech you that ye walk worthy of the vocation wherewith ye are called, with all lowliness and meekness, with long-suffering, forbearing one another in love, endeavouring to keep the unity of the Spirit in the bond of peace. There is one body, and one Spirit, even as ye are called in one hope of your calling: one Lord, one faith, one baptism, one God and Father of all, who is above all and through all and in you all.

The Gospel. St. Luke 14:1-11.

IT came to pass, as Jesus went into the house of one of the chief Pharisees to eat bread on the Sabbath day, that they watched him. And behold, there was a certain man before him which had the dropsy.

And Jesus answering spake unto the lawyers and Pharisees, saying, 'Is it lawful to heal on the Sabbath day?' And they held their peace. And he took him, and healed him, and let him go, and answered them, saying, 'Which of you shall have an ass or an ox fallen into a pit, and will not straightway pull him out on the Sabbath day?' And they could not answer him again to these things.

And he put forth a parable to those which were bidden, when he marked how they chose out the chief rooms, saying unto them, 'When thou art bidden of any man to a wedding, sit not down in the highest room, lest a more honourable man than thou be bidden of him, and he that bade thee and him come and say to thee, "Give this man place", and thou begin with shame to take the lowest room. But when thou art bidden, go and sit down in the lowest room, that when he that bade thee cometh, he may say unto thee, "Friend, go up higher." Then shalt thou have worship in the presence of them that sit at meat with thee. For whosoever exalteth himself shall be abased, and he that humbleth himself shall be exalted.'

The Eighteenth Sunday after Trinity.
The Collect.

L ORD, we beseech thee, grant thy people grace to withstand the temptations of the world, the flesh, and the devil, and with pure hearts and minds to follow thee, the only God, through Jesus Christ our Lord. *Amen.*

The Epistle. 1 Corinthians 1:4-8.

I THANK my God always on your behalf for the grace of God which is given you by Jesus Christ, that in everything ye are enriched by him, in all utterance and in all knowledge, even as the testimony of Christ was confirmed

THE NINETEENTH SUNDAY AFTER TRINITY

in you, so that ye come behind in no gift, waiting for the coming of our Lord Jesus Christ, who shall also confirm you unto the end, that ye may be blameless in the day of our Lord Jesus Christ.

The Gospel. St. Matthew 22:34-46.

WHEN the Pharisees had heard that Jesus had put the Sadducees to silence, they were gathered together. Then one of them, who was a lawyer, asked him a question, tempting him and saying, 'Master, which is the great commandment in the law?' Jesus said unto him, '"Thou shalt love the Lord thy God with all thy heart, and with all thy soul, and with all thy mind." This is the first and great commandment. And the second is like unto it, "Thou shalt love thy neighbour as thyself." On these two commandments hang all the law and the prophets.'

While the Pharisees were gathered together, Jesus asked them, saying, 'What think ye of Christ? whose son is he?' They say unto him, 'The son of David.'

He saith unto them, 'How then doth David in spirit call him Lord, saying, "The Lord said unto my Lord, 'Sit thou on my right hand till I make thine enemies thy footstool'"? If David then call him Lord, how is he his son?' And no man was able to answer him a word, neither durst any man from that day forth ask him any more questions.

The Nineteenth Sunday after Trinity.
The Collect.

O GOD, forasmuch as without thee we are not able to please thee, mercifully grant that thy Holy Spirit may in all things direct and rule our hearts, through Jesus Christ our Lord. *Amen.*

The Epistle. Ephesians 4:17-32.

THIS I say therefore, and testify in the Lord, that ye henceforth walk not as other Gentiles walk, in the vanity of their mind, having the understanding darkened, being alienated from the life of God through the ignorance that is in them, because of the blindness of their heart – who, being past feeling, have given themselves over unto lasciviousness, to work all uncleanness with greediness.

But ye have not so learned Christ – if so be that ye have heard him, and have been taught by him, as the truth is in Jesus, that ye put off (concerning the former conversation) the old man, which is corrupt according to the deceitful lusts; and be renewed in the spirit of your mind; and that ye put on the new man, which after God is created in righteousness and true holiness.

Wherefore, putting away lying, speak every man truth with his neighbour, for we are members one of another. Be ye angry and sin not; let not the sun go down upon your wrath, neither give place to the devil. Let him that stole steal no more, but rather let him labour, working with his hands the thing which is good, that he may have to give to him that needeth.

Let no corrupt communication proceed out of your mouth, but that which is good to the use of edifying, that it may minister grace unto the hearers. And grieve not the Holy Spirit of God whereby ye are sealed unto the day of redemption.

THE TWENTIETH SUNDAY AFTER TRINITY

Let all bitterness, and wrath, and anger, and clamour, and evil speaking be put away from you, with all malice. And be ye kind one to another, tender-hearted, forgiving one another, even as God for Christ's sake hath forgiven you.

The Gospel. St. Matthew 9:1-8.

JESUS entered into a ship, and passed over, and came into his own city. And behold, they brought to him a man sick of the palsy, lying on a bed. And Jesus seeing their faith, said unto the sick of the palsy, 'Son, be of good cheer; thy sins be forgiven thee.' And behold, certain of the scribes said within themselves, 'This man blasphemeth.' And Jesus knowing their thoughts said, 'Wherefore think ye evil in your hearts? For whether is easier to say, "Thy sins be forgiven thee", or to say, "Arise and walk"? But that ye may know that the Son of Man hath power on earth to forgive sins' – then saith he to the sick of the palsy, 'Arise, take up thy bed, and go unto thine house.' And he arose and departed to his house. But when the multitude saw it, they marvelled and glorified God, who had given such power unto men.

The Twentieth Sunday after Trinity.
The Collect.

O ALMIGHTY and most merciful God, of thy bountiful goodness keep us, we beseech thee, from all things that may hurt us, that we, being ready both in body and soul, may cheerfully accomplish those things that thou wouldest have done, through Jesus Christ our Lord. *Amen.*

THE TWENTIETH SUNDAY AFTER TRINITY

The Epistle. Ephesians 5:15-21.

SEE then that ye walk circumspectly, not as fools, but as wise, redeeming the time, because the days are evil. Wherefore be ye not unwise, but understanding what the will of the Lord is. And be not drunk with wine, wherein is excess; but be filled with the Spirit, speaking to yourselves in psalms and hymns and spiritual songs, singing and making melody in your heart to the Lord, giving thanks always for all things unto God and the Father in the name of our Lord Jesus Christ, submitting yourselves one to another in the fear of God.

The Gospel. St. Matthew 22:1-14.

JESUS said, 'The kingdom of heaven is like unto a certain king, who made a marriage for his son, and sent forth his servants to call them that were bidden to the wedding, and they would not come. Again, he sent forth other servants, saying, "Tell them which are bidden, 'Behold, I have prepared my dinner; my oxen and my fatlings are killed, and all things are ready. Come unto the marriage.'" But they made light of it, and went their ways, one to his farm, another to his merchandise. And the remnant took his servants, and entreated them spitefully, and slew them. But when the king heard thereof, he was wroth, and he sent forth his armies, and destroyed those murderers, and burnt up their city.

'Then saith he to his servants, "The wedding is ready, but they who were bidden were not worthy. Go ye therefore into the highways, and as many as ye shall find, bid to the marriage." So those servants went out into the highways and gathered together all, as many as they found, both bad and good, and the wedding was furnished with guests.

'And when the king came in to see the guests, he saw there a man which had not on a wedding garment. And he saith unto him, "Friend, how camest thou in hither, not having a wedding garment?" And he was speechless. Then said the king to the servants, "Bind him hand and foot, and take him away, and cast him into outer darkness; there shall be weeping and gnashing of teeth." For many are called, but few are chosen.'

The Twenty-First Sunday after Trinity.
The Collect.

G RANT, we beseech thee, merciful Lord, to thy faithful people pardon and peace, that they may be cleansed from all their sins, and serve thee with a quiet mind, through Jesus Christ our Lord. *Amen.*

The Epistle. Ephesians 6:10-20.

M Y brethren, be strong in the Lord and in the power of his might. Put on the whole armour of God, that ye may be able to stand against the wiles of the devil. For we wrestle not against flesh and blood, but against principalities, against powers, against the rulers of the darkness of this world, against spiritual wickedness in high places. Wherefore take unto you the whole armour of God, that ye may be able to withstand in the evil day, and having done all, to stand.

Stand therefore, having your loins girt about with truth, and having on the breastplate of righteousness, and your feet shod with the preparation of the gospel of peace; above all, taking the shield of faith, wherewith ye shall be able to quench all the fiery darts of the wicked. And take the helmet of salvation, and the sword of the Spirit, which is the word of God – praying always with all prayer and supplication in the Spirit, and watching thereunto with all perseverance and supplication for all saints, and for me, that utterance may be given unto me, that I may open my mouth boldly to make known the mystery of the gospel, for which I am an ambassador in bonds, that therein I may speak boldly, as I ought to speak.

The Gospel. St. John 4:46-54.

THERE was a certain nobleman, whose son was sick at Capernaum. When he heard that Jesus was come out of Judea into Galilee, he went unto him, and besought him that he would come down and heal his son, for he was at the point of death. Then said Jesus unto him, 'Except ye see signs and wonders, ye will not believe.' The nobleman saith unto him, 'Sir, come down ere my child die.'

Jesus saith unto him, 'Go thy way; thy son liveth.' And the man believed the word that Jesus had spoken unto him, and he went his way. And as he was now going down, his servants met him and told him, saying, 'Thy son liveth.' Then inquired he of them the hour when he began to amend, and they said unto him, 'Yesterday at the seventh hour the fever left him.'

So the father knew that it was at the same hour in the which Jesus said unto him, 'Thy son liveth', and himself believed, and his whole house.

THE TWENTY-SECOND SUNDAY AFTER TRINITY

This is again the second miracle that Jesus did when he was come out of Judea into Galilee.

The Twenty-Second Sunday after Trinity.
The Collect.

LORD, we beseech thee to keep thy household the church in continual godliness, that through thy protection it may be free from all adversities, and devoutly given to serve thee in good works, to the glory of thy name, through Jesus Christ our Lord. *Amen.*

The Epistle. Philippians 1:3-11.

I THANK my God upon every remembrance of you, always in every prayer of mine for you all, making request with joy for your fellowship in the gospel from the first day until now, being confident of this very thing, that he who hath begun a good work in you will perform it until the day of Jesus Christ, even as it is meet for me to think this of you all, because I have you in my heart, inasmuch as both in my bonds, and in the defence and confirmation of the gospel, ye all are partakers of my grace.

For God is my record, how greatly I long after you all in the bowels of Jesus Christ. And this I pray, that your love may abound yet more and more in knowledge and in all judgement, that ye may approve things that are excellent – that ye may be sincere and without offence till the day of Christ, being filled with the fruits of righteousness, which are by Jesus Christ unto the glory and praise of God.

THE TWENTY-SECOND SUNDAY AFTER TRINITY

The Gospel. St. Matthew 18:21-35.

PETER said unto Jesus, 'Lord, how oft shall my brother sin against me and I forgive him? till seven times?'

Jesus saith unto him, 'I say not unto thee until seven times, but until seventy times seven.

'Therefore is the kingdom of heaven likened unto a certain king, which would take account of his servants. And when he had begun to reckon, one was brought unto him which owed him ten thousand talents. But forasmuch as he had not to pay, his lord commanded him to be sold, and his wife, and children, and all that he had, and payment to be made.

'The servant therefore fell down and worshipped him, saying, "Lord, have patience with me, and I will pay thee all."

'Then the lord of that servant was moved with compassion, and loosed him, and forgave him the debt. But the same servant went out, and found one of his fellow-servants which owed him an hundred pence, and he laid hands on him, and took him by the throat, saying, "Pay me that thou owest." And his fellow-servant fell down at his feet and besought him, saying, "Have patience with me, and I will pay thee all." And he would not, but went and cast him into prison till he should pay the debt.

'So when his fellow-servants saw what was done, they were very sorry, and came and told unto their lord all that was done.

'Then his lord, after that he had called him, said unto him, "O thou wicked servant! I forgave thee all that debt, because thou desiredst me. Shouldest not thou also have had compassion on thy fellow-servant, even as I had pity on thee?"

'And his lord was wroth, and delivered him to the tormentors till he should pay all that was due unto him. So likewise shall my heavenly Father do also unto you, if ye from your hearts forgive not every one his brother their trespasses.'

The Twenty-Third Sunday after Trinity.
The Collect.

O GOD, our refuge and strength, who art the author of all godliness: Be ready, we beseech thee, to hear the devout prayers of thy church, and grant that those things which we ask faithfully, we may obtain effectually, through Jesus Christ our Lord. *Amen.*

The Epistle. Philippians 3:17-21.

B RETHREN, be followers together of me, and mark them which walk so as ye have us for an ensample. (For many walk, of whom I have told you often, and now tell you even weeping, that they are the enemies of the cross of Christ, whose end is destruction, whose god is their belly, and whose glory is in their shame, who mind earthly things.) For our conversation is in heaven, from whence also we look for the Saviour, the Lord Jesus Christ, who shall change our vile body, that it may be fashioned like unto his glorious body, according to the working whereby he is able even to subdue all things unto himself.

THE TWENTY-FOURTH SUNDAY AFTER TRINITY

The Gospel. St. Matthew 22:15-22.

THEN went the Pharisees and took counsel how they might entangle him in his talk. And they sent out unto him their disciples, with the Herodians, saying, 'Master, we know that thou art true, and teachest the way of God in truth, neither carest thou for any man, for thou regardest not the person of men. Tell us therefore, what thinkest thou? Is it lawful to give tribute unto Caesar, or not?'

But Jesus perceived their wickedness and said, 'Why tempt ye me, ye hypocrites? Show me the tribute money.' And they brought unto him a penny. And he saith unto them, 'Whose is this image and superscription?' They say unto him, 'Caesar's.' Then saith he unto them, 'Render therefore unto Caesar the things which are Caesar's, and unto God the things that are God's.' When they had heard these words, they marvelled, and left him, and went their way.

The Twenty-Fourth Sunday after Trinity.
The Collect.

O LORD, we beseech thee, absolve thy people from their offences, that through thy bountiful goodness we may all be delivered from the bands of those sins which by our frailty we have committed. Grant this, O heavenly Father, for Jesus Christ's sake, our blessed Lord and Saviour. *Amen.*

The Epistle. Colossians 1:3-12.

WE give thanks to God and the Father of our Lord Jesus Christ – praying always for you, since we heard of your faith in Christ Jesus, and of the love which ye have to all the saints – for the hope which is laid up for you in heaven, whereof ye heard before in the word of the truth of the gospel, which is come unto you, as it is in all the world; and bringeth forth fruit, as it doth also in you, since the day ye heard of it and knew the grace of God in truth – as ye also learned of Epaphras, our dear fellow-servant, who is for you a faithful minister of Christ, who also declared unto us your love in the Spirit.

For this cause, we also, since the day we heard it, do not cease to pray for you, and to desire that ye might be filled with the knowledge of his will in all wisdom and spiritual understanding, that ye might walk worthy of the Lord unto all pleasing, being fruitful in every good work and increasing in the knowledge of God, strengthened with all might according to his glorious power, unto all patience and long-suffering with joyfulness, giving thanks unto the Father, which hath made us meet to be partakers of the inheritance of the saints in light.

The Gospel. St. Matthew 9:18-26.

WHILE Jesus spake these things unto John's disciples, behold, there came a certain ruler and worshipped him, saying, 'My daughter is even now dead, but come and lay thy hand upon her, and she shall live.' And Jesus arose and followed him, and so did his disciples. And behold, a woman, which was diseased with an issue of blood twelve years, came behind him and touched the hem of his garment. For she said within herself, 'If I may but touch his garment, I shall be whole.'

But Jesus turned him about, and when he saw her, he said, 'Daughter, be of good comfort, thy faith hath made thee whole.' And the woman was made whole from that hour. And when Jesus came into the ruler's house, and saw the minstrels and the people making a noise, he said unto them, 'Give place, for the maid is not dead, but sleepeth.' And they laughed him to scorn. But when the people were put forth, he went in, and took her by the hand, and the maid arose. And the fame hereof went abroad into all that land.

The Twenty-Fifth Sunday after Trinity.
The Collect.

STIR up, we beseech thee, O Lord, the wills of thy faithful people, that they, plenteously bringing forth the fruit of good works, may of thee be plenteously rewarded, through Jesus Christ our Lord. *Amen.*

For the Epistle. Jeremiah 23:5-8.

'BEHOLD, the days come', saith the LORD, 'that I will raise unto David a righteous branch, and a king shall reign and prosper, and shall execute judgement and justice in the earth. In his days Judah shall be saved, and Israel shall dwell safely; and this is his name whereby he shall be called, THE LORD OUR RIGHTEOUSNESS.

'Therefore behold, the days come', saith the LORD, 'that they shall no more say, "The LORD liveth, which brought up the children of Israel out of the land of Egypt", but, "The LORD liveth, which brought up and which led the seed of the house of Israel out of the north country", and from all countries whither I had driven them, and they shall dwell in their own land.'

The Gospel. St. John 6:5-14.

WHEN Jesus then lifted up his eyes and saw a great company come unto him, he saith unto Philip, 'Whence shall we buy bread that these may eat?' (And this he said to prove him, for he himself knew what he would do.) Philip answered him, 'Two hundred pennyworth of bread is not sufficient for them, that every one of them may take a little.'

One of his disciples, Andrew, Simon Peter's brother, saith unto him, 'There is a lad here, which hath five barley loaves and two small fishes, but what are they among so many?' And Jesus said, 'Make the men sit down.' Now there was much grass in the place. So the men sat down, in number about five thousand. And Jesus took the loaves, and when he had given thanks, he distributed to the disciples, and the disciples to them that were set down, and likewise of the fishes, as much as they would. When they were filled, he said unto his disciples, 'Gather up the fragments that remain, that nothing be lost.' Therefore they gathered them together, and filled twelve baskets with the fragments of the five barley loaves which remained over and above unto them that had eaten.

Then those men, when they had seen the miracle that Jesus did, said, 'This is of a truth that prophet that should come into the world.'

SAINT ANDREW'S DAY

¶ *If there are any more Sundays before Advent Sunday, the service of some of those Sundays that were omitted after the Epiphany shall be used to supply as many as are here wanting. And if there are fewer, the surplus may be omitted, provided that this last collect, epistle, and gospel shall always be used upon the Sunday next before Advent.*

Saint Andrew's Day.*
The Collect.

ALMIGHTY God, who didst give such grace unto thy holy apostle Saint Andrew, that he readily obeyed the calling of thy Son Jesus Christ, and followed him without delay: Grant unto us all, that we, being called by thy holy word, may forthwith give up ourselves obediently to fulfil thy holy commandments, through the same Jesus Christ our Lord. *Amen.*

The Epistle. Romans 10:9-21.

IF thou shalt confess with thy mouth the Lord Jesus, and shalt believe in thine heart that God hath raised him from the dead, thou shalt be saved. For with the heart man believeth unto righteousness, and with the mouth confession is made unto salvation.

For the Scripture saith, 'Whosoever believeth on him shall not be ashamed.' For there is no difference between the Jew and the Greek, for the same Lord over all is rich unto all that call upon him. For whosoever shall call upon the name of the Lord shall be saved.

How then shall they call on him in whom they have not

* November 30.

believed? And how shall they believe in him of whom they have not heard? And how shall they hear without a preacher? And how shall they preach except they be sent? As it is written, 'How beautiful are the feet of them that preach the gospel of peace, and bring glad tidings of good things!' But they have not all obeyed the gospel. For Isaiah saith, 'Lord, who hath believed our report?' So then faith cometh by hearing, and hearing by the word of God. But I say, have they not heard? Yes, verily – 'Their sound went into all the earth, and their words unto the ends of the world.' But I say, did not Israel know? First Moses saith, 'I will provoke you to jealousy by them that are no people, and by a foolish nation I will anger you.' But Isaiah is very bold and saith, 'I was found of them that sought me not; I was made manifest unto them that asked not after me.' But to Israel he saith, 'All day long I have stretched forth my hands unto a disobedient and gainsaying people.'

The Gospel. St. Matthew 4:18-22.

JESUS, walking by the sea of Galilee, saw two brethren, Simon called Peter, and Andrew his brother, casting a net into the sea (for they were fishers). And he saith unto them, 'Follow me, and I will make you fishers of men.' And they straightway left their nets and followed him. And going on from thence, he saw other two brethren, James the son of Zebedee, and John his brother, in a ship with Zebedee their father, mending their nets, and he called them. And they immediately left the ship and their father and followed him.

SAINT THOMAS THE APOSTLE

Saint Thomas the Apostle.*
The Collect.

ALMIGHTY and everliving God, who for the greater confirmation of the faith didst suffer thy holy apostle Thomas to be doubtful of thy Son's resurrection: Grant us so perfectly, and without all doubt, to believe in thy Son Jesus Christ, that our faith in thy sight may never be reproved. Hear us, O Lord, through the same Jesus Christ, to whom, with thee and the Holy Ghost, be all honour and glory, now and for evermore. *Amen.*

The Epistle. Ephesians 2:19-22.

NOW therefore ye are no more strangers and foreigners, but fellow citizens with the saints, and of the household of God, and are built upon the foundation of the apostles and prophets, Jesus Christ himself being the chief cornerstone, in whom all the building fitly framed together groweth unto an holy temple in the Lord, in whom ye also are builded together for an habitation of God through the Spirit.

The Gospel. St. John 20:24-31.

THOMAS, one of the twelve, called Didymus, was not with them when Jesus came. The other disciples therefore said unto him, 'We have seen the Lord.' But he said unto them, 'Except I shall see in his hands the print of the nails, and put my finger into the print of the nails, and thrust my hand into his side, I will not believe.'

And after eight days again his disciples were within, and

* December 21.

207

Thomas with them; then came Jesus, the doors being shut, and stood in the midst and said, 'Peace be unto you.' Then saith he to Thomas, 'Reach hither thy finger, and behold my hands; and reach hither thy hand, and thrust it into my side; and be not faithless, but believing.'

And Thomas answered and said unto him, 'My Lord, and my God!' Jesus saith unto him, 'Thomas, because thou hast seen me, thou hast believed; blessed are they that have not seen, and yet have believed.'

And many other signs truly did Jesus in the presence of his disciples, which are not written in this book. But these are written, that ye might believe that Jesus is the Christ, the Son of God, and that believing ye might have life through his name.

The Conversion of Saint Paul.*
The Collect.

O GOD, who, through the preaching of the blessed apostle Saint Paul, hast caused the light of the gospel to shine throughout the world: Grant, we beseech thee, that we, having his wonderful conversion in remembrance, may show forth our thankfulness unto thee for the same, by following the holy doctrine which he taught, through Jesus Christ our Lord. *Amen.*

For the Epistle. Acts 9:1-22.

A ND Saul, yet breathing out threatenings and slaughter against the disciples of the Lord, went unto the high priest and desired of him letters to Damascus to the

* January 25.

synagogues, that if he found any of this way, whether they were men or women, he might bring them bound unto Jerusalem. And as he journeyed, he came near Damascus, and suddenly there shined round about him a light from heaven. And he fell to the earth, and heard a voice saying unto him, 'Saul, Saul, why persecutest thou me?' And he said, 'Who art thou, Lord?' And the Lord said, 'I am Jesus whom thou persecutest; it is hard for thee to kick against the pricks.' And he trembling and astonished said, 'Lord, what wilt thou have me to do?' And the Lord said unto him, 'Arise and go into the city, and it shall be told thee what thou must do.' And the men which journeyed with him stood speechless, hearing a voice, but seeing no man. And Saul arose from the earth, and when his eyes were opened, he saw no man, but they led him by the hand and brought him into Damascus. And he was three days without sight, and neither did eat nor drink.

And there was a certain disciple at Damascus, named Ananias, and to him said the Lord in a vision, 'Ananias.' And he said, 'Behold, I am here, Lord.' And the Lord said unto him, 'Arise and go into the street which is called Straight, and inquire in the house of Judas for one called Saul, of Tarsus. For behold, he prayeth, and hath seen in a vision a man named Ananias coming in, and putting his hand on him, that he might receive his sight.'

Then Ananias answered, 'Lord, I have heard by many of this man, how much evil he hath done to thy saints at Jerusalem; and here he hath authority from the chief priests to bind all that call on thy name.'

But the Lord said unto him, 'Go thy way; for he is a

chosen vessel unto me, to bear my name before the Gentiles, and kings, and the children of Israel. For I will show him how great things he must suffer for my name's sake.'

And Ananias went his way and entered into the house, and putting his hands on him said, 'Brother Saul, the Lord – even Jesus that appeared unto thee in the way as thou camest – hath sent me, that thou mightest receive thy sight and be filled with the Holy Ghost.' And immediately there fell from his eyes as it had been scales, and he received sight forthwith, and arose and was baptized. And when he had received meat, he was strengthened.

Then was Saul certain days with the disciples which were at Damascus. And straightway he preached Christ in the synagogues, that he is the Son of God.

But all that heard him were amazed and said, 'Is not this he that destroyed them which called on this name in Jerusalem, and came hither for that intent, that he might bring them bound unto the chief priests?'

But Saul increased the more in strength, and confounded the Jews which dwelt at Damascus, proving that this is very Christ.

The Gospel. St. Matthew 19:27-30.

PETER answered and said unto Jesus, 'Behold, we have forsaken all and followed thee; what shall we have therefore?'

And Jesus said unto them, 'Verily I say unto you that ye which have followed me, in the regeneration when the Son of Man shall sit in the throne of his glory, ye also shall sit upon twelve thrones, judging the twelve tribes of Israel.

'And every one that hath forsaken houses, or brethren, or sisters, or father, or mother, or wife, or children, or lands, for my name's sake, shall receive an hundredfold, and shall inherit everlasting life.

'But many that are first shall be last, and the last shall be first.'

The Presentation of Christ in the Temple, Commonly Called the Purification of Saint Mary the Virgin.*
The Collect.

ALMIGHTY and everliving God, we humbly beseech thy Majesty, that as thy only-begotten Son was this day presented in the temple in substance of our flesh, so we may be presented unto thee with pure and clean hearts, by the same thy Son Jesus Christ our Lord. *Amen.*

For the Epistle. Malachi 3:1-5.

'BEHOLD, I will send my messenger, and he shall prepare the way before me. And the Lord, whom ye seek, shall suddenly come to his temple; even the messenger of the covenant, whom ye delight in – behold, he shall come', saith the LORD of hosts. But who may abide the day of his coming? and who shall stand when he appeareth? for he is like a refiner's fire, and like fullers' soap. And he shall sit as a refiner and purifier of silver, and he shall purify the sons of Levi, and purge them as gold and silver, that they may offer unto the LORD an offering in righteousness. Then shall the offerings of Judah and Jerusalem be pleasant unto the LORD, as in the days of old, and as in former

* February 2.

years. 'And I will come near to you to judgement, and I will be a swift witness against the sorcerers, and against the adulterers, and against false swearers, and against those that oppress the hireling in his wages, the widow, and the fatherless, and that turn aside the stranger from his right, and fear not me', saith the LORD of hosts.

The Gospel. St. Luke 2:22-40.

AND when the days of her purification according to the law of Moses were accomplished, they brought Jesus to Jerusalem, to present him to the Lord (as it is written in the law of the Lord, 'Every male that openeth the womb shall be called holy to the Lord'), and to offer a sacrifice according to that which is said in the law of the Lord, 'A pair of turtle doves, or two young pigeons'.

And behold, there was a man in Jerusalem, whose name was Simeon, and the same man was just and devout, waiting for the consolation of Israel, and the Holy Ghost was upon him. And it was revealed unto him by the Holy Ghost that he should not see death before he had seen the Lord's Christ. And he came by the Spirit into the temple, and when the parents brought in the child Jesus, to do for him after the custom of the law, then took he him up in his arms, and blessed God and said, 'Lord, now lettest thou thy servant depart in peace, according to thy word. For mine eyes have seen thy salvation, which thou hast prepared before the face of all people, a light to lighten the Gentiles, and the glory of thy people Israel.'

And Joseph and his mother marvelled at those things which were spoken of him. And Simeon blessed them, and said unto Mary his mother, 'Behold, this child is set for the fall and rising again of many in Israel, and for a sign which shall be spoken against – yea, a sword shall pierce through thy own soul also – that the thoughts of many hearts may be revealed.'

And there was one Anna, a prophetess, the daughter of Phanuel of the tribe of Asher; she was of a great age, and had lived with an husband seven years from her virginity; and she was a widow of about fourscore and four years, which departed not from the temple, but served God with fastings and prayers night and day. And she coming in that instant gave thanks likewise unto the Lord, and spake of him to all them that looked for redemption in Jerusalem.

And when they had performed all things according to the law of the Lord, they returned into Galilee, to their own city Nazareth.

And the child grew, and waxed strong in spirit, filled with wisdom, and the grace of God was upon him.

Saint Matthias's Day.*
The Collect.

O ALMIGHTY God, who into the place of the traitor Judas didst choose thy faithful servant Matthias to be of the number of the twelve apostles: Grant that thy church, being alway preserved from false apostles, may be ordered and guided by faithful and true pastors, through Jesus Christ our Lord. *Amen.*

* February 24.

SAINT MATTHIAS'S DAY

For the Epistle. Acts 1:15-26.

IN those days Peter stood up in the midst of the disciples and said (the number of the names together were about an hundred and twenty), 'Men and brethren, this Scripture must needs have been fulfilled, which the Holy Ghost by the mouth of David spake before concerning Judas, which was guide to them that took Jesus. For he was numbered with us, and had obtained part of this ministry. Now this man purchased a field with the reward of iniquity, and falling headlong, he burst asunder in the midst, and all his bowels gushed out. And it was known unto all the dwellers at Jerusalem, insomuch as that field is called in their proper tongue *Aceldama,* that is to say, "the field of blood". For it is written in the book of Psalms, "Let his habitation be desolate, and let no man dwell therein" and "His bishopric let another take." Wherefore, of these men which have companied with us all the time that the Lord Jesus went in and out among us, beginning from the baptism of John, unto that same day that he was taken up from us, must one be ordained to be a witness with us of his resurrection.' And they appointed two, Joseph called Barsabbas, who was surnamed Justus, and Matthias. And they prayed and said, 'Thou, Lord, which knowest the hearts of all men, show whether of these two thou hast chosen, that he may take part of this ministry and apostleship, from which Judas by transgression fell, that he might go to his own place.' And they gave forth their lots, and the lot fell upon Matthias, and he was numbered with the eleven apostles.

THE ANNUNCIATION OF THE VIRGIN MARY

The Gospel. St. Matthew 11:25-30.

AT that time Jesus answered and said, 'I thank thee, O Father, Lord of heaven and earth, because thou hast hid these things from the wise and prudent, and hast revealed them unto babes. Even so, Father, for so it seemed good in thy sight.

'All things are delivered unto me of my Father, and no man knoweth the Son but the Father. Neither knoweth any man the Father save the Son, and he to whomsoever the Son will reveal him.

'Come unto me, all ye that labour and are heavy laden, and I will give you rest. Take my yoke upon you, and learn of me, for I am meek and lowly in heart, and ye shall find rest unto your souls. For my yoke is easy, and my burden is light.'

The Annunciation of the Blessed Virgin Mary.*
The Collect.

WE beseech thee, O Lord, pour thy grace into our hearts, that as we have known the incarnation of thy Son Jesus Christ by the message of an angel, so by his cross and passion we may be brought unto the glory of his resurrection, through the same Jesus Christ our Lord. *Amen.*

For the Epistle. Isaiah 7:10-15.

MOREOVER the LORD spake again unto Ahaz, saying, 'Ask thee a sign of the LORD thy God; ask it either in the depth or in the height above.' But Ahaz said, 'I will not

* March 25.

215

ask, neither will I tempt the LORD.' And he said, 'Hear ye now, O house of David; is it a small thing for you to weary men, but will ye weary my God also? Therefore the Lord himself shall give you a sign: Behold, a virgin shall conceive, and bear a son, and shall call his name *Emmanuel*. Butter and honey shall he eat, that he may know to refuse the evil, and choose the good.'

The Gospel. St. Luke 1:26-38.

AND in the sixth month the angel Gabriel was sent from God unto a city of Galilee named Nazareth, to a virgin espoused to a man whose name was Joseph, of the house of David, and the virgin's name was Mary.

And the angel came in unto her and said, 'Hail, thou that art highly favoured, the Lord is with thee; blessed art thou among women.' And when she saw him, she was troubled at his saying, and cast in her mind what manner of salutation this should be. And the angel said unto her, 'Fear not, Mary, for thou hast found favour with God. And behold, thou shalt conceive in thy womb, and bring forth a son, and shalt call his name JESUS. He shall be great, and shall be called the Son of the Highest, and the Lord God shall give unto him the throne of his father David. And he shall reign over the house of Jacob for ever, and of his kingdom there shall be no end.'

Then said Mary unto the angel, 'How shall this be, seeing I know not a man?'

And the angel answered and said unto her, 'The Holy Ghost shall come upon thee, and the power of the Highest shall overshadow thee; therefore also that holy thing which shall be born of thee shall be called the Son of God. And behold, thy cousin Elisabeth, she hath also conceived a son in her old age, and this is the sixth month with her who was called barren, for with God nothing shall be impossible.'

And Mary said, 'Behold the handmaid of the Lord; be it unto me according to thy word.' And the angel departed from her.

Saint Mark's Day.*
The Collect.

O ALMIGHTY God, who hast instructed thy holy church with the heavenly doctrine of thy evangelist Saint Mark: Give us grace, that, being not like children carried away with every blast of vain doctrine, we may be established in the truth of thy holy gospel, through Jesus Christ our Lord. *Amen.*

The Epistle. Ephesians 4:7-16.

U NTO every one of us is given grace, according to the measure of the gift of Christ. Wherefore he saith, 'When he ascended up on high, he led captivity captive and gave gifts unto men.' (Now that he ascended, what is it but that he also descended first into the lower parts of the earth? He that descended is the same also that ascended up far above all heavens, that he might fill all things.) And he gave some, apostles; and some, prophets; and some, evangelists; and some, pastors and teachers; for the perfecting of the saints for the work of the ministry,

* April 25.

for the edifying of the body of Christ, till we all come, in the unity of the faith and of the knowledge of the Son of God, unto a perfect man, unto the measure of the stature of the fulness of Christ, that we henceforth be no more children, tossed to and fro, and carried about with every wind of doctrine, by the sleight of men and cunning craftiness, whereby they lie in wait to deceive, but speaking the truth in love may grow up into him in all things, which is the head, even Christ – from whom the whole body fitly joined together and compacted by that which every joint supplieth, according to the effectual working in the measure of every part, maketh increase of the body, unto the edifying of itself in love.

The Gospel. St. John 15:1-11.

I AM the true vine, and my Father is the husbandman. Every branch in me that beareth not fruit he taketh away; and every branch that beareth fruit, he purgeth it, that it may bring forth more fruit. Now ye are clean through the word which I have spoken unto you.

Abide in me, and I in you. As the branch cannot bear fruit of itself, except it abide in the vine, no more can ye, except ye abide in me. I am the vine; ye are the branches. He that abideth in me, and I in him, the same bringeth forth much fruit, for without me ye can do nothing. If a man abide not in me, he is cast forth as a branch, and is withered; and men gather them, and cast them into the fire, and they are burned. If ye abide in me, and my words abide in you, ye shall ask what ye will, and it shall be done unto you. Herein is my Father glorified, that ye bear much fruit; so shall ye be my disciples. As the Father hath loved me, so have I loved you: continue ye in my love. If ye keep my commandments, ye shall abide in my love, even as I have kept my Father's commandments and abide in his love.

These things have I spoken unto you that my joy might remain in you, and that your joy might be full.

Saint Philip and Saint James's Day.*
The Collect.

O ALMIGHTY God, whom truly to know is everlasting life: Grant us perfectly to know thy Son Jesus Christ to be the way, the truth, and the life, that, following the steps of thy holy apostles, Saint Philip and Saint James, we may steadfastly walk in the way that leadeth to eternal life, through the same thy Son Jesus Christ our Lord. *Amen.*

The Epistle. James 1:1-12.

J AMES, a servant of God and of the Lord Jesus Christ, to the twelve tribes which are scattered abroad, greeting. My brethren, count it all joy when ye fall into divers temptations, knowing this, that the trying of your faith worketh patience. But let patience have her perfect work, that ye may be perfect and entire, wanting nothing. If any of you lack wisdom, let him ask of God, that giveth to all men liberally and upbraideth not, and it shall be given him. But let him ask in faith, nothing wavering, for he that wavereth is like a wave of the sea, driven with the wind and tossed. For let not that man think that he shall

* May 1.

receive anything of the Lord. A double-minded man is unstable in all his ways. Let the brother of low degree rejoice in that he is exalted; but the rich, in that he is made low, because as the flower of the grass he shall pass away. For the sun is no sooner risen with a burning heat, but it withereth the grass, and the flower thereof falleth, and the grace of the fashion of it perisheth; so also shall the rich man fade away in his ways. Blessed is the man that endureth temptation, for when he is tried, he shall receive the crown of life, which the Lord hath promised to them that love him.

The Gospel. St. John 14:1-14.

AND Jesus said unto his disciples, 'Let not your heart be troubled. Ye believe in God; believe also in me. In my Father's house are many mansions; if it were not so, I would have told you. I go to prepare a place for you; and if I go and prepare a place for you, I will come again and receive you unto myself, that where I am, there ye may be also. And whither I go ye know, and the way ye know.'

Thomas saith unto him, 'Lord, we know not whither thou goest, and how can we know the way?' Jesus saith unto him, 'I am the way, the truth, and the life: no man cometh unto the Father but by me. If ye had known me, ye should have known my Father also; and from henceforth ye know him, and have seen him.' Philip saith unto him, 'Lord, show us the Father, and it sufficeth us.' Jesus saith unto him, 'Have I been so long time with you and yet hast thou not known me, Philip? He that hath seen me hath seen the Father, and how sayest thou then, "Show us the Father"? Believest thou not that I am in the Father, and the Father in me? The words that I speak unto you I speak not of myself; but the Father that dwelleth in me, he doeth the works. Believe me that I am in the Father, and the Father in me, or else believe me for the very works' sake.

'Verily, verily I say unto you, he that believeth on me, the works that I do shall he do also, and greater works than these shall he do, because I go unto my Father. And whatsoever ye shall ask in my name, that will I do, that the Father may be glorified in the Son. If ye shall ask any thing in my name, I will do it.'

Saint Barnabas the Apostle.*
The Collect.

O LORD God almighty, who didst endue thy holy apostle Barnabas with singular gifts of the Holy Ghost: Leave us not, we beseech thee, destitute of thy manifold gifts, nor yet of grace to use them alway to thy honour and glory, through Jesus Christ our Lord. *Amen.*

For the Epistle. Acts 11:22-30.

T IDINGS of these things came unto the ears of the church which was in Jerusalem, and they sent forth Barnabas, that he should go as far as Antioch. Who, when he came, and had seen the grace of God, was glad, and exhorted them all, that with purpose of heart they would cleave unto the Lord. For he was a good man, and full of the Holy Ghost and of faith, and much people was added

* June 11.

unto the Lord. Then departed Barnabas to Tarsus, for to seek Saul. And when he had found him, he brought him unto Antioch. And it came to pass that a whole year they assembled themselves with the church and taught much people; and the disciples were called Christians first in Antioch.

And in these days came prophets from Jerusalem unto Antioch. And there stood up one of them named Agabus, and signified by the Spirit that there should be great dearth throughout all the world, which came to pass in the days of Claudius Caesar. Then the disciples, every man according to his ability, determined to send relief unto the brethren which dwelt in Judea, which also they did, and sent it to the elders by the hands of Barnabas and Saul.

The Gospel. St. John 15:12-16.

THIS is my commandment, that ye love one another, as I have loved you. Greater love hath no man than this, that a man lay down his life for his friends. Ye are my friends, if ye do whatsoever I command you. Henceforth I call you not servants, for the servant knoweth not what his lord doeth; but I have called you friends, for all things that I have heard of my Father I have made known unto you.

Ye have not chosen me, but I have chosen you, and ordained you, that ye should go and bring forth fruit, and that your fruit should remain, that whatsoever ye shall ask of the Father in my name, he may give it you.

Saint John the Baptist's Day.*

The Collect.

ALMIGHTY God, by whose providence thy servant John the Baptist was wonderfully born, and sent to prepare the way of thy Son our Saviour by preaching of repentance: Make us so to follow his doctrine and holy life, that we may truly repent according to his preaching; and after his example constantly speak the truth, boldly rebuke vice, and patiently suffer for the truth's sake, through Jesus Christ our Lord. *Amen.*

For the Epistle. Isaiah 40:1-11.

'COMFORT ye, comfort ye my people', saith your God. Speak ye comfortably to Jerusalem, and cry unto her, that her warfare is accomplished, that her iniquity is pardoned, for she hath received of the LORD's hand double for all her sins.

The voice of him that crieth in the wilderness, 'Prepare ye the way of the LORD, make straight in the desert a highway for our God. Every valley shall be exalted, and every mountain and hill shall be made low, and the crooked shall be made straight, and the rough places plain. And the glory of the LORD shall be revealed, and all flesh shall see it together, for the mouth of the LORD hath spoken it.'

The voice said, 'Cry.' And he said, 'What shall I cry?' 'All flesh is grass, and all the goodliness thereof is as the flower of the field. The grass withereth, the flower fadeth, because the Spirit of the LORD bloweth upon it; surely the

* June 24.

people is grass. The grass withereth, the flower fadeth, but the word of our God shall stand for ever.'

O Zion, that bringest good tidings, get thee up into the high mountain. O Jerusalem, that bringest good tidings, lift up thy voice with strength – lift it up; be not afraid. Say unto the cities of Judah, 'Behold your God.' Behold, the Lord GOD will come with strong hand, and his arm shall rule for him. Behold, his reward is with him, and his work before him. He shall feed his flock like a shepherd; he shall gather the lambs with his arm, and carry them in his bosom, and shall gently lead those that are with young.

The Gospel. St. Luke 1:57-80.

ELIZABETH'S full time came that she should be delivered, and she brought forth a son. And her neighbours and her cousins heard how the Lord had showed great mercy upon her, and they rejoiced with her.

And it came to pass that on the eighth day they came to circumcise the child, and they called him Zacharias, after the name of his father. And his mother answered and said, 'Not so, but he shall be called John.' And they said unto her, 'There is none of thy kindred that is called by this name.' And they made signs to his father, how he would have him called. And he asked for a writing tablet and wrote, saying, 'His name is John.' And they marvelled all.

And his mouth was opened immediately and his tongue loosed, and he spake and praised God. And fear came on all that dwelt round about them, and all these sayings were noised abroad throughout all the hill country of Judea. And all they that heard them laid them up in

their hearts, saying, 'What manner of child shall this be?'
And the hand of the Lord was with him. And his father
Zacharias was filled with the Holy Ghost, and prophe-
sied, saying, 'Blessed be the Lord God of Israel, for he
hath visited and redeemed his people, and hath raised
up an horn of salvation for us in the house of his servant
David, as he spake by the mouth of his holy prophets,
which have been since the world began: that we should
be saved from our enemies, and from the hand of all that
hate us, to perform the mercy promised to our fathers,
and to remember his holy covenant, the oath which he
sware to our father Abraham: that he would grant unto
us, that we, being delivered out of the hand of our enemies, might serve him without fear, in holiness and righteousness before him all the days of our life.

'And thou, child, shalt be called the prophet of the Highest, for thou shalt go before the face of the Lord to prepare
his ways, to give knowledge of salvation unto his people,
by the remission of their sins, through the tender mercy
of our God, whereby the dayspring from on high hath visited us, to give light to them that sit in darkness and in the
shadow of death, to guide our feet into the way of peace.'

And the child grew and waxed strong in spirit, and was
in the deserts till the day of his showing unto Israel.

Saint Peter's Day.*
The Collect.

O ALMIGHTY God, who by thy Son Jesus Christ didst
give to thy apostle Saint Peter many excellent gifts,
* June 29.

and commandedst him earnestly to feed thy flock: Make, we beseech thee, all bishops and pastors diligently to preach thy holy word, and the people obediently to follow the same, that they may receive the crown of everlasting glory, through Jesus Christ our Lord. *Amen.*

For the Epistle. Acts 12:1-11.

ABOUT that time Herod the king stretched forth his hands to vex certain of the church. And he killed James the brother of John with the sword. And because he saw it pleased the Jews, he proceeded further to take Peter also. (Then were the days of unleavened bread.) And when he had apprehended him, he put him in prison, and delivered him to four quaternions of soldiers to keep him, intending after Easter to bring him forth to the people.

Peter therefore was kept in prison, but prayer was made without ceasing of the church unto God for him. And when Herod would have brought him forth, the same night Peter was sleeping between two soldiers, bound with two chains, and the keepers before the door kept the prison. And behold, the angel of the Lord came upon him, and a light shined in the prison; and he smote Peter on the side, and raised him up, saying, 'Arise up quickly.' And his chains fell off from his hands. And the angel said unto him, 'Gird thyself and bind on thy sandals.' And so he did. And he saith unto him, 'Cast thy garment about thee and follow me.' And he went out and followed him, and wist not that it was true which was done by the angel, but thought he saw a vision. When they were past the first and the second ward, they came unto the iron gate that leadeth unto the city, which opened to them of his own accord; and they went out and passed on through one street, and forthwith the angel departed from him. And when Peter was come to himself, he said, 'Now I know of a surety that the Lord hath sent his angel, and hath delivered me out of the hand of Herod, and from all the expectation of the people of the Jews.'

The Gospel. St. Matthew 16:13-19.

WHEN Jesus came into the coasts of Caesarea Philippi, he asked his disciples, saying, 'Whom do men say that I, the Son of Man, am?' And they said, 'Some say that thou art John the Baptist; some, Elijah; and others, Jeremiah, or one of the prophets.' He saith unto them, 'But whom say ye that I am?'

And Simon Peter answered and said, 'Thou art the Christ, the Son of the living God.'

And Jesus answered and said unto him, 'Blessed art thou, Simon Bar-Jonah, for flesh and blood hath not revealed it unto thee, but my Father which is in heaven. And I say also unto thee that thou art Peter, and upon this rock I will build my church, and the gates of hell shall not prevail against it. And I will give unto thee the keys of the kingdom of heaven, and whatsoever thou shalt bind on earth shall be bound in heaven, and whatsoever thou shalt loose on earth shall be loosed in heaven.

Saint James the Apostle.*

The Collect.

GRANT, O merciful God, that as thy holy apostle Saint James, leaving his father and all that he had, without delay was obedient unto the calling of thy Son Jesus Christ, and followed him, so we, forsaking all worldly and carnal affections, may be evermore ready to follow thy holy commandments, through Jesus Christ our Lord. *Amen.*

For the Epistle. Acts 11:27-12:3.

IN those days came prophets from Jerusalem unto Antioch. And there stood up one of them named Agabus, and signified by the Spirit that there should be great dearth throughout all the world, which came to pass in the days of Claudius Caesar. Then the disciples, every man according to his ability, determined to send relief unto the brethren which dwelt in Judea, which also they did, and sent it to the elders by the hands of Barnabas and Saul.

Now about that time Herod the king stretched forth his hands to vex certain of the church. And he killed James the brother of John with the sword. And because he saw it pleased the Jews, he proceeded further to take Peter also.

The Gospel. St. Matthew 20:20-28.

THEN came to him the mother of Zebedee's children with her sons, worshipping him, and desiring a certain thing of him.

* July 25.

And he said unto her, 'What wilt thou?' She saith unto him, 'Grant that these, my two sons, may sit the one on thy right hand and the other on the left in thy kingdom.'

But Jesus answered and said, 'Ye know not what ye ask. Are ye able to drink of the cup that I shall drink of, and to be baptized with the baptism that I am baptized with?' They say unto him, 'We are able.'

And he saith unto them, 'Ye shall drink indeed of my cup, and be baptized with the baptism that I am baptized with. But to sit on my right hand and on my left is not mine to give, but it shall be given to them for whom it is prepared of my Father.'

And when the ten heard it, they were moved with indignation against the two brethren.

But Jesus called them unto him and said, 'Ye know that the princes of the Gentiles exercise dominion over them, and they that are great exercise authority upon them. But it shall not be so among you, but whosoever will be great among you, let him be your minister; and whosoever will be chief among you, let him be your servant; even as the Son of Man came not to be ministered unto, but to minister, and to give his life a ransom for many.'

Saint Bartholomew the Apostle.*
The Collect.

Oalmighty and everlasting God, who didst give to thine apostle Bartholomew grace truly to believe and to preach thy word: Grant, we beseech thee, unto thy church, to love that word which he believed, and both

* August 24.

to preach and receive the same, through Jesus Christ our Lord. *Amen.*

For the Epistle. Acts 5:12-16.

B Y the hands of the apostles were many signs and wonders wrought among the people – and they were all with one accord in Solomon's porch; and of the rest durst no man join himself to them, but the people magnified them; and believers were the more added to the Lord, multitudes both of men and women – insomuch that they brought forth the sick into the streets, and laid them on beds and couches, that at the least the shadow of Peter passing by might overshadow some of them. There came also a multitude out of the cities round about unto Jerusalem, bringing sick folks, and them which were vexed with unclean spirits, and they were healed every one.

The Gospel. St. Luke 22:24-30.

A ND there was also a strife among them, which of them should be accounted the greatest. And he said unto them, 'The kings of the Gentiles exercise lordship over them, and they that exercise authority upon them are called benefactors. But ye shall not be so, but he that is greatest among you, let him be as the younger; and he that is chief, as he that doth serve. For whether is greater, he that sitteth at meat or he that serveth? is not he that sitteth at meat? But I am among you as he that serveth. Ye are they which have continued with me in my temptations. And I appoint unto you a kingdom, as my Father hath appointed unto me, that ye may eat and drink at my table in my kingdom, and sit on thrones judging the twelve tribes of Israel.'

Saint Matthew the Apostle.*
The Collect.

O ALMIGHTY God, who by thy blessed Son didst call Matthew from the receipt of custom to be an apostle and evangelist: Grant us grace to forsake all covetous desires and inordinate love of riches, and to follow the same thy Son Jesus Christ, who liveth and reigneth with thee and the Holy Ghost, one God, world without end. *Amen.*

The Epistle. 2 Corinthians 4:1-6.

T HEREFORE seeing we have this ministry, as we have received mercy, we faint not, but have renounced the hidden things of dishonesty, not walking in craftiness, nor handling the word of God deceitfully, but by manifestation of the truth commending ourselves to every man's conscience in the sight of God. But if our gospel be hid, it is hid to them that are lost: in whom the god of this world hath blinded the minds of them which believe not, lest the light of the glorious gospel of Christ, who is the image of God, should shine unto them.

For we preach not ourselves but Christ Jesus the Lord, and ourselves your servants for Jesus' sake. For God, who commanded the light to shine out of darkness, hath shined in our hearts, to give the light of the knowledge of the glory of God in the face of Jesus Christ.

* September 21.

The Gospel. St. Matthew 9:9-13.

AND as Jesus passed forth from thence, he saw a man named Matthew, sitting at the receipt of custom, and he saith unto him, 'Follow me.' And he arose and followed him. And it came to pass, as Jesus sat at meat in the house, behold, many publicans and sinners came and sat down with him and his disciples. And when the Pharisees saw it, they said unto his disciples, 'Why eateth your master with publicans and sinners?' But when Jesus heard that, he said unto them, 'They that be whole need not a physician, but they that are sick. But go ye and learn what that meaneth, "I will have mercy, and not sacrifice", for I am not come to call the righteous, but sinners to repentance.'

Saint Michael and All Angels.*
The Collect.

O EVERLASTING God, who hast ordained and constituted the services of angels and men in a wonderful order: Mercifully grant that as thy holy angels alway do thee service in heaven, so by thy appointment they may succour and defend us on earth, through Jesus Christ our Lord. *Amen.*

For the Epistle. Revelation 12:7-12.

T HERE was war in heaven: Michael and his angels fought against the dragon, and the dragon fought and his angels, and prevailed not, neither was their place found anymore in heaven. And the great dragon was cast out, that old serpent, called the devil and Satan, which deceiveth

* September 29.

the whole world; he was cast out into the earth, and his angels were cast out with him. And I heard a loud voice saying in heaven, 'Now is come salvation, and strength, and the kingdom of our God, and the power of his Christ, for the accuser of our brethren is cast down, which accused them before our God day and night. And they overcame him by the blood of the Lamb, and by the word of their testimony, and they loved not their lives unto the death. Therefore rejoice, ye heavens, and ye that dwell in them. Woe to the inhabiters of the earth and of the sea, for the devil is come down unto you, having great wrath, because he knoweth that he hath but a short time.'

The Gospel. St. Matthew 18:1-10.

AT the same time came the disciples unto Jesus, saying, 'Who is the greatest in the kingdom of heaven?' And Jesus called a little child unto him, and set him in the midst of them and said, 'Verily I say unto you, except ye be converted and become as little children, ye shall not enter into the kingdom of heaven. Whosoever therefore shall humble himself as this little child, the same is greatest in the kingdom of heaven. And whoso shall receive one such little child in my name, receiveth me. But whoso shall offend one of these little ones which believe in me, it were better for him that a millstone were hanged about his neck, and that he were drowned in the depth of the sea.

'Woe unto the world because of offences. For it must needs be that offences come, but woe to that man by whom the offence cometh. Wherefore if thy hand or thy foot offend thee, cut them off, and cast them from thee.

It is better for thee to enter into life halt or maimed, rather than having two hands or two feet to be cast into everlasting fire. And if thine eye offend thee, pluck it out, and cast it from thee. It is better for thee to enter into life with one eye, rather than having two eyes to be cast into hellfire. Take heed that ye despise not one of these little ones, for I say unto you that in heaven their angels do always behold the face of my Father which is in heaven.'

Saint Luke the Evangelist.*
The Collect.

ALMIGHTY God, who calledst Luke the physician, whose praise is in the gospel, to be an evangelist and physician of the soul: May it please thee that, by the wholesome medicines of the doctrine delivered by him, all the diseases of our souls may be healed, through the merits of thy Son Jesus Christ our Lord. *Amen.*

The Epistle. 2 Timothy 4:5-15.

WATCH thou in all things, endure afflictions, do the work of an evangelist, make full proof of thy ministry.

For I am now ready to be offered, and the time of my departure is at hand. I have fought a good fight, I have finished my course, I have kept the faith. Henceforth there is laid up for me a crown of righteousness, which the Lord the righteous judge shall give me at that day, and not to me only, but unto all them also that love his appearing.

Do thy diligence to come shortly unto me, for Demas

* October 18.

hath forsaken me, having loved this present world, and is departed unto Thessalonica, Crescens to Galatia, Titus unto Dalmatia. Only Luke is with me. Take Mark and bring him with thee, for he is profitable to me for the ministry. And Tychicus have I sent to Ephesus.

The cloak that I left at Troas with Carpus, when thou comest bring with thee, and the books, but especially the parchments.

Alexander the coppersmith did me much evil; the Lord reward him according to his works. Of whom be thou ware also, for he hath greatly withstood our words.

The Gospel. St. Luke 10:1-7.

THE Lord appointed other seventy also, and sent them two and two before his face into every city and place, whither he himself would come. Therefore said he unto them, 'The harvest truly is great, but the labourers are few. Pray ye therefore the Lord of the harvest, that he would send forth labourers into his harvest.

'Go your ways: behold, I send you forth as lambs among wolves. Carry neither purse, nor scrip, nor shoes, and salute no man by the way. And into whatsoever house ye enter, first say, "Peace be to this house." And if the son of peace be there, your peace shall rest upon it; if not, it shall turn to you again. And in the same house remain, eating and drinking such things as they give, for the labourer is worthy of his hire.'

SAINT SIMON AND SAINT JUDE, APOSTLES

Saint Simon and Saint Jude, Apostles.*

The Collect.

O ALMIGHTY God, who hast built thy church upon the foundation of the apostles and prophets, Jesus Christ himself being the head cornerstone: Grant us so to be joined together in unity of spirit by their doctrine, that we may be made a holy temple acceptable unto thee, through Jesus Christ our Lord. *Amen.*

The Epistle. Jude 1-8.

J UDE, the servant of Jesus Christ, and brother of James, to them that are sanctified by God the Father, and preserved in Jesus Christ, and called: Mercy unto you, and peace and love be multiplied.

Beloved, when I gave all diligence to write unto you of the common salvation, it was needful for me to write unto you and exhort you that ye should earnestly contend for the faith which was once delivered unto the saints. For there are certain men crept in unawares, who were before of old ordained to this condemnation, ungodly men, turning the grace of our God into lasciviousness, and denying the only Lord God and our Lord Jesus Christ.

I will therefore put you in remembrance, though ye once knew this, how that the Lord, having saved the people out of the land of Egypt, afterward destroyed them that believed not. And the angels which kept not their first estate, but left their own habitation, he hath reserved in everlasting chains under darkness unto the judgement of the great day. Even as Sodom and Gomorrah and the cities

* October 28.

about them, in like manner giving themselves over to fornication and going after strange flesh, are set forth for an example, suffering the vengeance of eternal fire. Likewise also these filthy dreamers defile the flesh, despise dominion, and speak evil of dignities.

The Gospel. St. John 15:17-27.

THESE things I command you, that ye love one another. If the world hate you, ye know that it hated me before it hated you. If ye were of the world, the world would love his own; but because ye are not of the world, but I have chosen you out of the world, therefore the world hateth you.

Remember the word that I said unto you, 'The servant is not greater than his lord.' If they have persecuted me, they will also persecute you; if they have kept my saying, they will keep yours also. But all these things will they do unto you for my name's sake, because they know not him that sent me.

If I had not come and spoken unto them, they had not had sin, but now they have no cloak for their sin. He that hateth me hateth my Father also. If I had not done among them the works which none other man did, they had not had sin, but now have they both seen and hated both me and my Father. But this cometh to pass, that the word might be fulfilled that is written in their law, 'They hated me without a cause.'

But when the Comforter is come, whom I will send unto you from the Father, even the Spirit of truth, which proceedeth from the Father, he shall testify of me. And ye also shall bear witness, because ye have been with me from the beginning.

All Saints' Day.*
The Collect.

O ALMIGHTY God, who hast knit together thine elect in one communion and fellowship, in the mystical body of thy Son Christ our Lord: Grant us grace so to follow thy blessed saints in all virtuous and godly living, that we may come to those unspeakable joys, which thou hast prepared for those who unfeignedly love thee, through Jesus Christ our Lord. *Amen.*

For the Epistle. Revelation 7:2-12.

A ND I saw another angel ascending from the east, having the seal of the living God; and he cried with a loud voice to the four angels, to whom it was given to hurt the earth and the sea, saying, 'Hurt not the earth, neither the sea, nor the trees, till we have sealed the servants of our God in their foreheads.'

And I heard the number of them which were sealed, and there were sealed an hundred and forty and four thousand, of all the tribes of the children of Israel.

Of the tribe of Judah were sealed twelve thousand.

Of the tribe of Reuben were sealed twelve thousand.

Of the tribe of Gad were sealed twelve thousand.

Of the tribe of Asher were sealed twelve thousand.

Of the tribe of Naphtali were sealed twelve thousand.

Of the tribe of Manasseh were sealed twelve thousand.

* November 1.

Of the tribe of Simeon were sealed twelve thousand.
Of the tribe of Levi were sealed twelve thousand.
Of the tribe of Issachar were sealed twelve thousand.
Of the tribe of Zebulun were sealed twelve thousand.
Of the tribe of Joseph were sealed twelve thousand.
Of the tribe of Benjamin were sealed twelve thousand.

After this I beheld, and lo, a great multitude, which no man could number, of all nations and kindreds and peoples and tongues, stood before the throne and before the Lamb, clothed with white robes, and palms in their hands, and cried with a loud voice, saying, 'Salvation to our God which sitteth upon the throne and unto the Lamb.' And all the angels stood round about the throne, and about the elders and the four living creatures, and fell before the throne on their faces and worshipped God, saying, 'Amen. Blessing, and glory, and wisdom, and thanksgiving, and honour, and power, and might be unto our God for ever and ever. Amen.'

The Gospel. St. Matthew 5:1-12.

JESUS, seeing the multitudes, went up into a mountain; and when he was set, his disciples came unto him. And he opened his mouth and taught them, saying,

'Blessed are the poor in spirit, for theirs is the kingdom of heaven.

'Blessed are they that mourn, for they shall be comforted.

'Blessed are the meek, for they shall inherit the earth.

'Blessed are they which do hunger and thirst after righteousness, for they shall be filled.

'Blessed are the merciful, for they shall obtain mercy.

'Blessed are the pure in heart, for they shall see God.

'Blessed are the peacemakers, for they shall be called the children of God.

'Blessed are they which are persecuted for righteousness' sake, for theirs is the kingdom of heaven.

'Blessed are ye, when men shall revile you and persecute you, and shall say all manner of evil against you falsely for my sake. Rejoice, and be exceeding glad, for great is your reward in heaven, for so persecuted they the prophets which were before you.'

The Order for the Administration of the Lord's Supper, or Holy Communion.

¶ *As many as intend to be partakers of the holy communion shall signify their names to the pastor at least some time the day before.*

¶ *And if any of these liveth in open and notorious sin or hath done any wrong to his neighbours by word or deed, so that the congregation is thereby offended, the pastor, having knowledge thereof, shall call him and advise him not to come to the Lord's table until he have openly declared himself to have truly repented and amended his former evil life, that the congregation may thereby be satisfied which before were offended; and have recompensed the parties to whom he hath done wrong, or at least declare himself to be in full purpose so to do as soon as he conveniently may.*

¶ *The same order shall the pastor use with those between whom he perceiveth malice and hatred to reign, not suffering them to be partakers of the Lord's table until he know them to be reconciled. And if one of the parties thus opposed is content to forgive from the bottom of his heart all that the other hath trespassed against him, and to make amends for what he himself hath offended, yet the other party will not be persuaded to a godly unity but remain still in his contrariness and malice, the minister in that case ought to admit the penitent person to the holy communion and not him that is obstinate. Provided that every minister so repelling anyone, as is specified in this paragraph or the preceding paragraph of this rubric, shall be obliged to give an account of the same to the ordinary within fourteen days after at the farthest. And the ordinary shall proceed against the offending person according to the canons.*

¶ *At the communion time, the table, having a fair white linen cloth upon it, shall stand in the body of the church or in the chancel, where Morning and Evening Prayer are appointed to be said. And the priest, standing at the north side of the table, shall say the Lord's Prayer with the collect following, the people kneeling.*

OUR Father, who art in heaven, Hallowed be thy name. Thy kingdom come. Thy will be done, On earth as it is in heaven. Give us this day our daily bread. And forgive us our trespasses, As we forgive those who trespass against us. And lead us not into temptation, But deliver us from evil. Amen.

The Collect.

ALMIGHTY God, unto whom all hearts are open, all desires known, and from whom no secrets are hid: Cleanse the thoughts of our hearts by the inspiration of thy Holy Spirit, that we may perfectly love thee, and worthily magnify thy holy name, through Christ our Lord. *Amen.*

¶ *Then shall the priest, turning to the people, rehearse distinctly all the Ten Commandments. And the people (still kneeling) shall after every commandment ask God for mercy for their transgression thereof for the time past and grace to keep the same for the time to come, as followeth.*

G OD spake these words and said: 'I am the LORD thy God; thou shalt have none other gods but me.'

Lord, have mercy upon us, and incline our hearts to keep this law.

'Thou shalt not make to thyself any graven image, nor the likeness of anything that is in heaven above, or in the earth beneath, or in the water under the earth. Thou shalt not bow down to them, nor worship them. For I, the LORD thy God, am a jealous God, and visit the sins of the fathers upon the children unto the third and fourth generation of them that hate me, and show mercy unto thousands of them that love me and keep my commandments.'

Lord, have mercy upon us, and incline our hearts to keep this law.

'Thou shalt not take the name of the LORD thy God in vain. For the LORD will not hold him guiltless that taketh his name in vain.'

Lord, have mercy upon us, and incline our hearts to keep this law.

'Remember that thou keep holy the Sabbath day. Six days shalt thou labour, and do all that thou hast to do, but the seventh day is the Sabbath of the LORD thy God. In it thou shalt do no manner of work – thou, and thy son, and thy daughter, thy manservant, and thy maidservant, thy cattle, and the stranger that is within thy gates. For in six days the LORD made heaven and earth, the sea, and all that in them is, and rested the seventh day; wherefore the LORD blessed the seventh day, and hallowed it.'

Lord, have mercy upon us, and incline our hearts to keep this law.

'Honour thy father and thy mother, that thy days may be long in the land which the LORD thy God giveth thee.'

Lord, have mercy upon us, and incline our hearts to keep this law.

'Thou shalt do no murder.'

Lord, have mercy upon us, and incline our hearts to keep this law.

'Thou shalt not commit adultery.'

Lord, have mercy upon us, and incline our hearts to keep this law.

'Thou shalt not steal.'

Lord, have mercy upon us, and incline our hearts to keep this law.

'Thou shalt not bear false witness against thy neighbour.'

Lord, have mercy upon us, and incline our hearts to keep this law.

'Thou shalt not covet thy neighbour's house, thou shalt not covet thy neighbour's wife, nor his servant, nor his maid, nor his ox, nor his ass, nor anything that is his.'

Lord, have mercy upon us, and write all these thy laws in our hearts, we beseech thee.

THE COMMUNION

¶ *Then shall follow one of these two collects for all those in civil authority, the priest standing as before and saying,* Let us pray.

ALMIGHTY and everlasting God, we are taught by thy holy word that the hearts of rulers are in thy governance, and that thou dost dispose and turn them as it seemeth best to thy godly wisdom: We humbly beseech thee so to dispose and govern the hearts of thy servants, whom thou hast placed in civil authority, that in all their thoughts, words, and works, they may ever seek thy honour and glory, and study to preserve this people committed to their charge, in wealth, peace, and godliness. Grant this, O merciful Father, for thy dear Son's sake, Jesus Christ our Lord. *Amen.*

¶ *Or this.*

O LORD our governor, whose glory is in all the world: We commend this nation to thy merciful care, that, being guided by thy providence, we may dwell secure in thy peace. Grant to [*title of the head of state or government,*] and to all in authority, both wisdom and strength to know and to do thy will. Fill them with the love of truth and righteousness, and make them ever mindful of their calling to serve this people in thy fear, through Jesus Christ our Lord, who liveth and reigneth with thee and the Holy Ghost, one God, world without end. *Amen.*

¶ *Then shall be said the collect of the day (p. 49). And immediately after the collect, the priest shall read the epistle, saying,* The epistle *(or* The portion of Scripture appointed for the epistle) is written in the — chapter of —, beginning at the — verse. *And the epistle ended, he shall say,* Here endeth the epistle. *Then shall he read the gospel (the people all standing up), saying,* The holy gospel is written in the — chapter of —, beginning at the — verse. *And the gospel ended, the creed following shall be sung or said, the people still standing as before.*

I BELIEVE in one God the Father almighty, Maker of heaven and earth, And of all things visible and invisible;

And in one Lord Jesus Christ, the only-begotten Son of God, Begotten of his Father before all worlds, God of God, Light of Light, Very God of very God, Begotten, not made, Being of one substance with the Father, By whom all things were made, Who for us men and for our salvation came down from heaven, And was incarnate by the Holy Ghost of the Virgin Mary, And was made man, And was crucified also for us under Pontius Pilate. He suffered and was buried, And the third day he rose again according to the Scriptures, And ascended into heaven, And sitteth on the right hand of the Father. And he shall come again with glory to judge both the quick and the dead, Whose kingdom shall have no end.

And I believe in the Holy Ghost, The Lord, and giver of life, Who proceedeth from the Father and the Son, Who with the Father and the Son together is worshipped and glorified, Who spake by the prophets. And I believe one catholic and apostolic church. I acknowledge one baptism for the remission of sins. And I look for the resurrection of the dead, And the life of the world to come. Amen.

¶ *Then the minister shall declare unto the people what holy days or fasting days are to be observed in the week following. And then (if there is occasion) shall notice be given of the communion; and the banns of matrimony published; and briefs, citations, and excommunications read. And nothing shall be proclaimed or published in the church during the time of divine service but by the minister, nor by him anything but what is prescribed in the rules of this book or enjoined by the ordinary of the place.*

¶ *Then shall follow the sermon, or one of the homilies set forth by authority.*

¶ *Then shall the priest return to the Lord's table and begin the offertory, saying one or more of these sentences following, as he thinketh most convenient in his discretion.*

LET your light so shine before men that they may see your good works, and glorify your Father which is in heaven. *St. Matthew 5:16.*

Lay not up for yourselves treasure upon the earth, where rust and moth doth corrupt, and where thieves break through and steal; but lay up for yourselves treasures in heaven, where neither rust nor moth doth corrupt, and where thieves do not break through and steal. *St. Matthew 6:19-20.*

Whatsoever ye would that men should do unto you, even so do unto them, for this is the law and the prophets. *St. Matthew 7:12.*

Not everyone that saith unto me 'Lord, Lord' shall enter into the kingdom of heaven, but he that doeth the will of my Father which is in heaven. *St. Matthew 7:21.*

Zacchaeus stood forth and said unto the Lord, 'Behold, Lord, the half of my goods I give to the poor; and if I have done any wrong to any man, I restore fourfold.' *St. Luke 19:8.*

What soldier goeth a warfare at any time of his own cost? Who planteth a vineyard, and eateth not of the fruit thereof? Or who feedeth a flock, and eateth not of the milk of the flock? *1 Corinthians 9:7.*

If we have sown unto you spiritual things, is it a great matter if we shall reap your worldly things? *1 Corinthians 9:11.*

Do ye not know that they who minister about holy things live of the sacrifice, and they who wait at the altar are partakers with the altar? Even so hath the Lord also ordained, that they who preach the gospel should live of the gospel. *1 Corinthians 9:13-14.*

He that soweth little shall reap little, and he that soweth plenteously shall reap plenteously. Let every man do according as he is disposed in his heart, not grudgingly, or of necessity, for God loveth a cheerful giver. *2 Corinthians 9:6-7.*

Let him that is taught in the word minister unto him that teacheth in all good things. Be not deceived; God is not mocked, for whatsoever a man soweth, that shall he reap. *Galatians 6:6-7.*

While we have time, let us do good unto all men, and

especially unto them that are of the household of faith. *Galatians 6:10.*

Godliness is great riches, if a man be content with what he hath, for we brought nothing into the world, neither may we carry anything out. *1 Timothy 6:6-7.*

Charge them who are rich in this world, that they be ready to give and glad to distribute, laying up in store for themselves a good foundation against the time to come, that they may attain eternal life. *1 Timothy 6:17-19.*

God is not unrighteous, that he will forget your works and labour that proceedeth of love, which love ye have showed for his name's sake, who have ministered unto the saints, and yet do minister. *Hebrews 6:10.*

To do good and to distribute, forget not, for with such sacrifices God is pleased. *Hebrews 13:16.*

Whoso hath this world's good, and seeth his brother have need, and shutteth up his compassion from him, how dwelleth the love of God in him? *1 John 3:17.*

Give alms of thy goods, and never turn thy face from any poor man, and then the face of the Lord shall not be turned away from thee. *Tobit 4:7.*

Be merciful after thy power. If thou hast much, give plenteously; if thou hast little, do thy diligence gladly to give of that little, for so gatherest thou thyself a good reward in the day of necessity. *Tobit 4:8-9.*

He that hath pity upon the poor lendeth unto the LORD; and look, what he layeth out, it shall be paid him again. *Proverbs 19:17.*

Blessed be the man that provideth for the sick and

needy; the LORD shall deliver him in the time of trouble. *Psalm 41:1.*

¶ *Whilst these sentences are read, the deacons, churchwardens, or other fit persons appointed for that purpose shall receive the alms for the poor and other devotions of the people in a decent basin (to be provided by the parish for that purpose), and reverently bring it to the priest, who shall humbly present and place it upon the holy table.*

¶ *When there is a communion, the priest shall then place upon the table as much bread and wine as he shall think sufficient. After which, the priest shall say,*

> Let us pray for the whole state of Christ's
> church militant here on earth.

ALMIGHTY and everliving God, who by thy holy apostle hast taught us to make prayers and supplications, and to give thanks, for all men: We humbly beseech thee most mercifully [* *to accept our alms and oblations, and*] to receive these our prayers which we offer unto thy Divine Majesty, beseeching thee to inspire continually the universal church with the spirit of truth, unity, and concord. And grant that all those who do confess thy holy name

* If there are no alms or oblations, then shall the words of accepting our alms and oblations be left unsaid.

may agree in the truth of thy holy word, and live in unity and godly love. We beseech thee also so to direct and dispose the hearts of all Christian rulers, that they may truly and impartially administer justice, to the punishment of wickedness and vice, and to the maintenance of thy true religion, and virtue.

Give grace, O heavenly Father, to all bishops and pastors, that they may, both by their life and doctrine, set forth thy true and lively word, and rightly and duly administer thy holy sacraments. And to all thy people give thy heavenly grace, and especially to this congregation here present, that, with meek heart and due reverence, they may hear and receive thy holy word, truly serving thee in holiness and righteousness all the days of their life. And we most humbly beseech thee of thy goodness, O Lord, to comfort and succour all those, who in this transitory life are in trouble, sorrow, need, sickness, or any other adversity. And we also bless thy holy name for all thy servants departed this life in thy faith and fear, beseeching thee to give us grace so to follow their good examples, that with them we may be partakers of thy heavenly kingdom. Grant this, O Father, for Jesus Christ's sake, our only mediator and advocate. *Amen.*

¶ *When the minister giveth warning for the celebration of the holy communion (which he shall always do upon the Sunday or some holy day immediately preceding), after the sermon or homily is ended, he shall read this exhortation following.*

DEARLY beloved, on — day next I purpose, through God's assistance, to administer to all those who shall be religiously and devoutly disposed the most comfortable sacrament of the body and blood of Christ, to be received by them in remembrance of his meritorious cross and passion, whereby alone we obtain remission of our sins and are made partakers of the kingdom of heaven.

Wherefore it is our duty to render most humble and hearty thanks to almighty God, our heavenly Father, because he hath given his Son our Saviour Jesus Christ, not only to die for us, but also to be our spiritual food and sustenance in that holy sacrament. Which, being so divine and comfortable a thing to those who receive it worthily, and so dangerous to those who will presume to receive it unworthily, my duty is to exhort you, in the meantime, to consider the dignity of that holy mystery, and the great peril of the unworthy receiving thereof, and so to search and examine your own consciences – and that not lightly, and after the manner of dissemblers with God, but so that ye may come holy and clean to such a heavenly feast, in the marriage garment required by God in holy Scripture, and be received as worthy partakers of that holy table.

The way and means thereto is: First, to examine your life and conduct by the rule of God's commandments, and in whatsoever ye shall perceive yourselves to have offended, either by will, word, or deed, there to bewail your own sinfulness, and to confess yourselves to almighty God, with full purpose of amendment of life. And if ye shall perceive your offences to be such as are not only against God, but also against your neighbours, then ye shall reconcile yourselves unto them, being ready to make restitution and satisfaction (according to the uttermost of your powers) for all injuries and wrongs done by you to any other; and being likewise ready to forgive others who have offended you, as you would have forgiveness of your offences at God's hand. For otherwise the receiving of the holy communion doth nothing else but increase your condemnation. Therefore if any of you be a blasphemer of God, a hinderer or slanderer of his word, an adulterer, or be in malice, or envy, or in any other grievous crime, repent you of your sins, or else come not to that holy table – lest, after the taking of that holy sacrament, the devil enter into you, as he entered into Judas, and fill you full of all iniquities, and bring you to destruction both of body and soul.

And because it is requisite that no man should come to the holy communion, but with a full trust in God's mercy, and with a quiet conscience, therefore if there be any of you who by this means cannot quiet his own conscience, but requireth further comfort or counsel, let him come to me, or to some other discreet and learned minister of God's word, and open his grief, that by the ministry of God's holy word he may receive the benefit of absolution, together with spiritual counsel and advice, to the quieting of his conscience and removing of all scruple and doubtfulness.

¶ *Or, in case he shall see the people negligent to come to the holy communion, instead of the former he shall use this exhortation.*

Dearly beloved brethren, on — I intend, by God's grace, to celebrate the Lord's supper. Unto which, on God's behalf, I bid you all who are here present, and beseech you, for the Lord Jesus Christ's sake, that ye will not refuse to come thereto, being so lovingly called and bidden by God himself. Ye know how grievous and unkind a thing it is, when a man hath prepared a rich feast – decked his table with all kind of provision, so that there lacketh nothing but the guests to sit down – and yet those who are called (without any cause) most unthankfully refuse to come. Which of you in such a case would not be moved? Who would not think a great ingratitude and wrong done unto him? Wherefore, most dearly beloved in Christ, take ye good heed, lest ye, withdrawing yourselves from this holy supper, provoke God's indignation against you. It is an easy matter for a man to say, 'I will not communicate, because I am otherwise hindered with worldly business.' But such excuses are not so easily accepted and allowed before God. If any man say, 'I am a grievous sinner, and therefore am afraid to come', why then do ye not repent and amend? When God calleth you, are ye not ashamed to say ye will not come? When ye should return to God, will ye excuse yourselves, and say ye are not ready? Consider earnestly with yourselves how little such feigned excuses will avail before God. Those who refused the feast in the gospel, because they had bought a farm, or would try their yokes of oxen, or because they were married, were not so excused, but counted unworthy of the heavenly feast.

I, for my part, shall be ready. And according to mine office I bid you in the name of God, I call you on Christ's behalf, I exhort you, as ye love your own salvation, that ye will be partakers of this holy communion. And as the Son of God did vouchsafe to yield up his soul by death upon the cross for your salvation, so it is your duty to receive the communion in remembrance of the sacrifice of his death, as he himself hath commanded – which if ye shall neglect to do, consider with yourselves how great is your ingratitude to God, and what sore punishment hangeth over your heads for the same, when ye willfully abstain from the Lord's table, and separate from your brethren who come to feed on the banquet of that most heavenly food.

These things if ye earnestly consider, ye will by God's grace return to a better mind, for the obtaining of which we shall not cease to make our humble petitions unto almighty God our heavenly Father.

¶ *At the time of the celebration of the communion, the communicants being conveniently placed for the receiving of the holy sacrament, the priest shall say this exhortation.*

DEARLY beloved in the Lord, ye that mind to come to the holy communion of the body and blood of our Saviour Christ must consider how Saint Paul exhorteth all persons diligently to prove and examine themselves, before they presume to eat of that bread and drink of that cup. For as the benefit is great, if with a true penitent heart and lively faith we receive that holy sacrament – for then we spiritually eat the flesh of Christ and drink his blood; then we dwell in Christ, and Christ in us; we are one with Christ, and Christ with us – so is the danger great, if we receive the same unworthily. For then we are guilty of the body and blood of Christ our Saviour; we eat and drink our own condemnation, not considering the Lord's body. We kindle God's wrath against us. We provoke him to plague us with divers diseases and sundry kinds of death. Judge therefore yourselves, brethren, that ye be not judged by the Lord. Repent you truly for your sins past. Have a lively and steadfast faith in Christ our Saviour. Amend your lives, and be in perfect charity with all men. So shall ye be meet partakers of those holy mysteries.

And above all things, ye must give most humble and hearty thanks to God, the Father, the Son, and the Holy Ghost, for the redemption of the world by the death and passion of our Saviour Christ, both God and man, who did humble himself – even to the death upon the cross – for us miserable sinners, who lay in darkness and the shadow of death, that he might make us the children of God and exalt us to everlasting life. And to the end that we should alway remember the exceeding great love of our Master and only Saviour, Jesus Christ, thus dying for us, and the innumerable benefits which by his precious blood-shedding he hath obtained for us, he hath instituted and ordained holy mysteries as pledges of his love, and for a continual remembrance of his death, to our great and endless comfort.

To him therefore, with the Father and the Holy Ghost, let us give (as we are most bounden) continual thanks, submitting ourselves wholly to his holy will and pleasure, and studying to serve him in true holiness and righteousness all the days of our life. *Amen.*

THE COMMUNION

¶ *Then shall the priest say to those who come to receive the holy communion,*

YE who do truly and earnestly repent you of your sins, and are in love and charity with your neighbours, and intend to lead a new life, following the commandments of God and walking from henceforth in his holy ways, draw near with faith, and take this holy sacrament to your comfort, and make your humble confession to almighty God, meekly kneeling upon your knees.

¶ *Then shall this general confession be made in the name of all those who are minded to receive the holy communion by one of the ministers, both he and all the people kneeling humbly upon their knees and saying,*

ALMIGHTY God, Father of our Lord Jesus Christ, Maker of all things, Judge of all men: We acknowledge and bewail our manifold sins and wickedness, Which we from time to time most grievously have committed, By thought, word, and deed, Against thy Divine Majesty, Provoking most justly thy wrath and indignation against us. We do earnestly repent, And are heartily sorry for these our misdoings; The remembrance of them is grievous unto us; The burden of them is intolerable. Have mercy upon us; Have mercy upon us, most merciful Father. For thy Son our Lord Jesus Christ's sake, Forgive us all that is past, And grant that we may ever hereafter Serve and please thee In newness of life, To the honour and glory of thy name, Through Jesus Christ our Lord. Amen.

THE COMMUNION

¶ *Then shall the priest (or the bishop, being present) stand up, and, turning himself to the people, pronounce this absolution.*

ALMIGHTY God, our heavenly Father, who of his great mercy hath promised forgiveness of sins to all those who with hearty repentance and true faith turn unto him, have mercy upon you, pardon and deliver you from all your sins, confirm and strengthen you in all goodness, and bring you to everlasting life, through Jesus Christ our Lord. *Amen.*

¶ *Then shall the priest say,*

HEAR what comfortable words our Saviour Christ saith unto all who truly turn to him:

Come unto me, all that travail and are heavy laden, and I will refresh you. *St. Matthew 11:28.*

So God loved the world that he gave his only-begotten Son, to the end that all that believe in him should not perish, but have everlasting life. *St. John 3:16.*

HEAR also what Saint Paul saith:

This is a true saying and worthy of all men to be received, that Christ Jesus came into the world to save sinners. *1 Timothy 1:15.*

HEAR also what Saint John saith:

If any man sin, we have an advocate with the Father, Jesus Christ the righteous; and he is the propitiation for our sins. *1 John 2:1.*

¶ *After which, the priest shall proceed, saying,*
　　　　Lift up your hearts.
Answer.　We lift them up unto the Lord.
Priest.　Let us give thanks unto our Lord God.
Answer.　It is meet and right so to do.

¶ *Then shall the priest turn to the Lord's table and say,*
IT is very meet, right, and our bounden duty, that we should at all times and in all places give thanks unto thee, O Lord, * Holy Father, almighty everlasting God.

* *These words* Holy Father *must be omitted on Trinity Sunday.*

¶ *Here shall follow the proper preface (according to the time, if there is any specially appointed), or else immediately shall follow,*
THEREFORE with angels and archangels, and with all the company of heaven, we laud and magnify thy glorious name, evermore praising thee and saying:
　　'Holy, holy, holy, Lord God of hosts, heaven and earth are full of thy glory. Glory be to thee, O Lord Most High. Amen.'

Proper Prefaces.
¶ *Upon Christmas Day, and seven days after.*
BECAUSE thou didst give Jesus Christ, thine only Son, to be born as at this time for us, who, by the operation of the Holy Ghost, was made very man of the substance of the Virgin Mary his mother, and that without spot of sin, to make us clean from all sin. Therefore with angels, *&c.*

THE COMMUNION

¶ *Upon Easter Day, and seven days after.*

B UT chiefly are we bound to praise thee for the glorious resurrection of thy Son Jesus Christ our Lord, for he is the very Paschal Lamb which was offered for us, and hath taken away the sin of the world, who by his death hath destroyed death, and by his rising to life again hath restored to us everlasting life. Therefore with angels, *&c.*

¶ *Upon Ascension Day, and seven days after.*

T HROUGH thy most dearly beloved Son Jesus Christ our Lord, who, after his most glorious resurrection, manifestly appeared to all his apostles, and in their sight ascended up into heaven to prepare a place for us, that where he is, thither we might also ascend, and reign with him in glory. Therefore with angels, *&c.*

¶ *Upon Whitsunday, and six days after.*

T HROUGH Jesus Christ our Lord, according to whose most true promise the Holy Ghost came down as at this time from heaven, with a sudden great sound, as it had been a mighty wind, in the likeness of fiery tongues, lighting upon the apostles, to teach them and to lead them to all truth, giving them both the gift of divers languages and also boldness with fervent zeal constantly to preach the gospel unto all nations, whereby we have been brought out of darkness and error into the clear light and true knowledge of thee and of thy Son Jesus Christ. Therefore with angels, *&c.*

THE COMMUNION

¶ *Upon the Feast of Trinity only.*

Wно art one God, one Lord, not one person only, but three persons in one substance. For that which we believe of the glory of the Father, the same we believe of the Son, and of the Holy Ghost, without any difference or inequality. Therefore with angels, &c.

¶ *After each of which prefaces shall immediately be sung or said,*

THEREFORE with angels and archangels, and with all the company of heaven, we laud and magnify thy glorious name, evermore praising thee and saying:

'Holy, holy, holy, Lord God of hosts, heaven and earth are full of thy glory. Glory be to thee, O Lord Most High. Amen.'

¶ *Then shall the priest, kneeling down at the Lord's table, say in the name of all those who shall receive the communion this prayer following.*

WE do not presume to come to this thy table, O merciful Lord, trusting in our own righteousness, but in thy manifold and great mercies. We are not worthy so much as to gather up the crumbs under thy table. But thou art the same Lord, whose property is always to have mercy. Grant us therefore, gracious Lord, so to eat the flesh of thy dear Son Jesus Christ, and to drink his blood, that our sinful bodies may be made clean by his body, and our souls washed through his most precious blood, and that we may evermore dwell in him, and he in us. *Amen.*

THE COMMUNION

¶ *When the priest, standing before the table, hath so ordered the bread and wine that he may with the more readiness and decency break the bread before the people and take the cup into his hands, he shall say the prayer of consecration, as followeth.*

ALMIGHTY God, our heavenly Father, who, of thy tender mercy, didst give thine only Son Jesus Christ to suffer death upon the cross for our redemption, who made there – by his one oblation of himself once offered – a full, perfect, and sufficient sacrifice, oblation, and satisfaction, for the sins of the whole world; and did institute, and in his holy gospel command us to continue, a perpetual memory of that his precious death until his coming again: Hear us, O merciful Father, we most humbly beseech thee, and grant that we receiving these thy creatures of bread and wine, according to thy Son our Saviour Jesus Christ's holy institution, in remembrance of his death and passion, may be partakers of his most blessed body and blood: Who, in the same night that he was betrayed, [a] took bread, and, when he had given thanks, [b] he brake it, and gave it to his disciples, saying, 'Take, eat; [c] this is my body which is given for you: Do this in remembrance of me.' Likewise after supper [d] he took the cup, and, when

[a] *Here the priest is to take the paten into his hands.*

[b] *And here to break the bread.*

[c] *And here to lay his hand upon all the bread.*

[d] *Here he is to take the cup into his hand.*

[e] *And here to lay his hand upon every vessel (be it chalice or flagon) in which there is any wine to be consecrated.*

he had given thanks, he gave it to them, saying, 'Drink ye all of this, for [e] this is my blood of the new testament, which is shed for you and for many for the remission of sins: Do this, as oft as ye shall drink it, in remembrance of me.' *Amen.*

¶ *Then shall the minister himself first receive the communion in both kinds; and then proceed to deliver the same to the bishops, priests, and deacons in like manner (if any are present); and after that to the people also in order, into their hands, all meekly kneeling. And when he delivereth the bread to anyone, he shall say,*

THE body of our Lord Jesus Christ, which was given for thee, preserve thy body and soul unto everlasting life. Take and eat this in remembrance that Christ died for thee, and feed on him in thy heart by faith with thanksgiving.

¶ *And the minister who delivereth the cup to anyone shall say,*

THE blood of our Lord Jesus Christ, which was shed for thee, preserve thy body and soul unto everlasting life. Drink this in remembrance that Christ's blood was shed for thee, and be thankful.

¶ *If the consecrated bread or wine is all spent before all have communicated, the priest is to consecrate more according to the form before prescribed, beginning at* Our Saviour Christ in the same night, *&c. for the blessing of the bread; and at* Likewise after supper, *&c. for the blessing of the cup.*

THE COMMUNION

¶ *When all have communicated, the minister shall return to the Lord's table and reverently place upon it what remaineth of the consecrated elements, covering the same with a fair linen cloth.*

¶ *Then shall the priest say the Lord's Prayer, the people repeating after him every petition.*

OUR Father, who art in heaven, Hallowed be thy name. Thy kingdom come. Thy will be done, On earth as it is in heaven. Give us this day our daily bread. And forgive us our trespasses, As we forgive those who trespass against us. And lead us not into temptation, But deliver us from evil. For thine is the kingdom, the power, and the glory, For ever and ever. Amen.

¶ *After that shall be said as followeth.*

O LORD and heavenly Father, we thy humble servants entirely desire thy fatherly goodness mercifully to accept this our sacrifice of praise and thanksgiving, most humbly beseeching thee to grant, that by the merits and death of thy Son Jesus Christ, and through faith in his blood, we and all thy whole church may obtain remission of our sins, and all other benefits of his passion. And here we offer and present unto thee, O Lord, ourselves, our souls and bodies, to be a reasonable, holy, and lively sacrifice unto thee, humbly beseeching thee, that all we, who are partakers of this holy communion, may be fulfilled with thy grace and heavenly benediction. And although we are unworthy, through our manifold sins, to offer unto thee any sacrifice, yet we beseech thee to accept this our bounden duty and service, not weighing our merits, but pardoning our offences, through Jesus Christ our Lord, by whom, and with whom, in the unity of the Holy Ghost, all honour and glory be unto thee, O Father almighty, world without end. *Amen.*

¶ *Or this.*

ALMIGHTY and everliving God, we most heartily thank thee, for that thou dost vouchsafe to feed us, who have duly received these holy mysteries, with the spiritual food of the most precious body and blood of thy Son our Saviour Jesus Christ, and dost assure us thereby of thy favour and goodness towards us, and that we are very members incorporate in the mystical body of thy Son, which is the blessed company of all faithful people, and are also heirs through hope of thy everlasting kingdom, by the merits of the most precious death and passion of thy dear Son. And we most humbly beseech thee, O heavenly Father, so to assist us with thy grace, that we may continue in that holy fellowship, and do all such good works as thou hast prepared for us to walk in, through Jesus Christ our Lord, to whom, with thee and the Holy Ghost, be all honour and glory, world without end. *Amen.*

¶ *Then shall be said or sung,*

GLORY be to God on high, and on earth peace, good will towards men. We praise thee, we bless thee, we worship thee, we glorify thee, we give thanks to thee for thy great glory, O Lord God, heavenly king, God the Father almighty.

O Lord, the only-begotten Son, Jesu Christ; O Lord

God, Lamb of God, Son of the Father, that takest away the sins of the world, have mercy upon us. Thou that takest away the sins of the world, have mercy upon us. Thou that takest away the sins of the world, receive our prayer. Thou that sittest at the right hand of God the Father, have mercy upon us.

For thou only art holy; thou only art the Lord; thou only, O Christ, with the Holy Ghost, art most high in the glory of God the Father. Amen.

¶ *Then the priest (or bishop if he is present) shall let them depart with this blessing.*

THE peace of God, which passeth all understanding, keep your hearts and minds in the knowledge and love of God, and of his Son Jesus Christ our Lord. And the blessing of God almighty, the Father, the Son, and the Holy Ghost, be amongst you and remain with you always. *Amen.*

¶ *These collects are to be said after the offertory when there is no communion, on every such day one or more. The same may also be said, as often as occasion shall serve, after the collects either of Morning or Evening Prayer, Communion, or Litany, by the discretion of the minister.*

ASSIST us mercifully, O Lord, in these our supplications and prayers, and dispose the way of thy servants towards the attainment of everlasting salvation, that, among all the changes and chances of this mortal life, they may ever be defended by thy most gracious and ready help, through Jesus Christ our Lord. *Amen.*

O ALMIGHTY Lord and everlasting God, vouchsafe, we beseech thee, to direct, sanctify, and govern both our hearts and bodies, in the ways of thy laws and in the works of thy commandments, that, through thy most mighty protection, both here and ever, we may be preserved in body and soul, through our Lord and Saviour Jesus Christ. *Amen.*

G RANT, we beseech thee, almighty God, that the words which we have heard this day with our outward ears, may, through thy grace, be so grafted inwardly in our hearts, that they may bring forth in us the fruit of good living, to the honour and praise of thy name, through Jesus Christ our Lord. *Amen.*

P REVENT us, O Lord, in all our doings with thy most gracious favour, and further us with thy continual help, that in all our works – begun, continued, and ended in thee – we may glorify thy holy name, and finally by thy mercy obtain everlasting life, through Jesus Christ our Lord. *Amen.*

A LMIGHTY God, the fountain of all wisdom, who knowest our necessities before we ask and our ignorance in asking: We beseech thee to have compassion upon our infirmities; and those things which for our unworthiness we dare not, and for our blindness we cannot ask, vouchsafe to give us, for the worthiness of thy Son Jesus Christ our Lord. *Amen.*

ALMIGHTY God, who hast promised to hear the petitions of those who ask in thy Son's name: We beseech thee mercifully to incline thine ears to us who have made now our prayers and supplications unto thee, and grant that those things which we have faithfully asked according to thy will, may effectually be obtained, to the relief of our necessity and to the setting forth of thy glory, through Jesus Christ our Lord. *Amen.*

¶ *Upon Sundays and other holy days (if there is no communion) shall be said all that is appointed at the Communion until the end of the general prayer for the whole state of Christ's church militant here on earth (p. 251), together with one or more of the collects before rehearsed, concluding with the blessing.*

¶ *And there shall be no celebration of the Lord's supper unless there is a convenient number to communicate with the priest, according to his discretion.*

¶ *And if there are not above twenty persons in the parish of discretion to receive the communion, there shall be no communion unless four (or three at the least) communicate with the priest.*

¶ *And in cathedral and collegiate churches and colleges, where there are many priests and deacons, they shall all receive the communion with the priest every Sunday at the least, unless they have a reasonable cause to the contrary.*

¶ *And to take away all occasion of dissension and superstition which any person hath or might have concerning the bread and wine, it shall suffice that the bread is such as is usual to be eaten, but the best and purest wheat bread that conveniently may be gotten.*

¶ *And if any of the bread and wine remain unconsecrated, the pastor shall have it to his own use. But if any remain of that which was consecrated, it shall not be carried out of the church, but the priest, and such other of the communicants as he shall then call unto him, shall immediately after the blessing reverently eat and drink the same.*

¶ *The bread and wine for the communion shall be provided by the pastor and the churchwardens at the charge of the parish.*

¶ *And note that every parishioner shall communicate at least three times in the year, of which Easter shall be one.*

¶ *After the divine service is ended, the money given at the offertory shall be disposed of to such pious and charitable uses as the minister and churchwardens shall think fit. If they disagree, it shall be disposed of as the ordinary shall appoint.*

¶ *Whereas it is ordained in this Office for the Administration of the Lord's Supper that the communicants should receive the same kneeling – which order is well meant, for a signification of our humble and grateful acknowledgement of the benefits of Christ therein given to all worthy receivers, and for the avoiding of such profanation and disorder in the holy communion as might otherwise ensue – yet, lest the same kneeling should by any persons, either out of ignorance and infirmity or out of malice and obstinacy, be misconstrued and misunderstood: It is here declared that thereby no adoration is intended or ought to be done, either unto the sacramental bread or wine there bodily received or unto any corporal presence of Christ's natural flesh and blood. For the sacramental bread and wine remain still in their very natural substances, and therefore may not be adored – for that would be idolatry, to be abhorred by all faithful Christians – and the natural body and blood of our Saviour Christ are in heaven, and not here, it being against the truth of Christ's natural body to be at one time in more places than one.*

¶ *Instead of the collect for civil authorities (p. 245) may be said one of the collects for the King (p. 47).*
¶ *Instead of* We beseech thee also so to direct and dispose, *&c. (p. 250) may be said the following:*

We beseech thee also to save and defend all Christian kings, princes, and governors; and specially thy servant *CHARLES* our King; that under him we may be godly and quietly governed; and grant unto his whole council, and to all who are put in authority under him, that they may truly and impartially administer justice, to the punishment of wickedness and vice, and to the maintenance of thy true religion and virtue.

The Ministration of Public Baptism of Infants to Be Used in the Church.

¶ *The people are to be admonished that it is most convenient that baptism should not be administered but upon Sundays and other holy days, when the greatest number of people come together – not only so that the congregation there present may testify to the receiving of those who are newly baptized into the number of Christ's church, but also because in the baptism of infants every man present may be put in remembrance of his own profession made to God in his baptism. For which cause also it is expedient that baptism be ministered in the common tongue. Nevertheless – if necessity so require – children may be baptized upon any other day.*

¶ *And note that there shall be for every male child to be baptized two godfathers and one godmother; and for every female, one godfather and two godmothers.*

¶ *When there are children to be baptized, the parents shall give knowledge of it overnight, or in the morning before the beginning of Morning Prayer, to the pastor. And then the godfathers and godmothers and the people with the children must be ready at the font, either immediately after the last lesson at Morning Prayer or else immediately after the last lesson at Evening Prayer, as the pastor by his discretion shall appoint. And the priest coming to the font (which is then to be filled with pure water), and standing there, shall say,* Hath this child been already baptized, or no?

¶ *If they answer,* No, *then shall the priest proceed as followeth.*

DEARLY beloved, forasmuch as all men are conceived and born in sin, and that our Saviour Christ saith, 'None can enter into the kingdom of God, except he be regenerate and born anew of water and of the Holy Ghost': I beseech you to call upon God the Father, through our Lord Jesus Christ, that of his bounteous mercy he will grant to *this child* that thing which by nature *he* cannot have, that *he* may be baptized with water and the Holy Ghost, and received into Christ's holy church, and be made *a living member* of the same.

¶ *Then shall the priest say,*
Let us pray.

ALMIGHTY and everlasting God, who of thy great mercy didst save Noah and his family in the ark from perishing by water; and also didst safely lead the children of Israel thy people through the Red Sea, figuring thereby thy holy baptism; and by the baptism of thy well-beloved Son Jesus Christ, in the River Jordan, didst sanctify water to the mystical washing away of sin: We beseech thee, for thine infinite mercies, that thou wilt mercifully look upon *this child;* wash *him* and sanctify *him* with the Holy Ghost; that *he,* being delivered from thy wrath, may be received into the ark of Christ's church; and being steadfast in faith, joyful through hope, and rooted in charity, may so pass the waves of this troublesome world, that finally *he* may come to the land of everlasting life, there to reign with thee world without end, through Jesus Christ our Lord. *Amen.*

ALMIGHTY and immortal God, the aid of all who need, the helper of all who flee to thee for succour, the life of those who believe, and the resurrection of the dead: We call upon thee for *this infant,* that *he,* coming to thy holy baptism, may receive remission of *his* sins by spiritual regeneration. Receive *him,* O Lord, as thou hast promised by thy well-beloved Son, saying, 'Ask, and ye shall have; seek, and ye shall find; knock, and it shall be opened unto you.' So give now unto us who ask; let us who seek, find; open the gate unto us who knock; that *this infant* may enjoy the everlasting benediction of thy heavenly washing, and may come to the eternal kingdom which thou hast promised by Christ our Lord. *Amen.*

¶ *Then shall the people stand up, and the priest shall say,*
Hear the words of the Gospel written by Saint
Mark, in the tenth chapter, at the thirteenth verse:

THEY brought young children to Christ, that he should touch them, and his disciples rebuked those that brought them. But when Jesus saw it, he was much displeased and said unto them, 'Suffer the little children to come unto me, and forbid them not, for of such is the kingdom of God.

'Verily I say unto you, whosoever shall not receive the kingdom of God as a little child, he shall not enter therein.'

And he took them up in his arms, put his hands upon them, and blessed them.

¶ *After the gospel is read, the minister shall make this brief exhortation upon the words of the gospel.*

BELOVED, ye hear in this gospel the words of our Saviour Christ, that he commanded the children to be brought unto him, how he blamed those who would have kept them from him, how he exhorteth all men to follow their innocency. Ye perceive how, by his outward gesture and deed, he declared his good will toward them, for he embraced them in his arms, he laid his hands upon them, and blessed them. Doubt ye not therefore, but earnestly believe, that he will likewise favourably receive *this* present *infant,* that he will embrace *him* with the arms of his mercy, that he will give unto *him* the blessing of eternal life, and make *him partaker* of his everlasting kingdom.

Wherefore we being thus persuaded of the good will of our heavenly Father towards *this infant,* declared by his Son Jesus Christ, and nothing doubting but that he favourably accepteth this charitable work of ours in bringing *this infant* to his holy baptism, let us faithfully and devoutly give thanks unto him, and say,

ALMIGHTY and everlasting God, heavenly Father, we give thee humble thanks that thou hast vouchsafed to call us to the knowledge of thy grace and faith in thee: Increase this knowledge, and confirm this faith in us evermore. Give thy Holy Spirit to *this infant,* that *he* may be born again, and be made *an heir* of everlasting salvation, through our Lord Jesus Christ, who liveth and reigneth with thee and the Holy Spirit, now and for ever. *Amen.*

¶ *Then shall the priest speak thus unto the godfathers and godmothers.*

D EARLY beloved, ye have brought *this child* here to be baptized. Ye have prayed that our Lord Jesus Christ would vouchsafe to receive *him,* to release *him* of *his* sins, to sanctify *him* with the Holy Ghost, to give *him* the kingdom of heaven and everlasting life. Ye have heard also that our Lord Jesus Christ hath promised in his gospel, to grant all these things that ye have prayed for – which promise, he, for his part, will most surely keep and perform. Wherefore, after this promise made by Christ, *this infant* must also faithfully, for *his* part, promise by you that are *his* sureties – until *he* come of age to take it upon *himself* – that *he* will renounce the devil and all his works, and constantly believe God's holy word, and obediently keep his commandments. I demand therefore,

D OST thou, in the name of this child, renounce the devil and all his works, the vain pomp and glory of the world, with all covetous desires of the same, and the carnal desires of the flesh, so that thou wilt not follow nor be led by them?
Answer. I renounce them all.

¶ *Minister.*

D OST thou believe in God the Father almighty, maker of heaven and earth? And in Jesus Christ his only-begotten Son our Lord? And that he was conceived by the Holy Ghost, born of the Virgin Mary; that he suffered under Pontius Pilate, was crucified, dead, and buried; that he went down into hell, and also did rise again the third day; that he ascended into heaven, and sitteth on the right hand of God the Father almighty; and from thence shall come again at the end of the world, to judge the quick and the dead? And dost thou believe in the Holy Ghost, the holy catholic church, the communion of saints, the remission of sins, the resurrection of the flesh, and everlasting life after death?

Answer.   All this I steadfastly believe.

¶ *Minister.*

WILT thou be baptized in this faith?
Answer. That is my desire.

¶ *Minister.*

WILT thou then obediently keep God's holy will and commandments, and walk in the same all the days of thy life?

Answer.   I will.

¶ *Then shall the priest say,*

O MERCIFUL God, grant that the old Adam in *this child* may be so buried, that the new man may be raised up in *him. Amen.*

Grant that all carnal affections may die in *him,* and that all things belonging to the Spirit may live and grow in *him. Amen.*

Grant that *he* may have power and strength, to have victory and to triumph against the devil, the world, and the flesh. *Amen.*

Grant that whosoever is here dedicated to thee by our office and ministry, may also be endued with heavenly virtues, and everlastingly rewarded through thy mercy, O blessed Lord God, who dost live and govern all things, world without end. *Amen.*

ALMIGHTY, everliving God, whose most dearly beloved Son Jesus Christ, for the forgiveness of our sins, did shed out of his most precious side both water and blood, and gave commandment to his disciples, that they should go make disciples of all nations, and baptize them in the name of the Father, and of the Son, and of the Holy Ghost: Regard, we beseech thee, the supplications of thy congregation; sanctify this water to the mystical washing away of sin; and grant that *this child,* now to be baptized therein, may receive the fulness of thy grace, and ever remain in the number of thy faithful and elect children, through Jesus Christ our Lord. *Amen.*

¶ *Then the priest shall take the child into his hands, and shall say to the godfathers and godmothers,* Name this child. *And then naming it after them, (if they shall certify him that the child may well endure it) he shall dip it in the water discreetly and warily, saying,*

N. I BAPTIZE thee in the name of the Father, and of the Son, and of the Holy Ghost. Amen.

¶ *But if they certify that the child is weak, it shall suffice to pour water upon it, saying the foresaid words, N., I baptize* thee in the name of the Father, and of the Son, and of the Holy Ghost. Amen.

¶ *Then shall the priest say,*

WE receive this child into the congregation of Christ's flock, *and do sign *him* with the sign of the cross, in token that hereafter *he* shall not be ashamed to confess the faith of Christ crucified, and manfully to fight under his banner against sin, the world, and the devil, and to continue Christ's faithful soldier and servant unto *his* life's end. Amen.

* *Here the priest shall make a cross upon the child's forehead.*

¶ *Then shall the priest say,*

SEEING now, dearly beloved brethren, that *this child is regenerate* and grafted into the body of Christ's church, let us give thanks unto almighty God for these benefits, and with one accord make our prayers unto him, that *this child* may lead the rest of *his* life according to this beginning.

¶ *Then shall be said, all kneeling,*

OUR Father, who art in heaven, Hallowed be thy name. Thy kingdom come. Thy will be done, On earth as it is in heaven. Give us this day our daily bread. And forgive us our trespasses, As we forgive those who trespass against us. And lead us not into temptation, But deliver us from evil. Amen.

THE PUBLIC BAPTISM OF INFANTS

¶ *Then shall the priest say,*

WE yield thee hearty thanks, most merciful Father, that it hath pleased thee to regenerate *this infant* with thy Holy Spirit, to receive *him* for thine own *child* by adoption, and to incorporate *him* into thy holy church. And humbly we beseech thee to grant that *he,* being dead unto sin, and living unto righteousness, and being buried with Christ in his death, may crucify the old man, and utterly abolish the whole body of sin; and that, as *he is* made *partaker* of the death of thy Son, *he* may also be *partaker* of his resurrection; so that finally, with the rest of thy holy church, *he* may be *an inheritor* of thine everlasting kingdom, through Christ our Lord. *Amen.*

¶ *Then, all standing up, the priest shall say to the godfathers and godmothers this exhortation following.*

FORASMUCH as *this child hath* promised by you *his* sureties to renounce the devil and all his works, to believe in God, and to serve him, ye must remember that it is your parts and duties to see that *this infant is* taught, as soon as *he* shall be able to learn, what a solemn vow, promise, and profession *he hath* here made by you. And that *he* may know these things the better, ye shall call upon *him* to hear sermons; and chiefly ye shall provide that *he* may learn the Creed, the Lord's Prayer, and the Ten Commandments in the common tongue, and all other things which a Christian ought to know and believe to his soul's health; and that *this child* may be virtuously brought up to lead a godly and a Christian life, remembering always that baptism doth represent unto us our profession, which is to follow the example of our Saviour Christ and to be made like unto him, that as he died and rose again for us, so should we, who are baptized, die from sin and rise again unto righteousness, continually mortifying all our evil and corrupt affections, and daily proceeding in all virtue and godliness of living.

¶ *Then shall he add and say,*

YE are to take care that *this child* be brought to the bishop to be confirmed by him, as soon as *he* can say the Creed, the Lord's Prayer, and the Ten Commandments in the common tongue, and be further instructed in the church catechism set forth for that purpose.

¶ *It is certain by God's word that children who are baptized, dying before they commit actual sin, are undoubtedly saved.*

¶ *To take away all scruple concerning the use of the sign of the cross in baptism, the true explication of it and the just reasons for retaining it may be seen in Canon xxx, first published in the year 1604.*

The Ministration of Private Baptism of Children in Houses.

¶ *The pastors of every parish shall often admonish the people not to defer the baptism of their children longer than the first or second Sunday next after their birth (or other holy day falling between), unless with great and reasonable cause to be approved by the pastor.*

¶ *And also they shall warn them, without like great cause and necessity, not to procure their children to be baptized at home in their houses. But when need shall compel them to do so, then baptism shall be administered in this fashion:*

¶ *First let the minister of the parish (or, in his absence, any other lawful minister who can be procured) with those who are present call upon God, and say the Lord's Prayer and as many of the collects appointed to be said before in the Form of Public Baptism as the time and present exigence will suffer. And then, the child being named by someone who is present, the minister shall pour water upon it, saying these words:*

N. I BAPTIZE thee in the name of the Father, and of the Son, and of the Holy ◆ Ghost. Amen.

¶ *Then, all kneeling down, the minister shall give thanks unto God, and say,*

WE yield thee hearty thanks, most merciful Father, that it hath pleased thee to regenerate *this infant* with thy Holy Spirit, to receive *him* for thine own *child* by adoption, and to incorporate *him* into thy holy church. And humbly we beseech thee to grant, that as *he is* now made *partaker* of the death of thy Son, so *he* may be also of his resurrection; and that finally, with the rest of thy saints, *he* may inherit thine everlasting kingdom, through the same thy Son Jesus Christ our Lord. *Amen.*

¶ *And let them not doubt but that the child so baptized is lawfully and sufficiently baptized and ought not to be baptized again. Yet nevertheless, if the child which is baptized after this sort afterward lives, it is expedient that it be brought into the church, to the intent that if the minister of the same parish did himself baptize that child, the congregation may be certified of the true form of baptism that he privately before used. In which case he shall say thus,*

I CERTIFY you that according to the due and prescribed order of the church, *at such a time,* and *at such a place,* before divers witnesses, I baptized this child.

¶ *But if the child were baptized by any other lawful minister, then the minister of the parish where the child was born or christened shall examine and try whether the child was lawfully baptized, or no. In which case, if those who bring any child to the church answer that the same child was already baptized, then shall the minister examine them further, saying,*

BY whom was this child baptized? Who was present when this child was baptized? Because some things essential to this sacrament may happen to be omitted through fear or haste, in such times of extremity, therefore I demand further of you: With what matter was this child baptized? With what words was this child baptized?

¶ *And if the minister shall find, by the answers of those who bring the child, that all things were done as they ought to be, then shall he not christen the child again, but shall receive him as one of the flock of true Christian people, saying thus,*

I CERTIFY you that in this case all is well done, and according unto due order, concerning the baptizing of this child; who, being born in original sin and in the wrath of God, is now, by the laver of regeneration in baptism, received into the number of the children of God and heirs of everlasting life. For our Lord Jesus Christ doth not deny his grace and mercy unto such infants, but most lovingly doth call them unto him, as the holy gospel doth witness to our comfort in this manner:

St. Mark 10:13-16.

THEY brought young children to Christ, that he should touch them, and his disciples rebuked those that brought them. But when Jesus saw it, he was much displeased and said unto them, 'Suffer the little children to come unto me, and forbid them not, for of such is the kingdom of God.

'Verily I say unto you, whosoever shall not receive the kingdom of God as a little child, he shall not enter therein.' And he took them up in his arms, put his hands upon them, and blessed them.

¶ *After the gospel is read, the minister shall make this brief exhortation upon the words of the gospel.*

BELOVED, ye hear in this gospel the words of our Saviour Christ, that he commanded the children to be brought unto him, how he blamed those who would have kept them from him, how he exhorted all men to follow their innocency. Ye perceive how, by his outward gesture and deed, he declared his good will toward them, for he embraced them in his arms, he laid his hands upon them, and blessed them. Doubt ye not therefore, but earnestly believe, that he hath likewise favourably received *this* present *infant,* that he hath embraced *him* with the arms of his mercy, and (as he hath promised in his holy word) will give unto *him* the blessing of eternal life, and make *him partaker* of his everlasting kingdom. Wherefore, we being thus persuaded of the good will of our heavenly Father, declared by his Son Jesus Christ, towards *this infant,* let us faithfully and devoutly give thanks unto him, and say the prayer which the Lord himself taught us:

OUR Father, who art in heaven, Hallowed be thy name. Thy kingdom come. Thy will be done, On earth as it is in heaven. Give us this day our daily bread. And forgive us our trespasses, As we forgive those who trespass against us. And lead us not into temptation, But deliver us from evil. Amen.

ALMIGHTY and everlasting God, heavenly Father, we give thee humble thanks that thou hast vouchsafed to call us to the knowledge of thy grace and faith in thee: Increase this knowledge, and confirm this faith in us evermore. Give thy Holy Spirit to *this infant,* that *he,* being born again, and being made *an heir* of everlasting salvation, through our Lord Jesus Christ, may continue thy *servant* and attain thy promise, through the same our Lord Jesus Christ thy Son, who liveth and reigneth with thee and the Holy Spirit, now and for ever. *Amen.*

¶ *Then shall the priest demand the name of the child, which, being by the godfathers and godmothers pronounced, the minister shall say,*

DOST thou, in the name of this child, renounce the devil and all his works, the vain pomp and glory of this world, with all covetous desires of the same, and the carnal desires of the flesh, so that thou wilt not follow nor be led by them?

Answer. I renounce them all.

¶ *Minister.*

DOST thou believe in God the Father almighty, maker of heaven and earth? And in Jesus Christ his only-begotten Son our Lord? And that he was conceived by the Holy Ghost, born of the Virgin Mary; that he suffered under Pontius Pilate, was crucified, dead, and buried; that he went down into hell, and also did rise again the third day; that he ascended into heaven, and sitteth on the right hand of God the Father almighty; and from thence shall come again at the end of the world, to judge the quick and the dead? And dost thou believe in the Holy Ghost, the holy catholic church, the communion of saints, the remission of sins, the resurrection of the flesh, and everlasting life after death?

Answer. All this I steadfastly believe.

¶ *Minister.*

WILT thou then obediently keep God's holy will and commandments, and walk in the same all the days of thy life?

Answer. I will.

¶ *Then the priest shall say,*

WE receive this child into the congregation of Christ's flock, *and do sign *him* with the sign of the cross, in token that hereafter *he* shall not be ashamed to confess the faith of Christ crucified, and manfully to fight under his banner against sin, the world, and the devil, and to continue Christ's faithful soldier and servant unto *his* life's end. Amen.

Here the priest shall make a cross upon the child's forehead.

¶ *Then shall the priest say,*

SEEING now, dearly beloved brethren, that *this child is* by baptism regenerate and grafted into the body of Christ's church, let us give thanks unto almighty God for these benefits, and with one accord make our prayers unto him, that *he* may lead the rest of *his* life according to this beginning.

¶ *Then shall the priest say,*

WE yield thee most hearty thanks, most merciful Father, that it hath pleased thee to regenerate *this infant* with thy Holy Spirit, to receive *him* for thine own *child* by adoption, and to incorporate *him* into thy holy church. And humbly we beseech thee to grant that *he*, being dead unto sin, and living unto righteousness, and being buried with Christ in his death, may crucify the old man, and utterly abolish the whole body of sin; and that, as *he is* made *partaker* of the death of thy Son, *he* may also be *partaker* of his resurrection; so that finally, with the rest of thy holy church, *he* may be *an inheritor* of thine everlasting kingdom, through Christ our Lord. *Amen.*

¶ *Then, all standing up, the minister shall make this exhortation to the godfathers and godmothers.*

FORASMUCH as *this child hath* promised by you *his* sureties to renounce the devil and all his works, to believe in God, and to serve him, ye must remember that it is your parts and duties to see that *this infant* is taught, as soon as *he* shall be able to learn, what a solemn vow, promise, and profession *he hath* made by you. And that *he* may know these things the better, ye shall call upon *him* to hear sermons; and chiefly ye shall provide that *he* may learn the Creed, the Lord's Prayer, and the Ten

Commandments in the common tongue, and all other things which a Christian ought to know and believe to his soul's health; and that *this child* may be virtuously brought up to lead a godly and a Christian life, remembering always that baptism doth represent unto us our profession, which is to follow the example of our Saviour Christ and to be made like unto him, that as he died and rose again for us, so should we, who are baptized, die from sin and rise again unto righteousness, continually mortifying all our evil and corrupt affections, and daily proceeding in all virtue and godliness of living.

¶ *But if those who bring the infant to the church make such uncertain answers to the priest's questions that it cannot appear that the child was baptized with water in the name of the Father, and of the Son, and of the Holy Ghost – which are essential parts of baptism – then let the priest baptize it in the form before appointed for public baptism of infants (p. 271), except that at the dipping of the child in the font, he shall use this form of words.*

IF thou art not already baptized, *N.*, I baptize thee in the name of the Father, and of the Son, and of the Holy Ghost. Amen.

The Ministration of Baptism to Such as Are of Riper Years & Able to Answer for Themselves.

¶ *When any persons who are of riper years are to be baptized, timely notice shall be given to the bishop (or whomever he shall appoint for that purpose) by the parents or some other discreet persons, a week before at the least, that due care may be taken for their examination, whether they are sufficiently instructed in the principles of the Christian religion; and that they may be exhorted to prepare themselves with prayers and fasting for the receiving of this holy sacrament.*

¶ *And if they shall be found fit, then the godfathers and godmothers (the people being assembled upon the Sunday or holy day appointed) shall be ready to present them at the font immediately after the second lesson, either at Morning or Evening Prayer, as the pastor in his discretion shall think fit.*

¶ *And standing there, the priest shall ask whether any of the persons here presented are baptized, or no, and if they shall answer,* No, *then shall the priest say thus,*

DEARLY beloved, forasmuch as all men are conceived and born in sin; and that which is born of the flesh is flesh; and those who are in the flesh cannot please God, but live in sin, committing many actual transgressions; and that our Saviour Christ saith, 'None can enter into the kingdom of God, except he be regenerate and born anew of water and of the Holy Ghost': I beseech you to call upon God the Father, through our Lord Jesus Christ, that of his bounteous goodness he will grant to *these persons* that which by nature *they* cannot have, that *they* may be baptized with water and the Holy Ghost, and received into Christ's holy church, and be made *living members* of the same.

¶ *Then shall the priest say,*
Let us pray.

¶ *And here all the congregation shall kneel.*

A<small>LMIGHTY</small> and everlasting God, who of thy great mercy didst save Noah and his family in the ark from perishing by water; and also didst safely lead the children of Israel thy people through the Red Sea, figuring thereby thy holy baptism; and by the baptism of thy well-beloved Son Jesus Christ, in the River Jordan, didst sanctify the element of water to the mystical washing away of sin: We beseech thee, for thine infinite mercies, that thou wilt mercifully look upon *these* thy *servants;* wash *them* and sanctify *them* with the Holy Ghost; that *they,* being delivered from thy wrath, may be received into the ark of Christ's church; and being steadfast in faith, joyful through hope, and rooted in charity, may so pass the waves of this troublesome world, that finally *they* may come to the land of everlasting life, there to reign with thee, world without end, through Jesus Christ our Lord. *Amen.*

ALMIGHTY and immortal God, the aid of all who need, the helper of all who flee to thee for succour, the life of those who believe, and the resurrection of the dead: We call upon thee for *these persons,* that *they,* coming to thy holy baptism, may receive remission of *their* sins by spiritual regeneration. Receive *them,* O Lord, and as thou hast promised by thy well-beloved Son, saying, 'Ask, and ye shall receive; seek, and ye shall find; knock, and it shall be opened unto you', so give now unto us who ask; let us who seek, find; open the gate unto us who knock; that *these persons* may enjoy the everlasting benediction of thy heavenly washing, and may come to the eternal kingdom which thou hast promised by Christ our Lord. *Amen.*

¶ *Then shall the people stand up, and the priest shall say,*
Hear the words of the Gospel written by Saint John,
in the third chapter, beginning at the first verse:

THERE was a man of the Pharisees, named Nicodemus, a ruler of the Jews. The same came to Jesus by night and said unto him, 'Rabbi, we know that thou art a teacher come from God, for no man can do these miracles that thou doest, except God be with him.'

Jesus answered and said unto him, 'Verily, verily I say unto thee, except a man be born again, he cannot see the kingdom of God.'

Nicodemus saith unto him, 'How can a man be born when he is old? Can he enter the second time into his mother's womb, and be born?'

Jesus answered, 'Verily, verily I say unto thee, except a man be born of water and of the Spirit, he cannot enter into the kingdom of God.

'That which is born of the flesh is flesh, and that which is born of the Spirit is spirit. Marvel not that I said unto thee, "Ye must be born again." The wind bloweth where it listeth, and thou hearest the sound thereof, but canst not tell whence it cometh and whither it goeth. So is every one that is born of the Spirit.'

¶ *After which, he shall say this exhortation following.*

Beloved, ye hear in this gospel the express words of our Saviour Christ, that except a man be born of water and of the Spirit, he cannot enter into the kingdom of God. Whereby ye may perceive the great necessity of this sacrament, where it may be had. Likewise, immediately before his ascension into heaven, (as we read in the last chapter of Saint Mark's Gospel) he gave command to his disciples, saying, 'Go ye into all the world, and preach the gospel to every creature. He that believeth and is baptized shall be saved, but he that believeth not shall be condemned.' Which also showeth unto us the great benefit we reap thereby. For which cause Saint Peter the apostle, when upon his first preaching of the gospel many were pricked at the heart, and said to him and the rest of the apostles, 'Men and brethren, what shall we do?', replied and said unto them, 'Repent, and be baptized every one of you for the remission of sins, and ye shall receive the gift of the Holy Ghost. For the promise is to you and your children, and to all that are afar off, even as many as the

Lord our God shall call.' And with many other words exhorted he them, saying, 'Save yourselves from this untoward generation.' For (as the same apostle testifieth in another place) 'even baptism doth also now save us – not the putting away of the filth of the flesh, but the answer of a good conscience towards God – by the resurrection of Jesus Christ.' Doubt ye not therefore, but earnestly believe, that he will favourably receive *these* present *persons,* truly repenting, and coming unto him by faith; that he will grant *them* remission of *their* sins, and bestow upon *them* the Holy Ghost; that he will give *them* the blessing of eternal life, and make *them partakers* of his everlasting kingdom.

Wherefore we being thus persuaded of the good will of our heavenly Father towards *these persons,* declared by his Son Jesus Christ, let us faithfully and devoutly give thanks to him, and say,

ALMIGHTY and everlasting God, heavenly Father, we give thee humble thanks, because thou hast vouchsafed to call us to the knowledge of thy grace and faith in thee. Increase this knowledge, and confirm this faith in us evermore. Give thy Holy Spirit to *these persons,* that *they* may be born again, and be made *heirs* of everlasting salvation, through our Lord Jesus Christ, who liveth and reigneth with thee and the Holy Spirit, now and for ever. *Amen.*

¶ *Then the priest shall speak to the persons to be baptized in this manner.*

WELL-BELOVED, who are come hither desiring to receive holy baptism, *ye* have heard how the congregation hath prayed that our Lord Jesus Christ would vouchsafe to receive you and bless you, to release you of your sins, to give you the kingdom of heaven and everlasting life. *Ye* have heard also that our Lord Jesus Christ hath promised in his holy word, to grant all those things that we have prayed for – which promise, he, for his part, will most surely keep and perform.

Wherefore, after this promise made by Christ, *ye* must also faithfully, for your part, promise in the presence of these your witnesses, and this whole congregation, that *ye* will renounce the devil and all his works, and constantly believe God's holy word, and obediently keep his commandments.

¶ *Then shall the priest demand of each of the persons to be baptized, individually, these questions following.*

¶ *Question.*

DOST thou renounce the devil and all his works, the vain pomp and glory of the world, with all covetous desires of the same, and the carnal desires of the flesh, so that thou wilt not follow nor be led by them?

Answer. I renounce them all.

¶ *Question.*

Dost thou believe in God the Father almighty, maker of heaven and earth? And in Jesus Christ his only-begotten Son our Lord? And that he was conceived by the Holy Ghost, born of the Virgin Mary; that he suffered under Pontius Pilate, was crucified, dead, and buried; that he went down into hell, and also did rise again the third day; that he ascended into heaven, and sitteth on the right hand of God the Father almighty; and from thence shall come again at the end of the world, to judge the quick and the dead? And dost thou believe in the Holy Ghost, the holy catholic church, the communion of saints, the remission of sins, the resurrection of the flesh, and everlasting life after death?

Answer. All this I steadfastly believe.

¶ *Question.*

Wilt thou be baptized in this faith?
Answer. That is my desire.

¶ *Question.*

Wilt thou then obediently keep God's holy will and commandments, and walk in the same all the days of thy life?

Answer. I will endeavour so to do, God being my helper.

¶ *Then shall the priest say,*

OMERCIFUL God, grant that the old Adam in *these persons* may be so buried, that the new man may be raised up in *them. Amen.*

Grant that all carnal affections may die in *them,* and that all things belonging to the Spirit may live and grow in *them. Amen.*

Grant that *they* may have power and strength, to have victory and to triumph against the devil, the world, and the flesh. *Amen.*

Grant that *they,* being here dedicated to thee by our office and ministry, may also be endued with heavenly virtues, and everlastingly rewarded through thy mercy, O blessed Lord God, who dost live and govern all things, world without end. *Amen.*

ALMIGHTY, everliving God, whose most dearly beloved Son Jesus Christ, for the forgiveness of our sins, did shed out of his most precious side both water and blood, and gave commandment to his disciples, that they should go make disciples of all nations, and baptize them in the name of the Father, the Son, and the Holy Ghost: Regard, we beseech thee, the supplications of this congregation; sanctify this water to the mystical washing away of sin; and grant that the *persons* now to be baptized therein may receive the fulness of thy grace, and ever remain in the number of thy faithful and elect children, through Jesus Christ our Lord. *Amen.*

¶ *Then shall the priest take each person to be baptized by the right hand, and placing him conveniently by the font, according to his discretion, shall ask the godfathers and godmothers the name, and then shall dip him in the water, or pour water upon him, saying,*

N. I BAPTIZE thee in the name of the Father, and of the Son, and of the Holy Ghost. Amen.

¶ *Then shall the priest say,*

WE receive this person into the congregation of Christ's flock, and * do sign *him* with the sign of the cross, in token that hereafter *he* shall not be ashamed to confess the faith of Christ crucified, and manfully to fight under his banner against sin, the world, and the devil, and to continue Christ's faithful soldier and servant unto *his* life's end. Amen.

* *Here the priest shall make a cross upon the person's forehead.*

¶ *Then shall the priest say,*

SEEING now, dearly beloved brethren, that *these persons are* regenerate and grafted into the body of Christ's church, let us give thanks unto almighty God for these benefits, and with one accord make our prayers unto him, that *they* may lead the rest of *their* life according to this beginning.

¶ *Then shall be said the Lord's Prayer, all kneeling.*

OUR Father, who art in heaven, Hallowed be thy name. Thy kingdom come. Thy will be done, On earth as it is in heaven. Give us this day our daily bread. And forgive us our trespasses, As we forgive those who trespass against us. And lead us not into temptation, But deliver us from evil. Amen.

¶ Then shall the priest say,

WE yield thee humble thanks, O heavenly Father, that thou hast vouchsafed to call us to the knowledge of thy grace and faith in thee. Increase this knowledge, and confirm this faith in us evermore. Give thy Holy Spirit to *these persons,* that, being now born again, and made *heirs* of everlasting salvation, through our Lord Jesus Christ, *they* may continue thy *servants,* and attain thy promises, through the same Lord Jesus Christ thy Son, who liveth and reigneth with thee, in the unity of the same Holy Spirit, everlastingly. *Amen.*

¶ Then, all standing up, the priest shall use this exhortation following, speaking to the godfathers and godmothers first.

FORASMUCH as *these persons have* promised in your presence to renounce the devil and all his works, to believe in God, and to serve him: Ye must remember that it is your part and duty to put *them* in mind, what a solemn vow, promise, and profession *they have* now made before this congregation, and especially before you *their* chosen witnesses. And ye are also to call upon *them* to use all diligence to be rightly instructed in God's holy word, so that *they* may grow in grace and in the knowledge of our Lord Jesus Christ, and live godly, righteously, and soberly in this present world.

¶ *And then, speaking to the newly baptized persons, he shall proceed and say,*

AND as for you, who have now by baptism put on Christ, it is your part and duty also, being made the *children* of God and of the light by faith in Jesus Christ, to walk answerably to your Christian calling, and as becometh the children of light, remembering always that baptism representeth unto us our profession, which is to follow the example of our Saviour Christ, and to be made like unto him, that as he died and rose again for us, so should we, who are baptized, die from sin and rise again unto righteousness, continually mortifying all our evil and corrupt affections, and daily proceeding in all virtue and godliness of living.

¶ *It is expedient that every person thus baptized should be confirmed by the bishop as soon after his baptism as conveniently may be, so that he may be admitted to the holy communion.*

¶ *If any persons not baptized in their infancy shall be brought to be baptized before they come to years of discretion to answer for themselves, it may suffice to use the Office for Public Baptism of Infants, or (in case of extreme danger) the Office for Private Baptism, only changing the word* infant *for* child *or* person *as occasion requireth.*

A Catechism

*that is to say, an instruction to be learned
by every person before he is brought
to be confirmed by the bishop.*

Question. What is your name?

Answer. N.

Question. Who gave you this name?

Answer. My godfathers and godmothers in my baptism, wherein I was made a member of Christ, the child of God, and an inheritor of the kingdom of heaven.

Question. What did your godfathers and godmothers then do for you?

Answer. They did promise and vow three things in my name. First, that I should renounce the devil and all his works, the pomps and vanity of this wicked world, and all the sinful lusts of the flesh. Secondly, that I should believe all the articles of the Christian faith. And thirdly, that I should keep God's holy will and commandments, and walk in the same all the days of my life.

Question. Dost thou not think that thou art bound to believe and to do as they have promised for thee?

Answer. Yes, verily, and by God's help so I will. And I heartily thank our heavenly Father, that he hath called me to this state of salvation, through Jesus Christ our Saviour. And I pray unto God to give me his grace, that I may continue in the same unto my life's end.

A CATECHISM

CATECHIST. Rehearse the articles of thy belief.

Answer.   I believe in God the Father almighty, maker of heaven and earth; and in Jesus Christ his only Son our Lord, who was conceived by the Holy Ghost, born of the Virgin Mary, suffered under Pontius Pilate, was crucified, dead, and buried. He descended into hell. The third day he rose again from the dead. He ascended into heaven, and sitteth on the right hand of God the Father almighty. From thence he shall come to judge the quick and the dead. I believe in the Holy Ghost, the holy catholic church, the communion of saints, the forgiveness of sins, the resurrection of the body, and the life everlasting. Amen.

Question. What dost thou chiefly learn in these articles of thy belief?

Answer.   First, I learn to believe in God the Father, who hath made me and all the world. Secondly, in God the Son, who hath redeemed me and all mankind. Thirdly, in God the Holy Ghost, who sanctifieth me and all the elect people of God.

Question. You said that your godfathers and godmothers did promise for you, that you should keep God's commandments. Tell me how many there are.

Answer.   Ten.

Question. Which are they?

Answer.   The same which God spake in the twentieth chapter of Exodus, saying, I am the LORD thy God, who brought thee out of the land of Egypt, out of the house of bondage.

1.   Thou shalt have none other gods but me.

2. Thou shalt not make to thyself any graven image, nor the likeness of anything that is in heaven above, or in the earth beneath, or in the water under the earth. Thou shalt not bow down to them, nor worship them. For I, the LORD thy God, am a jealous God, and visit the sins of the fathers upon the children unto the third and fourth generation of them that hate me, and show mercy unto thousands of them that love me and keep my commandments.

3. Thou shalt not take the name of the LORD thy God in vain. For the LORD will not hold him guiltless that taketh his name in vain.

4. Remember that thou keep holy the Sabbath day. Six days shalt thou labour, and do all that thou hast to do, but the seventh day is the Sabbath of the LORD thy God. In it thou shalt do no manner of work – thou, and thy son, and thy daughter, thy manservant, and thy maidservant, thy cattle, and the stranger that is within thy gates. For in six days the LORD made heaven and earth, the sea, and all that in them is, and rested the seventh day; wherefore the LORD blessed the seventh day, and hallowed it.

5. Honour thy father and thy mother, that thy days may be long in the land which the LORD thy God giveth thee.

6. Thou shalt do no murder.

7. Thou shalt not commit adultery.

8. Thou shalt not steal.

9. Thou shalt not bear false witness against thy neighbour.

10. Thou shalt not covet thy neighbour's house, thou shalt not covet thy neighbour's wife, nor his servant, nor his maid, nor his ox, nor his ass, nor anything that is his.

Question. What dost thou chiefly learn by these commandments?

Answer. I learn two things – my duty towards God, and my duty towards my neighbour.

Question. What is thy duty towards God?

Answer. My duty towards God is to believe in him, to fear him, and to love him with all my heart, with all my mind, with all my soul, and with all my strength; to worship him, to give him thanks, to put my whole trust in him, to call upon him, to honour his holy name and his word, and to serve him truly all the days of my life.

Question. What is thy duty towards thy neighbour?

Answer. My duty towards my neighbour is to love him as myself, and to do to all men as I would they should do unto me; to love, honour, and succour my father and mother; to honour and obey all who are put in civil authority; to submit myself to all my governors, teachers, and spiritual pastors; to order myself with humility, showing reverence to whom it is due; to hurt nobody by word nor deed; to be true and just in all my dealing; to bear no malice nor hatred in my heart; to keep my hands from picking and stealing, and my tongue from evil-speaking, lying, and slandering; to keep my body in temperance, soberness, and chastity; not to covet nor desire other men's goods, but to learn and labour truly to get mine own living, and to do my duty in that state of life unto which it shall please God to call me.

CATECHIST. My good child, know this, that thou art not able to do these things of thyself, nor to walk in the commandments of God and to serve him, without his special grace, which thou must learn at all times to call for by diligent prayer. Let me hear therefore if thou canst say the Lord's Prayer.

Answer. Our Father, who art in heaven, hallowed be thy name. Thy kingdom come. Thy will be done, on earth as it is in heaven. Give us this day our daily bread. And forgive us our trespasses, as we forgive those who trespass against us. And lead us not into temptation, but deliver us from evil. Amen.

Question. What desirest thou of God in this prayer?

Answer. I desire my Lord God, our heavenly Father, who is the giver of all goodness, to send his grace unto me, and to all people, that we may worship him, serve him, and obey him as we ought to do. And I pray unto God, that he will send us all things that are needful both for our souls and bodies; and that he will be merciful unto us, and forgive us our sins; and that it will please him to save and defend us in all dangers ghostly and bodily; and that he will keep us from all sin and wickedness, and from our spiritual enemy, and from everlasting death. And this I trust he will do of his mercy and goodness, through our Lord Jesus Christ. And therefore I say, Amen, so be it.

QUESTION. How many sacraments hath Christ ordained in his church?

Answer. Two only, as generally necessary to salvation – that is to say, baptism and the supper of the Lord.

Question. What meanest thou by this word *sacrament*?

Answer. I mean an outward and visible sign of an inward and spiritual grace, given unto us, ordained by Christ himself, as a means by which we receive that grace, and a pledge to assure us thereof.

Question. How many parts are there in a sacrament?

Answer. Two – the outward, visible sign; and the inward, spiritual grace.

Question. What is the outward, visible sign or form in baptism?

Answer. Water, in which the person is baptized in the name of the Father, and of the Son, and of the Holy Ghost.

Question. What is the inward and spiritual grace?

Answer. A death unto sin and a new birth unto righteousness, for being by nature born in sin and the children of wrath, we are hereby made the children of grace.

Question. What is required of persons to be baptized?

Answer. Repentance, by which they forsake sin; and faith, by which they steadfastly believe the promises of God made to them in that sacrament.

Question. Why then are infants baptized, when by reason of their tender age they cannot perform them?

Answer. Because they promise both of them by their sureties – which promise, when they come to age, they are themselves bound to perform.

Question. Why was the sacrament of the Lord's supper ordained?

Answer. For the continual remembrance of the sacrifice of the death of Christ, and of the benefits which we receive by it.

Question. What is the outward part or sign of the Lord's supper?

Answer. Bread and wine, which the Lord hath commanded to be received.

Question. What is the inward part, or thing signified?

Answer. The body and blood of Christ, which are verily and indeed taken and received by the faithful in the Lord's supper.

Question. What are the benefits of which we are partakers in the Lord's supper?

Answer. The strengthening and refreshing of our souls by the body and blood of Christ, as our bodies are by the bread and wine.

Question. What is required of those who come to the Lord's supper?

Answer. To examine themselves – whether they truly repent of their former sins, steadfastly purposing to lead a new life; have a lively faith in God's mercy through Christ, with a thankful remembrance of his death; and are in charity with all men.

⁋ *The pastor of every parish shall diligently upon Sundays and holy days, after the second lesson at Evening Prayer, openly in the church instruct and examine as many children of his parish as are sent to him, as he shall think convenient, in some part of this catechism.*

⁋ *And all fathers and mothers shall cause their children who have not learned their catechism to come to the church at the time appointed, and obediently to hear and be instruct-*

ed by the pastor, until such time as they have learned all that is here appointed for them to learn.

¶ *As soon as children are come to a competent age and can say in their mother tongue the Creed, the Lord's Prayer, and the Ten Commandments, and also can answer to the other questions of this short catechism, they shall be brought to the bishop. And every one shall have a godfather or a godmother as a witness of their confirmation.*

¶ *And whenever the bishop shall give notice for children to be brought to him for their confirmation, the pastor of every parish shall either bring or send in writing the names of all persons within his parish that he shall think fit to be presented to the bishop to be confirmed. And if the bishop approves of them, he shall confirm them in the manner following.*

The Order of Confirmation

*or laying on of hands upon those who are
baptized and come to years of discretion.*

¶ *Upon the day appointed, all who are to be then confirmed
shall be placed and stand in order before the bishop. He
(or some other minister appointed by him) shall then read
this preface following.*

To the end that confirmation may be ministered
to the greater edifying of those who shall receive
it, the church hath thought good to order, that
none hereafter shall be confirmed, but such as
can say the Creed, the Lord's Prayer, and the Ten Commandments, and can also answer to such other questions
as in the short catechism are contained – which order is
very convenient to be observed, to the end that children
being now come to the years of discretion, and having
learned what their godfathers and godmothers promised
for them in baptism, they may themselves, with their own
mouth and consent, openly before the church ratify and
confirm the same, and also promise that, by the grace of
God, they will evermore endeavour themselves faithfully to observe such things, as they by their own confession
have assented unto.

¶ *Then shall the bishop say,*

Do ye here, in the presence of God and of this congregation, renew the solemn promise and vow that
was made in your name at your baptism, ratifying and

confirming the same in your own persons, and acknowledging yourselves bound to believe and to do all those things which your godfathers and godmothers then undertook for you?

¶ *And every one shall audibly answer,*
I do.

¶ *The bishop.*
Our help is in the name of the Lord,
Answer.   Who hath made heaven and earth.
Bishop.   Blessed be the name of the Lord,
Answer.   Henceforth, world without end.
Bishop.   Lord, hear our prayers,
Answer.   And let our cry come unto thee.

¶ *The bishop.*
Let us pray.

ALMIGHTY and everliving God, who hast vouchsafed to regenerate these thy servants by water and the Holy Ghost, and hast given unto them forgiveness of all their sins: Strengthen them, we beseech thee, O Lord, with the Holy Ghost the Comforter, and daily increase in them thy manifold gifts of grace – the spirit of wisdom and understanding, the spirit of counsel and ghostly strength, the spirit of knowledge and true godliness – and fill them, O Lord, with the spirit of thy holy fear, now and for ever. *Amen.*

THE ORDER OF CONFIRMATION

¶ *Then, all of them kneeling in order before the bishop, he shall lay his hand upon the head of every one individually, saying,*

D EFEND, O Lord, this thy child [or *this thy servant*] with thy heavenly grace, that *he* may continue thine for ever, and daily increase in thy Holy Spirit more and more until *he* come unto thy everlasting kingdom. Amen.

¶ *Then shall the bishop say,*
> The Lord be with you.

Answer.   And with thy spirit.

¶ *And all kneeling down, the bishop shall add,*
> Let us pray.

O UR Father, who art in heaven, Hallowed be thy name. Thy kingdom come. Thy will be done, On earth as it is in heaven. Give us this day our daily bread. And forgive us our trespasses, As we forgive those who trespass against us. And lead us not into temptation, But deliver us from evil. Amen.

¶ *And this collect.*

A LMIGHTY and everliving God, who makest us both to will and to do those things that are good and acceptable unto thy Divine Majesty: We make our humble supplications unto thee for these thy servants, upon whom (after the example of thy holy apostles) we have now laid our hands, to certify them (by this sign) of thy favour and gracious goodness towards them. Let thy fatherly hand, we beseech thee, ever be over them; let thy Holy Spirit ever be with them; and so lead them in the knowledge and obedience of thy word, that in the end they may obtain everlasting life, through our Lord Jesus Christ, who with thee and the Holy Ghost liveth and reigneth, ever one God, world without end. *Amen.*

O ALMIGHTY Lord and everlasting God, vouchsafe, we beseech thee, to direct, sanctify, and govern both our hearts and bodies, in the ways of thy laws and in the works of thy commandments, that through thy most mighty protection, both here and ever, we may be preserved in body and soul, through our Lord and Saviour Jesus Christ. *Amen.*

¶ *Then the bishop shall bless them, saying thus,*
THE blessing of God almighty, the Father, the Son, and the Holy Ghost, be upon you, and remain with you for ever. Amen.

¶ *And there shall none be admitted to the holy communion until such time as he is confirmed or is ready and desirous to be confirmed.*

The Form of Solemnization
of Matrimony.

¶ *First, the banns of all who are to be married together must be published in the church three different Sundays, during the time of morning service, or of evening service (if there is no morning service), immediately after the second lesson, the pastor saying after the accustomed manner,* I publish the banns of marriage between N. of — and N. of —. If any of you know cause or just impediment, why these two persons should not be joined together in holy matrimony, ye are to declare it. This is the first *(or* second *or* third*)* time of asking.

¶ *And if the persons that are to be married dwell in divers parishes, the banns must be asked in both parishes, and the pastor of the one parish shall not solemnize matrimony between them without a certificate of the banns being thrice asked from the pastor of the other parish.*

¶ *At the day and time appointed for solemnization of matrimony, the persons to be married shall come into the body of the church with their friends and neighbours, and there standing together, the man on the right hand and the woman on the left, the priest shall say,*

DEARLY beloved, we are gathered together here in the sight of God, and in the face of this congregation, to join together this man and this woman in holy matrimony, which is an honourable estate, instituted by God in the time of man's innocency, signifying unto us the mystical union that is between Christ and his church, which holy estate Christ adorned and beautified with his presence and first miracle that he wrought in Cana of Galilee, and is commended of Saint Paul to be honourable among all men, and therefore is not by any to be enterprised, nor taken in hand, unadvisedly, lightly, or wantonly, to satisfy men's carnal lusts and appetites, like brute beasts that have no understanding, but reverently, discreetly, advisedly, soberly, and in the fear of God, duly considering the causes for which matrimony was ordained.

First, it was ordained for the procreation of children, to be brought up in the fear and nurture of the Lord, and to the praise of his holy name.

Secondly, it was ordained for a remedy against sin, and to avoid fornication, that those persons who have not the gift of continency might marry, and keep themselves undefiled members of Christ's body.

Thirdly, it was ordained for the mutual society, help, and comfort, that the one ought to have of the other, both in prosperity and adversity.

Into which holy estate these two persons present come now to be joined. Therefore if any man can show any just cause, why they may not lawfully be joined together, let him now speak, or else hereafter for ever hold his peace.

¶ *And also, speaking unto the persons that shall be married, he shall say,*

I REQUIRE and charge you both, as ye will answer at the dreadful day of judgement, when the secrets of all hearts shall be disclosed, that if either of you know any impediment, why ye may not be lawfully joined together in matrimony, ye do now confess it. For be ye well assured, that as many as are coupled together otherwise than God's word doth allow are not joined together by God, neither is their matrimony lawful.

¶ *At which day of marriage, if any man alleges and declares any impediment why they may not be coupled together in matrimony – by God's law or the laws of the land – and will with sufficient sureties be bound to the parties, or else put in security to prove his allegation (to the full value of such charges as the persons to be married thereby sustain), then the solemnization must be deferred until such time as the truth is tried.*

¶ *If no impediment is alleged, then shall the pastor say unto the man,*

N. WILT thou have this woman to thy wedded wife, to live together after God's ordinance in the holy estate of matrimony? Wilt thou love her, comfort her, honour, and keep her, in sickness and in health; and, forsaking all others, keep thee only unto her, so long as ye both shall live?

¶ *The man shall answer,*
I will.

¶ *Then shall the priest say unto the woman,*

N. WILT thou have this man to thy wedded husband, to live together after God's ordinance in the holy estate of matrimony? Wilt thou obey him, and serve him, love, honour, and keep him, in sickness and in health; and, forsaking all others, keep thee only unto him, so long as ye both shall live?

¶ The woman shall answer,
I will.

¶ Then shall the minister say,
Who giveth this woman to be married to this man?

¶ Then shall they give their troth to each other in this manner. The minister, receiving the woman at her father's or friend's hands, shall cause the man with his right hand to take the woman by her right hand, and to say after him as followeth.

I N., TAKE thee, *N.*, to my wedded wife, to have and to hold from this day forward, for better for worse, for richer for poorer, in sickness and in health, to love and to cherish, till death us do part, according to God's holy ordinance, and thereto I plight thee my troth.

¶ Then shall they loose their hands, and the woman, with her right hand taking the man by his right hand, shall likewise say after the minister,

I N., TAKE thee, *N.*, to my wedded husband, to have and to hold from this day forward, for better for worse, for richer for poorer, in sickness and in health, to love, cherish, and to obey, till death us do part, according to God's holy ordinance, and thereto I give thee my troth.

THE SOLEMNIZATION OF MATRIMONY

¶ *Then shall they again loose their hands, and the man shall give unto the woman a ring, laying the same upon the book with the accustomed duty to the priest and clerk. And the priest, taking the ring, shall deliver it unto the man to put it upon the fourth finger of the woman's left hand. And the man holding the ring there, and taught by the priest, shall say,*

WITH this ring, I thee wed; with my body, I thee worship; and with all my worldly goods, I thee endow; in the name of the Father, and of the Son, and of the Holy Ghost. Amen.

¶ *Then the man leaving the ring upon the fourth finger of the woman's left hand, they shall both kneel down, and the minister shall say,*

Let us pray.

O ETERNAL God, creator and preserver of all mankind, giver of all spiritual grace, the author of everlasting life: Send thy blessing upon these thy servants, this man and this woman, whom we bless in thy name, that as Isaac and Rebecca lived faithfully together, so these persons may surely perform and keep the vow and covenant between them made – whereof this ring given and received is a token and pledge – and may ever remain in perfect love and peace together, and live according to thy laws, through Jesus Christ our Lord. *Amen.*

THE SOLEMNIZATION OF MATRIMONY

¶ *Then shall the priest join their right hands together and say,*

THOSE whom God hath joined together let no man put asunder.

¶ *Then shall the minister speak unto the people.*

FORASMUCH as *N.* and *N.* have consented together in holy wedlock, and have witnessed the same before God and this company, and thereto have given and pledged their troth, each to the other, and have declared the same by giving and receiving of a ring and by joining of hands, I pronounce that they are man and wife together, in the name of the Father, and of the Son, and of the Holy Ghost. Amen.

¶ *And the minister shall add this blessing.*

GOD the Father, God the Son, God the Holy Ghost, bless, preserve, and keep you; the Lord mercifully with his favour look upon you, and so fill you with all spiritual benediction and grace, that ye may so live together in this life, that in the world to come ye may have life everlasting. *Amen.*

¶ *Then the minister or clerks, going to the Lord's table, shall say or sing this psalm following.*

Beati omnes. Psalm 128.

BLESSED are all they that fear the LORD * and walk in his ways.

For thou shalt eat the labour of thine hands; * O well is thee and happy shalt thou be.

Thy wife shall be as the fruitful vine * upon the walls of thy house,

Thy children like the olive branches * round about thy table.

Lo, thus shall the man be blessed * that feareth the LORD.

The LORD from out of Sion shall so bless thee * that thou shalt see Jerusalem in prosperity all thy life long,

Yea, that thou shalt see thy children's children * and peace upon Israel.

Glory be to the Father, and to the Son, * and to the Holy Ghost;

As it was in the beginning, is now, and ever shall be, * world without end. Amen.

¶ *Or this psalm.*
Deus misereatur. Psalm 67.

GOD be merciful unto us and bless us, * and show us the light of his countenance and be merciful unto us,

That thy way may be known upon earth, * thy saving health among all nations.

Let the peoples praise thee, O God; * yea, let all the peoples praise thee.

O let the nations rejoice and be glad, * for thou shalt judge the folk righteously, and govern the nations upon earth.

Let the peoples praise thee, O God; * yea, let all the peoples praise thee.

Then shall the earth bring forth her increase, * and God, even our own God, shall give us his blessing.

God shall bless us, * and all the ends of the world shall fear him.

Glory be to the Father, and to the Son, * and to the Holy Ghost;

As it was in the beginning, is now, and ever shall be, * world without end. Amen.

¶ *The psalm ended, and the man and the woman kneeling before the Lord's table, the priest, standing at the table and turning his face towards them, shall say,*
Lord, have mercy upon us.
Answer. Christ, have mercy upon us.
Minister. Lord, have mercy upon us.

OUR Father, who art in heaven, Hallowed be thy name. Thy kingdom come. Thy will be done, On earth as it is in heaven. Give us this day our daily bread. And forgive us our trespasses, As we forgive those who trespass against us. And lead us not into temptation, But deliver us from evil. Amen.

Minister. O Lord, save thy servant and thy handmaid,
Answer. Who put their trust in thee.
Minister. O Lord, send them help from thy holy place,
Answer. And evermore defend them.
Minister. Be unto them a tower of strength,
Answer. From the face of their enemy.
Minister. O Lord, hear our prayer,
Answer. And let our cry come unto thee.

¶ *Minister.*

O GOD of Abraham, God of Isaac, God of Jacob: Bless these thy servants, and sow the seed of eternal life in their hearts, that whatsoever in thy holy word they shall profitably learn, they may in deed fulfil the same. Look, O Lord, mercifully upon them from heaven, and bless them. And as thou didst send thy blessing upon Abraham and Sarah, to their great comfort, so vouchsafe to send thy blessing upon these thy servants, that they, obeying thy will, and alway being in safety under thy protection, may abide in thy love unto their lives' end, through Jesus Christ our Lord. *Amen.*

¶ *This prayer next following shall be omitted where the woman is past childbearing.*

O MERCIFUL Lord and heavenly Father, by whose gracious gift mankind is increased: We beseech thee, assist with thy blessing these two persons, that they may both be fruitful in procreation of children, and also live together so long in godly love and honesty, that they may see their children Christianly and virtuously brought up, to thy praise and honour, through Jesus Christ our Lord. *Amen.*

O GOD, who by thy mighty power hast made all things of nothing, who also (after other things were set in order) didst appoint that out of man – created after thine own image and similitude – woman should take her beginning, and, knitting them together, didst teach that it should never be lawful to put asunder those whom thou by matrimony hadst made one; O God, who hast consecrated the state of matrimony to such an excellent mystery, that in it is signified and represented the spiritual marriage and unity between Christ and his church: Look mercifully upon these thy servants, that both this man may love his wife, according to thy word – as Christ did love his spouse the church, who gave himself for it, loving and cherishing it even as his own flesh – and also that this woman may be loving and amiable, faithful and obedient to her husband, and in all quietness, sobriety, and peace be a follower of holy and godly matrons. O Lord, bless them both, and grant them to inherit thy everlasting kingdom, through Jesus Christ our Lord. *Amen.*

¶ *Then shall the priest say,*

ALMIGHTY God, who at the beginning did create our first parents, Adam and Eve, and did sanctify and join them together in marriage, pour upon you the riches of his grace, sanctify and bless you, that ye may please him both in body and soul, and live together in holy love unto your lives' end. *Amen.*

¶ *After which, if there is no sermon declaring the duties of man and wife, the minister shall read as followeth.*

ALL ye that are married, or that intend to take the holy estate of matrimony upon you, hear what the holy Scripture doth say as touching the duty of husbands towards their wives, and wives towards their husbands.

THE SOLEMNIZATION OF MATRIMONY

Saint Paul, in his Epistle to the Ephesians, the fifth chapter, doth give this commandment to all married men: 'Husbands, love your wives, even as Christ also loved the church, and gave himself for it, that he might sanctify and cleanse it with the washing of water by the word; that he might present it to himself a glorious church, not having spot, or wrinkle, or any such thing, but that it should be holy and without blemish. So ought men to love their wives as their own bodies. He that loveth his wife loveth himself, for no man ever yet hated his own flesh, but nourisheth and cherisheth it, even as the Lord the church. For we are members of his body, of his flesh and of his bones. For this cause shall a man leave his father and mother, and shall be joined unto his wife, and they two shall be one flesh. This is a great mystery, but I speak concerning Christ and the church. Nevertheless, let every one of you in particular so love his wife, even as himself.'

Likewise the same Saint Paul, writing to the Colossians, speaketh thus to all men that are married: 'Husbands, love your wives, and be not bitter against them.'

Hear also what Saint Peter, the apostle of Christ, who was himself a married man, saith unto those who are married: 'Ye husbands, dwell with your wives according to knowledge, giving honour unto the wife, as unto the weaker vessel, and as being heirs together of the grace of life, that your prayers be not hindered.'

Hitherto ye have heard the duty of the husband toward the wife. Now likewise, ye wives, hear and learn your duties toward your husbands, even as it is plainly set forth in holy Scripture.

Saint Paul, in the aforenamed Epistle to the Ephesians, teacheth you thus: 'Wives, submit yourselves unto your own husbands, as unto the Lord. For the husband is the head of the wife, even as Christ is the head of the church, and he is the saviour of the body. Therefore as the church is subject unto Christ, so let the wives be to their own husbands in everything.' And again he saith: 'Let the wife see that she reverence her husband.'

And in his Epistle to the Colossians, Saint Paul giveth you this short lesson: 'Wives, submit yourselves unto your own husbands, as it is fit in the Lord.'

Saint Peter also doth instruct you very well, thus saying: 'Ye wives, be in subjection to your own husbands, that, if any obey not the word, they also may without the word be won by the conversation of the wives, while they behold your chaste conversation coupled with fear. Whose adorning, let it not be that outward adorning of plaiting the hair, and of wearing of gold, or of putting on of apparel, but let it be the hidden man of the heart, in that which is not corruptible, even the ornament of a meek and quiet spirit, which is in the sight of God of great price. For after this manner in the old time the holy women also, who trusted in God, adorned themselves, being in subjection unto their own husbands, even as Sarah obeyed Abraham, calling him lord, whose daughters ye are as long as ye do well, and are not afraid with any amazement.'

¶ *It is convenient that the newly married persons should receive the holy communion at the time of their marriage, or at the first opportunity after their marriage.*

The Order for the Visitation of the Sick.

¶ *When any person is sick, notice shall be given to the minister of the parish, who coming into the sick person's house shall say,*

Peace be to this house, and to all who dwell in it.

¶ *When he cometh into the sick man's presence he shall say, kneeling down,*

Remember not, Lord, our iniquities, nor the iniquities of our forefathers. Spare us, good Lord; spare thy people, whom thou hast redeemed with thy most precious blood, and be not angry with us for ever.

Answer. Spare us, good Lord.

¶ *Then the minister shall say,*
Let us pray.

Lord, have mercy upon us.
Christ, have mercy upon us.
Lord, have mercy upon us.

Our Father, who art in heaven, Hallowed be thy name. Thy kingdom come. Thy will be done, On earth as it is in heaven. Give us this day our daily bread. And forgive us our trespasses, As we forgive those who trespass against us. And lead us not into temptation, But deliver us from evil. Amen.

THE VISITATION OF THE SICK

Minister. O Lord, save thy servant,
Answer. Who putteth *his* trust in thee.
Minister. Send *him* help from thy holy place,
Answer. And evermore mightily defend *him.*
Minister. Let the enemy have no advantage of *him,*
Answer. Nor the wicked approach to hurt *him.*
Minister. Be unto *him,* O Lord, a strong tower,
Answer. From the face of *his* enemy.
Minister. O Lord, hear our prayers,
Answer. And let our cry come unto thee.

¶ *Minister.*

O LORD, look down from heaven, behold, visit, and relieve this thy servant. Look upon *him* with the eyes of thy mercy, give *him* comfort and sure confidence in thee, defend *him* from the danger of the enemy, and keep *him* in perpetual peace and safety, through Jesus Christ our Lord. *Amen.*

H EAR us, almighty and most merciful God and Saviour. Extend thy accustomed goodness to this thy servant, who is grieved with sickness. Sanctify, we beseech thee, this thy fatherly correction to *him,* that the sense of *his* weakness may add strength to *his* faith, and seriousness to *his* repentance, that, if it shall be thy good pleasure to restore *him* to *his* former health, *he* may lead the rest of *his* life in thy fear and to thy glory; or else give *him* grace so to take thy visitation, that, after this painful life is ended, *he* may dwell with thee in life everlasting, through Jesus Christ our Lord. *Amen.*

¶ *Then shall the minister exhort the sick person after this form (or another like it).*

DEARLY beloved, know this, that almighty God is the Lord of life and death, and of all things pertaining to them, such as youth, strength, health, age, weakness, and sickness. Wherefore, whatsoever your sickness is, know you certainly that it is God's visitation. And for whatsoever cause this sickness is sent unto you – whether it be to try your patience, for the example of others, and that your faith may be found in the day of the Lord laudable, glorious, and honourable, to the increase of glory and endless felicity; or else it be sent unto you to correct and amend in you whatsoever doth offend the eyes of your heavenly Father – know you certainly that if you truly repent you of your sins, and bear your sickness patiently, trusting in God's mercy for his dear Son Jesus Christ's sake, and render unto him humble thanks for his fatherly visitation, submitting yourself wholly unto his will, it shall turn to your profit, and help you forward in the right way that leadeth unto everlasting life.

¶ *If the person visited is very sick, then the pastor may end his exhortation in this place, or else proceed.*

TAKE therefore in good part the chastisement of the Lord. 'For' (as it is written in the twelfth chapter of the Epistle to the Hebrews) 'whom the Lord loveth he chasteneth, and scourgeth every son whom he receiveth. If ye endure chastening, God dealeth with you as with sons, for what son is he whom the father chasteneth not? But if ye be without chastisement, whereof all are partakers, then are ye bastards and not sons. Furthermore, we have had fathers of our flesh, which corrected us, and we gave them reverence. Shall we not much rather be in subjection unto the Father of spirits, and live? For they verily for a few days chastened us as seemed good to them, but he for our profit, that we might be partakers of his holiness.'

These words, good *brother*, are written in holy Scripture for our comfort and instruction, that we should patiently, and with thanksgiving, bear our heavenly Father's correction, whensoever by any manner of adversity it shall please his gracious goodness to visit us. And there should be no greater comfort to Christian persons than to be made like unto Christ, by suffering patiently adversities, troubles, and sicknesses. For he himself went not up to joy, but first he suffered pain; he entered not into his glory before he was crucified. So truly our way to eternal joy is to suffer here with Christ, and our door to enter into eternal life is gladly to die with Christ, that we may rise again from death and dwell with him in everlasting life.

Now therefore, taking your sickness – which is thus profitable for you – patiently, I exhort you in the name of God, to remember the profession which you made unto God in your baptism. And forasmuch as after this life there is an account to be given unto the righteous judge, by whom all must be judged without respect of persons, I require you to examine yourself and your estate, both toward God and man, so that, accusing and condemning yourself for your own faults, you may find mercy at our heavenly Father's hand for Christ's sake, and not be accused and condemned in that fearful judgement.

Therefore I shall rehearse to you the articles of our faith, that you may know whether you do believe as a Christian man should, or no.

¶ *Here the minister shall rehearse the articles of the faith, saying thus,*

Dost thou believe in God the Father almighty, maker of heaven and earth? And in Jesus Christ, his only-begotten Son our Lord? And that he was conceived by the Holy Ghost, born of the Virgin Mary; that he suffered under Pontius Pilate, was crucified, dead, and buried; that he went down into hell, and also did rise again the third day; that he ascended into heaven, and sitteth on the right hand of God the Father almighty; and from thence shall come again, at the end of the world, to judge the quick and the dead? And dost thou believe in the Holy Ghost, the holy catholic church, the communion of saints, the remission of sins, the resurrection of the flesh, and everlasting life after death?

¶ *The sick person shall answer,*
All this I steadfastly believe.

¶ *Then shall the minister examine whether he repents him truly of his sins and is in charity with all the world, exhorting him to forgive from the bottom of his heart all persons who have offended him, and if he hath offended any other to ask them forgiveness, and where he hath done injury or wrong to any man that he make amends to the uttermost of his power. And if he hath not before disposed of his goods, let him then be admonished to make his will and to declare his debts (what he oweth and what is owing unto him), for the better discharging of his conscience and the quietness of his executors. But men should often be put in remembrance to take order for the settling of their temporal estates whilst they are in health.*

¶ *These words before rehearsed may be said before the minister begins his prayer, as he shall see cause.*

¶ *The minister should not omit earnestly to move such sick persons as are of ability to be liberal to the poor.*

¶ *Here shall the sick person be moved to make a special confession of his sins, if he feel his conscience troubled with any weighty matter. After which confession, the priest shall absolve him – if he humbly and heartily desire it – after this sort.*

OUR Lord Jesus Christ, who hath left power to his church to absolve all sinners who truly repent and believe in him, of his great mercy forgive thee thine offences; and, by his authority committed to me, I absolve thee from all thy sins in the name of the Father, and of the Son, and of the Holy Ghost. Amen.

¶ *And then the priest shall say the collect following.*
Let us pray.

O MOST merciful God, who, according to the multitude of thy mercies, dost so put away the sins of those who truly repent, that thou rememberest them no more: Open thine eye of mercy upon this thy servant, who most earnestly desireth pardon and forgiveness. Renew in *him*, most loving Father, whatsoever hath been decayed by the fraud and malice of the devil, or by *his* own carnal will and frailness; preserve and continue this sick member in the unity of the church; consider *his* contrition; accept *his* tears; assuage *his* pain, as shall seem to thee most expedient for *him*. And forasmuch as *he* putteth *his* full trust only in thy mercy, impute not unto *him his* former sins, but strengthen *him* with thy blessed Spirit, and, when thou art pleased to take *him* hence, take *him* unto thy favour, through the merits of thy most dearly beloved Son, Jesus Christ our Lord. *Amen.*

¶ *Then shall the minister say this psalm.*
In te, Domine, speravi. Psalm 71.

I N thee, O LORD, have I put my trust; let me never be put to confusion; * but rid me and deliver me in thy righteousness; incline thine ear unto me and save me.

Be thou my stronghold, whereunto I may alway resort; * thou hast promised to help me, for thou art my house of defence and my castle.

Deliver me, O my God, out of the hand of the ungodly, * out of the hand of the unrighteous and cruel man.

For thou, O Lord GOD, art the thing that I long for; * thou art my hope even from my youth.

Through thee have I been holden up ever since I was born; * thou art he that took me out of my mother's womb; my praise shall alway be of thee.

I am become as it were a monster unto many, * but my sure trust is in thee.

O let my mouth be filled with thy praise, * that I may sing of thy glory and honour all the day long.

Cast me not away in the time of age; * forsake me not when my strength faileth me.

For mine enemies speak against me, and they that lay wait for my soul take their counsel together, saying, * 'God hath forsaken him; persecute him and take him, for there is none to deliver him.'

Go not far from me, O God; * my God, haste thee to help me.

Let them be confounded and perish that are against my soul; * let them be covered with shame and dishonour that seek to do me evil.

As for me, I will patiently abide alway, * and will praise thee more and more.

My mouth shall daily speak of thy righteousness and salvation, * for I know no end thereof.

I will go forth in the strength of the Lord GOD, * and will make mention of thy righteousness only.

Thou, O God, hast taught me from my youth up until now; * therefore will I tell of thy wondrous works.

Forsake me not, O God, in mine old age when I am gray-headed, * until I have showed thy strength unto this generation, and thy power to all them that are yet for to come.

Thy righteousness, O God, is very high, and great things are they that thou hast done; * O God, who is like unto thee?

Glory be to the Father, and to the Son, * and to the Holy Ghost;

As it was in the beginning, is now, and ever shall be, * world without end. Amen.

¶ *Adding this.*

O SAVIOUR of the world, who by thy cross and precious blood hast redeemed us: Save us and help us, we humbly beseech thee, O Lord.

¶ *Then shall the minister say,*

THE almighty Lord, who is a most strong tower to all those who put their trust in him, to whom all things in heaven, in earth, and under the earth do bow and obey, be now and evermore thy defence; and make thee know and feel, that there is none other name under heaven given to man, in whom and through whom, thou mayest receive health and salvation, but only the name of our Lord Jesus Christ. Amen.

¶ *And after that shall say,*

UNTO God's gracious mercy and protection we commit thee. The Lord bless thee, and keep thee. The Lord make his face to shine upon thee, and be gracious unto thee. The Lord lift up his countenance upon thee, and give thee peace, both now and evermore. *Amen.*

———————

A Prayer for a Sick Child.

O ALMIGHTY God and merciful Father, to whom alone belong the issues of life and death: Look down from heaven, we humbly beseech thee, with the eyes of mercy upon this child now lying upon the bed of sickness. Visit *him*, O Lord, with thy salvation; deliver *him* in thy good appointed time from *his* bodily pain, and save *his* soul for thy mercies' sake, that, if it shall be thy pleasure to prolong *his* days here on earth, *he* may live to thee, and be an instrument of thy glory, by serving thee faithfully and doing good in *his* generation; or else receive *him* into those heavenly habitations, where the souls of those who sleep in the Lord Jesus enjoy perpetual rest and felicity. Grant this, O Lord, for thy mercies' sake, in the same thy Son our Lord Jesus Christ, who liveth and reigneth with thee and the Holy Ghost, ever one God, world without end. *Amen.*

A Prayer for a Sick Person, When There Appeareth Small Hope of Recovery.

O FATHER of mercies, and God of all comfort, our only help in time of need: We fly unto thee for succour in behalf of this thy servant, here lying under thy hand in great weakness of body. Look graciously upon *him*, O Lord, and the more the outward man decayeth, strengthen *him*, we beseech thee, so much the more continually with thy grace and Holy Spirit in the inner man. Give *him* unfeigned repentance for all the errors of *his* life past, and steadfast faith in thy Son Jesus, that *his* sins may be done away by thy mercy, and *his* pardon sealed in heaven, before *he* go hence and be no more seen. We know, O Lord, that there is no word impossible with thee, and that, if thou wilt, thou canst even yet raise *him* up, and grant *him* a longer continuance amongst us. Yet, forasmuch as in all appearance the time of *his* dissolution draweth near, so fit and prepare *him*, we beseech thee, against the hour of death, that after *his* departure hence in peace and in thy favour, *his* soul may be received into thine everlasting kingdom, through the merits and mediation of Jesus Christ, thine only Son, our Lord and Saviour. *Amen.*

A Commendatory Prayer for a Sick Person at the Point of Departure.

O ALMIGHTY God, with whom do live the spirits of just men made perfect, after they are delivered from their earthly prisons: We humbly commend the soul of this thy servant, our dear *brother,* into thy hands, as into the hands of a faithful creator and most merciful saviour, most humbly beseeching thee that it may be precious in thy sight. Wash it, we pray thee, in the blood of that immaculate Lamb that was slain to take away the sins of the world, that whatsoever defilements it may have contracted in the midst of this miserable and wicked world, through the lusts of the flesh or the wiles of Satan, being purged and done away, it may be presented pure and without spot before thee. And teach us who survive, in this and other like daily spectacles of mortality, to see how frail and uncertain our own condition is, and so to number our days, that we may seriously apply our hearts to that holy and heavenly wisdom, whilst we live here, which may in the end bring us to life everlasting, through the merits of Jesus Christ, thine only Son our Lord. *Amen.*

THE VISITATION OF THE SICK

*A Prayer for Persons Troubled
in Mind or in Conscience.*

O BLESSED Lord, the Father of mercies, and the God of all comforts: We beseech thee, look down in pity and compassion upon this thy afflicted servant. Thou writest bitter things against *him,* and puttest *him* in mind of *his* former iniquities; thy wrath lieth hard upon *him,* and *his* soul is full of trouble. But, O merciful God – who hast written thy holy word for our learning, that we, through patience and comfort of thy holy Scriptures, might have hope – give *him* a right understanding of *himself,* and of thy threats and promises, that *he* may neither cast away *his* confidence in thee, nor place it anywhere but in thee. Give *him* strength against all *his* temptations, and heal all *his* distempers. Break not the bruised reed, nor quench the smoking flax. Shut not up thy tender mercies in displeasure, but make *him* to hear of joy and gladness, that the bones which thou hast broken may rejoice. Deliver *him* from fear of the enemy, and lift up the light of thy countenance upon *him,* and give *him* peace, through the merits and mediation of Jesus Christ our Lord. *Amen.*

The Communion of the Sick.

¶ *Forasmuch as all mortal men are subject to many sudden perils, diseases, and sicknesses, and ever uncertain what time they shall depart out of this life, therefore to the intent they may be always in a readiness to die whenever it shall please almighty God to call them, the pastors shall diligently from time to time (but especially in the time of pestilence or other infectious sickness) exhort their parishioners to often receive the holy communion of the body and blood of our Saviour Christ when it shall be publicly administered in the church, that so doing they may in case of sudden visitation have the less cause to be disquieted for lack of the same. But if the sick person is not able to come to the church, and yet is desirous to receive the communion in his house, then he must give timely notice to the pastor, signifying also how many there are to communicate with him (which shall be three, or two at the least). And having a convenient place in the sick man's house, with all things necessary so prepared that the pastor may reverently minister, he shall there celebrate the holy communion, beginning with the collect, epistle, and gospel here following.*

The Collect.

A LMIGHTY everliving God, maker of mankind, who dost correct those whom thou dost love, and chastise everyone whom thou dost receive: We beseech thee to have mercy upon this thy servant, visited with thy hand, and to grant that *he* may take *his* sickness patiently, and recover *his* bodily health – if it be thy gracious will – and whensoever *his* soul shall depart from the body, it may be without spot presented unto thee, through Jesus Christ our Lord. *Amen.*

The Epistle. Hebrews 12:5-6.

MY son, despise not thou the chastening of the Lord, nor faint when thou art rebuked of him. For whom the Lord loveth he chasteneth, and scourgeth every son whom he receiveth.

The Gospel. St. John 5:24.

VERILY, verily I say unto you, he that heareth my word, and believeth on him that sent me, hath everlasting life, and shall not come into condemnation, but is passed from death unto life.

¶ *After which, the priest shall proceed according to the form before prescribed for the holy communion, beginning at these words:* Ye who do truly, *&c. (p. 257).*

¶ *At the time of the distribution of the holy sacrament, the priest shall first receive the communion himself, and afterward minister unto those who are appointed to communicate with the sick, and last of all to the sick person.*

¶ *But if a man, either by reason of extremity of sickness, or for want of warning in due time to the pastor, or for lack of company to receive with him, or by any other just impediment, does not receive the sacrament of Christ's body and blood, the pastor shall instruct him that if he truly repents him of his sins, and steadfastly believes that Jesus Christ hath suffered death upon the cross for him and shed his blood for his redemption, earnestly remembering the benefits he hath thereby and giving him hearty thanks for the same, he doth eat and drink the body and blood of our Saviour Christ profitably to his soul's health, although he does not receive the sacrament with his mouth.*

¶ *When the sick person is visited and receiveth the holy communion all at one time, then the priest for more expedition shall cut off the Form of the Visitation at the psalm* In thee, O LORD, have I put my trust, *&c. (p. 330) and go straight to the Communion.*

¶ *In the time of the plague or such other like contagious times of sickness or diseases, when none of the parish or neighbours can be gotten to communicate with the sick in their houses, for fear of the infection, upon special request of the diseased the minister may communicate with him alone.*

The Order for the Burial of the Dead.

¶ *Here is to be noted that the office ensuing is not to be used for any who die unbaptized, or excommunicate, or have laid violent hands upon themselves.*

¶ *The priest and clerks, meeting the corpse at the entrance of the churchyard and going before it (either into the church or towards the grave), shall say or sing:*

'I AM the resurrection and the life', saith the Lord. 'He that believeth in me, though he were dead, yet shall he live. And whosoever liveth and believeth in me, shall never die.' *St. John 11:25-26.*

I KNOW that my Redeemer liveth, and that he shall stand at the latter day upon the earth. And though after my skin, worms destroy this body, yet in my flesh shall I see God; whom I shall see for myself, and mine eyes shall behold, and not another. *Job 19:25-27.*

WE brought nothing into this world, and it is certain we can carry nothing out. The LORD gave, and the LORD hath taken away; blessed be the name of the LORD. *1 Timothy 6:7; Job 1:21.*

¶ *After they have come into the church shall be read one or both of these psalms following.*

Dixi, Custodiam. Psalm 39.

I SAID, 'I will take heed to my ways, * that I offend not in my tongue;

I will keep my mouth as it were with a bridle, * while the ungodly is in my sight.'

I held my tongue and spake nothing; * I kept silence – yea, even from good words – but it was pain and grief to me.

My heart was hot within me, and while I was thus musing the fire kindled, * and at the last I spake with my tongue:

'LORD, let me know mine end and the number of my days, * that I may be certified how long I have to live.

Behold, thou hast made my days as it were a span long, * and mine age is even as nothing in respect of thee, and verily every man living is altogether vanity.

For man walketh in a vain shadow and disquieteth himself in vain; * he heapeth up riches and cannot tell who shall gather them.

And now, Lord, what is my hope? * truly my hope is even in thee.

Deliver me from all mine offences, * and make me not a rebuke unto the foolish.

I became dumb and opened not my mouth, * for it was thy doing.

Take thy plague away from me; * I am even consumed by means of thy heavy hand.

When thou with rebukes dost chasten man for sin, thou makest his beauty to consume away, like as it were a moth fretting a garment; * every man therefore is but vanity.

Hear my prayer, O LORD, and with thine ears consider my calling; * hold not thy peace at my tears.

For I am a stranger with thee, * and a sojourner as all my fathers were.

O spare me a little, that I may recover my strength, * before I go hence and be no more seen.'

Glory be to the Father, and to the Son, * and to the Holy Ghost;

As it was in the beginning, is now, and ever shall be, * world without end. Amen.

Domine, refugium. Psalm 90.

L ORD, thou hast been our refuge * from one generation to another.

Before the mountains were brought forth, or ever the earth and the world were made, * thou art God from everlasting, and world without end.

Thou turnest man to destruction; * again thou sayest, 'Come again, ye children of men.'

For a thousand years in thy sight are but as yesterday, * seeing it is past as a watch in the night.

As soon as thou scatterest them, they are even as a sleep, * and fade away suddenly like the grass.

In the morning it is green and groweth up, * but in the evening it is cut down, dried up, and withered.

For we consume away in thy displeasure, * and are afraid at thy wrathful indignation.

Thou hast set our misdeeds before thee, * and our secret sins in the light of thy countenance.

For when thou art angry, all our days are gone; * we bring our years to an end, as it were a tale that is told.

The days of our age are threescore years and ten, and though men be so strong that they come to fourscore years, * yet is their strength then but labour and sorrow, so soon passeth it away, and we are gone.

But who regardeth the power of thy wrath? * for even thereafter as a man feareth, so is thy displeasure.

O teach us to number our days, * that we may apply our hearts unto wisdom.

Turn thee again, O Lord, at the last, * and be gracious unto thy servants.

O satisfy us with thy mercy, and that soon; * so shall we rejoice and be glad all the days of our life.

Comfort us again now after the time that thou hast plagued us, * and for the years wherein we have suffered adversity.

Show thy servants thy work, * and their children thy glory.

And the glorious majesty of the Lord our God be upon us: * prosper thou the work of our hands upon us; O prosper thou our handiwork.

Glory be to the Father, and to the Son, * and to the Holy Ghost;

As it was in the beginning, is now, and ever shall be, * world without end. Amen.

¶ *Then shall follow the lesson taken out of the fifteenth chapter of the First Epistle of Saint Paul to the Corinthians.*
1 Corinthians 15:20-58.

Now is Christ risen from the dead, and become the first fruits of them that slept.

For since by man came death, by man came also the resurrection of the dead. For as in Adam all die, even so in Christ shall all be made alive. But every man in his own order: Christ the first fruits, afterward they that are Christ's at his coming. Then cometh the end, when he shall have delivered up the kingdom to God, even the Father, when he shall have put down all rule and all authority and power. For he must reign till he hath put all enemies under his feet. The last enemy that shall be destroyed is death. For he hath put all things under his feet. But when he saith 'all things are put under him', it is manifest that he is excepted which did put all things under him. And when all things shall be subdued unto him, then shall the Son also himself be subject unto him that put all things under him, that God may be all in all.

Else what shall they do which are baptized for the dead, if the dead rise not at all? why are they then baptized for the dead? And why stand we in jeopardy every hour? I protest by your rejoicing which I have in Christ Jesus our Lord: I die daily. If after the manner of men I have fought with beasts at Ephesus, what advantageth it me, if the dead rise not? let us eat and drink, for tomorrow we die. Be not deceived: evil communications corrupt good manners. Awake to righteousness, and sin not, for some have not the knowledge of God – I speak this to your shame.

But some man will say, 'How are the dead raised up? and with what body do they come?' Thou fool, that which thou sowest is not quickened, except it die. And that which thou sowest, thou sowest not that body that shall be, but bare grain (it may chance of wheat, or of some other grain); but God giveth it a body as it hath pleased him, and to every seed his own body.

All flesh is not the same flesh, but there is one kind of flesh of men, another flesh of beasts, another of fishes, and another of birds. There are also celestial bodies, and bodies terrestrial; but the glory of the celestial is one, and the glory of the terrestrial is another. There is one glory of the sun, and another glory of the moon, and another glory of the stars, for one star differeth from another star in glory.

So also is the resurrection of the dead. It is sown in corruption; it is raised in incorruption. It is sown in dishonour; it is raised in glory. It is sown in weakness; it is raised in power. It is sown a natural body; it is raised a spiritual body. There is a natural body, and there is a spiritual body. And so it is written, 'The first man Adam was made a living soul'; the last Adam was made a quickening spirit. Howbeit that was not first which is spiritual, but that which is natural, and afterward that which is spiritual.

The first man is of the earth, earthy; the second man is the Lord from heaven. As is the earthy, such are they that are earthy; and as is the heavenly, such are they also that are heavenly. And as we have borne the image of the earthy, we shall also bear the image of the heavenly.

Now this I say, brethren, that flesh and blood cannot inherit the kingdom of God, neither doth corruption inherit incorruption. Behold, I show you a mystery: we shall not all sleep, but we shall all be changed, in a moment, in the twinkling of an eye, at the last trump, for the trumpet shall sound, and the dead shall be raised incorruptible, and we shall be changed. For this corruptible must put on incorruption, and this mortal must put on immortality. So when this corruptible shall have put on incorruption, and this mortal shall have put on immortality, then shall be brought to pass the saying that is written, 'Death is swallowed up in victory.' O death, where is thy sting? O grave, where is thy victory? The sting of death is sin, and the strength of sin is the law.

But thanks be to God, which giveth us the victory through our Lord Jesus Christ. Therefore, my beloved brethren, be ye steadfast, immovable, always abounding in the work of the Lord, forasmuch as ye know that your labour is not in vain in the Lord.

¶ *When they come to the grave, while the corpse is made ready to be laid into the earth, the priest shall say, or the priest and clerks shall sing:*

MAN, that is born of a woman, hath but a short time to live, and is full of misery. He cometh up, and is cut down, like a flower; he fleeth as it were a shadow, and never continueth in one stay.

In the midst of life we are in death; of whom may we seek for succour, but of thee, O Lord, who for our sins art justly displeased?

Yet, O Lord God most holy, O Lord most mighty, O holy and most merciful Saviour, deliver us not into the bitter pains of eternal death.

Thou knowest, Lord, the secrets of our hearts. Shut not thy merciful ears to our prayer, but spare us, Lord most holy, O God most mighty, O holy and merciful Saviour, thou most worthy judge eternal. Suffer us not at our last hour, for any pains of death, to fall from thee.

¶ *Then, while the earth shall be cast upon the body by some standing by, the priest shall say,*

FORASMUCH as it hath pleased almighty God of his great mercy to take unto himself the soul of our dear *brother* here departed, we therefore commit *his* body to the ground, earth to earth, ashes to ashes, dust to dust, in sure and certain hope of the resurrection to eternal life, through our Lord Jesus Christ, who shall change our vile body, that it may be like unto his glorious body, according to the mighty working whereby he is able to subdue all things to himself.

¶ *Then shall be said or sung,*

I HEARD a voice from heaven, saying unto me, 'Write: From henceforth blessed are the dead which die in the Lord.' 'Even so', saith the Spirit, 'for they rest from their labours.'

¶ *Then the priest shall say,*
Lord, have mercy upon us.
Christ, have mercy upon us.
Lord, have mercy upon us.

OUR Father, who art in heaven, Hallowed be thy name. Thy kingdom come. Thy will be done, On earth as it is in heaven. Give us this day our daily bread. And forgive us our trespasses, As we forgive those who trespass against us. And lead us not into temptation, But deliver us from evil. Amen.

¶ *Priest.*

ALMIGHTY God, with whom do live the spirits of those who depart hence in the Lord, and with whom the souls of the faithful, after they are delivered from the burden of the flesh, are in joy and felicity: We give thee hearty thanks because it hath pleased thee to deliver this our *brother* out of the miseries of this sinful world, beseeching thee that it may please thee, of thy gracious goodness, shortly to accomplish the number of thine elect, and to hasten thy kingdom, that we, with all those who are departed in the true faith of thy holy name, may have our perfect consummation and bliss, both in body and soul, in thy eternal and everlasting glory, through Jesus Christ our Lord. *Amen.*

The Collect.

O MERCIFUL God, the Father of our Lord Jesus Christ, who is the resurrection and the life, in whom whosoever believeth shall live, though he die; and whosoever liveth, and believeth in him, shall not die eternally; who also hath taught us (by his holy apostle Saint Paul) not to be sorry, as men without hope, for those who sleep in him: We meekly beseech thee, O Father, to raise us from the death of sin unto the life of righteousness, that, when we shall depart this life, we may rest in him, as our hope is this our *brother* doth, and that, at the general resurrection in the last day, we may be found acceptable in thy sight, and receive that blessing which thy well-beloved Son shall then pronounce to all who love and fear thee, saying, 'Come, ye blessed children of my Father, receive the kingdom prepared for you from the beginning of the world.' Grant this, we beseech thee, O merciful Father, through Jesus Christ, our mediator and redeemer. *Amen.*

THE grace of our Lord Jesus Christ, and the love of God, and the fellowship of the Holy Ghost, be with us all evermore. *Amen.*

The Thanksgiving of Women after Childbirth, Commonly Called the Churching of Women.

¶ *The woman at the usual time after her delivery shall come into the church, and there shall kneel down in some convenient place, as hath been accustomed or as the ordinary shall direct. And then the priest shall say unto her,*

FORASMUCH as it hath pleased almighty God of his goodness to give you safe deliverance, and to preserve you in the great danger of childbirth, you shall therefore give hearty thanks unto God, and say,

¶ *Then shall the priest say the 116th Psalm.*
Dilexi quoniam.

I AM well pleased * that the LORD hath heard the voice of my prayer,

That he hath inclined his ear unto me; * therefore will I call upon him as long as I live.

The snares of death compassed me round about, * and the pains of hell gat hold upon me.

I found trouble and heaviness, and I called upon the name of the LORD: * 'O LORD, I beseech thee, deliver my soul.'

Gracious is the LORD and righteous; * yea, our God is merciful.

The LORD preserveth the simple; * I was in misery and he helped me.

Turn again then unto thy rest, O my soul, * for the LORD hath rewarded thee.

And why? thou hast delivered my soul from death, * mine eyes from tears, and my feet from falling.

I will walk before the LORD * in the land of the living.

I believed and therefore will I speak, but I was sore troubled; * I said in my haste, 'All men are liars.'

What reward shall I give unto the LORD * for all the benefits that he hath done unto me?

I will receive the cup of salvation, * and call upon the name of the LORD.

I will pay my vows now in the presence of all his people, * in the courts of the LORD's house, even in the midst of thee, O Jerusalem. Praise the LORD.

Glory be to the Father, and to the Son, * and to the Holy Ghost;

As it was in the beginning, is now, and ever shall be, * world without end. Amen.

¶ *Or Psalm 127.*
Nisi Dominus.

EXCEPT the LORD build the house, * their labour is but lost that build it.

Except the LORD keep the city, * the watchman waketh but in vain.

It is but lost labour that ye haste to rise up early, and so late take rest, and eat the bread of carefulness, * for so he giveth his beloved sleep.

Lo, children and the fruit of the womb * are an heritage and gift that cometh of the LORD.

Like as the arrows in the hand of the giant, * even so are the young children.

Happy is the man that hath his quiver full of them; * they shall not be ashamed when they speak with their enemies in the gate.

Glory be to the Father, and to the Son, * and to the Holy Ghost;

As it was in the beginning, is now, and ever shall be, * world without end. Amen.

¶ *Then shall the priest say,*
Let us pray.

Lord, have mercy upon us.
Christ, have mercy upon us.
Lord, have mercy upon us.

OUR Father, who art in heaven, Hallowed be thy name. Thy kingdom come. Thy will be done, On earth as it is in heaven. Give us this day our daily bread. And forgive us our trespasses, As we forgive those who trespass against us. And lead us not into temptation, But deliver us from evil. For thine is the kingdom, the power, and the glory, For ever and ever. Amen.

Minister. O Lord, save this woman thy servant,
Answer. Who putteth her trust in thee.

THE CHURCHING OF WOMEN

Minister. Be thou to her a strong tower,
Answer. From the face of her enemy.
Minister. Lord, hear our prayer,
Answer. And let our cry come unto thee.

¶ *Minister.*
Let us pray.

O ALMIGHTY God, we give thee humble thanks, that thou hast vouchsafed to deliver this woman thy servant from the great pain and peril of childbirth: Grant, we beseech thee, most merciful Father, that she through thy help may both faithfully live and walk according to thy will in this life present, and also may be a partaker of everlasting glory in the life to come, through Jesus Christ our Lord. *Amen.*

¶ *The woman who cometh to give her thanks must offer accustomed offerings; and if there is a communion, it is convenient that she receive the holy communion.*

A Commination

*or denouncing of God's anger and judgements
against sinners with certain prayers to be used
on the first day of Lent and at other times
as the ordinary shall appoint.*

¶ *After Morning Prayer, the Litany ended according to the
accustomed manner, the priest shall in the reading pew
or pulpit say,*

BRETHREN, in the primitive church there was a godly discipline that, at the beginning of Lent, those persons who stood convicted of notorious sin were put to open penance, and punished in this world, that their souls might be saved in the day of the Lord, and that others, admonished by their example, might be more afraid to offend.

Instead whereof, until that discipline may be restored again (which is much to be wished), it is thought good that at this time (in the presence of you all) should be read the general sentences of God's cursing against impenitent sinners, gathered out of the twenty-seventh chapter of Deuteronomy and other places of Scripture, and that ye should answer to every sentence 'Amen' – to the intent that, being admonished concerning the great indignation of God against sinners, ye may rather be moved to earnest and true repentance, and may walk more warily in these dangerous days, fleeing from these vices, for which ye affirm with your own mouths the curse of God is due.

CURSED is the man that maketh any carved or molten image, to worship it.

¶ *And the people shall answer and say,* Amen.

Cursed is he that curseth his father or mother. *Amen.*

Cursed is he that removeth his neighbour's landmark. *Amen.*

Cursed is he that maketh the blind to go out of his way. *Amen.*

Cursed is he that perverteth the judgement of the stranger, the fatherless, and widow. *Amen.*

Cursed is he that smiteth his neighbour secretly. *Amen.*

Cursed is he that lieth with his neighbour's wife. *Amen.*

Cursed is he that taketh reward to slay the innocent. *Amen.*

Cursed is he that putteth his trust in man, and taketh man for his defence, and in his heart goeth from the Lord. *Amen.*

Cursed are the unmerciful, fornicators and adulterers, covetous persons, idolaters, slanderers, drunkards, and extortioners. *Amen.*

¶ *Minister.*

NOW seeing that all they are accursed (as the prophet David beareth witness) who do err and go astray from the commandments of God, let us – remembering the dreadful judgement hanging over our heads and always ready to fall upon us – return unto our Lord God with all contrition and meekness of heart, bewailing and lamenting our sinful life, acknowledging and confessing our offences, and seeking to bring forth worthy fruits of penance.

For now is the axe put unto the root of the trees, so that every tree that bringeth not forth good fruit is hewn down and cast into the fire. It is a fearful thing to fall into the hands of the living God. He shall pour down rain upon the sinners – snares, fire and brimstone, storm and tempest; this shall be their portion to drink. For lo, the Lord is come out of his place to visit the wickedness of those who dwell upon the earth. But who may abide the day of his coming? Who shall be able to endure when he appeareth? His fan is in his hand, and he will purge his floor and gather his wheat into the barn, but he will burn the chaff with unquenchable fire. The day of the Lord cometh as a thief in the night, and when men shall say, 'Peace', and all things are safe, then shall sudden destruction come upon them, as sorrow cometh upon a woman travailing with child, and they shall not escape. Then shall appear the wrath of God in the day of vengeance, which obstinate sinners, through the stubbornness of their heart, have heaped unto themselves – who despised the goodness, patience, and long-sufferance of God, when he calleth them continually to repentance.

'Then shall they call upon me' (saith the Lord) 'but I will not hear; they shall seek me early, but they shall not find me; and that because they hated knowledge and received not the fear of the LORD, but abhorred my counsel and despised my correction.' Then shall it be too late to knock, when the door shall be shut; and too late to cry for mercy, when it is the time of justice. O terrible voice of most just judgement, which shall be pronounced upon them, when it shall be said unto them, 'Go, ye cursed, into the fire everlasting, which is prepared for the devil and his angels.'

Therefore, brethren, take we heed even now, while the day of salvation lasteth, for the night cometh when none can work. But let us, while we have the light, believe in the light, and walk as children of the light, that we may not be cast into utter darkness, where is weeping and gnashing of teeth. Let us not abuse the goodness of God, who calleth us mercifully to amendment, and of his endless pity promiseth us forgiveness of that which is past, if with a perfect and true heart we return unto him. For though our sins be as red as scarlet, they shall be made white as snow; and though they be like purple, yet they shall be made white as wool. 'Turn ye' (saith the Lord) 'from all your wickedness, and your sin shall not be your destruction. Cast away from you all your ungodliness that ye have done. Make you new hearts and a new spirit. Wherefore will ye die, O ye house of Israel? for I have no pleasure in the death of him that dieth, saith the Lord God. Turn ye then, and ye shall live.'

Although we have sinned, yet have we an advocate with the Father, Jesus Christ the righteous, and he is the propitiation for our sins. For he was wounded for our offences, and smitten for our wickedness. Let us therefore return unto him, who is the merciful receiver of all true penitent sinners, assuring ourselves that he is ready to receive us and most willing to pardon us, if we come unto him with faithful repentance, if we submit ourselves unto him and from henceforth walk in his ways, if we will take his easy yoke and light burden upon us, to follow him in lowliness, patience, and charity, and be ordered by the governance of his Holy Spirit, seeking always his glory, and serving him duly in our vocation with thanksgiving.

If we do this, Christ will deliver us from the curse of the law, and from the extreme malediction which shall light upon those who shall be set on the left hand, and he will set us on his right hand, and give us the gracious benediction of his Father, commanding us to take possession of his glorious kingdom. Unto which, may he vouchsafe to bring us all, for his infinite mercy. Amen.

¶ *Then shall they all kneel upon their knees; and the priest and clerks, kneeling in the place where they are accustomed to say the Litany, shall say this psalm.*

Miserere mei, Deus. Psalm 51.

HAVE mercy upon me, O God, after thy great goodness; * according to the multitude of thy mercies do away mine offences.

Wash me throughly from my wickedness, * and cleanse me from my sin.

For I acknowledge my faults, * and my sin is ever before me.

Against thee only have I sinned and done this evil in thy sight, * that thou mightest be justified in thy saying and clear when thou art judged.

Behold, I was shapen in wickedness, * and in sin hath my mother conceived me.

But lo, thou requirest truth in the inward parts, * and shalt make me to understand wisdom secretly.

Thou shalt purge me with hyssop, and I shall be clean; * thou shalt wash me, and I shall be whiter than snow.

Thou shalt make me hear of joy and gladness, * that the bones which thou hast broken may rejoice.

Turn thy face away from my sins, * and put out all my misdeeds.

Make me a clean heart, O God, * and renew a right spirit within me.

Cast me not away from thy presence, * and take not thy holy Spirit from me.

O give me the comfort of thy help again, * and stablish me with thy free Spirit.

Then shall I teach thy ways unto the wicked, * and sinners shall be converted unto thee.

Deliver me from blood-guiltiness, O God, thou that art the God of my health; * and my tongue shall sing of thy righteousness.

Thou shalt open my lips, O Lord, * and my mouth shall show thy praise.

For thou desirest no sacrifice, else would I give it thee, * but thou delightest not in burnt offering.

The sacrifice of God is a troubled spirit; * a broken and contrite heart, O God, shalt thou not despise.

O be favourable and gracious unto Sion; * build thou the walls of Jerusalem.

Then shalt thou be pleased with the sacrifice of righteousness, with the burnt offerings and oblations; * then shall they offer young bullocks upon thine altar.

A COMMINATION

Glory be to the Father, and to the Son, * and to the Holy Ghost;

Answer. As it was in the beginning, is now, and ever shall be, * world without end. Amen.

Lord, have mercy upon us.
Christ, have mercy upon us.
Lord, have mercy upon us.

OUR Father, who art in heaven, Hallowed be thy name. Thy kingdom come. Thy will be done, On earth as it is in heaven. Give us this day our daily bread. And forgive us our trespasses, As we forgive those who trespass against us. And lead us not into temptation, But deliver us from evil. Amen.

Minister. O Lord, save thy servants,
Answer. Who put their trust in thee.
Minister. Send unto them help from above,
Answer. And evermore mightily defend them.
Minister. Help us, O God our Saviour,
Answer. And for the glory of thy name deliver us; be merciful to us sinners for thy name's sake.
Minister. O Lord, hear our prayer,
Answer. And let our cry come unto thee.

¶ *Minister.*
Let us pray.

O LORD, we beseech thee, mercifully hear our prayers, and spare all those who confess their sins unto thee, that those whose consciences by sin are accused, by thy merciful pardon may be absolved, through Christ our Lord. *Amen.*

O MOST mighty God and merciful Father, who hast compassion upon all men and hatest nothing that thou hast made, who desirest not the death of a sinner, but that he should rather turn from his sin and be saved: Mercifully forgive us our trespasses; receive and comfort us, who are grieved and wearied with the burden of our sins. Thy property is always to have mercy; to thee only it appertaineth to forgive sins. Spare us therefore, good Lord; spare thy people, whom thou hast redeemed. Enter not into judgement with thy servants, who are vile earth and miserable sinners, but so turn thine anger from us, who meekly acknowledge our vileness and truly repent us of our faults, and so make haste to help us in this world, that we may ever live with thee in the world to come, through Jesus Christ our Lord. *Amen.*

¶ *Then shall the people say this that followeth, after the minister.*

T URN thou us, O good Lord, and so shall we be turned. Be favourable, O Lord, Be favourable to thy people, Who turn to thee in weeping, fasting, and praying. For thou art a merciful God, Full of compassion, long-suffering, and of great pity. Thou sparest when we deserve punishment, And in thy wrath thinkest upon mercy. Spare thy people, good Lord. Spare them, and let not thy heritage be brought to confusion. Hear us, O Lord, for thy mercy is great, And after the multitude of thy mercies look upon us, Through the merits and mediation of thy blessed Son, Jesus Christ our Lord. Amen.

¶ *Then the minister alone shall say,*

THE LORD bless us, and keep us; the LORD lift up the light of his countenance upon us, and give us peace, now and for evermore. *Amen.*

The Psalter or Psalms of David.

Day 1. Morning Prayer.

Psalm 1. *Beatus vir qui non abiit, &c.*

BLESSED is the man that hath not walked in the counsel of the ungodly, nor stood in the way of sinners, * and hath not sat in the seat of the scornful.

2 But his delight is in the law of the LORD, * and in his law will he exercise himself day and night.

3 And he shall be like a tree planted by the waterside, * that will bring forth his fruit in due season.

4 His leaf also shall not wither; * and look, whatsoever he doeth, it shall prosper.

5 As for the ungodly, it is not so with them; * but they are like the chaff, which the wind scattereth away from the face of the earth.

6 Therefore the ungodly shall not be able to stand in the judgement, * neither the sinners in the congregation of the righteous.

7 But the LORD knoweth the way of the righteous, * and the way of the ungodly shall perish.

Psalm 2. *Quare fremuerunt gentes?*

WHY do the heathen so furiously rage together, * and why do the peoples imagine a vain thing?

2 The kings of the earth stand up, and the rulers take counsel together, * against the LORD and against his anointed:

3 'Let us break their bonds asunder, * and cast away their cords from us.'

4 He that dwelleth in heaven shall laugh them to scorn; * the Lord shall have them in derision.

5 Then shall he speak unto them in his wrath, * and vex them in his sore displeasure:

6 'Yet have I set my king * upon my holy hill of Sion.'

7 I will preach the law * whereof the LORD hath said unto me, 'Thou art my Son; this day have I begotten thee.

8 Desire of me, and I shall give thee the heathen for thine inheritance, * and the utmost parts of the earth for thy possession.

9 Thou shalt bruise them with a rod of iron, * and break them in pieces like a potter's vessel.'

10 Be wise now therefore, O ye kings; * be learned, ye that are judges of the earth.

11 Serve the LORD in fear, * and rejoice unto him with reverence.

12 Kiss the Son, lest he be angry, and so ye perish from the right way, if his wrath be kindled (yea, but a little); * blessed are all they that put their trust in him.

Psalm 3. *Domine, quid multiplicati.*

LORD, how are they increased that trouble me; * many are they that rise against me.

2 Many one there be that say of my soul, * 'There is no help for him in his God.'

3 But thou, O LORD, art my defender; * thou art my worship and the lifter up of my head.

4 I did call upon the LORD with my voice, * and he heard me out of his holy hill.

5 I laid me down and slept, and rose up again, * for the LORD sustained me.

6 I will not be afraid for ten thousands of the people * that have set themselves against me round about.

7 Up, LORD, and help me, O my God, * for thou smitest all mine enemies upon the cheekbone; thou hast broken the teeth of the ungodly.

8 Salvation belongeth unto the LORD, * and thy blessing is upon thy people.

Psalm 4. *Cum invocarem.*

HEAR me when I call, O God of my righteousness. * Thou hast set me at liberty when I was in trouble; have mercy upon me and hearken unto my prayer.

2 O ye sons of men, how long will ye blaspheme mine honour, * and have such pleasure in vanity, and seek after lying?

3 Know this also, that the LORD hath chosen to himself the man that is godly; * when I call upon the LORD, he will hear me.

4 Stand in awe and sin not; * commune with your own heart, and in your chamber, and be still.

5 Offer the sacrifice of righteousness, * and put your trust in the LORD.

6 There be many that say, * 'Who will show us any good?'

7 LORD, lift thou up * the light of thy countenance upon us.

8 Thou hast put gladness in my heart * since the time that their corn and wine and oil increased.

9 I will lay me down in peace and take my rest, * for it is thou, LORD, only, that makest me dwell in safety.

Psalm 5. *Verba mea auribus.*

PONDER my words, O LORD; * consider my meditation.
2 O hearken thou unto the voice of my calling, my king and my God, * for unto thee will I make my prayer.

3 My voice shalt thou hear betimes, O LORD; * early in the morning will I direct my prayer unto thee and will look up.

4 For thou art the God that hast no pleasure in wickedness, * neither shall any evil dwell with thee.

5 Such as be foolish shall not stand in thy sight, * for thou hatest all them that work vanity.

6 Thou shalt destroy them that speak falsehood; * the LORD will abhor both the bloodthirsty and deceitful man.

7 But as for me, I will come into thine house, even upon the multitude of thy mercy, * and in thy fear will I worship toward thy holy temple.

8 Lead me, O LORD, in thy righteousness, because of mine enemies; * make thy way plain before my face.

9 For there is no faithfulness in his mouth; * their inward parts are very wickedness.

10 Their throat is an open sepulchre; * they flatter with their tongue.

11 Destroy thou them, O God; let them perish through their own imaginations; * cast them out in the multitude of their ungodliness, for they have rebelled against thee.

12 And let all them that put their trust in thee rejoice; * they shall ever be giving of thanks, because thou defendest them; they that love thy name shall be joyful in thee.

13 For thou, LORD, wilt give thy blessing unto the righteous, * and with thy favourable kindness wilt thou defend him as with a shield.

Day 1. Evening Prayer.

Psalm 6. *Domine, ne in furore.*

O LORD, rebuke me not in thine indignation, * neither chasten me in thy displeasure.

2 Have mercy upon me, O LORD, for I am weak; * O LORD, heal me, for my bones are vexed.

3 My soul also is sore troubled, * but LORD, how long wilt thou punish me?

4 Turn thee, O LORD, and deliver my soul; * O save me for thy mercy's sake.

5 For in death no man remembereth thee, * and who will give thee thanks in the pit?

6 I am weary of my groaning; every night wash I my bed, * and water my couch with my tears.

7 My beauty is gone for very trouble, * and worn away because of all mine enemies.

8 Away from me, all ye that work vanity, * for the LORD hath heard the voice of my weeping.

9 The LORD hath heard my petition; * the LORD will receive my prayer.

10 All mine enemies shall be confounded and sore vexed; * they shall be turned back and put to shame suddenly.

Psalm 7. *Domine, Deus meus.*

O LORD my God, in thee have I put my trust: * save me from all them that persecute me, and deliver me,

2 Lest he devour my soul like a lion, and tear it in pieces * while there is none to help.

3 O LORD my God, if I have done any such thing, * or if there be any wickedness in my hands,

4 If I have rewarded evil unto him that dealt friendly with me * (yea, I have delivered him that without any cause is mine enemy),

5 Then let mine enemy persecute my soul and take me; * yea, let him tread my life down upon the earth, and lay mine honour in the dust.

6 Stand up, O LORD, in thy wrath, and lift up thyself because of the indignation of mine enemies; * arise up for me in the judgement that thou hast commanded.

7 And so shall the congregation of the peoples come about thee. * For their sakes therefore lift up thyself again.

8 The LORD shall judge the peoples; give sentence with me, O LORD, * according to my righteousness and according to the innocency that is in me.

9 O let the wickedness of the ungodly come to an end, * but guide thou the just.

10 For the righteous God * trieth the very hearts and reins.

11 My help cometh of God, * who preserveth them that are true of heart.

12 God is a righteous judge, strong and patient, * and God is provoked every day.

13 If a man will not turn, he will whet his sword; * he hath bent his bow and made it ready.

14 He hath prepared for him the instruments of death; * he ordaineth his arrows against the persecutors.

15 Lo, the ungodly travaileth with mischief; * he hath conceived sorrow and brought forth iniquity.

16 He hath graven and digged up a pit, * and is fallen himself into the destruction that he made for others.

17 For his travail shall come upon his own head, * and his wickedness shall fall on his own pate.

18 I will give thanks unto the LORD according to his righteousness, * and I will praise the name of the LORD Most High.

Psalm 8. *Domine, Dominus noster.*

O LORD our governor, how excellent is thy name in all the world, * thou that hast set thy glory above the heavens!

2 Out of the mouth of very babes and sucklings hast thou ordained strength because of thine enemies, * that thou mightest still the enemy and the avenger.

3 For I will consider thy heavens, even the works of thy fingers: * the moon and the stars, which thou hast ordained.

4 What is man, that thou art mindful of him? * and the son of man, that thou visitest him?

5 Thou madest him lower than the angels, * to crown him with glory and worship.

6 Thou makest him to have dominion of the works of

thy hands, * and thou hast put all things in subjection under his feet:

7 All sheep and oxen, * yea, and the beasts of the field,

8 The fowls of the air, and the fishes of the sea, * and whatsoever walketh through the paths of the seas.

9 O LORD our governor, * how excellent is thy name in all the world!

Day 2. Morning Prayer.
Psalm 9. *Confitebor tibi.*

I WILL give thanks unto thee, O LORD, with my whole heart; * I will speak of all thy marvellous works.

2 I will be glad and rejoice in thee; * yea, my songs will I make of thy name, O thou Most Highest,

3 While mine enemies are driven back; * they shall fall and perish at thy presence.

4 For thou hast maintained my right and my cause; * thou art set in the throne that judgest right.

5 Thou hast rebuked the heathen and destroyed the ungodly; * thou hast put out their name for ever and ever.

6 O thou enemy, destructions are come to a perpetual end; * even as the cities which thou hast destroyed, their memorial is perished with them.

7 But the LORD shall endure for ever; * he hath also prepared his seat for judgement.

8 For he shall judge the world in righteousness, * and minister true judgement unto the peoples.

9 The LORD also will be a defence for the oppressed, * even a refuge in due time of trouble.

10 And they that know thy name will put their trust in thee, * for thou, LORD, hast never failed them that seek thee.

11 O praise the LORD, which dwelleth in Sion; * show the peoples of his doings.

12 For when he maketh inquisition for blood, he remembereth them, * and forgetteth not the complaint of the poor.

13 Have mercy upon me, O LORD; consider the trouble which I suffer of them that hate me, * thou that liftest me up from the gates of death,

14 That I may show all thy praises within the ports of the daughter of Sion; * I will rejoice in thy salvation.

15 The heathen are sunk down in the pit that they made; * in the same net which they hid privily is their foot taken.

16 The LORD is known to execute judgement; * the ungodly is trapped in the work of his own hands.

17 The wicked shall be turned into hell, * and all the peoples that forget God.

18 For the poor shall not alway be forgotten; * the patient abiding of the meek shall not perish for ever.

19 Up, LORD, and let not man have the upper hand; * let the heathen be judged in thy sight.

20 Put them in fear, O LORD, * that the heathen may know themselves to be but men.

Psalm 10. *Ut quid, Domine?*

WHY standest thou so far off, O LORD, * and hidest thy face in the needful time of trouble?

2 The ungodly for his own lust doth persecute the poor; * let them be taken in the crafty wiliness that they have imagined.

3 For the ungodly hath made boast of his own heart's desire, * and speaketh good of the covetous, whom GOD abhorreth.

4 The ungodly is so proud that he careth not for God, * neither is God in all his thoughts.

5 His ways are alway grievous; * thy judgements are far above out of his sight, and therefore defieth he all his enemies.

6 For he hath said in his heart, 'Tush, I shall never be cast down; * there shall no harm happen unto me.'

7 His mouth is full of cursing, deceit, and fraud; * under his tongue is ungodliness and vanity.

8 He sitteth lurking in the thievish corners of the streets, * and privily in his lurking dens doth he murder the innocent; his eyes are set against the poor.

9 For he lieth waiting secretly, even as a lion lurketh he in his den, * that he may ravish the poor.

10 He doth ravish the poor * when he getteth him into his net;

11 He falleth down and humbleth himself, * that the congregation of the poor may fall into the hands of his captains.

12 He hath said in his heart, 'Tush, God hath forgotten; * he hideth away his face, and he will never see it.'

13 Arise, O LORD God, and lift up thine hand; * forget not the poor.

14 Wherefore should the wicked blaspheme God, *

while he doth say in his heart, 'Tush, thou God carest not for it'?

15 Surely thou hast seen it, * for thou beholdest ungodliness and wrong,

16 That thou mayest take the matter into thy hand. * The poor committeth himself unto thee, for thou art the helper of the friendless.

17 Break thou the power of the ungodly and malicious; * take away his ungodliness, and thou shalt find none.

18 The LORD is king for ever and ever, * and the heathen are perished out of the land.

19 LORD, thou hast heard the desire of the poor; * thou preparest their heart, and thine ear hearkeneth thereto,

20 To help the fatherless and poor unto their right, * that the man of the earth be no more exalted against them.

Psalm 11. *In Domino confido.*

IN the LORD put I my trust; * how say ye then to my soul that she should flee as a bird unto the hill?

2 For lo, the ungodly bend their bow, and make ready their arrows within the quiver, * that they may privily shoot at them which are true of heart.

3 For the foundations will be cast down, * and what hath the righteous done?

4 The LORD is in his holy temple; * the LORD's seat is in heaven.

5 His eyes consider the poor, * and his eyelids try the children of men.

6 The LORD alloweth the righteous, * but the ungodly and him that delighteth in wickedness doth his soul abhor.

7 Upon the ungodly he shall rain snares, fire and brimstone, storm and tempest; * this shall be their portion to drink.

8 For the righteous LORD loveth righteousness; * his countenance will behold the thing that is just.

Day 2. Evening Prayer.
Psalm 12. *Salvum me fac.*

HELP me, LORD, for there is not one godly man left, * for the faithful are minished from among the children of men.

2 They talk of vanity every one with his neighbour; * they do but flatter with their lips, and dissemble in their double heart.

3 The LORD shall root out all deceitful lips, * and the tongue that speaketh proud things,

4 Which have said, 'With our tongue will we prevail; * we are they that ought to speak; who is lord over us?'

5 'Now for the comfortless trouble's sake of the needy, * and because of the deep sighing of the poor,

6 I will up', saith the LORD, * 'and will help every one from him that swelleth against him, and will set him at rest.'

7 The words of the LORD are pure words, * even as the silver which from the earth is tried and purified seven times in the fire.

8 Thou shalt keep them, O LORD; * thou shalt preserve him from this generation for ever.

9 The ungodly walk on every side, * and vileness is exalted among the children of men.

Psalm 13. *Usque quo, Domine?*

How long wilt thou forget me, O LORD – for ever? *
how long wilt thou hide thy face from me?

2 How long shall I seek counsel in my soul, and be so vexed in my heart? * how long shall mine enemies triumph over me?

3 Consider and hear me, O LORD my God; * lighten mine eyes, that I sleep not in death.

4 Lest mine enemy say, 'I have prevailed against him'; * for if I be cast down, they that trouble me will rejoice at it.

5 But my trust is in thy mercy, * and my heart is joyful in thy salvation.

6 I will sing of the LORD because he hath dealt so lovingly with me; * yea, I will praise the name of the Lord Most Highest. •

Psalm 14. *Dixit insipiens.*

The fool hath said in his heart, * 'There is no God.'
2 They are corrupt and become abominable in their doings; * there is none that doeth good, no, not one.

3 The LORD looked down from heaven upon the children of men, * to see if there were any that would understand and seek after God.

4 But they are all gone out of the way; they are altogether become abominable; * there is none that doeth good, no, not one.

5 Their throat is an open sepulchre; with their tongues have they deceived; * the poison of asps is under their lips.

6 Their mouth is full of cursing and bitterness; * their feet are swift to shed blood.

7 Destruction and unhappiness is in their ways, and the way of peace have they not known; * there is no fear of God before their eyes.

8 Have they no knowledge, that they are all such workers of mischief, * eating up my people as it were bread, and call not upon the LORD?

9 There were they brought in great fear, even where no fear was, * for God is in the generation of the righteous.

10 As for you, ye have made a mock at the counsel of the poor, * because he putteth his trust in the LORD.

11 Who shall give salvation unto Israel out of Sion? When the LORD turneth the captivity of his people, * then shall Jacob rejoice, and Israel shall be glad.

Day 3. Morning Prayer.
Psalm 15. *Domine, quis habitabit?*

LORD, who shall dwell in thy tabernacle? * or who shall rest upon thy holy hill?

2 Even he that leadeth an uncorrupt life, * and doeth the thing which is right, and speaketh the truth from his heart.

3 He that hath used no deceit in his tongue, nor done evil to his neighbour, * and hath not slandered his neighbour.

4 He that setteth not by himself, but is lowly in his own eyes, * and maketh much of them that fear the LORD.

5 He that sweareth unto his neighbour, and disappointeth him not, * though it were to his own hindrance.

6 He that hath not given his money upon usury, * nor taken reward against the innocent.

7 Whoso doeth these things * shall never fall.

Psalm 16. *Conserva me, Domine.*

PRESERVE me, O God, * for in thee have I put my trust.

2 O my soul, thou hast said unto the LORD, * 'Thou art my God; my goods are nothing unto thee.'

3 All my delight is upon the saints that are in the earth, * and upon such as excel in virtue.

4 But they that run after another god * shall have great trouble.

5 Their drink offerings of blood will I not offer, * neither make mention of their names within my lips.

6 The LORD himself is the portion of mine inheritance and of my cup; * thou shalt maintain my lot.

7 The lot is fallen unto me in a fair ground; * yea, I have a goodly heritage.

8 I will thank the LORD for giving me warning; * my reins also chasten me in the night season.

9 I have set GOD always before me, * for he is on my right hand; therefore I shall not fall.

10 Wherefore my heart was glad and my glory rejoiced; * my flesh also shall rest in hope.

11 For why? thou shalt not leave my soul in hell, * neither shalt thou suffer thy holy one to see corruption.

12 Thou shalt show me the path of life; in thy presence is the fulness of joy, * and at thy right hand there is pleasure for evermore.

Psalm 17. *Exaudi, Domine.*

HEAR the right, O LORD; consider my complaint; * and hearken unto my prayer that goeth not out of feigned lips.

2 Let my sentence come forth from thy presence, * and let thine eyes look upon the thing that is equal.

3 Thou hast proved and visited mine heart in the night season; thou hast tried me and shalt find no wickedness in me; * for I am utterly purposed that my mouth shall not offend,

4 Because of men's works that are done against the words of thy lips. * I have kept me from the ways of the destroyer;

5 O hold thou up my goings in thy paths, * that my footsteps slip not.

6 I have called upon thee, O God, for thou shalt hear me; * incline thine ear to me and hearken unto my words.

7 Show thy marvellous loving-kindness, thou that art the saviour of them which put their trust in thee, * from such as resist thy right hand.

8 Keep me as the apple of an eye; * hide me under the shadow of thy wings,

9 From the ungodly that trouble me; * mine enemies compass me round about to take away my soul.

10 They are enclosed in their own fat, * and their mouth speaketh proud things.

11 They lie waiting in our way on every side, * turning their eyes down to the ground,

12 Like as a lion that is greedy of his prey, * and as it were a lion's whelp lurking in secret places.

13 Up, LORD, disappoint him and cast him down; * deliver my soul from the ungodly, which is a sword of thine,

14 From the men of thy hand, O LORD – from the men (I say) and from the evil world, * which have their portion in this life, whose bellies thou fillest with thy hid treasure.

15 They have children at their desire, * and leave the rest of their substance for their babes.

16 But as for me, I will behold thy presence in righteousness; * and when I awake up after thy likeness, I shall be satisfied with it.

Day 3. Evening Prayer.
Psalm 18. *Diligam te, Domine.*

I WILL love thee, O LORD, my strength. The LORD is my stony rock and my defence; * my saviour, my God, and my might in whom I will trust; my buckler, the horn also of my salvation, and my refuge.

2 I will call upon the LORD, which is worthy to be praised; * so shall I be safe from mine enemies.

3 The sorrows of death compassed me, * and the overflowings of ungodliness made me afraid.

4 The pains of hell came about me; * the snares of death overtook me.

5 In my trouble I will call upon the LORD, * and complain unto my God.

6 So shall he hear my voice out of his holy temple, * and my complaint shall come before him; it shall enter even into his ears.

7 The earth trembled and quaked; * the very foundations also of the hills shook and were removed, because he was wroth.

8 There went a smoke out in his presence, * and a con-suming fire out of his mouth, so that coals were kindled at it.

9 He bowed the heavens also and came down, * and it was dark under his feet.

10 He rode upon the cherubim and did fly; * he came flying upon the wings of the wind.

11 He made darkness his secret place, * his pavilion round about him, with dark water and thick clouds to cover him.

12 At the brightness of his presence, his clouds re-moved: * hailstones and coals of fire.

13 The LORD also thundered out of heaven, and the Highest gave his thunder: * hailstones and coals of fire.

14 He sent out his arrows and scattered them; * he cast forth lightnings and destroyed them.

15 The springs of waters were seen, and the founda-tions of the round world were discovered, at thy chiding, O LORD, * at the blasting of the breath of thy displeasure.

16 He shall send down from on high to fetch me, * and shall take me out of many waters.

17 He shall deliver me from my strongest enemy and from them which hate me, * for they are too mighty for me.

18 They prevented me in the day of my trouble, * but the LORD was my upholder.

19 He brought me forth also into a place of liberty; * he brought me forth, even because he had a favour unto me.

20 The LORD shall reward me after my righteous deal-ing; * according to the cleanness of my hands shall he rec-ompense me.

21 Because I have kept the ways of the LORD, * and have not forsaken my God, as the wicked doth.

22 For I have an eye unto all his laws, * and will not cast out his commandments from me.

23 I was also uncorrupt before him, * and eschewed mine own wickedness.

24 Therefore shall the LORD reward me after my righteous dealing, * and according unto the cleanness of my hands in his eyesight.

25 With the holy, thou shalt be holy; * and with a perfect man, thou shalt be perfect.

26 With the clean, thou shalt be clean; * and with the froward, thou shalt learn frowardness.

27 For thou shalt save the people that are in adversity, * and shalt bring down the high looks of the proud.

28 Thou also shalt light my candle; * the LORD my God shall make my darkness to be light.

29 For in thee I shall discomfit an host of men; * and with the help of my God, I shall leap over the wall.

30 The way of God is an undefiled way; * the word of the LORD also is tried in the fire; he is the defender of all them that put their trust in him.

31 For who is God but the LORD? * or who hath any strength except our God?

32 It is God that girdeth me with strength of war, * and maketh my way perfect.

33 He maketh my feet like harts' feet, * and setteth me up on high.

34 He teacheth mine hands to fight, * and mine arms shall break even a bow of steel.

35 Thou hast given me the defence of thy salvation; *
thy right hand also shall hold me up, and thy loving correction shall make me great.

36 Thou shalt make room enough under me for to go, *
that my footsteps shall not slide.

37 I will follow upon mine enemies and overtake them, *
neither will I turn again till I have destroyed them.

38 I will smite them, that they shall not be able to stand, *
but fall under my feet.

39 Thou hast girded me with strength unto the battle; *
thou shalt throw down mine enemies under me.

40 Thou hast made mine enemies also to turn their
backs upon me, * and I shall destroy them that hate me.

41 They shall cry, but there shall be none to help them; *
yea, even unto the LORD shall they cry, but he shall not
hear them.

42 I will beat them as small as the dust before the wind; *
I will cast them out as the clay in the streets.

43 Thou shalt deliver me from the strivings of the people, * and thou shalt make me the head of the heathen;

44 A people whom I have not known * shall serve me.

45 As soon as they hear of me, they shall obey me; * but
the strange children shall dissemble with me.

46 The strange children shall fail, * and be afraid out
of their prisons.

47 The LORD liveth, and blessed be my strong helper, *
and praised be the God of my salvation,

48 Even the God that seeth that I be avenged, * and subdueth the peoples unto me.

49 It is he that delivereth me from my cruel enemies,

and setteth me up above mine adversaries. * Thou shalt
rid me from the wicked man.

50 For this cause will I give thanks unto thee, O LORD,
among the Gentiles; * and sing praises unto thy name.

51 Great prosperity giveth he unto his king, * and showeth loving-kindness unto David his anointed, and unto
his seed for evermore.

Day 4. Morning Prayer.
Psalm 19. *Caeli enarrant.*

THE heavens declare the glory of God, * and the firmament showeth his handiwork.

2 One day telleth another, * and one night certifieth
another.

3 There is neither speech nor language, * but their voices are heard among them.

4 Their sound is gone out into all lands, * and their
words into the ends of the world.

5 In them hath he set a tabernacle for the sun, * which
cometh forth as a bridegroom out of his chamber, and
rejoiceth as a giant to run his course.

6 It goeth forth from the uttermost part of the heaven,
and runneth about unto the end of it again, * and there is
nothing hid from the heat thereof.

7 The law of the LORD is an undefiled law, converting
the soul; * the testimony of the LORD is sure, and giveth
wisdom unto the simple;

8 The statutes of the LORD are right and rejoice the
heart; * the commandment of the LORD is pure and giveth
light unto the eyes;

9 The fear of the LORD is clean and endureth for ever; *
the judgements of the LORD are true and righteous altogether.

10 More to be desired are they than gold, yea, than
much fine gold; * sweeter also than honey and the honeycomb.

11 Moreover, by them is thy servant taught, * and in
keeping of them there is great reward.

12 Who can tell how oft he offendeth? * O cleanse thou
me from my secret faults.

13 Keep thy servant also from presumptuous sins, lest
they get the dominion over me; * so shall I be undefiled
and innocent from the great offence.

14 Let the words of my mouth, and the meditation of
my heart, * be alway acceptable in thy sight,

15 O LORD, * my strength and my redeemer.

Psalm 20. *Exaudiat te Dominus.*

THE LORD hear thee in the day of trouble; * the name
of the God of Jacob defend thee;

2 Send thee help from the sanctuary, * and strength-
en thee out of Sion;

3 Remember all thy offerings, * and accept thy burnt
sacrifice;

4 Grant thee thy heart's desire, * and fulfil all thy mind.

5 We will rejoice in thy salvation, and triumph in the
name of the LORD our God. * The LORD perform all thy
petitions.

6 Now know I that the LORD helpeth his anointed, and

will hear him from his holy heaven, * even with the wholesome strength of his right hand.

7 Some put their trust in chariots, and some in horses, * but we will remember the name of the LORD our God.

8 They are brought down and fallen, * but we are risen and stand upright.

9 Save, LORD; and hear us, O king of heaven, * when we call upon thee.

Psalm 21. *Domine, in virtute tua.*

THE king shall rejoice in thy strength, O LORD; * exceeding glad shall he be of thy salvation.

2 Thou hast given him his heart's desire, * and hast not denied him the request of his lips.

3 For thou shalt prevent him with the blessings of goodness, * and shalt set a crown of pure gold upon his head.

4 He asked life of thee, and thou gavest him a long life, * even for ever and ever.

5 His honour is great in thy salvation; * glory and great worship shalt thou lay upon him.

6 For thou shalt give him everlasting felicity, * and make him glad with the joy of thy countenance.

7 And why? because the king putteth his trust in the LORD, * and in the mercy of the Most Highest he shall not miscarry.

8 All thine enemies shall feel thine hand; * thy right hand shall find out them that hate thee.

9 Thou shalt make them like a fiery oven in time of thy wrath; * the LORD shall destroy them in his displeasure, and the fire shall consume them.

10 Their fruit shalt thou root out of the earth, * and their seed from among the children of men.

11 For they intended mischief against thee, * and imagined such a device as they are not able to perform.

12 Therefore shalt thou put them to flight, * and the strings of thy bow shalt thou make ready against the face of them.

13 Be thou exalted, LORD, in thine own strength; * so will we sing and praise thy power.

Day 4. Evening Prayer.
Psalm 22. *Deus, Deus meus.*

MY God, my God, look upon me – why hast thou forsaken me, * and art so far from my health, and from the words of my complaint?

2 O my God, I cry in the daytime, but thou hearest not; * and in the night season also I take no rest.

3 And thou continuest holy, * O thou Worship of Israel.

4 Our fathers hoped in thee; * they trusted in thee, and thou didst deliver them.

5 They called upon thee and were holpen; * they put their trust in thee and were not confounded.

6 But as for me, I am a worm and no man, * a very scorn of men and the outcast of the people.

7 All they that see me laugh me to scorn; * they shoot out their lips and shake their heads, saying,

8 'He trusted in GOD, that he would deliver him; * let him deliver him, if he will have him.'

9 But thou art he that took me out of my mother's

womb; * thou wast my hope when I hanged yet upon my mother's breasts.

10 I have been left unto thee ever since I was born; * thou art my God, even from my mother's womb.

11 O go not from me, for trouble is hard at hand, * and there is none to help me.

12 Many oxen are come about me; * fat bulls of Bashan close me in on every side.

13 They gape upon me with their mouths, * as it were a ramping and a roaring lion.

14 I am poured out like water, and all my bones are out of joint; * my heart also in the midst of my body is even like melting wax.

15 My strength is dried up like a potsherd, and my tongue cleaveth to my gums, * and thou shalt bring me into the dust of death.

16 For many dogs are come about me, * and the council of the wicked layeth siege against me.

17 They pierced my hands and my feet; I may tell all my bones; * they stand staring and looking upon me.

18 They part my garments among them, * and cast lots upon my vesture.

19 But be not thou far from me, O Lord; * thou art my succour; haste thee to help me.

20 Deliver my soul from the sword, * my darling from the power of the dog.

21 Save me from the lion's mouth; * thou hast heard me also from among the horns of the unicorns.

22 I will declare thy name unto my brethren; * in the midst of the congregation will I praise thee.

23 O praise the Lord, ye that fear him; * magnify him, all ye of the seed of Jacob; and fear him, all ye seed of Israel.

24 For he hath not despised nor abhorred the low estate of the poor; * he hath not hid his face from him, but when he called unto him, he heard him.

25 My praise is of thee in the great congregation; * my vows will I perform in the sight of them that fear him.

26 The poor shall eat and be satisfied; * they that seek after the Lord shall praise him; your heart shall live for ever.

27 All the ends of the world shall remember themselves and be turned unto the Lord, * and all the kindreds of the nations shall worship before him.

28 For the kingdom is the Lord's, * and he is the governor among the peoples.

29 All such as be fat upon earth * have eaten and worshipped.

30 All they that go down into the dust shall kneel before him, * and no man hath quickened his own soul.

31 My seed shall serve him; * they shall be counted unto the Lord for a generation.

32 They shall come, and the heavens shall declare his righteousness * unto a people that shall be born, whom the Lord hath made.

Psalm 23. *Dominus regit me.*

THE Lord is my shepherd; * therefore can I lack nothing.

2 He shall feed me in a green pasture, * and lead me forth beside the waters of comfort.

3 He shall convert my soul, * and bring me forth in the paths of righteousness, for his name's sake.

4 Yea, though I walk through the valley of the shadow of death, I will fear no evil, * for thou art with me; thy rod and thy staff comfort me.

5 Thou shalt prepare a table before me against them that trouble me; * thou hast anointed my head with oil, and my cup shall be full.

6 But thy loving-kindness and mercy shall follow me all the days of my life, * and I will dwell in the house of the LORD for ever.

Day 5. Morning Prayer.
Psalm 24. *Domini est terra.*

THE earth is the LORD's, and all that therein is; * the compass of the world, and they that dwell therein.

2 For he hath founded it upon the seas, * and prepared it upon the floods.

3 Who shall ascend into the hill of the LORD? * or who shall rise up in his holy place?

4 Even he that hath clean hands and a pure heart, * and that hath not lift up his mind unto vanity, nor sworn to deceive his neighbour.

5 He shall receive the blessing from the LORD, * and righteousness from the God of his salvation.

6 This is the generation of them that seek him, * even of them that seek thy face, O Jacob.

7 Lift up your heads, O ye gates, and be ye lift up, ye everlasting doors, * and the king of glory shall come in.

8 Who is the king of glory? * it is the LORD strong and mighty, even the LORD mighty in battle.

9 Lift up your heads, O ye gates, and be ye lift up, ye everlasting doors, * and the king of glory shall come in.

10 Who is the king of glory? * even the LORD of hosts, he is the king of glory.

Psalm 25. *Ad te, Domine, levavi.*

UNTO thee, O LORD, will I lift up my soul; my God, I have put my trust in thee. * O let me not be confounded, neither let mine enemies triumph over me.

2 For all they that hope in thee shall not be ashamed, * but such as transgress without a cause shall be put to confusion.

3 Show me thy ways, O LORD, * and teach me thy paths.

4 Lead me forth in thy truth and learn me, * for thou art the God of my salvation; in thee hath been my hope all the day long.

5 Call to remembrance, O LORD, thy tender mercies, * and thy loving-kindnesses, which have been ever of old.

6 O remember not the sins and offences of my youth; * but according to thy mercy think thou upon me, O LORD, for thy goodness.

7 Gracious and righteous is the LORD; * therefore will he teach sinners in the way.

8 Them that are meek shall he guide in judgement, * and such as are gentle, them shall he learn his way.

9 All the paths of the LORD are mercy and truth * unto such as keep his covenant and his testimonies.

10 For thy name's sake, O Lord, * be merciful unto my sin, for it is great.

11 What man is he that feareth the Lord? * him shall he teach in the way that he shall choose.

12 His soul shall dwell at ease, * and his seed shall inherit the land.

13 The secret of the Lord is among them that fear him, * and he will show them his covenant.

14 Mine eyes are ever looking unto the Lord, * for he shall pluck my feet out of the net.

15 Turn thee unto me and have mercy upon me, * for I am desolate and in misery.

16 The sorrows of my heart are enlarged; * O bring thou me out of my troubles.

17 Look upon my adversity and misery, * and forgive me all my sin.

18 Consider mine enemies, how many they are, * and they bear a tyrannous hate against me.

19 O keep my soul and deliver me; * let me not be confounded, for I have put my trust in thee.

20 Let perfectness and righteous dealing wait upon me, * for my hope hath been in thee.

21 Deliver Israel, O God, * out of all his troubles.

Psalm 26. *Judica me, Domine.*

Be thou my judge, O Lord, for I have walked innocently; * my trust hath been also in the Lord; therefore shall I not fall.

2 Examine me, O Lord, and prove me; * try out my reins and my heart.

3 For thy loving-kindness is ever before mine eyes, * and I will walk in thy truth.

4 I have not dwelt with vain persons, * neither will I have fellowship with the deceitful.

5 I have hated the congregation of the wicked, * and will not sit among the ungodly.

6 I will wash my hands in innocency, O LORD, * and so will I go to thine altar,

7 That I may show the voice of thanksgiving, * and tell of all thy wondrous works.

8 LORD, I have loved the habitation of thy house, * and the place where thine honour dwelleth.

9 O shut not up my soul with the sinners, * nor my life with the bloodthirsty,

10 In whose hands is wickedness, * and their right hand is full of gifts.

11 But as for me, I will walk innocently; * O deliver me and be merciful unto me.

12 My foot standeth right; * I will praise the LORD in the congregations.

Day 5. Evening Prayer.
Psalm 27. *Dominus illuminatio.*

THE LORD is my light and my salvation; whom then shall I fear? * the LORD is the strength of my life; of whom then shall I be afraid?

2 When the wicked, even mine enemies and my foes, came upon me to eat up my flesh, * they stumbled and fell.

3 Though an host of men were laid against me, yet shall not my heart be afraid; * and though there rose up war against me, yet will I put my trust in him.

4 One thing have I desired of the LORD, which I will require: * even that I may dwell in the house of the LORD all the days of my life, to behold the fair beauty of the LORD and to visit his temple.

5 For in the time of trouble he shall hide me in his tabernacle; * yea, in the secret place of his dwelling shall he hide me, and set me up upon a rock of stone.

6 And now shall he lift up mine head * above mine enemies round about me.

7 Therefore will I offer in his dwelling an oblation with great gladness; * I will sing and speak praises unto the LORD.

8 Hearken unto my voice, O LORD, when I cry unto thee; * have mercy upon me and hear me.

9 My heart hath talked of thee: 'Seek ye my face.' * 'Thy face, LORD, will I seek.'

10 O hide not thou thy face from me, * nor cast thy servant away in displeasure.

11 Thou hast been my succour; * leave me not, neither forsake me, O God of my salvation.

12 When my father and my mother forsake me, * the LORD taketh me up.

13 Teach me thy way, O LORD, * and lead me in the right way because of mine enemies.

14 Deliver me not over into the will of mine adversaries, * for there are false witnesses risen up against me, and such as speak wrong.

15 I should utterly have fainted, * but that I believe verily to see the goodness of the LORD in the land of the living.

16 O tarry thou the LORD's leisure; * be strong and he shall comfort thine heart, and put thou thy trust in the LORD.

Psalm 28. *Ad te, Domine.*

UNTO thee will I cry, O LORD my strength; * think no scorn of me, lest if thou make as though thou hearest not, I become like them that go down into the pit.

2 Hear the voice of my humble petitions when I cry unto thee, * when I hold up my hands towards the mercy seat of thy holy temple.

3 O pluck me not away, neither destroy me with the ungodly and wicked doers, * which speak friendly to their neighbours, but imagine mischief in their hearts.

4 Reward them according to their deeds, * and according to the wickedness of their own inventions.

5 Recompense them after the work of their hands; * pay them that they have deserved.

6 For they regard not in their mind the works of the LORD, nor the operation of his hands; * therefore shall he break them down and not build them up.

7 Praised be the LORD, * for he hath heard the voice of my humble petitions.

8 The LORD is my strength and my shield; my heart hath trusted in him and I am helped; * therefore my heart danceth for joy, and in my song will I praise him.

9 The LORD is my strength, * and he is the wholesome defence of his anointed.

10 O save thy people and give thy blessing unto thine inheritance; * feed them and set them up for ever.

Psalm 29. *Afferte Domino.*

BRING unto the LORD, O ye mighty, bring young rams unto the LORD; * ascribe unto the LORD worship and strength.

2 Give the LORD the honour due unto his name; * worship the LORD with holy worship.

3 It is the LORD that commandeth the waters; * it is the glorious God that maketh the thunder.

4 It is the LORD that ruleth the sea; the voice of the LORD is mighty in operation; * the voice of the LORD is a glorious voice.

5 The voice of the LORD breaketh the cedar trees; * yea, the LORD breaketh the cedars of Lebanon.

6 He maketh them also to skip like a calf; * Lebanon also, and Sirion, like a young unicorn.

7 The voice of the LORD divideth the flames of fire; the voice of the LORD shaketh the wilderness; * yea, the LORD shaketh the wilderness of Kadesh.

8 The voice of the LORD maketh the hinds to bring forth young and discovereth the thick bushes; * in his temple doth every man speak of his honour.

9 The LORD sitteth above the water-flood, * and the LORD remaineth a king for ever.

10 The LORD shall give strength unto his people; * the LORD shall give his people the blessing of peace.

Day 6. Morning Prayer.

Psalm 30. *Exaltabo te, Domine.*

I WILL magnify thee, O LORD, for thou hast set me up, *
and not made my foes to triumph over me.

2 O LORD my God, I cried unto thee, * and thou hast
healed me.

3 Thou, LORD, hast brought my soul out of hell; * thou
hast kept my life from them that go down to the pit.

4 Sing praises unto the LORD, O ye saints of his, * and
give thanks unto him for a remembrance of his holiness.

5 For his wrath endureth but the twinkling of an eye,
and in his pleasure is life; * heaviness may endure for a
night, but joy cometh in the morning.

6 And in my prosperity I said, 'I shall never be removed; *
thou, LORD, of thy goodness hast made my hill so strong.'

7 Thou didst turn thy face from me, * and I was troubled.

8 Then cried I unto thee, O LORD, * and gat me to my
Lord right humbly:

9 'What profit is there in my blood, * when I go down
to the pit?

10 Shall the dust give thanks unto thee? * or shall it
declare thy truth?

11 Hear, O LORD, and have mercy upon me; * LORD,
be thou my helper.'

12 Thou hast turned my heaviness into joy; * thou hast
put off my sackcloth and girded me with gladness.

13 Therefore shall every good man sing of thy praise
without ceasing; * O my God, I will give thanks unto thee
for ever.

Psalm 31. *In te, Domine, speravi.*

IN thee, O LORD, have I put my trust; * let me never be put to confusion; deliver me in thy righteousness.

2 Bow down thine ear to me; * make haste to deliver me.

3 And be thou my strong rock and house of defence, * that thou mayest save me.

4 For thou art my strong rock and my castle; * be thou also my guide, and lead me for thy name's sake.

5 Draw me out of the net that they have laid privily for me, * for thou art my strength.

• 6 Into thy hands I commend my spirit, * for thou hast redeemed me, O LORD, thou God of truth.

7 I have hated them that hold of superstitious vanities, * and my trust hath been in the LORD.

8 I will be glad and rejoice in thy mercy, * for thou hast considered my trouble, and hast known my soul in adversities.

9 Thou hast not shut me up into the hand of the enemy, * but hast set my feet in a large room.

10 Have mercy upon me, O LORD, for I am in trouble; * and mine eye is consumed for very heaviness, yea, my soul and my body.

11 For my life is waxen old with heaviness, * and my years with mourning.

12 My strength faileth me because of mine iniquity, * and my bones are consumed.

13 I became a reproof among all mine enemies, but especially among my neighbours; * and they of mine acquaintance were afraid of me, and they that did see me without conveyed themselves from me.

14 I am clean forgotten, as a dead man out of mind; *
I am become like a broken vessel.

15 For I have heard the blasphemy of the multitude, *
and fear is on every side, while they conspire together
against me and take their counsel to take away my life.

16 But my hope hath been in thee, O LORD; * I have
said, 'Thou art my God.'

17 My time is in thy hand; deliver me from the hand of
mine enemies * and from them that persecute me.

18 Show thy servant the light of thy countenance, * and
save me for thy mercy's sake.

19 Let me not be confounded, O LORD, for I have called
upon thee; * let the ungodly be put to confusion, and be
put to silence in the grave.

20 Let the lying lips be put to silence, * which cruelly,
disdainfully, and despitefully speak against the righteous.

21 O how plentiful is thy goodness, which thou hast
laid up for them that fear thee, * and that thou hast prepared for them that put their trust in thee, even before
the sons of men!

22 Thou shalt hide them privily by thine own presence
from the provoking of all men; * thou shalt keep them
secretly in thy tabernacle from the strife of tongues.

23 Thanks be to the LORD, * for he hath showed me
marvellous great kindness in a strong city.

24 And when I made haste, I said, * 'I am cast out of
the sight of thine eyes.'

25 Nevertheless, thou heardest the voice of my prayer *
when I cried unto thee.

26 O love the LORD, all ye his saints, * for the LORD

preserveth them that are faithful, and plenteously rewardeth the proud doer.

27 Be strong and he shall establish your heart, * all ye
that put your trust in the LORD.

Day 6. Evening Prayer.
Psalm 32. *Beati, quorum.*

BLESSED is he whose unrighteousness is forgiven, * and
whose sin is covered.

2 Blessed is the man unto whom the LORD imputeth
no sin, * and in whose spirit there is no guile.

3 For while I held my tongue, * my bones consumed
away through my daily complaining.

4 For thy hand is heavy upon me day and night, * and
my moisture is like the drought in summer.

5 I will acknowledge my sin unto thee, * and mine unrighteousness have I not hid.

6 I said, 'I will confess my sins unto the LORD', * and so
thou forgavest the wickedness of my sin.

7 For this shall everyone that is godly make his prayer
unto thee in a time when thou mayest be found; * therefore the great water-floods, they shall not come nigh him.

8 Thou art a place to hide me in; thou shalt preserve me
from trouble; * thou shalt compass me about with songs
of deliverance.

9 I will inform thee and teach thee in the way wherein
thou shalt go, * and I will guide thee with mine eye.

10 Be ye not like to horse and mule, which have no
understanding, * whose mouths must be held with bit
and bridle, lest they fall upon thee.

11 Great plagues remain for the ungodly, * but whoso putteth his trust in the LORD, mercy embraceth him on every side.

12 Be glad, O ye righteous, and rejoice in the LORD; * and be joyful, all ye that are true of heart.

Psalm 33. *Exultate, justi.*

REJOICE in the LORD, O ye righteous, * for it becometh well the just to be thankful.

2 Praise the LORD with harp; * sing praises unto him with the lute and instrument of ten strings.

3 Sing unto the LORD a new song; * sing praises lustily unto him with a good courage.

4 For the word of the LORD is true, * and all his works are faithful.

5 He loveth righteousness and judgement; * the earth is full of the goodness of the LORD.

6 By the word of the LORD were the heavens made, * and all the hosts of them by the breath of his mouth.

7 He gathereth the waters of the sea together as it were upon an heap, * and layeth up the deep as in a treasure house.

8 Let all the earth fear the LORD; * stand in awe of him, all ye that dwell in the world.

9 For he spake and it was done; * he commanded and it stood fast.

10 The LORD bringeth the counsel of the heathen to nought, * and maketh the devices of the peoples to be of none effect, and casteth out the counsels of princes.

11 The counsel of the LORD shall endure for ever, * and the thoughts of his heart from generation to generation.

12 Blessed are the people whose God is the Lord JEHO-VAH, * and blessed are the folk that he hath chosen to him to be his inheritance.

13 The LORD looked down from heaven and beheld all the children of men; * from the habitation of his dwelling he considereth all them that dwell on the earth.

14 He fashioneth all the hearts of them, * and understandeth all their works.

15 There is no king that can be saved by the multitude of an host, * neither is any mighty man delivered by much strength.

16 A horse is counted but a vain thing to save a man, * neither shall he deliver any man by his great strength.

17 Behold, the eye of the LORD is upon them that fear him, * and upon them that put their trust in his mercy,

18 To deliver their soul from death, * and to feed them in the time of dearth.

19 Our soul hath patiently tarried for the LORD, * for he is our help and our shield.

20 For our heart shall rejoice in him, * because we have hoped in his holy name.

21 Let thy merciful kindness, O LORD, be upon us, * like as we do put our trust in thee.

Psalm 34. *Benedicam Domino.*

I WILL alway give thanks unto the LORD; * his praise shall ever be in my mouth.

2 My soul shall make her boast in the LORD; * the humble shall hear thereof and be glad.

3 O praise the LORD with me, * and let us magnify his name together.

4 I sought the LORD and he heard me; * yea, he delivered me out of all my fear.

5 They had an eye unto him and were lightened, * and their faces were not ashamed.

6 Lo, the poor crieth and the LORD heareth him, * yea, and saveth him out of all his troubles.

7 The angel of the LORD tarrieth round about them that fear him * and delivereth them.

8 O taste and see how gracious the LORD is: * blessed is the man that trusteth in him.

9 O fear the LORD, ye that are his saints, * for they that fear him lack nothing.

10 The lions do lack and suffer hunger, * but they who seek the LORD shall want no manner of thing that is good.

11 Come, ye children, and hearken unto me; * I will teach you the fear of the LORD.

12 What man is he that lusteth to live, * and would fain see good days?

13 Keep thy tongue from evil, * and thy lips, that they speak no guile.

14 Eschew evil and do good; * seek peace and pursue it.

15 The eyes of the LORD are over the righteous, * and his ears are open unto their prayers.

16 The countenance of the LORD is against them that do evil, * to root out the remembrance of them from the earth.

17 The righteous cry and the LORD heareth them, * and delivereth them out of all their troubles.

18 The LORD is nigh unto them that are of a contrite heart, * and will save such as be of an humble spirit.

19 Great are the troubles of the righteous, * but the LORD delivereth him out of all.

20 He keepeth all his bones, * so that not one of them is broken.

21 But misfortune shall slay the ungodly, * and they that hate the righteous shall be desolate.

22 The LORD delivereth the souls of his servants, * and all they that put their trust in him shall not be destitute.

Day 7. Morning Prayer.
Psalm 35. *Judica, Domine.*

PLEAD thou my cause, O LORD, with them that strive with me, * and fight thou against them that fight against me.

2 Lay hand upon the shield and buckler, * and stand up to help me.

3 Bring forth the spear and stop the way against them that persecute me; * say unto my soul, 'I am thy salvation.'

4 Let them be confounded and put to shame that seek after my soul; * let them be turned back and brought to confusion that imagine mischief for me.

5 Let them be as the dust before the wind, * and the angel of the LORD scattering them.

6 Let their way be dark and slippery, * and let the angel of the LORD persecute them.

7 For they have privily laid their net to destroy me with-

out a cause; * yea, even without a cause have they made a pit for my soul.

8 Let a sudden destruction come upon him unawares, and his net, that he hath laid privily, catch himself, * that he may fall into his own mischief.

9 And, my soul, be joyful in the LORD; * it shall rejoice in his salvation.

10 All my bones shall say, 'LORD, who is like unto thee, who deliverest the poor from him that is too strong for him? * yea, the poor, and him that is in misery, from him that spoileth him?'

11 False witnesses did rise up; * they laid to my charge things that I knew not.

12 They rewarded me evil for good, * to the great discomfort of my soul.

13 Nevertheless, when they were sick, I put on sackcloth and humbled my soul with fasting, * and my prayer shall turn into mine own bosom.

14 I behaved myself as though it had been my friend or my brother; * I went heavily as one that mourneth for his mother.

15 But in mine adversity they rejoiced and gathered themselves together; * yea, the very abjects came together against me unawares, making mouths at me, and ceased not.

16 With the flatterers were busy mockers * who gnashed upon me with their teeth.

17 Lord, how long wilt thou look upon this? * O deliver my soul from the calamities which they bring on me, and my darling from the lions.

18 So will I give thee thanks in the great congregation; * I will praise thee among much people.

19 O let not them that are mine enemies triumph over me ungodly, * neither let them wink with their eyes that hate me without a cause.

20 And why? their communing is not for peace, * but they imagine deceitful words against them that are quiet in the land.

21 They gaped upon me with their mouths and said, * 'Fie on thee, fie on thee, we saw it with our eyes!'

22 This thou hast seen, O LORD; * hold not thy tongue then; go not far from me, O Lord.

23 Awake and stand up to judge my quarrel; * avenge thou my cause, my God and my Lord.

24 Judge me, O LORD my God, according to thy righteousness, * and let them not triumph over me.

25 Let them not say in their hearts, 'There, there, so would we have it'; * neither let them say, 'We have devoured him.'

26 Let them be put to confusion and shame together that rejoice at my trouble; * let them be clothed with rebuke and dishonour that boast themselves against me.

27 Let them be glad and rejoice that favour my righteous dealing; * yea, let them say alway, 'Blessed be the LORD, who hath pleasure in the prosperity of his servant.'

28 And as for my tongue, it shall be talking of thy righteousness * and of thy praise all the day long.

Psalm 36. *Dixit injustus.*

M Y heart showeth me the wickedness of the ungodly, *
that there is no fear of God before his eyes.

2 For he flattereth himself in his own sight, * until his abominable sin be found out.

3 The words of his mouth are unrighteous and full of deceit; * he hath left off to behave himself wisely and to do good.

4 He imagineth mischief upon his bed, and hath set himself in no good way, * neither doth he abhor anything that is evil.

5 Thy mercy, O LORD, reacheth unto the heavens, * and thy faithfulness unto the clouds.

6 Thy righteousness standeth like the strong mountains; * thy judgements are like the great deep.

7 Thou, LORD, shalt save both man and beast – how excellent is thy mercy, O God! – * and the children of men shall put their trust under the shadow of thy wings.

8 They shall be satisfied with the plenteousness of thy house, * and thou shalt give them drink of thy pleasures as out of the river.

9 For with thee is the well of life, * and in thy light shall we see light.

10 O continue forth thy loving-kindness unto them that know thee, * and thy righteousness unto them that are true of heart.

11 O let not the foot of pride come against me, * and let not the hand of the ungodly cast me down.

12 There are they fallen, all that work wickedness; * they are cast down and shall not be able to stand.

Day 7. Evening Prayer.
Psalm 37. *Noli aemulari.*

Fret not thyself because of the ungodly, * neither be thou envious against the evildoers.

2 For they shall soon be cut down like the grass, * and be withered even as the green herb.

3 Put thou thy trust in the Lord and be doing good; * dwell in the land and verily thou shalt be fed.

4 Delight thou in the Lord, * and he shall give thee thy heart's desire.

5 Commit thy way unto the Lord, and put thy trust in him, * and he shall bring it to pass.

6 He shall make thy righteousness as clear as the light, * and thy just dealing as the noonday.

7 Hold thee still in the Lord, and abide patiently upon him; * but grieve not thyself at him whose way doth prosper, against the man that doeth after evil counsels.

8 Leave off from wrath and let go displeasure; * fret not thyself, else shalt thou be moved to do evil.

9 Wicked doers shall be rooted out, * and they that patiently abide the Lord, those shall inherit the land.

10 Yet a little while and the ungodly shall be clean gone; * thou shalt look after his place, and he shall be away.

11 But the meek-spirited shall possess the earth, * and shall be refreshed in the multitude of peace.

12 The ungodly seeketh counsel against the just, * and gnasheth upon him with his teeth.

13 The Lord shall laugh him to scorn, * for he hath seen that his day is coming.

14 The ungodly have drawn out the sword and have bent their bow, * to cast down the poor and needy, and to slay such as are of a right conversation.

15 Their sword shall go through their own heart, * and their bow shall be broken.

16 A small thing that the righteous hath * is better than great riches of the ungodly.

17 For the arms of the ungodly shall be broken, * and the LORD upholdeth the righteous.

18 The LORD knoweth the days of the godly, * and their inheritance shall endure for ever.

19 They shall not be confounded in the perilous time, * and in the days of dearth they shall have enough.

20 As for the ungodly, they shall perish, and the enemies of the LORD shall consume as the fat of lambs; * yea, even as the smoke shall they consume away.

21 The ungodly borroweth and payeth not again, * but the righteous is merciful and liberal.

22 Such as are blessed of God shall possess the land, * and they that are cursed of him shall be rooted out.

23 The LORD ordereth a good man's going, * and maketh his way acceptable to himself.

24 Though he fall, he shall not be cast away, * for the LORD upholdeth him with his hand.

25 I have been young, and now am old, * and yet saw I never the righteous forsaken, nor his seed begging their bread.

26 The righteous is ever merciful and lendeth, * and his seed is blessed.

27 Flee from evil and do the thing that is good, * and dwell for evermore.

28 For the LORD loveth the thing that is right; * he forsaketh not his that be godly, but they are preserved for ever.

29 The unrighteous shall be punished; * as for the seed of the ungodly, it shall be rooted out.

30 The righteous shall inherit the land, * and dwell therein for ever.

31 The mouth of the righteous is exercised in wisdom, * and his tongue will be talking of judgement.

32 The law of his God is in his heart, * and his goings shall not slide.

33 The ungodly seeth the righteous, * and seeketh occasion to slay him.

34 The LORD will not leave him in his hand, * nor condemn him when he is judged.

35 Hope thou in the LORD and keep his way, and he shall promote thee, that thou shalt possess the land; * when the ungodly shall perish, thou shalt see it.

36 I myself have seen the ungodly in great power, * and flourishing like a green bay tree.

37 I went by, and lo, he was gone; * I sought him, but his place could nowhere be found.

38 Keep innocency and take heed unto the thing that is right, * for that shall bring a man peace at the last.

39 As for the transgressors, they shall perish together; * and the end of the ungodly is, they shall be rooted out at the last.

40 But the salvation of the righteous cometh of the LORD, * who is also their strength in the time of trouble.

41 And the LORD shall stand by them and save them; * he shall deliver them from the ungodly, and shall save them because they put their trust in him.

Day 8. Morning Prayer.
Psalm 38. *Domine, ne in furore.*

PUT me not to rebuke, O LORD, in thine anger, * neither chasten me in thy heavy displeasure.

2 For thine arrows stick fast in me, * and thy hand presseth me sore.

3 There is no health in my flesh, because of thy displeasure; * neither is there any rest in my bones, by reason of my sin.

4 For my wickednesses are gone over my head, * and are like a sore burden, too heavy for me to bear.

5 My wounds stink and are corrupt * through my foolishness.

6 I am brought into so great trouble and misery * that I go mourning all the day long.

7 For my loins are filled with a sore disease, * and there is no whole part in my body.

8 I am feeble and sore smitten; * I have roared for the very disquietness of my heart.

9 Lord, thou knowest all my desire, * and my groaning is not hid from thee.

10 My heart panteth, my strength hath failed me, * and the light of mine eyes is gone from me.

11 My lovers and my neighbours did stand looking upon my trouble, * and my kinsmen stood afar off.

12 They also that sought after my life laid snares for me, * and they that went about to do me evil talked of wickedness and imagined deceit all the day long.

13 As for me, I was like a deaf man and heard not, * and as one that is dumb, who doth not open his mouth.

14 I became even as a man that heareth not, * and in whose mouth are no reproofs.

15 For in thee, O LORD, have I put my trust; * thou shalt answer for me, O Lord my God.

16 I have desired that they, even mine enemies, should not triumph over me; * for when my foot slipped, they rejoiced greatly against me.

17 And I truly am set in the plague, * and my heaviness is ever in my sight.

18 For I will confess my wickedness, * and be sorry for my sin.

19 But mine enemies live and are mighty, * and they that hate me wrongfully are many in number.

20 They also that reward evil for good are against me, * because I follow the thing that good is.

21 Forsake me not, O LORD my God; * be not thou far from me.

22 Haste thee to help me, * O Lord God of my salvation.

Psalm 39. *Dixi, Custodiam.*

I SAID, 'I will take heed to my ways, * that I offend not in my tongue;

2 I will keep my mouth as it were with a bridle, * while the ungodly is in my sight.'

3 I held my tongue and spake nothing; * I kept silence – yea, even from good words – but it was pain and grief to me.

4 My heart was hot within me, and while I was thus musing the fire kindled, * and at the last I spake with my tongue:

5 'LORD, let me know mine end and the number of my days, * that I may be certified how long I have to live.

6 Behold, thou hast made my days as it were a span long, * and mine age is even as nothing in respect of thee, and verily every man living is altogether vanity.

7 For man walketh in a vain shadow and disquieteth himself in vain; * he heapeth up riches and cannot tell who shall gather them.

8 And now, Lord, what is my hope? * truly my hope is even in thee.

9 Deliver me from all mine offences, * and make me not a rebuke unto the foolish.

10 I became dumb and opened not my mouth, * for it was thy doing.

11 Take thy plague away from me; * I am even consumed by the means of thy heavy hand.

12 When thou with rebukes dost chasten man for sin, thou makest his beauty to consume away, like as it were a moth fretting a garment; * every man therefore is but vanity.

13 Hear my prayer, O LORD, and with thine ears consider my calling; * hold not thy peace at my tears.

14 For I am a stranger with thee, * and a sojourner as all my fathers were.

15 O spare me a little, that I may recover my strength, * before I go hence and be no more seen.'

Psalm 40. *Expectans expectavi.*

I WAITED patiently for the LORD, * and he inclined unto me and heard my calling.

2 He brought me also out of the horrible pit, out of the mire and clay; * and set my feet upon the rock; and ordered my goings.

3 And he hath put a new song in my mouth, * even a thanksgiving unto our God.

4 Many shall see it and fear, * and shall put their trust in the LORD.

5 Blessed is the man that hath set his hope in the LORD, * and turned not unto the proud and to such as go about with lies.

6 O LORD my God, great are the wondrous works which thou hast done, like as be also thy thoughts which are to us-ward, * and yet there is no man that ordereth them unto thee.

7 If I should declare them and speak of them, * they should be more than I am able to express.

8 Sacrifice and meat offering thou wouldest not, * but mine ears hast thou opened.

9 Burnt offerings and sacrifice for sin hast thou not required; * then said I, 'Lo, I come;

10 In the volume of the book it is written of me that I

should fulfil thy will, O my God. * I am content to do it; yea, thy law is within my heart.'

11 I have declared thy righteousness in the great congregation; * lo, I will not refrain my lips, O LORD, and that thou knowest.

12 I have not hid thy righteousness within my heart; * my talk hath been of thy truth and of thy salvation.

13 I have not kept back thy loving mercy and truth * from the great congregation.

14 Withdraw not thou thy mercy from me, O LORD; * let thy loving-kindness and thy truth alway preserve me.

15 For innumerable troubles are come about me; my sins have taken such hold upon me that I am not able to look up; * yea, they are more in number than the hairs of my head, and my heart hath failed me.

16 O LORD, let it be thy pleasure to deliver me; * make haste, O LORD, to help me.

17 Let them be ashamed and confounded together that seek after my soul to destroy it; * let them be driven backward and put to rebuke that wish me evil.

18 Let them be desolate and rewarded with shame * that say unto me, 'Fie upon thee, fie upon thee!'

19 Let all those that seek thee be joyful and glad in thee, * and let such as love thy salvation say alway, 'The LORD be praised.'

20 As for me, I am poor and needy, * but the Lord careth for me.

21 Thou art my helper and redeemer; * make no long tarrying, O my God.

Day 8. Evening Prayer.

Psalm 41. *Beatus qui intelligit.*

BLESSED is he that considereth the poor and needy; *
the LORD shall deliver him in the time of trouble.

2 The LORD preserve him and keep him alive, that he
may be blessed upon earth; * and deliver not thou him
into the will of his enemies.

3 The LORD comfort him when he lieth sick upon his
bed; * make thou all his bed in his sickness.

4 I said, 'LORD, be merciful unto me; * heal my soul, for
I have sinned against thee.'

5 Mine enemies speak evil of me, * 'When shall he die,
and his name perish?'

6 And if he come to see me, he speaketh vanity, * and
his heart conceiveth falsehood within himself, and when
he cometh forth he telleth it.

7 All mine enemies whisper together against me, * even
against me do they imagine this evil:

8 'Let the sentence of guiltiness proceed against him; *
and now that he lieth, let him rise up no more.'

9 Yea, even mine own familiar friend, whom I trusted, *
who did also eat of my bread, hath laid great wait for me.

10 But be thou merciful unto me, O LORD; * raise thou
me up again, and I shall reward them.

11 By this I know thou favourest me: * that mine enemy
doth not triumph against me.

12 And when I am in my health, thou upholdest me, *
and shalt set me before thy face for ever.

13 Blessed be the LORD God of Israel, * world without
end. Amen.

Psalm 42. *Quemadmodum.*

LIKE as the hart desireth the water-brooks, * so longeth my soul after thee, O God.

2 My soul is athirst for God, yea, even for the living God; * when shall I come to appear before the presence of God?

3 My tears have been my meat day and night, * while they daily say unto me, 'Where is now thy God?'

4 Now when I think thereupon, I pour out my heart by myself – * for I went with the multitude, and brought them forth into the house of God,

5 In the voice of praise and thanksgiving * among such as keep holy day.

6 Why art thou so full of heaviness, O my soul? * and why art thou so disquieted within me?

7 Put thy trust in God, * for I will yet give him thanks for the help of his countenance.

8 My God, my soul is vexed within me; * therefore will I remember thee from the land of Jordan and the little hill of Hermon.

9 One deep calleth another, because of the noise of the water-pipes; * all thy waves and storms are gone over me.

10 The LORD hath granted his loving-kindness in the daytime; * and in the night season did I sing of him, and made my prayer unto the God of my life.

11 I will say unto the God of my strength, 'Why hast thou forgotten me? * why go I thus heavily, while the enemy oppresseth me?'

12 My bones are smitten asunder as with a sword, * while mine enemies that trouble me cast me in the teeth,

13 Namely, while they say daily unto me, * 'Where is now thy God?'

14 Why art thou so vexed, O my soul? * and why art thou so disquieted within me?

15 O put thy trust in God, * for I will yet thank him, which is the help of my countenance and my God.

Psalm 43. *Judica me, Deus.*

GIVE sentence with me, O God, and defend my cause against the ungodly people; * O deliver me from the deceitful and wicked man.

2 For thou art the God of my strength; why hast thou put me from thee? * and why go I so heavily, while the enemy oppresseth me?

3 O send out thy light and thy truth, that they may lead me, * and bring me unto thy holy hill and to thy dwelling;

4 And that I may go unto the altar of God, even unto the God of my joy and gladness; * and upon the harp will I give thanks unto thee, O God, my God.

5 Why art thou so heavy, O my soul? * and why art thou so disquieted within me?

6 O put thy trust in God, * for I will yet give him thanks, which is the help of my countenance and my God.

Day 9. Morning Prayer.
Psalm 44. *Deus, auribus.*

WE have heard with our ears, O God, our fathers have told us, * what thou hast done in their time of old:

2 How thou hast driven out the heathen with thy hand,

and planted them in; * how thou hast destroyed the nations and cast them out.

3 For they gat not the land in possession through their own sword, * neither was it their own arm that helped them,

4 But thy right hand, and thine arm, and the light of thy countenance, * because thou hadst a favour unto them.

5 Thou art my king, O God; * send help unto Jacob.

6 Through thee will we overthrow our enemies, * and in thy name will we tread them under that rise up against us.

7 For I will not trust in my bow; * it is not my sword that shall help me;

8 But it is thou that savest us from our enemies, * and puttest them to confusion that hate us.

9 We make our boast of God all day long, * and will praise thy name for ever.

10 But now thou art far off, and puttest us to confusion, * and goest not forth with our armies.

11 Thou makest us to turn our backs upon our enemies, * so that they which hate us spoil our goods.

12 Thou lettest us be eaten up like sheep, * and hast scattered us among the heathen.

13 Thou sellest thy people for nought, * and takest no money for them.

14 Thou makest us to be rebuked of our neighbours, * to be laughed to scorn, and had in derision of them that are round about us.

15 Thou makest us to be a byword among the heathen, * and that the peoples shake their heads at us.

16 My confusion is daily before me, * and the shame of my face hath covered me,

17 For the voice of the slanderer and blasphemer, * for the enemy and avenger.

18 And though all this be come upon us, yet do we not forget thee, * nor behave ourselves frowardly in thy covenant.

19 Our heart is not turned back, * neither our steps gone out of thy way;

20 No, not when thou hast smitten us into the place of dragons, * and covered us with the shadow of death.

21 If we have forgotten the name of our God, and holden up our hands to any strange god, * shall not God search it out? for he knoweth the very secrets of the heart.

22 For thy sake also are we killed all the day long, * and are counted as sheep appointed to be slain.

23 Up, Lord, why sleepest thou? * awake and be not absent from us for ever.

24 Wherefore hidest thou thy face, * and forgettest our misery and trouble?

25 For our soul is brought low, even unto the dust; * our belly cleaveth unto the ground.

26 Arise and help us, * and deliver us for thy mercy's sake.

Psalm 45. *Eructavit cor meum.*

MY heart is inditing of a good matter; * I speak of the things which I have made unto the king.

2 My tongue is the pen * of a ready writer.

3 Thou art fairer than the children of men; * full of grace are thy lips, because God hath blessed thee for ever.

4 Gird thee with thy sword upon thy thigh, O thou most mighty, * according to thy worship and renown.

5 Good luck have thou with thine honour: * ride on because of the word of truth, of meekness, and righteousness; and thy right hand shall teach thee terrible things.

6 Thy arrows are very sharp (and the peoples shall be subdued unto thee), * even in the midst among the king's enemies.

7 Thy seat, O God, endureth for ever; * the sceptre of thy kingdom is a right sceptre.

8 Thou hast loved righteousness and hated iniquity; * wherefore God, even thy God, hath anointed thee with the oil of gladness above thy fellows.

9 All thy garments smell of myrrh, aloes, and cassia, * out of the ivory palaces whereby they have made thee glad.

10 Kings' daughters were among thy honourable women; * upon thy right hand did stand the queen in a vesture of gold, wrought about with divers colours.

11 Hearken, O daughter, and consider; incline thine ear; * forget also thine own people and thy father's house.

12 So shall the king have pleasure in thy beauty, * for he is thy Lord God, and worship thou him.

13 And the daughter of Tyre shall be there with a gift, * like as the rich also among the people shall make their supplication before thee.

14 The king's daughter is all glorious within; * her clothing is of wrought gold.

15 She shall be brought unto the king in raiment of

needlework; * the virgins that be her fellows shall bear her company, and shall be brought unto thee.

16 With joy and gladness shall they be brought, * and shall enter into the king's palace.

17 Instead of thy fathers thou shalt have children, * whom thou mayest make princes in all lands.

18 I will remember thy name from one generation to another; * therefore shall the peoples give thanks unto thee, world without end.

Psalm 46. *Deus noster refugium.*

GOD is our hope and strength, * a very present help in trouble.

2 Therefore will we not fear, though the earth be moved, * and though the hills be carried into the midst of the sea,

3 Though the waters thereof rage and swell, * and though the mountains shake at the tempest of the same.

4 The rivers of the flood thereof shall make glad the city of God, * the holy place of the tabernacle of the Most Highest.

5 God is in the midst of her; therefore shall she not be removed; * God shall help her, and that right early.

6 The heathen make much ado and the kingdoms are moved, * but God hath showed his voice, and the earth shall melt away.

7 The LORD of hosts is with us; * the God of Jacob is our refuge.

8 O come hither and behold the works of the LORD, * what destruction he hath brought upon the earth.

9 He maketh wars to cease in all the world; * he breaketh the bow, and knappeth the spear in sunder, and burneth the chariots in the fire.

10 Be still then and know that I am God: * I will be exalted among the heathen, and I will be exalted in the earth.

11 The LORD of hosts is with us; * the God of Jacob is our refuge.

Day 9. Evening Prayer.
Psalm 47. *Omnes gentes, plaudite.*

O CLAP your hands together, all ye peoples; * O sing unto God with the voice of melody.

2 For the LORD is high and to be feared; * he is the great king upon all the earth.

3 He shall subdue the peoples under us, * and the nations under our feet.

4 He shall choose out an heritage for us, * even the worship of Jacob, whom he loved.

5 God is gone up with a merry noise, * and the LORD with the sound of the trump.

6 O sing praises, sing praises unto our God; * O sing praises, sing praises unto our king.

7 For God is the king of all the earth: * sing ye praises with understanding.

8 God reigneth over the heathen; * God sitteth upon his holy seat.

9 The princes of the peoples are joined unto the people of the God of Abraham; * for God, which is very high exalted, doth defend the earth as it were with a shield.

Psalm 48. *Magnus Dominus.*

G REAT is the LORD and highly to be praised * in the
city of our God, even upon his holy hill.

2 The hill of Sion is a fair place and the joy of the whole earth; * upon the north side lieth the city of the great king; God is well known in her palaces as a sure refuge.

3 For lo, the kings of the earth * are gathered and gone by together.

4 They marvelled to see such things; * they were astonished and suddenly cast down.

5 Fear came there upon them, and sorrow * as upon a woman in her travail.

6 Thou shalt break the ships of the sea * through the east wind.

7 Like as we have heard, so have we seen in the city of the LORD of hosts, in the city of our God: * God upholdeth the same for ever.

8 We wait for thy loving-kindness, O God, * in the midst of thy temple.

9 O God, according to thy name, so is thy praise unto the world's end; * thy right hand is full of righteousness.

10 Let the Mount Sion rejoice and the daughters of Judah be glad, * because of thy judgements.

11 Walk about Sion and go round about her, * and tell the towers thereof.

12 Mark well her bulwarks; count up her houses, * that ye may tell them that come after.

13 For this God is our God for ever and ever; * he shall be our guide unto death.

Psalm 49. *Audite haec, omnes.*

O HEAR ye this, all ye peoples; * ponder it with your ears, all ye that dwell in the world,

2 High and low, rich and poor, * one with another.

3 My mouth shall speak of wisdom, * and my heart shall muse of understanding.

4 I will incline mine ear to the parable, * and show my dark speech upon the harp.

5 Wherefore should I fear in the days of wickedness, * and when the wickedness at my heels compasseth me round about?

6 There be some that put their trust in their goods, * and boast themselves in the multitude of their riches.

7 But no man may deliver his brother, * nor make agreement unto God for him;

8 For it cost more to redeem their souls, * so that he must let that alone for ever,

9 Yea, though he live long * and see not the grave.

10 For he seeth that wise men also die and perish together, * as well as the ignorant and foolish, and leave their riches for others.

11 And yet they think that their houses shall continue for ever, * and that their dwelling places shall endure from one generation to another, and call the lands after their own names.

12 Nevertheless, man will not abide in honour, * seeing he may be compared unto the beasts that perish; this is the way of them.

13 This is their foolishness, * and their posterity praise their sayings.

14 They lie in the hell like sheep; death gnaweth upon them, and the righteous shall have domination over them in the morning; * their beauty shall consume in the sepulchre out of their dwelling.

15 But God hath delivered my soul from the place of hell, * for he shall receive me.

16 Be not thou afraid, though one be made rich, * or if the glory of his house be increased;

17 For he shall carry nothing away with him when he dieth, * neither shall his pomp follow him.

18 For while he lived, he counted himself an happy man; * and so long as thou doest well unto thyself, men will speak good of thee.

19 He shall follow the generation of his fathers, * and shall never see light.

20 Man being in honour hath no understanding, * but is compared unto the beasts that perish.

Day 10. Morning Prayer.
Psalm 50. *Deus deorum.*

THE LORD, even the most mighty God, hath spoken, * and called the world from the rising up of the sun unto the going down thereof.

2 Out of Sion hath God appeared * in perfect beauty.

3 Our God shall come, and shall not keep silence; * there shall go before him a consuming fire, and a mighty tempest shall be stirred up round about him.

4 He shall call the heaven from above, * and the earth, that he may judge his people:

5 'Gather my saints together unto me, * those that have made a covenant with me with sacrifice.'

6 And the heavens shall declare his righteousness, * for God is judge himself.

7 'Hear, O my people, and I will speak; * I myself will testify against thee, O Israel, for I am God, even thy God.

8 I will not reprove thee because of thy sacrifices or for thy burnt offerings, * because they were not alway before me.

9 I will take no bullock out of thine house, * nor he-goat out of thy folds.

10 For all the beasts of the forest are mine, * and so are the cattle upon a thousand hills.

11 I know all the fowls upon the mountains, * and the wild beasts of the field are in my sight.

12 If I be hungry, I will not tell thee, * for the whole world is mine and all that is therein.

13 Thinkest thou that I will eat bulls' flesh * and drink the blood of goats?

14 Offer unto God thanksgiving, * and pay thy vows unto the Most Highest.

15 And call upon me in the time of trouble; * so will I hear thee, and thou shalt praise me.'

16 But unto the ungodly said God, * 'Why dost thou preach my laws, and takest my covenant in thy mouth;

17 Whereas thou hatest to be reformed, * and hast cast my words behind thee?

18 When thou sawest a thief, thou consentedst unto him, * and hast been partaker with the adulterers.

19 Thou hast let thy mouth speak wickedness, * and with thy tongue thou hast set forth deceit.

20 Thou satest and spakest against thy brother, * yea, and hast slandered thine own mother's son.

21 These things hast thou done and I held my tongue, and thou thoughtest wickedly that I am even such a one as thyself, * but I will reprove thee and set before thee the things that thou hast done.

22 O consider this, ye that forget God, * lest I pluck you away and there be none to deliver you.

23 Whoso offereth me thanks and praise, he honoureth me, * and to him that ordereth his conversation right will I show the salvation of God.'

Psalm 51. *Miserere mei, Deus.*

Have mercy upon me, O God, after thy great good-ness; * according to the multitude of thy mercies do away mine offences.

2 Wash me throughly from my wickedness, * and cleanse me from my sin.

3 For I acknowledge my faults, * and my sin is ever be-fore me.

4 Against thee only have I sinned and done this evil in thy sight, * that thou mightest be justified in thy saying and clear when thou art judged.

5 Behold, I was shapen in wickedness, * and in sin hath my mother conceived me.

6 But lo, thou requirest truth in the inward parts, * and shalt make me to understand wisdom secretly.

7 Thou shalt purge me with hyssop, and I shall be clean; *
thou shalt wash me, and I shall be whiter than snow.

8 Thou shalt make me hear of joy and gladness, * that
the bones which thou hast broken may rejoice.

9 Turn thy face from my sins, * and put out all my misdeeds.

10 Make me a clean heart, O God, * and renew a right
spirit within me.

11 Cast me not away from thy presence, * and take not
thy holy Spirit from me.

12 O give me the comfort of thy help again, * and stablish me with thy free Spirit.

13 Then shall I teach thy ways unto the wicked, * and
sinners shall be converted unto thee.

14 Deliver me from blood-guiltiness, O God, thou that
art the God of my health; * and my tongue shall sing of
thy righteousness.

15 Thou shalt open my lips, O Lord, * and my mouth
shall show thy praise.

16 For thou desirest no sacrifice, else would I give it
thee, * but thou delightest not in burnt offerings.

17 The sacrifice of God is a troubled spirit; * a broken
and contrite heart, O God, shalt thou not despise.

18 O be favourable and gracious unto Sion; * build thou
the walls of Jerusalem.

19 Then shalt thou be pleased with the sacrifice of righteousness, with the burnt offerings and oblations; * then
shall they offer young bullocks upon thine altar.

Psalm 52. *Quid gloriaris?*

WHY boastest thou thyself, thou tyrant, * that thou canst do mischief,

2 Whereas the goodness of God * endureth yet daily?

3 Thy tongue imagineth wickedness, * and with lies thou cuttest like a sharp razor.

4 Thou hast loved unrighteousness more than goodness, * and to talk of lies more than righteousness.

5 Thou hast loved to speak all words that may do hurt, * O thou false tongue.

6 Therefore shall God destroy thee for ever; * he shall take thee and pluck thee out of thy dwelling, and root thee out of the land of the living.

7 The righteous also shall see this and fear, * and shall laugh him to scorn:

8 'Lo, this is the man that took not God for his strength, * but trusted unto the multitude of his riches, and strengthened himself in his wickedness.'

9 As for me, I am like a green olive tree in the house of God; * my trust is in the tender mercy of God for ever and ever.

10 I will always give thanks unto thee, for that thou hast done; * and I will hope in thy name, for thy saints like it well.

Day 10. Evening Prayer.
Psalm 53. *Dixit insipiens.*

THE foolish body hath said in his heart, * 'There is no God.'

2 Corrupt are they and become abominable in their wickedness; * there is none that doeth good.

3 God looked down from heaven upon the children of men, * to see if there were any that would understand and seek after God.

4 But they are all gone out of the way; they are altogether become abominable; * there is also none that doeth good, no, not one.

5 Are not they without understanding that work wickedness, * eating up my people as if they would eat bread? they have not called upon God.

6 They were afraid where no fear was, * for God hath broken the bones of him that besieged thee; thou hast put them to confusion, because God hath despised them.

7 O that the salvation were given unto Israel out of Sion! * O that the Lord would deliver his people out of captivity!

8 Then should Jacob rejoice, * and Israel should be right glad.

Psalm 54. *Deus, in nomine.*

SAVE me, O God, for thy name's sake, * and avenge me in thy strength.

2 Hear my prayer, O God, * and hearken unto the words of my mouth.

3 For strangers are risen up against me; * and tyrants, which have not God before their eyes, seek after my soul.

4 Behold, God is my helper; * the Lord is with them that uphold my soul.

5 He shall reward evil unto mine enemies; * destroy thou them in thy truth.

6 An offering of a free heart will I give thee, and praise thy name, O LORD, * because it is so comfortable.

7 For he hath delivered me out of all my trouble, * and mine eye hath seen his desire upon mine enemies.

Psalm 55. *Exaudi, Deus.*

Hear my prayer, O God, * and hide not thyself from my petition.

2 Take heed unto me and hear me, * how I mourn in my prayer and am vexed.

3 The enemy crieth so and the ungodly cometh on so fast, * for they are minded to do me some mischief, so maliciously are they set against me.

4 My heart is disquieted within me, * and the fear of death is fallen upon me.

5 Fearfulness and trembling are come upon me, * and an horrible dread hath overwhelmed me.

6 And I said, 'O that I had wings like a dove! * for then would I flee away and be at rest.

7 Lo, then would I get me away far off, * and remain in the wilderness.

8 I would make haste to escape, * because of the stormy wind and tempest.'

9 Destroy their tongues, O Lord, and divide them, * for I have spied unrighteousness and strife in the city.

10 Day and night they go about within the walls thereof; * mischief also and sorrow are in the midst of it.

11 Wickedness is therein; * deceit and guile go not out of their streets.

12 For it is not an open enemy that hath done me this dishonour, * for then I could have borne it;

13 Neither was it mine adversary that did magnify himself against me, * for then peradventure I would have hid myself from him.

14 But it was even thou, my companion, * my guide, and mine own familiar friend;

15 We took sweet counsel together, * and walked in the house of God as friends.

16 Let death come hastily upon them, and let them go down quick into hell, * for wickedness is in their dwellings and among them.

17 As for me, I will call upon God, * and the LORD shall save me.

18 In the evening and morning and at noonday will I pray, and that instantly, * and he shall hear my voice.

19 It is he that hath delivered my soul in peace from the battle that was against me, * for there were many with me.

20 Yea, even God, that endureth for ever, shall hear me and bring them down, * for they will not turn, nor fear God.

21 He laid his hands upon such as be at peace with him, * and he brake his covenant.

22 The words of his mouth were softer than butter, having war in his heart; * his words were smoother than oil, and yet be they very swords.

23 O cast thy burden upon the LORD, and he shall nourish thee, * and shall not suffer the righteous to fall for ever.

24 And as for them: * thou, O God, shalt bring them into the pit of destruction.

25 The bloodthirsty and deceitful men shall not live out half their days; * nevertheless, my trust shall be in thee, O Lord.

Day 11. Morning Prayer.
Psalm 56. *Miserere mei, Deus.*

B E merciful unto me, O God, for man goeth about to devour me; * he is daily fighting and troubling me.

2 Mine enemies are daily at hand to swallow me up, * for they be many that fight against me, O thou Most Highest.

3 Nevertheless, though I am sometime afraid, * yet put I my trust in thee.

4 I will praise God because of his word; * I have put my trust in God, and will not fear what flesh can do unto me.

5 They daily mistake my words; * all that they imagine is to do me evil.

6 They hold all together and keep themselves close, * and mark my steps when they lay wait for my soul.

7 Shall they escape for their wickedness? * thou, O God, in thy displeasure shalt cast them down.

8 Thou tellest my flittings; put my tears into thy bottle; * are not these things noted in thy book?

9 Whensoever I call upon thee, then shall mine enemies be put to flight; * this I know, for God is on my side.

10 In God's word will I rejoice; * in the LORD's word will I comfort me.

11 Yea, in God have I put my trust; * I will not be afraid what man can do unto me.

12 Unto thee, O God, will I pay my vows; * unto thee will I give thanks.

13 For thou hast delivered my soul from death and my feet from falling, * that I may walk before God in the light of the living.

Psalm 57. *Miserere mei, Deus.*

BE merciful unto me, O God, be merciful unto me, for my soul trusteth in thee, * and under the shadow of thy wings shall be my refuge until this tyranny be overpast.

2 I will call unto the most high God, * even unto the God that shall perform the cause which I have in hand.

3 He shall send from heaven, * and save me from the reproof of him that would eat me up.

4 God shall send forth his mercy and truth; * my soul is among lions.

5 And I lie even among the children of men that are set on fire, * whose teeth are spears and arrows, and their tongue a sharp sword.

6 Set up thyself, O God, above the heavens, * and thy glory above all the earth.

7 They have laid a net for my feet and pressed down my soul; * they have digged a pit before me, and are fallen into the midst of it themselves.

8 My heart is fixed, O God, my heart is fixed: * I will sing and give praise.

9 Awake up, my glory; awake, lute and harp! * I myself will awake right early.

10 I will give thanks unto thee, O Lord, among the peoples, * and I will sing unto thee among the nations.

11 For the greatness of thy mercy reacheth unto the heavens, * and thy truth unto the clouds.

12 Set up thyself, O God, above the heavens, * and thy glory above all the earth.

Psalm 58. *Si vere utique.*

ARE your minds set upon righteousness, O ye congregation? * and do ye judge the thing that is right, O ye sons of men?

2 Yea, ye imagine mischief in your heart upon the earth, * and your hands deal with wickedness.

3 The ungodly are froward, even from their mother's womb; * as soon as they are born, they go astray and speak lies.

4 They are as venomous as the poison of a serpent, * even like the deaf adder that stoppeth her ears,

5 Which refuseth to hear the voice of the charmer, * charm he never so wisely.

6 Break their teeth, O God, in their mouths; smite the jawbones of the lions, O LORD. * Let them fall away like water that runneth apace, and when they shoot their arrows, let them be rooted out.

7 Let them consume away like a snail, and be like the untimely fruit of a woman, * and let them not see the sun.

8 Or ever your pots be made hot with thorns, * let him carry them away raw in his wrath.

9 The righteous shall rejoice when he seeth the vengeance; * he shall wash his footsteps in the blood of the ungodly,

10 So that a man shall say, 'Verily there is a reward for

the righteous; * doubtless there is a God that judgeth the earth.'

Day 11. Evening Prayer.
Psalm 59. *Eripe me de inimicis.*

DELIVER me from mine enemies, O God; * defend me from them that rise up against me.

2 O deliver me from the wicked doers, * and save me from the bloodthirsty men.

3 For lo, they lie waiting for my soul; * the mighty men are gathered against me, without any offence or fault of me, O LORD.

4 They run and prepare themselves without my fault; * arise thou therefore to help me, and behold.

5 Stand up, O LORD God of hosts, thou God of Israel, to visit all the heathen; * and be not merciful unto them that offend of malicious wickedness.

6 They go to and fro in the evening; * they grin like a dog and run about through the city.

7 Behold, they speak with their mouth, and swords are in their lips: * 'For who doth hear?'

8 But thou, O LORD, shalt have them in derision, * and thou shalt laugh all the heathen to scorn.

9 My strength will I ascribe unto thee, * for thou art the God of my refuge.

10 God showeth me his goodness plenteously, * and God shall let me see my desire upon mine enemies.

11 Slay them not, lest my people forget it, * but scatter them abroad by thy power, and put them down, O Lord our defence.

12 For the sin of their mouth and for the words of their lips, they shall be taken in their pride; * and why? their preaching is of cursing and lies.

13 Consume them in thy wrath; consume them, that they may perish * and know that it is God that ruleth in Jacob and unto the ends of the world.

14 And in the evening they will return, * grin like a dog, and will go about the city.

15 They will run here and there for meat, * and grudge if they be not satisfied.

16 As for me, I will sing of thy power, and will praise thy mercy betimes in the morning, * for thou hast been my defence and refuge in the day of my trouble.

17 Unto thee, O my strength, will I sing; * for thou, O God, art my refuge and my merciful God.

Psalm 60. *Deus, repulisti nos.*

O GOD, thou hast cast us out and scattered us abroad; * thou hast also been displeased; O turn thee unto us again.

2 Thou hast moved the land and divided it; * heal the sores thereof, for it shaketh.

3 Thou hast showed thy people heavy things; * thou hast given us a drink of deadly wine.

4 Thou hast given a token for such as fear thee, * that they may triumph because of the truth.

5 Therefore were thy beloved delivered; * help me with thy right hand and hear me.

6 God hath spoken in his holiness: 'I will rejoice and divide Shechem, * and mete out the valley of Succoth.

7 Gilead is mine and Manasseh is mine; * Ephraim also is the strength of my head; Judah is my lawgiver;

8 Moab is my wash-pot; over Edom will I cast out my shoe; * Philistia, be thou glad of me.'

9 Who will lead me into the strong city? * who will bring me into Edom?

10 Hast not thou cast us out, O God? * wilt not thou, O God, go out with our hosts?

11 O be thou our help in trouble, * for vain is the help of man.

12 Through God will we do great acts, * for it is he that shall tread down our enemies.

Psalm 61. *Exaudi, Deus.*

HEAR my crying, O God; * give ear unto my prayer.
2 From the ends of the earth will I call upon thee, * when my heart is in heaviness.

3 O set me up upon the rock that is higher than I, * for thou hast been my hope, and a strong tower for me against the enemy.

4 I will dwell in thy tabernacle for ever, * and my trust shall be under the covering of thy wings.

5 For thou, O Lord, hast heard my desires, * and hast given an heritage unto those that fear thy name.

6 Thou shalt grant the king a long life, * that his years may endure throughout all generations;

7 He shall dwell before God for ever. * O prepare thy loving mercy and faithfulness, that they may preserve him;

8 So will I always sing praise unto thy name, * that I may daily perform my vows.

Day 12. Morning Prayer.
Psalm 62. *Nonne Deo?*

M Y soul truly waiteth still upon God, * for of him cometh my salvation.

2 He verily is my strength and my salvation; * he is my defence, so that I shall not greatly fall.

3 How long will ye imagine mischief against every man? * Ye shall be slain all the sort of you; yea, as a tottering wall shall ye be, and like a broken hedge.

4 Their device is only how to put him out whom God will exalt; * their delight is in lies; they give good words with their mouth, but curse with their heart.

5 Nevertheless, my soul, wait thou still upon God, * for my hope is in him.

6 He truly is my strength and my salvation; * he is my defence, so that I shall not fall.

7 In God is my health and my glory, * the rock of my might, and in God is my trust.

8 O put your trust in him alway, ye people; * pour out your hearts before him, for God is our hope.

9 As for the children of men, they are but vanity; * the children of men are deceitful; upon the weights they are altogether lighter than vanity itself.

10 O trust not in wrong and robbery; give not yourselves unto vanity; * if riches increase, set not your heart upon them.

11 God spake once, and twice I have also heard the same: * that power belongeth unto God;

12 And that thou, Lord, art merciful, * for thou rewardest every man according to his work.

Psalm 63. *Deus, Deus meus.*

O GOD, thou art my God; * early will I seek thee.

2 My soul thirsteth for thee; my flesh also longeth after thee * in a barren and dry land where no water is.

3 Thus have I looked for thee in holiness, * that I might behold thy power and glory.

4 For thy loving-kindness is better than the life itself; * my lips shall praise thee.

5 As long as I live will I magnify thee in this manner, * and lift up my hands in thy name.

6 My soul shall be satisfied, even as it were with marrow and fatness, * when my mouth praiseth thee with joyful lips.

7 Have I not remembered thee in my bed, * and thought upon thee when I was waking?

8 Because thou hast been my helper, * therefore under the shadow of thy wings will I rejoice.

9 My soul hangeth upon thee; * thy right hand hath upholden me.

10 These also that seek the hurt of my soul, * they shall go under the earth.

11 Let them fall upon the edge of the sword, * that they may be a portion for foxes.

12 But the king shall rejoice in God; all they also that

swear by him shall be commended, * for the mouth of them that speak lies shall be stopped.

Psalm 64. *Exaudi, Deus.*

HEAR my voice, O God, in my prayer; * preserve my life from fear of the enemy.

2 Hide me from the gathering together of the froward, * and from the insurrection of wicked doers,

3 Who have whet their tongue like a sword, * and shoot out their arrows, even bitter words,

4 That they may privily shoot at him that is perfect – * suddenly do they hit him, and fear not.

5 They encourage themselves in mischief, * and commune among themselves how they may lay snares, and say that no man shall see them.

6 They imagine wickedness and practise it, * that they keep secret among themselves, every man in the deep of his heart.

7 But God shall suddenly shoot at them with a swift arrow, * that they shall be wounded.

8 Yea, their own tongues shall make them fall, * insomuch that whoso seeth them shall laugh them to scorn.

9 And all men that see it shall say, 'This hath God done', * for they shall perceive that it is his work.

10 The righteous shall rejoice in the LORD, and put his trust in him, * and all they that are true of heart shall be glad.

Day 12. Evening Prayer.

Psalm 65. *Te decet hymnus.*

THOU, O God, art praised in Sion, * and unto thee shall the vow be performed in Jerusalem.

2 Thou that hearest the prayer, * unto thee shall all flesh come.

3 My misdeeds prevail against me; * O be thou merciful unto our sins.

4 Blessed is the man whom thou choosest and receivest unto thee; * he shall dwell in thy court and shall be satisfied with the pleasures of thy house, even of thy holy temple.

5 Thou shalt show us wonderful things in thy righteousness, O God of our salvation, * thou that art the hope of all the ends of the earth, and of them that remain in the broad sea,

6 Who in his strength setteth fast the mountains, * and is girded about with power,

7 Who stilleth the raging of the sea, * and the noise of his waves, and the madness of the peoples.

8 They also that dwell in the uttermost parts of the earth shall be afraid at thy tokens, * thou that makest the outgoings of the morning and evening to praise thee.

9 Thou visitest the earth and blessest it; * thou makest it very plenteous.

10 The river of God is full of water; * thou preparest their corn, for so thou providest for the earth.

11 Thou waterest her furrows; thou sendest rain into the little valleys thereof; * thou makest it soft with the drops of rain and blessest the increase of it.

12 Thou crownest the year with thy goodness, * and thy clouds drop fatness.

13 They shall drop upon the dwellings of the wilderness, * and the little hills shall rejoice on every side.

14 The folds shall be full of sheep; * the valleys also shall stand so thick with corn that they shall laugh and sing.

Psalm 66. *Jubilate Deo.*

O BE joyful in God, all ye lands; * sing praises unto the honour of his name; make his praise to be glorious.

2 Say unto God, 'O how wonderful art thou in thy works! * through the greatness of thy power shall thine enemies be found liars unto thee.

3 For all the world shall worship thee, * sing of thee, and praise thy name.'

4 O come hither and behold the works of God, * how wonderful he is in his doing toward the children of men.

5 He turned the sea into dry land, * so that they went through the water on foot; there did we rejoice thereof.

6 He ruleth with his power for ever, his eyes behold the peoples, * and such as will not believe shall not be able to exalt themselves.

7 O praise our God, ye peoples, * and make the voice of his praise to be heard,

8 Who holdeth our soul in life * and suffereth not our feet to slip.

9 For thou, O God, hast proved us; * thou also hast tried us, like as silver is tried.

10 Thou broughtest us into the snare, * and laidest trouble upon our loins.

11 Thou sufferedst men to ride over our heads; * we went through fire and water, and thou broughtest us out into a wealthy place.

12 I will go into thine house with burnt offerings, * and will pay thee my vows, which I promised with my lips and spake with my mouth when I was in trouble.

13 I will offer unto thee fat burnt sacrifices with the incense of rams; * I will offer bullocks and goats.

14 O come hither and hearken, all ye that fear God, * and I will tell you what he hath done for my soul.

15 I called unto him with my mouth, * and gave him praises with my tongue.

16 If I incline unto wickedness with mine heart, * the Lord will not hear me.

17 But God hath heard me, * and considered the voice of my prayer.

18 Praised be God, who hath not cast out my prayer, * nor turned his mercy from me.

Psalm 67. *Deus misereatur.*

G OD be merciful unto us and bless us, * and show us the light of his countenance and be merciful unto us,

2 That thy way may be known upon earth, * thy saving health among all nations.

3 Let the peoples praise thee, O God; * yea, let all the peoples praise thee.

4 O let the nations rejoice and be glad, * for thou shalt judge the folk righteously, and govern the nations upon earth.

5 Let the peoples praise thee, O God; * let all the peoples praise thee.

6 Then shall the earth bring forth her increase, * and God, even our own God, shall give us his blessing.

7 God shall bless us, * and all the ends of the world shall fear him.

Day 13. Morning Prayer.
Psalm 68. *Exurgat Deus.*

LET God arise and let his enemies be scattered; * let them also that hate him flee before him.

2 Like as the smoke vanisheth, so shalt thou drive them away; * and like as wax melteth at the fire, so let the ungodly perish at the presence of God.

3 But let the righteous be glad and rejoice before God; * let them also be merry and joyful.

4 O sing unto God and sing praises unto his name; * magnify him that rideth upon the heavens as it were upon an horse; praise him in his name JAH and rejoice before him.

5 He is a father of the fatherless and defendeth the cause of the widows, * even God in his holy habitation.

6 He is the God that maketh men to be of one mind in an house, and bringeth the prisoners out of captivity, * but letteth the runagates continue in scarceness.

7 O God, when thou wentest forth before the people, * when thou wentest through the wilderness,

8 The earth shook and the heavens dropped at the presence of God, * even as Sinai also was moved at the presence of God, who is the God of Israel.

9 Thou, O God, sentest a gracious rain upon thine inheritance, * and refreshedst it when it was weary.

10 Thy congregation shall dwell therein, * for thou, O God, hast of thy goodness prepared for the poor.

11 The Lord gave the word; * great was the company of the preachers.

12 Kings with their armies did flee and were discomfited, * and they of the household divided the spoil.

13 Though ye have lain among the pots, yet shall ye be as the wings of a dove * that is covered with silver wings, and her feathers like gold.

14 When the Almighty scattered kings for their sake, * then were they as white as snow in Salmon.

15 As the hill of Bashan, so is God's hill; * even an high hill, as the hill of Bashan.

16 Why hop ye so, ye high hills? this is God's hill, in the which it pleaseth him to dwell; * yea, the Lord will abide in it for ever.

17 The chariots of God are twenty thousand, even thousands of angels; * and the Lord is among them, as in the holy place of Sinai.

18 Thou art gone up on high; thou hast led captivity captive and received gifts for men, * yea, even for thine enemies, that the Lord God might dwell among them.

19 Praised be the Lord daily, * even the God who helpeth us and poureth his benefits upon us.

20 He is our God, even the God of whom cometh salvation; * God is the Lord, by whom we escape death.

21 God shall wound the head of his enemies, * and the hairy scalp of such a one as goeth on still in his wickedness.

22 The Lord hath said, 'I will bring my people again as I did from Bashan; * mine own will I bring again as I did sometime from the deep of the sea,

23 That thy foot may be dipped in the blood of thine enemies, * and that the tongue of thy dogs may be red through the same.'

24 It is well seen, O God, how thou goest; * how thou, my God and king, goest in the sanctuary.

25 The singers go before, the players follow after; * in the midst are the damsels playing with the timbrels:

26 'Give thanks, O Israel, unto God, the LORD in the congregations, * from the ground of the heart.'

27 There is little Benjamin their ruler, and the princes of Judah their counsel, * the princes of Zebulun and the princes of Naphtali.

28 Thy God hath sent forth strength for thee; * stablish the thing, O God, that thou hast wrought in us,

29 For thy temple's sake at Jerusalem; * so shall kings bring presents unto thee.

30 Rebuke the wild beasts of the reeds, the congregation of mighty bulls with the calves of the peoples, so that they humbly bring pieces of silver; * scatter thou the peoples that delight in war.

31 Then shall the princes come out of Egypt; * Ethiopia shall soon stretch out her hands unto God.

32 Sing unto God, O ye kingdoms of the earth; * O sing praises unto the Lord,

33 Who sitteth in the heavens over all from the beginning – * lo, he doth send out his voice, yea, and that a mighty voice.

34 Ascribe ye the power to God over Israel; * his worship and strength is in the clouds.

35 O God, wonderful art thou in thy holy places; * even
the God of Israel, he will give strength and power unto
his people. Blessed be God.

Day 13. Evening Prayer.
Psalm 69. *Salvum me fac.*

S AVE me, O God, * for the waters are come in, even unto my soul.

2 I stick fast in the deep mire where no ground is; * I
am come into deep waters, so that the floods run over me.

3 I am weary of crying; my throat is dry; * my sight
faileth me for waiting so long upon my God.

4 They that hate me without a cause are more than the
hairs of my head; * they that are mine enemies and would
destroy me guiltless are mighty.

5 I paid them the things that I never took; * God, thou
knowest my simpleness and my faults are not hid from
thee.

6 Let not them that trust in thee, O Lord GOD of hosts,
be ashamed for my cause; * let not those that seek thee be
confounded through me, O Lord God of Israel.

7 And why? for thy sake have I suffered reproof; * shame
hath covered my face.

8 I am become a stranger unto my brethren, * even an
alien unto my mother's children.

9 For the zeal of thine house hath even eaten me, * and
the rebukes of them that rebuked thee are fallen upon
me.

10 I wept and chastened myself with fasting, * and that was turned to my reproof.

11 I put on sackcloth also, * and they jested upon me.

12 They that sit in the gate speak against me, * and the drunkards make songs upon me.

13 But, LORD, I make my prayer unto thee * in an acceptable time.

14 Hear me, O God, in the multitude of thy mercy, * even in the truth of thy salvation.

15 Take me out of the mire, that I sink not; * O let me be delivered from them that hate me, and out of the deep waters.

16 Let not the water-flood drown me, neither let the deep swallow me up, * and let not the pit shut her mouth upon me.

17 Hear me, O LORD, for thy loving-kindness is comfortable; * turn thee unto me according to the multitude of thy mercies.

18 And hide not thy face from thy servant, for I am in trouble; * O haste thee and hear me.

19 Draw nigh unto my soul and save it; * O deliver me because of mine enemies.

20 Thou hast known my reproof, my shame, and my dishonour; * mine adversaries are all in thy sight.

21 Thy rebuke hath broken my heart; I am full of heaviness; * I looked for some to have pity on me, but there was no man, neither found I any to comfort me.

22 They gave me gall to eat, * and when I was thirsty they gave me vinegar to drink.

23 Let their table be made a snare to take themselves

withal, * and let the things that should have been for their wealth be unto them an occasion of falling.

24 Let their eyes be blinded, that they see not, * and ever bow thou down their backs.

25 Pour out thine indignation upon them, * and let thy wrathful displeasure take hold of them.

26 Let their habitation be void, * and no man to dwell in their tents.

27 For they persecute him whom thou hast smitten, * and they talk how they may vex them whom thou hast wounded.

28 Let them fall from one wickedness to another, * and not come into thy righteousness.

29 Let them be wiped out of the book of the living, * and not be written among the righteous.

30 As for me, when I am poor and in heaviness, * thy help, O God, shall lift me up.

31 I will praise the name of God with a song, * and magnify it with thanksgiving.

32 This also shall please the LORD * better than a bullock that hath horns and hoofs.

33 The humble shall consider this and be glad; * seek ye after God, and your soul shall live.

34 For the LORD heareth the poor, * and despiseth not his prisoners.

35 Let heaven and earth praise him, * the sea and all that moveth therein.

36 For God will save Sion and build the cities of Judah, * that men may dwell there and have it in possession.

37 The posterity also of his servants shall inherit it, *
and they that love his name shall dwell therein.

Psalm 70. *Deus, in adjutorium.*

HASTE thee, O God, to deliver me; * make haste to
help me, O LORD.

2 Let them be ashamed and confounded that seek after
my soul; * let them be turned backward and put to confusion that wish me evil.

3 Let them for their reward be soon brought to shame *
that cry over me, 'There, there!'

4 But let all those that seek thee be joyful and glad in
thee, * and let all such as delight in thy salvation say alway,
'The Lord be praised.'

5 As for me, I am poor and in misery; * haste thee unto
me, O God.

6 Thou art my helper and my redeemer; * O LORD,
make no long tarrying.

Day 14. Morning Prayer.
Psalm 71. *In te, Domine, speravi.*

IN thee, O LORD, have I put my trust; let me never be put
to confusion, * but rid me and deliver me in thy righteousness; incline thine ear unto me and save me.

2 Be thou my stronghold, whereunto I may alway resort; * thou hast promised to help me, for thou art my
house of defence and my castle.

3 Deliver me, O my God, out of the hand of the ungodly, * out of the hand of the unrighteous and cruel man.

4 For thou, O Lord GOD, art the thing that I long for; * thou art my hope even from my youth.

5 Through thee have I been holden up ever since I was born; * thou art he that took me out of my mother's womb; my praise shall be always of thee.

6 I am become as it were a monster unto many, * but my sure trust is in thee.

7 O let my mouth be filled with thy praise, * that I may sing of thy glory and honour all the day long.

8 Cast me not away in the time of age; * forsake me not when my strength faileth me.

9 For mine enemies speak against me, and they that lay wait for my soul take their counsel together, saying, * 'God hath forsaken him; persecute him and take him, for there is none to deliver him.'

10 Go not far from me, O God; * my God, haste thee to help me.

11 Let them be confounded and perish that are against my soul; * let them be covered with shame and dishonour that seek to do me evil.

12 As for me, I will patiently abide alway, * and will praise thee more and more.

13 My mouth shall daily speak of thy righteousness and salvation, * for I know no end thereof.

14 I will go forth in the strength of the Lord GOD, * and will make mention of thy righteousness only.

15 Thou, O God, hast taught me from my youth up until now; * therefore will I tell of thy wondrous works.

16 Forsake me not, O God, in mine old age when I am gray-headed, * until I have showed thy strength unto this

generation, and thy power to all them that are yet for to come.

17 Thy righteousness, O God, is very high, * and great things are they that thou hast done; O God, who is like unto thee?

18 O what great troubles and adversities hast thou showed me, and yet didst thou turn and refresh me, * yea, and broughtest me from the deep of the earth again.

19 Thou hast brought me to great honour, * and comforted me on every side.

20 Therefore will I praise thee and thy faithfulness, O God, playing upon an instrument of music; * unto thee will I sing upon the harp, O thou Holy One of Israel.

21 My lips will be fain when I sing unto thee, * and so will my soul whom thou hast delivered.

22 My tongue also shall talk of thy righteousness all the day long, * for they are confounded and brought unto shame that seek to do me evil.

Psalm 72. *Deus, judicium.*

GIVE the king thy judgements, O God, * and thy righteousness unto the king's son.

2 Then shall he judge thy people according unto right, * and defend the poor.

3 The mountains also shall bring peace, * and the little hills righteousness unto the people.

4 He shall keep the simple folk by their right, * defend the children of the poor, and punish the wrongdoer.

5 They shall fear thee as long as the sun and moon endureth, * from one generation to another.

6 He shall come down like the rain into a fleece of wool, *
even as the drops that water the earth.

7 In his time shall the righteous flourish, * yea, and
abundance of peace so long as the moon endureth.

8 His dominion shall be also from the one sea to the
other, * and from the flood unto the world's end.

9 They that dwell in the wilderness shall kneel before
him; * his enemies shall lick the dust.

10 The kings of Tarshish and of the isles shall give presents; * the kings of Arabia and Saba shall bring gifts.

11 All kings shall fall down before him; * all nations
shall do him service.

12 For he shall deliver the poor when he crieth; * the
needy also, and him that hath no helper.

13 He shall be favourable to the simple and needy, * and
shall preserve the souls of the poor.

14 He shall deliver their souls from falsehood and
wrong, * and dear shall their blood be in his sight.

15 He shall live and unto him shall be given of the gold
of Arabia; * prayer shall be made ever unto him, and daily shall he be praised.

16 There shall be an heap of corn in the earth, high upon
the hills; * his fruit shall shake like Lebanon, and shall be
green in the city like grass upon the earth.

17 His name shall endure for ever; his name shall remain under the sun among the posterities, * which shall
be blessed through him, and all the heathen shall praise
him.

18 Blessed be the LORD God, even the God of Israel, *
which only doeth wondrous things,

19 And blessed be the name of his majesty for ever, *
and all the earth shall be filled with his majesty. Amen,
Amen.

Day 14. Evening Prayer.
Psalm 73. *Quam bonus Israel!*

TRULY God is loving unto Israel, * even unto such as
are of a clean heart.

2 Nevertheless, my feet were almost gone; * my tread-
ings had well-nigh slipped.

3 And why? I was grieved at the wicked; * I do also see
the ungodly in such prosperity.

4 For they are in no peril of death, * but are lusty and
strong.

5 They come in no misfortune like other folk, * neither
are they plagued like other men,

6 And this is the cause that they are so holden with
pride * and overwhelmed with cruelty.

7 Their eyes swell with fatness, * and they do even what
they lust.

8 They corrupt others, and speak of wicked blasphemy; * their talking is against the Most High.

9 For they stretch forth their mouth unto the heaven, *
and their tongue goeth through the world.

10 Therefore fall the people unto them, * and thereout
suck they no small advantage.

11 'Tush', say they, 'how should God perceive it? * is
there knowledge in the Most High?'

12 Lo, these are the ungodly, these prosper in the world,
and these have riches in possession; * and I said, 'Then

have I cleansed my heart in vain and washed my hands in innocency.'

13 All the day long have I been punished, * and chastened every morning.

14 Yea, and I had almost said even as they; * but lo, then I should have condemned the generation of thy children.

15 Then thought I to understand this, * but it was too hard for me,

16 Until I went into the sanctuary of God; * then understood I the end of these men,

17 Namely, how thou dost set them in slippery places, * and castest them down, and destroyest them.

18 O how suddenly do they consume, * perish, and come to a fearful end!

19 Yea, even like as a dream when one awaketh, * so shalt thou make their image to vanish out of the city.

20 Thus my heart was grieved, * and it went even through my reins;

21 So foolish was I and ignorant, * even as it were a beast before thee.

22 Nevertheless, I am alway by thee, * for thou hast holden me by my right hand.

23 Thou shalt guide me with thy counsel, * and after that receive me with glory.

24 Whom have I in heaven but thee? * and there is none upon earth that I desire in comparison of thee.

25 My flesh and my heart faileth, * but God is the strength of my heart and my portion for ever.

26 For lo, they that forsake thee shall perish; * thou hast destroyed all them that commit fornication against thee.

27 But it is good for me to hold me fast by God, to put my trust in the Lord GOD, * and to speak of all thy works in the gates of the daughter of Sion.

Psalm 74. *Ut quid, Deus?*

O GOD, wherefore art thou absent from us so long? * why is thy wrath so hot against the sheep of thy pasture?

2 O think upon thy congregation, * whom thou hast purchased and redeemed of old.

3 Think upon the tribe of thine inheritance, * and Mount Sion, wherein thou hast dwelt.

4 Lift up thy feet, that thou mayest utterly destroy every enemy * which hath done evil in thy sanctuary.

5 Thine adversaries roar in the midst of thy congregations, * and set up their banners for tokens.

6 He that hewed timber afore out of the thick trees * was known to bring it to an excellent work,

7 But now they break down all the carved work thereof * with axes and hammers.

8 They have set fire upon thy holy places, * and have defiled the dwelling place of thy name, even unto the ground.

9 Yea, they said in their hearts, 'Let us make havoc of them altogether'; * thus have they burnt up all the houses of God in the land.

10 We see not our tokens; there is not one prophet more; * no, not one is there among us that understandeth anymore.

11 O God, how long shall the adversary do this dishonour? * how long shall the enemy blaspheme thy name – for ever?

12 Why withdrawest thou thy hand? * why pluckest thou not thy right hand out of thy bosom to consume the enemy?

13 For God is my king of old; * the help that is done upon earth, he doeth it himself.

14 Thou didst divide the sea through thy power; * thou brakest the heads of the dragons in the waters.

15 Thou smotest the heads of Leviathan in pieces, * and gavest him to be meat for the people of the wilderness.

16 Thou broughtest out fountains and waters out of the hard rocks; * thou driedst up mighty waters.

17 The day is thine and the night is thine; * thou hast prepared the light and the sun.

18 Thou hast set all the borders of the earth; * thou hast made summer and winter.

19 Remember this, O Lord, how the enemy hath rebuked, * and how the foolish people hath blasphemed thy name.

20 O deliver not the soul of thy turtle dove unto the multitude of the enemies, * and forget not the congregation of the poor for ever.

21 Look upon the covenant, * for all the earth is full of darkness and cruel habitations.

22 O let not the simple go away ashamed, * but let the poor and needy give praise unto thy name.

23 Arise, O God, maintain thine own cause; * remember how the foolish man blasphemeth thee daily.

24 Forget not the voice of thine enemies; * the presumption of them that hate thee increaseth ever more and more.

Day 15. Morning Prayer.

Psalm 75. *Confitebimur tibi.*

UNTO thee, O God, do we give thanks; * yea, unto thee do we give thanks.

2 Thy name also is so nigh, * and that do thy wondrous works declare:

3 'When I receive the congregation, * I shall judge according unto right.

4 The earth is weak, and all the inhabiters thereof; * I bear up the pillars of it.

5 I said unto the fools, "Deal not so madly"; * and to the ungodly, "Set not up your horn."'

6 Set not up your horn on high, * and speak not with a stiff neck.

7 For promotion cometh neither from the east, nor from the west, * nor yet from the south.

8 And why? God is the judge; * he putteth down one and setteth up another.

9 For in the hand of the LORD there is a cup, and the wine is red; * it is full mixed, and he poureth out of the same.

10 As for the dregs thereof, * all the ungodly of the earth shall drink them and suck them out.

11 But I will talk of the God of Jacob, * and praise him for ever.

12 All the horns of the ungodly also will I break, * and the horns of the righteous shall be exalted.

Psalm 76. *Notus in Judaea.*

IN Judah is God known; * his name is great in Israel.

2 At Salem is his tabernacle, * and his dwelling in Sion.

3 There brake he the arrows of the bow, * the shield, the sword, and the battle.

4 Thou art of more honour and might * than the hills of the robbers.

5 The proud are robbed; they have slept their sleep; * and all the men whose hands were mighty have found nothing.

6 At thy rebuke, O God of Jacob, * both the chariot and horse are fallen.

7 Thou, even thou, art to be feared, * and who may stand in thy sight when thou art angry?

8 Thou didst cause thy judgement to be heard from heaven; * the earth trembled and was still,

9 When God arose to judgement * and to help all the meek upon earth.

10 The fierceness of man shall turn to thy praise, * and the fierceness of them shalt thou refrain.

11 Promise unto the LORD your God and keep it, all ye that are round about him; * bring presents unto him that ought to be feared.

12 He shall refrain the spirit of princes, * and is wonderful among the kings of the earth.

Psalm 77. *Voce mea ad Dominum.*

I WILL cry unto God with my voice, * even unto God will I cry with my voice, and he shall hearken unto me.

2 In the time of my trouble I sought the Lord; * my sore

ran and ceased not in the night season; my soul refused comfort.

3 When I am in heaviness, I will think upon God; * when my heart is vexed, I will complain.

4 Thou holdest mine eyes waking; * I am so feeble that I cannot speak.

5 I have considered the days of old, * and the years that are past.

6 I call to remembrance my song, * and in the night I commune with mine own heart and search out my spirit.

7 Will the Lord absent himself for ever, * and will he be no more entreated?

8 Is his mercy clean gone for ever, * and is his promise come utterly to an end for evermore?

9 Hath God forgotten to be gracious, * and will he shut up his loving-kindness in displeasure?

10 And I said, 'It is mine own infirmity'; * but I will remember the years of the right hand of the Most Highest.

11 I will remember the works of the LORD, * and call to mind thy wonders of old time.

12 I will think also of all thy works, * and my talking shall be of thy doings.

13 Thy way, O God, is holy; * who is so great a god as our God?

14 Thou art the God that doeth wonders, * and hast declared thy power among the peoples.

15 Thou hast mightily delivered thy people, * even the sons of Jacob and Joseph.

16 The waters saw thee, O God, the waters saw thee, and were afraid; * the depths also were troubled.

17 The clouds poured out water, the air thundered, * and thine arrows went abroad.

18 The voice of thy thunder was heard round about; * the lightnings shone upon the ground; the earth was moved and shook withal.

19 Thy way is in the sea and thy paths in the great waters, * and thy footsteps are not known.

20 Thou leddest thy people like sheep * by the hand of Moses and Aaron.

Day 15. Evening Prayer.
Psalm 78. *Attendite, popule.*

H EAR my law, O my people; * incline your ears unto the words of my mouth.

2 I will open my mouth in a parable; * I will declare hard sentences of old,

3 Which we have heard and known, * and such as our fathers have told us,

4 That we should not hide them from the children of the generations to come, * but to show the honour of the LORD, his mighty and wonderful works that he hath done.

5 He made a covenant with Jacob, and gave Israel a law, * which he commanded our forefathers to teach their children,

6 That their posterity might know it, * and the children which were yet unborn,

7 To the intent that when they came up, * they might show their children the same,

8 That they might put their trust in God, * and not to forget the works of God, but to keep his commandments,

9 And not to be as their forefathers, a faithless and stubborn generation, * a generation that set not their heart aright, and whose spirit cleaved not steadfastly unto God,

10 Like as the children of Ephraim, * who, being harnessed and carrying bows, turned themselves back in the day of battle.

11 They kept not the covenant of God, * and would not walk in his law,

12 But forgat what he had done, * and the wonderful works that he had showed for them.

13 Marvellous things did he in the sight of our forefathers in the land of Egypt, * even in the field of Zoan.

14 He divided the sea and let them go through; * he made the waters to stand on an heap.

15 In the daytime also he led them with a cloud, * and all the night through with a light of fire.

16 He clave the hard rocks in the wilderness, * and gave them drink thereof, as it had been out of the great depth.

17 He brought waters out of the stony rock, * so that it gushed out like the rivers.

18 Yet for all this they sinned more against him, * and provoked the Most Highest in the wilderness.

19 They tempted God in their hearts, * and required meat for their lust.

20 They spake against God also, saying, * 'Shall God prepare a table in the wilderness?

21 He smote the stony rock indeed, that the waters gushed out and the streams flowed withal, * but can he give bread also or provide flesh for his people?'

22 When the LORD heard this, he was wroth; * so the

fire was kindled in Jacob, and there came up heavy displeasure against Israel,

23 Because they believed not in God, * and put not their trust in his help.

24 So he commanded the clouds above, * and opened the doors of heaven.

25 He rained down manna also upon them for to eat, * and gave them food from heaven.

26 So man did eat angels' food, * for he sent them meat enough.

27 He caused the east wind to blow under heaven, * and through his power he brought in the southwest wind.

28 He rained flesh upon them as thick as dust, * and feathered fowls like as the sand of the sea.

29 He let it fall among their tents, * even round about their habitation.

30 So they did eat and were well filled, for he gave them their own desire; * they were not disappointed of their lust.

31 But while the meat was yet in their mouths, the heavy wrath of God came upon them, and slew the wealthiest of them; * yea, and smote down the chosen men that were in Israel.

32 But for all this they sinned yet more, * and believed not his wondrous works.

33 Therefore their days did he consume in vanity, * and their years in trouble.

34 When he slew them, they sought him, * and turned them early and inquired after God.

35 And they remembered that God was their strength, * and that the high God was their redeemer.

36 Nevertheless, they did but flatter him with their mouth, * and dissembled with him in their tongue.

37 For their heart was not whole with him, * neither continued they steadfast in his covenant.

38 But he was so merciful that he forgave their misdeeds, * and destroyed them not.

39 Yea, many a time turned he his wrath away, * and would not suffer his whole displeasure to arise.

40 For he considered that they were but flesh, * and that they were even a wind that passeth away and cometh not again.

41 Many a time did they provoke him in the wilderness, * and grieved him in the desert.

42 They turned back and tempted God, * and moved the Holy One in Israel.

43 They thought not of his hand, * and of the day when he delivered them from the hand of the enemy,

44 How he had wrought his miracles in Egypt, * and his wonders in the field of Zoan.

45 He turned their waters into blood, * so that they might not drink of the rivers.

46 He sent lice among them and devoured them up, * and frogs to destroy them.

47 He gave their fruit unto the caterpillar, * and their labour unto the grasshopper.

48 He destroyed their vines with hailstones, * and their mulberry trees with the frost.

49 He smote their cattle also with hailstones, * and their flocks with hot thunderbolts.

50 He cast upon them the furiousness of his wrath,

anger, displeasure, and trouble; * and sent evil angels among them.

51 He made a way for his indignation, and spared not their soul from death, * but gave their life over to the pestilence,

52 And smote all the firstborn in Egypt, * the most principal and mightiest in the dwellings of Ham.

53 But as for his own people, he led them forth like sheep, * and carried them in the wilderness like a flock.

54 He brought them out safely, that they should not fear, * and overwhelmed their enemies with the sea,

55 And brought them within the borders of his sanctuary, * even to his mountain which he purchased with his right hand.

56 He cast out the heathen also before them, * caused their land to be divided among them for an heritage, and made the tribes of Israel to dwell in their tents.

57 So they tempted and displeased the Most High God, * and kept not his testimonies,

58 But turned their backs, and fell away like their forefathers, * starting aside like a broken bow.

59 For they grieved him with their hill-altars, * and provoked him to displeasure with their images.

60 When God heard this, he was wroth, * and took sore displeasure at Israel.

61 So that he forsook the tabernacle in Shiloh, * even the tent that he had pitched among men.

62 He delivered their power into captivity, * and their beauty into the enemy's hand.

63 He gave his people over also unto the sword, * and was wroth with his inheritance.

64 The fire consumed their young men, * and their maidens were not given in marriage.

65 Their priests were slain with the sword, * and there were no widows to make lamentation.

66 So the Lord awaked as one out of sleep, * and like a giant refreshed with wine.

67 He smote his enemies backward, * and put them to a perpetual shame.

68 He refused the tabernacle of Joseph, * and chose not the tribe of Ephraim,

69 But chose the tribe of Judah, * even the hill of Sion which he loved.

70 And there he built his temple on high, * and laid the foundation of it like the ground which he hath made continually.

71 He chose David also his servant, * and took him away from the sheepfolds.

72 As he was following the ewes great with young ones, he took him, * that he might feed Jacob his people and Israel his inheritance.

73 So he fed them with a faithful and true heart, * and ruled them prudently with all his power.

Day 16. Morning Prayer.
Psalm 79. *Deus, venerunt.*

O GOD, the heathen are come into thine inheritance; * thy holy temple have they defiled, and made Jerusalem an heap of stones.

2 The dead bodies of thy servants have they given to be meat unto the fowls of the air, * and the flesh of thy saints unto the beasts of the land.

3 Their blood have they shed like water on every side of Jerusalem, * and there was no man to bury them.

4 We are become an open shame to our enemies, * a very scorn and derision unto them that are round about us.

5 LORD, how long wilt thou be angry? * shall thy jealousy burn like fire for ever?

6 Pour out thine indignation upon the heathen that have not known thee, * and upon the kingdoms that have not called upon thy name.

7 For they have devoured Jacob, * and laid waste his dwelling place.

8 O remember not our old sins, but have mercy upon us, and that soon, * for we are come to great misery.

9 Help us, O God of our salvation, for the glory of thy name; * O deliver us and be merciful unto our sins, for thy name's sake.

10 Wherefore do the heathen say, * 'Where is now their God?'

11 O let the vengeance of thy servants' blood that is shed * be openly showed upon the heathen in our sight.

12 O let the sorrowful sighing of the prisoners come before thee; * according to the greatness of thy power, preserve thou those that are appointed to die.

13 And for the blasphemy wherewith our neighbours have blasphemed thee, * reward thou them, O Lord, sevenfold into their bosom.

14 So we, that are thy people and sheep of thy pasture,

shall give thee thanks for ever, * and will alway be showing forth thy praise from generation to generation.

Psalm 80. *Qui regis Israel.*

HEAR, O thou Shepherd of Israel, thou that leadest Joseph like a sheep; * show thyself also, thou that sittest upon the cherubim.

2 Before Ephraim, Benjamin, and Manasseh, * stir up thy strength, and come, and help us.

3 Turn us again, O God; * show the light of thy countenance and we shall be whole.

4 O LORD God of hosts, * how long wilt thou be angry with thy people that prayeth?

5 Thou feedest them with the bread of tears, * and givest them plenteousness of tears to drink.

6 Thou hast made us a very strife unto our neighbours, * and our enemies laugh us to scorn.

7 Turn us again, thou God of hosts; * show the light of thy countenance and we shall be whole.

8 Thou hast brought a vine out of Egypt; * thou hast cast out the heathen and planted it.

9 Thou madest room for it, * and when it had taken root, it filled the land.

10 The hills were covered with the shadow of it, * and the boughs thereof were like the goodly cedar trees.

11 She stretched out her branches unto the sea, * and her boughs unto the river.

12 Why hast thou then broken down her hedge, * that all they that go by pluck off her grapes?

13 The wild boar out of the wood doth root it up, * and the wild beasts of the field devour it.

14 Turn thee again, thou God of hosts; look down from heaven; * behold and visit this vine,

15 And the place of the vineyard that thy right hand hath planted, * and the branch that thou madest so strong for thyself.

16 It is burnt with fire and cut down, * and they shall perish at the rebuke of thy countenance.

17 Let thy hand be upon the man of thy right hand, * and upon the son of man, whom thou madest so strong for thine own self.

18 And so will not we go back from thee; * O let us live, and we shall call upon thy name.

19 Turn us again, O LORD God of hosts; * show the light of thy countenance and we shall be whole.

Psalm 81. *Exultate Deo.*

SING we merrily unto God our strength; * make a cheerful noise unto the God of Jacob.

2 Take the psalm; bring hither the tabret, * the merry harp with the lute.

3 Blow up the trumpet in the new moon, * even in the time appointed and upon our solemn feast day.

4 For this was made a statute for Israel, * and a law of the God of Jacob.

5 This he ordained in Joseph for a testimony, * when he came out of the land of Egypt, and had heard a strange language.

6 I eased his shoulder from the burden, * and his hands were delivered from making the pots.

7 Thou calledst upon me in troubles, and I delivered thee, * and heard thee what time as the storm fell upon thee.

8 I proved thee also * at the waters of strife:

9 'Hear, O my people, and I will assure thee, O Israel, * if thou wilt hearken unto me.

10 There shall no strange god be in thee, * neither shalt thou worship any other god.

11 I am the LORD thy God, who brought thee out of the land of Egypt; * open thy mouth wide and I shall fill it.'

12 But my people would not hear my voice, * and Israel would not obey me.

13 So I gave them up unto their own hearts' lusts, * and let them follow their own imaginations.

14 O that my people would have hearkened unto me! * for if Israel had walked in my ways,

15 I should soon have put down their enemies, * and turned my hand against their adversaries;

16 The haters of the LORD should have been found liars, * and their time should have endured for ever.

17 He should have fed them also with the finest wheat flour, * and with honey out of the stony rock should I have satisfied thee.

Day 16. Evening Prayer.
Psalm 82. *Deus stetit.*

G OD standeth in the congregation of princes; * he is a judge among gods:

2 'How long will ye give wrong judgement, * and accept the persons of the ungodly?

3 Defend the poor and fatherless; * see that such as are in need and necessity have right.

4 Deliver the outcast and poor; * save them from the hand of the ungodly.'

5 They will not be learned nor understand, but walk on still in darkness; * all the foundations of the earth are out of course.

6 I have said, 'Ye are gods, * and ye are all the children of the Most Highest,

7 But ye shall die like men, * and fall like one of the princes.'

8 Arise, O God, and judge thou the earth, * for thou shalt take all heathen to thine inheritance.

Psalm 83. *Deus, quis similis?*

HOLD not thy tongue, O God; keep not still silence; * refrain not thyself, O God.

2 For lo, thine enemies make a murmuring, * and they that hate thee have lift up their head.

3 They have imagined craftily against thy people, * and taken counsel against thy secret ones.

4 They have said, 'Come, and let us root them out, that they be no more a people, * and that the name of Israel may be no more in remembrance.'

5 For they have cast their heads together with one consent, * and are confederate against thee:

6 The tabernacles of the Edomites and the Ishmaelites, * the Moabites and Hagarenes,

7 Gebal and Ammon and Amalek, * the Philistines with them that dwell at Tyre;

8 Assur also is joined with them, * and have holpen the children of Lot.

9 But do thou to them as unto the Midianites, * unto Sisera and unto Jabin at the brook of Kison,

10 Who perished at Endor, * and became as the dung of the earth.

11 Make them and their princes like Oreb and Zeeb; * yea, make all their princes like as Zebah and Zalmunna,

12 Who say, 'Let us take to ourselves * the houses of God in possession.'

13 O my God, make them like unto a wheel, * and as the stubble before the wind.

14 Like as the fire that burneth up the wood, * and as the flame that consumeth the mountains,

15 Persecute them even so with thy tempest, * and make them afraid with thy storm.

16 Make their faces ashamed, O LORD, * that they may seek thy name.

17 Let them be confounded and vexed ever more and more; * let them be put to shame and perish.

18 And they shall know that thou, whose name is JEHOVAH, * art only the Most Highest over all the earth.

Psalm 84. *Quam dilecta!*

O HOW amiable are thy dwellings, * thou LORD of hosts!

2 My soul hath a desire and longing to enter into the

courts of the LORD; * my heart and my flesh rejoice in the living God.

3 Yea, the sparrow hath found her an house, and the swallow a nest where she may lay her young, * even thy altars, O LORD of hosts, my king and my God.

4 Blessed are they that dwell in thy house; * they will be alway praising thee.

5 Blessed is the man whose strength is in thee, * in whose heart are thy ways.

6 Going through the vale of misery, they use it for a well, * and the pools are filled with water.

7 They will go from strength to strength, * and unto the God of gods appeareth every one of them in Sion.

8 O LORD God of hosts, hear my prayer; * hearken, O God of Jacob.

9 Behold, O God our defender, * and look upon the face of thine anointed.

10 For one day in thy courts * is better than a thousand.

11 I had rather be a doorkeeper in the house of my God, * than to dwell in the tents of ungodliness.

12 For the LORD God is a light and defence; * the LORD will give grace and worship, and no good thing shall he withhold from them that live a godly life.

13 O LORD God of hosts, * blessed is the man that putteth his trust in thee.

Psalm 85. *Benedixisti, Domine.*

LORD, thou art become gracious unto thy land; * thou hast turned away the captivity of Jacob.

2 Thou hast forgiven the offence of thy people, * and covered all their sins.

3 Thou hast taken away all thy displeasure, * and turned thyself from thy wrathful indignation.

4 Turn us then, O God our saviour, * and let thine anger cease from us.

5 Wilt thou be displeased at us for ever? * and wilt thou stretch out thy wrath from one generation to another?

6 Wilt thou not turn again and quicken us, * that thy people may rejoice in thee?

7 Show us thy mercy, O LORD, * and grant us thy salvation.

8 I will hearken what the LORD God will say concerning me, * for he shall speak peace unto his people and to his saints, that they turn not again.

9 For his salvation is nigh them that fear him, * that glory may dwell in our land.

10 Mercy and truth are met together; * righteousness and peace have kissed each other.

11 Truth shall flourish out of the earth, * and righteousness hath looked down from heaven.

12 Yea, the LORD shall show loving-kindness, * and our land shall give her increase.

13 Righteousness shall go before him, * and shall direct his going in the way.

Day 17. Morning Prayer.
Psalm 86. *Inclina, Domine.*

Bow down thine ear, O LORD, and hear me, * for I am poor and in misery.

2 Preserve thou my soul, for I am holy; * my God, save thy servant that putteth his trust in thee.

3 Be merciful unto me, O Lord, * for I will call daily upon thee.

4 Comfort the soul of thy servant, * for unto thee, O Lord, do I lift up my soul.

5 For thou, Lord, art good and gracious, * and of great mercy unto all them that call upon thee.

6 Give ear, LORD, unto my prayer, * and ponder the voice of my humble desires.

7 In the time of my trouble I will call upon thee, * for thou hearest me.

8 Among the gods there is none like unto thee, O Lord; * there is not one that can do as thou doest.

9 All nations whom thou hast made shall come and worship thee, O Lord, * and shall glorify thy name.

10 For thou art great and doest wondrous things; * thou art God alone.

11 Teach me thy way, O LORD, and I will walk in thy truth; * O knit my heart unto thee, that I may fear thy name.

12 I will thank thee, O Lord my God, with all my heart, * and will praise thy name for evermore.

13 For great is thy mercy toward me, * and thou hast delivered my soul from the nethermost hell.

14 O God, the proud are risen against me; * and the congregations of mighty men have sought after my soul, and have not set thee before their eyes.

15 But thou, O Lord God, art full of compassion and mercy, * long-suffering, plenteous in goodness and truth.

16 O turn thee then unto me and have mercy upon me; *
give thy strength unto thy servant, and help the son of
thine handmaid.

17 Show some token upon me for good, that they who
hate me may see it and be ashamed, * because thou, LORD,
hast holpen me and comforted me.

Psalm 87. *Fundamenta ejus.*

HER foundations are upon the holy hills; * the LORD
loveth the gates of Sion more than all the dwellings
of Jacob.

2 Very excellent things are spoken of thee, * thou city
of God.

3 I will think upon Rahab and Babylon * with them that
know me.

4 Behold ye the Philistines also, * and they of Tyre, with
the Ethiopians – lo, there was he born.

5 And of Sion it shall be reported that many were born
in her, * and the Most High shall stablish her.

6 The LORD shall rehearse it when he writeth up the
peoples, * that he was born there.

7 The singers also and trumpeters shall he rehearse: *
'All my fresh springs shall be in thee.'

Psalm 88. *Domine Deus.*

O LORD God of my salvation, I have cried day and night
before thee: * O let my prayer enter into thy presence; incline thine ear unto my calling.

2 For my soul is full of trouble, * and my life draweth
nigh unto hell.

3 I am counted as one of them that go down into the pit, * and I have been even as a man that hath no strength,

4 Free among the dead, like unto them that are wounded and lie in the grave, * who are out of remembrance and are cut away from thy hand.

5 Thou hast laid me in the lowest pit, * in a place of darkness, and in the deep.

6 Thine indignation lieth hard upon me, * and thou hast vexed me with all thy storms.

7 Thou hast put away mine acquaintance far from me, * and made me to be abhorred of them.

8 I am so fast in prison * that I cannot get forth.

9 My sight faileth for very trouble; * Lord, I have called daily upon thee; I have stretched forth my hands unto thee.

10 Dost thou show wonders among the dead? * or shall the dead rise up again and praise thee?

11 Shall thy loving-kindness be showed in the grave? * or thy faithfulness in destruction?

12 Shall thy wondrous works be known in the dark? * and thy righteousness in the land where all things are forgotten?

13 Unto thee have I cried, O Lord, * and early shall my prayer come before thee.

14 Lord, why abhorrest thou my soul, * and hidest thou thy face from me?

15 I am in misery, and like unto him that is at the point to die; * even from my youth up, thy terrors have I suffered with a troubled mind.

16 Thy wrathful displeasure goeth over me, * and the fear of thee hath undone me.

17 They came round about me daily like water, * and compassed me together on every side.

18 My lovers and friends hast thou put away from me, * and hid mine acquaintance out of my sight.

Day 17. Evening Prayer.

Psalm 89. *Misericordias Domini.*

M Y song shall be alway of the loving-kindness of the LORD; * with my mouth will I ever be showing thy truth from one generation to another.

2 For I have said, 'Mercy shall be set up for ever; * thy truth shalt thou stablish in the heavens.'

3 'I have made a covenant with my chosen; * I have sworn unto David my servant:

4 "Thy seed will I stablish for ever, * and set up thy throne from one generation to another."'

5 O LORD, the very heavens shall praise thy wondrous works, * and thy truth in the congregation of the saints.

6 For who is he among the clouds * that shall be compared unto the LORD?

7 And what is he among the gods * that shall be like unto the LORD?

8 God is very greatly to be feared in the council of the saints, * and to be had in reverence of all them that are round about him.

9 O LORD God of hosts, who is like unto thee? * thy truth, most mighty LORD, is on every side.

10 Thou rulest the raging of the sea; * thou stillest the waves thereof when they arise.

11 Thou hast subdued Egypt and destroyed it; * thou hast scattered thine enemies abroad with thy mighty arm.

12 The heavens are thine; the earth also is thine; * thou hast laid the foundation of the round world and all that therein is.

13 Thou hast made the north and the south; * Tabor and Hermon shall rejoice in thy name.

14 Thou hast a mighty arm; * strong is thy hand, and high is thy right hand.

15 Righteousness and equity are the habitation of thy seat; * mercy and truth shall go before thy face.

16 Blessed is the people, O LORD, that can rejoice in thee; * they shall walk in the light of thy countenance.

17 Their delight shall be daily in thy name, * and in thy righteousness shall they make their boast.

18 For thou art the glory of their strength, * and in thy loving-kindness thou shalt lift up our horns.

19 For the LORD is our defence; * the Holy One of Israel is our king.

20 Thou spakest sometime in visions unto thy saints and saidst, * 'I have laid help upon one that is mighty; I have exalted one chosen out of the people.

21 I have found David my servant; * with my holy oil have I anointed him.

22 My hand shall hold him fast, * and my arm shall strengthen him.

23 The enemy shall not be able to do him violence; * the son of wickedness shall not hurt him.

24 I will smite down his foes before his face, * and plague them that hate him.

25 My truth also and my mercy shall be with him, * and in my name shall his horn be exalted.

26 I will set his dominion also in the sea, * and his right hand in the floods.

27 He shall call me, "Thou art my Father, * my God, and my strong salvation."

28 And I will make him my firstborn, * higher than the kings of the earth.

29 My mercy will I keep for him for evermore, * and my covenant shall stand fast with him.

30 His seed also will I make to endure for ever, * and his throne as the days of heaven.

31 But if his children forsake my law, * and walk not in my judgements;

32 If they break my statutes and keep not my commandments, * I will visit their offences with the rod and their sin with scourges.

33 Nevertheless my loving-kindness will I not utterly take from him, * nor suffer my truth to fail.

34 My covenant will I not break, nor alter the thing that is gone out of my lips: * I have sworn once by my holiness that I will not fail David.

35 His seed shall endure for ever, * and his seat is like as the sun before me.

36 He shall stand fast for evermore as the moon, * and as the faithful witness in heaven.'

37 But thou hast abhorred and forsaken thine anointed, * and art displeased at him.

38 Thou hast broken the covenant of thy servant, * and cast his crown to the ground.

39 Thou hast overthrown all his hedges, * and broken down his strongholds.

40 All they that go by spoil him, * and he is become a reproach to his neighbours.

41 Thou hast set up the right hand of his enemies, * and made all his adversaries to rejoice.

42 Thou hast taken away the edge of his sword, * and givest him not victory in the battle.

43 Thou hast put out his glory, * and cast his throne down to the ground.

44 The days of his youth hast thou shortened, * and covered him with dishonour.

45 LORD, how long wilt thou hide thyself – for ever? * and shall thy wrath burn like fire?

46 O remember how short my time is; * wherefore hast thou made all men for nought?

47 What man is he that liveth and shall not see death? * and shall he deliver his soul from the hand of hell?

48 Lord, where are thy old loving-kindnesses, * which thou swarest unto David in thy truth?

49 Remember, Lord, the rebuke that thy servants have, * and how I do bear in my bosom the rebukes of many people,

50 Wherewith thine enemies have blasphemed thee, and slandered the footsteps of thine anointed. * Praised be the LORD for evermore. Amen and Amen.

Day 18. Morning Prayer.

Psalm 90. *Domine, refugium.*

LORD, thou hast been our refuge * from one generation to another.

2 Before the mountains were brought forth, or ever the earth and the world were made, * thou art God from everlasting, and world without end.

3 Thou turnest man to destruction; * again thou sayest, 'Come again, ye children of men.'

4 For a thousand years in thy sight are but as yesterday, * seeing it is past as a watch in the night.

5 As soon as thou scatterest them, they are even as a sleep, * and fade away suddenly like the grass.

6 In the morning it is green and groweth up, * but in the evening it is cut down, dried up, and withered.

7 For we consume away in thy displeasure, * and are afraid at thy wrathful indignation.

8 Thou hast set our misdeeds before thee, * and our secret sins in the light of thy countenance.

9 For when thou art angry, all our days are gone; * we bring our years to an end, as it were a tale that is told.

10 The days of our age are threescore years and ten, and though men be so strong that they come to fourscore years, * yet is their strength then but labour and sorrow, so soon passeth it away, and we are gone.

11 But who regardeth the power of thy wrath? * for even thereafter as a man feareth, so is thy displeasure.

12 So teach us to number our days, * that we may apply our hearts unto wisdom.

13 Turn thee again, O LORD, at the last, * and be gracious unto thy servants.

14 O satisfy us with thy mercy, and that soon; * so shall we rejoice and be glad all the days of our life.

15 Comfort us again now after the time that thou hast plagued us, * and for the years wherein we have suffered adversity.

16 Show thy servants thy work, * and their children thy glory.

17 And the glorious majesty of the Lord our God be upon us: * prosper thou the work of our hands upon us; O prosper thou our handiwork.

Psalm 91. *Qui habitat.*

WHOSO dwelleth under the defence of the Most High * shall abide under the shadow of the Almighty.

2 I will say unto the LORD, 'Thou art my hope and my stronghold; * my God, in him will I trust.'

3 For he shall deliver thee from the snare of the hunter, * and from the noisome pestilence.

4 He shall defend thee under his wings, and thou shalt be safe under his feathers; * his faithfulness and truth shall be thy shield and buckler.

5 Thou shalt not be afraid for any terror by night, * nor for the arrow that flieth by day,

6 For the pestilence that walketh in darkness, * nor for the sickness that destroyeth in the noonday.

7 A thousand shall fall beside thee, and ten thousand at thy right hand, * but it shall not come nigh thee.

8 Yea, with thine eyes shalt thou behold * and see the reward of the ungodly.

9 For thou, LORD, art my hope; * thou hast set thine house of defence very high.

10 There shall no evil happen unto thee, * neither shall any plague come nigh thy dwelling.

11 For he shall give his angels charge over thee, * to keep thee in all thy ways.

12 They shall bear thee in their hands, * that thou hurt not thy foot against a stone.

13 Thou shalt go upon the lion and adder; * the young lion and the dragon shalt thou tread under thy feet.

14 'Because he hath set his love upon me, therefore will I deliver him; * I will set him up, because he hath known my name.

15 He shall call upon me, and I will hear him; * yea, I am with him in trouble; I will deliver him and bring him to honour.

16 With long life will I satisfy him, * and show him my salvation.'

Psalm 92. *Bonum est confiteri.*

IT is a good thing to give thanks unto the LORD, * and to sing praises unto thy name, O Most Highest;

2 To tell of thy loving-kindness early in the morning, * and of thy truth in the night season,

3 Upon an instrument of ten strings and upon the lute, * upon a loud instrument and upon the harp.

4 For thou, LORD, hast made me glad through thy

works, * and I will rejoice in giving praise for the operations of thy hands.

5 O Lord, how glorious are thy works; * thy thoughts
are very deep.

6 An unwise man doth not well consider this, * and a
fool doth not understand it.

7 When the ungodly are green as the grass, and when
all the workers of wickedness do flourish, * then shall they
be destroyed for ever; but thou, Lord, art the Most Highest for evermore.

8 For lo, thine enemies, O Lord; lo, thine enemies
shall perish, * and all the workers of wickedness shall be
destroyed.

9 But mine horn shall be exalted like the horn of an
unicorn, * for I am anointed with fresh oil.

10 Mine eye also shall see his lust on mine enemies, *
and mine ear shall hear his desire of the wicked that arise
up against me.

11 The righteous shall flourish like a palm tree, * and
shall spread abroad like a cedar in Lebanon.

12 Such as are planted in the house of the Lord * shall
flourish in the courts of the house of our God.

13 They also shall bring forth more fruit in their age, *
and shall be fat and well-pleasing,

14 That they may show how true the Lord my strength
is, * and that there is no unrighteousness in him.

Day 18. Evening Prayer.

Psalm 93. *Dominus regnavit.*

THE LORD is king and hath put on glorious apparel; *
the LORD hath put on his apparel and girded himself
with strength.

2 He hath made the round world so sure * that it cannot be moved.

3 Ever since the world began hath thy seat been prepared; * thou art from everlasting.

4 The floods are risen, O LORD; the floods have lift up
their voice; * the floods lift up their waves.

5 The waves of the sea are mighty and rage horribly, *
but yet the LORD, who dwelleth on high, is mightier.

6 Thy testimonies, O LORD, are very sure; * holiness
becometh thine house for ever.

Psalm 94. *Deus ultionum.*

O LORD God, to whom vengeance belongeth; * thou
God, to whom vengeance belongeth, show thyself.

2 Arise, thou judge of the world, * and reward the proud
after their deserving.

3 LORD, how long shall the ungodly, * how long shall
the ungodly triumph?

4 How long shall all wicked doers speak so disdainfully, * and make such proud boasting?

5 They smite down thy people, O LORD, * and trouble
thine heritage.

6 They murder the widow and the stranger, * and put
the fatherless to death.

7 And yet they say, 'Tush, the Lord shall not see, * neither shall the God of Jacob regard it.'

8 Take heed, ye unwise among the people; * O ye fools, when will ye understand?

9 He that planted the ear, shall he not hear? * or he that made the eye, shall he not see?

10 Or he that nurtureth the heathen, * it is he that teacheth man knowledge – shall not he punish?

11 The Lord knoweth the thoughts of man, * that they are but vain.

12 Blessed is the man whom thou chastenest, O Lord, * and teachest him in thy law,

13 That thou mayest give him patience in time of adversity, * until the pit be digged up for the ungodly.

14 For the Lord will not fail his people, * neither will he forsake his inheritance.

15 Until righteousness turn again unto judgement, * all such as are true in heart shall follow it.

16 Who will rise up with me against the wicked? * or who will take my part against the evildoers?

17 If the Lord had not helped me, * it had not failed but my soul had been put to silence.

18 But when I said, 'My foot hath slipped', * thy mercy, O Lord, held me up.

19 In the multitude of the sorrows that I had in my heart, * thy comforts have refreshed my soul.

20 Wilt thou have anything to do with the throne of wickedness, * which imagineth mischief as a law?

21 They gather them together against the soul of the righteous, * and condemn the innocent blood.

22 But the Lord is my refuge, * and my God is the strength of my confidence.

23 He shall recompense them their wickedness, and destroy them in their own malice; * yea, the Lord our God shall destroy them.

Day 19. Morning Prayer.
Psalm 95. *Venite, exultemus.*

O COME, let us sing unto the Lord; * let us heartily rejoice in the strength of our salvation.

2 Let us come before his presence with thanksgiving, * and show ourselves glad in him with psalms.

3 For the Lord is a great God, * and a great king above all gods.

4 In his hand are all the corners of the earth, * and the strength of the hills is his also.

5 The sea is his and he made it, * and his hands prepared the dry land.

6 O come, let us worship and fall down, * and kneel before the Lord our maker.

7 For he is the Lord our God, * and we are the people of his pasture and the sheep of his hand.

8 Today if ye will hear his voice – 'Harden not your hearts * as in the provocation, and as in the day of temptation in the wilderness,

9 When your fathers tempted me, * proved me, and saw my works.

10 Forty years long was I grieved with this generation and said, * "It is a people that do err in their hearts, for they have not known my ways",

11 Unto whom I sware in my wrath * that they should not enter into my rest.'

Psalm 96. *Cantate Domino.*

O SING unto the LORD a new song; * sing unto the LORD, all the whole earth.

2 Sing unto the LORD and praise his name; * be telling of his salvation from day to day.

3 Declare his honour unto the heathen, * and his wonders unto all peoples.

4 For the LORD is great and cannot worthily be praised; * he is more to be feared than all gods.

5 As for all the gods of the heathen, they are but idols, * but it is the LORD that made the heavens.

6 Glory and worship are before him; * power and honour are in his sanctuary.

7 Ascribe unto the LORD, O ye kindreds of the peoples, * ascribe unto the LORD worship and power.

8 Ascribe unto the LORD the honour due unto his name; * bring presents and come into his courts.

9 O worship the LORD in the beauty of holiness; * let the whole earth stand in awe of him.

10 Tell it out among the heathen that the LORD is king, * and that it is he who hath made the round world so fast that it cannot be moved, and how that he shall judge the peoples righteously.

11 Let the heavens rejoice, and let the earth be glad; * let the sea make a noise and all that therein is.

12 Let the field be joyful and all that is in it; * then shall all the trees of the wood rejoice before the LORD.

13 For he cometh, for he cometh to judge the earth, * and with righteousness to judge the world, and the peoples with his truth.

Psalm 97. *Dominus regnavit.*

THE LORD is king – the earth may be glad thereof; * yea, the multitude of the isles may be glad thereof.

2 Clouds and darkness are round about him; * righteousness and judgement are the habitation of his seat.

3 There shall go a fire before him, * and burn up his enemies on every side.

4 His lightnings gave shine unto the world; * the earth saw it and was afraid.

5 The hills melted like wax at the presence of the LORD, * at the presence of the Lord of the whole earth.

6 The heavens have declared his righteousness, * and all the peoples have seen his glory.

7 Confounded be all they that worship carved images, and that delight in vain gods; * worship him, all ye gods.

8 Sion heard of it and rejoiced, * and the daughters of Judah were glad because of thy judgements, O LORD.

9 For thou, LORD, art higher than all that are in the earth; * thou art exalted far above all gods.

10 O ye that love the LORD, see that ye hate the thing which is evil; * the Lord preserveth the souls of his saints; he shall deliver them from the hand of the ungodly.

11 There is sprung up a light for the righteous, * and joyful gladness for such as are true-hearted.

12 Rejoice in the LORD, ye righteous, * and give thanks for a remembrance of his holiness.

Day 19. Evening Prayer.

Psalm 98. *Cantate Domino.*

O SING unto the LORD a new song, * for he hath done marvellous things.

2 With his own right hand, and with his holy arm, * hath he gotten himself the victory.

3 The LORD declared his salvation; * his righteousness hath he openly showed in the sight of the heathen.

4 He hath remembered his mercy and truth toward the house of Israel, * and all the ends of the world have seen the salvation of our God.

5 Show yourselves joyful unto the LORD, all ye lands; * sing, rejoice, and give thanks.

6 Praise the LORD upon the harp; * sing to the harp with a psalm of thanksgiving.

7 With trumpets also, and shawms, * O show yourselves joyful before the LORD the king.

8 Let the sea make a noise and all that therein is; * the round world, and they that dwell therein.

9 Let the floods clap their hands, and let the hills be joyful together before the LORD, * for he is come to judge the earth.

10 With righteousness shall he judge the world, * and the peoples with equity.

Psalm 99. *Dominus regnavit.*

T HE LORD is king, be the peoples never so impatient; * he sitteth between the cherubim, be the earth never so unquiet.

2 The LORD is great in Sion, * and high above all peoples.

3 They shall give thanks unto thy name, * which is great, wonderful, and holy.

4 The king's power loveth judgement; thou hast prepared equity; * thou hast executed judgement and righteousness in Jacob.

5 O magnify the LORD our God, * and fall down before his footstool, for he is holy.

6 Moses and Aaron among his priests, and Samuel among such as call upon his name: * these called upon the LORD and he heard them.

7 He spake unto them out of the cloudy pillar, * for they kept his testimonies and the law that he gave them.

8 Thou heardest them, O LORD our God; * thou forgavest them, O God, and punishedst their own inventions.

9 O magnify the LORD our God, and worship him upon his holy hill, * for the LORD our God is holy.

Psalm 100. *Jubilate Deo.*

O BE joyful in the LORD, all ye lands; * serve the LORD with gladness, and come before his presence with a song.

2 Be ye sure that the LORD he is God; * it is he that hath made us and not we ourselves; we are his people and the sheep of his pasture.

3 O go your way into his gates with thanksgiving, and into his courts with praise; * be thankful unto him, and speak good of his name.

4 For the LORD is gracious, his mercy is everlasting, * and his truth endureth from generation to generation.

Psalm 101. *Misericordiam et judicium.*

MY song shall be of mercy and judgement; * unto thee, O LORD, will I sing.

2 O let me have understanding * in the way of godliness.

3 When wilt thou come unto me? * I will walk in my house with a perfect heart.

4 I will take no wicked thing in hand; I hate the sins of unfaithfulness; * there shall no such cleave unto me.

5 A froward heart shall depart from me; * I will not know a wicked person.

6 Whoso privily slandereth his neighbour, * him will I destroy.

7 Whoso hath also a proud look and a high heart, * I will not suffer him.

8 Mine eyes look upon such as are faithful in the land, * that they may dwell with me.

9 Whoso leadeth a godly life, * he shall be my servant.

10 There shall no deceitful person dwell in my house; * he that telleth lies shall not tarry in my sight.

11 I shall soon destroy all the ungodly that are in the land, * that I may root out all wicked doers from the city of the LORD.

Day 20. Morning Prayer.
Psalm 102. *Domine, exaudi.*

HEAR my prayer, O LORD, * and let my crying come unto thee.

2 Hide not thy face from me in the time of my trouble; * incline thine ear unto me when I call; O hear me, and that right soon.

3 For my days are consumed away like smoke, * and my bones are burnt up as it were a firebrand.

4 My heart is smitten down and withered like grass, * so that I forget to eat my bread.

5 For the voice of my groaning, * my bones will scarce cleave to my flesh.

6 I am become like a pelican in the wilderness, * and like an owl that is in the desert.

7 I have watched, and am even as it were a sparrow * that sitteth alone upon the housetop.

8 Mine enemies revile me all the day long, * and they that are mad upon me are sworn together against me.

9 For I have eaten ashes as it were bread, * and mingled my drink with weeping,

10 And that because of thine indignation and wrath, * for thou hast taken me up and cast me down.

11 My days are gone like a shadow, * and I am withered like grass.

12 But thou, O Lord, shalt endure for ever, * and thy remembrance throughout all generations.

13 Thou shalt arise and have mercy upon Sion, * for it is time that thou have mercy upon her; yea, the time is come.

14 And why? thy servants think upon her stones, * and it pitieth them to see her in the dust.

15 The heathen shall fear thy name, O Lord, * and all the kings of the earth thy majesty,

16 When the Lord shall build up Sion, * and when his glory shall appear,

17 When he turneth him unto the prayer of the poor destitute, * and despiseth not their desire.

18 This shall be written for those that come after, * and the people which shall be born shall praise the LORD.

19 For he hath looked down from his sanctuary; * out of the heaven did the LORD behold the earth,

20 That he might hear the mournings of such as are in captivity, * and deliver them that are appointed unto death,

21 That they may declare the name of the LORD in Sion, * and his worship at Jerusalem,

22 When the peoples are gathered together, * and the kingdoms also, to serve the LORD.

23 He brought down my strength in my journey, * and shortened my days.

24 But I said, 'O my God, take me not away in the midst of mine age; * as for thy years, they endure throughout all generations.'

25 Thou, Lord, in the beginning hast laid the foundation of the earth, * and the heavens are the work of thy hands.

26 They shall perish, but thou shalt endure; * they all shall wax old as doth a garment,

27 And as a vesture shalt thou change them, and they shall be changed; * but thou art the same and thy years shall not fail.

28 The children of thy servants shall continue, * and their seed shall stand fast in thy sight.

Psalm 103. *Benedic, anima mea.*

PRAISE the LORD, O my soul, * and all that is within me praise his holy name.

2 Praise the LORD, O my soul, * and forget not all his benefits:

3 Who forgiveth all thy sin, * and healeth all thine infirmities;

4 Who saveth thy life from destruction, * and crowneth thee with mercy and loving-kindness;

5 Who satisfieth thy mouth with good things, * making thee young and lusty as an eagle.

6 The LORD executeth righteousness and judgement * for all them that are oppressed with wrong.

7 He showed his ways unto Moses, * his works unto the children of Israel.

8 The LORD is full of compassion and mercy, * long-suffering and of great goodness.

9 He will not alway be chiding, * neither keepeth he his anger for ever.

10 He hath not dealt with us after our sins, * nor rewarded us according to our wickednesses.

11 For look how high the heaven is in comparison of the earth; * so great is his mercy also toward them that fear him.

12 Look how wide also the east is from the west; * so far hath he set our sins from us.

13 Yea, like as a father pitieth his own children, * even so is the LORD merciful unto them that fear him.

14 For he knoweth whereof we are made; * he remembereth that we are but dust.

15 The days of man are but as grass, * for he flourisheth as a flower of the field.

16 For as soon as the wind goeth over it, it is gone, * and the place thereof shall know it no more.

17 But the merciful goodness of the LORD endureth for ever and ever upon them that fear him, * and his righteousness upon children's children,

18 Even upon such as keep his covenant, * and think upon his commandments to do them.

19 The LORD hath prepared his seat in heaven, * and his kingdom ruleth over all.

20 O praise the LORD, ye angels of his, ye that excel in strength, * ye that fulfil his commandment and hearken unto the voice of his words.

21 O praise the LORD, all ye his hosts, * ye servants of his that do his pleasure.

22 O speak good of the LORD, all ye works of his in all places of his dominion. * Praise thou the LORD, O my soul.

Day 20. Evening Prayer.
Psalm 104. *Benedic, anima mea.*

PRAISE the LORD, O my soul. * O LORD my God, thou art become exceeding glorious; thou art clothed with majesty and honour.

2 Thou deckest thyself with light as it were with a garment, * and spreadest out the heavens like a curtain,

3 Who layeth the beams of his chambers in the waters, * and maketh the clouds his chariot, and walketh upon the wings of the wind.

4 He maketh his angels spirits, * and his ministers a flaming fire.

5 He laid the foundations of the earth, * that it never should move at any time.

6 Thou coveredst it with the deep like as with a garment; * the waters stand in the hills.

7 At thy rebuke they flee; * at the voice of thy thunder they are afraid.

8 They go up as high as the hills, and down to the valleys beneath, * even unto the place which thou hast appointed for them.

9 Thou hast set them their bounds which they shall not pass, * neither turn again to cover the earth.

10 He sendeth the springs into the rivers, * which run among the hills.

11 All beasts of the field drink thereof, * and the wild asses quench their thirst.

12 Beside them shall the fowls of the air have their habitation, * and sing among the branches.

13 He watereth the hills from above; * the earth is filled with the fruit of thy works.

14 He bringeth forth grass for the cattle, * and green herb for the service of men;

15 That he may bring food out of the earth, and wine that maketh glad the heart of man, * and oil to make him a cheerful countenance, and bread to strengthen man's heart.

16 The trees of the Lord also are full of sap, * even the cedars of Lebanon which he hath planted,

17 Wherein the birds make their nests; * and the fir trees are a dwelling for the stork.

18 The high hills are a refuge for the wild goats, * and so are the stony rocks for the conies.

19 He appointed the moon for certain seasons, * and the sun knoweth his going down.

20 Thou makest darkness that it may be night, * wherein all the beasts of the forest do move.

21 The lions, roaring after their prey, * do seek their meat from God.

22 The sun ariseth and they get them away together, * and lay them down in their dens.

23 Man goeth forth to his work, and to his labour * until the evening.

24 O LORD, how manifold are thy works! * in wisdom hast thou made them all; the earth is full of thy riches.

25 So is the great and wide sea also, * wherein are things creeping innumerable, both small and great beasts.

26 There go the ships, and there is that Leviathan, * whom thou hast made to take his pastime therein.

27 These wait all upon thee, * that thou mayest give them meat in due season.

28 When thou givest it them, they gather it; * and when thou openest thy hand, they are filled with good.

29 When thou hidest thy face, they are troubled; * when thou takest away their breath, they die and are turned again to their dust.

30 When thou lettest thy breath go forth, they shall be made, * and thou shalt renew the face of the earth.

31 The glorious majesty of the LORD shall endure for ever; * the LORD shall rejoice in his works.

32 The earth shall tremble at the look of him; * if he do but touch the hills, they shall smoke.

33 I will sing unto the LORD as long as I live; * I will praise my God while I have my being.

34 And so shall my words please him; * my joy shall be in the LORD.

35 As for sinners, they shall be consumed out of the earth, and the ungodly shall come to an end. * Praise thou the LORD, O my soul; praise the LORD.

Day 21. Morning Prayer.
Psalm 105. *Confitemini Domino.*

O GIVE thanks unto the LORD, and call upon his name; * tell the peoples what things he hath done.

2 O let your songs be of him and praise him, * and let your talking be of all his wondrous works.

3 Rejoice in his holy name; * let the heart of them rejoice that seek the LORD.

4 Seek the LORD and his strength; * seek his face evermore.

5 Remember the marvellous works that he hath done, * his wonders and the judgements of his mouth,

6 O ye seed of Abraham his servant, * ye children of Jacob his chosen.

7 He is the LORD our God; * his judgements are in all the world.

8 He hath been alway mindful of his covenant and promise * that he made to a thousand generations,

9 Even the covenant that he made with Abraham, * and the oath that he sware unto Isaac,

10 And appointed the same unto Jacob for a law, * and to Israel for an everlasting testament,

11 Saying, 'Unto thee will I give the land of Canaan, * the lot of your inheritance.'

12 When there were yet but a few of them, * and they strangers in the land,

13 What time as they went from one nation to another, * from one kingdom to another people,

14 He suffered no man to do them wrong, * but reproved even kings for their sakes:

15 'Touch not mine anointed, * and do my prophets no harm.'

16 Moreover, he called for a dearth upon the land, * and destroyed all the provision of bread.

17 But he had sent a man before them, * even Joseph, who was sold to be a bondservant,

18 Whose feet they hurt in the stocks; * the iron entered into his soul.

19 Until the time came that his cause was known, * the word of the Lord tried him.

20 The king sent and delivered him; * the prince of the people let him go free.

21 He made him lord also of his house, * and ruler of all his substance,

22 That he might inform his princes after his will, * and teach his senators wisdom.

23 Israel also came into Egypt, * and Jacob was a stranger in the land of Ham.

24 And he increased his people exceedingly, * and made them stronger than their enemies,

25　Whose heart turned so that they hated his people, * and dealt untruly with his servants.

26　Then sent he Moses his servant, * and Aaron whom he had chosen.

27　And these showed his tokens among them, * and wonders in the land of Ham.

28　He sent darkness and it was dark, * and they were not obedient unto his word.

29　He turned their waters into blood, * and slew their fish.

30　Their land brought forth frogs, * yea, even in their kings' chambers.

31　He spake the word and there came all manner of flies, * and lice in all their quarters.

32　He gave them hailstones for rain, * and flames of fire in their land.

33　He smote their vines also and fig trees, * and destroyed the trees that were in their coasts.

34　He spake the word and the grasshoppers came, and caterpillars innumerable, * and did eat up all the grass in their land and devoured the fruit of their ground.

35　He smote all the firstborn in their land, * even the chief of all their strength.

36　He brought them forth also with silver and gold; * there was not one feeble person among their tribes.

37　Egypt was glad at their departing, * for they were afraid of them.

38　He spread out a cloud to be a covering, * and fire to give light in the night season.

39 At their desire he brought quails, * and he filled them with the bread of heaven.

40 He opened the rock of stone, and the waters flowed out, * so that rivers ran in the dry places.

41 For why? he remembered his holy promise, * and Abraham his servant.

42 And he brought forth his people with joy, * and his chosen with gladness;

43 And gave them the lands of the heathen, * and they took the labours of the peoples in possession,

44 That they might keep his statutes * and observe his laws.

Day 21. Evening Prayer.
Psalm 106. *Confitemini Domino.*

O GIVE thanks unto the LORD, for he is gracious, * and his mercy endureth for ever.

2 Who can express the noble acts of the LORD, * or show forth all his praise?

3 Blessed are they that alway keep judgement * and do righteousness.

4 Remember me, O LORD, according to the favour that thou bearest unto thy people; * O visit me with thy salvation,

5 That I may see the felicity of thy chosen, * and rejoice in the gladness of thy people, and give thanks with thine inheritance.

6 We have sinned with our fathers; * we have done amiss and dealt wickedly.

7 Our fathers regarded not thy wonders in Egypt, neither kept they thy great goodness in remembrance, * but were disobedient at the sea, even at the Red Sea.

8 Nevertheless, he helped them for his name's sake, * that he might make his power to be known.

9 He rebuked the Red Sea also and it was dried up; * so he led them through the deep as through a wilderness.

10 And he saved them from the adversaries' hand, * and delivered them from the hand of the enemy.

11 As for those that troubled them, the waters overwhelmed them; * there was not one of them left.

12 Then believed they his words, * and sang praise unto him.

13 But within a while they forgat his works, * and would not abide his counsel.

14 But lust came upon them in the wilderness, * and they tempted God in the desert.

15 And he gave them their desire, * and sent leanness withal into their soul.

16 They angered Moses also in the tents, * and Aaron the saint of the LORD.

17 So the earth opened and swallowed up Dathan, * and covered the congregation of Abiram.

18 And the fire was kindled in their company; * the flame burnt up the ungodly.

19 They made a calf in Horeb, * and worshipped the molten image.

20 Thus they turned their glory * into the similitude of a calf that eateth hay.

21 And they forgat God their saviour, * who had done so great things in Egypt,

22 Wondrous works in the land of Ham, * and fearful things by the Red Sea.

23 So he said he would have destroyed them, had not Moses his chosen stood before him in the gap, * to turn away his wrathful indignation, lest he should destroy them.

24 Yea, they thought scorn of that pleasant land, * and gave no credence unto his word,

25 But murmured in their tents, * and hearkened not unto the voice of the LORD.

26 Then lift he up his hand against them * to overthrow them in the wilderness,

27 To cast out their seed among the nations, * and to scatter them in the lands.

28 They joined themselves unto Baal-Peor, * and ate the offerings of the dead.

29 Thus they provoked him to anger with their own inventions, * and the plague was great among them.

30 Then stood up Phinehas and prayed, * and so the plague ceased.

31 And that was counted unto him for righteousness, * among all posterities for evermore.

32 They angered him also at the waters of strife, * so that he punished Moses for their sakes,

33 Because they provoked his spirit, * so that he spake unadvisedly with his lips.

34 Neither destroyed they the heathen * as the LORD commanded them,

35 But were mingled among the heathen * and learned their works,

36 Insomuch that they worshipped their idols, which turned to their own decay; * yea, they offered their sons and their daughters unto devils,

37 And shed innocent blood, even the blood of their sons and of their daughters, * whom they offered unto the idols of Canaan; and the land was defiled with blood.

38 Thus were they stained with their own works, * and went a-whoring with their own inventions.

39 Therefore was the wrath of the LORD kindled against his people, * insomuch that he abhorred his own inheritance.

40 And he gave them over into the hands of the heathen, * and they that hated them were lords over them.

41 Their enemies oppressed them, * and had them in subjection.

42 Many a time did he deliver them, * but they rebelled against him with their own inventions, and were brought down in their wickedness.

43 Nevertheless, when he saw their adversity, * he heard their complaint.

44 He thought upon his covenant, and pitied them according unto the multitude of his mercies; * yea, he made all those that led them away captive to pity them.

45 Deliver us, O LORD our God, and gather us from among the heathen, * that we may give thanks unto thy holy name and make our boast of thy praise.

46 Blessed be the LORD God of Israel, from everlast-

ing and world without end, * and let all the people say,
'Amen.'

Day 22. Morning Prayer.
Psalm 107. *Confitemini Domino.*

O GIVE thanks unto the LORD, for he is gracious, * and
his mercy endureth for ever.

2 Let them give thanks whom the LORD hath redeemed *
and delivered from the hand of the enemy,

3 And gathered them out of the lands, from the east
and from the west, * from the north and from the south.

4 They went astray in the wilderness out of the way, *
and found no city to dwell in.

5 Hungry and thirsty, * their soul fainted in them.

6 So they cried unto the LORD in their trouble, * and
he delivered them from their distress.

7 He led them forth by the right way, * that they might
go to the city where they dwelt.

8 O that men would therefore praise the LORD for his
goodness, * and declare the wonders that he doeth for
the children of men!

9 For he satisfieth the empty soul, * and filleth the hungry soul with goodness.

10 Such as sit in darkness and in the shadow of death, *
being fast bound in misery and iron,

11 Because they rebelled against the words of the Lord, *
and lightly regarded the counsel of the Most Highest,

12 He also brought down their heart through heaviness; * they fell down, and there was none to help them.

13 So when they cried unto the LORD in their trouble, *
he delivered them out of their distress.

14 For he brought them out of darkness and out of the
shadow of death, * and brake their bonds in sunder.

15 O that men would therefore praise the LORD for his
goodness, * and declare the wonders that he doeth for
the children of men!

16 For he hath broken the gates of brass, * and smitten
the bars of iron in sunder.

17 Foolish men are plagued for their offence * and because of their wickedness.

18 Their soul abhorred all manner of meat, * and they
were even hard at death's door.

19 So when they cried unto the LORD in their trouble, *
he delivered them out of their distress.

20 He sent his word and healed them, * and they were
saved from their destruction.

21 O that men would therefore praise the LORD for his
goodness, * and declare the wonders that he doeth for the
children of men!

22 That they would offer unto him the sacrifice of
thanksgiving, * and tell out his works with gladness!

23 They that go down to the sea in ships, * and occupy
their business in great waters,

24 These men see the works of the LORD * and his wonders in the deep.

25 For at his word the stormy wind ariseth, * which
lifteth up the waves thereof.

26 They are carried up to the heaven, and down again

to the deep; * their soul melteth away because of the trouble.

27 They reel to and fro, and stagger like a drunken man, * and are at their wits' end.

28 So when they cry unto the LORD in their trouble, * he delivereth them out of their distress.

29 For he maketh the storm to cease, * so that the waves thereof are still.

30 Then are they glad because they are at rest, * and so he bringeth them unto the haven where they would be.

31 O that men would therefore praise the LORD for his goodness, * and declare the wonders that he doeth for the children of men!

32 That they would exalt him also in the congregation of the people, * and praise him in the seat of the elders!

33 He turneth the floods into a wilderness, * and drieth up the water-springs.

34 A fruitful land maketh he barren, * for the wickedness of them that dwell therein.

35 Again he maketh the wilderness a standing water, * and water-springs of a dry ground.

36 And there he setteth the hungry, * that they may build them a city to dwell in,

37 That they may sow their land and plant vineyards, * to yield them fruits of increase.

38 He blesseth them so that they multiply exceedingly, * and suffereth not their cattle to decrease.

39 And again, when they are minished and brought low * through oppression, through any plague or trouble,

40 Though he poureth contempt upon tyrants, * and letteth them wander out of the way in the wilderness,

41 Yet helpeth he the poor out of misery, * and maketh him households like a flock of sheep.

42 The righteous will consider this and rejoice, * and the mouth of all wickedness shall be stopped.

43 Whoso is wise will ponder these things, * and they shall understand the loving-kindness of the LORD.

Day 22. Evening Prayer.
Psalm 108. *Paratum cor meum.*

O GOD, my heart is ready, my heart is ready; * I will sing and give praise with the noblest part that I have.

2 Awake, thou lute and harp! * I myself will awake right early.

3 I will give thanks unto thee, O LORD, among the peoples; * I will sing praises unto thee among the nations.

4 For thy mercy is greater than the heavens, * and thy truth reacheth unto the clouds.

5 Set up thyself, O God, above the heavens, * and thy glory above all the earth.

6 That thy beloved may be delivered, * let thy right hand save them, and hear thou me.

7 God hath spoken in his holiness: * 'I will rejoice therefore, and divide Shechem, and mete out the valley of Succoth.

8 Gilead is mine, and Manasseh is mine; * Ephraim also is the strength of my head;

9 Judah is my lawgiver; Moab is my wash-pot; * over Edom will I cast out my shoe; upon Philistia will I triumph.'

10 Who will lead me into the strong city? * and who will bring me into Edom?

11 Hast not thou forsaken us, O God? * and wilt not thou, O God, go forth with our hosts?

12 O help us against the enemy, * for vain is the help of man.

13 Through God we shall do great acts, * and it is he that shall tread down our enemies.

Psalm 109. *Deus, laudem.*

HOLD not thy tongue, O God of my praise, * for the mouth of the ungodly, yea, the mouth of the deceitful, is opened upon me.

2 And they have spoken against me with false tongues; * they compassed me about also with words of hatred, and fought against me without a cause.

3 For the love that I had unto them, lo, they take now my contrary part, * but I give myself unto prayer.

4 Thus have they rewarded me evil for good, * and hatred for my good will.

5 Set thou an ungodly man to be ruler over him, * and let Satan stand at his right hand.

6 When sentence is given upon him, let him be condemned, * and let his prayer be turned into sin.

7 Let his days be few, * and let another take his office.

8 Let his children be fatherless * and his wife a widow.

9 Let his children be vagabonds and beg their bread; * let them seek it also out of desolate places.

10 Let the extortioner consume all that he hath, * and let the stranger spoil his labour.

11 Let there be no man to pity him, * nor to have compassion upon his fatherless children.

12 Let his posterity be destroyed, * and in the next generation let his name be clean put out.

13 Let the wickedness of his fathers be had in remembrance in the sight of the LORD, * and let not the sin of his mother be done away.

14 Let them alway be before the LORD, * that he may root out the memorial of them from off the earth;

15 And that because his mind was not to do good, * but persecuted the poor helpless man, that he might slay him that was vexed at the heart.

16 His delight was in cursing, and it shall happen unto him; * he loved not blessing, therefore shall it be far from him.

17 He clothed himself with cursing like as with a raiment, * and it shall come into his bowels like water, and like oil into his bones.

18 Let it be unto him as the cloak that he hath upon him, * and as the girdle that he is alway girded withal.

19 Let it thus happen from the LORD unto mine enemies, * and to those that speak evil against my soul.

20 But deal thou with me, O LORD God, according unto thy name, * for sweet is thy mercy.

21 O deliver me, for I am helpless and poor, * and my heart is wounded within me.

22 I go hence like the shadow that departeth, * and am driven away as the grasshopper.

23 My knees are weak through fasting; * my flesh is dried up for want of fatness.

24 I became also a reproach unto them; * they that looked upon me shaked their heads.

25 Help me, O LORD my God; * O save me according to thy mercy.

26 And they shall know, how that this is thy hand, * and that thou, LORD, hast done it.

27 Though they curse, yet bless thou; * and let them be confounded that rise up against me, but let thy servant rejoice.

28 Let mine adversaries be clothed with shame, * and let them cover themselves with their own confusion as with a cloak.

29 As for me, I will give great thanks unto the LORD with my mouth, * and praise him among the multitude.

30 For he shall stand at the right hand of the poor, * to save his soul from unrighteous judges.

Day 23. Morning Prayer.
Psalm 110. *Dixit Dominus.*

THE LORD said unto my lord, * 'Sit thou on my right hand until I make thine enemies thy footstool.'

2 The LORD shall send the rod of thy power out of Sion; * be thou ruler, even in the midst among thine enemies.

3 In the day of thy power shall the people offer thee free-will offerings with an holy worship; * the dew of thy birth is of the womb of the morning.

4 The LORD sware and will not repent, * 'Thou art a priest for ever after the order of Melchizedek.'

5 The Lord upon thy right hand * shall wound even kings in the day of his wrath.

6 He shall judge among the heathen; he shall fill the places with the dead bodies, * and smite in sunder the heads over divers countries.

7 He shall drink of the brook in the way; * therefore shall he lift up his head.

Psalm 111. *Confitebor tibi.*

I WILL give thanks unto the LORD with my whole heart, * secretly among the faithful and in the congregation.

2 The works of the LORD are great, * sought out of all them that have pleasure therein.

3 His work is worthy to be praised and had in honour, * and his righteousness endureth for ever.

4 The merciful and gracious LORD hath so done his marvellous works * that they ought to be had in remembrance.

5 He hath given meat unto them that fear him; * he shall ever be mindful of his covenant.

6 He hath showed his people the power of his works, * that he may give them the heritage of the heathen.

7 The works of his hands are verity and judgement; * all his commandments are true.

8 They stand fast for ever and ever, * and are done in truth and equity.

9 He sent redemption unto his people; * he hath commanded his covenant for ever; holy and reverend is his name.

10 The fear of the LORD is the beginning of wisdom; * a good understanding have all they that do thereafter. The praise of him endureth for ever.

Psalm 112. *Beatus vir.*

BLESSED is the man that feareth the LORD; * he hath great delight in his commandments.

2 His seed shall be mighty upon earth; * the generation of the faithful shall be blessed.

3 Riches and plenteousness shall be in his house, * and his righteousness endureth for ever.

4 Unto the godly there ariseth up light in the darkness; * he is merciful, loving, and righteous.

5 A good man is merciful and lendeth, * and will guide his words with discretion.

6 For he shall never be moved, * and the righteous shall be had in everlasting remembrance.

7 He will not be afraid of any evil tidings, * for his heart standeth fast and believeth in the LORD.

8 His heart is established, and will not shrink * until he see his desire upon his enemies.

9 He hath dispersed abroad and given to the poor, * and his righteousness remaineth for ever; his horn shall be exalted with honour.

10 The ungodly shall see it and it shall grieve him; * he shall gnash with his teeth and consume away; the desire of the ungodly shall perish.

Psalm 113. *Laudate, pueri.*

PRAISE the LORD, ye servants; * O praise the name of the LORD.

2 Blessed be the name of the LORD, * from this time forth for evermore.

3 The LORD's name is praised, * from the rising up of the sun unto the going down of the same.

4 The LORD is high above all heathen, * and his glory above the heavens.

5 Who is like unto the LORD our God, that hath his dwelling so high, * and yet humbleth himself to behold the things that are in heaven and earth?

6 He taketh up the simple out of the dust, * and lifteth the poor out of the mire,

7 That he may set him with the princes, * even with the princes of his people.

8 He maketh the barren woman to keep house, * and to be a joyful mother of children.

Day 23. Evening Prayer.
Psalm 114. *In exitu Israel.*

WHEN Israel came out of Egypt, * and the house of Jacob from among the strange people,

2 Judah was his sanctuary * and Israel his dominion.

3 The sea saw that and fled; * Jordan was driven back.

4 The mountains skipped like rams, * and the little hills like young sheep.

5 What aileth thee, O thou sea, that thou fleddest? * and thou Jordan, that thou wast driven back?

6 Ye mountains, that ye skipped like rams? * and ye little hills, like young sheep?

7 Tremble, thou earth, at the presence of the Lord, * at the presence of the God of Jacob,

8 Who turned the hard rock into a standing water, * and the flintstone into a springing well.

Psalm 115. *Non nobis, Domine.*

Not unto us, O Lord, not unto us, but unto thy name give the praise, * for thy loving mercy and for thy truth's sake.

2 Wherefore shall the heathen say, * 'Where is now their God?'

3 As for our God, he is in heaven; * he hath done whatsoever pleased him.

4 Their idols are silver and gold, * even the work of men's hands.

5 They have mouths and speak not; * eyes have they, and see not.

6 They have ears and hear not; * noses have they, and smell not.

7 They have hands and handle not; feet have they, and walk not, * neither speak they through their throat.

8 They that make them are like unto them, * and so are all such as put their trust in them.

9 But thou, house of Israel, trust thou in the Lord: * he is their succour and defence.

10 Ye house of Aaron, put your trust in the Lord: * he is their helper and defender.

11 Ye that fear the Lord, put your trust in the Lord: * he is their helper and defender.

12 The Lord hath been mindful of us, and he shall bless us; * even he shall bless the house of Israel; he shall bless the house of Aaron.

13 He shall bless them that fear the Lord, * both small and great.

14 The LORD shall increase you more and more, * you and your children.

15 Ye are the blessed of the LORD, * who made heaven and earth.

16 All the whole heavens are the LORD's; * the earth hath he given to the children of men.

17 The dead praise not thee, O LORD, * neither all they that go down into silence.

18 But we will praise the LORD, * from this time forth for evermore. Praise the LORD.

Day 24. Morning Prayer.
Psalm 116. *Dilexi, quoniam.*

I AM well pleased * that the LORD hath heard the voice of my prayer,

2 That he hath inclined his ear unto me; * therefore will I call upon him as long as I live.

3 The snares of death compassed me round about, * and the pains of hell gat hold upon me.

4 I shall find trouble and heaviness, and I will call upon the name of the LORD: * 'O LORD, I beseech thee, deliver my soul.'

5 Gracious is the LORD and righteous; * yea, our God is merciful.

6 The LORD preserveth the simple; * I was in misery and he helped me.

7 Turn again then unto thy rest, O my soul, * for the LORD hath rewarded thee.

8 And why? thou hast delivered my soul from death, * mine eyes from tears, and my feet from falling.

9 I will walk before the LORD * in the land of the living.

10 I believed and therefore will I speak, but I was sore troubled; * I said in my haste, 'All men are liars.'

11 What reward shall I give unto the LORD * for all the benefits that he hath done unto me?

12 I will receive the cup of salvation, * and call upon the name of the LORD.

13 I will pay my vows now in the presence of all his people; * right dear in the sight of the LORD is the death of his saints.

14 Behold, O LORD, how that I am thy servant; * I am thy servant and the son of thine handmaid; thou hast broken my bonds in sunder.

15 I will offer to thee the sacrifice of thanksgiving, * and will call upon the name of the LORD.

16 I will pay my vows unto the LORD in the sight of all his people, * in the courts of the LORD's house, even in the midst of thee, O Jerusalem. Praise the LORD.

Psalm 117. *Laudate Dominum.*

O PRAISE the LORD, all ye heathen; * praise him, all ye nations.

2 For his merciful kindness is ever more and more towards us, * and the truth of the LORD endureth for ever. Praise the LORD.

Psalm 118. *Confitemini Domino.*

O GIVE thanks unto the LORD, for he is gracious, * because his mercy endureth for ever.

2 Let Israel now confess that he is gracious, * and that his mercy endureth for ever.

3 Let the house of Aaron now confess * that his mercy endureth for ever.

4 Yea, let them now that fear the LORD confess * that his mercy endureth for ever.

5 I called upon the LORD in trouble, * and the LORD heard me at large.

6 The LORD is on my side; * I will not fear what man doeth unto me.

7 The LORD taketh my part with them that help me; * therefore shall I see my desire upon mine enemies.

8 It is better to trust in the LORD * than to put any confidence in man.

9 It is better to trust in the LORD * than to put any confidence in princes.

10 All nations compassed me round about, * but in the name of the LORD will I destroy them.

11 They kept me in on every side; they kept me in, I say, on every side, * but in the name of the LORD will I destroy them.

12 They came about me like bees, and are extinct even as the fire among the thorns, * for in the name of the LORD I will destroy them.

13 Thou hast thrust sore at me, that I might fall, * but the LORD was my help.

14 The LORD is my strength and my song, * and is become my salvation.

15 The voice of joy and health is in the dwellings of the

righteous; * the right hand of the LORD bringeth mighty things to pass.

16 The right hand of the LORD hath the preeminence; * the right hand of the LORD bringeth mighty things to pass.

17 I shall not die, but live * and declare the works of the LORD.

18 The LORD hath chastened and corrected me, * but he hath not given me over unto death.

19 Open me the gates of righteousness, * that I may go into them and give thanks unto the LORD.

20 This is the gate of the LORD; * the righteous shall enter into it.

21 I will thank thee, for thou hast heard me, * and art become my salvation.

22 The same stone which the builders refused * is become the headstone in the corner.

23 This is the LORD's doing, * and it is marvellous in our eyes.

24 This is the day which the LORD hath made; * we will rejoice and be glad in it.

25 Help me now, O LORD; * O LORD, send us now prosperity.

26 Blessed be he that cometh in the name of the LORD; * we have wished you good luck, ye that are of the house of the LORD.

27 God is the LORD, who hath showed us light; * bind the sacrifice with cords, yea, even unto the horns of the altar.

28 Thou art my God, and I will thank thee; * thou art my God, and I will praise thee.

29 O give thanks unto the LORD, for he is gracious, *
and his mercy endureth for ever.

Day 24. Evening Prayer.
Psalm 119:1-8. *Beati immaculati.*

B LESSED are those that are undefiled in the way, * and
walk in the law of the LORD.

2 Blessed are they that keep his testimonies, * and seek
him with their whole heart,

3 For they who do no wickedness * walk in his ways.

4 Thou hast charged * that we shall diligently keep thy
commandments.

5 O that my ways were made so direct * that I might
keep thy statutes!

6 So shall I not be confounded, * while I have respect
unto all thy commandments.

7 I will thank thee with an unfeigned heart, * when I
shall have learned the judgements of thy righteousness.

8 I will keep thy statutes; * O forsake me not utterly.

Psalm 119:9-16. *In quo corriget?*

W HEREWITHAL shall a young man cleanse his way? *
even by ruling himself after thy word.

10 With my whole heart have I sought thee; * O let me
not go wrong out of thy commandments.

11 Thy words have I hid within my heart, * that I should
not sin against thee.

12 Blessed art thou, O LORD; * O teach me thy statutes.

13 With my lips have I been telling * of all the judgements of thy mouth.

14 I have had as great delight in the way of thy testimonies * as in all manner of riches.

15 I will talk of thy commandments, * and have respect unto thy ways.

16 My delight shall be in thy statutes, * and I will not forget thy word.

Psalm 119:17-24. *Retribue servo tuo.*

O DO well unto thy servant, * that I may live and keep thy word.

18 Open thou mine eyes, * that I may see the wondrous things of thy law.

19 I am a stranger upon earth; * O hide not thy commandments from me.

20 My soul breaketh out for the very fervent desire * that it hath alway unto thy judgements.

21 Thou hast rebuked the proud, * and cursed are they that do err from thy commandments.

22 O turn from me shame and rebuke, * for I have kept thy testimonies.

23 Princes also did sit and speak against me, * but thy servant is occupied in thy statutes.

24 For thy testimonies are my delight * and my counsellors.

Psalm 119:25-32. *Adhaesit pavimento.*

M Y soul cleaveth to the dust; * O quicken thou me according to thy word.

26 I have acknowledged my ways, and thou heardest me; * O teach me thy statutes.

27 Make me to understand the way of thy commandments, * and so shall I talk of thy wondrous works.

28 My soul melteth away for very heaviness; * comfort thou me according unto thy word.

29 Take from me the way of lying, * and cause thou me to make much of thy law.

30 I have chosen the way of truth, * and thy judgements have I laid before me.

31 I have stuck unto thy testimonies; * O LORD, confound me not.

32 I will run the way of thy commandments, * when thou hast set my heart at liberty.

Day 25. Morning Prayer.
Psalm 119:33-40. *Legem pone.*

TEACH me, O LORD, the way of thy statutes, * and I shall keep it unto the end.

34 Give me understanding, and I shall keep thy law; * yea, I shall keep it with my whole heart.

35 Make me to go in the path of thy commandments, * for therein is my desire.

36 Incline my heart unto thy testimonies, * and not to covetousness.

37 O turn away mine eyes, lest they behold vanity, * and quicken thou me in thy way.

38 O stablish thy word in thy servant, * that I may fear thee.

39 Take away the rebuke that I am afraid of, * for thy judgements are good.

40 Behold, my delight is in thy commandments; * O quicken me in thy righteousness.

Psalm 119:41-48. *Et veniat super me.*

L ET thy loving mercy come also unto me, O LORD, * even thy salvation, according unto thy word.

42 So shall I make answer unto my blasphemers, * for my trust is in thy word.

43 O take not the word of thy truth utterly out of my mouth, * for my hope is in thy judgements.

44 So shall I alway keep thy law, * yea, for ever and ever.

45 And I will walk at liberty, * for I seek thy commandments.

46 I will speak of thy testimonies also, even before kings, * and will not be ashamed.

47 And my delight shall be in thy commandments, * which I have loved.

48 My hands also will I lift up unto thy commandments, which I have loved, * and my study shall be in thy statutes.

Psalm 119:49-56. *Memor esto verbi tui.*

O THINK upon thy servant, as concerning thy word, * wherein thou hast caused me to put my trust.

50 The same is my comfort in my trouble, * for thy word hath quickened me.

51 The proud have had me exceedingly in derision, * yet have I not shrinked from thy law.

52 For I remembered thine everlasting judgements, O LORD, * and received comfort.

53 I am horribly afraid, * for the ungodly that forsake thy law.

54 Thy statutes have been my songs * in the house of my pilgrimage.

55 I have thought upon thy name, O LORD, in the night season, * and have kept thy law.

56 This I had * because I kept thy commandments.

Psalm 119:57-64. *Portio mea, Domine.*

THOU art my portion, O LORD; * I have promised to keep thy law.

58 I made my humble petition in thy presence with my whole heart; * O be merciful unto me according to thy word.

59 I called mine own ways to remembrance, * and turned my feet unto thy testimonies.

60 I made haste and prolonged not the time * to keep thy commandments.

61 The congregations of the ungodly have robbed me, * but I have not forgotten thy law.

62 At midnight I will rise to give thanks unto thee, * because of thy righteous judgements.

63 I am a companion of all them that fear thee * and keep thy commandments.

64 The earth, O LORD, is full of thy mercy; * O teach me thy statutes.

Psalm 119:65-72. *Bonitatem fecisti.*

O LORD, thou hast dealt graciously with thy servant, * according unto thy word.

66 O learn me true understanding and knowledge, *
for I have believed thy commandments.

67 Before I was troubled I went wrong, * but now have
I kept thy word.

68 Thou art good and gracious; * O teach me thy statutes.

69 The proud have imagined a lie against me, * but I will
keep thy commandments with my whole heart.

70 Their heart is as fat as boars' flesh, * but my delight
hath been in thy law.

71 It is good for me that I have been in trouble, * that I
may learn thy statutes.

72 The law of thy mouth is dearer unto me * than thousands of gold and silver.

Day 25. Evening Prayer.
Psalm 119:73-80. *Manus tuae fecerunt me.*

THY hands have made me and fashioned me; * O give
me understanding, that I may learn thy commandments.

74 They that fear thee will be glad when they see me, *
because I have put my trust in thy word.

75 I know, O Lord, that thy judgements are right, *
and that thou of very faithfulness hast caused me to be
troubled.

76 O let thy merciful kindness be my comfort, * according to thy word unto thy servant.

77 O let thy loving mercies come unto me, that I may
live, * for thy law is my delight.

78 Let the proud be confounded, for they go wickedly

about to destroy me, * but I will be occupied in thy commandments.

79 Let such as fear thee and have known thy testimonies * be turned unto me.

80 O let my heart be sound in thy statutes, * that I be not ashamed.

Psalm 119:81-88. *Defecit anima mea.*

MY soul hath longed for thy salvation, * and I have a good hope because of thy word.

82 Mine eyes long sore for thy word, * saying, 'O when wilt thou comfort me?'

83 For I am become like a bottle in the smoke, * yet do I not forget thy statutes.

84 How many are the days of thy servant? * when wilt thou be avenged of them that persecute me?

85 The proud have digged pits for me, * which are not after thy law.

86 All thy commandments are true; * they persecute me falsely; O be thou my help.

87 They had almost made an end of me upon earth, * but I forsook not thy commandments.

88 O quicken me after thy loving-kindness, * and so shall I keep the testimonies of thy mouth.

Psalm 119:89-96. *In aeternum, Domine.*

O LORD, thy word * endureth for ever in heaven.

90 Thy truth also remaineth from one generation to another; * thou hast laid the foundation of the earth, and it abideth.

91 They continue this day according to thine ordinance, * for all things serve thee.

92 If my delight had not been in thy law, * I should have perished in my trouble.

93 I will never forget thy commandments, * for with them thou hast quickened me.

94 I am thine; O save me, * for I have sought thy commandments.

95 The ungodly laid wait for me to destroy me, * but I will consider thy testimonies.

96 I see that all things come to an end, * but thy commandment is exceeding broad.

Psalm 119:97-104. *Quomodo dilexi!*

LORD, what love have I unto thy law! * all the day long is my study in it.

98 Thou through thy commandments hast made me wiser than mine enemies, * for they are ever with me.

99 I have more understanding than my teachers, * for thy testimonies are my study.

100 I am wiser than the aged, * because I keep thy commandments.

101 I have refrained my feet from every evil way, * that I may keep thy word.

102 I have not shrunk from thy judgements, * for thou teachest me.

103 O how sweet are thy words unto my throat, * yea, sweeter than honey unto my mouth.

104 Through thy commandments I get understanding; * therefore I hate all evil ways.

Day 26. Morning Prayer.
Psalm 119:105-112. *Lucerna pedibus meis.*

THY word is a lantern unto my feet, * and a light unto my paths.

106 I have sworn and am steadfastly purposed * to keep thy righteous judgements.

107 I am troubled above measure; * quicken me, O LORD, according to thy word.

108 Let the free-will offerings of my mouth please thee, O LORD, * and teach me thy judgements.

109 My soul is alway in my hand, * yet do I not forget thy law.

110 The ungodly have laid a snare for me, * but yet I swerved not from thy commandments.

111 Thy testimonies have I claimed as mine heritage for ever; * and why? they are the very joy of my heart.

112 I have applied my heart to fulfil thy statutes alway, * even unto the end.

Psalm 119:113-120. *Iniquos odio habui.*

I HATE them that imagine evil things, * but thy law do I love.

114 Thou art my defence and shield, * and my trust is in thy word.

115 Away from me, ye wicked; * I will keep the commandments of my God.

116 O stablish me according to thy word, that I may live, * and let me not be disappointed of my hope.

117 Hold thou me up, and I shall be safe; * yea, my delight shall be ever in thy statutes.

118 Thou hast trodden down all them that depart from thy statutes, * for they imagine but deceit.

119 Thou puttest away all the ungodly of the earth like dross; * therefore I love thy testimonies.

120 My flesh trembleth for fear of thee, * and I am afraid of thy judgements.

Psalm 119:121-128. *Feci judicium.*

I DEAL with the thing that is lawful and right; * O give me not over unto mine oppressors.

122 Make thou thy servant to delight in that which is good, * that the proud do me no wrong.

123 Mine eyes are wasted away with looking for thy health, * and for the word of thy righteousness.

124 O deal with thy servant according unto thy loving mercy, * and teach me thy statutes.

125 I am thy servant; O grant me understanding, * that I may know thy testimonies.

126 It is time for thee, LORD, to lay to thine hand, * for they have destroyed thy law.

127 For I love thy commandments * above gold and precious stone.

128 Therefore hold I straight all thy commandments, * and all false ways I utterly abhor.

Psalm 119:129-136. *Mirabilia.*

T HY testimonies are wonderful; * therefore doth my soul keep them.

130 When thy word goeth forth, * it giveth light and understanding unto the simple.

131 I opened my mouth and drew in my breath, * for my delight was in thy commandments.

132 O look thou upon me and be merciful unto me, * as thou usest to do unto those that love thy name.

133 Order my steps in thy word, * and so shall no wickedness have dominion over me.

134 O deliver me from the wrongful dealings of men, * and so shall I keep thy commandments.

135 Show the light of thy countenance upon thy servant, * and teach me thy statutes.

136 Mine eyes gush out with water, * because men keep not thy law.

Psalm 119:137-144. *Justus es, Domine.*

RIGHTEOUS art thou, O LORD, * and true is thy judgement.

138 The testimonies that thou hast commanded * are exceeding righteous and true.

139 My zeal hath even consumed me, * because mine enemies have forgotten thy words.

140 Thy word is tried to the uttermost, * and thy servant loveth it.

141 I am small and of no reputation, * yet do I not forget thy commandments.

142 Thy righteousness is an everlasting righteousness, * and thy law is the truth.

143 Trouble and heaviness have taken hold upon me, * yet is my delight in thy commandments.

144 The righteousness of thy testimonies is everlasting; * O grant me understanding and I shall live.

Day 26. Evening Prayer.

Psalm 119:145-152. *Clamavi in toto corde meo.*

I CALL with my whole heart; * hear me, O LORD; I will keep thy statutes.

146 Yea, even unto thee do I call; * help me, and I shall keep thy testimonies.

147 Early in the morning do I cry unto thee, * for in thy word is my trust.

148 Mine eyes prevent the night watches, * that I might be occupied in thy words.

149 Hear my voice, O LORD, according unto thy loving-kindness; * quicken me, according as thou art wont.

150 They draw nigh that of malice persecute me * and are far from thy law.

151 Be thou nigh at hand, O LORD, * for all thy commandments are true.

152 As concerning thy testimonies, I have known long since * that thou hast grounded them for ever.

Psalm 119:153-160. *Vide humilitatem.*

O CONSIDER mine adversity and deliver me, * for I do not forget thy law.

154 Avenge thou my cause and deliver me; * quicken me according to thy word.

155 Health is far from the ungodly, * for they regard not thy statutes.

156 Great is thy mercy, O LORD; * quicken me, as thou art wont.

157 Many there are that trouble me and persecute me, * yet do I not swerve from thy testimonies.

158 It grieveth me when I see the transgressors, * because they keep not thy law.

159 Consider, O Lᴏʀᴅ, how I love thy commandments; * O quicken me according to thy loving-kindness.

160 Thy word is true from everlasting; * all the judgements of thy righteousness endure for evermore.

Psalm 119:161-168. *Principes persecuti sunt.*

Pʀɪɴᴄᴇs have persecuted me without a cause, * but my heart standeth in awe of thy word.

162 I am as glad of thy word * as one that findeth great spoils.

163 As for lies, I hate and abhor them, * but thy law do I love.

164 Seven times a day do I praise thee, * because of thy righteous judgements.

165 Great is the peace that they have who love thy law, * and they are not offended at it.

166 Lᴏʀᴅ, I have looked for thy saving health, * and done after thy commandments.

167 My soul hath kept thy testimonies, * and loved them exceedingly.

168 I have kept thy commandments and testimonies, * for all my ways are before thee.

Psalm 119:169-176. *Appropinquet deprecatio.*

Lᴇᴛ my complaint come before thee, O Lᴏʀᴅ: * give me understanding according to thy word.

170 Let my supplication come before thee: * deliver me according to thy word.

171 My lips shall speak of thy praise, * when thou hast taught me thy statutes.

172 Yea, my tongue shall sing of thy word, * for all thy commandments are righteous.

173 Let thine hand help me, * for I have chosen thy commandments.

174 I have longed for thy saving health, O LORD, * and in thy law is my delight.

175 O let my soul live, and it shall praise thee, * and thy judgements shall help me.

176 I have gone astray like a sheep that is lost; * O seek thy servant, for I do not forget thy commandments.

Day 27. Morning Prayer.
Psalm 120. *Ad Dominum.*

WHEN I was in trouble I called upon the LORD, * and he heard me.

2 Deliver my soul, O LORD, from lying lips, * and from a deceitful tongue.

3 What reward shall be given or done unto thee, thou false tongue? * even mighty and sharp arrows, with hot burning coals.

4 Woe is me, that I am constrained to dwell with Meshech, * and to have my habitation among the tents of Kedar.

5 My soul hath long dwelt among them * that are enemies unto peace.

6 I labour for peace, but when I speak unto them thereof, * they make them ready to battle.

Psalm 121. *Levavi oculos.*

I WILL lift up mine eyes unto the hills; * from whence cometh my help?

2 My help cometh even from the LORD, * who hath made heaven and earth.

3 He will not suffer thy foot to be moved, * and he that keepeth thee will not sleep.

4 Behold, he that keepeth Israel * shall neither slumber nor sleep.

5 The LORD himself is thy keeper; * the LORD is thy defence upon thy right hand,

6 So that the sun shall not burn thee by day, * neither the moon by night.

7 The LORD shall preserve thee from all evil; * yea, it is even he that shall keep thy soul.

8 The LORD shall preserve thy going out and thy coming in, * from this time forth for evermore.

Psalm 122. *Laetatus sum.*

I WAS glad when they said unto me, * 'We will go into the house of the LORD.'

2 Our feet shall stand in thy gates, * O Jerusalem.

3 Jerusalem is built as a city * that is at unity in itself.

4 For thither the tribes go up, even the tribes of the LORD, * to testify unto Israel, to give thanks unto the name of the LORD.

5 For there is the seat of judgement, * even the seat of the house of David.

6 O pray for the peace of Jerusalem; * they shall prosper that love thee.

7 Peace be within thy walls, * and plenteousness within thy palaces.

8 For my brethren and companions' sakes, * I will wish thee prosperity.

9 Yea, because of the house of the LORD our God, * I will seek to do thee good.

Psalm 123. *Ad te levavi oculos meos.*

UNTO thee lift I up mine eyes, * O thou that dwellest in the heavens.

2 Behold, even as the eyes of servants look unto the hand of their masters, and as the eyes of a maiden unto the hand of her mistress, * even so our eyes wait upon the LORD our God until he have mercy upon us.

3 Have mercy upon us, O LORD, have mercy upon us, * for we are utterly despised.

4 Our soul is filled with the scornful reproof of the wealthy, * and with the despitefulness of the proud.

Psalm 124. *Nisi quia Dominus.*

IF the LORD himself had not been on our side, now may Israel say, * if the LORD himself had not been on our side, when men rose up against us,

2 They had swallowed us up quick, * when they were so wrathfully displeased at us.

3 Yea, the waters had drowned us, * and the stream had gone over our soul;

4 The deep waters of the proud * had gone even over our soul.

5 But praised be the LORD, * who hath not given us over for a prey unto their teeth.

6 Our soul is escaped even as a bird out of the snare of the fowler; * the snare is broken and we are delivered.

7 Our help standeth in the name of the LORD, * who hath made heaven and earth.

Psalm 125. *Qui confidunt.*

THEY that put their trust in the LORD shall be even as the Mount Sion, * which may not be removed, but standeth fast for ever.

2 The hills stand about Jerusalem; * even so standeth the LORD round about his people, from this time forth for evermore.

3 For the rod of the ungodly cometh not into the lot of the righteous, * lest the righteous put their hand unto wickedness.

4 Do well, O LORD, * unto those that are good and true of heart.

5 As for such as turn back unto their own wickedness, * the LORD shall lead them forth with the evildoers, but peace shall be upon Israel.

Day 27. Evening Prayer.
Psalm 126. *In convertendo.*

WHEN the LORD turned again the captivity of Sion, * then were we like unto them that dream.

2 Then was our mouth filled with laughter * and our tongue with joy.

3 Then said they among the heathen, * 'The LORD hath done great things for them.'

4 Yea, the LORD hath done great things for us already, * whereof we rejoice.

5 Turn our captivity, O LORD, * as the rivers in the south.

6 They that sow in tears * shall reap in joy.

7 He that now goeth on his way weeping, and beareth forth good seed, * shall doubtless come again with joy, and bring his sheaves with him.

Psalm 127. *Nisi Dominus.*

EXCEPT the LORD build the house, * their labour is but lost that build it.

2 Except the LORD keep the city, * the watchman waketh but in vain.

3 It is but lost labour that ye haste to rise up early, and so late take rest, and eat the bread of carefulness, * for so he giveth his beloved sleep.

4 Lo, children and the fruit of the womb * are an heritage and gift that cometh of the LORD.

5 Like as the arrows in the hand of the giant, * even so are the young children.

6 Happy is the man that hath his quiver full of them; * they shall not be ashamed when they speak with their enemies in the gate.

Psalm 128. *Beati omnes.*

BLESSED are all they that fear the LORD * and walk in his ways.

2 For thou shalt eat the labours of thine hands; * O well is thee and happy shalt thou be.

3 Thy wife shall be as the fruitful vine * upon the walls of thine house,

4 Thy children like the olive branches * round about thy table.

5 Lo, thus shall the man be blessed * that feareth the LORD.

6 The LORD from out of Sion shall so bless thee * that thou shalt see Jerusalem in prosperity all thy life long,

7 Yea, that thou shalt see thy children's children * and peace upon Israel.

Psalm 129. *Saepe expugnaverunt.*

MANY a time have they fought against me from my youth up, * may Israel now say;

2 Yea, many a time have they vexed me from my youth up, * but they have not prevailed against me.

3 The plowers plowed upon my back * and made long furrows.

4 But the righteous LORD * hath hewn the snares of the ungodly in pieces.

5 Let them be confounded and turned backward, * as many as have evil will at Sion.

6 Let them be even as the grass growing upon the housetops, * which withereth afore it be plucked up,

7 Whereof the mower filleth not his hand, * neither he that bindeth up the sheaves his bosom.

8 So that they who go by say not so much as, 'The LORD

prosper you; * we wish you good luck in the name of the
Lord.'

Psalm 130. *De profundis.*

OUT of the deep have I called unto thee, O Lord; *
Lord, hear my voice.

2 O let thine ears consider well * the voice of my complaint.

3 If thou, Lord, wilt be extreme to mark what is done
amiss, * O Lord, who may abide it?

4 For there is mercy with thee; * therefore shalt thou
be feared.

5 I look for the Lord; my soul doth wait for him; * in
his word is my trust.

6 My soul fleeth unto the Lord * before the morning
watch, I say, before the morning watch.

7 O Israel, trust in the Lord, for with the Lord there
is mercy, * and with him is plenteous redemption.

8 And he shall redeem Israel * from all his sins.

Psalm 131. *Domine, non est.*

LORD, I am not high-minded; * I have no proud looks.
2 I do not exercise myself in great matters * which
are too high for me.

3 But I refrain my soul and keep it low, like as a child
that is weaned from his mother; * yea, my soul is even as
a weaned child.

4 O Israel, trust in the Lord, * from this time forth for
evermore.

Day 28. Morning Prayer.

Psalm 132. *Memento, Domine.*

LORD, remember David * and all his trouble,

2 How he sware unto the LORD, * and vowed a vow unto the almighty God of Jacob:

3 'I will not come within the tabernacle of mine house, * nor climb up into my bed;

4 I will not suffer mine eyes to sleep, nor mine eyelids to slumber, * neither the temples of my head to take any rest,

5 Until I find out a place for the temple of the LORD, * an habitation for the mighty God of Jacob.'

6 Lo, we heard of the same at Ephrathah, * and found it in the wood.

7 We will go into his tabernacle, * and fall low on our knees before his footstool.

8 Arise, O LORD, into thy resting place, * thou and the ark of thy strength.

9 Let thy priests be clothed with righteousness, * and let thy saints sing with joyfulness.

10 For thy servant David's sake, * turn not away the presence of thine anointed.

11 The LORD hath made a faithful oath unto David, * and he shall not shrink from it:

12 'Of the fruit of thy body * shall I set upon thy seat.

13 If thy children will keep my covenant, and my testimonies that I shall learn them, * their children also shall sit upon thy seat for evermore.'

14 For the LORD hath chosen Sion to be an habitation for himself; * he hath longed for her:

15 'This shall be my rest for ever; * here will I dwell, for I have a delight therein.

16 I will bless her victuals with increase, * and will satisfy her poor with bread.

17 I will deck her priests with health, * and her saints shall rejoice and sing.

18 There shall I make the horn of David to flourish; * I have ordained a lantern for mine anointed.

19 As for his enemies, I shall clothe them with shame, * but upon himself shall his crown flourish.'

Psalm 133. *Ecce, quam bonum!*

BEHOLD, how good and joyful a thing it is, * brethren, to dwell together in unity!

2 It is like the precious ointment upon the head that ran down unto the beard, * even unto Aaron's beard, and went down to the skirts of his clothing;

3 Like as the dew of Hermon, * which fell upon the hill of Sion.

4 For there the LORD promised his blessing * and life for evermore.

Psalm 134. *Ecce nunc.*

BEHOLD now, praise the LORD, * all ye servants of the LORD,

2 Ye that by night stand in the house of the LORD, * even in the courts of the house of our God.

3 Lift up your hands in the sanctuary, * and praise the LORD.

4 The LORD that made heaven and earth * give thee blessing out of Sion.

Psalm 135. *Laudate Nomen.*

O PRAISE the LORD. Laud ye the name of the LORD; * praise it, O ye servants of the LORD,

2 Ye that stand in the house of the LORD, * in the courts of the house of our God.

3 O praise the LORD, for the LORD is gracious; * O sing praises unto his name, for it is lovely.

4 For why? the LORD hath chosen Jacob unto himself, * and Israel for his own possession.

5 For I know that the LORD is great, * and that our Lord is above all gods.

6 Whatsoever the LORD pleased, that did he in heaven and in earth, * and in the sea and in all deep places.

7 He bringeth forth the clouds from the ends of the world, * and sendeth forth lightnings with the rain, bringing the winds out of his treasures.

8 He smote the firstborn of Egypt, * both of man and beast.

9 He hath sent tokens and wonders into the midst of thee, O thou land of Egypt, * upon Pharaoh and all his servants.

10 He smote divers nations * and slew mighty kings –

11 Sihon king of the Amorites, and Og the king of Bashan, * and all the kingdoms of Canaan –

12 And gave their land to be an heritage, * even an heritage unto Israel his people.

13 Thy name, O Lord, endureth for ever; * so doth thy memorial, O Lord, from one generation to another.

14 For the Lord will avenge his people, * and be gracious unto his servants.

15 As for the images of the heathen, they are but silver and gold, * the work of men's hands.

16 They have mouths and speak not; * eyes have they, but they see not.

17 They have ears and yet they hear not, * neither is there any breath in their mouths.

18 They that make them are like unto them, * and so are all they that put their trust in them.

19 Praise the Lord, ye house of Israel; * praise the Lord, ye house of Aaron.

20 Praise the Lord, ye house of Levi; * ye that fear the Lord, praise the Lord.

21 Praised be the Lord out of Sion, * who dwelleth at Jerusalem.

Day 28. Evening Prayer.
Psalm 136. *Confitemini.*

O GIVE thanks unto the Lord, for he is gracious, * and his mercy endureth for ever.

2 O give thanks unto the God of all gods, * for his mercy endureth for ever.

3 O thank the Lord of all lords, * for his mercy endureth for ever;

4 Who only doeth great wonders, * for his mercy endureth for ever;

5 Who by his excellent wisdom made the heavens, * for his mercy endureth for ever;

6 Who laid out the earth above the waters, * for his mercy endureth for ever;

7 Who hath made great lights, * for his mercy endureth for ever;

8 The sun to rule the day, * for his mercy endureth for ever;

9 The moon and the stars to govern the night, * for his mercy endureth for ever;

10 Who smote Egypt with their firstborn, * for his mercy endureth for ever;

11 And brought out Israel from among them, * for his mercy endureth for ever;

12 With a mighty hand and stretched-out arm, * for his mercy endureth for ever;

13 Who divided the Red Sea in two parts, * for his mercy endureth for ever;

14 And made Israel to go through the midst of it, * for his mercy endureth for ever;

15 But as for Pharaoh and his host, he overthrew them in the Red Sea, * for his mercy endureth for ever;

16 Who led his people through the wilderness, * for his mercy endureth for ever;

17 Who smote great kings, * for his mercy endureth for ever;

18 Yea, and slew mighty kings, * for his mercy endureth for ever;

19 Sihon king of the Amorites, * for his mercy endureth for ever;

20 And Og the king of Bashan, * for his mercy endureth for ever;

21 And gave away their land for an heritage, * for his mercy endureth for ever;

22 Even for an heritage unto Israel his servant, * for his mercy endureth for ever;

23 Who remembered us when we were in trouble, * for his mercy endureth for ever;

24 And hath delivered us from our enemies, * for his mercy endureth for ever;

25 Who giveth food to all flesh, * for his mercy endureth for ever.

26 O give thanks unto the God of heaven, * for his mercy endureth for ever.

27 O give thanks unto the Lord of lords, * for his mercy endureth for ever.

Psalm 137. *Super flumina.*

B Y the waters of Babylon we sat down and wept, * when we remembered thee, O Sion.

2 As for our harps, we hanged them up * upon the trees that are therein.

3 For they that led us away captive required of us then a song, and melody in our heaviness: * 'Sing us one of the songs of Sion.'

4 How shall we sing the LORD's song * in a strange land?

5 If I forget thee, O Jerusalem, * let my right hand forget her cunning.

6 If I do not remember thee, let my tongue cleave to

the roof of my mouth, * yea, if I prefer not Jerusalem in my mirth.

7　Remember the children of Edom, O LORD, in the day of Jerusalem, * how they said, 'Down with it, down with it, even to the ground.'

8　O daughter of Babylon, wasted with misery, * yea, happy shall he be that rewardeth thee as thou hast served us.

9　Blessed shall he be that taketh thy children * and throweth them against the stones.

Psalm 138. *Confitebor tibi.*

I WILL give thanks unto thee, O Lord, with my whole heart; * even before the gods will I sing praise unto thee.

2　I will worship toward thy holy temple and praise thy name, because of thy loving-kindness and truth, * for thou hast magnified thy name and thy word above all things.

3　When I called upon thee, thou heardest me, * and enduedst my soul with much strength.

4　All the kings of the earth shall praise thee, O LORD, * for they have heard the words of thy mouth.

5　Yea, they shall sing in the ways of the LORD * that great is the glory of the LORD.

6　For though the LORD be high, yet hath he respect unto the lowly; * as for the proud, he beholdeth them afar off.

7　Though I walk in the midst of trouble, yet shalt thou refresh me; * thou shalt stretch forth thy hand upon the furiousness of mine enemies, and thy right hand shall save me.

8 The LORD shall make good his loving-kindness toward me. * Yea, thy mercy, O LORD, endureth for ever; despise not then the works of thine own hands.

Day 29. Morning Prayer.
Psalm 139. *Domine, probasti.*

O LORD, thou hast searched me out and known me; * thou knowest my down-sitting and mine up-rising; thou understandest my thoughts long before.

2 Thou art about my path and about my bed, * and spiest out all my ways.

3 For lo, there is not a word in my tongue, * but thou, O LORD, knowest it altogether.

4 Thou hast fashioned me behind and before, * and laid thine hand upon me.

5 Such knowledge is too wonderful and excellent for me; * I cannot attain unto it.

6 Whither shall I go then from thy Spirit? * or whither shall I go then from thy presence?

7 If I climb up into heaven, thou art there; * if I go down to hell, thou art there also.

8 If I take the wings of the morning, * and remain in the uttermost parts of the sea,

9 Even there also shall thy hand lead me, * and thy right hand shall hold me.

10 If I say, 'Peradventure the darkness shall cover me', * then shall my night be turned to day.

11 Yea, the darkness is no darkness with thee, but the night is as clear as the day; * the darkness and light to thee are both alike.

12 For my reins are thine; * thou hast covered me in my mother's womb.

13 I will give thanks unto thee, for I am fearfully and wonderfully made; * marvellous are thy works, and that my soul knoweth right well.

14 My bones are not hid from thee, * though I be made secretly and fashioned beneath in the earth.

15 Thine eyes did see my substance yet being imperfect, * and in thy book were all my members written,

16 Which day by day were fashioned, * when as yet there was none of them.

17 How dear are thy counsels unto me, O God; * O how great is the sum of them!

18 If I tell them, they are more in number than the sand; * when I wake up, I am present with thee.

19 Wilt thou not slay the wicked, O God? * depart from me, ye bloodthirsty men.

20 For they speak unrighteously against thee, * and thine enemies take thy name in vain.

21 Do not I hate them, O Lord, that hate thee? * and am not I grieved with those that rise up against thee?

22 Yea, I hate them right sore, * even as though they were mine enemies.

23 Try me, O God, and seek the ground of my heart; * prove me and examine my thoughts.

24 Look well if there be any way of wickedness in me, * and lead me in the way everlasting.

Psalm 140. *Eripe me, Domine.*

DELIVER me, O LORD, from the evil man, * and pre-serve me from the wicked man,

2 Who imagine mischief in their hearts, * and stir up strife all the day long.

3 They have sharpened their tongues like a serpent; * adders' poison is under their lips.

4 Keep me, O LORD, from the hands of the ungodly; * preserve me from the wicked men who are purposed to overthrow my goings.

5 The proud have laid a snare for me and spread a net abroad with cords, * yea, and set traps in my way.

6 I said unto the LORD, 'Thou art my God; * hear the voice of my prayers, O LORD.'

7 O LORD God, thou strength of my health, * thou hast covered my head in the day of battle.

8 Let not the ungodly have his desire, O LORD; * let not his mischievous imagination prosper, lest they be too proud.

9 Let the mischief of their own lips fall upon the head of them * that compass me about.

10 Let hot burning coals fall upon them; * let them be cast into the fire and into the pit, that they never rise up again.

11 A man full of words shall not prosper upon the earth; * evil shall hunt the wicked person to overthrow him.

12 Sure I am that the LORD will avenge the poor * and maintain the cause of the helpless.

13 The righteous also shall give thanks unto thy name, * and the just shall continue in thy sight.

Psalm 141. *Domine, clamavi.*

Lord, I call upon thee; haste thee unto me, * and consider my voice when I cry unto thee.

2 Let my prayer be set forth in thy sight as the incense, * and let the lifting up of my hands be an evening sacrifice.

3 Set a watch, O Lord, before my mouth, * and keep the door of my lips.

4 O let not mine heart be inclined to any evil thing; * let me not be occupied in ungodly works with the men that work wickedness, lest I eat of such things as please them.

5 Let the righteous rather smite me friendly * and reprove me.

6 But let not their precious balms break my head; * yea, I will pray yet against their wickedness.

7 Let their judges be overthrown in stony places, * that they may hear my words, for they are sweet.

8 Our bones lie scattered before the pit, * like as when one breaketh and heweth wood upon the earth.

9 But mine eyes look unto thee, O Lord God; * in thee is my trust; O cast not out my soul.

10 Keep me from the snare that they have laid for me, * and from the traps of the wicked doers.

11 Let the ungodly fall into their own nets together, * and let me ever escape them.

Day 29. Evening Prayer.
Psalm 142. *Voce mea ad Dominum.*

I cried unto the Lord with my voice; * yea, even unto the Lord did I make my supplication.

2 I poured out my complaints before him, * and showed him of my trouble.

3 When my spirit was in heaviness, thou knewest my path; * in the way wherein I walked have they privily laid a snare for me.

4 I looked also upon my right hand, * and saw there was no man that would know me.

5 I had no place to flee unto, * and no man cared for my soul.

6 I cried unto thee, O LORD, and said, * 'Thou art my hope, and my portion in the land of the living.'

7 Consider my complaint, * for I am brought very low.

8 O deliver me from my persecutors, * for they are too strong for me.

9 Bring my soul out of prison, that I may give thanks unto thy name * – which thing if thou wilt grant me, then shall the righteous resort unto my company.

Psalm 143. *Domine, exaudi.*

HEAR my prayer, O LORD, and consider my desire; * hearken unto me for thy truth and righteousness' sake.

2 And enter not into judgement with thy servant, * for in thy sight shall no man living be justified.

3 For the enemy hath persecuted my soul; he hath smitten my life down to the ground; * he hath laid me in the darkness, as the men that have been long dead.

4 Therefore is my spirit vexed within me, * and my heart within me is desolate.

5 Yet do I remember the time past; I muse upon all thy works; * yea, I exercise myself in the works of thy hands.

6 I stretch forth my hands unto thee; * my soul gaspeth unto thee as a thirsty land.

7 Hear me, O LORD, and that soon, for my spirit waxeth faint; * hide not thy face from me, lest I be like unto them that go down into the pit.

8 O let me hear thy loving-kindness betimes in the morning, for in thee is my trust; * show thou me the way that I should walk in, for I lift up my soul unto thee.

9 Deliver me, O LORD, from mine enemies, * for I flee unto thee to hide me.

10 Teach me to do the thing that pleaseth thee, for thou art my God; * let thy loving Spirit lead me forth into the land of righteousness.

11 Quicken me, O LORD, for thy name's sake, * and for thy righteousness' sake bring my soul out of trouble.

12 And of thy goodness slay mine enemies, * and destroy all them that vex my soul, for I am thy servant.

Day 30. Morning Prayer.

Psalm 144. Benedictus Dominus.

BLESSED be the LORD my strength, * who teacheth my hands to war and my fingers to fight,

2 My hope and my fortress, my castle and deliverer, my defender in whom I trust, * who subdueth my people that is under me.

3 LORD, what is man, that thou hast such respect unto him? * or the son of man, that thou so regardest him?

4 Man is like a thing of nought; * his time passeth away like a shadow.

5 Bow thy heavens, O LORD, and come down; * touch the mountains, and they shall smoke.

6 Cast forth thy lightning and tear them; * shoot out thine arrows and consume them.

7 Send down thine hand from above; * deliver me and take me out of the great waters, from the hand of strange children,

8 Whose mouth talketh of vanity, * and their right hand is a right hand of wickedness.

9 I will sing a new song unto thee, O God, * and sing praises unto thee upon a ten-stringed lute.

10 Thou hast given victory unto kings, * and hast delivered David thy servant from the peril of the sword.

11 Save me, and deliver me from the hand of strange children, * whose mouth talketh of vanity, and their right hand is a right hand of iniquity,

12 That our sons may grow up as the young plants, * and that our daughters may be as the polished corners of the temple,

13 That our garners may be full and plenteous with all manner of store, * that our sheep may bring forth thousands and ten thousands in our streets,

14 That our oxen may be strong to labour, that there be no decay, * no leading into captivity, and no complaining in our streets.

15 Happy are the people that are in such a case; * yea, blessed are the people who have the LORD for their God.

Psalm 145. *Exaltabo te, Deus.*

I WILL magnify thee, O God my king, * and I will praise thy name for ever and ever.

2 Every day will I give thanks unto thee, * and praise thy name for ever and ever.

3 Great is the LORD and marvellous worthy to be praised; * there is no end of his greatness.

4 One generation shall praise thy works unto another, * and declare thy power.

5 As for me, I will be talking of thy worship, * thy glory, thy praise, and wondrous works,

6 So that men shall speak of the might of thy marvellous acts; * and I will also tell of thy greatness.

7 The memorial of thine abundant kindness shall be showed, * and men shall sing of thy righteousness.

8 The LORD is gracious and merciful, * long-suffering and of great goodness.

9 The LORD is loving unto every man, * and his mercy is over all his works.

10 All thy works praise thee, O LORD, * and thy saints give thanks unto thee.

11 They show the glory of thy kingdom, * and talk of thy power,

12 That thy power, thy glory, and mightiness of thy kingdom * might be known unto men.

13 Thy kingdom is an everlasting kingdom, * and thy dominion endureth throughout all ages.

14 The LORD upholdeth all such as fall, * and lifteth up all those that are down.

15 The eyes of all wait upon thee, O Lord, * and thou givest them their meat in due season.

16 Thou openest thine hand, * and fillest all things living with plenteousness.

17 The LORD is righteous in all his ways, * and holy in all his works.

18 The LORD is nigh unto all them that call upon him, * yea, all such as call upon him faithfully.

19 He will fulfil the desire of them that fear him; * he also will hear their cry, and will help them.

20 The LORD preserveth all them that love him, * but scattereth abroad all the ungodly.

21 My mouth shall speak the praise of the LORD, * and let all flesh give thanks unto his holy name for ever and ever.

Psalm 146. *Lauda, anima mea.*

PRAISE the LORD, O my soul. While I live will I praise the LORD; * yea, as long as I have any being, I will sing praises unto my God.

2 O put not your trust in princes, nor in any child of man, * for there is no help in them.

3 For when the breath of man goeth forth, he shall turn again to his earth, * and then all his thoughts perish.

4 Blessed is he that hath the God of Jacob for his help, * and whose hope is in the LORD his God,

5 Who made heaven and earth, the sea and all that therein is, * who keepeth his promise for ever,

6 Who helpeth them to right that suffer wrong, * who feedeth the hungry.

7 The LORD looseth men out of prison; * the LORD giveth sight to the blind.

8 The LORD helpeth them that are fallen; * the LORD careth for the righteous.

9 The LORD careth for the strangers; he defendeth the fatherless and widow; * as for the way of the ungodly, he turneth it upside down.

10 The LORD thy God, O Sion, shall be king for evermore * and throughout all generations.

Day 30. Evening Prayer.
Psalm 147. *Laudate Dominum.*

O PRAISE the LORD, for it is a good thing to sing praises unto our God; * yea, a joyful and pleasant thing it is to be thankful.

2 The LORD doth build up Jerusalem, * and gather together the outcasts of Israel.

3 He healeth those that are broken in heart, * and giveth medicine to heal their sickness.

4 He telleth the number of the stars, * and calleth them all by their names.

5 Great is our Lord and great is his power; * yea, and his wisdom is infinite.

6 The LORD setteth up the meek, * and bringeth the ungodly down to the ground.

7 O sing unto the LORD with thanksgiving; * sing praises upon the harp unto our God;

8 Who covereth the heaven with clouds, and prepareth rain for the earth, * and maketh the grass to grow upon the mountains and herb for the use of men;

9 Who giveth fodder unto the cattle, * and feedeth the young ravens that call upon him.

10 He hath no pleasure in the strength of an horse, * neither delighteth he in any man's legs.

11 But the LORD's delight is in them that fear him * and put their trust in his mercy.

12 Praise the LORD, O Jerusalem; * praise thy God, O Sion.

13 For he hath made fast the bars of thy gates, * and hath blessed thy children within thee.

14 He maketh peace in thy borders, * and filleth thee with the flour of wheat.

15 He sendeth forth his commandment upon earth, * and his word runneth very swiftly.

16 He giveth snow like wool, * and scattereth the hoar frost like ashes.

17 He casteth forth his ice like morsels; * who is able to abide his frost?

18 He sendeth out his word and melteth them; * he bloweth with his wind and the waters flow.

19 He showeth his word unto Jacob, * his statutes and ordinances unto Israel.

20 He hath not dealt so with any nation, * neither have the heathen knowledge of his laws.

Psalm 148. *Laudate Dominum.*

O PRAISE the LORD of heaven; * praise him in the height.

2 Praise him, all ye angels of his; * praise him, all his host.

3 Praise him, sun and moon; * praise him, all ye stars and light.

4 Praise him, all ye heavens, * and ye waters that are above the heavens.

5 Let them praise the name of the LORD, * for he spake the word and they were made; he commanded and they were created.

6 He hath made them fast for ever and ever; * he hath given them a law which shall not be broken.

7 Praise the LORD upon earth, * ye dragons and all deeps,

8 Fire and hail, snow and vapours, * wind and storm fulfilling his word,

9 Mountains and all hills, * fruitful trees and all cedars,

10 Beasts and all cattle, * worms and feathered fowls,

11 Kings of the earth and all peoples, * princes and all judges of the world,

12 Young men and maidens, old men and children – praise the name of the LORD, * for his name only is excellent, and his praise above heaven and earth.

13 He shall exalt the horn of his people; all his saints shall praise him, * even the children of Israel, even the people that serveth him.

Psalm 149. *Cantate Domino.*

O SING unto the LORD a new song; * let the congregation of saints praise him.

2 Let Israel rejoice in him that made him, * and let the children of Sion be joyful in their king.

3 Let them praise his name in the dance; * let them sing praises unto him with tabret and harp.

4 For the LORD hath pleasure in his people, * and helpeth the meek-hearted.

5 Let the saints be joyful with glory; * let them rejoice
in their beds.

6 Let the praises of God be in their mouth, * and a two-
edged sword in their hands,

7 To be avenged of the heathen, * and to rebuke the
peoples,

8 To bind their kings in chains, * and their nobles with
links of iron,

9 That they may be avenged of them, as it is written, *
'Such honour have all his saints.'

Psalm 150. *Laudate Dominum.*

O PRAISE God in his holiness; * praise him in the firmament of his power.

2 Praise him in his noble acts; * praise him according
to his excellent greatness.

3 Praise him in the sound of the trumpet; * praise him
upon the lute and harp.

4 Praise him in the cymbals and dances; * praise him
upon the strings and pipe.

5 Praise him upon the well-tuned cymbals; * praise him
upon the loud cymbals.

6 Let everything that hath breath * praise the LORD.

Forms of Prayer to Be Used at Sea.

¶ *The morning and evening service to be used daily at sea shall be the same as appointed in the Book of Common Prayer (pp. 1, 17).*

¶ *These two following prayers may be used in ships of war.*

O ETERNAL Lord God, who alone spreadest out the heavens and rulest the raging of the sea, who hast compassed the waters with bounds until day and night come to an end: Be pleased to receive into thy almighty and most gracious protection the persons of us thy servants, and the fleet in which we serve. Preserve us from the dangers of the sea and from the violence of the enemy, that we may be a safeguard unto our nation, and a security for all who pass on the seas upon their lawful occasions, that the inhabitants of every nation may in peace and quietness serve thee our God, and that we may return in safety to enjoy the blessings of the land, with the fruits of our labours, and with a thankful remembrance of thy mercies to praise and glorify thy holy name, through Jesus Christ our Lord. *Amen.*

The Collect.

PREVENT us, O Lord, in all our doings with thy most gracious favour, and further us with thy continual help, that in all our works – begun, continued, and ended in thee – we may glorify thy holy name, and finally by thy mercy obtain everlasting life, through Jesus Christ our Lord. *Amen.*

FORMS OF PRAYER TO BE USED AT SEA

Prayers to Be Used in Storms at Sea.

O MOST powerful and glorious Lord God, at whose command the winds blow and lift up the waves of the sea, and who stillest the rage thereof: We thy creatures, but miserable sinners, do in this our great distress cry unto thee for help. Save, Lord, or else we perish. We confess when we have been safe and seen all things quiet about us, we have forgot thee our God, and refused to hearken to the still voice of thy word and to obey thy commandments. But now we see how terrible thou art in all thy works of wonder, the great God to be feared above all. And therefore we adore thy Divine Majesty, acknowledging thy power and imploring thy goodness. Help, Lord, and save us for thy mercy's sake in Jesus Christ thy Son, our Lord. *Amen.*

¶ *Or this.*

O MOST glorious and gracious Lord God, who dwellest in heaven but beholdest all things below: Look down, we beseech thee, and hear us, calling out of the depth of misery, and out of the jaws of this death which is ready now to swallow us up. Save, Lord, or else we perish. The living, the living shall praise thee. O send thy word of command to rebuke the raging winds and the roaring sea, that we, being delivered from this distress, may live to serve thee and to glorify thy name all the days of our life. Hear, Lord, and save us, for the infinite merits of our blessed Saviour, thy Son, our Lord Jesus Christ. *Amen.*

FORMS OF PRAYER TO BE USED AT SEA

The Prayer to Be Said before a Fight
at Sea against Any Enemy.

O MOST powerful and glorious Lord God, the Lord of hosts, who rulest and commandest all things: Thou sittest on the throne judging right, and therefore we make our address to thy Divine Majesty in this our necessity, that thou wouldest take the cause into thine own hand, and judge between us and our enemies. Stir up thy strength, O Lord, and come and help us, for thou givest not alway the battle to the strong, but canst save by many or by few. O let not our sins now cry against us for vengeance, but hear us thy poor servants begging mercy and imploring thy help, and that thou wouldest be a defence unto us against the face of the enemy. Make it appear that thou art our saviour and mighty deliverer, through Jesus Christ our Lord. *Amen.*

General Prayers.
Short Prayers for a Single Person Who Cannot
Meet to Join in Prayer with Others by
Reason of the Fight or Storm.

L ORD, be merciful to us sinners, and save us for thy mercy's sake.

Thou art the great God who hast made and rulest all things: O deliver us for thy name's sake.

Thou art the great God to be feared above all: O save us, that we may praise thee.

FORMS OF PRAYER TO BE USED AT SEA

Special Prayers with Respect to the Enemy.

THOU, O Lord, art just and powerful: O defend our cause against the face of the enemy.

O God, thou art a strong tower of defence to all who flee unto thee: O save us from the violence of the enemy.

O Lord of hosts, fight for us, that we may glorify thee.

O suffer us not to sink under the weight of our sins, or the violence of the enemy.

O Lord, arise, help us, and deliver us for thy name's sake.

Short Prayers in Respect of a Storm.

THOU, O Lord, who stillest the raging of the sea: Hear, hear us, and save us, that we perish not.

O blessed Saviour, who didst save thy disciples ready to perish in a storm: Hear us and save us, we beseech thee.

Lord, have mercy upon us.
Christ, have mercy upon us.
Lord, have mercy upon us.

O Lord, hear us. O Christ, hear us.

God the Father, God the Son, God the Holy Ghost, have mercy upon us; save us now and evermore. Amen.

OUR Father, who art in heaven, Hallowed be thy name. Thy kingdom come. Thy will be done, On earth as it is in heaven. Give us this day our daily bread. And forgive us our trespasses, As we forgive those who trespass against us. And lead us not into temptation, But deliver us from evil. For thine is the kingdom, the power, and the glory, For ever and ever. Amen.

¶ *When there shall be imminent danger, as many as can be spared from necessary service in the ship shall be called together and make a humble confession of their sin to God, in which everyone ought seriously to reflect upon those particular sins of which his conscience shall accuse him, saying as followeth.*

The Confession.

ALMIGHTY God, Father of our Lord Jesus Christ, Maker of all things, Judge of all men: We acknowledge and bewail our manifold sins and wickedness, Which we from time to time most grievously have committed, By thought, word, and deed, Against thy Divine Majesty, Provoking most justly thy wrath and indignation against us. We do earnestly repent, And are heartily sorry for these our misdoings; The remembrance of them is grievous unto us; The burden of them is intolerable. Have mercy upon us, Have mercy upon us, most merciful Father. For thy Son our Lord Jesus Christ's sake, Forgive us all that is past, And grant that we may ever hereafter Serve and please thee In newness of life, To the honour and glory of thy name, Through Jesus Christ our Lord. Amen.

¶ *Then shall the priest (if there is any in the ship) pronounce this absolution.*

ALMIGHTY God, our heavenly Father, who of his great mercy hath promised forgiveness of sins to all those who with hearty repentance and true faith turn unto him, have mercy upon you, pardon and deliver you from all your sins, confirm and strengthen you in all goodness, and bring you to everlasting life, through Jesus Christ our Lord. *Amen.*

Thanksgiving after a Storm.
Jubilate Deo. Psalm 66.

O BE joyful in God, all ye lands; * sing praises unto the honour of his name; make his praise to be glorious.

Say unto God, 'O how wonderful art thou in thy works! * through the greatness of thy power shall thine enemies be found liars unto thee.

For all the world shall worship thee, * sing of thee, and praise thy name.'

O come hither and behold the works of God, * how wonderful he is in his doing toward the children of men.

He turned the sea into dry land, * so that they went through the water on foot; there did we rejoice thereof.

He ruleth with his power for ever, his eyes behold the peoples, * and such as will not believe shall not be able to exalt themselves.

O praise our God, ye peoples, * and make the voice of his praise to be heard,

Who holdeth our soul in life * and suffereth not our feet to slip.

For thou, O God, hast proved us; * thou also hast tried us, like as silver is tried.

Thou broughtest us into the snare, * and laidest trouble upon our loins.

Thou sufferedst men to ride over our heads; * we went through fire and water, and thou broughtest us out into a wealthy place.

I will go into thine house with burnt offerings, * and will pay thee my vows, which I promised with my lips and spake with my mouth when I was in trouble.

I will offer unto thee fat burnt sacrifices with the incense of rams; * I will offer bullocks and goats.

O come hither and hearken, all ye that fear God, * and I will tell you what he hath done for my soul.

I called unto him with my mouth, * and gave him praises with my tongue.

If I incline unto wickedness with mine heart, * the Lord will not hear me.

But God hath heard me, * and considered the voice of my prayer.

Praised be God, who hath not cast out my prayer, * nor turned his mercy from me.

Glory be to the Father, and to the Son, * and to the Holy Ghost;

As it was in the beginning, is now, and ever shall be, * world without end. Amen.

Confitemini Domino. Psalm 107.

O GIVE thanks unto the LORD, for he is gracious, * and his mercy endureth for ever.

Let them give thanks whom the LORD hath redeemed * and delivered from the hand of the enemy,

And gathered them out of the lands, from the east and from the west, * from the north and from the south.

They went astray in the wilderness out of the way, * and found no city to dwell in.

Hungry and thirsty, * their soul fainted in them.

So they cried unto the LORD in their trouble, * and he delivered them from their distress.

He led them forth by the right way, * that they might go to the city where they dwelt.

O that men would therefore praise the LORD for his goodness, * and declare the wonders that he doeth for the children of men!

For he satisfieth the empty soul, * and filleth the hungry soul with goodness.

Such as sit in darkness and in the shadow of death, * being fast bound in misery and iron,

Because they rebelled against the words of the Lord, * and lightly regarded the counsel of the Most High,

He also brought down their heart through heaviness; * they fell down, and there was none to help them.

So when they cried unto the LORD in their trouble, * he delivered them out of their distress.

For he brought them out of darkness and out of the shadow of death, * and brake their bonds in sunder.

O that men would therefore praise the LORD for his goodness, * and declare the wonders that he doeth for the children of men!

For he hath broken the gates of brass, * and smitten the bars of iron in sunder.

Foolish men are plagued for their offence * and because of their wickedness.

Their soul abhorred all manner of meat, * and they were even hard at death's door.

So when they cried unto the LORD in their trouble, * he delivered them out of their distress.

He sent his word and healed them, * and they were saved from their destruction.

O that men would therefore praise the LORD for his goodness, * and declare the wonders that he doeth for the children of men!

That they would offer unto him the sacrifice of thanksgiving, * and tell out his works with gladness!

They that go down to the sea in ships, * and occupy their business in great waters,

These men see the works of the LORD * and his wonders in the deep.

For at his word the stormy wind ariseth, * which lifteth up the waves thereof.

They are carried up to the heaven, and down again to the deep; * their soul melteth away because of the trouble.

They reel to and fro, and stagger like a drunken man, * and are at their wits' end.

So when they cry unto the LORD in their trouble, * he delivereth them out of their distress.

For he maketh the storm to cease, * so that the waves thereof are still.

Then are they glad because they are at rest, * and so he bringeth them unto the haven where they would be.

O that men would therefore praise the LORD for his

goodness, * and declare the wonders that he doeth for the children of men!

That they would exalt him also in the congregation of the people, * and praise him in the seat of the elders!

He turneth the floods into a wilderness, * and drieth up the water-springs.

A fruitful land maketh he barren, * for the wickedness of them that dwell therein.

Again he maketh the wilderness a standing water, * and water-springs of a dry ground.

And there he setteth the hungry, * that they may build them a city to dwell in,

That they may sow their land and plant vineyards, * to yield them fruits of increase.

He blesseth them so that they multiply exceedingly, * and suffereth not their cattle to decrease.

And again, when they are minished and brought low * through oppression, through any plague or trouble,

Though he poureth contempt upon tyrants, * and letteth them wander out of the way in the wilderness,

Yet helpeth he the poor out of misery, * and maketh him households like a flock of sheep.

The righteous will consider this and rejoice, * and the mouth of all wickedness shall be stopped.

Whoso is wise will ponder these things, * and they shall understand the loving-kindness of the LORD.

Glory be to the Father, and to the Son, * and to the Holy Ghost;

As it was in the beginning, is now, and ever shall be, * world without end. Amen.

Collects of Thanksgiving.

O MOST blessed and glorious Lord God, who art of infinite goodness and mercy: We thy poor creatures, whom thou hast made and preserved, holding our souls in life and now rescuing us out of the jaws of death, humbly present ourselves again before thy Divine Majesty, to offer a sacrifice of praise and thanksgiving, because thou heardest us when we called in our trouble, and didst not cast out our prayer which we made before thee in our great distress. Even when we gave all for lost – our ship, our goods, our lives – then didst thou mercifully look upon us, and wonderfully command a deliverance, for which we, now being in safety, do give all praise and glory to thy holy name, through Jesus Christ our Lord. *Amen.*

¶ *Or this.*

O MOST mighty and gracious good God, thy mercy is over all thy works, but in special manner hath been extended toward us, whom thou hast so powerfully and wonderfully defended. Thou hast showed us terrible things and wonders in the deep, that we might see how powerful and gracious a God thou art, how able and ready to help those who trust in thee. Thou hast showed us how both winds and seas obey thy command, that we may learn, even from them, hereafter to obey thy voice and to do thy will. We therefore bless and glorify thy name, for this thy mercy in saving us when we were ready to perish. And, we beseech thee, make us as truly sensible now of thy mercy, as we were then of the danger; and give us hearts always ready to express our thankfulness, not only by words, but also by our lives, in being more obedient to thy holy commandments. Continue, we beseech thee, this thy goodness to us, that we, whom thou hast saved, may serve thee in holiness and righteousness all the days of our life, through Jesus Christ our Lord and Saviour. *Amen.*

A Hymn of Praise and Thanksgiving after a Dangerous Tempest.

O COME, let us give thanks unto the Lord, for he is gracious, * and his mercy endureth for ever.

Great is the Lord and greatly to be praised; let the redeemed of the Lord say so, * whom he hath delivered from the merciless rage of the sea.

The Lord is gracious and full of compassion, * slow to anger and of great mercy.

He hath not dealt with us according to our sins, * neither rewarded us according to our iniquities.

But as the heaven is high above the earth, * so great hath been his mercy towards us.

We found trouble and heaviness; * we were even at death's door.

The waters of the sea had well-nigh covered us; * the proud waters had well-nigh gone over our soul.

The sea roared, * and the stormy wind lifted up the waves thereof.

We were carried up as it were to heaven, and then down again into the deep; * our soul melted within us because of trouble.

Then cried we unto thee, O Lord, * and thou didst deliver us out of our distress.

Blessed be thy name, who didst not despise the prayer of thy servants, * but didst hear our cry and hast saved us.

Thou didst send forth thy commandment, * and the windy storm ceased and was turned into a calm.

O let us therefore praise the Lord for his goodness, * and declare the wonders that he hath done, and still doeth, for the children of men.

Praised be the Lord daily, * even the Lord that helpeth us and poureth his benefits upon us.

He is our God, even the God of whom cometh salvation; * God is the Lord by whom we have escaped death.

Thou, Lord, hast made us glad through the operation of thy hands, * and we will triumph in thy praise.

Blessed be the Lord God, * even the Lord God who only doeth wondrous things,

And blessed be the name of his Majesty for ever, * and let every one of us say, 'Amen, Amen.'

Glory be to the Father, and to the Son, * and to the Holy Ghost;

As it was in the beginning, is now, and ever shall be, * world without end. Amen.

2 Corinthians 13:14.

THE grace of our Lord Jesus Christ, and the love of God, and the fellowship of the Holy Ghost, be with us all evermore. *Amen.*

After Victory or Deliverance from an Enemy.

A Psalm or Hymn of Praise and
Thanksgiving after Victory.

I F the Lord had not been on our side, now may we say, *
if the Lord himself had not been on our side, when men
rose up against us,

They had swallowed us up quick, * when they were so
wrathfully displeased at us.

Yea, the waters had drowned us, and the stream had
gone over our soul; * the deep waters of the proud had
gone over our soul.

But praised be the Lord, * who hath not given us over
as a prey unto them.

The Lord hath wrought * a mighty salvation for us.

We gat not this by our own sword, neither was it our
own arm that saved us, * but thy right hand, and thine
arm, and the light of thy countenance, because thou hadst
a favour unto us.

The Lord hath appeared for us; * the Lord hath covered our heads and made us to stand in the day of battle.

The Lord hath appeared for us; * the Lord hath overthrown our enemies and dashed in pieces those that rose
up against us.

Therefore not unto us, O Lord, not unto us, * but unto
thy name be given the glory.

The Lord hath done great things for us; * the Lord hath
done great things for us, for which we rejoice.

Our help standeth in the name of the Lord, * who hath
made heaven and earth.

Blessed be the name of the Lord, * from this time forth for evermore.

Glory be to the Father, and to the Son, * and to the Holy Ghost;

As it was in the beginning, is now, and ever shall be, * world without end. Amen.

¶ *After this hymn may be sung the Te Deum (p. 6).*
¶ *Then this collect.*

O ALMIGHTY God, the sovereign commander of all the world, in whose hand is power and might which none is able to withstand: We bless and magnify thy great and glorious name for this happy victory, the whole glory whereof we do ascribe to thee, who art the only giver of victory. And, we beseech thee, give us grace to improve this great mercy to thy glory, the advancement of thy gospel, the honour of our nation, and, as much as in us lieth, to the good of all mankind. And, we beseech thee, give us such a sense of this great mercy, as may engage us to a true thankfulness, such as may appear in our lives by a humble, holy, and obedient walking before thee all our days, through Jesus Christ our Lord, to whom, with thee and the Holy Spirit, as for all thy mercies, so in particular for this victory and deliverance, be all glory and honour, world without end. *Amen.*

2 Corinthians 13:14.

T HE grace of our Lord Jesus Christ, and the love of God, and the fellowship of the Holy Ghost, be with us all evermore. *Amen.*

FORMS OF PRAYER TO BE USED AT SEA

At the Burial of Their Dead at Sea.

¶ *The office in the Common Prayer Book may be used, only instead of these words* – we therefore commit *his* body to the ground, earth to earth, *&c. (p. 346) – say,*

WE therefore commit *his* body to the deep, to be turned into corruption, looking for the resurrection of the body – when the sea shall give up her dead – and the life of the world to come, through our Lord Jesus Christ, who at his coming shall change our vile body, that it may be like his glorious body, according to the mighty working whereby he is able to subdue all things to himself.

¶ *Instead of* that we may be a safeguard unto our nation *(p. 562) may be said* that we may be a safeguard unto our most gracious Sovereign Lord, King CHARLES, and his dominions.

¶ *Instead of* the honour of our nation *(p. 576) may be said* the honour of our Sovereign.

The Ordinal

The form and manner of making, ordaining, and consecrating of bishops, priests, and deacons.

The Preface.

IT is evident unto all men diligently reading holy Scripture and ancient authors that from the apostles' time there have been these orders of ministers in Christ's church: bishops, priests, and deacons. Which offices were evermore had in such reverend estimation that no man might presume to execute any of them except he were first called, tried, examined, and known to have such qualities as are requisite for the same, and also by public prayer with imposition of hands were approved and admitted thereunto by lawful authority. And therefore, to the intent that these orders may be continued and reverently used and esteemed in *this church:* No man shall be accounted or taken to be a lawful bishop, priest, or deacon in *this church,* or suffered to execute any of the said functions, except he is called, tried, examined, and admitted thereunto, according to the form hereafter following, or hath had formerly episcopal consecration or ordination.

And none shall be admitted a deacon except he shall be full twenty-three years of age, unless he has a faculty. And every man which is to be admitted a priest shall be full twenty-four years of age, unless being over twenty-three years of age he has a faculty. And every man which is to be ordained or consecrated bishop shall be full thirty years of age.

And the bishop, knowing, either by himself or by sufficient testimony, any person to be a person of virtuous conversation and without crime, and after examination and trial finding him learned in the Latin tongue and sufficiently instructed in holy Scripture, may at the times appointed in the canon; or else on urgent occasion upon some other Sunday or holy day, before the face of the church; admit him a deacon in such manner and form as hereafter followeth.

The Form & Manner of
Making of Deacons.

¶ *When the day appointed by the bishop is come, after Morning Prayer is ended, there shall be a sermon or exhortation declaring the duty and office of such as come to be admitted deacons, how necessary that order is in the church of Christ, and also how the people ought to esteem them in their office.*

¶ *First, the archdeacon or his deputy shall present unto the bishop (sitting in his chair, near to the holy table) such as desire to be ordained deacons (each of them being decently habited), saying these words.*

REVEREND father in God, I present unto you these persons present to be admitted deacons.

¶ *The bishop.*

TAKE heed that the persons whom ye present unto us are apt and meet, for their learning and godly conversation, to exercise their ministry duly to the honour of God and the edifying of his church.

¶ *The archdeacon shall answer,*

I HAVE inquired of them and also examined them, and think them so to be.

THE ORDERING OF DEACONS

¶ *Then the bishop shall say unto the people,*

BRETHREN, if there be any of you who knoweth any impediment or notable crime in any of these persons presented to be ordered deacons, for which he ought not to be admitted to that office, let him come forth in the name of God and show what the crime or impediment is.

¶ *And if any great crime or impediment is given as an objection, the bishop shall cease from ordering that person until such time as the party accused shall be found clear of that crime.*

¶ *Then the bishop (commending to the prayers of the congregation such as shall be found meet to be ordered) shall, with the clergy and people present, sing or say the Litany, with the prayers, as followeth.*

The Litany and Suffrages.

O GOD the Father of heaven, have mercy upon us miserable sinners.

O God the Father of heaven, have mercy upon us miserable sinners.

O God the Son, Redeemer of the world, have mercy upon us miserable sinners.

O God the Son, Redeemer of the world, have mercy upon us miserable sinners.

O God the Holy Ghost, proceeding from the Father and the Son, have mercy upon us miserable sinners.

O God the Holy Ghost, proceeding from the Father and the Son, have mercy upon us miserable sinners.

O holy, blessed, and glorious Trinity, three persons and one God, have mercy upon us miserable sinners.

O holy, blessed, and glorious Trinity, three persons and one God, have mercy upon us miserable sinners.

REMEMBER not, Lord, our offences, nor the offences of our forefathers; neither take thou vengeance of our sins. Spare us, good Lord; spare thy people, whom thou hast redeemed with thy most precious blood, and be not angry with us for ever.

Spare us, good Lord.

FROM all evil and mischief; from sin, from the crafts and assaults of the devil; from thy wrath, and from everlasting damnation,

Good Lord, deliver us.

From all blindness of heart; from pride, vainglory, and hypocrisy; from envy, hatred, and malice, and all uncharitableness,

Good Lord, deliver us.

From fornication, and all other deadly sin; and from all the deceits of the world, the flesh, and the devil,

Good Lord, deliver us.

From lightning and tempest; from plague, pestilence, and famine; from battle and murder, and from sudden death,

Good Lord, deliver us.

From all sedition, privy conspiracy, and rebellion; from all false doctrine, heresy, and schism; from hardness of

heart, and contempt of thy word and commandment,
Good Lord, deliver us.

By the mystery of thy holy incarnation; by thy holy nativity and circumcision; by thy baptism, fasting, and temptation,
Good Lord, deliver us.

By thine agony and bloody sweat; by thy cross and passion; by thy precious death and burial; by thy glorious resurrection and ascension; and by the coming of the Holy Ghost,
Good Lord, deliver us.

In all time of our tribulation, in all time of our wealth, in the hour of death, and in the day of judgement,
Good Lord, deliver us.

WE sinners do beseech thee to hear us, O Lord God, and that it may please thee to rule and govern thy holy church universal in the right way,
We beseech thee to hear us, good Lord.

* That it may please thee to rule the heart of thy servant, —, and all others in authority, that under them we may lead a quiet and peaceable life in all godliness and honesty,
We beseech thee to hear us, good Lord.

That it may please thee to be their defender and keeper,
We beseech thee to hear us, good Lord.

---

* The next two suffrages may be replaced with the suffrages for the King and the royal family on p. 38.

That it may please thee to endue the *legislators,* and the *ministers of state,* with grace, wisdom, and understanding,
We beseech thee to hear us, good Lord.

That it may please thee to bless and keep the *judges* and *magistrates,* giving them grace to execute justice and to maintain truth,
We beseech thee to hear us, good Lord.

That it may please thee to illuminate all bishops, priests, and deacons, with true knowledge and understanding of thy word; and that both by their preaching and living they may set it forth and show it accordingly,
We beseech thee to hear us, good Lord.

That it may please thee to bless these thy servants now to be admitted to the order of deacons [or *priests*] and to pour thy grace upon them, that they may duly execute their office to the edifying of thy church and the glory of thy holy name,
We beseech thee to hear us, good Lord.

That it may please thee to bless and keep all thy people,
We beseech thee to hear us, good Lord.

That it may please thee to give to all nations unity, peace, and concord,
We beseech thee to hear us, good Lord.

That it may please thee to give us a heart to love and dread thee, and diligently to live after thy commandments,
We beseech thee to hear us, good Lord.

That it may please thee to give to all thy people increase of grace, to hear meekly thy word, and to receive it with pure affection, and to bring forth the fruits of the Spirit,
We beseech thee to hear us, good Lord.

That it may please thee to bring into the way of truth all such as have erred and are deceived,

We beseech thee to hear us, good Lord.

That it may please thee to strengthen such as do stand, and to comfort and help the weak-hearted, and to raise up those who fall, and finally to beat down Satan under our feet,

We beseech thee to hear us, good Lord.

That it may please thee to succour, help, and comfort all who are in danger, necessity, and tribulation,

We beseech thee to hear us, good Lord.

That it may please thee to preserve all who travel by land, by water, or by air; all women labouring with child, all sick persons, and young children, and to show thy pity upon all prisoners and captives,

We beseech thee to hear us, good Lord.

That it may please thee to defend and provide for the fatherless children, and widows, and all who are desolate and oppressed,

We beseech thee to hear us, good Lord.

That it may please thee to have mercy upon all men,

We beseech thee to hear us, good Lord.

That it may please thee to forgive our enemies, persecutors, and slanderers, and to turn their hearts,

We beseech thee to hear us, good Lord.

That it may please thee to give and preserve to our use the kindly fruits of the earth, so that in due time we may enjoy them,

We beseech thee to hear us, good Lord.

That it may please thee to give us true repentance; to forgive us all our sins, negligences, and ignorances; and to endue us with the grace of thy Holy Spirit, to amend our lives according to thy holy word,

We beseech thee to hear us, good Lord.

Son of God, we beseech thee to hear us.

Son of God, we beseech thee to hear us.

O Lamb of God, that takest away the sins of the world,

Grant us thy peace.

O Lamb of God, that takest away the sins of the world,

Have mercy upon us.

O Christ, hear us.

O Christ, hear us.

Lord, have mercy upon us.

Lord, have mercy upon us.

Christ, have mercy upon us.

Christ, have mercy upon us.

Lord, have mercy upon us.

Lord, have mercy upon us.

¶ *Then shall the priest and the people say the Lord's Prayer.*

OUR Father, who art in heaven, Hallowed be thy name. Thy kingdom come. Thy will be done, On earth as it is in heaven. Give us this day our daily bread. And forgive us our trespasses, As we forgive those who trespass against us. And lead us not into temptation, But deliver us from evil. Amen.

Priest.   O Lord, deal not with us after our sins,
Answer.   Neither reward us after our iniquities.

THE ORDERING OF DEACONS

Let us pray.

O GOD, merciful Father, who despisest not the sighing of a contrite heart, nor the desire of such as are sorrowful: Mercifully assist our prayers that we make before thee in all our troubles and adversities, whensoever they oppress us, and graciously hear us, that those evils which the craft and subtlety of the devil or man worketh against us may be brought to nought, and by the providence of thy goodness they may be dispersed, that we thy servants, being hurt by no persecutions, may evermore give thanks unto thee in thy holy church, through Jesus Christ our Lord.

O Lord, arise, help us, and deliver us for thy name's sake.

O GOD, we have heard with our ears, and our fathers have declared unto us, the noble works that thou didst in their days, and in the old time before them.

O Lord, arise, help us, and deliver us for thine honour.

G LORY be to the Father, and to the Son, and to the Holy Ghost;

As it was in the beginning, is now, and ever shall be, world without end. Amen.

From our enemies defend us, O Christ.

Graciously look upon our afflictions.

Pitifully behold the sorrows of our hearts.

Mercifully forgive the sins of thy people.

Favourably with mercy hear our prayers.

O Son of David, have mercy upon us.

Both now and ever vouchsafe to hear us, O Christ.
*Graciously hear us, O Christ; graciously hear us, O Lord
Christ.*

Priest. O Lord, let thy mercy be showed upon us,
Answer. As we do put our trust in thee.

Let us pray.

WE humbly beseech thee, O Father, mercifully to look
upon our infirmities, and for the glory of thy name,
turn from us all those evils that we most justly have deserved, and grant that in all our troubles we may put our
whole trust and confidence in thy mercy, and evermore
serve thee in holiness and pureness of living, to thy honour and glory, through our only mediator and advocate,
Jesus Christ our Lord. *Amen.*

¶ *Then shall be sung or said the service for the Communion
(p. 241), with the collect, epistle, and gospel as followeth.*
The Collect.

ALMIGHTY God, who by thy divine providence hast appointed divers orders of ministers in thy church, and
didst inspire thine apostles to choose into the order of
deacons the first martyr, Saint Stephen, with others: Mercifully behold these thy servants now called to the like office and administration; replenish them so with the truth
of thy doctrine, and adorn them with innocency of life,
that, both by word and good example, they may faithfully
serve thee in this office, to the glory of thy name and the

edification of thy church, through the merits of our Saviour Jesus Christ, who liveth and reigneth with thee and the Holy Ghost, now and for ever. *Amen.*

The Epistle. 1 Timothy 3:8-13.

LIKEWISE must the deacons be grave, not double-tongued, not given to much wine, not greedy of filthy lucre, holding the mystery of the faith in a pure conscience. And let these also first be proved; then let them use the office of a deacon, being found blameless.

Even so must their wives be grave, not slanderers, sober, faithful in all things. Let the deacons be the husbands of one wife, ruling their children and their own houses well. For they that have used the office of a deacon well purchase to themselves a good degree and great boldness in the faith which is in Christ Jesus.

¶ *Or else this, out of the sixth chapter of the Acts of the Apostles.*

Acts 6:2-7.

THEN the twelve called the multitude of the disciples unto them and said, 'It is not reason that we should leave the word of God and serve tables. Wherefore, brethren, look ye out among you seven men of honest report, full of the Holy Ghost and wisdom, whom we may appoint over this business. But we will give ourselves continually to prayer and to the ministry of the word.' And the saying pleased the whole multitude, and they chose Stephen, a man full of faith and of the Holy Ghost; and Philip, and Prochorus, and Nicanor, and Timon, and Parmenas, and

Nicolaus a proselyte of Antioch; whom they set before the apostles, and when they had prayed, they laid their hands on them.

And the word of God increased, and the number of the disciples multiplied in Jerusalem greatly, and a great company of the priests were obedient to the faith.

¶ *And before the gospel, the bishop, sitting in his chair, shall examine every one of those who are to be ordered in the presence of the people after this manner following.*

Do you trust that you are inwardly moved by the Holy Ghost to take upon you this office and ministration, to serve God, for the promoting of his glory and the edifying of his people?

Answer. I trust so.

¶ *The bishop.*

Do you think that you are truly called, according to the will of our Lord Jesus Christ and the due order of this church, to the ministry of the church?

Answer. I think so.

¶ *The bishop.*

Do you unfeignedly believe all the canonical Scriptures of the Old and New Testament?

Answer. I do believe them.

¶ *The bishop.*

WILL you diligently read the same unto the people assembled in the church where you shall be appointed to serve?

Answer. I will.

¶ *The bishop.*

IT appertaineth to the office of a deacon, in the church where he shall be appointed to serve, to assist the priest in divine service, and especially when he ministereth the holy communion, and to help him in the distribution thereof; and to read holy Scriptures and homilies in the church; and to instruct the youth in the catechism; in the absence of the priest to baptize infants; and to preach, if he is admitted thereto by the bishop. And furthermore, it is his office, where provision is so made, to search for the sick, poor, and destitute people of the parish, to intimate their estates, names, and places where they dwell unto the pastor, that by his exhortation they may be relieved with the alms of the parishioners or others. Will you do this gladly and willingly?

Answer. I will so do, by the help of God.

¶ *The bishop.*

WILL you apply all your diligence to frame and fashion your own lives, and the lives of your families, according to the doctrine of Christ; and to make both yourselves and them, as much as in you lieth, wholesome examples of the flock of Christ?

Answer. I will so do, the Lord being my helper.

THE ORDERING OF DEACONS

¶ *The bishop.*

WILL you reverently obey your ordinary, and other chief ministers of the church, and those to whom the charge and government over you is committed, following with a glad mind and will their godly admonitions?

Answer. I will endeavour myself, the Lord being my helper.

¶ *Then the bishop, laying his hands individually upon the head of every one of those humbly kneeling before him, shall say,*

TAKE thou authority to execute the office of a deacon in the church of God committed unto thee, in the name of the Father, and of the Son, and of the Holy Ghost. Amen.

¶ *Then shall the bishop deliver to every one of them the New Testament, saying,*

TAKE thou authority to read the gospel in the church of God, and to preach the same, if thou be thereto licensed by the bishop himself.

¶ *Then one of them, as appointed by the bishop, shall read the gospel.*

St. Luke 12:35-38.

LET your loins be girded about, and your lights burning, and ye yourselves like unto men that wait for their lord, when he will return from the wedding, that when he cometh and knocketh, they may open unto him immediately. Blessed are those servants whom the lord when he cometh shall find watching. Verily I say unto you that he shall gird himself, and make them to sit down to meat, and will come forth and serve them. And if he shall come in the second watch, or come in the third watch, and find them so, blessed are those servants.

¶ *Then shall the bishop proceed in the Communion, and all who are ordered shall tarry and receive the holy communion the same day with the bishop. The communion ended, after the last collect and immediately before the benediction shall be said these collects following.*

ALMIGHTY God, giver of all good things, who of thy great goodness hast vouchsafed to accept and take these thy servants unto the office of deacons in thy church: Make them, we beseech thee, O Lord, to be modest, humble, and constant in their ministration, to have a ready will to observe all spiritual discipline, that they, having always the testimony of a good conscience, and continuing ever stable and strong in thy Son Christ, may so well behave themselves in this inferior office, that they may be found worthy to be called unto the higher ministries in thy church, through the same thy Son our Saviour Jesus Christ, to whom be glory and honour, world without end. *Amen.*

PREVENT us, O Lord, in all our doings with thy most gracious favour, and further us with thy continual help, that in all our works – begun, continued, and ended in thee – we may glorify thy holy name, and finally by thy mercy obtain everlasting life, through Jesus Christ our Lord. *Amen.*

THE peace of God, which passeth all understanding, keep your hearts and minds in the knowledge and love of God, and of his Son Jesus Christ our Lord. And the blessing of God almighty, the Father, the Son, and the Holy Ghost, be amongst you and remain with you always. *Amen.*

¶ *And here it must be declared unto the deacon that he must continue in that office of a deacon the space of a whole year (except for reasonable causes which shall otherwise seem good unto the bishop), to the intent that he may be perfect and well expert in the things appertaining to the ecclesiastical administration. In executing whereof, if he is found faithful and diligent, he may be admitted by his diocesan to the order of priesthood at the times appointed in the canon; or else on urgent occasion upon some other Sunday or holy day, before the face of the church, in such manner and form as hereafter followeth.*

The Form & Manner of Ordering of Priests.

¶ *When the day appointed by the bishop is come, after Morning Prayer is ended, there shall be a sermon or exhortation declaring the duty and office of such as come to be admitted priests, how necessary that order is in the church of Christ, and also how the people ought to esteem them in their office.*

¶ *First, the archdeacon or in his absence one appointed in his stead shall present unto the bishop (sitting in his chair, near to the holy table) all those who shall receive the order of priesthood that day (each of them being decently habited), and say,*

REVEREND father in God, I present unto you these persons present to be admitted to the order of priesthood.

¶ *The bishop.*

TAKE heed that the persons whom ye present unto us are apt and meet, for their learning and godly conversation, to exercise their ministry duly to the honour of God and the edifying of his church.

¶ *The archdeacon shall answer,*

I HAVE inquired of them and also examined them, and think them so to be.

¶ *Then the bishop shall say unto the people,*

GOOD people, these are the ones whom we purpose, God willing, to receive this day unto the holy office of priesthood. For after due examination, we find not to the contrary, but that they are lawfully called to their function and ministry, and that they are persons meet for the same. But yet if there be any of you who knoweth any impediment or notable crime in any of them for which he ought not to be received into this holy ministry, let him come forth in the name of God and show what the crime or impediment is.

¶ *And if any great crime or impediment be objected, the bishop shall cease from ordering that person until such time as the party accused shall be found clear of that crime.*

¶ *Then the bishop (commending such as shall be found meet to be ordered to the prayers of the congregation) shall, with the clergy and people present, sing or say the Litany, with the prayers, as is before appointed in the Form of Ordering Deacons (p. 583), save only that in the proper suffrage there added (p. 586) the word* deacons *shall be omitted and the word* priests *inserted instead of it.*

¶ *Then shall be sung or said the service for the Communion (p. 241), with the collect, epistle, and gospel as followeth.*

The Collect.

ALMIGHTY God, giver of all good things, who by thy Holy Spirit hast appointed divers orders of ministers in thy church: Mercifully behold these thy servants now called to the office of priesthood, and replenish them so with the truth of thy doctrine, and adorn them with innocency of life, that, both by word and good example, they may faithfully serve thee in this office, to the glory of thy name and the edification of thy church, through the merits of our Saviour Jesus Christ, who liveth and reigneth with thee and the Holy Ghost, world without end. *Amen.*

The Epistle. Ephesians 4:7-13.

UNTO every one of us is given grace according to the measure of the gift of Christ. Wherefore he saith, 'When he ascended up on high, he led captivity captive and gave gifts unto men.' (Now that he ascended, what is it but that he also descended first into the lower parts of the earth? He that descended is the same also that ascended up far above all heavens, that he might fill all things.) And he gave some, apostles; and some, prophets; and some, evangelists; and some, pastors and teachers; for the perfecting of the saints for the work of the ministry, for the edifying of the body of Christ, till we all come, in the unity of the faith and of the knowledge of the Son of God, unto a perfect man, unto the measure of the stature of the fulness of Christ.

¶ *After this shall be read for the gospel part of the ninth chapter of St. Matthew, as followeth.*

St. Matthew 9:36-38.

WHEN Jesus saw the multitudes, he was moved with compassion on them, because they fainted, and were scattered abroad, as sheep having no shepherd.

Then saith he unto his disciples, 'The harvest truly is

plenteous, but the labourers are few. Pray ye therefore the Lord of the harvest, that he will send forth labourers into his harvest.'

¶ *Or else this, out of the tenth chapter of St. John.*
St. John 10:1-16.

'VERILY, verily I say unto you, he that entereth not by the door into the sheepfold, but climbeth up some other way, the same is a thief and a robber. But he that entereth in by the door is the shepherd of the sheep. To him the porter openeth, and the sheep hear his voice, and he calleth his own sheep by name, and leadeth them out. And when he putteth forth his own sheep, he goeth before them, and the sheep follow him, for they know his voice. And a stranger will they not follow, but will flee from him, for they know not the voice of strangers.'

This parable spake Jesus unto them, but they understood not what things they were which he spake unto them.

Then said Jesus unto them again, 'Verily, verily I say unto you, I am the door of the sheep. All that ever came before me are thieves and robbers, but the sheep did not hear them. I am the door: by me if any man enter in, he shall be saved, and shall go in and out, and find pasture. The thief cometh not but for to steal, and to kill, and to destroy; I am come that they might have life, and that they might have it more abundantly.

'I am the good shepherd; the good shepherd giveth his life for the sheep. But he that is a hireling, and not the shepherd, whose own the sheep are not, seeth the wolf coming, and leaveth the sheep, and fleeth; and the wolf catcheth them, and scattereth the sheep. The hireling fleeth because he is a hireling, and careth not for the sheep.

'I am the good shepherd, and know my sheep, and am known of mine. As the Father knoweth me, even so know I the Father, and I lay down my life for the sheep. And other sheep I have which are not of this fold; them also I must bring, and they shall hear my voice, and there shall be one fold and one shepherd.'

¶ *Then the bishop, sitting in his chair, shall say unto them as hereafter followeth.*

Y OU have heard, brethren, as well in your private examination, as in the exhortation which was now made to you, and in the holy lessons taken out of the gospel and the writings of the apostles, of what dignity and of how great importance this office is whereunto ye are called. And now again we exhort you, in the name of our Lord Jesus Christ, that you have in remembrance into how high a dignity and to how weighty an office and charge ye are called – that is to say, to be messengers, watchmen, and stewards of the Lord; to teach and to forewarn, to feed and provide for the Lord's family; to seek for Christ's sheep that are dispersed abroad, and for his children who are in the midst of this wicked world, that they may be saved through Christ for ever.

Have always therefore printed in your remembrance how great a treasure is committed to your charge. For they are the sheep of Christ, which he bought with his death, and for whom he shed his blood. The church and congregation whom you must serve is his spouse and his body. And if it shall happen that the same church, or any member thereof, do take any hurt or hindrance by reason of your negligence, ye know the greatness of the fault and also the horrible punishment that will ensue. Wherefore consider with yourselves the end of your ministry towards the children of God, towards the spouse and body of Christ, and see that you never cease your labour, your care and diligence, until you have done all that lieth in you, according to your bounden duty, to bring all such as are or shall be committed to your charge, unto that agreement in the faith and knowledge of God, and to that ripeness and perfectness of age in Christ, that there be no place left among you, either for error in religion or for viciousness in life.

Forasmuch then as your office is both of so great excellency and of so great difficulty, ye see with how great care and study ye ought to apply yourselves, as well that ye may show yourselves dutiful and thankful unto that Lord, who hath placed you in so high a dignity, as also to beware that neither you yourselves offend, nor be occasion that others offend. Howbeit ye cannot have a mind and will thereto of yourselves, for that will and ability is given of God alone. Therefore ye ought, and have need, to pray earnestly for his Holy Spirit. And seeing that you cannot by any other means compass the doing of so weighty a work, pertaining to the salvation of man, but with doctrine and exhortation taken out of the holy Scriptures, and with a life agreeable to the same, consider how studious ye ought to be in reading and learning the Scriptures, and in framing the manners both of yourselves and of those who especially pertain unto you, according to the rule of the same Scriptures; and for this selfsame cause, how ye ought to forsake and set aside (as much as you may) all worldly cares and studies.

We have good hope that you have well weighed and pondered these things with yourselves long before this time, and that you have clearly determined, by God's grace, to give yourselves wholly to this office, whereunto it hath pleased God to call you – so that, as much as lieth in you, you will apply yourselves wholly to this one thing, and draw all your cares and studies this way, and that you will continually pray to God the Father, by the mediation of our only Saviour Jesus Christ, for the heavenly assistance of the Holy Ghost, that, by daily reading and weighing of the Scriptures, ye may wax riper and stronger in your ministry, and that ye may so endeavour yourselves, from time to time to sanctify the lives of you and yours, and to fashion them after the rule and doctrine of Christ, that ye may be wholesome and godly examples and patterns for the people to follow.

And now, that this present congregation of Christ here assembled may also understand your minds and wills in these things, and that this your promise may the more move you to do your duties, ye shall answer plainly to these things which we, in the name of God and of his church, shall demand of you touching the same.

Do you think in your heart that you are truly called, according to the will of our Lord Jesus Christ and the order of *this church,* to the order and ministry of priesthood?

Answer. I think it.

¶ *The bishop.*

ARE you persuaded that the holy Scriptures contain sufficiently all doctrine required of necessity for eternal salvation through faith in Jesus Christ? And are you determined out of the said Scriptures to instruct the people committed to your charge, and to teach nothing (as required of necessity to eternal salvation) but that which you shall be persuaded may be concluded and proved by the Scripture?

Answer. I am so persuaded, and have so determined by God's grace.

¶ *The bishop.*

WILL you then give your faithful diligence always so to minister the doctrine and sacraments, and the discipline of Christ, as the Lord hath commanded, and as *this church* hath received the same, according to the commandments of God, so that you may teach the people committed to your cure and charge with all diligence to keep and observe the same?

Answer. I will so do, by the help of the Lord.

¶ *The bishop.*

WILL you be ready, with all faithful diligence, to banish and drive away all erroneous and strange doctrines contrary to God's word, and to use both public and private admonitions and exhortations, as well to the sick as to the whole within your cures, as need shall require and occasion shall be given?

Answer. I will, the Lord being my helper.

¶ *The bishop.*

WILL you be diligent in prayers, and in reading of the holy Scriptures, and in such studies as help to the knowledge of the same, laying aside the study of the world and the flesh?

Answer. I will endeavour myself so to do, the Lord being my helper.

¶ *The bishop.*

WILL you be diligent to frame and fashion your own selves, and your families, according to the doctrine of Christ, and to make both yourselves and them, as much as in you lieth, wholesome examples and patterns to the flock of Christ?

Answer. I will apply myself thereto, the Lord being my helper.

¶ *The bishop.*

WILL you maintain and set forward, as much as lieth in you, quietness, peace, and love among all Christian people, and especially among those who are or shall be committed to your charge?

Answer. I will so do, the Lord being my helper.

THE ORDERING OF PRIESTS

¶ *The bishop.*

WILL you reverently obey your ordinary and other chief ministers unto whom is committed the charge and government over you, following with a glad mind and will their godly admonitions, and submitting yourselves to their godly judgements?

Answer. I will so do, the Lord being my helper.

¶ *Then shall the bishop, standing up, say,*

ALMIGHTY God, who hath given you this will to do all these things, grant also unto you strength and power to perform the same, that he may accomplish his work which he hath begun in you, through Jesus Christ our Lord. *Amen.*

¶ *After this the congregation shall be desired to make their humble supplications to God for all these things secretly in their prayers, for which prayers there shall be silence kept for a space.*

¶ *After which shall be sung or said by the bishop (the persons to be ordained priests all kneeling) Veni, Creator Spiritus, the bishop beginning, and the priests and others that are present answering by verses, as followeth.*

COME, Holy Ghost, our souls inspire,
And lighten with celestial fire.
Thou the anointing Spirit art,
Who dost thy sevenfold gifts impart.
Thy blessed unction from above
Is comfort, life, and fire of love.

Enable with perpetual light
The dullness of our blinded sight.
Anoint and cheer our soiled face
With the abundance of thy grace.
Keep far our foes; give peace at home;
Where thou art guide, no ill can come.
Teach us to know the Father, Son,
And thee, of both, to be but one,
That through the ages all along,
This may be our endless song:
Praise to thy eternal merit,
Father, Son, and Holy Spirit.

¶ *Or this.*

Come, Holy Ghost, eternal God, * proceeding from above,
 *Both from the Father and the Son, * the God of peace and love;*
Visit our minds; into our hearts * thy heavenly grace inspire,
 *That truth and godliness we may * pursue with full desire.*
Thou art the very comforter * in grief and all distress;
 *The heav'nly gift of God most high, * no tongue can it express;*
The fountain and the living spring * of joy celestial;
 *The fire so bright, the love so sweet, * the unction spiritual.*
Thou in thy gifts art manifold; * by them Christ's church doth stand;
 *In faithful hearts thou writ'st thy law, * the finger of God's hand.*

According to thy promise, Lord, * thou givest speech with grace,
*That through thy help God's praises may * resound in every place.*
O Holy Ghost, into our minds * send down thy heav'nly light;
*Kindle our hearts with fervent zeal * to serve God day and night.*
Our weakness strengthen and confirm – * for, Lord, thou know'st us frail –
*That neither devil, world, nor flesh * against us may prevail.*
Put back our enemy far from us, * and help us to obtain
*Peace in our hearts with God and man – * the best, the truest gain –*
And grant that thou, being, O Lord, * our leader and our guide,
*We may escape the snares of sin, * and never from thee slide.*
Such measures of thy powerful grace, * grant, Lord, to us, we pray,
*That thou may'st be our comforter * at the last dreadful day.*
Of strife and of dissension, * dissolve, O Lord, the bands,
*And knit the knots of peace and love * throughout all Christian lands.*
Grant us the grace that we may know * the Father of all might,
*That we of his beloved Son * may gain the blissful sight,*

And that we may with perfect faith * ever acknowledge thee,

The Spirit of Father and of Son, * one God in persons three.

To God the Father laud and praise, * and to his blessed Son,

And to the Holy Spirit of grace, * co-equal three in one.

And pray we that our only Lord * would please his Spirit to send

On all that shall profess his name, * from hence to the world's end. Amen.

¶ *That done, the bishop shall pray in this manner and say,*
Let us pray.

ALMIGHTY God and heavenly Father, who of thine infinite love and goodness towards us hast given to us thy only and most dearly beloved Son Jesus Christ, to be our redeemer and the author of everlasting life, who, after he had made perfect our redemption by his death, and was ascended into heaven, sent abroad into the world his apostles, prophets, evangelists, doctors, and pastors, by whose labour and ministry he gathered together a great flock in all the parts of the world, to set forth the eternal praise of thy holy name: For such great benefits of thy eternal goodness, and because thou hast vouchsafed to call these thy servants here present to the same office and ministry, appointed for the salvation of mankind, we render unto thee most hearty thanks, we praise and worship thee, and we humbly beseech thee, by the same thy blessed Son, to grant unto all, who either here or else-where call upon thy holy name, that we may continue to show ourselves thankful unto thee for these and all thy other benefits, and that we may daily increase and go forward in the knowledge and faith of thee and thy Son, by the Holy Spirit. So that as well by these thy ministers, as by those over whom they shall be appointed thy ministers, thy holy name may be for ever glorified, and thy blessed kingdom enlarged, through the same thy Son Jesus Christ our Lord, who liveth and reigneth with thee in the unity of the same Holy Spirit, world without end. *Amen.*

¶ *When this prayer is done, the bishop with the priests present shall lay their hands severally upon the head of every one who receiveth the order of priesthood, the receivers humbly kneeling upon their knees, and the bishop saying,*
RECEIVE the Holy Ghost for the office and work of a priest in the church of God, now committed unto thee by the imposition of our hands. Whose sins thou dost forgive, they are forgiven; and whose sins thou dost retain, they are retained. And be thou a faithful dispenser of the word of God and of his holy sacraments, in the name of the Father, and of the Son, and of the Holy Ghost. Amen.

¶ *Then the bishop shall deliver to every one of them (kneeling) the Bible into his hand, saying,*
TAKE thou authority to preach the word of God, and to minister the holy sacraments in the congregation, where thou shalt be lawfully appointed thereunto.

¶ *When this is done, the Nicene Creed shall be sung or said (p. 246); and the bishop shall after that go on in the service of the Communion, which all those who receive orders shall take together, and remain in the same place where hands were laid upon them until such time as they have received the communion. The communion being done, after the last collect and immediately before the benediction shall be said these collects.*

M OST merciful Father, we beseech thee to send upon these thy servants thy heavenly blessing, that they may be clothed with righteousness, and that thy word spoken by their mouths may have such success, that it may never be spoken in vain. Grant also that we may have grace to hear and receive what they shall deliver out of thy most holy word, or agreeable to the same, as the means of our salvation, that in all our words and deeds we may seek thy glory and the increase of thy kingdom, through Jesus Christ our Lord. *Amen.*

P REVENT us, O Lord, in all our doings with thy most gracious favour, and further us with thy continual help, that in all our works – begun, continued, and ended in thee – we may glorify thy holy name, and finally by thy mercy obtain everlasting life, through Jesus Christ our Lord. *Amen.*

T HE peace of God, which passeth all understanding, keep your hearts and minds in the knowledge and love of God, and of his Son Jesus Christ our Lord. And the blessing of God almighty, the Father, the Son, and the Holy Ghost, be amongst you and remain with you always. *Amen.*

¶ *And if on the same day the order of deacons be given to some and the order of priesthood to others, the deacons shall be first presented and then the priests, and it shall suffice that the Litany be once said for both. The collects shall both be used, first that for deacons, then that for priests. The epistle shall be Ephesians 4:7-13, as before in this office. Immediately after which, those who are to be made deacons shall be examined and ordained, as is above prescribed. Then, one of them having read the gospel (which shall be either out of St. Matthew 9:36-38, as before in this office; or else St. Luke 12:35-38, as before in the Form for the Ordering of Deacons), those who are to be made priests shall likewise be examined and ordained, as is in this office before appointed.*

The Form of Ordaining or Consecrating of an Archbishop or Bishop

which is always to be performed upon some Sunday or holy day unless for weighty and urgent reasons some other day be appointed.

¶ *When all things are duly prepared in the church and set in order, after Morning Prayer is ended, the archbishop (or some other bishop appointed) shall begin the Communion service, in which this shall be*

The Collect.

ALMIGHTY God, who by thy Son Jesus Christ didst give to thy holy apostles many excellent gifts, and didst charge them to feed thy flock: Give grace, we beseech thee, to all bishops, the pastors of thy church, that they may diligently preach thy word, and duly administer the godly discipline thereof, and grant to the people that they may obediently follow the same, that all may receive the crown of everlasting glory, through Jesus Christ our Lord. *Amen.*

¶ *And another bishop shall read the epistle.*
1 Timothy 3:1-7.

THIS is a true saying, 'If a man desire the office of a bishop, he desireth a good work.' A bishop then must be blameless, the husband of one wife, vigilant, sober, of good behaviour, given to hospitality, apt to teach, not given to wine, no striker, not greedy of filthy lucre, but patient, not a brawler, not covetous; one that ruleth well his own house, having his children in subjection with all gravity – for if a man know not how to rule his own house, how shall he take care of the church of God? – not a novice, lest being lifted up with pride he fall into the condemnation of the devil. Moreover, he must have a good report of them which are without, lest he fall into reproach and the snare of the devil.

¶ *Or this for the epistle.*
Acts 20:17-35.

FROM Miletus Paul sent to Ephesus, and called the elders of the church. And when they were come to him, he said unto them, 'Ye know, from the first day that I came into Asia, after what manner I have been with you at all seasons, serving the Lord with all humility of mind, and with many tears and temptations, which befell me by the lying in wait of the Jews; and how I kept back nothing that was profitable unto you, but have showed you and have taught you publicly, and from house to house, testifying both to the Jews and also to the Greeks, repentance toward God and faith toward our Lord Jesus Christ.

'And now behold, I go bound in the Spirit unto Jerusalem, not knowing the things that shall befall me there, save that the Holy Ghost witnesseth in every city, saying that bonds and afflictions abide me. But none of these things move me, neither count I my life dear unto myself, so that I might finish my course with joy, and the ministry which I have received of the Lord Jesus, to testify the gospel of the grace of God. And now behold, I know that ye all, among whom I have gone preaching the kingdom of God, shall see my face no more. Wherefore I take you to record this day, that I am pure from the blood of all men. For I have not shunned to declare unto you all the counsel of God. Take heed therefore unto yourselves, and to all the flock over the which the Holy Ghost hath made you overseers, to feed the church of God, which he hath purchased with his own blood.

'For I know this, that after my departing shall grievous wolves enter in among you, not sparing the flock. Also of your own selves shall men arise speaking perverse things, to draw away disciples after them. Therefore watch, and remember that by the space of three years I ceased not to warn every one night and day with tears. And now, brethren, I commend you to God, and to the word of his grace, which is able to build you up, and to give you an inheritance among all them which are sanctified. I have coveted no man's silver or gold or apparel. Yea, ye yourselves know that these hands have ministered unto my necessities, and to them that were with me. I have showed you all things, how that so labouring ye ought to support the weak, and to remember the words of the Lord Jesus, how he said, "It is more blessed to give than to receive."'

¶ *Then another bishop shall read the gospel.*
St. John 21:15-17.

JESUS saith to Simon Peter, 'Simon, son of John, lovest thou me more than these?' He saith unto him, 'Yea, Lord, thou knowest that I love thee.' He saith unto him, 'Feed my lambs.' He saith to him again the second time, 'Simon, son of John, lovest thou me?' He saith unto him, 'Yea, Lord, thou knowest that I love thee.' He saith unto him, 'Feed my sheep.' He saith unto him the third time, 'Simon, son of John, lovest thou me?' Peter was grieved because he said unto him the third time, 'Lovest thou me?' And he said unto him, 'Lord, thou knowest all things; thou knowest that I love thee.' Jesus saith unto him, 'Feed my sheep.'

¶ *Or else this.*
St. John 20:19-23.

THE same day at evening, being the first day of the week, when the doors were shut where the disciples were assembled for fear of the Jews, came Jesus and stood in the midst and saith unto them, 'Peace be unto you.' And when he had so said, he showed unto them his hands and his side. Then were the disciples glad when they saw the Lord. Then said Jesus to them again, 'Peace be unto you. As my Father hath sent me, even so send I you.'

And when he had said this, he breathed on them and saith unto them, 'Receive ye the Holy Ghost. Whose soever sins ye remit, they are remitted unto them; and whose soever sins ye retain, they are retained.'

¶ *Or this.*
St. Matthew 28:18-20.

JESUS came and spake unto them, saying, 'All power is given unto me in heaven and in earth. Go ye therefore and teach all nations, baptizing them in the name of the

Father, and of the Son, and of the Holy Ghost; teaching them to observe all things whatsoever I have commanded you. And lo, I am with you alway, even unto the end of the world.'

¶ *After the gospel, the Nicene Creed, and the sermon are ended, the elected bishop (vested with his rochet) shall be presented by two bishops unto the archbishop of that province (or to some other bishop appointed by lawful commission), the archbishop sitting in his chair, near the holy table, and the bishops who present him saying,*

MOST reverend father in God, we present unto you this godly and well-learned man to be ordained and consecrated bishop.

¶ *Then shall the archbishop demand the mandate for the consecration and cause it to be read. And then shall be ministered unto them the oath of due obedience to the archbishop, as followeth.*

The Oath of Due Obedience to the Archbishop.

IN the name of God, Amen. I, *N.,* chosen bishop of the church and see of *N.,* do profess and promise all due reverence and obedience to the archbishop and to the metropolitical church of *N.* and to their successors, so help me God, through Jesus Christ.

¶ *This oath shall not be made at the consecration of an archbishop.*

¶ *Then the archbishop shall move the congregation present to pray, saying thus to them:*

BRETHREN, it is written in the Gospel of Saint Luke that our Saviour Christ continued the whole night in prayer, before he did choose and send forth his twelve apostles. It is written also in the Acts of the Apostles, that the disciples who were at Antioch did fast and pray, before they laid hands on Paul and Barnabas and sent them forth. Let us therefore, following the example of our Saviour Christ and his apostles, first fall to prayer, before we admit and send forth this person presented unto us, to the work whereunto we trust the Holy Ghost hath called him.

¶ *And then shall be said the Litany, as before in the Form Ordering Deacons (p. 583), save only that after this place – That it may please thee to illuminate all bishops, &c. – the proper suffrage there following (p. 586) shall be omitted and this inserted instead of it.*

THAT it may please thee to bless this our brother elected, and to send thy grace upon him, that he may duly execute the office whereunto he is called, to the edifying of thy church, and to the honour, praise, and glory of thy name, *We beseech thee to hear us, good Lord.*

¶ *Then shall be said this prayer following.*

ALMIGHTY God, giver of all good things, who by thy Holy Spirit hast appointed divers orders of ministers in thy church: Mercifully behold this thy servant now called to the work and ministry of a bishop, and so replenish him with the truth of thy doctrine, and adorn him with innocency of life, that both by word and deed he may faithfully serve thee in this office, to the glory of thy name, and the edifying and well-governing of thy church, through the merits of our Saviour Jesus Christ, who liveth and reigneth with thee and the Holy Ghost, world without end. *Amen.*

¶ *Then the archbishop, sitting in his chair, shall say to him who is to be consecrated,*

BROTHER, forasmuch as the holy Scripture and the ancient canons command that we should not be hasty in laying on hands, and admitting any person to government in the church of Christ, which he hath purchased with no less price than the effusion of his own blood: Before I admit you to this administration, I will examine you in certain articles, to the end that the congregation present may have a trial and bear witness how you are minded to behave yourself in the church of God.

ARE you persuaded that you are truly called to this ministration, according to the will of our Lord Jesus Christ and the order of this church?

Answer. I am so persuaded.

¶ *The archbishop.*

ARE you persuaded that the holy Scriptures contain sufficiently all doctrine required of necessity for eternal salvation through faith in Jesus Christ? And are you determined out of the same holy Scriptures to instruct the people committed to your charge, and to teach or maintain nothing as required of necessity to eternal salvation, but that which you shall be persuaded may be concluded and proved by the same?

Answer. I am so persuaded and determined, by God's grace.

¶ *The archbishop.*

WILL you then faithfully exercise yourself in the same holy Scriptures, and call upon God by prayer, for the true understanding of the same, so that ye may be able by them to teach and exhort with wholesome doctrine, and to withstand and convince the gainsayers?

Answer. I will so do, by the help of God.

¶ *The archbishop.*

ARE you ready, with all faithful diligence, to banish and drive away all erroneous and strange doctrine contrary to God's word, and both privately and openly to call upon and encourage others to the same?

Answer. I am ready, the Lord being my helper.

¶ *The archbishop.*

WILL you deny all ungodliness and worldly lusts, and live soberly, righteously, and godly in this present world, that you may show yourself in all things an example of good works unto others, that the adversary may be ashamed, having nothing to say against you?

Answer. I will so do, the Lord being my helper.

THE CONSECRATION OF BISHOPS

¶ *The archbishop.*

WILL you maintain and set forward (as much as shall lie in you) quietness, love, and peace among all men; and those who are unquiet, disobedient, and lawless within your diocese, correct and punish, according to such authority as ye have by God's word, and as to you shall be committed by the ordinance of this church?

Answer. I will so do, by the help of God.

¶ *The archbishop.*

WILL you be faithful in ordaining, sending, or laying hands upon others?

Answer. I will so be, by the help of God.

¶ *The archbishop.*

WILL you show yourself gentle, and be merciful for Christ's sake to poor and needy people, and to all strangers destitute of help?

Answer. I will so show myself, by God's help.

¶ *Then the archbishop, standing up, shall say,*

ALMIGHTY God, our heavenly Father, who hath given you a good will to do all these things, grant also unto you strength and power to perform the same, that he accomplishing in you the good work which he hath begun, ye may be found perfect and irreproachable at the latter day, through Jesus Christ our Lord. *Amen.*

THE CONSECRATION OF BISHOPS

¶ *Then shall the bishop-elect put on the rest of the episcopal habit, and kneeling down, Veni, Creator Spiritus shall be sung or said over him, the archbishop beginning, and the bishops with others that are present answering by verses, as followeth.*

COME, Holy Ghost, our souls inspire,
And lighten with celestial fire.
Thou the anointing Spirit art,
Who dost thy sevenfold gifts impart.
Thy blessed unction from above
Is comfort, life, and fire of love.
Enable with perpetual light
The dullness of our blinded sight.
Anoint and cheer our soiled face
With the abundance of thy grace.
Keep far our foes; give peace at home;
Where thou art guide, no ill can come.
Teach us to know the Father, Son,
And thee, of both, to be but one,
That through the ages all along,
This may be our endless song:
Praise to thy eternal merit,
Father, Son, and Holy Spirit.

¶ *Or this, as before in the Form for Ordering Priests (p. 607).*

COME, Holy Ghost, eternal God, *&c.*

THE CONSECRATION OF BISHOPS

¶ *That ended, the archbishop shall say*

O Lord, hear our prayer,

Answer.   And let our cry come unto thee.

Let us pray.

ALMIGHTY God and most merciful Father, who of thine infinite goodness hast given thine only and dearly beloved Son Jesus Christ, to be our redeemer and the author of everlasting life, who, after he had made perfect our redemption by his death, and was ascended into heaven, poured down his gifts abundantly upon men, making some apostles, some prophets, some evangelists, some pastors and doctors, to the edifying and making perfect of his church: Grant, we beseech thee, to this thy servant such grace, that he may evermore be ready to spread abroad thy gospel, the glad tidings of reconciliation with thee, and use the authority given him, not to destruction, but to salvation; not to hurt, but to help; so that as a wise and faithful servant, giving to thy family their portion in due season, he may at last be received into everlasting joy, through Jesus Christ our Lord, who with thee and the Holy Ghost liveth and reigneth, one God, world without end. *Amen.*

¶ *Then the archbishop and bishops present shall lay their hands upon the head of the elected bishop (kneeling before them upon his knees), the archbishop saying,*

RECEIVE the Holy Ghost for the office and work of a bishop in the church of God, now committed unto thee by the imposition of our hands, in the name of the Father, and of the Son, and of the Holy Ghost. Amen. And remember that thou stir up the grace of God which is given thee by this imposition of our hands, for God hath not given us the spirit of fear, but of power and love and soberness.

¶ *Then the archbishop shall deliver him the Bible, saying,*

GIVE heed unto reading, exhortation, and doctrine. Think upon the things contained in this book. Be diligent in them, that the increase coming thereby may be manifest unto all men. Take heed unto thyself, and to doctrine, and be diligent in doing them, for by so doing thou shalt both save thyself and those who hear thee. Be to the flock of Christ a shepherd, not a wolf. Feed them; devour them not. Hold up the weak; heal the sick; bind up the broken; bring again the outcasts; seek the lost. Be so merciful that ye be not too remiss; so minister discipline, that you forget not mercy, that when the chief shepherd shall appear, ye may receive the never-fading crown of glory, through Jesus Christ our Lord. *Amen.*

¶ *Then the archbishop shall proceed in the Communion service, with whom the new consecrated bishop (with others) shall also communicate. And for the last collect, immediately before the benediction, shall be said these prayers.*

MOST merciful Father, we beseech thee to send down upon this thy servant thy heavenly blessing; and so endue him with thy Holy Spirit, that he, preaching thy word, may not only be earnest to reprove, beseech, and rebuke with all patience and doctrine, but also may be to such as believe a wholesome example – in word, in conversation, in love, in faith, in chastity, and in purity – that, faithfully fulfilling his course, at the latter day he may receive the crown of righteousness laid up by the Lord the righteous judge, who liveth and reigneth one God with the Father and the Holy Ghost, world without end. *Amen.*

Prevent us, O Lord, in all our doings with thy most gracious favour, and further us with thy continual help, that in all our works – begun, continued, and ended in thee – we may glorify thy holy name, and finally by thy mercy obtain everlasting life, through Jesus Christ our Lord. *Amen.*

The peace of God, which passeth all understanding, keep your hearts and minds in the knowledge and love of God, and of his Son Jesus Christ our Lord. And the blessing of God almighty, the Father, the Son, and the Holy Ghost, be amongst you and remain with you always. *Amen.*

Articles of Religion

*Agreed upon by the archbishops and bishops
of both provinces and the whole clergy in the
convocation held at London in the year 1562
for the avoiding of diversities of opinions
and for the establishing of consent
touching true religion.*

Articles of Religion.

1. Of Faith in the Holy Trinity.

THERE is but one living and true God, everlasting, without body, parts, or passions; of infinite power, wisdom, and goodness; the maker and preserver of all things both visible and invisible. And in unity of this Godhead there be three persons, of one substance, power, and eternity: the Father, the Son, and the Holy Ghost.

2. Of the Word or Son of God, Which Was Made Very Man.

THE Son, which is the Word of the Father, begotten from everlasting of the Father, the very and eternal God, of one substance with the Father, took man's nature in the womb of the Blessed Virgin, of her substance; so that two whole and perfect natures, that is to say, the Godhead and manhood, were joined together in one person, never to be divided, whereof is one Christ, very God and very man, who truly suffered, was crucified, dead, and buried, to reconcile his Father to us, and to be a sacrifice, not only for original guilt, but also for all actual sins of men.

3. Of the Going Down of Christ into Hell.

As Christ died for us, and was buried, so also is it to be believed that he went down into hell.

4. Of the Resurrection of Christ.

CHRIST did truly rise again from death, and took again his body, with flesh, bones, and all things appertaining to the perfection of man's nature, wherewith he ascended into heaven, and there sitteth until he return to judge all men at the last day.

5. Of the Holy Ghost.

THE Holy Ghost, proceeding from the Father and the Son, is of one substance, majesty, and glory with the Father and the Son, very and eternal God.

6. Of the Sufficiency of the Holy Scriptures for Salvation.

HOLY Scripture containeth all things necessary to salvation; so that whatsoever is not read therein, nor may be proved thereby, is not to be required of any man, that it should be believed as an article of the faith, or be thought requisite or necessary to salvation.

In the name of the holy Scripture we do understand those canonical books of the Old and New Testament, of whose authority was never any doubt in the church.

Of the Names & Number of the Canonical Books.

Genesis	Joshua
Exodus	Judges
Leviticus	Ruth
Numbers	The First Book of Samuel
Deuteronomy	The Second Book of Samuel

The First Book of Kings
The Second Book of Kings
The First Book of Chronicles
The Second Book of
Chronicles
The First Book of Esdras
The Second Book of Esdras
The Book of Esther

The Book of Job
The Book of Psalms
The Book of Proverbs
Ecclesiastes, or Preacher
Cantica, or Songs of
Solomon
Four Prophets the Greater
Twelve Prophets the Less

And the other books (as Jerome saith) the church doth read for example of life and instruction of manners, but yet doth it not apply them to establish any doctrine. Such are these following:

The Third Book of Esdras
The Fourth Book of Esdras
The Book of Tobias
The Book of Judith
The rest of the Book of Esther
The Book of Wisdom
Jesus the Son of Sirach
Baruch the Prophet

The Song of the Three
Children
The Story of Susanna
Of Bel and the Dragon
The Prayer of Manasses
The First Book of Maccabees
The Second Book of
Maccabees

All the books of the New Testament, as they are commonly received, we do receive and account them canonical.

7. Of the Old Testament.

THE Old Testament is not contrary to the New, for both in the Old and New Testament everlasting life is offered to mankind by Christ, who is the only mediator between God and man, being both God and man. Wherefore they are not to be heard which feign that the old Fathers did look only for transitory promises. Although the law given from God by Moses, as touching ceremonies and rites, do not bind Christian men, nor the civil precepts thereof ought of necessity to be received in any commonwealth, yet notwithstanding, no Christian man whatsoever is free from the obedience of the commandments which are called moral.

8. Of the Three Creeds.

THE three creeds, Nicene Creed, Athanasius' Creed, and that which is commonly called the Apostles' Creed, ought thoroughly to be received and believed, for they may be proved by most certain warrants of holy Scripture.

9. Of Original or Birth Sin.

ORIGINAL sin standeth not in the following of Adam (as the Pelagians do vainly talk), but it is the fault and corruption of the nature of every man that naturally is engendered of the offspring of Adam, whereby man is very far gone from original righteousness, and is of his own nature inclined to evil, so that the flesh lusteth always contrary to the spirit; and therefore in every person born into this world it deserveth God's wrath and damnation. And this infection of nature doth remain, yea in them that are regenerated; whereby the lust of the flesh, called in the Greek φρόνημα σαρκὸς (which some do expound the wisdom, some sensuality, some the affection, some the desire of the flesh), is not subject to the law of

God. And although there is no condemnation for them that believe and are baptized, yet the apostle doth confess that concupiscence and lust hath of itself the nature of sin.

10. Of Free Will.

THE condition of man after the fall of Adam is such that he cannot turn and prepare himself, by his own natural strength and good works, to faith and calling upon God. Wherefore we have no power to do good works pleasant and acceptable to God, without the grace of God by Christ preventing us that we may have a good will, and working with us when we have that good will.

11. Of the Justification of Man.

WE are accounted righteous before God only for the merit of our Lord and Saviour Jesus Christ, by faith, and not for our own works or deservings. Wherefore, that we are justified by faith only is a most wholesome doctrine, and very full of comfort, as more largely is expressed in the homily of justification.

12. Of Good Works.

ALBEIT that good works, which are the fruits of faith, and follow after justification, cannot put away our sins, and endure the severity of God's judgement; yet are they pleasing and acceptable to God in Christ, and do spring out necessarily of a true and lively faith; insomuch that by them a lively faith may be as evidently known as a tree discerned by the fruit.

13. Of Works before Justification.

WORKS done before the grace of Christ and the inspiration of his Spirit are not pleasant to God, forasmuch as they spring not of faith in Jesus Christ, neither do they make men meet to receive grace, or (as the School Authors say) deserve grace of congruity; yea rather, for that they are not done as God hath willed and commanded them to be done, we doubt not but they have the nature of sin.

14. Of Works of Supererogation.

VOLUNTARY works besides, over, and above God's commandments, which they call 'works of supererogation,' cannot be taught without arrogancy and impiety. For by them men do declare that they do not only render unto God as much as they are bound to do, but that they do more for his sake than of bounden duty is required; whereas Christ saith plainly, 'When ye have done all that are commanded to you, say, "We be unprofitable servants."'

15. Of Christ Alone without Sin.

CHRIST in the truth of our nature was made like unto us in all things, sin only except, from which he was clearly void, both in his flesh and in his spirit. He came to be the Lamb without spot, who, by sacrifice of himself once made, should take away the sins of the world; and sin, as Saint John saith, was not in him. But all we the rest, although baptized and born again in Christ, yet offend in many things; and if we say we have no sin, we deceive ourselves, and the truth is not in us.

16. Of Sin after Baptism.

NOT every deadly sin willingly committed after baptism is sin against the Holy Ghost and unpardonable. Wherefore the grant of repentance is not to be denied to such as fall into sin after baptism. After we have received the Holy Ghost, we may depart from grace given and fall into sin, and by the grace of God we may arise again and amend our lives. And therefore they are to be condemned which say they can no more sin as long as they live here, or deny the place of forgiveness to such as truly repent.

17. Of Predestination and Election.

PREDESTINATION to life is the everlasting purpose of God, whereby – before the foundations of the world were laid – he hath constantly decreed by his counsel secret to us, to deliver from curse and damnation those whom he hath chosen in Christ out of mankind, and to bring them by Christ to everlasting salvation, as vessels made to honour. Wherefore, they which be endued with so excellent a benefit of God be called according to God's purpose by his Spirit working in due season; they through grace obey the calling; they be justified freely; they be made sons of God by adoption; they be made like the image of his only-begotten Son Jesus Christ; they walk religiously in good works; and at length, by God's mercy, they attain to everlasting felicity.

As the godly consideration of predestination and our election in Christ is full of sweet, pleasant, and unspeakable comfort to godly persons, and such as feel in themselves the working of the Spirit of Christ, mortifying the works of the flesh and their earthly members, and drawing up their mind to high and heavenly things, as well because it doth greatly establish and confirm their faith of eternal salvation to be enjoyed through Christ, as because it doth fervently kindle their love towards God; so, for curious and carnal persons, lacking the Spirit of Christ, to have continually before their eyes the sentence of God's predestination is a most dangerous downfall, whereby the devil doth thrust them either into desperation or into wretchlessness of most unclean living, no less perilous than desperation.

Furthermore, we must receive God's promises in such wise as they be generally set forth to us in holy Scripture; and in our doings that will of God is to be followed which we have expressly declared unto us in the word of God.

18. Of Obtaining Eternal Salvation Only by the Name of Christ.

THEY also are to be had accursed that presume to say that every man shall be saved by the law or sect which he professeth, so that he be diligent to frame his life according to that law and the light of nature. For holy Scripture doth set out to us only the name of Jesus Christ, whereby men must be saved.

19. Of the Church.

THE visible church of Christ is a congregation of faithful men, in the which the pure word of God is preached, and the sacraments be duly ministered according to

Christ's ordinance in all those things that of necessity are requisite to the same.

As the Church of Jerusalem, Alexandria, and Antioch have erred; so also the Church of Rome hath erred, not only in their living and manner of ceremonies, but also in matters of faith.

20. Of the Authority of the Church.

THE church hath power to decree rites or ceremonies, and authority in controversies of faith; and yet it is not lawful for the church to ordain anything that is contrary to God's word written, neither may it so expound one place of Scripture that it be repugnant to another. Wherefore, although the church be a witness and a keeper of holy writ, yet, as it ought not to decree anything against the same, so besides the same ought it not to enforce anything to be believed for necessity of salvation.

21. Of the Authority of General Councils.

GENERAL councils may not be gathered together without the commandment and will of princes. And when they be gathered together – forasmuch as they be an assembly of men, whereof all be not governed with the Spirit and word of God – they may err, and sometimes have erred, even in things pertaining unto God. Wherefore things ordained by them as necessary to salvation have neither strength nor authority, unless it may be declared that they be taken out of holy Scripture.

22. Of Purgatory.

THE Romish doctrine concerning purgatory, pardons, worshipping and adoration as well of images as of relics, and also invocation of saints, is a fond thing vainly invented, and grounded upon no warranty of Scripture, but rather repugnant to the word of God.

23. Of Ministering in the Congregation.

IT is not lawful for any man to take upon him the office of public preaching or ministering the sacraments in the congregation before he be lawfully called and sent to execute the same. And those we ought to judge lawfully called and sent which be chosen and called to this work by men who have public authority given unto them in the congregation to call and send ministers into the Lord's vineyard.

24. Of Speaking in the Congregation in Such a Tongue as the People Understandeth.

IT is a thing plainly repugnant to the word of God, and the custom of the primitive church, to have public prayer in the church or to minister the sacraments in a tongue not understood of the people.

25. Of the Sacraments.

SACRAMENTS ordained of Christ be not only badges or tokens of Christian men's profession, but rather they be certain sure witnesses and effectual signs of grace and God's good will towards us, by the which he doth work invisibly in us, and doth not only quicken, but also strengthen and confirm, our faith in him.

There are two sacraments ordained of Christ our Lord in the gospel, that is to say, baptism and the supper of the Lord.

Those five commonly called sacraments, that is to say, confirmation, penance, orders, matrimony, and extreme unction, are not to be counted for sacraments of the gospel – being such as have grown partly of the corrupt following of the apostles, partly are states of life allowed in the Scriptures; but yet have not like nature of sacraments with baptism and the Lord's supper, for that they have not any visible sign or ceremony ordained of God.

The sacraments were not ordained of Christ to be gazed upon, or to be carried about, but that we should duly use them. And in such only as worthily receive the same they have a wholesome effect or operation; but they that receive them unworthily purchase to themselves damnation, as Saint Paul saith.

26. Of the Unworthiness of the Ministers, Which Hinders Not the Effect of the Sacraments.

ALTHOUGH in the visible church the evil be ever mingled with the good, and sometime the evil have chief authority in the ministration of the word and sacraments, yet forasmuch as they do not the same in their own name, but in Christ's, and do minister by his commission and authority, we may use their ministry, both in hearing the word of God and in the receiving of the sacraments. Neither is the effect of Christ's ordinance taken away by their wickedness, nor the grace of God's gifts diminished from such as by faith and rightly do receive the sacraments ministered unto them, which be effectual because of Christ's institution and promise, although they be ministered by evil men.

Nevertheless, it appertaineth to the discipline of the church that inquiry be made of evil ministers; and that they be accused by those that have knowledge of their offences; and finally, being found guilty by just judgement, be deposed.

27. Of Baptism.

BAPTISM is not only a sign of profession and mark of difference, whereby Christian men are discerned from others that be not christened, but it is also a sign of regeneration or new birth, whereby, as by an instrument, they that receive baptism rightly are grafted into the church; the promises of the forgiveness of sin and of our adoption to be the sons of God by the Holy Ghost are visibly signed and sealed; faith is confirmed, and grace increased by virtue of prayer unto God.

The baptism of young children is in any wise to be retained in the church as most agreeable with the institution of Christ.

28. Of the Lord's Supper.

THE supper of the Lord is not only a sign of the love that Christians ought to have among themselves, one to another, but rather it is a sacrament of our redemption by Christ's death; insomuch that to such as rightly, worthily, and with faith receive the same, the bread which we break is a partaking of the body of Christ, and likewise the cup of blessing is a partaking of the blood of Christ.

Transubstantiation (or the change of the substance of bread and wine) in the supper of the Lord cannot be proved by holy writ; but is repugnant to the plain words of Scripture, overthroweth the nature of a sacrament, and hath given occasion to many superstitions.

The body of Christ is given, taken, and eaten in the supper only after a heavenly and spiritual manner. And the means whereby the body of Christ is received and eaten in the supper is faith.

The sacrament of the Lord's supper was not by Christ's ordinance reserved, carried about, lifted up, or worshipped.

29. Of the Wicked, Which Do Not Eat the Body of Christ in the Use of the Lord's Supper.

THE wicked and such as be void of a lively faith, although they do carnally and visibly press with their teeth (as Saint Augustine saith) the sacrament of the body and blood of Christ, yet in no wise are they partakers of Christ, but rather to their condemnation do eat and drink the sign or sacrament of so great a thing.

30. Of Both Kinds.

THE cup of the Lord is not to be denied to the lay people; for both the parts of the Lord's sacrament, by Christ's ordinance and commandment, ought to be ministered to all Christian men alike.

31. Of the One Oblation of Christ
Finished upon the Cross.

THE offering of Christ once made is the perfect redemption, propitiation, and satisfaction for all the sins of the whole world, both original and actual; and there is none other satisfaction for sin, but that alone. Wherefore the sacrifices of masses, in the which it was commonly said that the priest did offer Christ for the quick and the dead, to have remission of pain or guilt, were blasphemous fables and dangerous deceits.

32. Of the Marriage of Priests.

BISHOPS, priests, and deacons are not commanded by God's law either to vow the estate of single life or to abstain from marriage. Therefore it is lawful for them, as for all other Christian men, to marry at their own discretion, as they shall judge the same to serve better to godliness.

33. Of Excommunicate Persons, How
They Are to Be Avoided.

THAT person which by open denunciation of the church is rightly cut off from the unity of the church and excommunicated ought to be taken of the whole multitude of the faithful as a heathen and publican, until he be openly reconciled by penance and received into the church by a judge that hath authority thereunto.

34. Of the Traditions of the Church.

IT is not necessary that traditions and ceremonies be in all places one or utterly like; for at all times they have been divers, and may be changed according to the diversity of countries, times, and men's manners, so that nothing be ordained against God's word.

Whosoever through his private judgement, willingly and purposely, doth openly break the traditions and ceremonies of the church which be not repugnant to the word of God, and be ordained and approved by common authority, ought to be rebuked openly (that others may fear to do the like), as he that offendeth against the common order of the church, and hurteth the authority of the magistrate, and woundeth the consciences of the weak brethren.

Every particular or national church hath authority to ordain, change, and abolish ceremonies or rites of the church ordained only by man's authority, so that all things be done to edifying.

35. Of Homilies.

THE second Book of Homilies, the several titles whereof we have joined under this article, doth contain a godly and wholesome doctrine and necessary for these times, as doth the former Book of Homilies, which were set forth in the time of Edward the Sixth; and therefore we judge them to be read in churches by the ministers diligently, and distinctly, that they may be understood of the people.

Of the Names of the Homilies.

1. *Of the right use of the church.*
2. *Against peril of idolatry.*

3. *Of repairing and keeping clean of churches.*
4. *Of good works: first of fasting.*
5. *Against gluttony and drunkenness.*
6. *Against excess of apparel.*
7. *Of prayer.*
8. *Of the place and time of prayer.*
9. *That common prayers and sacraments ought to be ministered in a known tongue.*
10. *Of the reverend estimation of God's word.*
11. *Of alms-doing.*
12. *Of the nativity of Christ.*
13. *Of the passion of Christ.*
14. *Of the resurrection of Christ.*
15. *Of the worthy receiving of the sacrament of the body and blood of Christ.*
16. *Of the gifts of the Holy Ghost.*
17. *For the Rogation Days.*
18. *Of the state of matrimony.*
19. *Of repentance.*
20. *Against idleness.*
21. *Against rebellion.*

36. *Of Consecration of Bishops and Ministers.*

THE Book of Consecration of Archbishops and Bishops and Ordering of Priests and Deacons, lately set forth in the time of Edward the Sixth and confirmed at the same time by authority of Parliament, doth contain all things necessary to such consecration and ordering, neither hath it anything that of itself is superstitious and ungodly. And therefore whosoever are consecrated or ordered according to the rites of that book, since the second year of the forenamed King Edward unto this time, or hereafter shall be consecrated or ordered according to the same rites; we decree all such to be rightly, orderly, and lawfully consecrated and ordered.

37. Of the Civil Magistrates.

THE Queen's Majesty hath the chief power in this realm of England and other her dominions, unto whom the chief government of all estates of this realm, whether they be ecclesiastical or civil, in all causes doth appertain, and is not, nor ought to be, subject to any foreign jurisdiction.

Where we attribute to the Queen's Majesty the chief government, by which titles we understand the minds of some slanderous folks to be offended, we give not to our princes the ministering either of God's word or of the sacraments, the which thing the injunctions also lately set forth by Elizabeth our Queen do most plainly testify, but that only prerogative which we see to have been given always to all godly princes in holy Scriptures by God himself – that is, that they should rule all estates and degrees committed to their charge by God, whether they be ecclesiastical or temporal, and restrain with the civil sword the stubborn and evildoers.

The bishop of Rome hath no jurisdiction in this realm of England.

The laws of the realm may punish Christian men with death for heinous and grievous offences.

It is lawful for Christian men, at the commandment of the magistrate, to wear weapons and serve in the wars.

38. Of Christian Men's Goods, Which Are Not Common.

THE riches and goods of Christians are not common, as touching the right, title, and possession of the same, as certain Anabaptists do falsely boast. Notwithstanding, every man ought of such things as he possesseth liberally to give alms to the poor, according to his ability.

39. Of a Christian Man's Oath.

As we confess that vain and rash swearing is forbidden Christian men by our Lord Jesus Christ, and James his apostle, so we judge that Christian religion doth not prohibit but that a man may swear when the magistrate requireth, in a cause of faith and charity, so it be done according to the prophet's teaching in justice, judgement, and truth.

The Ratification.

THIS Book of Articles before rehearsed is again approved, and allowed to be holden and executed within the realm, by the assent and consent of our Sovereign Lady *ELIZABETH*, by the grace of God, of England, France, and Ireland, Queen, Defender of the Faith, &c. Which Articles were deliberately read, and confirmed again by the subscription of the hands of the archbishop and bishops of the upper house, and by the subscription of the whole clergy of the nether house in their convocation, in the year of our Lord 1571.

Addenda

The Editors to the Reader.

IN the last three and a half centuries, the Church of England and her daughter churches have developed and diverged. But this family of churches has developed from a common point. A key expression of that shared Anglican identity is the Book of Common Prayer (1662), along with the texts customarily appended to it: the Psalter, the Ordinal, and the Thirty-Nine Articles. This prayer book remains widely used in public worship around the world, and some judge it to excel recent alternatives in simplicity as well as in the gravity of both its language and theology.

But for those who wish to use it today, especially outside England, three problems arise. First, some elements of the classic prayer book, such as the state prayers, are specific to England. Second, developments in the English language have made some words and phrases into obstacles for a contemporary user. Third, the 1662 prayer book lacks some later prayers that have become a treasured part of the Anglican tradition. Each of these problems can be addressed. The classic prayer book – with its simplicity, language, and theology intact – can be presented for use today. That is the editors' aim. A few examples will illustrate our approach.

I. Where the prayer book has prayers for the Queen and the royal family, we substituted prayers from other Anglican prayer books, with modest revisions to keep the prayers from being tied to any one country's polity.

In Morning and Evening Prayer, for example, the prayers for the Queen and the royal family are replaced by state prayers from later prayer books (US 1928, Ghana 1960). The excised prayers are shifted but retained in the book to allow their continued use in Commonwealth countries. Note that we have left unaltered the English political references in the Thirty-Nine Articles.

II. Our linguistic updating has been modest. *Cherubins* becomes *cherubim; Apostolick, apostolic.* This updating of capitalization, punctuation, and orthography has ample precedent in the prayer book printing tradition. Beyond this, we revised some overly obscure words and phrases, in the manner of the Irish 1926, US 1928, and Canadian 1962 editions of the prayer book. For example, in a prayer after the third collect in Morning and Evening Prayer, *curates* becomes *pastors.* In a prayer in the Communion service, *indifferently* becomes *impartially.* In one of the exhortations to be read before a Communion service, *in the mean season* becomes *in the meantime.*

We followed the traditional form of the Lord's Prayer most familiar around the world today: *who art* instead of *which art,* and *those who trespass* instead of *them that trespass.* In other places, too, we updated pronouns and determiners, though not always – in each case we have given weight to rhythm, euphony, and the preservation of familiar expressions. In short, we updated the language of rubrics most; prayers less; and psalms, canticles, and biblical texts least of all. Thus, for example, a phrase like 'them that' usually survives in a canticle or psalm, but in a prayer it becomes 'those who.'

THE EDITORS TO THE READER

Our aim was to remove a few of the higher hurdles for those who have not used the classic prayer book but would like to do so. Our anchor was a desire to preserve the prayer book's linguistic character (which was already consciously old-fashioned in 1662). The language of the prayer book is from a time when spoken and written English were in closer connection, with the ear having priority over the eye. Its distinctive liturgical register aids memorization and allows for continuity in worship across time and space. For many people today – both young and old – its language is a positive aid to worship and catechesis.

The language of the Psalter required particular attention because it is older than the rest of the prayer book. In all essentials, the prayer book Psalter is Miles Coverdale's edition of the Psalms in the Great Bible (1539). Some adaptations of Coverdale's work are freewheeling, but our revision is much more modest, along the lines of the Irish 1926 and US 1928 prayer books. We have made occasional alterations for clarity or accuracy, but we have not departed from Coverdale's penchant for paraphrase and his frequent reliance on the Greek and Latin versions. Nor has there been any shift in his register and idiom. In addition, because we wished to avoid any rupture with the Anglican choral tradition, our revisions preserve the rhythms of the words or phrases they replace whenever it is possible to do so without straying from Coverdale's idiom. For example, in 4:2 *leasing* becomes the metrically identical *lying,* which also preserves the initial consonant. An instance where we did change the syllable count is 119:70, where the prayer book Psalter says of the wicked, 'Their heart is as fat as brawn.' Readers now take *brawn* as a reference to strength (preserved in the alliterative phrase 'brains and brawn'). But Coverdale likely has in mind a different and quite specific image, for in early modern usage *brawn* could refer to a boar that had been fattened for a feast. We preserve his striking image with 'Their heart is as fat as boars' flesh.' Note that a list of every alteration to the spoken text of the prayer book, Psalter, and Ordinal, beyond punctuation and the merely orthographic, will be published separately.

III. We include an appendix of additional prayers. Our principles of selection were as follows. First, we included prayers that have become so well known as part of the Anglican tradition that their absence would be keenly felt (e.g. the Compline prayer that begins 'Be present, O merciful God, and protect us through the silent hours of this night'). Second, later Anglican prayer books usually include a wide range of occasional prayers. We included ones drawn out of prayer books from Canada, England, Ireland, Japan, Kenya, Nigeria, Scotland, South Africa, South India, Uganda, the United States, and the West Indies. Third, we sought to recover some prayers from earlier editions of the prayer book (e.g. St. Mary Magdalene's Day) and from Anglican devotional manuals (e.g. preparation for communion). Finally, we included a few prayers by individuals who express the breadth of the Anglican theological tradition. Across these categories, where necessary we have made alterations for stylistic consistency and felicity. In doing so, our guide was the main text in this volume. Many more prayers could of course have been included, but restraint was essential; this book is not an encyclopedia of prayers old and new.

There are other appendices. One is a sermon on justification from the first of the two authorized books of homilies. These homilies are commended in Article xxxv and the 1604 Canons 'for the confirmation of the true faith, and for the good instruction and edification of the people' (Canon xlix). Uniquely among the official homilies, this sermon is also cross-referenced in the Articles of Religion: Article xi directs readers to this sermon for a fuller expression of the doctrine of justification by faith alone.

Another appendix contains rubrics drawn from later prayer books. These distill centuries of customs regarding the use of the Book of Common Prayer (1662).

Yet another appendix offers an additional lectionary for Morning and Evening Prayer. The 1662 table of lessons, organized according to the civil calendar year, provides for continuous reading through the Scriptures with only occasional breaks for red-letter days. The alternative lectionary in the appendix is the Church of England's 1961 revised table of lessons, which is organized by the church year. Its selection of lessons aims to wed the principle of continuous reading to alignment with the sequence of greater festivals.

The final appendix is a glossary, after which there is a page of instructions for following the services of Morning Prayer, Holy Communion, and Evening Prayer.

In all these decisions, our purpose has been to let the text speak for itself. The Book of Common Prayer (1662) is an instrument of unity, the shared heritage of Anglicans around the world. We have sought to avoid any trace of idiosyncrasy in our editorial judgements. Indeed, it is not our place as editors to indulge in theological or ethical adjustments to the prayer book, nor to explicate it with commentary. As has been true for three and a half centuries, this book will be taught and explained, by turns justified and criticized, interrogated patiently or impatiently, and rightly so. Criticism and interrogation are the fate of every human work and the health of every living tradition. But those tasks are for the users, not the editors, of this volume.

The various versions of the Book of Common Prayer, from the earliest versions to the culminating one of 1662, 'will always be acknowledged as historical documents of the first order, and masterpieces of English prose, but that is not what they want or mean to be. Their goal ... is to be living words in the mouths of those who have a living faith.'* So, too, with this edition. It is not for antiquarian interest, nor for academic study, but for use: it is for those who desire to pray.

SLB

DNK

21 March 2020

---

* Alan Jacobs, *The Book of Common Prayer: A Biography* (Princeton University Press, 2013), pp. 193-94.

Appendix I.*

A Sermon of the Salvation of Mankind by Only Christ Our Saviour from Sin & Death Everlasting (1547).

BECAUSE all men are sinners and offenders against God, and breakers of his law and commandments, therefore can no man, by his own acts, works, and deeds – seem they never so good – be justified and made righteous before God. But every man of necessity is constrained to seek for another righteousness or justification, to be received at God's own hands, that is to say, the remission, pardon, and forgiveness of his sins and trespasses in such things as he hath offended. And this justification or righteousness, which we so receive by God's mercy and Christ's merits, embraced by faith, is taken, accepted, and allowed of God for our perfect and full justification. For the more full understanding hereof it is our parts and duties ever to remember the great mercy of God: how that all the world being wrapped in sin by breaking of the law, God sent his only Son our Saviour Christ into this world to fulfil the law for us, and by shedding of his most precious blood to make a sacrifice and satisfaction or (as it may be called) amends to his

---

* Article xi calls justification by faith alone 'a most wholesome doctrine, and very full of comfort, as more largely is expressed in the homily of justification' (p. 632). It is printed here.

Father for our sins, to assuage his wrath and indignation conceived against us for the same.

The efficacy of Christ's passion and oblation. Insomuch that infants, being baptized and dying in their infancy, are by this sacrifice washed from their sins, brought to God's favour, and made his children and inheritors of his kingdom of heaven. And those who actually do sin after their baptism, when they convert and turn again to God unfeignedly, they are likewise washed by this sacrifice from their sins in such sort that there remaineth not any spot of sin that shall be imputed to their damnation. This is that justification or righteousness which St. Paul speaketh of when he saith, 'No man is justified by the works of the law, but freely by faith in Jesus Christ.' * And again he saith, 'We believe in Christ Jesu, that we are justified freely by the faith of Christ, and not by the works of the law, because that no man shall be justified by the works of the law.' † And although this justification is free unto us, yet it cometh not so freely unto us that there is no ransom paid therefore at all.

An objection. But here may man's reason be astonished, reasoning after this fashion: 'If a ransom be paid for our redemption, then is it not given us freely. For a prisoner that paid his ransom is not let go freely. For if he go freely, then he goeth without ransom; for what is it else to go freely, than to be set at liberty without payment of ransom?'

Answer. This reason is satisfied by the great wisdom of

* Romans 3:20.
† Galatians 2:16.

God in this mystery of our redemption, who hath so tempered his justice and mercy together, that he would neither by his justice condemn us unto the perpetual captivity of the devil and his prison of hell, remediless for ever without mercy, nor by his mercy deliver us clearly without justice or payment of a just ransom, but with his endless mercy he joined his most upright and equal justice. His great mercy he showed unto us in delivering us from our former captivity, without requiring of any ransom to be paid or amends to be made upon our parts, which thing by us had been impossible to be done. And whereas it lay not in us that to do, he provided a ransom for us that was the most precious body and blood of his own most dear and best beloved Son Jesu Christ, who besides this ransom, fulfilled the law for us perfectly. And so the justice of God and his mercy did embrace together and fulfilled the mystery of our redemption. And of this justice and mercy of God knit together speaketh St. Paul in the third chapter to the Romans, 'All have offended, and have need of the glory of God, but are justified freely by his grace by redemption which is in Jesu Christ, whom God hath sent forth to us for a reconciler and peacemaker through faith in his blood, to show his righteousness.' * And in the tenth chapter, 'Christ is the end of the law unto righteousness to every man that believeth.' † And in the eighth chapter, 'That which was impossible by the law, inasmuch as it was weak by the flesh, God sending his own Son in the similitude of sinful flesh by sin damned sin in the flesh, that the

* Romans 3:23-25.
† Romans 10:4.

righteousness of the law might be fulfilled in us, which walk not after the flesh but after the Spirit.' *

Three things must go together in our justification. In these foresaid places, the apostle toucheth specially three things which must concur and go together in our justification: upon God's part, his great mercy and grace; upon Christ's part, justice, that is, the satisfaction of God's justice, or the price of our redemption by the offering of his body and shedding of his blood with fulfilling of the law perfectly and throughly; and upon our part, true and lively faith in the merits of Jesus Christ, which yet is not ours, but by God's working in us.

How it is to be understood that faith justifieth without works. So that in our justification is not only God's mercy and grace, but also his justice, which the apostle calleth the justice of God, and it consisteth in paying our ransom and fulfilling of the law. And so the grace of God doth not exclude the justice of God in our justification, but only excludeth out the justice of man, that is to say, the justice of our works, as to be merits of deserving our justification. And therefore St. Paul declareth here nothing upon the behalf of man, concerning his justification, but only a true and lively faith, which nevertheless is the gift of God, and not man's only work without God. And yet that faith doth not exclude repentance, hope, love, dread, and the fear of God, to be joined with faith in every man that is justified, but it excludeth them out from the office of justifying. So that although they be all present together in him that is justified, yet they justify not all together.

* Romans 8:3-4.

Nor also doth faith exclude the justice of our good works, necessarily to be done afterwards of duty towards God – for we are most bounden to serve God in doing good deeds, commanded by him in his holy Scripture, all the days of our life. But it excludeth them, so that we may not do them to this intent, to be made good by doing of them. For all the good works that we can do are imperfect, and therefore not able to deserve our justification. But our justification doth come freely by the mere mercy of God, and of so great and free mercy, that whereas all the world was not able of themselves to pay any part towards their ransom, it pleased our heavenly Father of his infinite mercy, without any of our desert or deserving, to prepare for us the most precious jewels of Christ's body and blood, whereby our ransom might be fully paid, the law fulfilled, and his justice fully satisfied. So that Christ is now the righteousness of all them that truly do believe in him. He for them paid their ransom by his death. He for them fulfilled the law in his life. So that now in him and by him every true Christian man may be called a fulfiller of the law, forasmuch as that which their infirmity lacketh, Christ's justice hath supplied.

Before was declared at large that no man can be justified by his own good works, because that no man fulfilleth the law according to the full request of the law. And St. Paul in his Epistle to the Galatians proveth the same, saying thus, 'If there had been any law given which could have justified, verily righteousness should have been by the law.'* And again he saith, 'If righteousness is by the

* Galatians 3:21.

law, then Christ died in vain.'* And again he saith, 'You
that are justified by the law, are fallen away from grace.' †
And furthermore he writeth to the Ephesians on this wise,
'By grace are ye saved through faith, and that not of yourselves, for it is the gift of God, and not of works, lest any
man should glory.' ‡ And to be short, the sum of all Paul's
disputation is this, that if justice come of works, then it
cometh not of grace; and if it come of grace, then it cometh not of works. And to this end tendeth all the prophets, as St. Peter saith in the tenth of the Acts. Of Christ
'all the prophets', saith St. Peter, 'do witness that through
his name all they that believe in him shall receive the
remission of sins.' §

Faith only justifieth is the doctrine of the old doctors. And
after this wise, to be justified only by this true and lively
faith in Christ, speaketh all the old and ancient authors,
both Greek and Latin. Of whom I will specially rehearse
three: Hilary, Basil, and Ambrose. St. Hilary saith these
words plainly in the ninth canon upon Matthew, 'Faith
only justifieth.' And St. Basil, a Greek author, writeth thus,
'This is a perfect and a whole rejoicing in God, when a
man advanceth not himself for his own righteousness,
but knoweth himself to lack true justice and righteousness, and to be justified by the only faith in Christ. And
Paul,' saith he, 'doth glory in the contempt of his own righteousness, and that he looketh for the righteousness of

---

* Galatians 2:21.
† Galatians 5:4.
‡ Ephesians 2:8-9.
§ Acts 10:43.

God by faith.'* These be the very words of St. Basil. And St. Ambrose, a Latin author, saith these words, 'This is the ordinance of God, that he which believeth in Christ should be saved without works, by faith only, freely receiving remission of their sins.' Consider diligently these words, 'by faith only, freely we receive remission of our sins.' What can be spoken more plainly than to say that freely without works, by faith only, we obtain remission of our sins? These and other like sentences – that we are justified by faith only, freely, and without works – we do read oft-times in the most best and ancient writers. As beside Hilary, Basil, and St. Ambrose before rehearsed, we read the same in Origen, St. Chrysostom, St. Cyprian, St. Augustine, Prosper, Oecumenius, Photius, Bernardus, Anselm, and many other authors, Greek and Latin.

Faith alone, how it is to be understood. Nevertheless, this sentence – that we are justified by faith only – is not so meant of them that the said justifying faith is alone in man, without true repentance, hope, charity, dread, and the fear of God, at any time and season. Nor, when they say that we are justified freely, do they mean that we should or might afterward be idle, and that nothing should be required on our part afterward; neither they mean not so to be justified without our good works that we should do no good works at all, like as shall be more expressed at large hereafter. But this proposition – that we are justified by faith only, freely, and without works – is spoken for to take away clearly all merit of our works, as being insufficient to deserve our justification at God's hands,

* Philippians 3:9.

660

and thereby most plainly to express the weakness of man and the goodness of God, the great infirmity of ourselves and the might and power of God, the imperfectness of our own works and the most abundant grace of our Saviour Christ, and thereby wholly to ascribe the merit and deserving of our justification unto Christ only and his most precious bloodshedding.

The profit of the doctrine of faith only justifieth. This faith the holy Scripture teacheth; this is the strong rock and foundation of Christian religion; this doctrine all old and ancient authors of Christ's church do approve; this doctrine advanceth and setteth forth the true glory of Christ and beateth down the vainglory of man.

Who they are that impugn the doctrine of faith only justifieth. This, whosoever denieth is not be counted for a true Christian man, nor for a setter-forth of Christ's glory, but for an adversary of Christ and his gospel, and for a setter-forth of man's vainglory.

And although this doctrine is never so true, as it is most true indeed, that we are justified freely without all merit of our own good works (as St. Paul doth express it) and freely by this lively and perfect faith in Christ only (as the ancient authors use to speak it), yet this true doctrine must be also truly understood and most plainly declared, lest carnal men should take unjustly occasion thereby to live carnally, after the appetite and will of the world, the flesh, and the devil. And because no man should err by mistaking of this doctrine, I shall plainly and shortly so declare the right understanding of the same, that no man shall justly think that he may thereby take any occasion of carnal liberty, to follow the desires of the flesh, or that thereby any kind of sin shall be committed, or any ungodly living the more used.

A declaration of this doctrine of faith without works justifieth. First you shall understand that in our justification by Christ it is not all one thing, the office of God unto man and the office of man unto God. Justification is not the office of man but of God. For man cannot justify himself by his own works – neither in part, nor in the whole – for that were the greatest arrogance and presumption of man that antichrist could erect against God, to affirm that a man might by his own works take away and purge his own sins, and so justify himself.

Justification is the office of God only. But justification is the office of God only and is not a thing which we render unto him, but which we receive of him – not which we give to him, but which we take of him, by his free mercy, and by the only merits of his most dearly beloved Son, our only Redeemer, Saviour, and Justifier Jesus Christ, so that the true understanding of this doctrine (we are justified freely by faith without works, or that we are justified by faith in Christ only) is not that this our own act, to believe in Christ, or this our faith in Christ, which is within us, doth justify us and deserve our justification unto us – for that were to count ourselves to be justified by some act or virtue that is within ourselves. But the true understanding and meaning thereof is that although we hear God's word and believe it, although we have faith, hope, charity, repentance, dread, and fear of God within us, and do never so many works thereunto, yet we must renounce the merit of all our said virtues – of faith, hope, charity, and all other virtues and good deeds, which we either have done, shall do, or can do – as things that are far too weak and insufficient and imperfect to merit remission of our sins and our justification. And therefore we must trust only in God's mercy, and that sacrifice which our high priest and Saviour Christ Jesus, the Son of God, once offered for us upon the cross, to obtain thereby God's grace and remission as well of our original sin in baptism as of all actual sin committed by us after our baptism, if we truly repent and turn unfeignedly to him again. So that as St. John the Baptist, although he were never so virtuous and godly a man, yet in this matter of forgiving of sin, he did put the people from him, and appointed them unto Christ, saying thus unto them, 'Behold, yonder is the Lamb of God, which taketh away the sins of the world.' * Even so, as great and as godly a virtue as the lively faith is, yet it putteth us from itself, and remitteth or appointeth us unto Christ, for to have only by him remission of our sins or justification. So that our faith in Christ (as it were) saith unto us thus, 'It is not I that take away your sins, but it is Christ only, and to him only I send you for that purpose, renouncing therein all your good virtues, words, thoughts, and works, and only putting your trust in Christ.'

Thus do you see the very true sense of this proposition – 'We are justified by faith in Christ only' – according to the meaning of the old ancient authors is this: We put our faith in Christ, that we are justified by him only, that we are justified by God's free mercy, and the merits of our

* St. John 1:29.

Saviour Christ only and by no virtue or good works of our own, that is in us, or that we are able to have or to do, for to deserve the same, Christ himself only being the meritorious cause thereof.

Here you perceive many words are used to avoid contention in words with those that delight to brawl about words, and also to show the true meaning, to avoid evil taking and misunderstanding. And yet peradventure all will not serve with them that are contentious, but contenders will ever forge matters of contention, even when they have no occasion thereto. Not withstanding, such are the less to be passed upon, so that the rest may profit, which are more desirous to know the truth than (when it is plain enough) to contend about it, and with contentious and captious cavillation to obscure and darken it.

True it is, that our own works do not justify us, to speak properly of our justification – that is to say, our works do not merit or deserve remission of our sins, and make us, being unjust, just before God. But God, of his mere mercy, through the only merits and deservings of his Son Jesus Christ, doth justify us. Nevertheless, because faith doth directly send us to Christ for remission of our sins, and that by faith given us of God we embrace the promise of God's mercy, and of the remission of our sins – which thing no other of our virtues or works properly doth – therefore Scripture useth to say that faith without works doth justify. And forasmuch that it is all one sentence, in effect to say, faith without works, and only faith doth justify us; therefore the old ancient Fathers of the church from time to time have uttered our justification with this speech, 'Only faith justifieth us', meaning no other thing than St. Paul meant when he said, 'Faith without works justifieth us.'

And because all this brought to pass through the only merits and deservings of our Saviour Christ, and not through our merits, or through the merit of any virtue that we have within us, or of any work that cometh from us, therefore in that respect of merit and deserving, we renounce (as it were) altogether again faith, works, and all other virtues. For our own imperfection is so great, through the corruption of original sin, that all is imperfect that is within us – faith, charity, hope, dread, thoughts, words, and works – and therefore not apt to merit and deserve any part of our justification for us. And this form of speaking we use, in the humbling of ourselves to God, and to give all the glory to our Saviour Christ, who is most worthy to have it.

Here you have heard the office of God in our justification, and how we receive it of him freely, by his mercy, without our deserts, through true and lively faith. Now you shall hear the office and duty of a Christian man unto God, what we ought on our part to render unto God again, for his great mercy and goodness.

They that preach faith only justifieth do not teach carnal liberty or that we should do no good works. Our office is not to pass the time of this present life unfruitfully and idly, after that we are baptized or justified, not caring how few good works we do to the glory of God and profit of our neighbours. Much less is it our office, after that we are once made Christ's members, to live contrary to the same, making ourselves members of the devil, walking after his enticements, and after the suggestions of the world and the flesh, whereby we know that we do serve the world and the devil and not God.

The devils have faith, but not true faith. For that faith which bringeth forth, without repentance, either evil works or no good works is not a right, pure, and lively faith, but a dead, devilish, counterfeit, and feigned faith, as St. Paul and St. James call it. For even the devils know and believe that Christ was born of a virgin, that he fasted forty days and forty nights without meat and drink, that he wrought all kind of miracles, declaring himself very God. They believe also that Christ for our sakes suffered most painful death to redeem from everlasting death, and that he rose again from death the third day. They believe that he ascended into heaven, and that he sitteth on the right hand of the Father, and at the last end of this world shall come again, and judge both the quick and the dead. These articles of our faith the devils believe, and so they believe all things that be written in the New and Old Testament to be true. And yet for all this faith, they be but devils, remaining still in their damnable estate, lacking the very true Christian faith.

What is true and justifying faith. For the right and true Christian faith is not only to believe that holy Scripture and all the foresaid articles of our faith are true, but also to have a sure trust and confidence in God's merciful promises to be saved from everlasting damnation by Christ, whereof doth follow a loving heart to obey his commandments. And this true Christian faith neither any devil hath, nor yet any man which in the outward profession of his mouth, and in his outward receiving of the sacraments, in coming to the church, and in all other outward appearances, seemeth to be a Christian man, and yet in his living and deeds showeth the contrary.

They that continue in evil living have not true faith. For how can a man have this true faith – this sure trust and confidence in God that by the merits of Christ his sins are remitted, and that he is reconciled to the favour of God, and to be partaker of the kingdom of heaven by Christ – when he liveth ungodly, and denieth Christ in his deeds? Surely no such ungodly man can have this faith and trust in God. For as they know Christ to be the only Saviour of the world, so they know also that wicked men shall not enjoy the kingdom of God. * They know that God hateth unrighteousness, that he will destroy all those that speak untruly, † that those which have done good works – which cannot be done without a lively faith in Christ – shall come forth into the resurrection of life, and those that have done evil shall come unto the resurrection of judgement. Very well they know also, that to those that are contentious, and to those that will not be obedient unto the truth, but will obey unrighteousness, shall come indignation, wrath, and affliction, and so forth.

Therefore to conclude, considering the infinite benefits of God showed and exhibited unto us mercifully without our deserts, who hath not only created us of nothing, and from a piece of vile clay of his infinite goodness hath

* Psalm 25.
† Psalm 5:5-6.

exalted us (as touching our soul) unto his own similitude and likeness, but also, whereas we were condemned to hell and death eternal, hath given his own natural Son, being God eternal, immortal, and equal unto himself in power and glory, to be incarnated and to take our mortal nature upon him, with the infirmities of the same, and in the same nature to suffer most shameful and painful death for our offences, to the intent to justify us, and to restore us to life everlasting, so making us also his dear beloved children, brethren unto his only Son our Saviour Christ, and inheritors for ever with him of his eternal kingdom of heaven.

These great and merciful benefits of God, if well considered, do neither minister unto us occasion to be idle, and to live without doing any good works, neither yet stirreth us by any means to do evil things; but contrariwise, if we are not desperate persons, and our hearts harder than stones, they move us to render ourselves unto God wholly with all our will, hearts, might, and power, to serve him in all good deeds, obeying his commandments during our lives, to seek in all things his glory and honour, not our sensual pleasures and vainglory, evermore dreading willingly to offend such a merciful God and loving Redeemer in word, thought, or deed. And the said benefits of God, deeply considered, do move us for his sake also to be ever ready to give ourselves to our neighbours, and as much as lieth in us, to study with all our endeavour to do good to every man.

These are the fruits of true faith: to do good, as much as lieth in us, to every man; and above all things and in all things to advance the glory of God, of whom only we have our sanctification, justification, salvation, and redemption, to whom be ever glory, praise, and honour, world without end. Amen.

Appendix II.

Additional Prayers & Thanksgivings.

Society and State.
For Fruitful Seasons.

O GRACIOUS Father, who openest thy hand and fillest all things living with plenteousness: We beseech thee of thine infinite goodness to hear us, who now make our prayers and supplications unto thee. Remember not our sins, but thy promises of mercy. Vouchsafe to bless the lands and multiply the harvests of the world. Let thy breath go forth that it may renew the face of the earth. Show thy loving-kindness, that our land may give her increase; and so fill us with good things, that the poor and needy may give thanks unto thy name, through Christ our Lord. *Amen.*

For Joy in God's Creation.

O HEAVENLY Father, who hast filled the world with beauty: Open, we beseech thee, our eyes to behold thy gracious hand in all thy works, that, rejoicing in thy whole creation, we may learn to serve thee with gladness, for the sake of him by whom all things were made, thy Son, Jesus Christ our Lord. *Amen.*

ADDITIONAL PRAYERS

For Schools.

ALMIGHTY God, of whose gift alone cometh wisdom and understanding: We beseech thee with thy gracious favour to behold our universities, colleges, and schools, that knowledge may be increased among us, and all good learning flourish and abound. Bless all who teach and all who learn, and grant that in humility of heart they may ever look unto thee, who art the fount of all wisdom, through Jesus Christ our Lord. *Amen.*

For Our Country.

ALMIGHTY God, from whom all power in heaven and earth is derived: Accept the prayers we offer thee for our nation, granting virtue unto its citizens and wisdom unto those in authority, that, through obedience to thy will, justice and truth may be more firmly established among us, through Jesus Christ our Lord. *Amen.*

¶ Or this.

ALMIGHTY God, who hast given us this good land for our heritage: We humbly beseech thee that we may always prove ourselves a people mindful of thy favour and glad to do thy will. Bless our land with honourable industry, sound learning, and pure manners. Save us from violence, discord, and confusion, from pride and arrogancy, and from every evil way. Defend our liberties, and fashion into one united people all our many kindreds and tongues. Endue with the spirit of wisdom those to whom in thy name we entrust the authority of government, that there may be justice and peace at home, and that, through obedience to thy law, we may show forth thy praise among the nations of the earth. In the time of prosperity, fill our hearts with thankfulness, and in the day of trouble, suffer not our trust in thee to fail, all which we ask through Jesus Christ our Lord. *Amen.*

In a Time of Calamity.

O GOD, merciful and compassionate, who art ever ready to hear the prayers of those who put their trust in thee: Graciously hearken to us who call upon thee, and grant us thy help in this our need, through Jesus Christ our Lord. *Amen.*

In a Time of War.

O ALMIGHTY Lord, who art a most strong tower to all those who put their trust in thee: Be now and evermore our defence. Grant us victory, if it be thy will. Look in pity upon the wounded and the prisoners, cheer the anxious, comfort the bereaved, succour the dying, and hasten the time when war shall cease in all the world, through Jesus Christ our Lord. *Amen.*

For the Armed Forces.

O LORD God of hosts, stretch forth (we pray thee) thine almighty arm to strengthen and protect the soldiers, sailors, and airmen of our country. Support them in the day of battle, and in the time of peace keep them safe from all evil. Endue them with courage and loyalty, and grant that in all things they may serve without reproach, through Jesus Christ our Lord. *Amen.*

ADDITIONAL PRAYERS

¶ *Or this.*

ALMIGHTY God, the strong tower and refuge of thy people: We entreat thy favour upon the officers and all who are enlisted in the service of defence of our country, upon land, and on the water, and in the air. Ever spare them from being ordered into a war of conquest or ambition. Use them, if need be, as thine instruments, in the defence of our national life and liberty. But restrain, we beseech thee, the greed and wrath of man, that wars may cease in all the earth. Deepen in the hearts of our defenders the spirit of peace, and may they ever love and serve the Prince of Peace, our Lord and Saviour Jesus Christ. *Amen.*

In a Time of Great Sickness.

O ALMIGHTY God, the Lord of life and death, of health and sickness, have pity upon us miserable sinners now visited with great sickness [*and mortality*]. Withdraw from us this grievous affliction. Sanctify to us, we beseech thee, this thy fatherly correction. Enlarge our charity to relieve those who need our help. Bless the remedies applied to assist them. Give us prudence to see, and vigour to use, those means which thy providence affords for preventing and alleviating such calamities. And, above all, teach us to know how frail and uncertain our condition is, and so to number our days that we may seriously apply our hearts to that holy and heavenly wisdom, whilst we live here, which may in the end bring us to life everlasting, through the merits and mediation of Jesus Christ, thine only Son our Lord. *Amen.*

¶ *Or this.*

O MOST mighty and merciful God, in this time of griev-ous sickness, we flee unto thee for succour. Deliver us, we beseech thee, from our peril. Give strength and skill to all those who minister to the sick; prosper the means made use of for their cure; and grant that, perceiving how frail and uncertain our life is, we may apply our hearts unto that heavenly wisdom which leadeth to eternal life, through Jesus Christ our Lord. *Amen.*

For an Election.

A LMIGHTY God, the fountain of all wisdom: Guide, we beseech thee, the minds of all those who are called at this time to exercise the duty of electing fit persons to serve in public office, that their choices may promote thy glory and the welfare of this people. And to all those who shall be elected, give the spirit of wisdom, courage, and true godliness. And this we ask in the name of Jesus Christ our Lord. *Amen.*

For the Courts of Justice.

A LMIGHTY God, who sittest on the throne judging right: We humbly beseech thee to bless the courts of justice and the magistrates throughout *this whole land,* and to give unto them the spirit of wisdom and understanding, that they may discern the truth, and that they may impartially administer the law in the fear of thee alone, through him who shall come to be our judge, thy Son, our Saviour, Jesus Christ. *Amen.*

ADDITIONAL PRAYERS

For Justice.

O GOD, who wilt set thy glory among the nations and cause all the peoples to see the judgements of thy right hand: Have mercy upon those who are persecuted by the wicked and unrighteous, and so cause justice to prevail among men, that the meek may inherit the earth and the redeemed praise thee for thy deliverance, through Jesus Christ our Lord. *Amen.*

For the Peace of the World.

O GOD our Father, look with mercy upon all thy children; purify our hearts from all hatred, falsehood, and prejudice; and so guide us by thy loving wisdom that peace and righteousness may be established among all men, through Jesus Christ our Lord. *Amen.*

For the Reign of Christ.

A LMIGHTY and everlasting God, whose will it is to restore all things in thy well-beloved Son, the King of kings and Lord of lords: Mercifully grant that all the peoples of the earth, though now divided and in bondage to sin, may be made free and brought together under his most gracious rule, who liveth and reigneth with thee and the Holy Ghost, one God, now and for ever. *Amen.*

The Church.
For the Church.

M OST gracious God, we humbly beseech thee for thy holy catholic church: Fill it with all truth, in all peace. Where it is corrupt, purge it; where it is in error, direct it; where anything is amiss, reform it; where it is right, strengthen and confirm it; where it is in want, furnish it; where it is divided and rent asunder, make up the breaches of it, through Jesus Christ our Lord. *Amen.*

¶ *Or this.*

O GOD of unchangeable power and light eternal: Look favourably upon the body of thy whole church, and by thy eternal providence accomplish the salvation of man, that all the world may see and know that what was fallen has been lifted up, and what was grown old has been made new, and that all things are restored by him through whom they were made, even thy Son Jesus Christ our Lord. *Amen.*

¶ *Or this.*

O LORD, we beseech thee to maintain thy church in truth and patience, that her pastors may be faithful, her watchmen vigilant, her flock loyal, her camp united, her war spiritual, her weapons heavenly, her lamp burning and shining; and as thy Son Jesus Christ hath given so great a price for us, let us not count it a hard thing to give up all for him, and to spend and be spent for the souls he hath redeemed, who liveth and reigneth with thee and the Holy Ghost, now and for evermore. *Amen.*

¶ *Or this.*

E TERNAL and gracious God, who art slow to anger and of great kindness: Have mercy upon thy faithless and backsliding church. We mourn and confess to thee our sins, the poverty of our devotion, and the weakness of our testimony. Pardon, cleanse, and restore us, we humbly beseech thee. Fill us with the power of thy Holy Spirit, that we thy people may be humbled and sanctified, and that the multitudes who are lost to thee may be convicted of their sins and converted to their Saviour, for the glory of his saving name. *Amen.*

For the Spread of the Gospel.

ALMIGHTY God, who by thy Son Jesus Christ didst give commandment to the apostles, that they should go into all the world and preach the gospel to every creature: Grant to us, whom thou hast called into thy church, a ready will to obey thy word, and fill us with a hearty desire to make thy way known upon earth, thy saving health among all nations. Look with compassion upon the peoples that have not known thee, and upon the multitudes that are scattered abroad as sheep having no shepherd, and gather them into thy fold, through the same Jesus Christ our Lord. *Amen.*

¶ *Or this.*

GOD, who by sending the Spirit at Pentecost didst endue thine apostles with power to witness to thy Son and to make disciples of all the nations: Pour out abundantly, we beseech thee, the same Holy Spirit upon thy church, that it may bring the good tidings of great joy to all people, and that every man may hear in his own tongue thy wonderful works, through the same Jesus Christ our Lord. *Amen.*

ADDITIONAL PRAYERS

For Missionaries.

O GOD our Saviour, who willest that all men should be saved and come to the knowledge of the truth: Prosper, we pray thee, those who labour in distant lands, [*especially those for whom our prayers are desired*]. Protect them in all perils, and supply their every need. Give them grace to bear faithful witness unto thee, and endue them with burning zeal and love, that they may turn many to righteousness, and finally obtain a crown of glory, through Jesus Christ our Lord. *Amen.*

For the Persecuted Church.

O GOD, whose arm is mighty to save: Uphold and deliver all those who suffer for thy name, bearing in their bodies the dying of our Lord Jesus, and as they have known the fellowship of his sufferings, make them to know the power of his resurrection, through the same Jesus Christ our Lord. *Amen.*

¶ *Or this.*

O LORD God of our salvation, in whose hands are the issues of life and death, of good and evil, and without whose aid the wisest counsels of frail men, and the multitude of a host, and all the instruments of war are but weak and vain: Incline thine ear, we pray thee, to the earnest and devout supplications of thy servants, who, not confiding in the splendour of anything that is great, nor the stability of anything that is strong here below, do most humbly flee, O Lord, unto thee for succour, and put their trust under the shadow of thy wings. Be thou to *us* a tower of defence against the assaults of *our* enemies, *our* shield and buckler in the day of battle, that *we,* being preserved by thy help and goodness from all perils and disasters, may joyfully laud and magnify thy glorious name, and serve thee from generation to generation in all godliness and quietness, through Jesus Christ our Lord. *Amen.*

For the Diocese.

O GOD, who by thy grace hast called us in this diocese to a godly fellowship of faith: Bless our bishop, clergy, and all our people. Grant that thy word may be truly preached and truly heard, thy sacraments faithfully administered and faithfully received. By thy Spirit, fashion our lives according to the example of thy Son, and grant that we may show the power of thy love to all among whom we live, through Jesus Christ our Lord. *Amen.*

For the Parish.

A LMIGHTY God, we beseech thee to bless this our parish. Forgive us our many and grievous sins. Draw us nearer to thyself, and cause true religion to increase and abound among us. Prosper the reading and preaching of thy word, and bless all the ministrations of thy church. Give patience to the sick and afflicted, and make their sufferings a blessing to them. Visit with thy favour the schools, that both those who teach and those who learn may grow in grace and in the knowledge of thee and of thy dear Son, whom to know is life eternal. Hear us for the sake of him who died for us, Jesus Christ our Lord. *Amen.*

ADDITIONAL PRAYERS

¶ *Or this.*

ALMIGHTY and everliving God, ruler of all things in heaven and earth: Hear our prayers for this parish family. Strengthen the faithful, stir up the careless, and restore the penitent. Grant us all things necessary for our common life, and bring us all to be of one heart and mind within thy holy church, through Jesus Christ our Lord. *Amen.*

For Preaching.

GRANT, O Lord, that by thy holy word which *shall be* read and preached in this place, and by thy Holy Spirit grafting it inwardly in the heart, the hearers of it may both perceive and know what things they ought to do, and also have power and strength to fulfil the same. *Amen.*

For the Anniversary of a Parish or Church Building.

O GOD, by whose providence we celebrate the *establishing* of this *parish:* Send down upon us, we beseech thee, thy heavenly blessing; and, because holiness becometh thy house for ever, make us living temples, holy and acceptable unto thee, through Jesus Christ our Lord. *Amen.*

For Christian Service.

O LORD, our heavenly Father, whose blessed Son came not to be ministered unto, but to minister: We beseech thee to bless all who, following in his steps, give themselves to the service of their fellow men. Endue them with wisdom, patience, and courage, to strengthen the weak and raise up those who fall, that, being inspired by thy love, they may worthily minister in thy name to the suffering, the friendless, and the needy, for the sake of him who laid down his life for us, the same thy Son our Saviour Jesus Christ. *Amen.*

¶ *Or this.*

REMEMBER, O Lord, what thou hast wrought in us, and not what we deserve, and as thou hast called us to thy service, make us worthy of our calling, through Jesus Christ our Lord. *Amen.*

For the Unity of the Church.

O GOD, the Father of our Lord Jesus Christ, our only Saviour, the Prince of Peace: Give us grace seriously to lay to heart the great dangers we are in by our unhappy divisions. Take away all hatred and prejudice, and whatsoever else may hinder us from godly union and concord, that as there is but one body and one Spirit and one hope of our calling, one Lord, one faith, one baptism, one God and Father of us all, so we may be all of one heart and of one soul, united in one holy bond of truth and peace, of faith and charity, and may with one mind and one mouth glorify thee, through Jesus Christ our Lord. *Amen.*

For the Meeting of a Church Council or Synod.

ALMIGHTY and everlasting God, who, by thy Holy Spirit, didst preside in the councils of the blessed apostles, and hast promised, through thy Son Jesus Christ, to be with thy church to the end of the world: We beseech thee to be with the council of thy church [*here*] assembled in thy name and presence. Save *us* from all error, ignorance, pride, and prejudice; and of thy great mercy vouchsafe, we beseech thee, so to direct, sanctify, and govern *us* in *our* work, by the mighty power of the Holy Ghost, that the comfortable gospel of Christ may be truly preached, truly received, and truly followed in all places to the breaking down of the kingdom of sin, Satan, and death, till at length the whole of thy dispersed sheep, being gathered into one fold, shall become partakers of everlasting life, through the merits and death of Jesus Christ our Saviour. *Amen.*

For Theological Schools.

O GOD, who through thy Holy Spirit dost illuminate the minds and sanctify the lives of those whom thou dost call to serve as pastors and teachers: Look favourably upon all places devoted to their instruction and discipline, [*especially* —,] and equip them for the sacred ministry of thy church. Bless those who teach and those who learn, that they may diligently apply themselves to that knowledge which is able to make men wise unto salvation, and also submit themselves with ready obedience to the law of Christ, and so fulfil their ministry with joy and singleness of heart, though the same Lord Jesus Christ. *Amen.*

Throughout the Day.
A Litany for the Morning.

G LORY be to thee, O Lord, glory to thee. Glory to thee who givest me sleep to refresh my weakness, and to remit the toils of this fretful flesh. To this day and all days, a perfect, holy, peaceful, healthy, sinless course,

Vouchsafe, O Lord.

The angel of peace, a faithful guide, guardian of souls and bodies, to encamp around me, and ever to prompt what is salutary,

Vouchsafe, O Lord.

To our souls what is good and convenient, and peace to the world,

Vouchsafe, O Lord.

Repentance and strictness for the rest of our life, and health and peace to the end,

Vouchsafe, O Lord.

Whatever is true, whatever is honest, whatever just, whatever pure, whatever lovely, whatever of good report, if there be any virtue, if any praise, such thoughts, such deeds,

Vouchsafe, O Lord.

A Christian close, without sin, without shame, and should it please thee, without pain, and a good answer at the dreadful and fearful judgement seat of Jesus Christ our Lord,

Vouchsafe, O Lord.

In the Morning.

O LORD, who hast brought us through the darkness of night to the light of morning, and who by thy Holy Spirit dost illumine the darkness of ignorance and sin:

We beseech thee of thy loving-kindness to pour thy holy light into our souls, that we may be ever devoted to thee, by whose wisdom we were created, by whose mercy we were redeemed, and by whose providence we are governed, to the honour and glory of thy great name. *Amen.*

Prayers at Midday.

BLESSED Saviour, who at this hour didst hang upon the cross, stretching out thy loving arms: Grant that all mankind may look unto thee and be saved, who livest and reignest with the Father and the Holy Ghost, ever one God, world without end. *Amen.*

ALMIGHTY Saviour, who at midday didst call thy servant Saint Paul to be an apostle to the Gentiles: We beseech thee to illumine the world with the radiance of thy glory, that all nations may come and worship thee, who art, with the Father and the Holy Ghost, one God, world without end. *Amen.*

FATHER of mercies, who to thine apostle Saint Peter didst reveal in threefold vision thy boundless compassion: Forgive, we pray thee, our unbelief, and so enlarge our hearts and enkindle our zeal, that we may fervently desire the salvation of all men, and with more ready diligence labour in the extension of thy kingdom, for his sake, who gave himself for the life of the world, thy Son our Saviour Jesus Christ. *Amen.*

ADDITIONAL PRAYERS

Prayers in the Evening.

BE present, O merciful God, and protect us through the silent hours of this night, so that we who are wearied by the changes and chances of this fleeting world, may repose upon thy eternal changelessness, through Jesus Christ our Lord. *Amen.*

KEEP watch, dear Lord, with those who work, or watch, or weep this night, and give thine angels charge over those who sleep. Tend the sick, Lord Christ, give rest to the weary, bless the dying, soothe the suffering, pity the afflicted, shield the joyous, and all for thy love's sake. *Amen.*

O MERCIFUL Lord God, heavenly Father, whether we sleep or wake, live or die, we are always thine. Wherefore I beseech thee heartily to take care and charge of me, not suffering me to perish in the works of darkness, but kindling the light of thy countenance in my heart, that thy godly knowledge may daily increase in me, through a right and pure faith, and that I may always be found to walk and live after thy wisdom and pleasure, through Jesus Christ our Lord and Saviour. Amen.

Phos hilaron.

O GRACIOUS light,
pure brightness of the everliving Father in heaven,
O Jesus Christ, holy and blessed!

Now as we come to the setting of the sun,
and our eyes behold the vesper light,
we sing thy praises, O God: Father, Son, and Holy Spirit.

Thou art worthy at all times to be praised by happy voices,
O Son of God, O giver of life,
and to be glorified through all the worlds. Amen.

At Home and Work.
For Families.

Almighty God, our heavenly Father, who settest the solitary in families: Bless our homes, and put far from us, we beseech thee, all bitterness, the desire of vainglory, and the pride of life. Fill us with faith, virtue, knowledge, temperance, patience, godliness. Knit together in constant affection those who, in holy wedlock, have been made one flesh; turn the heart of the fathers to the children, and the heart of the children to the fathers; and so enkindle fervent charity among us all, through Jesus Christ our Lord. *Amen.*

For an Expectant Mother.

O Lord and giver of life, receive our prayer for *N.* and for the child she is carrying, that they may safely come to the time of birth, and serving thee in all things may rejoice in thy tender care, through Jesus Christ our Lord. *Amen.*

ADDITIONAL PRAYERS

For Children.

O LORD Jesus Christ, who dost embrace children with the arms of thy mercy, and dost make them living members of thy church: Give them grace, we pray thee, to stand fast in thy faith, to obey thy word, and to abide in thy love, that, being made strong by thy Holy Spirit, they may resist temptation and overcome evil, and may rejoice in the life that now is, and dwell with thee in the life that is to come, through thy merits, O merciful Saviour, who with the Father and the Holy Ghost livest and reignest one God, world without end. *Amen.*

¶ *Or this.*

A LMIGHTY God, heavenly Father, who hast blessed us with the joy and care of children: Give us light and strength so to train them, that they may love whatsoever things are true and pure and lovely and of good report, following the example of their Saviour Jesus Christ. *Amen.*

For a Birthday.

W ATCH over thy child, O Lord, as *his* days increase; bless and guide *him* wherever *he* may be, keeping *him* unspotted from the world. Strengthen *him* when *he* stands; comfort *him* when discouraged or sorrowful; raise *him* up if *he* should fall; and may thy peace which passeth understanding abide in *his* heart all the days of *his* life, through Jesus Christ our Lord. *Amen.*

ADDITIONAL PRAYERS

In Our Work.

ALMIGHTY God, our heavenly Father, who declarest thy glory and showest forth thy handiwork in the heavens and in the earth: Deliver us, we beseech thee, in our several callings, from the service of mammon, that we may do the work which thou givest us to do, in truth, in beauty, and in righteousness, with singleness of heart as thy servants, and to the benefit of our fellow men, for the sake of him who came among us as one that serveth, thy Son, Jesus Christ our Lord. *Amen.*

¶ *Or this.*

MERCIFUL God, who hast given unto us all things that pertain unto life and godliness: Grant that we may be faithful in the exercise of our duties; and that whatsoever thou givest us to do, we may do it heartily, as unto thee, O Lord, and not unto men, through him who hast called us to glory and virtue, Jesus Christ, thy Son, our Lord. *Amen.*

¶ *Or this.*

O GOD, who hast made man and woman to be companions in labour and joint heirs of the gift of life: Grant that each may find the tasks to perform for which nature and grace have been furnished; that the work of each may earn its just praise, and each may eat of the fruit thereof; that each may have confidence in the other and be clothed in strength and dignity, for Jesus Christ's sake. *Amen.*

ADDITIONAL PRAYERS

For Protection.

VISIT, we beseech thee, O Lord, this place, and drive from it all the snares of the enemy. Let thy holy angels dwell herein to preserve us in peace, and may thy blessing be upon us evermore, through Jesus Christ our Lord. *Amen.*

A Holy Life.
For True Devotion.

GRANT us, O Lord, not to mind earthly things, but to love things heavenly; and, while we sojourn among things that are passing away, to cleave to these that shall abide, through Jesus Christ our Lord. *Amen.*

¶ Or this.

FIX our hearts on thee, O God, in pure devotion, that the vain pursuits of this world may have no hold upon us, and that we may be changed, by the consuming fire of thy Spirit, into the image and likeness of thy Son, Jesus Christ our Lord, to whom, with thee and the same Spirit, be all honour and glory, world without end. *Amen.*

¶ Or this.

TAKE our minds, and think through them. Take our lips, and speak through them. Take our hearts, and set them on fire with love for thee. What we know not, teach us. What we have not, give us. What we are not, make us. For Jesus Christ's sake. *Amen.*

ADDITIONAL PRAYERS

For Wisdom.

O GOD of our fathers and Lord of mercy, thou that hast made all things with thy word and ordained that mankind, through thy wisdom, should have dominion over the creatures which thou hast made, ordering the world according to equity and righteousness, and executing judgement with a true heart: Give me wisdom, who is ever about thy seat, and put me not out from among thy children, for I thy servant am a feeble person, of a short time, with too little understanding of thy judgement and laws. Yea, though one is never so perfect among the children of men, yet if thy wisdom is not with him, he shall be nothing worth. O send thy wisdom out of thy holy heavens, and from the throne of thy Majesty, that she may be with me and labour with me, that I may know what is acceptable in thy sight, for she knoweth and understandeth all things, and she shall conduct me soberly in all my works, and preserve me in her power. So shall my works be acceptable in thy sight, O Lord my God. Amen.

For Humility.

INCLINE us, O God, to think humbly of ourselves, to be severe only in the examination of our own conduct, to consider our fellow creatures with kindness, and to judge of all they say and do with that charity which we would desire from them ourselves. Grant this, most merciful Father, for the sake of our blessed Saviour, who hast set us an example of such a temper of forbearance and patience, to whom with thee and the Holy Ghost be all honour and glory, world without end. *Amen.*

ADDITIONAL PRAYERS

For Illumination.

O LORD God, who hast left unto us thy holy word to be a lantern unto our feet and a light unto our steps: Give unto us thy Holy Spirit, that out of that word we may learn what is thy righteous will, and frame our lives in all holy obedience to the same, to thy honour and glory and the increase of our faith, through Jesus Christ our Lord. *Amen.*

For Right Use of the Scriptures.

O GRACIOUS God and most merciful Father, who hast vouchsafed to us the rich and precious jewel of thy most holy word, assist us with thy Spirit, that it may be written in our hearts to our everlasting comfort, to reform us, to renew us according to thine image, to build us up and edify us into the perfect building of thy Christ, sanctifying and increasing in us all heavenly virtues. Grant this, O heavenly Father, for the sake of the same Jesus Christ our Lord. *Amen.*

For Right Use of the Sacraments.

O LORD Jesus Christ, who hast ordained the signs whereby we are assured of thy gracious work in us: Grant that, being born anew of water and the Spirit, we may by faith receive thy precious body and blood, and, in union with thee, offer ourselves a living sacrifice, holy and acceptable to the Father, who liveth and reigneth with thee and the Holy Spirit, ever one God, world without end. *Amen.*

ADDITIONAL PRAYERS

For Right Use of the Lord's Day.

ALMIGHTY God, who hast given a day of rest to thy people, and, through thy Spirit in the church, hast consecrated the first day of the week to be a perpetual memorial of thy Son's resurrection: Grant that we may so use thy gift, that, being refreshed and strengthened in soul and body, we may serve thee faithfully all the days of our life, through the same Jesus Christ our Lord. *Amen.*

For Daily Bread.

O MERCIFUL God, at whose bidding the earth withholdeth her increase, or rendereth her fruits in their season: Give us grace that we may learn, both from thy mercies and thy judgements, our entire dependence upon thee for the supply of our daily bread. And grant that we, remembering that thy blessings are for our trial as well as for our comfort, with thankful hearts may give unto thee of thine own, ministering gladly to the maintenance of thy church, and to the relief of the poor and the afflicted, the widow and the orphan, to the glory of thy holy name, through Jesus Christ our Lord. *Amen.*

For Quiet Confidence.

O GOD of peace, who hast taught us that in returning and rest we shall be saved, in quietness and in confidence shall be our strength: By the might of thy Spirit lift us, we pray thee, to thy presence, where we may be still and know that thou art God, through Jesus Christ our Lord. *Amen.*

ADDITIONAL PRAYERS

For Guidance.

O GOD, by whom the meek are guided in judgement, and light riseth up in darkness for the godly: Grant us, in all our doubts and uncertainties, the grace to ask what thou wouldest have us to do, that the Spirit of wisdom may save us from all false choices, and that in thy light we may see light, and in thy straight path may not stumble, through Jesus Christ our Lord. *Amen.*

For Trustfulness.

O MOST loving Father, who willest us to give thanks for all things, to dread nothing but the loss of thee, and to cast all our care on thee, who carest for us: Preserve us from faithless fears and worldly anxieties, and grant that no clouds of this mortal life may hide from us the light of that love which is immortal, and which thou hast manifested unto us in thy Son, Jesus Christ our Lord. *Amen.*

For Holiness.

O LORD Jesus Christ, who art the true sun of the world, evermore arising and never going down, who, by thy most wholesome appearing and light, dost bring forth, preserve, nourish, and refresh all things – those that are in heaven and those that are on earth – we beseech thee mercifully and favourably to shine into our hearts, that the night and darkness of sins and the mists of errors on every side being driven away (thou brightly shining within our hearts), we may go without stumbling or offence all our life long, and may walk decently and seemly as in the daytime, being pure and clean from the works of darkness, and abounding in all good works which God hath prepared for us to walk in, who with the Father and the Holy Ghost livest and reignest for ever and ever. *Amen.*

For Right Use of This World's Goods.

ALMIGHTY God, whose loving hand hath given us all that we possess: Grant us grace that we may honour thee with our substance, and, remembering the account which we must one day give, may be faithful stewards of thy bounty, through Jesus Christ our Lord. *Amen.*

In Preparation for the Communion.

O GRACIOUS and merciful God, the almighty Father, look down from heaven, the throne of thy great glory, upon me thine unworthy creature, with the eyes of thy covenanted mercy and compassion. O Lord my God, I disclaim all merit; I renounce all righteousness of my own, either inherent in my nature or acquired by my own industry; and I fly for refuge, for pardon and sanctification, to the righteousness of thy Christ. For his sake, for the sake of the blessed Jesus, thy Son, whom thou hast set forth to be a propitiation for fallen man, and in whom alone thou art well pleased, have mercy upon me, receive my prayers, pardon my infirmities, strengthen my weak resolutions, guide my steps to thy holy table, and there feed me by thy Holy Spirit with the meat which perisheth not, but endureth to everlasting life. Amen.

¶ *Or this.*

O GOD most holy, O Lord most righteous, O Father most merciful, who in thy tender bowels of compassion towards me hast freely given me thine only Son, to perform for me in mercy that which thou requirest of me in justice: Look not upon me, I meekly beseech thee, as I am in myself, in my frailties of sinful nature, but graciously behold me in the beauties and perfections of thy blessed Son. O Lord, give me such holy hungering and thirsting after thee, that my longings may be earnest for thee; let thy holy table be delightful to me, and sweeter than all outward enjoyments, that I may truly love it, and joyfully possess thy heavenly comforts by it. Amen.

¶ *Or this.*

O LORD, who for me was wheeled as a lamb to the slaughter; and as a sheep before the shearer is dumb, so thou opened'st not thy mouth; thou didst good to thy enemies, and didst pray earnestly for thy persecutors: O plant in my heart gentleness, patience, and meekness, that I may not be transported with the violent passion of anger, disordered by peevishness or thoughts of revenge, but patiently bear all crosses, and with charity may return blessing for cursing, keeping peace with all men, and so loving my neighbour as myself, and thee more than myself and more than all the world, I may at last come to the place of peace and eternal charity where thou livest, who lovest all men and wouldest have none to perish but all to be saved through thee, O most merciful Saviour and Redeemer.

O thou who sitteth between the cherubim, and whose throne is in the highest heavens: Purge me from all filthiness of the flesh and spirit, that I may perfectly love thee and worthily magnify thy holy name all the days of my life. For thou art gracious and full of compassion, and givest meat unto them that fear thee, and drink from the wells of eternal salvation. Thou preparest a table for us, and anointest our heads with thy heavenly unction, and our cup runneth over. Let thy precious blood which was shed for me, and the water which gushed from thy side, wash me clean, that I may, with a pure heart and a clean soul, come to eat of that best sacrifice, the Lamb slain from the beginning of the world.

O Lord, in the wonders of this holy sacrament thou givest thyself to be the food of our souls in the faith of thy word, in the blessings and graces of thy Holy Spirit. Enkindle in my heart a bright devotion, and extinguish all the fires of hell. Pardon all my sins, and fill me with thy Holy Spirit, that by obedience and love I may adore and honour thee all the days of my life.

Thou hast opened unto me the fountains of thy mercy, and hast invited all penitent sinners to come and receive pardon, the oppressed to be eased, and the sorrowful to be comforted. Admit me, O Lord, to this great celebration of thy loving-kindness, that I may be comforted in all my griefs, healed of all the wounds of my soul and the bruises of my spirit, and finish my journey through this valley of tears until I come to my portion of thy heavenly kingdom. Amen.

ADDITIONAL PRAYERS

¶ *Or this, adding and omitting as needed.*

O MOST holy Lord God, I thy unworthy servant do here prostrate myself before thee in all humility, acknowledging and confessing my manifold sins and wickedness. My whole life has abounded with actual transgressions against every one of thy commandments. I have, O Lord, lived in contempt of thy providence, committing idolatry with thy creatures, taking thy glorious name in vain, profaning thy most holy Sabbath. I have not shown reverence to those to whom it was due; I have envied my brethren, defiled my soul with unchaste desires, laboured to be rich by unlawful means. I have slandered my neighbour, and have coveted his wealth. I have heard thy word, O Lord, but have not believed it. I have known thy word, but have not practiced it. I have come into thy house without reverence, and approached to thy holy table without repentance. I have practiced many sins without remorse. And when I read thy sacred Scriptures, it is not as sweet to me as the honeycomb, but my delight is more in ungodliness, profaneness, and atheism. I have by gluttony and drunkenness pampered my body; I am guilty of pride in my appearance; I am negligent in my calling by mispending my time; I have spoken vainly at my table, and have sinned out of measure against all those means of grace which thou hast been pleased to afford me from time to time. I have wandering eyes, wanton lusts, an ambitious mind, and covetous desires which have no bounds nor limits. I have lascivious ears, unsavoury speeches, and censorious reproaches.

I am still adding sin unto sin, and transgression unto transgression, and am altogether unfaithful in my life, and forgetful of my death and of the day of judgement. My abusing of thy mercies and despising of thy judgements is testified against me, yet, O Lord, I am not ashamed, nor confess myself guilty, but still run on in a course of sinning against the works of thy Holy Spirit and the checks of my own conscience, and have refused thy calls and my own purposes and vows of amendment. O what shall I say, or how shall I open my mouth, O thou that art the preserver of all men? I know that the wages of sin is death, but thy gift, O God, is eternal life, through Jesus Christ our Lord. O enter not into judgement with thy servant, O Lord, for in thy sight is no flesh righteous.

Be merciful, O Lord, be merciful unto my sins for they are great, out of thine abundant mercy forgive me all that is past, and be gracious unto me in preventing sins to come. Correct me, O Lord, but with mercy, not in thy judgement, for then shall I be consumed and brought to nothing. Destroy in me, O Lord, the cursed works of the devil, increase in me daily the gifts of thy Spirit, fit me for that calling in which thou hast placed me, and make me to employ the strength of my body, the gifts of my mind, and whatsoever grace thou hast already or wilt hereafter bestow upon me, to the glory of thy holy name and the eternal salvation of my own soul. And grant in the remainder of the time which I shall live in this present evil world, that my conversation may be in heaven, and that whether I eat or drink or whatsoever I do, I may hear always this voice sounding in my ears: 'Arise you dead and come to judgement.' Many other things, O Lord, I have to beg – things that my ignorance knoweth not how to ask, or my forgetfulness remembereth not – but accept, O Lord, this my humble confession unto thee at this time, and whatever else thou knowest needful for me, supply it by the merits of thy dear Son, my only Lord and Saviour, who taught me thus to pray, Our Father, *&c.*

Before the Communion.

O LORD Jesus Christ, who hast ordained this holy sacrament to be a pledge of thy love, and a continual remembrance of thy passion: Grant that we, who partake thereof in faith, may grow up into thee in all things until we come to thy eternal joy, who with the Father and the Holy Ghost livest and reignest, one God, world without end. *Amen.*

A Confession of Sin.

WE confess to God almighty, the Father, the Son, and the Holy Ghost, that we have sinned in thought, word, and deed, through our own grievous fault. Wherefore we pray God to have mercy upon us.

Almighty God, have mercy upon us, forgive us all our sins, deliver us from all evil, confirm and strengthen us in all goodness, and bring us to life everlasting, through Jesus Christ our Lord. *Amen.*

On Fast Days.

O GOD, who didst command thy people Israel of old to fast and afflict their souls, humbling themselves before thee in weeping and fasting, and who, by the forty days' fast of thy dear Son in the desert, hast both sanctified and taught fasting, and by whose divine inspiration thy church hath in all succeeding ages appointed times of fasting and humiliation before thee: Help us now, O Lord, * give us grace rightly to use these blessed means, and as much as our bodies are subdued, by so much and more may our souls be sanctified and refreshed in thee, O blessed Jesus, to the glory of thy holy name. *Amen.*

* *On Fridays:* while in humble sorrow for our sins, we gratefully call to mind his sufferings who was bruised for our iniquities, wounded for our transgressions, and by whose stripes we are healed,

* *On vigils:* the better to prepare our minds to commemorate, not with worldly but with spiritual joy, the manifestation of thy grace which we are called on by thy church to join in remembering with praise and thanksgiving before thee tomorrow,

* *When fasting for a particular purpose:* and as thou hast shown how powerfully prayer and fasting, when offered from sincere and contrite hearts, avail with thee,

For the Spirit of Prayer.

O ALMIGHTY God, from whom every good prayer cometh, and who pourest out on all who desire it the spirit of grace and supplication: Deliver us, when we draw nigh to thee, from coldness of heart and wanderings of mind, that with steadfast thoughts and kindled affection we may worship thee in spirit and in truth, through Jesus Christ our Lord. *Amen.*

ADDITIONAL PRAYERS

In Sorrow and Suffering.
For the Recovery of the Sick.

O HEAVENLY Father, watch with us, we pray thee, over *N.*, for whom our prayers are offered, and grant that *he* may be restored to that perfect health which it is thine alone to give, through Jesus Christ our Lord. *Amen.*

¶ *Or this.*

O FATHER of mercies and God of all comfort, our only help in time of need: We humbly beseech thee to behold, visit, and relieve thy sick *servant N.*, for whom our prayers are desired. Look upon *him* with the eyes of thy mercy, comfort *him* with a sense of thy goodness, preserve *him* from the temptations of the enemy, and give *him* patience under *his* affliction. In thy good time, restore *him* to health, and enable *him* to lead the rest of *his* life in thy fear and to thy glory, and grant that finally *he* may dwell with thee in life everlasting, through Jesus Christ our Lord. *Amen.*

¶ *Other suitable prayers are found in the Visitation of the Sick; the collects for the third, fourth, and sixth Sundays after the Epiphany; the second and fourth Sundays in Lent; the Sunday next before Easter; the fourth Sunday after Easter; the Sunday after Ascension Day; the second, third, fourth, sixth, eighth, twelfth, and twentieth Sundays after Trinity; and St. Michael and All Angels; as well as the second and fifth of the collects following the Order for the Administration of the Lord's Supper.*

ADDITIONAL PRAYERS

For Those in Anxiety.

ALMIGHTY God, who art afflicted in the afflictions of thy people: Regard with thy tender compassion those in anxiety and distress, bear their sorrows and their cares, supply all their manifold needs, and help both them and us to put our whole trust and confidence in thee, through Jesus Christ our Lord. *Amen.*

For Divine Aid.

GRANT *us,* O Lord, in all *our* duties thy help, in all *our* perplexities thy counsel, in all *our* dangers thy protection, and in all *our* sorrows thy peace, for the sake of Jesus Christ our Saviour. *Amen.*

For Submission to the Will of God.

O GOD our heavenly Father, in whom we live, and move, and have our being: Grant to this thy servant grace to desire only thy most holy will, that whether living or dying *he* may be thine, for his sake who loved us and gave himself for us, Jesus Christ our Lord. *Amen.*

For Those Who Grieve.

O HEAVENLY Father, whose blessed Son Jesus Christ did weep at the grave of Lazarus his friend: Look, we beseech thee, with compassion upon those who are now in sorrow and affliction. Comfort them, O Lord, with thy gracious consolations; make them to know that all things work together for good to those who love thee; and grant them a sure trust and confidence in thy fatherly care, through the same Jesus Christ our Lord. *Amen.*

ADDITIONAL PRAYERS

¶ *Or this.*

ALMIGHTY God, Father of all mercies and giver of all comfort: Deal graciously, we pray thee, with those who mourn, that, casting every care upon thee, they may know the consolation of thy love, through Jesus Christ our Lord. *Amen.*

In Any Kind of Trouble.

O MERCIFUL God and heavenly Father, who hast taught us in thy holy word that thou dost not willingly afflict nor grieve the children of men: Look with pity upon the sorrows of thy servant for whom our prayers are offered. In thy wisdom thou hast seen fit to visit *him* with trouble, and to bring distress upon *him.* Remember *him,* O Lord, in mercy; nourish *his* soul with patience; comfort *him* with a sense of thy goodness; lift up thy countenance upon *him,* and give *him* peace, through Jesus Christ our Lord. *Amen.*

General Prayers.
A General Intercession.

BE mindful, O Lord, of thy people bowed before thee, and of those who are absent through age, sickness, or infirmity. Care for the infants, guide the young, support the aged, encourage the faint-hearted, collect the scattered, and bring the wandering to thy fold. Travel with the voyagers; defend the widows; shield the orphans; deliver the captives; heal the sick. Succour all who are in tribulation, necessity, or distress. Remember for good all those who love us, and those who hate us, and those who have desired us, unworthy as we are, to pray for them. And those whom we have forgotten, do thou, O Lord, remember. For thou art the helper of the helpless, the saviour of the lost, the refuge of the wanderer, the healer of the sick. Thou, who knowest each man's need, and hast heard his prayer, grant unto each according to thy merciful loving-kindness and thy eternal love, through Jesus Christ our Lord. *Amen.*

A Bidding Prayer.

¶ *To be used before sermons or on special occasions.*

¶ *And note that the minister in his discretion may omit any of the clauses in this prayer, or may add others, as the occasion may require.*

Good Christian people, I bid your prayers for Christ's holy catholic church, the blessed company of all faithful people, that it may please God to confirm and strengthen it in purity of faith, in holiness of life, and in perfectness of love, and to restore to it the witness of visible unity, and more especially for that branch of the same planted by God in this land, whereof we are members, that in all things it may work according to God's will, serve him faithfully, and worship him acceptably.

Let us pray for all those who bear authority in this land, that all and every one of them may serve truly in their several callings, to the glory of God and the edifying and well-governing of the people, remembering the account they shall be called upon to give at the last great day.

Let us also pray for the ministers of God's holy word and sacraments: for bishops, [*and more particularly for the*

704

bishop of this diocese,] that they may minister faithfully and wisely the discipline of Christ; likewise for all priests and deacons, [and more particularly for the clergy here residing,] that they may shine as lights in the world, and in all things may adorn the doctrine of God our Saviour.

And let us pray for a due supply of persons fitted to serve God in the ministry and in the state, and to that end, as well as for the good education of all the youth of this land, let us pray for all schools, colleges, and seminaries of sound and godly learning, and for all whose hands are open for their maintenance, that whatever tends to the advancement of true religion and useful learning may flourish and abound.

Let us pray for all the people of this land, that they may live in the true faith and fear of God, and in brotherly charity one towards another.

Let us pray also for all who travel by land or sea or air; for all prisoners and captives; for all who are in sickness or in sorrow; for all who have fallen into grievous sin; for all who – through temptation, ignorance, helplessness, grief, trouble, dread, or the near approach of death – especially need our prayers.

Let us also praise God for rain and sunshine; for the fruits of the earth; for the products of all honest industry; and for all his good gifts, temporal and spiritual, to us and to all men.

Finally, let us yield unto God Most High praise and hearty thanks for the wonderful grace and virtue declared in all his saints, who have been the choice vessels of his grace and the lights of the world in their generations; and pray unto God that we may have grace to direct our lives after their good examples, that, this life ended, we may be made partakers with them of the glorious resurrection and the life everlasting.

And now, brethren, summing up all our petitions and all our thanksgivings, in the words which Christ hath taught us, we make bold to say, Our Father, *&c.*

Additional Collects.
In Advent.

ALMIGHTY God, who in many and various ways didst speak to thy chosen people by the prophets, and hast given us, in thy Son our Saviour Jesus Christ, the fulfilment of the hope of Israel: Hasten, we beseech thee, the coming of the day when all things shall be subject to him, who liveth and reigneth with thee and the Holy Spirit, ever one God, world without end. *Amen.*

O LORD, we beseech thee, give ear to our prayers, and by thy gracious visitation lighten the darkness of our hearts, by our Lord Jesus Christ. *Amen.*

On St. Stephen's Day.

GRANT us, O Lord, to learn to love our enemies, by the example of thy martyr Saint Stephen, who prayed to thee for his persecutors, who livest and reignest with the Father and the Holy Ghost, one God, world without end. *Amen.*

ADDITIONAL PRAYERS

Between Christmas and the Circumcision.

O GOD, who makest us glad with the yearly remembrance of the birth of thine only Son Jesus Christ: Grant that as we joyfully receive him for our redeemer, so we may with sure confidence behold him when he shall come to be our judge, who liveth and reigneth with thee and the Holy Ghost, one God, world without end. *Amen.*

O GOD, who didst wonderfully create, and yet more wonderfully restore, the dignity of human nature: Grant that we may be partakers of the divine nature of thy Son Jesus Christ, even as he humbled himself to partake of our humanity, who liveth and reigneth with thee, in the unity of the Holy Spirit, one God, for ever and ever. *Amen.*

At the New Year.

O ALMIGHTY God, who alone art without variableness or shadow of turning, and hast safely brought us, through the changes of time, to the beginning of another year: We beseech thee to pardon the sins we have committed in the year which is past, and give us grace that we may spend the remainder of our days to thy honour and glory, through Jesus Christ our Lord. *Amen.*

Between the Circumcision and the Epiphany.

A LMIGHTY God, who hast poured upon us the new light of thine incarnate Word: Grant that the same light enkindled in our hearts may shine forth in our lives, through Jesus Christ our Lord. *Amen.*

ADDITIONAL PRAYERS

In Epiphany.

ALMIGHTY God, who by our Saviour Jesus Christ didst manifest thy great glory: We beseech thee to pour thy grace into our hearts, that we may show forth thy glory by word and deed, and lead many into thy presence, through the same thy Son, Jesus Christ our Lord, who liveth and reigneth with thee in the unity of the Holy Spirit, one God, world without end. *Amen.*

Between the Sunday next before Easter, Commonly Called Palm Sunday, and Good Friday.

ALMIGHTY God, whose most dear Son went not up to joy but first he suffered pain, and entered not into glory before he was crucified: Mercifully grant that we, walking in the way of the cross, may find it none other than the way of life and peace, through the same thy Son Jesus Christ our Lord. *Amen.*

GRANT, we beseech thee, almighty God, that we, who celebrate with reverence the Paschal feast, may be found worthy to attain to everlasting joys, through Jesus Christ our Lord. *Amen.*

ASSIST us mercifully with thy help, O Lord God of our salvation, that we may enter with joy upon the meditation of those mighty acts whereby thou hast given unto us life and immortality, through Jesus Christ our Lord. *Amen.*

ADDITIONAL PRAYERS

On the Thursday before Easter, Commonly Called Maundy Thursday.

ALMIGHTY Father, whose dear Son on the night before he suffered death did institute the sacrament of his body and blood: Mercifully grant that we may receive it thankfully in remembrance of the same Jesus Christ our Lord, who in these holy mysteries giveth us a pledge of eternal life, who now liveth and reigneth with thee and the Holy Spirit, ever one God, world without end. *Amen.*

ALMIGHTY Father, whose Son Jesus Christ hast taught us that whatsoever we do for the least of our brethren, we do also unto him: Grant unto us the will to be the servant of others, as he was the servant of all, who didst give up his life and died for us, yet now liveth and reigneth with thee and the Holy Spirit, ever one God, world without end. *Amen.*

Between Easter Day and Ascension Day.

O GOD, who for our redemption didst give thine only-begotten Son to the death of the cross, and by his glorious resurrection hast delivered us from the power of our enemy: Grant us so to die daily unto sin, that we may evermore live with him in the joy of his resurrection, through the same Jesus Christ our Lord. *Amen.*

O LORD God almighty, whose blessed Son, our Saviour, Jesus Christ, did on the third day rise triumphant over death: Raise us, we beseech thee, from the death of sin unto the life of righteousness, that we may seek those things which are above, where he sitteth on thy right hand in glory, and this we beg for the sake of the same thy Son, Jesus Christ our Lord. *Amen.*

In Whitsun Week.

SEND, we beseech thee, almighty God, thy Holy Spirit into our hearts, that he may direct and rule us according to thy will, comfort us in all our afflictions, defend us from all error, and lead us into all truth, through Jesus Christ our Lord, who with thee and the same Holy Spirit liveth and reigneth, one God, world without end. *Amen.*

In Trinitytide.

O GOD, who hast taught us that by loving thee and our neighbour we keep all thy holy commandments: Grant unto us the spirit of grace and peace, that we may be devoted to thee with our whole heart and united to each other with a pure will, through Jesus Christ our Lord. *Amen.*

GRANT us, O Lord, to trust in thee with all our hearts, for as thou confoundest the proud, who confide in their own strength, so dost thou never forsake those who make their boast in thy mercy, through Jesus Christ our Lord, who liveth and reigneth with thee and the Holy Spirit, one God, now and forever. *Amen.*

ADDITIONAL PRAYERS

*On St. Mary Magdalene's Day.**

Merciful Father, give us grace that we may never presume to sin through the example of any creature, but if it shall happen at any time that we offend thy Divine Majesty, that we may then truly repent and lament the same, after the example of Mary Magdalene, and by lively faith obtain remission of all our sins, through the merit alone of thy Son, our Saviour Christ. *Amen.*

On the Transfiguration.†

Almighty Father, whose most dear Son, before he suffered death upon the cross, was revealed in majesty: Grant unto us thy servants faith to behold the light of his countenance, that we may be strengthened to bear the cross, and be changed into his likeness from glory to glory, who liveth and reigneth with thee and the Holy Ghost, one God, now and for ever. *Amen.*

Prayers for the Commemoration of a Saint.

O almighty God, who hast called us to faith in thee, and hast compassed us about with so great a cloud of witnesses: Grant that we, encouraged by the good examples of thy saints, and especially of thy servant *N.*, may persevere in running the race that is set before us, until at length, through thy mercy, we, with them, attain to thine eternal joy, through him who is the author and finisher of our faith, thy Son Jesus Christ our Lord. *Amen.*

* July 22.
† August 6.

Almighty God, who dost choose thine elect out of every nation, and dost show forth thy glory in their lives: Grant, we pray thee, that, following the example of thy servant *N.*, we may be fruitful in good works to the praise of thy holy name, through Jesus Christ our Lord. *Amen.*

Almighty God, who didst raise up thy servant *N.* to proclaim thy grace in the church: Keep all thy faithful people, that they may not be tempted away by any human conceit, nor avarice, nor worldly wisdom, but remain steadfast and immovable in the gospel of Jesus Christ, our only mediator and advocate. *Amen.*

O God, who didst show forth the light of thy gospel in the land of —, through thy faithful servant *N.*: Enlighten our hearts, that we may receive with faith thy promises, and so be numbered with thy saints in glory everlasting, through Jesus Christ our Lord. *Amen.*

For Feasts of Apostles and Evangelists.

Almighty God, who by thy Son didst call the apostles [or *evangelists*], giving them grace to preach the gospel to the ends of the earth: Grant to us also thy grace, that we may hold fast their doctrine, and, following their example, set forward thy kingdom, through the same Jesus Christ, thy Son our Lord, who liveth and reigneth with thee in the unity of the Holy Spirit, one God, world without end. *Amen.*

ADDITIONAL PRAYERS

For the Feast of a National Martyr.

BLESSED Lord, in whose sight the death of thy saints is precious: We magnify thy name for the abundant grace bestowed upon *N.*, by which *he* was enabled so cheerfully to follow the steps of *his* blessed Master and Saviour, in a constant meek suffering of all barbarous indignities, and at last resisting unto blood; and even then, according to the same pattern, praying for *his* murderers. Let *his* memory, O Lord, be ever blessed among us, that we may follow the example of *his* courage and constancy, *his* meekness and patience, and great charity. And grant that this our land may be freed from the vengeance of *his* righteous blood, and thy mercy glorified in the forgiveness of our sins, and all for Jesus Christ's sake, our only mediator and advocate. *Amen.*

For a Day of National Commemoration.

ALMIGHTY and everlasting God, by whom the whole world is governed and sanctified: Receive our humble supplications, we beseech thee, for this our nation, that it may be ruled evermore in righteousness and equity, and that we thy people may serve and glorify thy holy name, through the power of thy blessed Son Jesus Christ, who with thee and the Holy Spirit liveth and reigneth, ever one God, world without end. *Amen.*

Concluding Prayers.
After Any Service.

Now the God of peace, who brought again from the dead our Lord Jesus, that great shepherd of the sheep, through the blood of the everlasting covenant, make you perfect in every good work to do his will, working in you that which is well-pleasing in his sight, through Jesus Christ, to whom be glory for ever and ever. *Amen.*

After the Communion.

ALMIGHTY God, eternal Father, we have sat at thy feet, learned from thy word, and eaten from thy table. We give thee thanks and praise for accepting us into thy family. Send us out with thy blessing, to live and to witness for thee in the power of thy Spirit, through Jesus Christ, the firstborn from the dead. *Amen.*

¶ *Or this.*

STRENGTHEN us for thy service, O Lord; and may the ears which have heard thy word be deaf to clamour and dispute; may the tongues which have sung thy praise be free from deceit; and may the bodies which have been fed with thy body be refreshed with the fulness of thy life; glory be to thee, world without end. *Amen.*

After Intercessions.

HEAR us and help us, O God of our salvation, and answer us graciously in these our suits and petitions, for Jesus Christ's sake, to whom, with thee and thy Holy Spirit, be rendered of us and of thy whole church, all glory and praise, power and dominion, both now and evermore. *Amen.*

After an Offering.

A LMIGHTY God, we humbly beseech thee to accept the offerings which we have presented unto thee, and mercifully to receive our supplications and prayers, and grant that those things which we have faithfully asked according to thy will, may effectually be obtained, to the relief of our necessity and to the setting forth of thy glory, through Jesus Christ our Lord. *Amen.*

Thanksgivings.
For Fruitful Seasons and on National Days of Thanksgiving.

O ALMIGHTY and everlasting God, who crownest the year with thy goodness, and hast given unto us the fruits of the earth in their season: We yield thee humble and hearty thanks for these thy bounties, beseeching thee to give us grace to use them rightly, to thy glory and the relief of those in need, through Jesus Christ our Lord. *Amen.*

In a Lean Year.

A LMIGHTY God and heavenly Father, who hast in wisdom seen fit to withhold from us at this time thine accustomed bounty: We most humbly praise thee for still bestowing upon us far more than we deserve. Make us truly thankful for our many blessings, and increase in us more and more a lively faith and love, and a humble submission to thy blessed will, through Jesus Christ our Lord. *Amen.*

For Use on Memorial Days.

ALMIGHTY God, our heavenly Father, in whose hands are the living and the dead: We give thanks unto thee for all thy servants who have laid down their lives in the service of our country. Grant, we beseech thee, that as they have laboured to defend our liberties, so we and all the people of this land may have grace to maintain these liberties in righteousness and peace, through Jesus Christ our Lord. *Amen.*

For the Church.

ALMIGHTY God, whose mercy is over all thy works: We praise thee for the blessings which have been brought to mankind by thy holy church throughout all the world. We bless thee for drawing us into fellowship with thy Son, Jesus Christ our Lord, by the operation of thy Spirit in the preaching of the gospel, the teaching of the Scriptures, and the faithful use of the sacraments, whereby we are made one body and each of us members one of another. We thank thee for the holy example of thy saints in all ages, for thy servants departed this life in thy faith and fear, and for the memory and example of all that has been true and good in their lives. And we humbly beseech thee that we may be numbered with them in the great company of the redeemed in heaven, through Jesus Christ our Lord. *Amen.*

ADDITIONAL THANKSGIVINGS

For the Spread of the Gospel.

ALMIGHTY and everlasting God, who in days of old didst cause thy word to grow mightily and to prevail: We praise and magnify thy holy name for the manifestation of thy presence in this our day, and we beseech thee to pour out thy Spirit upon the church, that thy way may be known upon earth and thy saving health among all nations, through Jesus Christ our Lord. *Amen.*

A Commemoration of the Faithful Departed.

O LORD Jesus Christ, Son of the living God, who hast opened unto us the gate of everlasting life, and art the peace and light of those who rest in thee: In company with thy holy apostles, prophets, and martyrs, and with all the faithful departed, we praise and glorify thee for the fulness of joy which thou givest to all who put their trust in thee, who with the Father and the Holy Spirit livest and reignest, one God, world without end. *Amen.*

For an Offering.

BLESSED be thou, O Lord God, for ever and ever. Thine, O Lord, is the greatness, and the glory, and the victory, and the majesty, for all that is in the heaven and in the earth is thine; thine is the kingdom, O Lord, and thou art exalted as head above all; both riches and honour come of thee, and of thine own do we give unto thee. *Amen.*

For Deliverance in Peril.

ALMIGHTY God, who art a strong tower of defence unto thy servants in the time of trouble: We yield thee praise and hearty thanks for our deliverance from the dangers which lately encompassed us [*and for thy gracious gift of peace*]. We confess that it is of thy goodness alone that we are preserved, and we beseech thee still to continue thy mercies towards us, that we may always acknowledge thee as our saviour and mighty deliverer, through Jesus Christ our Lord. *Amen.*

For Recovery from Sickness.

ALMIGHTY God and heavenly Father, we give thee humble thanks, that thou hast been graciously pleased to deliver *N.* from *his* bodily sickness, in whose behalf we bless and praise thy name, in the presence of all thy people. Grant, we beseech thee, O gracious Father, that *he*, through thy help, may both faithfully live in this world according to thy will, and be *a partaker* of everlasting glory in the life to come, through Jesus Christ our Lord. *Amen.*

For All Blessings.

O MOST merciful Father, we humbly thank thee for all thy gifts so freely bestowed upon us. For life and health and safety, for power to work and leisure to rest, for all that is beautiful in creation and in the lives of men, we praise and magnify thy holy name. But above all, we thank thee for our spiritual mercies in Christ Jesus our Lord, for the means of grace, and for the hope of glory. Fill our hearts with all joy and peace in believing, through Jesus Christ our Lord. *Amen.*

Appendix III.*

Additional Rubrics.

The Order for Morning and Evening Prayer.

¶ *A hymn, anthem, or psalm may be sung before the opening sentences (pp. 1, 17).*

¶ *On any day other than a Sunday, the exhortation (pp. 2, 18) may be shortened at the discretion of the minister.*

¶ *The Venite may be omitted on Ash Wednesday and Good Friday.*

¶ *In the Benedicite, omnia opera the words* praise him and magnify him for ever *may be sung or said following each group of verses instead of at the end of each verse.*

¶ *The Benedicite, omnia opera is suitable for use in place of the Te Deum laudamus in Advent, from Septuagesima till Easter Even, on Ember Days outside Whitsun Week, on Rogation Days, and when the third chapter of the Book of Daniel is read as the first lesson.*

¶ *The proper collect, epistle, and gospel for the Epiphany and the Ascension may serve for the days after until the following Sunday, except when a holy day falls between Ascen-*

---

* These rubrics are from later editions of the Book of Common Prayer authorized for use in various Anglican churches; they reflect customs from long years of use and adaptation of the prayer book liturgies. These rubrics do not follow verbatim the source texts, which themselves differ, but are instead a distillation that avoids repetition and aims for consistency of style. They may appear prescriptive, but the editors disclaim any such authority; permission to follow them in public worship may be granted only by the appropriate ecclesiastical authority.

sion Day and the Sunday after Ascension Day (in which case the collect for Ascension Day may also be used following the proper collect for the holy day).

¶ *If any of the holy days for which proper lessons are appointed in the table (p. xxxi) fall upon a Sunday which is the First Sunday in Advent, Easter Day, Whitsunday, or Trinity Sunday, the lessons appointed for such Sunday shall be read; but if it fall upon any other Sunday, the lessons appointed either for the Sunday or for the holy day may be read at the discretion of the minister.*

¶ *Upon any Sunday or holy day, the minister may read the epistle or the gospel in place of the second lesson.*

¶ *The people may join with the priest in saying the general thanksgiving (p. 44).*

¶ *A sermon may be preached after the anthem (pp. 14, 24) or the grace (pp. 16, 26). If a sermon is preached after the grace, it may be preceded by an anthem or hymn.*

¶ *At the conclusion of the service, the offerings of the people may be received and presented at the Lord's table.*

¶ *Morning Prayer may be abbreviated when followed by the Communion. It may begin with the versicle,* O Lord, open thou our lips *(p. 4) and proceed through the first canticle (p. 10). Then may be omitted the second lesson, second canticle, and Apostles' Creed (pp. 10-12). The rest of Morning Prayer may then be said, except for the collect of the day (p. 13) and the prayers after the third collect (pp. 14-16). The Lord's Prayer at the start of the Communion may be omitted (p. 242). Morning Prayer may be similarly abbreviated when followed by the Ante-Communion, except that it may begin with the sentences (p. 1).*

ADDITIONAL RUBRICS

The Litany.

¶ *On the days appointed for its use, the Litany may be said after Morning Prayer or before the Communion service.*

¶ *When the Litany precedes the Communion, the Litany may end with the Lord's Prayer (p. 35), after which the Communion may begin with the collect for purity (p. 242).*

¶ *When the prayers of the congregation are desired on behalf of any person, the minister may give notice before the Litany and may insert the words* especially those for whom our prayers are desired *in the appropriate suffrage.*

¶ *After the suffrage beginning* That it may please thee to illuminate all bishops, &c. *(p. 33) may be added:*

That it may please thee to send forth labourers into thy harvest,

We beseech thee to hear us, good Lord.

The Lord's Supper, or Holy Communion.

¶ *A hymn, anthem, or psalm may be sung before the Lord's Prayer (p. 242).*

¶ *The summary of the law may be substituted for the Ten Commandments (which, however, shall always be said at least once a month):*

OUR Lord Jesus Christ said: 'Hear, O Israel, the Lord our God is one Lord; and thou shalt love the Lord thy God with all thy heart, and with all thy soul, and with all thy mind, and with all thy strength. This is the first commandment. And the second is like, namely this: Thou shalt love thy neighbour as thyself. There is none other commandment greater than these. On these two commandments hang all the law and the prophets.'

Lord, have mercy upon us, and write these thy laws in our hearts, we beseech thee.

¶ *In addition to the Ten Commandments or summary of the law may be sung or said,*

Lord, have mercy upon us.
Christ, have mercy upon us.
Lord, have mercy upon us.

¶ *The Greek Kyrie, eleison and Christe, eleison may be used (in threefold or ninefold form) instead of the English.*

¶ *In place of a collect for all those in civil authority (p. 245) may be said the collect on p. 267 beginning* O almighty Lord and everlasting God.

¶ *When an Old Testament lesson is desired, the proper first lesson for the Sunday or holy day (p. xxix) may be read before the epistle.*

¶ *A hymn, anthem, or psalm may be sung after the epistle.*

¶ *After the announcement of the gospel may be said or sung,* Glory be to thee, O Lord; *and after the gospel is ended,* Thanks be to thee, O Lord, *or* Hallelujah.

¶ *Those who do not intend to communicate may withdraw from the service at the end of the prayer for the whole state of Christ's church militant (p. 251).*

¶ *The exhortations may be shortened or omitted, provided that the exhortation in the Communion service is read to the people at least three times in the year and always on the First Sundays in Advent and Lent.*

¶ *The people may join with the priest in saying the prayer commonly called the prayer of humble access (p. 261).*

ADDITIONAL RUBRICS

¶ *During the distribution, one or more hymns or anthems may be sung.*

¶ *The words appointed to be said upon delivering the bread and the cup may be said once to every two communicants, or once to as many as shall kneel together for receiving the communion.*

¶ *The two post-communion prayers (pp. 264, 265) may be said in succession at the same service.*

¶ *Before the benediction (p. 266), the minister may say one or more of the collects from pp. 266-268, or other prayers.*

The Ministration of Baptism.

¶ *The people may join with the minister in saying the prayer that begins* Almighty and everlasting God, heavenly Father, we give thee humble thanks *(pp. 274, 285, 293).*

The Visitation of the Sick.

¶ *Instead of the short litany beginning* Remember not, Lord *(p. 324), the minister may read the comfortable words from the Communion service (p. 258).*

¶ *When a shorter service is desired, after the prayer beginning* O Lord, look down from heaven *(p. 325), the minister may read Psalm 23 or another appropriate psalm (e.g. Psalm 20, 27, 30, 42, 43, 71:1-17, 77, 86, 91, 103, 121, 138, 142, or 146), continuing with* O Saviour of the world *(p. 332).*

The Order for the Burial of the Dead.

¶ *If there is no Communion, the minister may dismiss those who are gathered together, saying* Let us pray, *followed by the collect beginning* O almighty Lord and everlasting God, vouchsafe, we beseech thee *(p. 267) and the grace (p. 16).*

¶ *If question arise as to whether this office should be used for the burial of any person, reference shall be made to the ordinary.*

General Rubrics.

¶ *If the people are instructed to say a text after the minister, it may be said with the minister.*

¶ *One or more of the offertory sentences provided in the Communion service (p. 247) may be used on any other occasion of public worship when the offerings of the people are received.*

¶ *Rubrics that use male pronouns are construed as generic, that is, as referring to men and women, where consistent with the appropriate ecclesiastical constitution and canons.*

¶ *At the discretion of the minister, Morning or Evening Prayer, the Litany, and Communion may be used as separate services or in any combination, subject to the permission of the ordinary, to whom due notice shall be given of any proposed change.*

Appendix IV.*

An Alternative Table of Lessons.

¶ *When the First Sunday in Advent occurs in a year with an even number the lessons appointed for Year I shall be read, and when it occurs in a year with an odd number the lessons appointed for Year II shall be read, for the whole of that ecclesiastical year.*

¶ *It is convenient that, to assist the congregation, the minister shall say before every lesson: 'The first (or second) lesson is written in (such a book) in (such a chapter) beginning at (such a verse).'*

¶ *When a lesson begins with a pronoun, the reader shall substitute the appropriate noun.*

¶ *In this table, verses are stated inclusively.*

¶ *Verses printed within brackets are permissive additions to the appointed passages.*

¶ *The letter a after the number of a verse signifies the first part of that verse, and the letter b the second part.*

¶ *When only a single verse is given, the lesson continues to the end of the chapter.*

¶ *In any church where Morning or Evening Prayer only is said on successive Sundays it is convenient that the sequence of lessons for either Morning or Evening Prayer should be adopted when necessary to preserve continuity.*

ALTERNATIVE TABLE OF LESSONS

	Morning Prayer		Evening Prayer	
	1 Lesson	*2 Lesson*	*1 Lesson*	*2 Lesson*

THE FIRST SUNDAY IN ADVENT

I	Isa. 1:1-20	Matt. 24:1-28	Isa. 2:10-22	1 Thess. 5
II	Isa. 1:1-20	Rev. 14:13–15:4	Isa. 2:10-22	John 3:1-21
M	Isa. 3:1-15	Mark 1:1-20	Isa. 4:2-6	Rev. 6
T	5:1-17	1:21-45	5:18-30	7
W	6	2:1-22	8:16–9:7	8
T	9:8–10:4	2:23–3:12	10:5-23	9
F	10:24–11:9	3:13-35	11:10–12:6	10
S	13:1–14:2	4:1-20	14:3-27	11

THE SECOND SUNDAY IN ADVENT

I	Isa. 5:1-16	Matt. 24:29-51	Isa. 5:18-30	2 Tim. 3:14–4:8
II	Isa. 11:1-9	Rev. 20:11–21:7	Isa. 11:10–12:6	Luke 1:1-25
M	Isa. 17	Mark 4:21-41	Isa. 18	Rev. 12
T	19:1-17	5:1-20	19:18-25	13
W	21:1-12	5:21-43	22:1-14	14
T	24	6:1-13	28:1-13	15
F	28:14-29	6:14-29	29:1-14	16
S	29:15-24	6:30-56	30:1-18	17

THE THIRD SUNDAY IN ADVENT

I	Isa. 25:1-9	Matt. 25:1-30	Isa. 26:1-13	1 Tim. 1:12–2:8
II	Isa. 28:9-22	Rev. 21:9–22:5	Isa. 30:8-21	Matt. 3
M	Isa. 30:19-33	Mark 7:1-23	Isa. 31	Rev. 18
T	38:1-20	7:24–8:10	40:1-11	19
W	40:12-31	8:11–9:1	41	20
T	42:1-17	9:2-32	42:18–43:13	21:1-14
F	43:14–44:5	9:33-50	44:6-23	21:15–22:5
S	44:24–45:13	10:1-31	45:14-25	22:6-21

THE FOURTH SUNDAY IN ADVENT

I	Isa. 32:1-8	Matt. 25:31	Isa. 40:1-11	2 Pet. 3:1-14
II	Isa. 35	Rev. 22:6	Isa. 40:1-11	Luke 1:26-45

ALTERNATIVE TABLE OF LESSONS

	Morning Prayer		Evening Prayer	
	1 Lesson	*2 Lesson*	*1 Lesson*	*2 Lesson*
M	Isa. 46	Mark 10:32	Isa. 47	Jude 1-16 [17-25]
T	48	11:1-26	50:4-10	[1-16] 17-25
W	51:1-16	11:27–12:12	51:17–52:12	2 Pet. 1
T	52:13–53:12	12:13-34	54	2
F	56:1-8	12:35–13:13	57:15-21	3
S	59	13:14-37	- · -	- · -

CHRISTMAS EVE

I·II	- · -	- · -	Zech. 2:10-13	Titus 2:11–3:7

CHRISTMAS DAY

I·II	Isa. 9:2-7	Luke 2:1-20	Isa. 7:10-14	1 John 4:7-21

ST. STEPHEN

I·II	Gen. 4:1-10	Acts 6	2 Chr. 24:15-22	Acts 7:59–8:8

ST. JOHN THE EVANGELIST

I·II	Exod. 33:9-19	John 13:21-35	Isa. 6:1-8	1 John 5:1-12

THE INNOCENTS' DAY

I·II	Jer. 31:1-17	Matt. 18:1-10	Bar. 4:21-27	Mark 10:13-16

SUNDAY AFTER CHRISTMAS DAY*

I·II	Isa. 41:8-20	Col. 1:1-20	Isa. 12	Phil. 2:1-11

DECEMBER

29	Isa. 55	John 1:14-18	Isa. 60:1-12	Matt. 11:2-6
30	60:13-22	3:16-21	61	16:13-20
31	62	6:41-58	Deut. 10:12–11:1	Luke 21:25-36

CIRCUMCISION OF CHRIST

I·II	Gen. 17:1-13	Rom. 2:17-29	Deut. 30	Col. 2:8-15

* Note: The lessons of the First Sunday after Christmas will be read only when 29, 30, or 31 December is a Sunday.

ALTERNATIVE TABLE OF LESSONS

	Morning Prayer		Evening Prayer	
	1 Lesson	2 Lesson	1 Lesson	2 Lesson

SECOND SUNDAY AFTER CHRISTMAS*

I·II	Isa. 41:21-29	1 John 1:1–2:6	Isa. 12	Phil. 2:1-11

JANUARY

2	Isa. 63:1-6	Matt. 1:18-25	Isa. 63:7-19	1 Thess. 1
3	64	2	65:1-16	2:1-16
4	65:17-25	3:1–4:11	66:1-9	2:17–3:13
5	66:10	4:12–5:16	60:1-7	Rom. 15:8-21

THE EPIPHANY

I·II	Isa. 49:1-13	Luke 3:15-22	Isa. 60:9-22	John 2:1-11

WEEKDAYS AFTER EPIPHANY

M	Hos. 2:14–3:5	Matt. 5:17-48	Hos. 4:1-11	1 Thess. 4:1-12
T	5:8–6:6	6:1-18	8	4:13–5:11
W	9	6:19-34	10	5:12-28
T	11	7	12	2 Thess. 1
F	13:1-14	8:1-17	14	2
S	Joel 1	8:18-34	Joel 2:1-14	3

THE FIRST SUNDAY AFTER EPIPHANY

I	Isa. 49:13-23	Matt. 17:1-13	Isa. 61	Matt. 2
II	Isa. 42:1-12	John 4:1-26 [27-42]	Isa. 43:1-13	John 12:20-36a
M	Joel 2:15-32	Matt. 9:1-17	Joel 3	Gal. 1
T	Amos 1	9:18-34	Amos 2	2
W	3	9:35–10:23	4	3
T	5	10:24-42	6	4:1–5:1
F	7	11	8	5:2-26
S	9	12:1-21	Obad.	6

* Note: The lessons of the Second Sunday after Christmas will be read only when 2, 3, 4, or 5 January is a Sunday, and in the last case the Morning Lessons only.

ALTERNATIVE TABLE OF LESSONS

	Morning Prayer		Evening Prayer	
	1 Lesson	*2 Lesson*	*1 Lesson*	*2 Lesson*

THE SECOND SUNDAY AFTER EPIPHANY

I	Isa. 43:14–44:5	Eph. 1	Isa. 44:6-23	Mark 1:35-45
II	Amos 3	John 6:22-40	Mic. 3:5-12	John 4:43–5:9
M	Jonah 1 & 2	Matt. 12:22-50	Jonah 3 & 4	1 Cor. 1:1-25
T	Mic. 1	13:1-23	Mic. 2	1:26–2:16
W	3	13:24-43	4:1–5:1	3
T	5:2-15	13:44-58	6	4:1-17
F	7	14	Nah. 1	4:18–5:13
S	Nah. 2	15:1-28	3	6

THE THIRD SUNDAY AFTER EPIPHANY

I	Isa. 45:9-25	Eph. 2	Isa. 46:3-13	Mark 7:24-37
II	Amos 5:6-24	John 6:41-71	Mic. 4:1-7	John 9
M	Hab. 1	1 Cor. 7	Hab. 2	1 Cor. 8
T	3:2-19	9	Zeph. 1	10:1–11:1
W	Zeph. 2	11:2-34	3	12:1-27
T	Zech. 11	12:27–13:13	Zech. 13	14:1-19
F	Mal. 1	14:20-40	Mal. 2:1-16	15:1-34
S	2:17–3:12	15:35-58	3:13–4:6	16

THE FOURTH SUNDAY AFTER EPIPHANY

I	Isa. 48:12-22	Eph. 3	Isa. 54:1-14	Luke 13:1-17
II	Amos 7:1-15	John 8:1-11	Mic. 5:2-7	John 10:1-18
M	Jer. 1	2 Cor. 1:1–2:11	Jer. 2:1-13	2 Cor. 2:12–3:18
T	4:1-18	4	5:1-19	5
W	5:20-31	5:20–7:1	6:1-21	7:2-16
T	7:1-28	8	8	9
F	9:1-24	10	10	11
S	14	12:1-13	15	12:14–13:14

THE FIFTH SUNDAY AFTER EPIPHANY

I	Isa. 59:12-20	Eph. 5:15–6:9	Isa. 60	Mark 2:1-12
II	Amos 8:4-12	John 7:14-36	Mic. 6:1-8	John 5:19-29 [30-40]

ALTERNATIVE TABLE OF LESSONS

	Morning Prayer		Evening Prayer	
	1 Lesson	*2 Lesson*	*1 Lesson*	*2 Lesson*
M	Jer. 17:1-18	Acts 15:1-29	Jer. 17:19-27	Acts 15:30–16:5
T	18:1-17	16:6-40	20	17:1-15
W	23:9-32	17:16-34	30:1-22	18:1-23
T	31:1-20	18:24–19:7	31:23-40	19:8-20
F	33:1-13	19:21-41	33:14-26	20:1-16
S	35:1-11	20:17-38	35:12-19	21:1-16

THE SIXTH SUNDAY AFTER EPIPHANY

I	Isa. 63:7-16	Eph. 6:10-24	Isa. 64	Luke 7:1-10
II	Amos 9:5-15	John 7:37-52	Mic. 7:1-9	John 8:12-30
M	Tob. 4:5-19	Acts 21:17-36	Tob. 13	Acts 21:37–22:22
T	Bar. 1:15–2:10	22:23–23:11	Bar. 2:11-35	23:12-35
W	3:1-8	24:1-23	3:9-37	24:24–25:12
T	4:21-30	25:13-27	4:36–5:9	26
F	2 Macc. 4:7–17	27:1-26	2 Macc. 6:12-31	27:27-44
S	7:1-19	28:1-15	7:20-41	28:16-31

SEPTUAGESIMA SUNDAY

I	Gen. 1:1–2:3	John 1:1-18	Gen. 2:4-25	Rev. 4
II	Gen. 1:1–2:3	Rev. 21:1-7	Gen. 2:4-25	Mark 10:1-16
M	Gen. 3	Matt. 15:29–16:12	Gen. 4:1-16	Rom. 1
T	6:5-22	16:13-28	7	2
W	8:1-14	17:1-23	8:15–9:17	3
T	11:1-9	17:24–18:14	11:27–12:10	4
F	13	18:15-35	14	5
S	15	19:1-15	16	6

SEXAGESIMA SUNDAY

I	Gen. 3	1 Cor. 10:1-13 [14-24]	Gen. 4:1-16	1 John 3:1-15
II	Gen. 3	1 Cor. 6:12-20	Gen. 37	Luke 10:25-37
M	Gen. 17:1-22	Matt. 19:16–20:16	Gen. 18	Rom. 7

ALTERNATIVE TABLE OF LESSONS

	Morning Prayer		Evening Prayer	
	1 Lesson	2 Lesson	1 Lesson	2 Lesson
T	19:1-3, 12-29	20:17-34	21	8:1-17
W	22:1-19	21:1-22	23	8:18-39
T	24:1-28	21:23-46	24:29-67	9
F	25:7-11, 19-34	22:1-33	27:1-40	10
S	27:41–28:22	22:34–23:12	29:1-20	11

QUINQUAGESIMA SUNDAY

I	Gen. 12:1-9	1 Cor. 12:4-31	Gen. 6:5-22	Luke 17:20-37
II	Gen. 12:1-9	1 Cor. 12:4-31	Gen. 41:1-40	1 John 4:7-21
M	Gen. 31:1-9, 14-21	Matt. 23:13-39	Gen. 31:22–32:2	Rom. 12
T	32:3-30	24:1-28	33	13
W	Isa. 58	Mark 2:13-22	Dan. 9:3-19	Heb. 3:12–4:13
T	Gen. 35:1-20	Matt. 24:29-51	Gen. 37	Rom. 14
F	39	25:1-30	40	15
S	41:1-40	25:31-46	41:41-57	16

THE FIRST SUNDAY IN LENT

I	Gen. 13	Luke 15:1-10	Gen. 8:15–9:17	Mark 14:1-26
II	Gen. 27:1-40	Heb. 4:14–5:10	Gen. 42	Luke 22:1-23
M*	Gen. 42	Matt. 26:1-30	Gen. 43	Phil. 1
M	Gen. 43:1-14	Matt. 26:1-30	Gen. 43:15-34	Phil. 1
T	44	26:31-56	45:1-15	2
W	45:16–46:7	26:57-75	46:26–47:12	3
T	47:13	27:1-26	48	4
F	49:1-32	27:27-56	49:33–50:26	Col. 1:1-20
S	Exod. 1:1-14, 22–2:10	27:57–28:20	Exod. 2:11-22	1:21–2:7

THE SECOND SUNDAY IN LENT

I	Gen. 18:1-16	Luke 15:11-32	Gen. 11:1-9	Mark 14:27-52
II	Gen. 28:10-22	Heb. 10:19-39	Gen. 43:1-15 [16-26], 27-34	Luke 22:24-53

* Two sets of lessons are provided for the Monday after the First Sunday in Lent, the first for use in Year I and the second for use in Year II.

ALTERNATIVE TABLE OF LESSONS

	Morning Prayer		Evening Prayer	
	1 Lesson	*2 Lesson*	*1 Lesson*	*2 Lesson*
M	Exod. 2:23–3:22	John 1:1-28	Exod. 4:1-23	Col. 2:8–3:11
T	4:27–6:1	1:29-51	6:2-13 & 7:1-7	3:12–4:1
W	7:8-25	2	8:1-19	4:2-18
T	8:20–9:12	3:1-21	9:13-35	Phlm.
F	10:1-20	3:22-36	10:21–11:10	Eph. 1
S	12:1-20	4:1-26	12:21-36	2

THE THIRD SUNDAY IN LENT

I	Gen. 18:17-33	Luke 18:1-14	Gen. 24:1-28	Mark 14:53-72
II	Gen. 29:1-20	Heb. 12:14-29	Gen. 44:1–45:8	Luke 22:54-71
M	Exod. 12:37-51	John 4:27-54	Exod. 13:1-16	Eph. 3
T	13:17–14:14	5:1-23	14:15-31	4:1-16
W	15:1-26	5:24-47	15:27–16:35	4:17-30
T	17	6:1-21	18	4:31–5:21
F	19	6:22-40	20:1-21	5:22–6:9
S	22:20–23:17	6:41-71	23:20-33	6:10-24

THE FOURTH SUNDAY IN LENT

I	Exod. 1:8-14, 22–2:10	Luke 18:35–19:10	Gen. 24:29-67	Mark 15:1-21
II	Gen. 32:3-30	Heb. 13:1-21	Gen. 45:16–46:7	Luke 23:1-25
M	Exod. 24	John 7:1-24	Exod. 25:1-22	1 Tim. 1:1-17
T	28:1-4 & 29:1-9	7:25-53	29:38–30:16	1:18–2:15
W	32	8:1-30	33	3
T	34	8:31-59	35:20–36:7	4
F	40:17	9	Lev. 6:8-30	5
S	Lev. 19:1-18, 30-37	10:1-21	25:1-24	6

THE FIFTH SUNDAY IN LENT

I	Exod. 2:23–3:20	Matt. 20:17-28	Exod. 4:27–6:1	Mark 15:22-39
II	Exod. 2:23–3:20	Matt. 20:17-28	Exod. 6:2-13	Luke 23:26-49
M	Num. 6	John 10:22-42	Num. 9:15-23 & 10:29-36	Titus 1:1–2:8

ALTERNATIVE TABLE OF LESSONS

	Morning Prayer		Evening Prayer	
	1 Lesson	*2 Lesson*	*1 Lesson*	*2 Lesson*
T	11:10-23	11:1-44	12	2:9–3:15
W	13:1-3, 17-33	11:45-57	14:1-25	2 Tim. 1
T	16:1-35	12:1-19	16:36–17:13	2
F	20	12:20-50	22:1-35	3
S	22:36–23:26	13	23:27–24:25	4

THE SUNDAY NEXT BEFORE EASTER

I·II	Exod. 11	Matt. 26	Isa. 52:13–53:12	Luke 19:29-48
M	Lam. 1:1-12	John 14:1-14	Lam. 2:8-19	John 14:15-31
T	3:1-30	15:1-16	3:40-51	15:17-27
W	Isa. 42:1-9	16:1-15	Num. 21:4-9	16:16-33
T	Exod. 24:1-11	17	Lev. 16:2-24	13:1-35
F	Gen. 22:1-18	18	Isa. 50:4-10	19:38-42
S	Zech. 9:9-12	1 Pet. 2:19-25	Job 19:21-27	2:13-22

EASTER DAY

I·II	Exod. 12:1-14	Rev. 1:4-18	Exod. 14:5-31	John 20:11-23
M	Exod. 15:1-18	Luke 24:1-12	Isa. 12	Rev. 7:9-17
T	Isa. 25:1-9	1 Pet. 1:1-12	26:1-19	Matt. 28:1-15
W	61	1:13-25	Song 2:8-17	28:16-20
T	Job 14:1-15	1 Thess. 4:13-18	Dan. 12	Mark 16
F	Zeph. 3:14-20	Acts 17:16-31	2 Kgs. 4:8-37	John 21:1-14
S	Jer. 31:1-14	26:1-23	Mic. 7:7-20	21:15-25

THE FIRST SUNDAY AFTER EASTER

I	Isa. 51:1-16	Luke 24:13-35	Exod. 15:1-18	John 20:24-31
II	Ezek. 37:1-14	Luke 24:13-35	1 Kgs. 17:8-24	John 20:24-31
M	Deut. 1:3-18	Acts 1:1-14	Deut. 1:19-46	Acts 1:15-26
T	2:1-25	2:1-21	2:26–3:5	2:22-47
W	3:18-29	3:1–4:4	4:1-24	4:5-31
T	4:25-40	4:32–5:11	5:1-21	5:12-42
F	5:22-33	6:1–7:16	6	7:17-34
S	7:1-11	7:35–8:4	7:12-26	8:4-25

ALTERNATIVE TABLE OF LESSONS

	Morning Prayer		Evening Prayer	
	1 Lesson	*2 Lesson*	*1 Lesson*	*2 Lesson*

THE SECOND SUNDAY AFTER EASTER

	1 Lesson	*2 Lesson*	*1 Lesson*	*2 Lesson*
I	Exod. 16:2-15	1 Cor. 15:1-26	Exod. 24	John 21:1-14
II	Isa. 55	Mark 5:21-43	Deut. 4:25-40	Rev. 2:1-17
M	Deut. 8	Acts 8:26-40	Deut. 9:1-10	Acts 9:1-31
T	9:11-29	9:32-43	10	10:1-23
W	11:1-12	10:24-48	11:13-32	11:1-18
T	12:1-14	11:19-30	15:1-18	12:1-24
F	16:1-20	12:25−13:12	17:8-20	13:13-43
S	18:9-22	13:44−14:7	19	14:8-28

THE THIRD SUNDAY AFTER EASTER

I	Exod. 32:1-14, 30-35	1 Cor. 15:35-58	Exod. 33:7-23	John 21:15-25
II	Num. 13:1-2, 17-33	Luke 7:11-17	Deut. 5:1-21	Rev. 2:18−3:6
M	Deut. 21:22−22:8	Acts 15:1-21	Deut. 24:5-22	Acts 15:22-35
T	26	15:36−16:5	28:58-68	16:6-40
W	29:10-29	17:1-15	30	17:16-34
T	31:1-13	18:1-23	31:14-29	18:24−19:7
F	31:30−32:14	19:8-20	32:15-47	19:21-41
S	33	20:1-16	32:48-52 & 34	20:17-38

THE FOURTH SUNDAY AFTER EASTER

I	Exod. 34:1-10	1 Pet. 3:8-22	Exod. 35:30−36:1	Luke 16:19-31
II	Num. 22:1-35	John 11:1-44	Deut. 10:12−11:1	Rev. 3:7-22
M	Josh. 1	Acts 21:1-16	Josh. 2	Acts 21:17-36
T	3	21:37−22:22	4:1−5:1	22:23−23:11
W	5:13−6:20	23:12-35	7	24:1-23
T	9:3-27	24:24−25:12	10:1-15	25:13-27
F	21:43−22:8	26	22:9-34	27
S	23	28:1-15	24:1-28	28:16-31

ALTERNATIVE TABLE OF LESSONS

	Morning Prayer		Evening Prayer	
	1 Lesson	2 Lesson	1 Lesson	2 Lesson

THE FIFTH SUNDAY AFTER EASTER

	1 Lesson	2 Lesson	1 Lesson	2 Lesson
I	Deut. 34	Acts 13:26-43	Deut. 6	Luke 10:38–11:13
II	Num. 22:36–23:12	Rom. 6:1-14	Deut. 28:1-14	Mark 4:1-20
M	Deut. 7:6-13	Matt. 6:5-18	Deut. 8	Matt. 6:19-34
T	11:8-21	Luke 5:1-11	1 Kgs. 8:22-43	Jas. 5:1-18
W	Joel 2:21-27	John 6:22-40	Sg. III 29-37	Matt. 28:16-20
T	2 Kgs. 2:1-15	17	Dan. 7:9-10, 13-14	Heb. 1
F	Judg. 2:6-23	Heb. 2	Judg. 4	3
S	5	4:1-13	6:1-24	4:14–5:10

THE SUNDAY AFTER ASCENSION DAY

	1 Lesson	2 Lesson	1 Lesson	2 Lesson
I	Isa. 65:17-25	Luke 24:36-53	Jer. 31:1-13	John 14:1-14
II	Isa. 52:1-12	Eph. 4:1-16	Isa. 62	Rev. 5
M	Judg. 6:25-40	Heb. 5:11–6:20	Judg. 7	Heb. 7
T	10:17–11:28	8	11:29–12:7	9:1-14
W	13	9:15-28	14	10:1-18
T	16:4-31	10:19-39	Ruth 1	11
F	Ruth 2	12:1-13	3	12:14-29
S	4:1-17	13	Deut. 16:9-12	Acts 18:24–19:7

WHITSUNDAY

	1 Lesson	2 Lesson	1 Lesson	2 Lesson
I·II	Joel 2:28-32	Rom. 8:1-17	Isa. 11:1-9	Rom. 8:18-39
M	Ezek. 11:14-20	Acts 2:12-36	Wis. 1:1-7	Acts 2:37-47
T	37:1-14	1 Cor. 12:1-13	7:15–8:1	1 Cor. 12:27–13:13
W	1 Kgs. 19:1-18	2	9	3
T	2 Sam. 23:1-5	Eph. 6:10-20	Exod. 35:30–36:1	Gal. 5:13-26
F	Num. 11:16-17, 24-29	2 Cor. 5:14–6:10	Jer. 31:31-34	2 Cor. 3
S	27:15-23	Matt. 9:35–10:20	Isa. 61	2 Tim. 1:3-14

ALTERNATIVE TABLE OF LESSONS

	Morning Prayer		Evening Prayer	
	1 Lesson	*2 Lesson*	*1 Lesson*	*2 Lesson*
		TRINITY SUNDAY		
I·II	Isa. 6:1-8	Mark 1:1-13	Isa. 40:12-31	1 Pet. 1:3-12
M	1 Sam. 1	Jas. 1	1 Sam. 2:1-21	Mark 1:14-31
T	2:22-36	2:1-13	3	1:32-45
W	4	2:14-26	7	2:1-22
T	8	3	9:1-25	2:23–3:12
F	9:26—10:16	4	10:17-27	3:13-35
S	11	5	12	4:1-34
		THE FIRST SUNDAY AFTER TRINITY		
I	Josh. 1:1-9	Mark 1:21-34	Hos. 6:1-6	Acts 1:1-14
II	Jer. 5:1-19	Acts 9:1-22 [23-31]	1 Kgs. 3:5-14	John 13:1-20
M	1 Sam. 13	1 Pet. 1:1-21	1 Sam. 14:1-23	Mark 4:35–5:20
T	14:24-48	1:22–2:10	15	5:21-43
W	16	2:11–3:7	17:1-30	6:1-9
T	17:31-54	3:8–4:6	17:55—18:16	6:30-56
F	19	4:7-19	20:1-17	7:1-23
S	20:18-42	5	21:1—22:5	7:24—8:10
		THE SECOND SUNDAY AFTER TRINITY		
I	Josh. 2	Mark 2:23–3:19	Hos. 11:1-9a	Acts 2:1-21
II	Jer. 7:1-16	Acts 13:1-13 [14-26]	1 Kgs. 8:22-30 [9:1-3]	John 13:21-38
M	1 Sam. 22:6-23	2 Pet. 1	1 Sam. 23	Mark 8:11–9:1
T	24	2	25:2-42	9:2-29
W	26	3	28:3-25	9:30-50
T	31	Jude	2 Sam. 1	10:1-31
F	2:1–3:1	1 John 1:1–2:6	3:17-39	10:32-52
S	5:1-12	2:7-29	6	11:1-26
		THE THIRD SUNDAY AFTER TRINITY		
I	Josh. 3	Mark 3:20-35	Hos. 14	Acts 2:22-42 [43-47]

ALTERNATIVE TABLE OF LESSONS

	Morning Prayer		Evening Prayer	
	1 Lesson	*2 Lesson*	*1 Lesson*	*2 Lesson*
II	Jer. 17:5-14	Acts 16:6-34	1 Kgs. 10:1-13	John 14:1-14
M	2 Sam. 7	1 John 3:1-12	2 Sam. 9	Mark 11:27– 12:12
T	11	3:13–4:6	12:1-23	12:13-34
W	13:38–14:24	4:7-21	14:25–15:12	12:35–13:13
T	15:13-37	5	16:1-19	13:14-37
F	17:1-23	2 John	17:24–18:18	14:1-26
S	18:19-33	3 John	19:1-23	14:27-52

THE FOURTH SUNDAY AFTER TRINITY

I	Josh. 5:13–6:20	Mark 4:21-41	Joel 2:1-14	Acts 3:1-16 [17-26]
II	Jer. 18:1-17	Acts 17:16-34	1 Kgs. 12:1-20	John 14:15-31
M	2 Sam. 19:24-43	Rom. 1	2 Sam. 23:1-17	Mark 14:53-72
T	24	2:1-16	1 Kgs. 1:5-31	15:1-41
W	1 Kgs. 1:32-53	2:17-29	1 Chr. 22:2-19	15:42–16:20
T	1 Chr. 28:1-10	3	28:20–29:9	Luke 1:1-23
F	29:10-30	4	1 Kgs. 3	1:24-56
S	1 Kgs. 4:21-34	5	5	1:57-80

THE FIFTH SUNDAY AFTER TRINITY

I	Josh. 24:1-5, 13-25	Mark 6:7-32	Joel 2:15-27	Acts 4:1-22 [23-31]
II	Jer. 26:1-16	Acts 19:21-41	1 Kgs. 18:17-39	John 15:1-16
M	1 Kgs. 6:1-14	Rom. 6	1 Kgs. 8:1-21	Luke 2:1-21
T	8:22-53	7	8:54–9:9	2:22-52
W	10	8:1-17	11:1-13	3:1-22
T	11:26-43	8:18-39	12:1-24	4:1-30
F	12:25–13:10	9	13:11	4:31
S	14:1-20	10	2 Chr. 12	5:1-16

THE SIXTH SUNDAY AFTER TRINITY

I	Judg. 5	Mark 6:53–7:23	Zech. 2	Acts 6
II	Jer. 30:1-3, 10-22	Acts 20:17-38	1 Kgs. 19:1-18	John 15:17-27

ALTERNATIVE TABLE OF LESSONS

	Morning Prayer		Evening Prayer	
	1 Lesson	*2 Lesson*	*1 Lesson*	*2 Lesson*
M	2 Chr. 13	Rom. 11:1-24	2 Chr. 14	Luke 5:17-39
T	15	11:25-36	16	6:1-19
W	1 Kgs. 16:15-34	12	1 Kgs. 17	6:20-38
T	18:1-16	13	18:17-46	6:39—7:10
F	19	14	21	7:11-35
S	22:1-40	15:1-13	2 Chr. 20:1-30	7:36-50

THE SEVENTH SUNDAY AFTER TRINITY

	Morning Prayer		Evening Prayer	
I	Judg. 7:1-23	Mark 9:14-29	Zech. 8:1-17	Acts 8:4-17
II	Jer. 31:27-34	Acts 21:15-36	1 Kgs. 21:1-23 [24-29]	John 16:1-15
M	2 Kgs. 1	Rom. 15:14-33	2 Kgs. 2:1-22	Luke 8:1-21
T	4:1-37	16	5	8:22-56
W	6:1-23	1 Cor. 1:1-25	6:24—7:2	9:1-17
T	7:3-20	1:26—2:16	8:1-15	9:18-50
F	9	3	11:1-20	9:51
S	11:21—12:21	4:1-17	13	10:1-24

THE EIGHTH SUNDAY AFTER TRINITY

	Morning Prayer		Evening Prayer	
I	Judg. 16:4	Mark 9:30	Jonah 1 & 2	Acts 8:26-39
II	Jer. 36:1-26	Acts 25:1-12 [13-27]	1 Kgs. 22:1-38	John 16:16-22
M	2 Kgs. 14	1 Cor. 4:18—5:13	2 Chr. 26	Luke 10:25-42
T	15:17-38	6	2 Kgs. 16	11:1-28
W	Isa. 7:1-17	7	Isa. 8:1-18	11:29-54
T	2 Kgs. 17:1-23	8	2 Kgs. 17:24-41	12:1-34
F	18:1-8	9	2 Chr. 30	12:35-53
S	18:13-37	10:1—11:1	2 Kgs. 19	12:54—13:9

THE NINTH SUNDAY AFTER TRINITY

	Morning Prayer		Evening Prayer	
I	1 Sam. 1:1-20	Mark 10:17-31	Jonah 3 & 4	Acts 11:1-18
II	Jer. 38:1-13	Acts 27	2 Kgs. 4:8-37	John 16:23-33
M	2 Kgs. 20	1 Cor. 11:2-34	2 Chr. 33	Luke 13:10-35
T	22	12:1-27	2 Kgs. 23:1-20	14:1-24

ALTERNATIVE TABLE OF LESSONS

	Morning Prayer		Evening Prayer	
	1 Lesson	*2 Lesson*	*1 Lesson*	*2 Lesson*
W	23:21-35	12:27–13:13	23:36–24:17	14:25–15:10
T	24:18–25:7	14:1-19	25:8-30	15:11-32
F	Jer. 19	14:20-40	Jer. 21:1-10	16
S	22:20–23:8	15:1-34	24	17:1-19

THE TENTH SUNDAY AFTER TRINITY

I	1 Sam. 3:1–4:1*a*	Mark 12:18-44	Prov. 1:20-33	Acts 15:1-31
II	Jer. 52:1-11	Acts 28:11-31	2 Kgs. 5:1-19 [20-30]	John 17
M	Jer. 25:1-14	1 Cor. 15:35-58	Jer. 27:2-22	Luke 17:20-37
T	28	16	29:1-20	18:1-30
W	32:1-25	2 Cor. 1:1-22	32:26-44	18:31–19:10
T	33	1:23–2:17	34:8-22	19:11-28
F	37	3	38:1-13	19:29-48
S	38:14-28	4	39	20:1-26

THE ELEVENTH SUNDAY AFTER TRINITY

I	1 Sam. 9:1–10:1	Rom. 1:1-25 [26-32]	Prov. 8:1-17	Matt. 4:23–5:20
II	Ezek. 11:14-20	Luke 4:1-15	2 Kgs. 17:1-23	Gal. 1
M	Jer. 40	2 Cor. 5:1-19	Jer. 41	Luke 20:27–21:4
T	42	5:20–7:1	43	21:5-38
W	44:1-14	7:2-16	44:15-30	22:1-38
T	Ezek. 1:1-14	8	Ezek. 2:1–3:3	22:39-53
F	3:4-27	9	8	22:54-71
S	11:14-25	10	12:17-28	23:1-25

THE TWELFTH SUNDAY AFTER TRINITY

I	1 Sam. 16:1-13	Rom. 5:1-11	Prov. 8:1, 22-36	Matt. 5:21-48
II	Ezek. 18:1-4, 19-32	Luke 4:16-30	2 Kgs. 18:17-22 & 28–19:7	Gal. 6:1-10
M	Ezek. 13:1-16	2 Cor. 11	Ezek. 14:1-11	Luke 23:26-49
T	14:12-23	12:1-13	20:1-20	23:50–24:12

ALTERNATIVE TABLE OF LESSONS

	Morning Prayer		Evening Prayer	
	1 Lesson	*2 Lesson*	*1 Lesson*	*2 Lesson*
W	20:27-44	12:14–13:14	33:21-33	24:13-53
T	34:1-16	Gal. 1	34:17-31	John 1:1-28
F	36:22-36	2	37:1-14	1:29-51
S	37:15-28	3	47:1-12	2

THE THIRTEENTH SUNDAY AFTER TRINITY

I	1 Sam. 17:1-11, 32-51	Rom. 12	Prov. 14:31–15:17	Matt. 6:1-18
II	Ezek. 33:1-11	Luke 6:20-38	2 Kgs. 19:8-35	1 Cor. 1:1-25
M	Ezra 1	Gal. 4:1–5:1	Ezra 3	John 3:1-21
T	4	5:2-26	Hag. 1:1–2:9	3:22-36
W	Zech. 1:1-17	6	Zech. 1:18–2:13	4:1-26
T	3	Eph. 1:1-14	4	4:27-54
F	6:9-15	1:15-23	Hag. 2:10-23	5:1-23
S	Ezra 5	2:1-10	Ezra 6	5:24-47

THE FOURTEENTH SUNDAY AFTER TRINITY

I	1 Sam. 18:1-16	Rom. 14:1–15:3	Prov. 31:10-31	Matt. 6:19-34
II	Ezek. 33:21-33	Luke 6:39-49	2 Kgs. 22	1 Cor. 1:26–2:9 [10-16]
M	Zech. 7	Eph. 2:11-22	Zech. 8	John 6:1-21
T	Ezra 7	3	Ezra 8:15-36	6:22-40
W	9	4:1-16	10:1-19	6:41-71
T	Neh. 1	4:17-30	Neh. 2	7:1-24
F	4	4:31–5:21	5	7:25-53
S	6:1–7:4	5:22-33	8	8:1-30

THE FIFTEENTH SUNDAY AFTER TRINITY

I	1 Sam. 26	1 Pet. 1:13-25	Job 1	Matt. 7:1-14
II	Ezek. 34:1-16	Luke 7:36–8:3	Ezra 1:1-8	1 Cor. 3
M	Neh. 9:1-23	Eph. 6:1-9	Neh. 9:24-38	John 8:31-59
T	13	6:10-24	Dan. 1	9
W	Dan. 2:1-24	Phil. 1:1-11	2:25-49	10:1-21
T	4:1-18	1:12-30	4:19-37	10:22-42

ALTERNATIVE TABLE OF LESSONS

	Morning Prayer		Evening Prayer	
	1 Lesson	*2 Lesson*	*1 Lesson*	*2 Lesson*
F	7:9-28	2:1-11	9	11:1-44
S	10	2:12-30	12	11:45-57

THE SIXTEENTH SUNDAY AFTER TRINITY

I	1 Sam. 28:3-25	1 Pet. 2:1-17	Job 2	Matt. 7:15-29
II	Ezek. 36:22-28, 34-36	Luke 9:46-62	Ezra 3	1 Cor. 13
M	Esth. 1	Phil. 3	Esth. 2:5-11, 15-23	John 12:1-19
T	3	4	4	12:20-50
W	5	Col. 1:1-20	6 & 7	13
T	1 Macc. 1:1-19	1:21−2:7	1 Macc. 1:20-40	14
F	1:41-64	2:8-19	2:1-28	15
S	2:29-48	2:20−3:11	2:49-70	16

THE SEVENTEENTH SUNDAY AFTER TRINITY

I	2 Sam. 1	1 Pet. 4	Job 4:1 & 5:6-27	Matt. 11:2-19
II	Ezek. 37:15-28	Luke 10:1-24	Neh. 1	Phil. 1:12-30
M	1 Macc. 3:1-26	Col. 3:12−4:1	1 Macc. 3:27-41	John 17
T	3:42-60	4:2-18	4:1-25	18:1-27
W	4:26-35	Phlm.	4:36-61	18:28-40
T	6:1-17	1 Thess. 1	6:18-47	19:1-30
F	7:1-20	2:1-16	7:21-50	19:31-42
S	9:1-22	2:17−3:13	13:41 & 14:4-15	20

THE EIGHTEENTH SUNDAY AFTER TRINITY

I	2 Sam. 7	1 Pet. 5:1-11	Job 19:1-27*a*	Matt. 11:20-30
II	Dan. 3	Luke 11:37-54	Neh. 2	Phil. 2:1-18
M	Job 1	1 Thess. 4:1-12	Job 2	John 21
T	3	4:13−5:11	4	Heb. 1
W	5	5:12-28	6	2
T	7	2 Thess. 1	8	3
F	9	2	10	4:1-13
S	11	3	12	4:14−5:10

ALTERNATIVE TABLE OF LESSONS

	Morning Prayer		Evening Prayer	
	1 Lesson	*2 Lesson*	*1 Lesson*	*2 Lesson*

THE NINETEENTH SUNDAY AFTER TRINITY

I	2 Sam. 12:1-23	Col. 1:21–2:7	Job 28	Matt. 12:22-45
II	Dan. 5	Luke 12:1-21	Ruth 1	Phil. 3:1-16
M	Job 13	1 Tim. 1:1-17	Job 14	Heb. 5:11–6:20
T	15:1-16	1:18–2:15	16:1–17:2	7
W	17:3-16	3	18	8
T	19	4	21	9:1-14
F	22	5	23	9:15-28
S	24	6	25 & 26	10:1-18

THE TWENTIETH SUNDAY AFTER TRINITY

I	1 Sam. 18	Col. 3:12–4:6	Job 38 & 42:1-6	Matt. 13:44-58
II	Dan. 6:1-23	Luke 12:22-34	Ruth 2:1-20a & 4:13-17	Phil. 4
M	Job 27	Titus 1:1–2:8	Job 28	Heb. 10:19-39
T	29:1–30:1	2:9–3:15	31:13-40	11:1-16
W	32	2 Tim. 1	33	11:17-40
T	38:1-21	2	38:22-41	12:1-13
F	39	3	40	12:14-29
S	41	4	42	13

THE TWENTY-FIRST SUNDAY AFTER TRINITY

I	Wis. 2	Phlm.	Bar. 3:1-14	Matt. 14:13-33
II	1 Macc. 2:1-22	Luke 12:35-59	Sir. 3:17-29	2 Cor. 1:1-22
M	Prov. 1:1-19	Jas. 1:1-11	Prov. 1:20-33	Jas. 1:12-27
T	2	2:1-13	3:1-26	2:14-26
W	3:27–4:19	3	4:20–5:14	4
T	6:1-19	5	8	1 Pet. 1:1-12
F	9	1 Pet. 1:13-25	10:1-22	2:1-10
S	11:1-25	2:11–3:7	12:10-28	3:8-22

THE TWENTY-SECOND SUNDAY AFTER TRINITY

I	Wis. 4:7-17	Jas. 1:1-18 [19-27]	Bar. 4:36–5:9	Matt. 16:13-28

ALTERNATIVE TABLE OF LESSONS

| | Morning Prayer | | Evening Prayer | |
	1 Lesson	2 Lesson	1 Lesson	2 Lesson
II	1 Macc. 2:49-69	Luke 13:18-35	Sir. 4:11-28	1 Cor. 4
M	Prov. 14:9-27	1 Pet. 4:1-11	Prov. 15:18-33	1 Pet. 4:12-19
T	16:31—17:17	5	18:10-24	1 John 1:1—2:6
W	20:1-22	1 John 2:7-17	22:1-16	2:18-29
T	24:23-34	3:1-18	25	3:19—4:6
F	26:12-28	4:7-21	27:1-22	5
S	30:1-16	2 John	31:10-31	3 John

THE TWENTY-THIRD SUNDAY AFTER TRINITY

| | Morning Prayer | | Evening Prayer | |
	1 Lesson	2 Lesson	1 Lesson	2 Lesson
I	Wis. 6:1-21	Jas. 2:1-13 [14-26]	Prayer of Manasseh	Matt. 18:1-20
II	1 Macc. 3:42-60	Luke 14:15-35	Sir. 4:29—6:1	2 Cor. 5
M	Sir. 1:1-10	Acts 1	Sir. 1:11-30	Acts 2:1-21
T	2	2:22-47	3:17-29	3:1—4:4
W	4:11-28	4:5-31	4:29—6:1	4:32—5:11
T	6:14-31	5:12-42	7:27-36	6:1—7:16
F	10:6-8, 12-24	7:17-34	11:7-28	7:35—8:4
S	14:20—15:10	8:4-25	15:11-20	8:26-40

THE TWENTY-FOURTH SUNDAY AFTER TRINITY

| | Morning Prayer | | Evening Prayer | |
	1 Lesson	2 Lesson	1 Lesson	2 Lesson
I	Wis. 7:15—8:1	Jas. 3	2 Esd. 16:53-67	Matt. 21:12-32
II	1 Macc. 14:4-15	Luke 15:1-10	Sir. 11:7-28	2 Cor. 9
M	Sir. 16:17-30	Acts 9:1-31	Sir. 17:1-24	Acts 9:32-43
T	18:1-14	10:1-23	19:13-30	10:24-48
W	21:1-17	11:1-18	22:6-22	11:19-30
T	22:27—23:15	12:1-24	24:1-22	12:25—13:12
F	24:23-34	13:13-43	27:30—28:9	13:44—14:7
S	31:1-11	14:8-28	34:9-31	15:1-21

THE TWENTY-FIFTH SUNDAY AFTER TRINITY

| | Morning Prayer | | Evening Prayer | |
	1 Lesson	2 Lesson	1 Lesson	2 Lesson
I	Wis. 9	Jas. 4	Sir. 18:1-13	Matt. 21:33-46
II	Sir. 15:11-20	Luke 17:1-10	Sir. 27:30—28:9	1 Tim. 6:1-16 [17-21]
M	Sir. 35	Acts 15:22-35	Sir. 37:7-15	Acts 15:36—16:5

ALTERNATIVE TABLE OF LESSONS

	Morning Prayer		Evening Prayer	
	1 Lesson	2 Lesson	1 Lesson	2 Lesson
T	38:1-14	16:6-40	38:24-34	17:1-15
W	39:1-11	17:16-34	39:13-35	18:1-23
T	42:15-25	18:24–19:7	43:1-12	19:8-20
F	43:13-33	19:21-41	50:1-24	20:1-16
S	51:1-12	20:17-38	51:13-30	21:1-16

THE TWENTY-SIXTH SUNDAY AFTER TRINITY

I	Wis. 11:21–12:2	Jas. 5:[1-6] 7-20	Sir. 38:24-34	Matt. 23:1-22
II	Sir. 42:15-25	Luke 20:1-19	Sir. 43:13-26	2 Tim. 1:1-14 [15–2:7]
M	Eccl. 1*	Acts 21:17-36	Eccl. 2:1-20*	Acts 21:37–22:22
T	3:1-15	22:23–23:11	3:16–4:6	23:12-35
W	4:7-16	24:1-23	5	24:24–25:12
T	6	25:13-27	7:1-14	26
F	7:15-29	27:1-26	8	27:27-44
S	9	28:1-15	10:5-18	28:16-31

THE SUNDAY NEXT BEFORE ADVENT

I·II	Eccl. 11 & 12	Heb. 11:1-16	Mal. 3:1-6 & 4	Heb. 11:17–12:2
M	Wis. 1	Matt. 5:1-16	Wis. 2	Rev. 1
T	3:1-9	5:17-48	4:7-20	2:1-17
W	5:1-16	6:1-18	6:1-21	2:18–3:6
T	7:15–8:4	6:19-34	8:5-18	3:7-22
F	8:21–9:18	7:1-14	10:15–11:10	4
S	11:21–12:2	7:15-29	12:12-21	5

* These first lessons from Ecclesiastes shall always be read in the week previous to the Sunday next before Advent.

ALTERNATIVE TABLE OF LESSONS

Alternative Sunday Lessons for Certain Sundays after Trinity.*

	Year I		Year II	
	Morning Prayer	*Evening Prayer*	*Morning Prayer*	*Evening Prayer*
21	Job 39:1–40:4	Jer. 5:20-31	Prov. 2	Dan. 1
22	Hab. 1:1-14	Jer. 10:1-16	Prov. 9:1-11	Dan. 2:1-23
23	Hab. 2:1-14	Jer. 11:1-14	Prov. 16:9-20	Dan. 2:24-45
24	Hab. 3:2-19	Jer. 22:1-9	Prov. 25:11-28	Dan. 9:1-19
25	Amos 2:4-16	Ezek. 14:1-11	Zech. 1:7-21	Zech. 9:9-12 & 16
26	Amos 4:4-13	Ezek. 14:12-23	Zech. 11	Zech. 13

Lessons Proper for Holy Days Not Included in the Foregoing Table.

Morning Prayer		*Evening Prayer*	
1 Lesson	*2 Lesson*	*1 Lesson*	*2 Lesson*
ST. ANDREW		Sir. 14:20-27	1 Cor. 4:9-16
Zech. 8:20-23	John 1:35-42	Ezek. 47:1-12	John 12:20-32
ST. THOMAS		2 Sam. 15:17-21	John 11:1-16
Job 42:1-6	John 14:1-7	Sir. 2	1 Pet. 1:3-9
CONVERSION OF ST. PAUL		Jer. 1:4-10	Acts 26:1-23
Isa. 56:1-8	Gal. 1:11-24	Sir. 39:1-10	Phil. 3:1-14
PURIFICATION OF ST. MARY THE VIRGIN		Exod. 13:11-16	Gal. 4:1-7
1 Sam. 1:21-28	Heb. 10:1-10	Hag. 2:1-9	Rom. 12:1-5
ST. MATTHIAS		Isa. 22:15-22	John 15:1-16
1 Sam. 2:27-35	Matt. 7:15-27	1 Sam. 16:1-13	1 Cor. 4:1-8
ANNUNCIATION OF OUR LADY		Gen. 3:1-15	Rom. 5:12-21
Isa. 52:7-12	Heb. 2:5-18	1 Sam. 2:1-10	Matt. 1:18-23

* These first lessons may be used at the discretion of the minister in place of the lessons from the Apocrypha on Sundays.

ALTERNATIVE TABLE OF LESSONS

	Morning Prayer		Evening Prayer	
	1 Lesson	*2 Lesson*	*1 Lesson*	*2 Lesson*
ST. MARK			Ezek. 1:1-14	Acts 12:25–13:13
	Sir. 51:13-30	Acts 15:35-41	Isa. 62:6-12	2 Tim. 4:1-11
ST. PHILIP & ST. JAMES			Isa. 30:15-21	John 1:43-51
	Prov. 4:10-18	John 6:1-14	Job 23:1-12	John 17:1-8
ST. BARNABAS			Tob. 4:5-11	Acts 4:32-37
	Jer. 9:23-24	Acts 9:26-31	Job 29:11-16	Acts 14:8-28
NATIVITY OF ST. JOHN THE BAPTIST			Mal. 3:1-6	Matt. 3
	Judg. 13:1-7	Luke 1:5-25	Mal. 4	Matt. 11:2-19
ST. PETER			Ezek. 2:1-7	Acts 9:32-43
	Ezek. 3:4-11	Acts 11:1-18	Ezek. 34:11-16	John 21:15-22
ST. MARY MAGDALEN			1 Sam. 16:14-23	Luke 8:1-3
	Isa. 25:1-9	John 20:1-10	Zeph. 3:14-20	Mark 15:40–16:7
ST. JAMES			Jer. 26:1-15	Mark 1:14-20
	2 Kgs. 1:1-15	Luke 9:46-56	Jer. 45	Mark 14:32-42
TRANSFIGURATION OF OUR LORD			Exod. 24:12-18	Luke 9:28-45
	Exod. 34:29-35	2 Cor. 3	Sir. 48:1-10	2 Pet. 1:12-21
ST. BARTHOLOMEW			Gen. 28:10-17	John 1:43-51
	Deut. 18:15-19	Matt. 10:1-15	Isa. 49:1-13	Matt. 10:16-22
ST. MATTHEW			1 Kgs. 19:15-21	Matt. 6:19-34
	Prov. 3:1-17	Matt. 19:16-30	1 Chr. 29:9-18	1 Tim. 6:6-19
ST. MICHAEL & ALL ANGELS			Dan. 10:4-21	Rev. 5
	2 Kgs. 6:8-17	Acts 12:1-11	Dan. 12:1-4	Rev. 8:1-6
ST. LUKE			Isa. 55	Luke 1:1-4
	Isa. 61:1-6	2 Tim. 3:10-17	Sir. 38:1-14	Col. 4:7-18
ST. SIMON & ST. JUDE			Isa. 28:9-16	Eph. 2:11-22
	Isa. 45:18-25	Luke 6:12-19	Wis. 5:1-16	John 14:15-24
ALL SAINTS			2 Esd. 2:42-48	Heb. 11:32–12:2
	Wis. 3:1-9	Rev. 19:6-10	Sir. 44:1-15	Rev. 7:9-17

Appendix V.

Glossary.

ABJECTS refers to 'the outcasts' or 'the downtrodden'.
AFTER can have its sense of being later in time, but it also has other senses in the prayer book. It can mean 'according to' (e.g. 'to live after thy commandments', p. 33). Or it can mean 'in proportion to', as in Psalm 90:15: 'Comfort us again now after the time that thou hast plagued us.'

ALLEGE, as used in the Solemnization of Matrimony (p. 314), means not merely 'to claim' but 'to offer evidence, to testify on oath'.

ALLOW can mean 'to approve' or 'to praise' (e.g. Psalm 11:6).

ALWAY is an old variant of *always*.

ANTE PORTAM LATINAM, 'before the Latin gate', appears on 6 May in the calendar. It refers to the tradition that St. John the Divine miraculously survived immersion in a vat of boiling oil before the Latin gate in Rome.

ANTHEM refers to a short text (usually of Scripture) that is said or sung, or more generally to a piece of sung sacred music.

APACE means 'at a good pace, swiftly'.

BANNS means a public proclamation of a forthcoming marriage, from the French *ban* (used for a proclamation or summons, including the proclamation of a person as an outlaw, which aligns with the sense of the more common English word *ban*).

GLOSSARY

BATTLE usually refers to fighting between armies, but it can also refer to the armies themselves, especially when arrayed for fighting (as in Psalm 76:3).

BECOME can mean 'to agree with, to be suitable to.'

BETIMES means 'early', 'quickly', or 'before it is too late.'

BEWAIL means 'to mourn, to express great sorrow.'

BEWRAY means 'to expose' or 'to accuse.'

BOUNDEN is an old variant of *bound*, in the sense of being pledged or obligated.

BOWELS means 'intestines, gut', or metaphorically the seat of sympathetic emotions, especially pity and mercy.

BRIEFS, CITATIONS, AND EXCOMMUNICATIONS is a phrase in a rubric in the Order for the Administration of the Lord's Supper. *Briefs* refers to royal instructions to collect alms and oblations for specific purposes; *citations*, to a notice for certain persons to appear on a given day in court; and *excommunications*, to the decisions of ecclesiastical tribunals that certain persons are to be put out of the church. The phrase is illustrative of parish notices.

CANON is from the Greek χανών, *kanon*, meaning 'rule, standard.' It is used in two senses in the prayer book. The first is the books of the Old and New Testaments accepted as holy Scripture ('the canon'); the second is ecclesiastical laws (often 'the canons'). References on pp. 242 and 280 are to the 1604 Constitutions and Canons Ecclesiastical, one of the historic formularies of the Church of England (remaining in effect until the 1960s).

CARNAL, from the Latin *carnalis* ('fleshly'), refers to the body, especially as a source of human appetites.

CATHOLIC means 'universal'. In the creeds it is used for the church (or the Christian faith) throughout the whole world and all ages.

CEREMONY refers to an outward act or external observance, especially in connection with religious services. The 'old ceremonies ... retained still' (xviii) in the prayer book include kneeling for confession, standing for the gospel, and the casting of earth in the Burial Service.

CERTIFY can have its older meaning of 'to inform' (e.g. Psalm 19:2).

CHAMBERING refers to lewd or promiscuous behaviour.

CHANCEL (from Latin *cancelli*, 'lattice screen') refers to the part of the church building that before the Reformation contained the high altar and was reserved for clergy. It is to the east of the part of the church where the congregation assembles, which is called the 'nave' or 'the body of the church'.

CHOIR, in the phrase 'choirs and places where they sing' (pp. 14, 24), refers to churches that maintain a staff of singers, such as cathedral churches, collegiate chapels, and the Chapel Royal.

CLERK (pronounced 'CLARK') refers to a lay officer who leads the people's responses in the liturgy and otherwise assists the clergy. *Clerk, cleric,* and *clergy* are all derived from the Ecclesiastical Latin *clericus* (a transliteration of the Greek κληρϊκός). Because in medieval Europe literacy was often concentrated in the clergy, the word came to refer to any person able to read, and thus was used of literate lay persons.

COMFORT means 'to strengthen or encourage'. Thus the 'comfortable words' in the Communion service are 'strengthening, encouraging words'.

COMMUNICANT refers to a person receiving communion.

COMPLAIN means 'to lament or cry', or otherwise to express sorrow or suffering.

CONCUPISCENCE (from Latin *concupere*, 'to covet'), has the sense of 'desire' or 'inclination', particularly for sinful or worldly things.

CONEY means 'a mature rabbit'.

CONTINENCY can mean 'abstinence from illicit sexual activity' or 'abstinence from all sexual activity'.

CONTINUALLY can have its current sense of something that happens unceasingly. An older sense, found in Psalm 78:70, is 'for ever'.

CONVENIENT is used throughout the prayer book in its older sense of 'appropriate, fitting'.

CONVERSATION refers to 'common life' in several senses, including the sense of living with others in the same place; of being in the company of others; and of a certain person's way of life, conduct, or behaviour among others.

CORN is a generic word for any kind of grain.

CURATE, as used in Concerning the Service of the Church, refers to the person responsible for the 'cure of souls' in a parish or other ecclesiastical charge (from Latin *cura*, 'care'), that is, the pastor of a congregation.

CURE comes from the Latin *cura*, meaning 'care'. It can refer to the spiritual care that pastors exercise over their flocks or to the sphere of a pastor's oversight, for example, the parish or other ecclesiastical charge. Both senses are used in the Ordering of Priests (*cure* and *cures* on pp. 604-605). See *curate.*

COUNTENANCE means 'face'.

DISCOVER does not mean 'to find', but 'to reveal' (in the Preface) or 'to expose' (in Psalm 18:15).

DRAGON is a word transliterated from Latin that can refer to any large (and often frightening) land or sea animal, particularly a large serpent. In Psalm 148:7, for example, 'ye dragons and all deeps' uses the Anglicized form of the Vulgate's *dracones* (from Greek δράκοντες).

ESCHEW means 'to shun', both in the sense of rejecting and of avoiding.

ESTATE means 'condition', and it takes its colour from its context. It may refer to the interior condition of mind or soul, as in 'their damnable estate, lacking the very true Christian faith' (p. 666); exterior circumstances generally, as in 'afflicted or distressed, in mind, body, or estate' (p. 43); property and possessions, as in 'take order for the settling of their temporal estates' (p. 329); a particular condition of one's life, as in 'the holy estate of matrimony' (p. 314) or 'the estate of single life' (p. 641); the state of one's relationship with another, as in 'examine yourself and your estate, both toward God and man' (p. 327); and social position or rank, as in 'all estates of this realm, whether they be ecclesiastical or civil' (p. 644; also p. 128).

EVENSONG is another name for Evening Prayer; the two names are used interchangeably in the prayer book. The word *evensong* originated in English as a translation of the Latin *vesperas* (from which we get the English word *vespers*), the name of the evening office in the monastic cycle of daily prayer.

FACULTY means 'a dispensation, license, or permission granted by an ecclesiastical authority'.

FAIN means 'glad, gladly', from an Old English word meaning 'to rejoice' (*fægen*).

FIE is an exclamation of reproach.

FLOOD refers to any water, but especially flowing water such as a tide or river (e.g. in the *Benedicite, omnia opera*). In Psalm 72:8, 'the flood' refers to the Euphrates, which the Scriptures call 'the great river' (e.g. Genesis 15:18).

FOND means 'foolish', in the sense of silly or naive.

FROWARD means 'perverse' or 'difficult', particularly with reference to a person. It has an older sense of 'moving away from' and is derived from the Middle English word *fraward*, equivalent to *from-ward* (as opposed to *to-ward*). *Froward* and *untoward* are overlapping.

FRUITION refers to the enjoyment of a thing, or to the pleasure of possessing something desirable.

GARNER means 'granary', a storehouse for grain.

GHOST is the Old English word for soul or spirit. Hence 'ghostly strength' in Confirmation is 'spiritual strength'.

GODS has a wide range of reference, from idols and false gods to heavenly beings such as angels.

GRAVEN, as used in Psalm 7:16, is the past participle of *grave*, a verb meaning 'dig' (from which we get the noun *grave*). This word is not to be confused with *graven* in the Second Commandment, which comes from a different root and means 'hewn' or 'carved'.

GRIN means, most literally, 'to draw back the lips and

bare the teeth'. Now associated with joy or amusement, in older usage the word often referred to baring the teeth in anger or pain, as of a snarling dog (e.g. Psalm 59:5).

GRUDGE means 'to grumble, to murmur complaints'.

HART means 'a male deer', that is, a stag (see *hind*).

HEALTH refers to soundness, whether of body or soul. In the Psalter, it is often used for restoring to soundness (that is, salvation). In Morning and Evening Prayer, 'There is no health in us' has both the sense of soundness ('we are not spiritually sound') and of restoring to soundness ('we cannot save ourselves').

HELL refers to the place of departed spirits generally, or specifically to the place of eternal punishment.

HIND means 'a female deer', that is, a doe (see *hart*).

HOLDEN is an old verb form meaning 'held' or 'held back'.

HOLPEN is an old verb form meaning 'helped'.

HORN appears in the Psalms in the figure of speech metonymy (one thing standing for another). In horned animals, the horn is usually a means of defence; thus the horn symbolizes might, strength, and power.

HUMOURS refers to whims or inclinations, especially ones that are idiosyncratic.

INCOMPREHENSIBLE (from Latin *incomprehensibilis*) is used in the Athanasian Creed with the meaning 'that which cannot be contained', that is, 'infinite'.

INDITE is a verb meaning 'to write or compose'.

INSPIRATION can mean 'breathing into', with reference to the Holy Spirit's influence.

INSTANT(LY) means 'urgently' or 'persistently' (or both 'urgently and persistently').

GLOSSARY

INTERCALATED means 'inserted within the calendar year'. In the instructions for finding Easter Day, it refers to the day added at the end of February in leap years (also called 'the bissextile day').

INVENTION can mean 'finding, discovery'. On 3 May in the calendar, 'Invention of the Cross' refers to the legend of the discovery of the cross in AD 326 by Helena, the mother of Constantine.

JESU is a variant of *Jesus;* it is pronounced 'JEE-*su*' in English. This form comes from the Latin vocative case; it is occasionally used as a kind of intimate address.

KINDLY can mean 'naturally, according to nature'.

KNAP is a verb that means 'to strike' or 'break off'.

LAVER refers to a vessel for washing, including a baptismal font.

LEARN can mean 'to teach', just as *learned* can mean 'taught'.

LEG in the ancient world stood for a person's strength, both in terms of stability and swiftness (by the figure of speech metonymy, that is, one thing standing for another; compare *horn*). An example is Psalm 147:10: 'He hath no pleasure in the strength of an horse, neither delighteth he in any man's legs'.

LESSON means 'a text read aloud' or 'a reading'. It is an Anglicization of the Latin *lectio.*

LET can mean 'hinder', which is nearly the opposite of its present meaning of 'allow'.

LEVIATHAN is an untranslated Hebrew word referring to a large, frightening sea animal, and is associated with chaos and destruction, as is the sea itself.

LIKE AS can mean 'in the same manner that' (e.g. Psalm 45:13).

LIVELY means 'animate'. Like that word, it can mean both 'alive, living' as well as 'moving, active', often without any sharp differentiation between those two senses.

LUST in older usage refers to any appetite or desire, not merely to those that are sexual. It can be a noun (meaning 'a desire' or 'the thing desired') or a verb (meaning 'to desire, long for, incline towards'). Its range of meaning includes both friendly inclination (as in Coverdale's translation of Numbers 14:8, 'If the Lord have lust unto us') and immoderate or reckless desire. The verb *lust* was used interchangeably in the sixteenth century with *list* (meaning 'to like', 'wish', 'desire', or 'be pleased to'). The adjective *lusty* can mean 'cheerful', as well as 'vigorous' (e.g. Psalm 103:5, 'lusty as an eagle'). The adverb *lustily* similarly means 'with vigour' or 'with delight'.

MAGNIFY means 'to honour or praise'.

MARVEL means 'miracle' (from Latin *mirabilia* via Old French). By extension, it refers to any good occurrence sufficiently unexpected that it seems like a miracle.

MATTINS is an alternative name for Morning Prayer. It derives from the Latin *matutinus*, 'of the early morning', and was used in the monastic cycle of daily prayer to refer to the office usually occurring two hours after midnight.

MEET, as in 'meet and right', means 'appropriate, just'.

METROPOLITICAL CHURCH, as used in the Consecration of Bishops (p. 617), refers to the jurisdiction of a metropolitan, that is, an archbishop, or a bishop who oversees other bishops.

MINISHED is a truncation of *diminished*. Compared to the longer form, it can be used more intensively and actively, having the sense of 'to cause a diminution' or 'to take away' (e.g. Psalm 12:1; Exodus 5:19 in the Authorized Version, 'Ye shall not minish ought from your bricks of your daily task').

MISERABLE means 'in need of mercy'. It refers not to a feeling of unhappiness but to an objective condition.

MYSTERY is now used of something hidden, but in biblical and prayer book usage it usually refers to something that was once hidden but is now revealed (e.g. Ephesians 3:1-12 in the Authorized Version).

NOBLE, as used in the *Te Deum*, may have its more common sense of 'illustrious' or an older sense that is now obsolete: 'not destroyed by fire'.

NURTURE, as a verb and a noun, refers to discipline or moral training (e.g. 'the fear and nurture of the Lord' in the Solemnization of Matrimony; Psalm 94:10).

O SAPIENTIA is Latin for 'O, Wisdom'. These are the first words of the old proper anthem for Vespers on 17 December; the anthem, said before and after the *Magnificat*, was the first of seven proper antiphons that marked the last seven days of Advent. These antiphons are the basis for the Advent hymn *Veni, Veni Emmanuel*.

OBLATION means 'an offering, a sacrifice'. The prayer book follows an old distinction between thank offerings and sin offerings. A thank offering is something of value (typically money) given in gratitude to God and for charitable uses, such as relief of the poor and support of the ministry (e.g. 'We humbly beseech thee most mercifully to accept our alms and oblations', p. 250). A sin offering, or propitiation, is an offering that reconciles or restores a right relationship between conflicting parties. Preeminently, this refers to Jesus Christ's 'death upon the cross for our redemption, who made there – by his one oblation of himself once offered – a full, perfect, and sufficient sacrifice, oblation, and satisfaction, for the sins of the whole world' (p. 262).

OFFEND means 'to strike one's foot against something' and so 'to stumble', and by extension 'to cause to stumble'. Metaphorically, it refers to all kinds of mistakes and transgressions, especially injurious ones, as well as to becoming the cause of another's mistakes and transgressions.

OFFICE (from Latin *officium*) means 'a task or duty'. It can refer to a church service (or liturgy) such as Morning Prayer or the Communion. It is also used in the prayer book for a position or role to which certain services or duties are attached (e.g. the prayer on p. 42 for those 'called to any office and administration' in the church).

ONLY can mean 'alone'. The word often has this sense in the homily in Appendix I (e.g. 'Faith only justifieth' = 'Faith alone justifieth').

THE ORDINARY refers to the bishop of the diocese.

PATEN is an old word for 'a plate'.

PERADVENTURE means 'perhaps'.

PERSECUTE means 'to pursue in order to capture or harm', and by extension it can mean 'to act with hostility toward someone'.

PICKING is an old word for stealing, and it survives in the word *pickpocket.*

PIE refers to one of several medieval books regulating the liturgies of the church. This particular book provided instructions for determining feast days.

PLANTATION has an older sense of 'settlement, colony'.

PLIGHT THEE MY TROTH refers to a pledge or promise of loyalty.

PREACH can be used for any kind of oral declaration, from promulgating a decree (Psalm 2:7) to bearing news (Psalm 68:12) to speech generally (Psalm 59:12).

PREVENT means 'to precede', often with a purpose (whether good or ill).

PRIVILY mean 'in private' or 'in secret'.

PROPITIATION refers to the conciliation of anger, especially of divine wrath, and thus to the reconciliation of God and man.

PUBLICAN refers, in biblical usage, to those in first-century Judea who collected taxes for Rome; they were considered both thieves and traitors. By extension, the word can refer to any dishonourable person.

QUICK means 'living'.

RAMP refers to an animal rearing up on its hind legs while the other legs are raised in front. It is typically used of a lion (e.g. Psalm 22:13, as well as the lion rampant in heraldry).

REBUKE as a verb means 'to chastise, reprimand'. As a noun, it can mean 'chastisement' or 'shame, disgrace'. These two senses are used in close conjunction in Psalm 39:9, 12. Compare *reproof.*

REDUCING, as used in Of Ceremonies, has its literal sense of 'bringing back'.

REFRAIN has an older meaning of 'to keep in check, to place a restraint upon' (from Latin *frenum*, 'a bridle').

REHEARSE means 'to tell, give an account', and it can refer to the activities of describing, reporting, or tabulating. It can also mean 'to practice for performance', as in the modern sense of rehearsing a play or piece of music. Both senses appear in Psalm 87.

REINS refers to the kidneys, which are portrayed in ancient literature as the source of feelings or pleasures. The word is often paired with 'heart', understood as the seat of the intellect and will.

REPROOF can refer to a rebuke, a cause for rebuke (that is, something shameful or disgraceful), or an object of rebuke (that is, a disgraced person). Compare *rebuke.*

RESPONDS, VERSES, VAIN REPETITIONS, COMMEMORATIONS, AND SYNODALS (at p. xiv) refers to the large number of pre-Reformation liturgical texts appointed for a particular day (called 'propers'). In the medieval liturgies, these texts interrupted the continuous, day-by-day, reading of the Scriptures. Because the instructions for finding these texts were in various books, 'many times there was more business to find out what should be read, than to read it when it was found out' (p. xv).

RID means 'to make clear' or 'to set free'. This usage survives today in the reflexive – 'rid myself of' means 'to free myself from' a nuisance.

ROOM refers to space and can be used figuratively (e.g. Psalm 31:9).

RUBRIC refers to instructions in the prayer book. It is

from the Latin *rubrica* ('red'), from the tradition of using red ink for instructions in liturgical books.

RUNAGATE is from the Latin *renegare* (from which the English *renegade* is also derived), with influence from the English *run*. It refers generally to a wanderer or fugitive; more narrowly, it can refer to an apostate or one who has abandoned the faith. Both senses probably contribute to its meaning in Psalm 68:6.

SABAOTH is an untranslated Hebrew word that means 'hosts' or 'armies', especially the angelic armies of heaven. It is sometimes confused with *sabbath,* another Hebrew word that is often left untranslated in Christian usage, which means 'rest', with particular reference to the weekly day of rest appointed in the Ten Commandments.

SAINTS means 'holy ones' or 'those set apart'. It can refer to the people whom God has set apart as his own (e.g. Psalm 116:13) or to angels or celestial beings (e.g. Psalm 89:8; Jude 14 in the Authorized Version; compare *gods*). It can also be an adjective before the name of a holy person commemorated by the church, either human or angelic (e.g. St. Mary the Virgin, St. Michael the Archangel).

SEPTUAGESIMA, SEXAGESIMA, and QUINQUAGESIMA are untranslated Latin words meaning seventieth, sixtieth, and fiftieth (respectively). They are used in the prayer book to refer to the three Sundays before the beginning of Lent (called *quadragesima*), because they are roughly (though not exactly) seventy, sixty, and fifty days before Easter Day. These three Sundays are a time of preparation for Lent.

SHAWM refers to a wind instrument.

SIMPLE means 'without guile, pretense, or design'. It can refer to the innocent and honest, but can also refer to those who are easily deceived by others. By extension, it can refer to victims of fraud and oppression who are the special object of divine vindication.

SO can introduce an action or idea that follows from what precedes it. Used this way, *so* means 'accordingly, therefore, in this manner' (e.g. Psalm 13:6). But in older usage it can also be used to introduce an action or idea that is simply the next in a sequence, where it is equivalent to 'then' (e.g. Psalm 18:6); or as an expression of surprise, where it is equivalent to 'but, yet, nevertheless' (e.g. Psalm 78:57).

STABLISH is a variant of *establish*. It means 'to make firm or strong' and so it has a range of usage from 'shore up' and 'stabilize' to 'set up' and 'found'. It has a connotation of permanence.

STRANGE CHILDREN is used in the prayer book Psalter to mean 'the descendants of foreigners' in contrast to the children of Israel. Compare the Psalter's references to the 'heathen' and the 'Gentiles' – those who worship 'strange' (that is, foreign) gods.

SUCCOUR means 'help, assistance' or 'shelter, protection'. In a martial context, it refers to military reinforcements (e.g. in the collect for St. Michael and All Angels).

SUPEREROGATION means 'beyond what is commanded or required'.

TABRET (like *timbrel*) is a variant of *tabor*, a small drum.

TELL can mean 'to count', 'to list', or 'to report'.

GLOSSARY

TEMPTATION can refer to any testing, and not merely to an enticing to sin.

THROUGHLY means either 'through and through' or 'all throughout'.

TOKEN means 'a sign' – something that represents, indicates, or is evidence of something else.

TRANSLATION refers to a transfer or removal from one place or condition to another. The calendar marks the 'translation' of certain saints to commemorate the day on which their remains were removed from one burial place to another. For example, Edward the Martyr, King of the West Saxons is commemorated on 18 March, the day of his martyrdom, and on 20 June, the day on which his remains were relocated to Shaftesbury Abbey.

TUSH is an exclamation of annoyance or contempt.

UNCTION means 'anointing', from the Latin *unctio* ('anointing' or 'ointment').

UNICORN is the word that early modern English Bibles use for the Hebrew *re'em,* which referred to a wild bull with two horns. But there is a long-standing tradition that the word referred to a one-horned animal. The ancient Greek translators of the Psalms rendered the word with μονόκερως (*monokeros*), meaning 'single-horned [animal]'. The Vulgate followed suit with *unicornis,* 'one horn'. Like the Greek and Latin renderings, the English *unicorn* emphasizes the horns of these fearsome beasts, a symbol of their strength (see *horn*).

USE can refer to the liturgical forms of a particular place, as in the Preface: 'some following Salisbury Use, some Hereford Use, and some the Use of Bangor, some of York, some of Lincoln – now from henceforth all the whole realm shall have but one Use' (p. xvi).

USURY refers to lending (typically of money) at interest, especially in an exploitative sense. It may also refer to the interest earned on a loan.

VERY means 'true, genuine'.

VICTUALS (pronounced VIT-*uls*) is food of any kind or, in an overlapping sense, the fruit of the ground.

VILE means 'of low condition, base' (e.g. the contrast between 'our vile body' and 'his glorious body' on pp. 200, 346, 577).

VOUCHSAFE means 'to give, graciously and without compulsion'. It usually has an implication of gracious condescension because the gift is from a superior to an inferior (especially from God to man).

WATER-PIPE refers to a torrent of water, such as a waterfall or geyser.

WEALTH can refer to prosperity, strength, or abundance of any kind, and not only to money or possessions.

WHITSUNDAY is another name for Pentecost, the feast commemorating the descent of the Holy Spirit upon the apostles after the Ascension of Jesus (described in Acts 2). *Whit* is likely a contraction of *white,* and may refer to the white robes worn by those who were baptized on this day. Later writers sometimes associated the word with the 'wit' (knowledge, intellect) given by the Holy Spirit to the apostles.

WITHAL means 'likewise' or 'in addition'.

WONDER and WONDERFUL refer to something that is a cause of astonishment or profound admiration. Especially used for divine deeds, these words can be associated with dread or terror (e.g. Psalm 76:12; 78:44). Compare *marvel*.

WORSHIP means 'praise' or 'honour', that is, 'a public acknowledgement of respect, allegiance, or fealty'. As a verb, it is used for the activity of honouring (in the Solemnization of Matrimony, 'with my body, I thee worship'). As a noun, it is used for the honour that is rendered (e.g. Psalm 8:5). By extension, it can mean 'source or cause of honour', which is probably the sense it has in Psalm 3:3, where 'thou art my worship' is paired with 'the lifter up of my head'.

How to Follow the Services.

MORNING PRAYER

1. Begin on p. 1 and continue to the end of the *Venite* (p. 6).
2. Find the psalms appointed for the morning of the day of the month (pp. 362-561).
3. Find the first lesson in the calendar (pp. xxxiv-lvii); then turn to the *Te Deum* (p. 6).
4. Find the second lesson in the calendar (pp. xxxiv-lvii); then turn to the *Benedictus* (p. 11), after which continue to the end of Morning Prayer.
5. When the Litany is used, after the third collect (p. 14) turn to p. 31.

HOLY COMMUNION

1. Begin on p. 242 and continue to the end of the collect for all those in civil authority (p. 245).
2. Turn to the collect, epistle, and gospel for the Sunday (pp. 49-204) or holy day (pp. 205-240).
3. After the gospel, turn to the creed (p. 246), after which continue to the end of the Communion office.

EVENING PRAYER

1. Begin on p. 17 and continue to the end of the response 'The Lord's name be praised' (p. 20).
2. Find the psalms appointed for the evening of the day of the month (pp. 362-561).
3. Find the first lesson in the calendar (pp. xxxiv-lvii); then turn to the *Magnificat* (p. 21).
4. Find the second lesson in the calendar (pp. xxxiv-lvii); then turn to the *Nunc Dimittis* (p. 22), after which continue to the end of Evening Prayer.

THIS BOOK IS SET IN ROBERT SLIMBACH'S
WARNOCK PRO, A TYPEFACE WHOSE
STURDY, VIGOROUS SIMPLICITY
IS SUITED TO THE WORDS.